Country Living
Volume 1

A Bible-based Blueprint for Leaving the City and an Encyclopedia of Country Living

A work book to stimulate discussion and help you and your family make plans to move to and thrive while living in the country.

Crystal Whitten, Ph.D.

Published by Amazon
for Build A Better You, LLC

2021

Country Living, Volume 1
A Bible-based Blueprint for Leaving the City and an Encyclopedia of Country Living
A work book to stimulate discussion and help you and your family make plans to move to and thrive while living in the country.

ISBN
978-1-7352988-4-9

Library of Congress Control Number
1735298840

Copyright © 2021, 2022, 2023, 2024, 2025, 2026   Crystal Whitten, USA
This edition is copyrighted under the Universal Copyright Convention. All rights are reserved. No portion of this book may be reproduced, stored in a retrieval system, or transmitted in any form or by any means (electronic, mechanical, photocopy, recording, scanning, or other), except for brief quotations in critical reviews or articles, without the prior written permission of the author.

This book was partially edited by Wesley Whitten (1932-2023), Professional Engineer

To reference the food and lifestyle guidance graphics known as:

"Plant-based food guidance – meals matter: take your pick" ©,
Take your pick! Sample plant-based menus ©,
"Lifestyle guidance – make each lifestyle habit count: take your pick!" ©

Developed and published by Crystal Whitten, at Build a Better You (www.buildabetteryou.us)."
Send correspondence to: phytochemwhitten@yahoo.com with subject title: Country Living
Use the above titles as part of the graphic and reference.

Published by
Amazon

Date of Original Publication: April 2021
Current modifications as of: October 2025

Front Cover Photo Credit
by Lucas Ludwig (Unsplash.com), Horse, Montana, USA
I would like to thank God for this beautiful and magnificent animal and thank Mr. Ludwig for the lovely photo!

Poem (back cover) – Woods (1967)
by Hallie Tressie Spraggins Whitten, (1914 – 2012)

Back Cover Photo Credit
by Mick Haupt (Unsplash.com), Yosemite, USA
I would like to thank God for this beautiful scene and
thank Mr. Haupt for capturing a beautiful moment in time!

Contents

Acknowledgements, 7

About this book, 9

The educational process, 13

Home school activities, 19

Section 1: Spiritual Preparation

Chapter 1: Introduction, 20 Steps for moving to the country, 31

Chapter 2: Bible and other country living quotes, 47

Chapter 3: Special equations, 53

Chapter 4: Simplicity principle, 55

Chapter 5: Downsizing for country living, 61

Chapter 6: Character development, 71

Chapter 7: Your brain, what it means to be human, and the frontal lobes, 75

Section 2: Country Living Health and Lifestyle

Chapter 8: Clean up your living environment, 95

Chapter 9: Time spent outdoors, etc., 105

Chapter 10: Chronobiology and country living, 113

Chapter 11: 5G – Electromagnetic pollution and country living, 121

Chapter 12: Take down inflammation, 129

Chapter 13: Hydrotherapy, 133

Chapter 14: Lymphatics, 141

Section 3: Country Living Nutrition

Chapter 15: Restore normal gut functions, 149

Chapter 16: Top off vitamins, minerals and antioxidants, 157

Chapter 17: Plant-based food guidance, 167

Meals Matter: Take Your Pick ©, 183

Take your pick! Sample plant-based menus ©, 186

Lifestyle guidance—make each lifestyle habit count: take your pick! ©, 189

Chapter 18: Vaccine detoxificatioRen: before and after, 193

Chapter 19: Immunity, covid-19 and other pathologic microorganisms, 201

Five Natural Plant-based Covid-19 Prevention, Treatment and Recovery Protocols

1. Prevention Protocol
2. Mild Symptoms, Early Viral Stage Protocol (no hospitalization required)
3. Major Symptoms, Late Viral Stage, Early Host Immune Response Stage with Cytokine Storm and Oxidative Stress Protocol
4. Major Symptoms, Ongoing Host Inflammatory Response Stage with Cytokine Storm, Oxidative Stress and Multi-system Organ Dysfunction Syndrome (MODS) Protocol (usually hospitalized)
5. Recovery Protocol (quick recovery and long hauler's)
   Chapter 20: Health parties, 241

Section 4: Country Living Plant-based Culinary Arts
Chapter 21: The green smoothie, 245
Chapter 22: Fresh juices as part of a healthy lifestyle, 251
Chapter 23: Using and preserving the harvest, 257
Chapter 24: Plant-based food for 4 for a Year, 259
Chapter 25: Learn to cook: the choir of flavors and flavor corrections, 265

Section 5: The Country Living Medicine Cabinet and Essential Skills
Chapter 26: Country living medicine cabinet essentials, 275
Chapter 27: Make herbal teas, infusions and elixirs, 281
Chapter 28: Make oxymels, cordials, shrubs and electuaries, 289
Chapter 29: Make electrolyte water, 295
Chapter 30: Make alkaline water and nebulizing formulas, 297
Chapter 31: Make charcoal, clay, diatomaceous earth (DE), or zeolite water, 299
Chapter 32: When and how to make antibiotic type juices, 301
Chapter 33: Make natural quinine-containing syrup, 305
Chapter 34: Make decoctions, tinctures, bitters and extracts, 307
Chapter 35: Make plant powders, 311
Chapter 36: Make plasters, poultices, compresses and fomentations, 313
Chapter 37: Make clay masks, add clay to soaps, shampoo bars, etc., 317
Chapter 38: Make a face wash and hand sanitizer, 319
Chapter 39: Make sinus rinses and nasal sprays, 321
Chapter 40: Make natural gargling liquids, throat sprays and room sprays, 323
Chapter 41: Make natural hair shampoo, rinse and detangler, 325
Chapter 42: Make laundry, hand soaps and deodorants, 327
Chapter 43: Make herbal bath bombs, sugar scrub and exfoliating paste, 329
Chapter 44: Make herbal mineral soaking water, 331
Chapter 45: Make a salve, balm, ointment or liniment, 333
Chapter 46: Make lozenges and gummy swallows, 337
Chapter 47: Make a natural toothpaste and tooth wash, 339
Chapter 48: Make colloidal silver, 341
Chapter 49: Activated charcoal, 343
Chapter 50: Medicine cabinet herbs and other items, 345
Chapter 51: Basic medical equipment to have on hand, 363

Section 6: Country Living Land & Homes
Chapter 52: Find and evaluate the land and the location, 367
Chapter 53: Evaluate the homestead and other structures, 379

Section 7: Potential Country Living Income Streams
Chapter 54: Monetize your country home, 393

Section 8: Country Living Gardens and Landscaping
Chapter 55: "Am I ready to garden?", 405
Chapter 56: Basic gardening terminology and techniques, 407
Chapter 57: Long-term garden and outdoor planning, 415
Chapter 58: What and how much to plant, 427
Chapter 59: High yield fast-growing fruits and vegetables, 429
Chapter 60: A word about tomatoes, 443
Chapter 61: Edible Plants, Bushes, Vines and Trees, 447
Chapter 62: Edible Wild Plants, 463
Chapter 63: Herb garden: 20 essential herbs, 471
Chapter 64: Flower gardens, 475
Chapter 65: Orchards, 481
Chapter 66: The vineyard, 485
Chapter 67: Experimental, demonstration and test gardens, 491
Chapter 68: Green houses, orangeries, hoop houses, walipinis, high and low tunnels, 493
Chapter 69: Great plant combinations, 497
Chapter 70: Privacy hedgerows: vines and trees, 499
Chapter 71: Plants for repelling pests, 503

Section 9: Small building projects for consideration
Chapter 72: Small building projects, 507
Chapter 73: Solar and wind energy, 511
Chapter 74: Build a root cellar, 515
Chapter 75: Build a solar dehydrator, 519
Chapter 76: Build raised beds, 521
Chapter 77: Build a strawberry tower, 523
Chapter 78: Build a chicken coop, 525
Chapter 79: Build a small chapel on your property, 527

Section 10: Civil Unrest, Local and National Emergencies
Chapter 80: Make plans for civil unrest, local and national emergencies, 531

The Appendix

Section 1: Spiritual Preparation
My God Given Tasks, 534
Country Living Personal Skills Inventory (PSI), 535
A Collection of Scripture Promises, 543
Types of Cognitive Biases, 552
The Holmes-Rahe Life Stress Inventory, 558

Section 2: Country Living Health and Lifestyle
Hydrotherapy Methods and Techniques, 559

Section 3: Country Living Nutrition
Histamine Intolerance, 564

Section 4: Country Living Plant-based Culinary Arts

Section 5: The Country Living Medicine Cabinet and Essential Skills

Section 6: Country Living Land and Homes

Section 7: Potential Country Living Income Streams
Care Giver Daily Activity and Progress Note, 569

Section 8: Country Living Gardens and Landscaping
12 Months of Gardening Tasks, 571

Section 9: Small Building Projects

Section 10: Civil Unrest and Local and National Emergencies
Age Appropriate First Aid Kits, 573
Emergency Services Contact Numbers and Locations
- Construction, Fire, Local Utilities, Neighbors, Police, Utilities, 575
- Church and Clergy, 576
- Friends and Relatives, 576
- Websites and News Outlets, 576
- News Outlets: Radio Stations, TV Stations and HAM Radio Operators, 576
- Medical and Emergency Type Services Directory, 577

Emergency Supply List, 578
Contingency Group Plans, 580
Vital Document Checklist, 581

Back cover
Woods, by Hallie Tressie Spraggins Whitten, 1967

Acknowledgements

Evelyn Whitten (1934 – 2009) – The greatest inspiration for almost everything I do! I thank her for all the great stories she told us as we were growing up about how she hated living in the country. She did not enjoy trekking outside to an outhouse and using the Sears catalogue. She worried about running into snakes all the time. She had to wash, dry and iron all the laundry by hand using an iron heated on a hot wood burning stove. She watched in horror as her mother or grandmother would kill a chicken to cook and it would run around with its head cut off (definitely motivation for me to become a vegetarian at age 5), etc. For these reasons and more, Mother loved modernity and every modern appliance and device she ever met, therefore I loved the country. She was an English teacher who loved poetry, in particular, the American poets including Robert Frost, Emily Dickinson, John Keats, Henry David Thoreau, etc. I too share her love for poetry.

Wesley Whitten (1932 – 2023), Professional Engineer – Both my parents, Wes and Evelyn Whitten, were hard workers. However, Dad takes first place to anyone else I have ever known. By his admission, one of the keys to his success as a mechanical engineer who specialized in thermodynamics, was perseverance. When others had given up on a task, Dad found a way to make it happen. More recently, I have enjoyed working with Dad on a small electronic device, known as the venom desensitizer, which we hope to put into production soon. Dad has been a faithful editor and constructive critic of almost everything I have written since I began writing my dissertation – all 5,500 pages or so of my collective writings since 2007.

Mom (Margaret Belding Culpepper) – My maternal grandmother married very young and had my mother shortly after turning 17. When I was born, my grandmother did not want to be called "Grandma" so she became "Mom" and Mother became known as Mother. Mom was one of the greatest farm girls who ever lived. She married early, started a family right away, set up a large garden, cooked almost everything from scratch for most of her life, preserved food for the winter, prepped and used up all the animals and fish my grandpa hunted down for food, rescued innumerable cats and dogs, and sewed most of her clothes. She was the original "meals on wheels" service, delivering thousands of meals over many decades to anyone in need. Almost every day of the week she delivered her home-made meals to her home-bound friends. She decorated using mainly natural elements, arranged flowers, baked bread almost every day, made coffee for anyone who stopped by her country home between the hours of 4:30 am to 10 am, made the best pizza I have ever had, and managed to raise 4 kids – all while living a modest Christian life in the country on a meager income.

Hallie Spraggins Whitten (1912 – 2012) – My paternal grandmother had 7 children and lived her entire life in the country, much of that time she lived as a widow. She spent her days studying the Bible and listening to TV evangelists. She probably never weighed more than 100 pounds but could herd cattle, kill rattlesnakes, stay active in church events, study her Bible and keep up with 7 kids, 24 grand kids and lots of great grands!

My 4-legged children – God blessed me with four wonderful dogs, **Shelby** (1990-2007), **Speckles 1** (2004 – 2016) and **Jack** (2005 – 2020) – I have written 5 books and a 1,076 page dissertation (5,500+ pages total) with Shelby, Speckles and Jack by my side or at my feet (see page 382 for pics). Miss them! As of 4 Jan 2022, I found an an older **Speckles 2 eating a dead dear while I was driving** along a deserted stretch of I-70 in Oklahoma. She now occupies a huge place in my heart!

Grace Oh and Bob Iacono (1952 – 2007), MDs – Grace Oh, an ophthalmologist and retina specialist, has been a faithful and supportive "sister" and an incredible source of scientific information. For many years, her husband Bob Iacono, MD, FACS, a neurosurgeon and friend, provided mentoring and inspiration for learning about the brain and chronic neurodegenerative conditions associated with dysregulation of neurotransmitters and deficiency of vitamins and minerals. His philosophy, "make the brain so healthy it cannot harbor disease," drives my understanding of alternative approaches for achieving health and wellness. Together they have two amazing children, Robert and Rose.

Marlene Brewer, PhD – Thank you for box after box of tropical sorbet and the hours you spent critiquing this book.

Bozena and Paul Wentland, MS/MD – For hundreds of telephone calls, prayers and support of each other over the years! Bozena has been a faithful and loving friend, a "sister" in Christ. In part, her experiences while living in Croatia during the 1990s have helped to broaden my perspectives on the importance of promoting peace and shunning all forms of violence and war.

Leona and Norman Gulley, PhDs – "Focus on Christ and not the crisis." One of my favorite Norman Gulley quotes. This quote drives my philosophy on country living and preparing for troublous times ahead. Leona, another "sister" in Christ, has faithfully shown kindness, love and care to me since we met in 2013. The Gulley's are friends and colleagues. They provided invaluable insights into scriptures.

Jann and Stan Abrams, RN/MD – They are great friends and have always provided a place to crash and learn. They have been invaluable for listening and adding important content to my writing. Stan's knowledge of energy medicine has invaluably enriched my life. Have enjoyed learning about venom detoxification methods and working on the venom desensitizer with Stan and Dad. Since my mother's death, Jann's loving and kind nature has been a constant source of encouragement and blessings.

Janet and Neil Lovitt, RN/MD – For many hours of critiquing and our many discussions of these topics.

Sue and Ron Patterson – For their spiritual insights, loving care, and open arms!

Danielle Bunkley – A beautiful friend always willing to help with feedback.

Morris Venden (1932 – 2013) – As one of his Southern California parishioners from several decades ago, pastor Venden's words (written and spoken) and sermons have been a constant source of inspiration. He had a knack for making the mundane funny, for piercing honesty, and for planting in me a longing for a closer walk with the Lord.

Ellen G. White – From the time I began reading her books, I never doubted her inspiration and dedication to the Gospel! Her writings have shaped much of my thinking.

God and the Bible's Scribes – Nothing about life makes sense unless we consider it in the context of a loving Lord, Creator, Saviour, Friend, Redeemer, Father, Husband, Confidante, and Adonai-Jehovah! What a privilege it is to know Him through Scripture and through a close walk with Him! God (God the Father, Jesus Christ our Redeemer, and the Holy Spirit our Comforter and a perfect reflection of Christ) is love!

About this book

This book is for people attempting to move out of the crowded cities into a country setting. It is meant to be a general guide or even a blueprint. It is designed to encourage further exploration and research. It may be used in group settings such as camp meetings, self-help groups, church groups, etc., for stimulating interest in moving to the country. Each chapter could be further developed and used as the backbone for a seminar or informational session. It may also be used as a home school textbook. Most chapters end with discussion questions and serve to stimulate additional research.

As you read through this book, keep the following questions and comments in mind:

- How does this knowledge, action or theory promote the Gospel and the Kingdom of God?
- Will doing this make me a better person and increase my desire for a closer walk with God?
- Is it important to examine the moral issues and the spiritual lessons to be learned from our experiences?
- Are the fruits of the Spirit present and a driving force in my life and everything I do, including: love, kindness, gentleness, joy, peace, patience, goodness, faithfulness, long-suffering, and self-control? Is your ego or pride getting in the way of true conversion? Are you a humble servant or do you seek to be right, erudite, etc.? Do you seek to put others in their place or do you seek to preserve each man's dignity? Do you tend to unite or divide? Do you demand others serve you? Are you willing to serve those with whom you disagree with? Do you frequently speak negatively about people or situations? Are you polite to everyone? Are you classy? Do you do the right thing even when it is inconvenient?
- Is there an expanding or contracting element in my spiritual insights? In other words, do my insights into the character of God expand, enlighten and make me love Him even more, or do they restrict God to a limited narrative?
- Are you inwardly or outwardly focused? Are you more interested in your personal experiences, enriching your own spaces, or do you have an active outreach into the community?
- Are you willing to show compassion and care to animals in need?
- The number "7," as it is used in the Bible is used to reflect fulfillment, perfection, exoneration, etc. John, in Revelation 1:4 (7 Spirits before the throne of God), 3:1 (7 Spirits of God possessed by Christ), 4:5 (7 Spirits of God symbolized by the seven lamps of fire burning before the throne), and 5:6 (the Lamb's 7 eyes which are the 7 Spirits of God) uses the number "7" to illustrate perfection and completeness, both physical and spiritual. The number "7" is used 54 times just in the book of Revelation. Isaiah and John the Revelator, give us insight into the work of the Holy Spirit on earth. John mentions the 7 stars (angels of the 7 churches), 7 golden lampstands (churches), and the sevenfold activity of the Holy Spirit. Isaiah 11, confirms the work of the Holy Spirit in reflecting the life and atonement of Christ. Read about the seven

ways the Holy Spirit ministers in our lives and works through us, including: 1. the Spirit of the Lord in me, 2. increasing in wisdom, 3. gaining in understanding, 4. counsel of might in all matters of my life, 5. imparting to me strength, 6. acquiring knowledge, and 7. having the fear of the Lord.

- Is the Holy Spirit working in your life? Do you feel the Holy Spirit is impressing you to move to the country, acquire new skills, help others in their endeavors to move to the country, spend time in God's word, preach God's word, raise your children to live holy lives, etc.? If you do not feel the Holy Spirit is working in you, ask yourself why this might be the case.
- How do wisdom and knowledge reflect on God's loving character?
- Is this wisdom and knowledge a principle, something which holds true across all cultures, all times, and all peoples, or is this referring to a guideline, which is culturally specific and does not necessarily apply to everyone?
- Should we operate outside of our small sphere of influence? (Doing things for others which have no direct reward for us and our family other than we are acting as Christ's emissary on earth?)
- Is there a therapeutic principle involved in this information; if the answer is "yes," describe it.
- Is a healing principle revealed for those with spiritual eyesight; if the answer is "yes," describe it?
- Does this information or knowledge provide an "entering wedge" to win souls to Christ?

Love for Jesus and a passion to introduce others to Jesus motivates and drives the true Christian. The study of scriptures is the best preparation for life. Expensive and prestigious schools impress some, but Heavenly occupants are thrilled when we open the Bible for instruction and direction in life. Constant communication with the Father keeps us in the best position to make choices which reflect the will of the Father. Even when our choices are less than perfect, we can rely on our heavenly Father to be with us through the vagaries of life. At one time or another, everyone you love invariably disappoints or fails you in some way. In the final analysis, for Christians, the true constant in life is a growing relationship with Christ. Understanding how Christ and the cross intimately connect us for eternity is a critical spiritual milestone. Understanding the depth of God's love for every single human who has ever inhabited the earth is beyond our comprehension. When Christ died for us, he took our sins and infirmities and atoned for them. We have nothing to fear except we reject Him. He wants to teach us complete reliance upon him.

Transitions are hard. Make sure your move to the country is a God-filled journey. Just like any other aspect of life, it will include many trials and joys. Every chapter in this book addresses one or more aspects of country living. No one family's experience encompasses every challenge. A second volume is in progress and includes more in-depth information in the areas of health and wellness.

Originally, this information was to be presented at conferences in March and April of 2020. However, as you may recall, a worldwide pandemic ensued and indelibly changed our lives. The meetings were canceled due to an invisible 'viral' particle, known as a corona virus (SARS-Cov-2). The handouts were done and I was disappointed I would not be able to fellowship with other like-minded individuals over the content. One night it dawned on me, why not compile the handouts into a booklet and publish it. This way it could benefit a larger audience and hopefully be a blessing to many instead of a few. I hope you appreciate the content, which in many cases, is not necessarily mine, but is considered common knowledge, not attributable to a single source. An example of this is giving information about plant requirements and growing conditions. There are many sources which say the same thing and very few of the sources cite a primary reference. In such cases, I have used several sources to provide a range or have incorporated my experiences with a specific plant or technique.

Each chapter usually ends with several sections. One section is dedicated to resources. This is where you can explore references and sources, internet resources, books, movies related to the content of the chapter. In some chapters there is a section dedicated to discussion questions. This section is good for using with groups. The questions are designed to stimulate meaningful and relevant conversations about the content.

As a former university professor for over 20 years, I spent a good part of my professional life grading for style and content. However, this booklet does not have a professional editor and does not follow a specific style. I made the decision to forego editing services because at the time of this writing, I was working with an editor on another book. It did not seem feasible to take on a 2nd editing project. While it is never purposeful to publish something not 100% perfect, it is also a type of document which does not require complete perfection.

Most of this information comes from experience, research, discussions with key people, and hopefully a little heavenly inspiration! Some of the graphics are in the public domain and when copyrighted, are noted as such. They are not my documents. Most Bible texts are from the KJV, NIV and RSV. Ellen White quotes are from the search engine at this webpage: www.whiteestate.org

Other quotes are given attribution when possible. However, The Food and Lifestyle Guidance graphics as well as the Plant-based menus are under copyright protection. This is the first publication of these graphics; if you want to use them please give attribution as follows:

"Plant-based food guidance – meals matter: take your pick" ©,

Take your pick! Sample plant-based menus ©,

"Lifestyle guidance – make each lifestyle habit count: take your pick!" ©

Developed and published by Crystal Whitten, at Build a Better You (www.buildabetteryou.us)."
Send correspondence to: phytochemwhitten@yahoo.com with "Country Living" in the subject line.

The educational process

Most of my life has either been in the role of a student, as an educator, a researcher, or as a clinician. All roles are amazing! When it comes to education, it is critical to keep the end in mind as well as the process.

Either by choice or now due to Covid-19, more and more parents are choosing to educate their children at home while supplementing language lessons, sports sessions, music lessons, and science labs. The parent educator might be the most difficult position in the field of education. As an educator, you rapidly see where you have succeeded as well as failed in the parenting department. In a sense, this is a good outcome because it allows you to recalibrate early in the process. It is a sacred honor to be involved in the education process, especially when the targets of your education are your children and the goal of their education is Christ-centered.

Educators convey information as well as methods of interacting with information.

Education, while formally forced into an organized, time-constrained and linear classroom experience, is oftentimes chaotic, unique, and sometimes is unduly influenced by the times in which we live. Certain aspects of education tend to be experiential in nature. It is always a synthesis of the participants, the facilitators, and the unique time and place where education occurs. Many outside influences bring their forces to bear on the educational process. As public education significantly morphs away from historical standards and benchmarks, there is a push to examine alternatives to traditional public schools and universities. Information is readily available, but without context and experience, information is oftentimes not useful and serves as a flimsy construct of an "educated" person. Content needs anchors. If no anchors exist, what is considered standard content may constantly change. There is a lot to learn in this book. Whether or not you use this book as a homeschool textbook or whether you use it as a reference, the content is extensive. Some content may be new and some may be familiar. This short chapter is not meant to be an exhaustive treatise on what works and what does not work in the field of education. It is included because I believe others could possibly learn one or two critical nuggets from my experiences as well as from the experience of other educators. I am not the first person to make these observations. Most educators eventually land on this shore.

There is grave danger in constantly calibrating educational content to social constructs.

The content in this text is aimed at somewhere around a high school level but in some places, it is at a college level (e.g., Chapters 18 and 19). This means some content is more challenging than most. However, I have always found that when challenged, the human spirit usually rises to the occasion. If the information is too complex or detailed, skip through it. Others may have an appreciation for it. Hopefully there is something for everyone in this book. This book is appropriate for using as an introductory text on Country Living. It could be used as a primary or secondary text in the following types of classes and / or programs: religion, agriculture, general studies, nutrition, herbology, etc.

Intelligence is how we process information. Information may consist of processing numbers and developing and applying equations or it may consist of culturally specific ways of communicating or solving social problems. Keep in mind there are many types of intelligence. Howard Gardner's theory of multiple intelligences proposes up to 12 types of intelligence including mathematical (logic based), musical, intra-personal, interpersonal, linguistic, spatial, kinesthetic, naturalistic, spiritual, existential, and moral intelligences. Some people amass huge amounts of information and transform it into knowledge to help others. Some hone their knowledge to the extent they can rapidly find the information and present a simple, elegant lecture. Sometimes knowledge is complex and nuanced and sometimes it is straightforward. We can have endless debates about which type of intelligence is superior, but ultimately, each type of intelligence plays a role in an advanced society. It is important to learn to appreciate all types of intelligence and their anthropomorphic package.

You may be teaching a Bible study class, leading out in youth groups, teaching health and cooking classes, preaching weekly sermons, mentoring young people, teaching at the local community college or university, or you may be raising children. Everyone is an educator. Share your successes with others. We can all learn from each other. Education is critical to successful relationships, whether in the home, social, or work realms. We educate our family and friends about how to treat us, we define relationship boundaries, we educate our children in regards to acceptable behaviors, we educate high school students in reading, writing and arithmetic. The physician educates their patients about avoiding high risk behaviors. The dentist educates their patients about optimal oral care. A wife may need to educate her shy husband about how to demonstrate love and affection. A father may educate his daughter on how to trouble shoot car issues.

This reminds me of dad, who several months before I took off for my sophomore year of college with one of the family cars, spent several hours beginning at 8 am, every Sunday morning teaching me how to clean and adjust spark plug gaps, change the oil, change a tire, adjust the timing, tighten the belt, flush the radiator, etc. As a 19-year old college student, I was completely uninterested in car engines. I distinctly remember "failing" almost every session, much to Dad's frustration. Unbeknownst to me, before I left, he attached labels to some of the major parts of the car as a reminder. Later, this provided a humorous moment when I took the car to get gas and the attendant checked the oil (this was in Oregon at a time when only an attendant could pump your gas and even though I attended college in Washington state, many of the female students drove the few miles to Oregon to fill up). Fortunately, the car never broke down or needed anything but gas. Looking back on this experience, I think about how I could have been a better student and Dad could have used some positive motivators to snag my interest. Fast forward several decades, I am a little more comfortable around car engines and helping to troubleshoot car issues. It did not happen overnight, but the early exposure to car engines, as traumatic as it was, paved the way for a better relationship with cars. This also points to the fact that the education process is never complete and it is certainly never perfect.

If you are an educator, even if you are a home-schooling parent, you may find something of value in the following list of educational principles and practices (not in hierarchal order):

1. Start with an outline for each class and prepare, prepare, prepare!
2. Learn everyone's name (should not be difficult if you are homeschooling).
3. Make eye contact with every student in the room at some point during class time.
4. Try to speak to everyone in the classroom either before or after class time.
5. Remember to smile.
6. Appreciate the differences in each student.

7. Avoid the appearance of favoritism – even though you may have favorites.
8. Avoid non-classroom involvement with students unless everyone is involved.
9. Establish office hours right before and right after class times.
10. Establish acceptable classroom etiquette / boundaries.
11. Define success and failure in learning terms.
12. Always start at the beginning, describe the process of getting to the destination, and then define the destination; repeat at the beginning of every class period.
13. Require each student to turn off their phone and laptop computer during class time unless advised otherwise. It usually works best if they leave their electronic devices, including phones, at the front of the classroom.
14. Quickly "remove" the non-attenders and the ones who you believe may not successfully complete the course. Give them an opportunity to do something different such as spending time in the library reading books, working on inventions, etc.
15. Set up a regular communication schedule with the students.
16. Tell them what you plan to cover, then cover that material, then summarize what you covered.
17. Drop hooks which link the current class content to future and previous class topics.
18. If you can, teach people how to think, solve problems and process information.
19. In the nicest way possible, inform your students their feelings about a subject or topic are not necessarily critical to their educational process. For example, if they register for nursing school and hate needles, their feelings about needles while "real" are not hugely important to their instructors (unless they cannot overcome their "feelings" toward needles). They must learn to reform their feelings and successfully use needles if they want to complete nursing school. What is important is developing a skill and refining their feelings to include successful mastery of needles used in nursing. Too much emphasis on feelings has led to a "feeling and emotional autocracy" where feelings and emotions trump common sense, facts and truth. Some may prefer an empathetic instructor who spends hours listening to their "feelings" while others do better with a facts-oriented, humorous instructor. This is where temperament and personality converge with education to give it many memorable moments.
20. Learn to laugh at yourself.
21. Begin the year with giving the students the assignment to take the Myers-Briggs Type Indicator (MBTI) questionnaire. This gives you valuable information about each student and how you may interact with them. Here is a website to take the test: http://www.humanmetrics.com/cgi-win/jtypes2.asp
22. Your syllabus is a legal document – include everything relevant to successful completion of the class in the syllabus (i.e., class dates, attendance, test dates, objectives, goals, assignments, lecture topics).
23. Allow students to toss one low quiz score, but don't tell them until toward end of the grading period.
24. When appropriate, provide the opportunity to skip the final exam if they are at 99.8% or more of total points possible, but do not tell them until the end of the grading period. This may not apply to every teaching semester / quarter / unit.
25. Learn to love grading – it is the best feedback reflecting how well you are teaching.
26. Require at least one outside reading book from a list of acceptable books. Have them summarize this book as part of an exam.
27. To ensure fair grading, use at least two graders, each using a different colored ink. Keep in mind, grading is about sharpening their knowledge and not just criticizing their effort.
28. Offer one or two extra credit points on each exam for the over-achievers.

29. Plan something for everyone (if you are an educator, you know what I mean).
30. With complex ideas, it is impossible to go from A (the beginning) to Z (the end) in a short period of time. This is probably one of the most frustrating aspects of education. As an educator, I am happy to take a student from point D to point E or F, knowing that it may take decades to actually reach point Z. In fact, there might be several iterations of going from point A to point Z.
31. When possible, tell stories and case studies which illustrate your objectives.
32. Each step in the process has value.
33. Not all students begin at the same place or progress at the same rate and yet everyone sits in the same classroom, "hears" the same information, but assimilates the information differently.
34. Use medical or other types of riddles to pique interest. Solve the riddle during the next class period.
35. Knowing and understanding the terminology is critical to being on the same page. Review previous terminology and definitions and go over the new ones.
36. Don't assume the students hear or understand you.
37. Always start on time.
38. Pray before class starts (whether out loud, with the class, or silently).
39. Information is not knowledge (many young people do not understand this).
40. Information without a grid of experience and understanding is worthless.
41. Knowledge without application is worthless.
42. A knowledge seeker usually is good at "self-education."
43. A resistant student rarely gleans long-term knowledge, but just enough to satisfy the requirements.
44. Motivation can change in the blink of an eye (for better or worse).
45. Motivation is almost always internal.
46. Perseverance, combined with expert knowledge and strategy, usually wins the day.
47. To do lists are critical – they help organize the brain and establish critical and logical steps.
48. Always keep in mind the endpoint.
49. Sometimes it looks like you are going off track, but the diversion may be essential to the process.
50. Education is about teasing and building anticipation of what is to come through stories, analogy, and case studies.
51. **Competing values must be reconciled before education can proceed.**
52. Not everyone is educable. Trying to force education on this person at this time may result in harm.
53. Not everything of great value can be taught via lecture or even hands-on.
54. No part of the educational process should conflict with Biblical principles.
55. True education never demeans humanity or teaches methods and means of destroying it.
56. Yes, there are some dumb questions, but try to understand where the questioner is coming from.
57. Some of your students have minor limitations such as Asperger's syndrome (i.e., a mild, high functioning individual on the autism spectrum who may have social issues, difficulties with non-verbal communication, etc.). Seek to better understand functional approaches to their limitations.
58. Sometimes students act angry or disinterested but it is oftentimes largely unrelated to classroom interactions (i.e., usually something at home or a broken or stressful relationship). When possible, find out if they are "OK."
59. Most students have an elevated opinion of their abilities. This is ok. Don't convince them otherwise.
60. There may be one or two students in class whose intellectual abilities exceed that of the professor's. Let them make meaningful contributions!
61. Higher education coincides with the early stages of adulthood. Many educators today believe the "teenage" years extend into the late 20s to the early 30s. Behaviors typical of 17, 18 and 19 year old students are now common in students who are in their late 20's and even early 30's.

62. Just because someone doesn't seem to be smart doesn't mean they are hopeless. Even some "dummies," with the right inputs, can learn to think and succeed beyond expectations.
63. Hecklers are a valuable classroom asset. Learn how to effectively use them and to love them.
64. Never give the same test twice.
65. Good test questions are difficult to write. Use validated questions or slightly modified questions.
66. If re-using an exam, reword test questions and offer different answer options.
67. Ladies, never wear the exact same outfit over the course of a semester; for the male professors, vary what you wear by different suits, socks and ties.
68. Dress up and look professional. Kids need to see professionalism modeled.
69. Bring in guest speakers with a different perspective.
70. Always put at least one space between seats during exams and use several roaming test monitors to prevent cheating. Videotaping the exam is even better.
71. Offer exam review sessions if necessary.
72. Go over the exam answers – this is an excellent teaching moment.
73. If a student must take the exam at a different time their exam grade must be docked by one letter grade for each change of schedule. No exceptions.
74. Invest in the student's success while realizing you cannot push them over the finish line.
75. Be kinder than you oftentimes feel.
76. In like a lion, out like a lamb.
77. Maintain high standards.
78. Treat everyone the same, knowing that personal interactions are highly variable and may require individualized interactions.
79. Do not allow students to bully or demean you or another student.
80. Anonymize your grading system.
81. The textbook may be inadequate; supplemental information is usually needed.
82. Group projects require excellent chemistry between the group participants and highly motivated and honest members. Unfortunately, they are oftentimes disastrous, unless you are dealing with upper classmen and even then...
83. Learn how to teach teamwork if you can pull it off (i.e., group assignments).
84. If possible, introduce novel technology to the class such as 3-D printing, holograms, etc.
85. You don't know everything. Show humility of thought and purpose.
86. Require attendance, connecting their grade to their attendance.
87. Give one assignment which requires they not attend one class. For example, require they do some kind of class-related activity such as observing athletic performance of elite athletes, cognitive testing on relatives, etc. Require video proof they completed the out-of-class assignment.
88. If you want to ascertain their writing level, spelling and grammar ability, give them a surprise in-class 15-minute writing assignment to use as a comparison for future writing assignments.
89. When it comes to content, understand the difference between "signal" and "noise."
90. If your class requires a pre-requisite, give a short exam to ensure this content requirement is met.
91. At least one time provide the class with a treat like donuts, cookies, granola bars, etc. Start out saying something like, "I have never done this before..." This may be true if you always provide them with something different.
92. Have fun with your class. This works better with grade school, middle school and high school students. This reminds me of a friend and fellow educator who planned a field trip for his high school students.

He obtained authorization, and the required paperwork from each student's parents. On the day of the field trip, 1 April, the students eagerly awaited the arrival of the buses, he emerged from the building and led them in several laps around the field – the field trip he had promised them, on April 1st. Only one parent called to query exactly where they were going and they were sworn to secrecy. It's good to keep the students' guessing and on their toes. The students learned a few good lessons that day.

93. Be memorable for the right reasons.
94. Do not assume you understand their questions – always clarify.
95. Give a one- or two-point quiz at the beginning of class. This discourages tardiness.
96. Clickers are a great way to monitor interest and learning during class times.
97. Pay attention to the prosody of your voice including the pitch, loudness, length of sounds, etc.
98. If you have a foreign accent or a heavy southern accent, work to improve your word pronunciation.
99. If you find it hard to get students to settle down and start class, stand at the front and do not say a single word. Don't look at them except maybe a quick glance but no direct eye contact – you can occupy yourself without having to speak. Maybe look at your notes, tap your index finger, sit on the table, file your nails, do whatever, but ignore the students. Within less than a minute, the class will be so quiet you could hear a pin drop. If that doesn't work, take out your gradebook and start placing zero's in everyone's column and then walk out. Never beg your students to be quiet. They may end up not respecting you. Hopefully this never happens to you, but be prepared if it gets to this point.
100. **Sometimes, the dog does eat their homework...** It was after midnight. As a doctoral graduate student, I had just finished up a long paper which included several hand-drawn biochemical pathways. I attached the stack of papers with a clamp, placed it on top of my laptop computer and put both away under my bed. Exhausted, I crawled into bed and slept a few short hours before I had to wake up, go to class, and turn in the paper. Upon waking, I noticed the paper was missing. I looked everywhere until I saw something in Speckles' bed, my 1-year old border collie full of energy and sometimes unresolved angst. She was my fearless companion and an endless source of entertainment and happiness, even when she destroyed my favorite purse or pair of shoes. I saw a few shreds of paper in her bed but I never found the rest. It was enough to indict and convict her in about half a second. Having been a professor for a number of years before this time, I had heard every excuse about what happened to homework, including the "dog ate my paper" excuse. I never believed these excuses until that morning when it happened to me. Speckles, my smart little border collie, put me in checkmate – my professor would never believe my excuse and I dared never to mention it. I quickly redrew the pathways and reprinted the paper and everything turned out ok.
101. Speaking of dogs, take your dog to class (if allowed). If you have a well-behaved dog who does not nip or cause a disturbance, taking the dog may calm frazzled students' nerves.
102. Don't let your students throw you off with their passive aggressive behaviors. Acknowledge them and keep moving on.

Home school activities

You may want to use this book as a home school textbook. This text contains 80 chapters of varying length. Each chapter contains dense content, worthy of study and additional research. Each chapter is focused on providing actionable content.

This section may be a good place to point out the difference between truth and facts. Facts are usually thought to be irrefutable, hard evidence of something, but unless we understand additional things such as context, motivation, history, etc., we may miss arriving at the real truth. Do the facts represent truth? Not always. Data is applied to situations where it belongs. Extrapolation of data is taking data and projecting it to a situation where it might apply, given the backdrop of experience, good judgment, clear thinking and the application of Biblical principles. Just because you glean information from a "www.xxxxx.org" web page does not make it credible. Just because an article is published in a journal and can be found as part of the PubMed data base, does not make it 100% truthful or even relevant to your situation. Data is always the product of human activity and is always subject to error, interpretation bias, and improper application. I certainly use the PubMed database but I integrate the information and sometimes I extrapolate the findings. Both are legitimate uses of data. I integrate data with my training, past clinical experience, best judgment, personal experience, other articles, and discussions with experts. In the case where no obvious harm is apparent and a possible benefit may be gleaned (which is largely the realm of nutrition and lifestyle approaches to achieving health), extrapolation of data is used to make decisions and achieve relevant progress. This is why it is important to do your own research based on your history and in the context of your life experiences. This is why many parents choose to home school their children.

If you are traveling and happen to have this book with you and your kids want to know what to do, the first activity is a search-and-find exercise. There are 219 words in this book which may be new or at least used in a different context (<u>Activity 1</u>). Learning definitions is fun and educational. See how many definitions you can collect. If the definition is not clearly spelled out in the book, look it up in a dictionary. Children oftentimes appear frustrated and give up on the educational moment or process when they do not fully understand a word or term. This is also true for reading the Bible when it comes to understanding words like "justification" and "sanctification." To the degree words cause confusion, children may reject the learning process. They may also reject values which are poorly defined or values they see in conflict with real life experiences.

Learning the terminology of any field is a large chunk of the educational process. Dwelling on the meaning of words can be done in casual moments with your family and as you go about your daily business. Start with small children and see how their minds grasp words and their meanings and then how they begin to use their new vocabulary to describe their surroundings. This reminds me of when my friends 5 year old son who, while he was sautéeing kale and garlic together one evening, described in detail how kale and garlic upregulated the CYP450 detoxification enzymes in the liver. Yes, this occurred when he was 5 years of age (both parents are physicians). Another time while sitting in church and listening to the children's story, the narrator asked the children if they had heard about photosynthesis. A small child stood up and proceeded to give an excellent definition of photosynthesis using scientific terms. After an incredible 30+ seconds of his definition, the audience (largely made up of medical professionals) broke out in thunderous applause. Childhood is the best time to insert as many words and definitions as possible into their verbal dictionary. Many 5- or 10-minute discussions about photosynthesis during the autumn months serve to cement the concept into their mind and lays the groundwork for even greater future insights and revelations.

Activity 2, includes using the PubMed database. When you see the letters "PMID," they stand for PubMed IDentifier number (see red arrow in Figure 1). Almost every scientific publication is logged in the PubMed database. Each article is given a unique identifier number, known as the PMID. When you go to the PubMed webpage, https://pubmed.ncbi.nlm.nih.gov/ you are able to enter the PMID number and pull up the reference article associated with that number (see Figure 1). Usually an abstract is available to read, but not always. An abstract is a short summary of the information in the research article. Some abstracts provide a link to read the entire article for free. Sometimes the article is available for a fee. In most cases, I primarily accessed abstracts and free articles as references.

When you read a research article, it usually is broken down into the following sections: The publication journal and date of publication, the title, authors, author affiliations, identifiers, the abstract (objectives, methods, results, conclusions, discussion), key words and acronyms, introduction, study design, findings, discussion, figures, acknowledgements, disclosures, and references. Activity 2, is a worksheet to fill out after you go to PubMed and enter 3 or more of the PMID identifiers found throughout this book, read the abstract or the article and then answer the questions on the Activity 2 Worksheet (PubMed is primarily links to abstracts but sometimes you can access the entire article for free). All pubmed logged research articles pertaining to Covid-19 (C19) offer free access to the entire article. I suggest keeping a record of all the scientific articles you and your child access using a subject / topic type method of organizing them. For example, you could start a spreadsheet file and place the subject or topic in one column with the PMID numbers listed below.

Other resources may include DOIs, ISBNs and ISSNs. If you see the acronym, DOI, it stands for digital object identifier. It is a string of numbers and symbols used to identify an article or document and link to it on the web. An ISBN number stands for International Standard Book Number. This number is linked to a specific book. ISSN stands for International Standard Serial Number, which is assigned to a specific publication such as a magazine. When you enter a number in the search box while on the internet, you link to the content referenced in this book. If you see the letters NCT followed by numbers, this is a publicly supported national clinical trial (NCT).

These two skills, understanding word definitions and how to use words and understanding how to navigate the PubMed data base are two excellent skills for everyone to develop, but especially young people. Practice using new words in sentences. Dazzle your teachers with brilliance. Ultimately, these two activities as well as participating in the discussion questions and interacting with the resources is a valuable skill contributing to an educated mind.

Activity 3, is reading chapter 54, Monetize Your Country Home. This chapter provides dozens of ideas for monetizing your country living lifestyle. Read through this chapter and choose one of the ideas or come up with a new idea. Outline the steps you would need to take to start earning an income from one or more of these ideas or another idea of your own. Steps could include: 1. Identify a way to monetize something you are passionate about; 2. Determine if there is a need for this service / product in your community (surveys, interviews, contact key people in the community, etc.); 3. Determine if there is potential to make money using this avenue (cost / benefit analysis); 4. Outline every step you need to take to reach the point of viability; 5. Set up a timeline to reach each goal and objective; 6. Advertise your program; 7. Plan to give your customers more than is expected; 8. Do it!; 9. Recalibrate as you go to maintain relevance and adjust to consumer and regulatory demands / requirements.

Activity 4, is picking one or more of the small building projects to complete. If you don't see anything in this chapter of interest, choose a different building project. Outline the equipment you need, a schedule for completion, the cost of each piece of equipment, the tools needed to build it, a blueprint, and the anticipated costs of the building project. Take a picture of the project and send it to me. I would love to see your completed projects: phytochemwhitten@yahoo.com, subject line: Country Living Home School Projects.

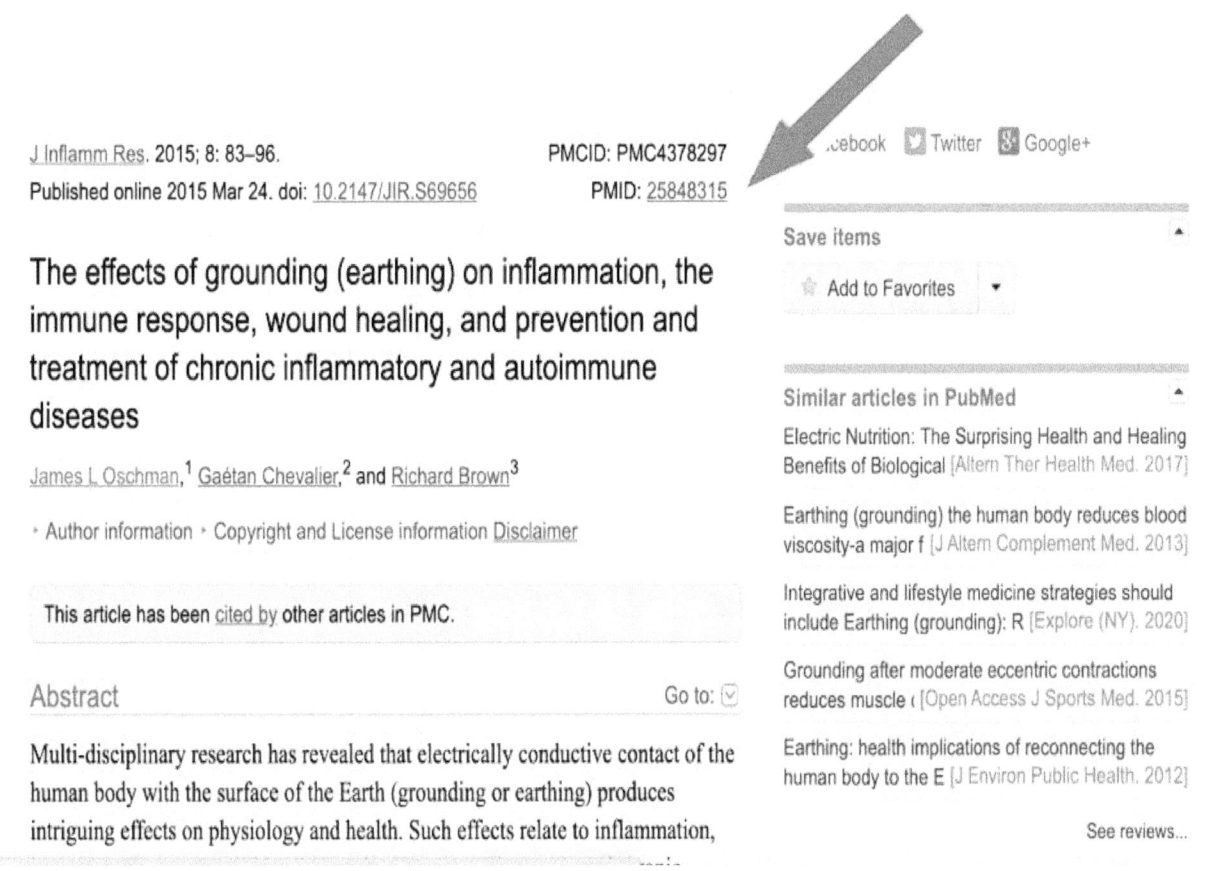

Figure 1. Home school activities. **Searching the PubMed database of scientific journals.**

Activity 1. Word Find and Define

Instructions: look for the following words in this text and when found, record the page number and a brief description of the context of using the word.

Word / Phrase	Definition	Page #	Context
5G		121	
A - B			
Abscisic acid		407, 437	
Alliances		423	
Almanac		518	
Alpha amylase		410	
Amanita phalloides		464	
Andrographis p.		503	
Annual		407	
Aquaponics		407	
Arborvitae		500	
Asbestos		275	
Ashwagandha		348	
Bee garden		440	
Begets		37	
Bioluminescence		431	
Black mold		385	
Blight		434	
Bolt		407	
Borborigmi		151	
Bramble berry patch		424	
Butterfly garden		440	
Butterfly pea flower		450	
C – D			
Caliper		370	
Calvin cycle		407	
Canavanine		407	
Cape gooseberries		441	
Carboxypeptidase		410	
Character		35	
Chelation		221	
Chlorophyll		245	
Chronobiology		113	
Chymotrypsin		410	
Cinchona tree		353	
Circadian		113	
Circannual		113	
Circa-septan		113	

Word / Phrase	Definition	Page #	Context
Clamp		515	
Cognitive bias		552	
Corral		508	
Cotyledons		408	
Covenant		376	
Cultivar		408	
Cuneiform script		61	
Dame's rocket		440	
Deadheading		408	
Dehydrator		519	
Delta		373	
Detoxification		143	
Diatomaceous earth (DE)		299	
Dilapidated		372	
Dittany of Crete		452	
Dominion		526	
Dopamine		83	
Dormancy		409	
Dragon fruit		452	
E – F			
Easement		376	
Egyptian walking onions		419	
Elastase		410	
Endosperm		409	
Enzymes		410	
Epigenetic		163	
Equanimity		35	
Espalier		409	
Ethylene gas		515	
Extrapolate		19	
Faithfulness		73	
Forbearance		73	
Fracked		377	
French drain		385	
Frontal lobes		75	
Fulvic acid		409	
G - H			
GABA		83	
Geothermal		377	
Germinate		409	
Giant hogweed		469	

Word / Phrase	Definition	Page #	Context
Gibberellin		409	
Ginko		222	
GMO		409	
Gnocchi		187	
Gourmet garlic		415	
Gratitude		76	
Greece		35	
Hairy vetch		408	
Hardening off		409	
Hardiness		409	
Hedgerow		417	
Heirloom		409	
Helichrysum		454	
Hemlock		454	
Herbicide		487	
Hoop house		495	
Humus		409	
Hydroponics		409	
Hyphae		436	
I - J			
Idaho blue spruce		476	
Ideographs		61	
Illimitable space		79	
Inanimate		79	
Indeterminate		409	
Indoles		431	
Infradian		113	
Interpret		61	
Inverter		370	
Joists		384	
Juane Flamme		444	
Jugulone		499	
K – L			
Lady bug garden		440	
Larder		515	
Lasagna gardening		409	
Latitude		114	
Legumes		130	
Lichens		420	
Loam		410	
Longevity		115	

Word / Phrase	Definition	Page #	Context
Low tunnel		411	
Luciferin / luciferase		431	
Lunar		113	
Luteinizing hormone		114	
M – N			
Manganese		317, 410	
Melatonin		114	
Mene mene tekel upharsin		61	
Microorganisms		96, 410	
Migration		376	
Millennia		431	
Millivolts, mV		83	
Mineral pitch		411	
Momotaro		444	
Mortgage		383	
Neuroplasticity		84/5	
Nigella sativa		238	
Nightshade crops		444	
Ninja turtle		65	
Nitrogen-fixing		408	
No-hunting purple		417	
Nootropic		204	
O – Q			
Orangerie		496	
Overconsumption		88	
Passover		476	
Patmos		81	
Pelargonium		480	
PERC test		376	
Perennial		410	
Perimeter		422	
Permaculture		410	
Pesticide		151	
Petroleum products		387	
pH		407	
Philistines		71	
Photosynthesis		245	
Phytic acid		407	
Phytoestrogen		465	
Pit house		515	

Word / Phrase	Definition	Page #	Context
Pollinator		410	
Pollinator garden		440	
Pom pom		440	
Princess		38	
Progesterone		113	
Prosody		17	
Proteinase inhibitors		410	
Psychosomatic		88	
Psyllium		146	
Purification		331	
Quinine		357	
R – S			
Radicchio		399	
Ramps		458	
Rechabites		486	
Red Clay Farm		523	
Reservation (Indian)		375	
Respirator		370	
Rhythm		76	
Riparian Zone		373	
Rivulets		379	
Rocket mass heater		425	
Rudimentary		134	
SAD		115	
Samson		71	
Scarification		411	
Scuppernong		415	
Serotonin		83	
Shilajit		213	
Solar oven		519	
Spirituality		75	
Stratification		411	
Strawberry tower		523	
Symbiotic		168	
T – V			
Tap root		412	
Tatsoi		437	
Telegraph plant		474	
Thuja		502	
Tidal rhythms		113	
Tom Landry		67	

Word / Phrase	Definition	Page #	Context
Topography		375	
Translate		61	
Trehalose		269	
Tumbleweed		477	
Ultradian		113	
Uncouple		88	
Universal edibility test		464	
Vagaries		10	
Variety		93	
Vector		101	
Voltage		83	
Voltage-gated calcium channels		83	
W – Z			
Walipini		418	
Warranty		376	
Winterizing		426	
Yuzu		462	
Zeer pot		515	
Zeitgebers		113	

Activity 2. PubMed Article Reviews		
Article name and publication date	Findings / new information I learned	How I will apply the information
1.	1. 2. 3.	1. 2. 3.
2.	1. 2. 3.	1. 2. 3.
3.	1. 2. 3.	1. 2. 3.
4.	1. 2. 3.	1. 2. 3.
5.	1. 2. 3.	1. 2. 3.
6.	1. 2. 3.	1. 2. 3.
7.	1. 2. 3.	1. 2. 3.
8.	1. 2. 3.	1. 2. 3.

Section 1

Spiritual Preparation

Chapter 1
Introduction

Why do you want to move to the country? Common answers to this question include, "The city got too big," or "I want to get away from having noisy neighbors," or "We believe the time has come to leave the large cities and their worldly influences on our family," or "We prefer country living values over city living values." Maybe your desire to move to the country is really God's calling on you to place your family in a safer place. There are various ministry options in the country as well as opportunities to refine and develop a loving and deeply spiritual character. Maybe the 2020 pandemic has opened your eyes to the dangers of city living. Will it take another seminal event such as 9/11, the riots of 2020, the Covid-19 pandemic, or are you ready to take the country living plunge today? If you have lived in the city your whole life, it can be difficult to conceptualize country living. However, with God's leading on your behalf, wise advice from friends, and inspiration from this workbook you can plan for and successfully make the transition.

Genesis 18, provides a sharp contrast between city and country living. It details heavenly beings during an earthly mission to visit Abram (i.e., Abraham before the promise) and Lot. Abraham, who allowed Lot to choose the more desirable land and the opportunity to reside in the city, received one of the most incredible promises in the Bible during this heavenly visit, while his city dwelling relative, Lot received a stern warning. Nomadic and country dwelling Abram and Sarai, when confronted with heavenly visitors, demonstrated respectful hospitality and care for the strangers. They cooked and fed the travelers and during this interaction, Abram, with increasing awareness of the nature of their visitors, was given one of the most incredible promises in the Bible, that his elderly wife Sarai would have a child and their descendants would be without number. God chose to directly give this prophecy to Abram.

Contrast their visit with Lot, who lived in the city of Sodom and Gomorrah. As the three men arrived in the city, they were immediately mobbed. Men actuated by evil demons knew heavenly hosts disguised in humanity, had come to their city to warn Lot and his family. Lot, while living in the city and trying to maintain his religious traditions also recognized the visitors "peril." In the course of their brief visit to the city, they would have apparently been in great danger had God not blinded the men of Sodom and Gomorrha seeking to abuse them. A similar scenario could happen in the future for those dwelling in the city. The story of Lot shows God will do anything to preserve those who love Him and are called according to His purposes. God, in the flesh, chose to rescue Lot and his family. At some point in the near future, there may be one last opportunity to leave with your family, but why wait for the last train out?

The contrast between country living and city dwelling is obvious. Living in cities is not safe anymore. It may seem safe because you have not personally experienced negative consequences, but it also can blind you to what is real and what is contrived and a construct of real life. If events over the past decade have not opened your eyes to where we are in prophetic times, then possibly nothing else short of angelic visitors and complete destruction will help. Think about Abram and Sarai living in the countryside. Did they have endless opportunities for fun and pleasure? Think about Lot, his wife and two daughters who at the last minute escaped from Sodom and Gomorrha. Even Lot's wife could not detach from the city and she gave her life for disobeying the Lord's instructions. Even Lot's virgin daughters, raised in the city, had seen enough to seduce their father into drunken sex – even as they had been saved, even as they could view the destruction of their beloved home. I think the contrasts and principles illustrated here are good things to contemplate as we prepare for the second coming.

You may have friends who criticize or mock you for your decision to move to the country. They may call you a "fanatic." Don't be offended. Show a level of grace and class which exceeds their words and actions toward you. Accept their criticisms without argument. They are not going to change their mind without their own personal season of prayer and fasting. Obviously, not everyone is going to move to the country. Some people are better suited to live in the city until otherwise influenced. The best way to combat criticism is to pray and continue on your path. Do not make rash and irrational decisions, but well-thought-out ones. When your friends see that you are taking reasonable measures in making plans they may be less critical and may even learn to support your decision. If you plan to live in a tent for a year with small children in diapers, their criticisms may be legitimate. But, if you are a young couple and plan to live in an RV for a year while you build a cabin, this may be a reasonable plan. If you are making reasonable and legitimate plans, then keep those to yourself; otherwise you may be inviting criticism. Instead of telling everyone about your plans, seek the advice of those who have already made the move to the country. Learn from their experience.

Many believe the cities are becoming more and more dangerous. This appears to be true. Country living provides an advantage over the large cities for this reason. Those who are able to live partially or fully off-the-grid also have an advantage over those who completely rely on public utilities. Maybe you have seen your utility bills double or even triple over the past several years. Being off-the-grid sounds like a good plan to avoid higher bills in the future. Even with the initial investment in equipment, it is good to know you are somewhat, if not completely independent of the utility companies. Especially during during extreme weather conditions which may interrupt the flow of energy to your home. A large battery bank of stored energy provides peace of mind when the utility companies are negatively impacted by inclement weather and other disasters such as fires and hurricanes.

Those who can plant from seeds and grow a garden will have an advantage over those who completely rely on shopping at grocery stores and markets. Country living folks definitely have an edge over city folks who know nothing about country living. Even if you live in the city, you can learn some country living skills such as growing seeds in a greenhouse, keeping chickens, composting, learning how to preserve fresh food, planting a medicinal garden, learning about natural remedies, setting up a small solar system, etc.

Let's visit the book of Matthew, chapter 24 (KJV) for a glimpse into the future – which is happening now. If you believe the Lord is coming soon, you may appreciate the narrative in Matthew 24. Matthew wrote this book around the year 85 A.D., more than 1,935+ years ago. As you read through these verses spanning from the time of the Flood until now, reflect on how various aspects of this chapter are a metaphor. For example, in verse 41, Matthew describes two women grinding at the mill and one is taken and the other is left. This is not necessarily a literal event but a figurative description. Sometimes, the words 'women' or 'woman' in the Bible represent the church. In this verse, two churches are represented. One church (not any specific denomination) is spreading the gospel and working for the salvation of souls and the other church is more concerned about appearances and superficial acts. This is consistent with a remnant of Christians who are found in every church. God's church does not have a denominational designation. His followers are from all walks of life. "I press on toward the goal for the prize of the upward call of God in Christ Jesus." Philippians 3:14.

While this chapter may cause some to feel anxious about the future, hopefully most see this chapter as a glorious description of how God's people triumph. We see the sweep of human history come alive and begin to understand the significance of the times in which we live. "For God so loved the world that he gave his only Son, that whoever believes in him shall not perish but have eternal life." John 3:16. Instead of fearing the future, we should embrace the news His coming is near!

Matthew 24/1 And Jesus went out, and departed from the temple: and his disciples came to him for to shew him the buildings of the temple.

2 And Jesus said unto them, See ye not all these things? verily I say unto you, There shall not be left here one stone upon another, that shall not be thrown down.

3 And as he sat upon the mount of Olives, the disciples came unto him privately, saying, tell us, when shall these things be? and what shall be the sign of thy coming, and of the end of the world?

4 And Jesus answered and said unto them, **take heed that no man deceive you.**

5 For many shall come in my name, saying, I am Christ; and shall deceive many.

6 And ye shall hear of wars and rumors of wars: see that ye be not troubled: for all these things must come to pass, but the end is not yet.

7 For nation shall rise against nation, and kingdom against kingdom: and there shall be famines, and pestilences, and earthquakes, in divers [diverse] places.

8 All these are the beginning of sorrows.

9 Then shall they deliver you up to be afflicted, and shall kill you: and ye shall be hated of all nations for my name's sake.

10 And then shall many be offended, and shall betray one another, and shall hate one another.

11 And many false prophets shall rise, and shall deceive many.

12 **And because iniquity shall abound, the love of many shall wax cold.**

13 But he that shall endure unto the end, the same shall be saved.

14 And this gospel of the kingdom shall be preached in all the world for a witness unto all nations; and then shall the end come.

15 When ye therefore shall see the abomination of desolation, spoken of by Daniel the prophet, stand in the holy place, whoso readeth, let him understand:

16 Then let them which be in Judaea flee into the mountains:

17 Let him which is on the housetop not come down to take anything out of his house:

18 Neither let him which is in the field return back to take his clothes.

19 And woe unto them that are with child, and to them that give suck in those days!

20 But pray ye that your flight be not in the winter, neither on the sabbath day:

21 For then shall be the great tribulation, such as was not since the beginning of the world to this time, no, nor ever shall be.

22 And except those days should be shortened, there should no flesh be saved: but for the elect's sake those days shall be shortened.

23 Then if any man shall say unto you, Lo, here is Christ, or there; believe it not.

24 For there shall arise false Christs, and false prophets, and shall shew great signs and wonders; insomuch that, if it were possible, they shall deceive the very elect.

25 Behold, I have told you before.

26 Wherefore if they shall say unto you, Behold, he is in the desert; go not forth: behold, he is in the secret chambers; believe it not.

²⁷ For as the lightning cometh out of the east, and shineth even unto the west; so shall also the coming of the Son of man be.
²⁸ For wheresoever the carcase is, there will the eagles be gathered together.
²⁹ Immediately after the tribulation of those days shall the sun be darkened, and the moon shall not give her light, and the stars shall fall from heaven, and the powers of the heavens shall be shaken:
³⁰ And then shall appear the sign of the Son of man in heaven: and then shall all the tribes of the earth mourn, and they shall see the Son of man coming in the clouds of heaven with power and great glory.
³¹ And he shall send his angels with a great sound of a trumpet, and they shall gather together his elect from the four winds, from one end of heaven to the other.
³² Now learn a parable of the fig tree; When his branch is yet tender, and putteth forth leaves, ye know that summer is nigh:
³³ So likewise ye, when ye shall see all these things, know that it is near, even at the doors.
³⁴ Verily I say unto you, this generation shall not pass, till all these things be fulfilled.
³⁵ **Heaven and earth shall pass away, but my words shall not pass away.**
³⁶ But of that day and hour knoweth no man, no, not the angels of heaven, but my Father only.
³⁷ But as the days of Noah were, so shall also the coming of the Son of man be.
³⁸ For as in the days that were before the flood they were eating and drinking, marrying and giving in marriage, until the day that Noe entered into the ark,
³⁹ And knew not until the flood came, and took them all away; so shall also the coming of the Son of man be.
⁴⁰ Then shall two be in the field; the one shall be taken, and the other left.
⁴¹ Two women shall be grinding at the mill; the one shall be taken, and the other left.
⁴² Watch therefore: for ye know not what hour your Lord doth come.
⁴³ But know this, that if the good man of the house had known in what watch the thief would come, he would have watched, and would not have suffered his house to be broken up.
⁴⁴ Therefore be ye also ready: for in such an hour as ye think not the Son of man cometh.
⁴⁵ Who then is a faithful and wise servant, whom his lord hath made ruler over his household, to give them meat in due season?
⁴⁶ Blessed is that servant, whom his lord when he cometh shall find so doing.
⁴⁷ Verily I say unto you, that he shall make him ruler over all his goods.
⁴⁸ But and if that evil servant shall say in his heart, My lord delayeth his coming;
⁴⁹ And shall begin to smite his fellow servants, and to eat and drink with the drunken;
⁵⁰ The lord of that servant shall come in a day when he looketh not for him, and in an hour that he is not aware of,
⁵¹ And shall cut him asunder, and appoint him his portion with the hypocrites: there shall be weeping and gnashing of teeth.

The signs written about in Matthew 24 are occurring today with greater frequency and intensity. For many, now is a good time to leave the big cities and move to the country before it becomes more difficult to move and acquire land. If you are watching with spiritual discernment, the signs are before us. **Riots, pestilence, food shortages, violence, one calamity after another is occurring in the big cities.** Our homes are not safe from lawless rioters and violent protesters. The food supply is becoming less and less safe. Utilities and property taxes continue to rise. What happens if the economy crashes and the banks close? Inflation snowballs. What happens if cash is no longer accepted? Have we been lulled to sleep in believing we can safely remain in the city? Again, not everyone reading this book is going to move to the country. God can work with us in every situation. Some Christians may want to live near enough to the city to retain an influence on or keep up a ministry for those who remain in the city.

The harvest in the cities is large. As Christians, one of our deepest desires is to spread the Gospel to everyone, including people in the large cities. Recently, three of us visited Bourbon Street in New Orleans. Our visit there was in part to meet the street people and get to know them while inviting them to get to know Jesus as their Saviour. We met prostitutes, card readers, Satanists, and mostly people who had no plans for their life. Most of those we met desired to be somewhere else. The street life we saw reflected the Biblical account of the Prodigal Son. "And not many days after the younger son gathered all together, and took his journey into a far country, and there wasted his substance with riotous living. And when he had spent all, there arose a mighty famine in that land; and he began to be in want. <u>And he went and joined himself to a citizen of that country</u>; and he sent him into his fields to feed swine. And he would fain [with pleasure] have filled his belly with the husks that the swine did eat: and no man gave unto him. <u>And when he came to himself</u>, he said, how many hired servants of my father's have bread enough and to spare, and I perish with hunger!" **Luke 15:13-17**. As a citizen of this earth, to whom should we "join" to ourselves? What happens when we open our eyes and come to our senses (i.e., "... and when he came to himself...")?" If we are connected to the God of the universe, we fully understand the meaning of life. We embrace the opportunity to cooperate with God in the salvation of others.

Every homeless or desperate person walking the streets in New Orleans probably has someone praying for them. When we choose to cooperate with God and meet the "prodigal sons and daughters" where they are, we may be used by God to answer a mother's or father's prayer for their child. None of us lived in New Orleans, but we visited and desired to spread God's Word there. It is not necessary to live in a big city to have a Christian influence in the city. It does take motivation, thoughtful consideration, and preparation to meet others where they are.

The latter rain is coming. The power of the Holy Spirit will carry the day. If you have successfully moved to the country, start a ministry to help others move to the country. Teach others how to grow their own provisions. Describe the benefits of getting water from a well or tapping into power sources found in the sun's rays, wind, or the continuous movement of water? In the final analysis, Christians rely on the Lord for their provisions, for protection, for spiritual eyesight, for truth, and for life. It is only through the provisions of the Creator, that we wake up in the morning and experience peace and equanimity. It is only through knowing Christ as our Saviour, we find hope in a world full of strife. It is critical to pray for spiritual eyesight about where to move, when to move, how to move, why to move, etc. For many Christians, the time has come to move out of the big cities and into smaller towns and even the countryside.

It is easy to rationalize remaining in large cities. Just as it was in the days of Noah, it is the same before the Son of Man returns. The second coming is a worldwide event. Every eye shall see Him. He does not touch the earth but gathers his people to Him in the clouds. "For this we declare to you by the word of the Lord, that we who are alive, who are left until the coming of the Lord, shall not precede those who have fallen asleep. For the Lord himself will descend from heaven with a cry of command, with the archangel's call, and with the sound of the trumpet of God. <u>And the dead in Christ will rise first; then we who are alive, who are left, shall be caught up together with them in the clouds to meet the Lord in the air</u>; and so we shall always be with the Lord." **1 Thessalonians 4:15-17**

Take time to pray about your living situation. If you are inspired, begin making plans to move to the country. Not everyone is able to move or desires to move. Maybe you are just where the Lord needsyou to be. If you cannot move, you may be able to take steps to become self-sufficient. Steps such as learning to garden, installing solar panels, etc. If you feel the Lord has impressed you to move to the country, you may want to be near a big city but living in a semi-rural setting. Most of us are not ready to move to a mountainous, isolated, or remote location, but somewhere in between living in a crowded city and living in a remote location may be a good option.

What are you preparing for? As you plan to transition to the country, think about issues such as: how much land do you need; what types of food will you grow; will you build your home or do you want to find land with a home; how far out do you want to be; how will you support your family; what about schools; what are your useful skill sets; and, are you willing to downsize? These are some of the common issues, but there are deeper issues to consider such as: interruptions in the food supply; bank holidays; widespread surveillance; the possibility of forced vaccinations; rolling blackouts; local and civil unrest; increasing lawlessness; and, natural disasters, etc. Having no plan is planning to fail.

Even a simple plan is better than no plan. For example, if you have a relative who lives in the country and is willing to let you build on their property, set up a contractual agreement to build a small cabin or set up a place to park your RV (when someone is doing you a favor – always take extreme care to keep your area clean and tidy and be generous with your gratitude). If the plan is in place, it is easier to execute than if no plan exists. If we believe the Lord is coming to redeem us, we realize these final days are not going to be a picnic, but a time of great injustice and trials. It is also a time to exercise and grow our faith. Setting up a place in the country does not insulate us against the trials ahead, but it allows us to refine our character and keep our family safe from unnecessary worldly influences.

If you are an older adult with one or more medical conditions, consider the story of Stamatis Moraitis. In the 1970s, he received a terminal diagnosis: lung cancer. He visited nine different physicians looking for hope. None of his physicians gave him any chance for a long life. They advised him to spend time with his family and prepare to die. Instead of dying in the USA, he preferred to die in his homeland, Greece. Not just Greece, but Ikaria, a Greek island in the eastern Aegean Sea where he was born and grew up before he left to fight in WWII. When he first arrived to his island home, he stayed in bed, believing he was about to die. After a short time, he felt better and started gardening around his home and visiting with the locals in the evening. Before long, he was living a full and happy life. One day he realized he had "forgotten to die." Instead of dying "young," he died when he had LIVED for over 100 years. While country living may not feel like living on a Greek island, it offers the opportunity to live in ways which promote health and wellness.

There are excellent reasons to move to the country but if you rely on weak motivators such as, "everyone else is doing it," you may struggle to make the transition. You may use every possible excuse including, "I cannot afford it," or "I don't know where to go," or even, "I won't have a job there." Each statement is legitimate. However, there are always reasons to hold back. When it comes to cost, you can invest in a used motorhome, travel trailer, or 5th wheel and make the move. You may have friends in the country who will let you park an RV on their property in exchange for rent or helping with chores until you are able to buy some land. Line up a job or identify your income stream(s) before you move to the country. You can usually find a way to earn money such as mowing lawns, working in agriculture, rural retail, etc. You can live in the country and work at the local market or farm supply store. If you can sew, start a business making quilts, aprons, clothing, etc. If you can bake or cook, make food products to sell in local retail outlets. If you can design web sites, start a consulting business. Children can learn to plant vegetable gardens and care for farm animals. If you have building skills, specialize in building unique structures such as solar arrays, solar furnaces, hydro-electric energy, etc. If you are waiting for the perfect plan to move, you may find yourself indefinitely living in the city.

If you are moving to the country out of fear, you may make expensive mistakes. Fear is never the best motivator for making major life changes. However, if you feel the Lord is calling you to separate you and your family from the city and worldly influences, your motivation may be inspired! Either way, if you are following a trend or just wanting to do what your friends are doing, you may find country living is difficult and not your thing.

Country living is an opportunity to minimize city influences on your values and focus on refining your character. City living may give you a false sense of security. You may be geographically close to supermarkets, malls, car parts stores, sports arenas, business centers, etc., but it also involves living where artificial passion and the whirl of excitement drive daily activities and entertainment choices. **In fact, city living sets up the false expectation we must be constantly entertained and satisfied.** We become slaves to materialism and hedonism and we are disconnected from knowing God through nature, His second bible. Moving from the city to the country liberates us from caustic prevailing attitudes such as that of entitlement, virtue signaling, shaming others, prideful boasting, unprovoked violence, laziness, drug-induced violence, addictions, etc. Country living shifts the focus from being fashion forward, adopting the latest trends and fads, spending money on non-essentials such as fancy meals and beverages, concerts, sporting events, etc., to caring for the land, participating in a lovely dominion over the animals, growing food, connecting with family and learning to enjoy nature, etc. Last time I checked, most of our food is grown in the country and most of our natural resources originate in the country. Proximity to these resources is vital.

Most Christians realize the earth is susceptible to destructive forces such as wide spread dumping, releasing toxic chemicals into waterways and the air, destroying natural resources, exploiting animals, squandering natural resources for non-essential purposes, etc. **Country living gives us the opportunity to reverse damage to the environment.** As Bible-loving Christians, we believe the earth was created for our enjoyment. Christians link enjoyment of the earth to caring for the earth in a way that preserves its natural beauty and functions. We see nature as God's second Bible. Spending time in nature not only revives our health but gives us greater insights into a loving Creator and Saviour. In my experience, many Christians are interested in preserving the natural resources of the earth by adopting the smallest "environmental footprint" when possible.

If you think country living is easy and pastoral, you may need to readjust your expectations. Country living requires a lot of hard work and planning, especially if you are aiming for any degree of self-sufficiency. A trip to the grocery store is not an impulsive quick trip but must be planned in advance and combined with other errands. When your plumbing goes out, you need to know how to repair it. When your tractor blades need sharpening, you do it. **One important benefit – when you work for yourself, you can never complain about the boss.**

A great benefit of country living is creating time with God in outdoor settings. Whether you are cutting hay or feeding animals, it's a great time to commune with God. These quiet moments are invaluable as we seek to understand the times in which we live. There is no better time to be alive than now! We have hundreds, if not thousands, of opportunities to share God's love for man with others. Live in the country and use your talents to help others and show people how Christians care for everyone, especially those who do not yet know the Lord.

God is faithful to His people. We may want to move to the country but unless we are making plans and moving forward, nothing happens. Take the first step or two. God honors our actions. This booklet is about stimulating your mind and prompting creative considerations. It is like a skeleton or a framework for additional investigation and study. Most of what is included here is either from experience or culled from a wide range of sources. This book does not always contain in-depth material but it is idea-rich. In each chapter you find a synthesis of information. In some cases, you may choose to do additional research. Each chapter may serve as a framework for an interactive presentation at church, camp meeting, workshops, seminars, or used to stimulate discussion in small groups. I recommend making notes on the pages and writing in additional resources on each topic.

Below is an outline of some of the initial steps you could take in moving to the country. Read through the steps and apply them in whatever ways suit your life situation (add or subtract what you feel is necessary). The first step is to pray about it. Involve your family and friends. Make it a daily prayer item. **Pray for divine wisdom in taking each step toward country living.** If you want to make reading these steps an activity, find one or more Bible verses which support each step. Perseverance is critical. Failure is assured, but failure oftentimes only requires a slight re-calibration before success is achieved. You may find and make offers on 10 different properties before God provides you with the perfect situation. A final word, actions speak louder than words! Take actions after praying and taking the counsel of wise and experienced people. One positive action begets another positive action until the huge task of relocating is accomplished. Break everything down into steps and then with prayer and careful study, move forward!

- **Step 1 – Spiritual preparation is essential**. Lack of spiritual preparation leads to doing things the hard way. When Christ is at the helm of your life, your problems and successes are assigned to Him. Insurmountable problems become insignificant and successes strengthen one's faith. The point of country living is learning complete dependence on Christ. Obedience is the mark of a mature Christian and results in blessings.

    Make it your goal to specifically pray about it both personally and corporately with friends and family. Pray that God leads you and your family to move to the country when the time is right. **Expect an answer. Pray for spiritual vision to see how God answers your prayer.** Prayer is the answer to every issue in our lives. Think about starting a prayer chain of families who want to move to the country.

    For those who call themselves Christ followers, are your actions consistent with being a Christ follower? Are you living in open rebellion against God? Are you shacking up, cheating at work or school, gossiping about your friends, using foul language, viewing porn, fantasizing about something that is not yours, are you prideful and unwilling to confess and reform your shortcomings, do you treat your spouse with love and respect, do your children see a loving parent or do they see someone who is out of control, do you claim the banner of Christ and yet live a hypocritical life, etc.? Do you expect God to bless you even in the midst of open rebellion against him?

Is rebellion against God something a mature Christian does or is it something a Christian in name only (CINO) would do? This is not about judgement, but about Christian maturity and growing in Christ. It is about moving from immaturity to maturity, becoming a true disciple. As a Christ follower, our lives must be consistent with the object of our hope and faith. Anything short of this is an affront to our Savior and Lord.

The first seven chapters of this book address several aspects of Christian maturity but there are many more aspects to learn that are not included in this book. Kohlberg's theory of moral development may be applied to Christians who grow and mature in Christ. This may be compared to how Christ's apostles grew in wisdom, understanding and maturity. As Christ called them to follow him, they could be categorized as "pre-conventional" or without a strong personal code of morality. This describes children who generally follow their parents' rules. They are oriented to obedience and punishment as directed by their parents and others in authority. As the disciples left their families and followed Jesus, their orientation to Christ's kingdom was possibly at this level. As they spent time with Christ, they came to understand a new form of morality and living that was in stark contrast to the commonly accepted norms of their time. Even so, they did not fully understand true discipleship until they were tested and failed at Christ's crucifixion. Judas betrayed Christ for 30 pieces of silver. Peter used foul language and gestures to deny Christ three times. None of the apostles stood by his side as he was condemned to death. This happened after spending three years with Christ on a daily basis. Only after Christ died, arose and ascended to heaven, did they mature to understand what they could not comprehend before his death. They moved from conventional morality to postconventional morality where they understood the spiritual stakes of every person's choices. At this point, they only wanted to spread the good news. They became singularly focused on one thing – the only thing of any importance in this life – and that is to know God and to live in a way to inspire others to want to know him!

Bible story or verse:

- **Step 2 – Take a personal skills inventory (PSI) assessment** (see appendix). Some people expect others to give them a job, allow them to live on their property, pay their bills, feed and clothe them, emotionally support them, financially support them, say only nice things, let their children and animals ruin the owner's property, etc., all while never offering to help or assist around the home or offer useful services in return for a place to stay. Some people have failed to care for their health, suffer from their poor habits of overindulgence and intemperance, and a host of other self-inflicted conditions. Sometimes people expect others to solve their problems they knowingly and willingly chose.

Recently, a dentist friend told me about a semi-homeless lady from her church she had examined and worked on for free. The lady needed additional dental work which my dentist friend did not do in her office. She spent some time, made a few phone calls, and located a low-cost clinic that would do the work for free. But because this dentist was a low-cost dentist, the patient refused to get the work done. Instead she chose to suffer in pain instead of going to a clinic that was in the 'wrong' section of town. Instead of being part of the solution, some people languish as being part of the problem. Some people have little capacity for self-introspection and acknowledgement of their weaknesses and how those weaknesses might be limiting their joy and success in life and may be sabotaging God's answers to their prayers.

There is a 12-section Country Living Personal Skills Inventory (PSI) assessment in the appendix. This may be used to assess your usefulness and utility for country living. There is no right or wrong assessment profile. However, honestly completing the form may lead you to reassess your ability to make meaningful contributions. To improve the usefulness of this assessment form, ask your spouse to fill out the form, evaluating your skills from their perspective. Add more questions if you desire.

The Country Living Personal Skills Inventory assessment is useful for those wishing to work as part of a group toward a common goal. This could be communal living, group building projects, bringing people onto your property, mission trips, etc. There are 12 evaluation categories: Christian walk with God; my health and wellness philosophy; work commitment and area(s) of expertise; work ethic; attitude toward work and others; work relationships; attention to detail and ability to follow instructions; how does your health or lack thereof affect your ability to contribute; what tangible and intangible things do you bring to the project; your children's habits and attitudes toward work; real, established skills I have and am willing to perform on a regular basis; and skills I am willing to learn and perform on a regular and long-term basis. Each category could be the focus of self-help groups or groups wanting to work together.

For example, you may think you like to garden, but can you hoe, rake, dig, prune, pull weeds, etc., for 4 hours? What about 8 hours? This may be a good time for meaningful introspection. Are you a complainer or are you pleasant? Are you an optimist or a pessimist? Do you like to talk about doing something or do you do it right away without needing to be asked a second time or frequently encouraged to complete a task? Do you find yourself making excuses to get out of hard work? Do you have a princess complex? Do you let your husband do all the difficult work while you are on the computer or telephone? Do you help your wife with chores or do you take time to play golf and basketball while your wife stays home with the kids?

Do not expect others to do anything for you. Do not approach people with your hands out. Sometimes people may choose to help you, but you need to show industriousness and the ability to be a significant contributor, whether that includes manual physical labor or other types of skills. Several years ago, some of my friends moved to the country. Shortly after moving they had to leave their homestead for an extended period of time. They thought they had found a suitable family to live on their property (they had not previously known the family and failed to ask for and check their references). A year or so later, they returned to find their property was almost destroyed. Their furniture had been burned, countertops ruined, every window treatment missing or non-functional, trees they had planted had been uprooted, tools were missing, etc. Experiences such as this make it more difficult to trust people to be legitimate contributors. When people take a risk on you, always give back more than you take.

Country living is hard work. It requires everything you have. **Most people living in the country cannot add a person or family who contributes little if anything to the economy of their household.** Most farming families do not have a wide margin of financial independence. Even their children work hard. If you join their team, you need to present them with needed and legitimate skills and the ability and desire to regularly perform those skills and required tasks. Provide them with references and evidence of the quality of your work / skills. If you have learned lazy habits, they need to be un-learned before you succeed in vibrant, mission-oriented country living.

Only God can help us! If you give your life to Jesus and ask Him to reform you into His likeness and fit you for country living, He does such a good work in you. **If you like to spend time watching sports, playing golf, shopping online, texting your friends, etc., you may not have useful skills for country living.** These habits may need to be pruned if not purged before you move to the country or during the transition process. Only God can change us into His likeness. Only God can take us from lazy and indolent to industrious and productive. When the goal is to work for His Kingdom, the means to do so are assured by Him.

God transforms us into useful people. **Romans 12:1-2** gives us this promise, "I beseech you therefore, brethren, by the mercies of God, that ye present your bodies a living sacrifice, holy, acceptable unto God, which is your reasonable service. And be not conformed to this world: but be ye transformed by the renewing of your mind, that ye may prove what is that good, and acceptable, and perfect, will of God."
Bible story or verse:

- **Step 3 – Make the commitment to moving to the country by taking purposeful steps.** Make a schedule. Look at the calendar and set a date to move to the country, which could be 6 months, 12 months, 18 months, etc. This date is preceded by many steps, some are outlined here. Set up a network with people who have moved to the country and also with people who desire to move to the country. Set up regular contact with these groups. This gives you early information about someone selling a piece of land, etc. Also, identify organizations which may assist you in moving to the country.
Bible story or verse:

- **Step 4 – If you know your target location, contact local real estate agents, bankers, church elders, business leaders and set up a line of communication** with them about any land and property which meets your needs. You may want to contact local bankers to explore foreclosed properties and online resources for properties going to auction. In some counties a notice of Substitute Trustee sale may be posted at the County Clerk's office and on the web site.
Bible story or verse:

- **Step 5 –** If you have no ties to a country location, **do some research** about state and local laws that might impact home schooling, gun ownership, self-defense, taxes, etc.
Bible story or verse:

- **Step 6 – Make a list of your "must haves / necessities"** and your "nice to haves / wants and desires." This list is critical for guiding your property selection. Modify it as often as necessary. Involve the entire family and anyone else impacted by this decision.
Bible story or verse:

- **Step 7 – Do a financial statement listing your assets and liabilities.** Define your budget, always set aside a year's worth of savings you never touch unless there is an emergency. If you do not have this much to set aside, plan to do this when you sell your belongings and property. If you are recently married, both should work and live on just one person's salary while saving the second person's salary for 5 years. If you want children, plan to have children after 5 years of marriage. After you have your first child, one parent can plan to stay home and raise the child while living on the other spouse's salary and the savings can be used for essential needs and emergencies. Factor these requirements into your budget for a country property.

Obtain necessary financial documentation for purchase of land and property. This could include bank statements, retirement savings statements, investment statements, etc. Now that you have an assets and liability statement, it is time to set up an approximate calendar to move to the country. Take every-thing into consideration and determine the best time to make the smoothest transition to the country. If possible, keep this calendar to one or two years due to the urgency of our times. For example, you may have $35,000 dollars left after you pay off debts and sell your house and have a garage sale. This means you could buy a small piece of land and start out by putting a 5th wheel or travel trailer on the property. Ultimately, as we cooperate with God, our actions line up with His will. Even when there seems to be no possible avenue of moving to the country, God can open the door!
Bible story or verse:

- **Step 8 – Pay off your debts!** If possible, move to the country without debt. This allows you to make a fresh start. Learn to pay as you go using cash without resorting to credit. This ties your labor to your purchases. You may even be able to barter your goods or services. Maybe you can plow a field in return for several farm animals.
  Bible story or verse:

- **Step 9 – Live BELOW your means** and not right at your means or above your means; plan to save at least 10% – 25% of your paycheck.
  Bible story or verse:

- **Step 10 – Sell everything but your basic necessities; set this money aside to pay off debts or save for your emergency fund.** If you are lucky, you may make a significant amount of money to go toward your move to the country. Utilize local social networks to make quick sales.
  Bible story or verse:

- **Step 11 – Read books, talk with others, and watch videos to learn country living skills** such as food preservation, gardening, building a house, electrical wiring, plumbing, solar wiring, wood working, etc. If you have small children, it is also a good time to begin collecting home school resources, etc.
  Bible story or verse:

- **Step 12 – Start to think about whether or not your vehicles are going to be useful in a country living setting?** You may need to sell a vehicle or two and buy a more functional one. If you are going to set up a 5th wheel on your property, you may need a ½ to 1-ton pick-up truck to pull the RV. Make sure your truck matches the weight and all of the specifications of the towed vehicle. Will you need vehicles such as an ATV or golf cart for moving around the property? What type of equipment will you need? Hitches? You may be able to trade or barter for equipment.
  Bible story or verse:

- **Step 13 – Have a BIG vision but learn to start small.** Write down your vision about where you want to live, what your homestead looks like, the setting of the property, the features of property, etc. Write down what God has placed in your heart.

  Only invest in what you can afford. This is being a good steward with what God provides. Most people's vision far exceeds their means. Stay within your means which gives you more freedom to grow and reach your goal. God rewards those who are good stewards of his resources, including money. Learn to minimize wasteful and unnecessary purchases. Even if your finances are 'unlimited,' it's wise conserve resources. **God does not give us a vision** without the means to achieve it if we are faithful to the talents he has given us such as education, training, work experiences, etc.
  Bible story or verse:

- **Step 14 – Match your skills and training with what you plan to do to earn a living and / or do outreach in the country. Seek to do no harm to others by your witness.** God gives everyone talents. You are likely blessed with many talents. This means everyone has a skill which is needed in the country. Take a skill inventory. If you are an English, Computer, Business or Education major (i.e., any major which does not involve formal medical / allied health type training), you probably don't want to open up a wellness center because you have absolutely no training or background in this area. If you are handing out nutrition information, you need to have nutrition training. In fact, most states have laws against providing nutritional advice unless you are registered or licensed with the state. A legitimate nutrition degree involves four to six or more years of studying biochemistry, anatomy and physiology, molecular biology, genetics, psychology, management and business practices, food science, etc.

This is true of any allied health - medical based training.

You cannot substitute reading a book for formal training and years of clinical experience. **Lack of training can hurt other legitimate outreach efforts when false, harmful, or inadequate information is conveyed.** If you are church affiliated, this lack of professionalism may hurt your church's reputation and impede other people's legitimate efforts.

Most people do not realize their ignorance in the area of health and wellness. Most people without formal training may have good intentions but ultimately, they have great potential and ability to negatively impact others with what they DO NOT KNOW and UNDERSTAND about the human body. I have seen a popular lay evangelist broadcast to the TV world that vegetarians do not need to worry about getting enough vitamin B12 (he is 100% WRONG)! I have seen extreme vegans pass along information which truly harms other people. It even harms their own family, but they are unable to see the damage because they are blinded by their own cognitive biases (see appendix for a description of cognitive biases). I have seen people into multi-level marketing essential oil businesses come to believe essential oils can heal every single symptom, every single disease, and every single condition known to man. I 100% support the use of essential oils, but I also know they are not a cure-all for everything. In fact, have seen plenty of families into essential oils, with poor health, declining health, lots of health problems, etc. Obviously, if you believe a little lavender oil can cure just about anything, you won't seek medical care even when your children or your spouse might need expert medical care.

If you are a car mechanic, you probably don't want to open up a day care business. **In each case, what you do not know can hurt other people.** God has not called us to operate outside of our areas of expertise. However, if you are an English major you can write, teach, help with marketing campaigns, etc. If you are a car mechanic, set up a repair shop and be a blessing to many people who are not mechanically minded. Farm equipment needs frequent repairs and restoration. If you are a computer person, help others with their computers.

Bible story or verse:

- **Step 15 – Get healthy!** If you have health issues, address those issues by making as many positive lifestyle changes as possible. Write goals, set up objectives which describe how you plan to reach your goals, and then transfer this to a calendar. For example, if you are obese, with hypertension, high cholesterol, bad feet, bad knees, shortness of breath, and swelling in your ankles and legs – you need to lose weight. Losing weight may solve some, if not almost all, of the aforementioned issues. In fact, you may need only to lose 10 to 20 pounds to jumpstart a turnaround in your health. This is motivation to continue to reach your health goals. It is a good idea to get a baseline exam for each member of the family. Make sure you understand each person's issues. It is interesting that when people move to the country their health usually improves. Obtaining baseline health data provides confirmation that country living is almost always healthy living.

Bible story or verse:

- **Step 16 – Be prepared for hard work!** If children and / or parents have learned lazy habits, country living, out of necessity, usually requires them to learn good work skills and habits. Ask each child in your family over the age of 5 or 6 to think of a way they could earn money or contribute to the family economy. Children have a great sense of industriousness and want to be useful. Take advantage of this before they learn lazy habits, which are difficult to reverse engineer. Make sure all computer games are off-limits and computer time is monitored and limited to 15 minutes or less per day. Set up a workplace specific to their activities such as a desk, table, workshop, etc. Let them make their own business cards, do their own marketing plan and even set production goals. Children using their hands in coordination with their eyes and brains, improves their frontal lobes and contributes to their spiritual development as well as their social and intellectual development.

Some activities contributing to an income include: making and selling jams, making and selling sweet rolls, mowing lawns, setting up sprinkler systems, dog sitting, plant-watering, weed pulling, sewing projects, wood working projects such as wooden spoons and bowls, seed saving and selling, selling artwork, website development, etc. Older kids can tutor, run a food truck, plant an orchard, transport elderly people to their appointments, set up a gardening business, repair farm equipment, build sheds, learn plumbing, do book-keeping, etc. This is a great way to teach them good work habits, time management, income management, quality control, etc.
Bible story or verse:

- **Step 17 – Learn to be content with what you have.** The 10th commandment states, "Thou shalt not covet thy neighbor's house, thou shalt not covet thy neighbor's wife, nor his manservant, nor his maidservant, nor his ox, nor his ass, nor anything that is thy neighbor's." **Let's add a few more things not to covet such as your neighbor's vacations, their clothes, their bank account, their cars, their hair style, their friends, their privilege, their status, their standing in the community, etc.** Do not compare yourself to others. This does not mean you don't advance and grow, it just means you have peace of mind in your situation.
Bible story or verse:

- **Step 18 –** If possible, **set up one or more income streams before you move to the country**. This could include a work-from-home job, income from book sales, small business income, passive income streams, start a blog, etc. Even small income streams are better than nothing at all. Maybe your current employer would allow you to work from home. This would be a blessing. If you know how much you might be earning, set up a budget and live below it.
Bible story or verse:

- **Step 19 – If your heart is open and your cup is full, be inclusive**! If there are other people you could include in your plans to move to the country, spend a season in prayer and if God impresses you to ask them to go along, follow His leading. More hands make for less work. It also refines our character as each person must rely on the Lord for inspiration and patience in dealing with others. Think about Jesus and his 12 disciples. It was quite the feat to bring together 12 strong-willed people and then travel together, eat together, sleep together and fellowship together. What are some of the life lessons we could learn from their experiences?

    If you are bringing other people to your country property, especially if you do not know them well and even if you know them well, it is advisable to set up a detailed written contract which covers daily, weekly and monthly required tasks and activities. What financial arrangements are necessary? What equipment can and cannot be used, the behavior of their children and pets, etc.? There are so many unknowns when you bring strangers onto your land and share living space with them. In my experience and observing others who do this, it has almost never been a successful adventure.

    It is usually advisable for each family unit to get their own land and maintain their own space vs. communal living but living close or next door may work.
Bible story or verse:

- **Step 20 – Spend daily time with God in prayer and study.** This is the key to hearing God's voice guiding you and to seeing answers to your prayers. God's answers are sometimes whispered to us. If we are not used to hearing His voice, we may miss an opportunity to experience a softly spoken answer to our prayers. Prayer keeps us connected and allows us greater freedom in moving forward.

You may add other steps to the 20 listed here. Every family may modify these steps and individualize them. The future is ahead of us and it will unfold in unexpected ways. Ultimately, God may supersede anything man has devised. It is only His word which matters.

Think about Enoch and how he walked with God every day. I doubt their conversations were desperate and one-sided. Enoch was not begging God for more money or a better job. This does not mean God and Enoch did not discuss the world's condition or specific people, but I imagine there was a lot of camaraderie and familiarity between the two.

Bible story or verse:

This book is not specific to any religious organization. Even those who are not religious and have never explored the Bible, are sensing a change in the world. Many have seen an uptick in unrestrained violence, indoctrination of children from kindergarten through college, civil unrest, rebellion, and lack of basic civility between strangers. We see increasing lawlessness, less accountability for one's actions, lack of compassion for the victim while the perpetrator is unjustly exonerated, racial intolerance, unbridled stupidity, misplaced respect, etc. Christians around the world are beginning to re-evaluate their lifestyle and living priorities. **People are leaving the cities because they are increasingly concerned about the safety aspects of their living situation.** Within the past week of writing this section, a violent criminal threw a brick through a friend's window as he watched just a few feet from where the brick shattered the window. In a different state and town, a bullet shattered a friend's car window as they drove through town (fortunately they were uninjured). Young children's school curriculums include unacceptable content such as perverse sex education, evolution, socialism, etc. History is being erased and re-written to be favorable to oppressive regimes while demonizing freedom-based governments and economies, which have built the largest and most successful economies in the world. The economy which everyone around the world envies is now being dismantled. Unrest is spreading across the globe. Is there anywhere that is safe? **The safest place in the world is living within God's will. When we pray to discern His will for us, He gives us the desires of our heart, maybe including a country home.**

In addition to promoting country living, the Christian church community could promote a number of healthy lifestyle habits such as plant-based nutrition, culturally specific healthy lifestyles, exercise, active hobbies, gardening, community outreach, missionary outreach, drinking adequate amounts of water, getting adequate rest every night, avoiding alcoholic and caffeinated beverages, use of natural approaches to achieve health and wellness, spending time outdoors, respect for all living creatures, temperance in all matters, fresh air, a high quality educational system, daily and weekly rest cycles, a set-aside a Sabbath day of worship, and trust in God. God is not only interested in our religious and spiritual condition, He's interested in our physical, social and even mental state. Christians should represent the healthiest and most vibrant sections of society. Our example should inspire others to follow our lead.

Country living is a lifestyle. It is a way to reclaim what may have been lost over the past several centuries. Maybe you have never had the pleasure of sleeping under a canopy of stars, or going to sleep with a bull frog serenade, or waking up to a herd of deer staring at you through your expansive bathroom window. If you have never retrieved a basket full of tomatoes and fresh basil and made fresh tomato sauce and pesto, you have truly missed out on several of the many luxuries of country living. **Finally, the** most important benefit, is carving out time and space for communing with God. This is the true benefit of country living.

Additional resources

- www.whiteestate.org
- https://text.egwwritings.org/publicationtoc.php?bookCode=CL&lang=en&collection=2&section=all
- https://m.egwwritings.org/en/book/25.3
- http://cheerministries.org/endtime-ministries-gateway - A collection of resource-rich links.
- https://www.countryliving.com/ - Secular magazine with articles about country living.
- https://www.haneyrealestate.org/homeeval - Evaluates property values.
- https://www.census.gov/programs-surveys/acs/ - find out more about the area of interest.
- Mountain Media Ministries
  https://www.youtube.com/playlist?list=PL9w14WheunFtVNmbIR8C-eI5i2MCleYLM
- Out of the cities: the threequel, an appeal to parents to leave the city, day 6 of 7. (Natalie and Roy) https://www.youtube.com/watch?v=G5Qv4fvMRo0

Discussion questions

1. What are your top reasons for moving to the country, in order of priority?
2. What does it mean to "have a full cup?"
3. What does it mean to bear the cross of Jesus?
4. What are you preparing for by moving to the country?
5. Are you willing to organize and outline each step to move to the country?
6. What personal skills would be useful in country living?

Bible verses to memorize

The mind should be restrained and not allowed to wander. It should be trained to dwell upon the Scriptures; even whole chapters may be committed to memory, to be repeated when satan comes in with temptations. The 58th chapter of Isaiah is profitable for this purpose. GW 92 418.2. E.G. White

- **Specific verse / books:**
  1 Corinthians 12, 13; Deuteronomy 32; Exodus 20; Isaiah 51, 53, 58; James 2, 4:5-12, 5:13-20; John 1:1-5, 6, 14, 17; Matthew 5, 6, 7; Psalm 1, 19, 46, 51, 66:1-5, 78, 91, 105, 106, 107; Revelation 14:6-20, 22
- **Promises (see appendix)**
- **Words of Christ**

Chapter 2
Bible and other country living quotes

He that dwelleth in the secret place of the Most High shall abide under the shadow of the Almighty. I will say of the LORD, He is my refuge and my fortress: my God; in him will I trust. Surely, he shall deliver thee from the snare of the fowler, and from the noisome pestilence. He shall cover thee with his feathers, and under his wings shalt thou trust: his truth shall be thy shield and buckler. Thou shalt not be afraid for the terror by night; nor for the arrow that flieth by day; nor for the pestilence that walketh in darkness; nor for the destruction that wasteth at noonday. **A thousand shall fall at thy side, and ten thousand at thy right hand; but it shall not come nigh thee.** Only with thine eyes shalt thou behold and see the reward of the wicked. Because thou hast made the LORD, which is my refuge, even the Most High, thy habitation; There shall no evil befall thee, neither shall any plague come nigh thy dwelling. For he shall give his angels charge over thee, to keep thee in all thy ways. They shall bear thee up in their hands, lest thou dash thy foot against a stone. Thou shalt tread upon the lion and adder: the young lion and the dragon shalt thou trample under feet. Because he hath set his love upon me, therefore will I deliver him: I will set him on high, because he hath known my name. He shall call upon me, and I will answer him: I will be with him in trouble; I will deliver him, and honor him. With long life will I satisfy him, and shew him my salvation. **Ps 91**

"... Make it your ambition to lead a quiet life." **1 Thessalonians 4:11**

Parents can secure small homes in the country, with land for cultivation, where they can have orchards and where they can raise vegetables and small fruits to take the place of flesh meat. On such places the children will not be surrounded with the corrupting influences of city life. God will help His people to find such homes outside the cities. —**Medical Ministry by E. G. White, 310 (1902)**

Come to me, all who labor and are heavy laden, and I will give you rest. Take my yoke upon you, and learn from me; for I am gentle and lowly in heart, and you will find rest for your souls. For my yoke is easy, and my burden is light. **Matthew 11:28-30 (RSV)**

Let everyone take time to consider carefully; and not be like the man in the parable who began to build, and was not able to finish. Not a move should be made but that movement and all that it portends are carefully considered — everything weighed... To every man was given his work according to his several ability[ies]. Then let him not move hesitatingly, but firmly, and yet humbly trusting in God. There may be individuals who will make a rush to do something, and enter into some business they know nothing about. This God does not require. Think candidly, prayerfully, studying the Word with all carefulness and prayerfulness, with mind and heart awake to hear the voice of God... To understand the will of God is a great thing. -**Country Living by E. G. White, page 26**

And when ye shall see Jerusalem compassed with armies, then know that the desolation thereof is nigh. Then let them which are in Judaea flee to the mountains; and let them which are in the midst of it depart out; and let not them that are in the countries enter thereinto. For these be the days of vengeance, that all things which are written may be fulfilled. But woe unto them that are with child, and to them that give suck, in those days! for there shall be great distress in the land, and wrath upon this people. And they shall fall by the edge of the sword, and shall be led away captive into all nations: and Jerusalem shall be trodden down of the Gentiles, until the times of the Gentiles be fulfilled. And there shall be signs in the sun, and in the moon, and in the stars; and upon the earth distress of nations, with perplexity; the sea and the waves roaring; men's hearts failing them for fear, and for looking after those things which are coming on the earth: for the powers of heaven shall be shaken. And then shall they see the Son of man coming in a cloud with power and great glory. And when these things begin to come to pass, then look up, and lift up your heads; for your redemption draweth nigh. **Luke 21:26**

"... To the person who pleases him, God gives wisdom, knowledge and happiness but to the sinner he gives the task of gathering and stiring up wealth to hand it over to the one who pleases God." **Ecclesiastes 2:26**

Or whether it were two days, or a month, or a year, that the cloud tarried upon the tabernacle, remaining thereon, the children of Israel abode in their tents, and journeyed not: but when it was taken up, they journeyed. **Numbers 9:22**

Many do not see the importance of having land to cultivate, and of raising fruit and vegetables, and their tables may be supplied with these things. I am instructed to say to every family and every church, God will bless you when you work out your own salvation with fear and trembling, fearing lest, by unwise treatment of the body, you will mar the Lord's plan for you. **-Letter 5, 1904 (Counsels on Diet and Foods by E. G. White 323.3)**

Out of the cities; out of the cities!" — this is the message the Lord has been giving me. The earthquakes will come; the floods will come; and we are not to establish ourselves in the cities, where the enemy is served in every way, and where God is so often forgotten. The Lord desires that we shall have clear spiritual eyesight... We must make wise plans to warn the cities, and at the same time live where we can shield our children and ourselves from the contaminating and demoralizing influences so prevalent in these places. —**Life Sketches, 409, 410 (1906) and Country Living, by E. G. White p 31**

Then Abram removed his tent, and came and dwelt in the plain of Mamre, which is in Hebron, and built there an altar unto the LORD. **Genesis 13:18**

One of the most subtle and dangerous temptations that assails the children and youth in the cities is the love of pleasure. Holidays are numerous; games and horse racing draw thousands, and the whirl of excitement and pleasure attracts them away from the sober duties of life. Money that should have been saved for better uses is frittered away for amusements. **-Country Living, E. G. White, pg 6**

Now is not the time for God's people to be fixing their affections or laying up their treasure in the world.
The time is near, when, like the early disciples, we shall be forced to seek a refuge in desolate and solitary places. The first siege of Jerusalem and then surprise retreat by the Roman army was the signal for Judean Christians to leave Jerusalem. The assumption of power on the part of our nation to enforce worship on Sunday will be a warning to us. It will then be time to leave the large cities, preparatory to leaving the smaller ones for retired homes in secluded Places among the mountains. And now, instead of seeking expensive dwellings here, we should be

preparing to move to a better country, even a heavenly. Instead of spending our means in self-gratification, we should be studying to economize. **-Testimonies for the Church Vol 5:464, 465 (1885) by E. G. White**

And there came two angels to Sodom at even; and Lot sat in the gate of Sodom: and Lot seeing them rose up to meet them; and he bowed himself with his face toward the ground; and he said, behold now, my lords, turn in, I pray you, into your servant's house, and tarry all night, and wash your feet, and ye shall rise up early, and go on your ways. And they said, nay; but we will abide in the street all night. And he pressed upon them greatly; and they turned in unto him, and entered into his house; and he made them a feast, and did bake unleavened bread, and they did eat.

But before they lay down, the men of the city, even the men of Sodom, compassed the house round, both old and young, all the people from every quarter: and they called unto Lot, and said unto him, where are the men which came in to thee this night? Bring them out unto us, that we may know them. And Lot went out at the door unto them, and shut the door after him, and said, I pray you, brethren, do not so wickedly. Behold now, I have two daughters which have not known man; let me, I pray you, bring them out unto you, and do ye to them as is good in your eyes: only unto these men do nothing; for therefore came they under the shadow of my roof.

And they said, stand back. And they said again, this one fellow came in to sojourn, and he will needs be a judge: now will we deal worse with thee, than with them. And they pressed sore upon the man, even Lot, and came near to break the door. But the men put forth their hand, and pulled Lot into the house to them, and shut to the door. And they smote the men that were at the door of the house with blindness, both small and great: so that they wearied themselves to find the door. And the men said unto Lot, Hast thou here any besides? Son in law, and thy sons, and thy daughters, and whatsoever thou hast in the city, bring them out of this place: for we will destroy this place, because the cry of them is waxen great before the face of the Lord; and the Lord hath sent us to destroy it. And Lot went out, and spake unto his sons in law, which married his daughters, and said, up, get you out of this place; for the Lord will destroy this city. But he seemed as one that mocked, unto his sons in law. And when the morning arose, then the angels hastened Lot, saying, arise, take thy wife, and thy two daughters, which are here; lest thou be consumed in the iniquity of the city. **And while he lingered, the men laid hold upon his hand, and upon the hand of his wife, and upon the hand of his two daughters; the Lord being merciful unto him: and they brought him forth, and set him without the city.**

And it came to pass, when they had brought them forth abroad, that he said, escape for thy life; look not behind thee, neither stay thou in all the plain; escape to the mountain, lest thou be consumed. And Lot said unto them, oh, not so, my Lord: behold now, thy servant hath found grace in thy sight, and thou hast magnified thy mercy, which thou hast shewed unto me in saving my life; and I cannot escape to the mountain, lest some evil take me, and I die: behold now, this city is near to flee unto, and it is a little one: Oh, let me escape thither, (is it not a little one?) and my soul shall live. And he said unto him, See, I have accepted thee concerning this thing also, that I will not overthrow this city, for the which thou hast spoken. Haste thee, escape thither; for I cannot do anything till thou become thither. Therefore, the name of the city was called Zoar. The sun was risen upon the earth when Lot entered into Zoar. Then the Lord rained upon Sodom and upon Gomorrah brimstone and fire from the Lord out of heaven; and he overthrew those cities, and all the plain, and all the inhabitants of the cities, and that which grew upon the ground. But his wife looked back from behind him, and she became a pillar of salt. And Abraham gat up early in the morning to the place where he stood before the LORD: and he looked toward Sodom and Gomorrah, and toward all the land of the plain, and beheld, and, lo, the smoke of the country went up as the smoke of a furnace. And it came to pass, when God destroyed the cities of the plain, that God remembered Abraham, and sent Lot out of the midst of the overthrow, when he overthrew the cities in the which Lot dwelt. **Genesis 19:1-29**

Except the LORD build the house, they labor in vain that build it: except the LORD keep the city, the watchman waketh but in vain. It is vain for you to rise up early, to sit up late, to eat the bread of sorrows: for so he giveth his beloved sleep. **Psalm 127:1-2**

The time has come, when, as God opens the way, families should move out of the cities. The children should be taken into the country. The parents should get as suitable a place as their means will allow. Though the dwelling may be small, yet there should be land in connection with it, that may be cultivated. -**Manuscript 50, 1903 (CL 24- C-24.2) E. G. White**

A prayer of Habakkuk the prophet. On Shigionoth. Lord, I have heard of your fame; I stand in awe of your deeds, Lord. Repeat them in our day, in our time make them known; in wrath remember mercy. God came from Teman, the Holy One from Mount Paran. His glory covered the heavens and his praise filled the earth. His splendor was like the sunrise; rays flashed from his hand, where his power was hidden. Plague went before him; pestilence followed his steps. He stood, and shook the earth; he looked, and made the nations tremble. The ancient mountains crumbled and the age-old hills collapsed – but he marches on forever. I saw the tents of Cushan in distress, the dwellings of Midian in anguish. Were you angry with the rivers, Lord? Was your wrath against the streams? Did you rage against the sea when you rode your horses and your chariots to victory? You uncovered your bow, you called for many arrows. You split the earth with rivers; the mountains saw you and writhed. Torrents of water swept by; the deep roared and lifted its waves on high. Sun and moon stood still in the heavens at the glint of your flying arrows, at the lightning of your flashing spear. In wrath you strode through the earth and in anger you threshed the nations. You came out to deliver your people, to save your anointed one. You crushed the leader of the land of wickedness, you stripped him from head to foot. With his own spear you pierced his head when his warriors stormed out to scatter us, gloating as though about to devour the wretched who were in hiding. You trampled the sea with your horses, churning the great waters. I heard and my heart pounded, my lips quivered at the sound; decay crept into my bones, and my legs trembled. Yet I will wait patiently for the day of calamity to come on the nation invading us. Though the fig tree does not bud and there are no grapes on the vines, though the olive crop fails and the fields produce no food, though there are no sheep in the pen and no cattle in the stalls, yet I will rejoice in the Lord, I will be joyful in God my Saviour. The Sovereign Lord is my strength; he makes my feet like the feet of a deer, he enables me to tread on the heights. **Habakkuk 3**

Again and again the Lord has instructed that our people are to take their families away from the cities, into the country, where they can raise their own provisions; for in the future the problem of buying and selling will be a very serious one. **Country Living, p 9, E. G. White**

Commit thy works unto the LORD, and thy thoughts shall be established. **Proverbs 6:3**

We assembled in the orchards and groves to commune with God and to offer up our petitions to Him, feeling more fully in His presence when surrounded by His natural works. -**Testimonies, Vol 1, p 55.2, E. G. White**

I sought the LORD, and he heard me, and delivered me from all my fears. **Psalm 34:4**

I can do all things through Christ who strengthens me. **Philippians 4:13**

But my God shall supply all your need according to his riches in glory by Christ Jesus. **Phil 4:19**

And Jesus said unto them, Because of your unbelief: for verily I say unto you, if ye have faith as a grain of mustard seed, ye shall say unto this mountain, remove hence to yonder place; and it shall remove; and nothing shall be impossible unto you. **Matthew 17:20**

We felt glad to leave the houses so thickly crowded together and go where houses have good space of ground; glad to leave behind the bad odor of open drains and poisonous, offensive smells. We felt so pleased to feel it our privilege to fill our lungs by inhaling good, pure, invigorating air, and to get into a house that had land adjoining it. There is a yard full of flowers of fine rich quality, but weeds are growing as I never thought possible... The ground is good, excellent soil. We have plenty of land around us, and we have the blessed privilege of full and deep without fear of being poisoned. - **Manuscripts 28, 1892, E. G. White**

The very best legacy parents can leave their children is a knowledge of useful labor and the example of a life characterized by disinterested benevolence. By such a life, they show the true value of money, that it is only to be appreciated for the good that it will accomplish in relieving their own wants and the necessities of others, and in advancing the cause of God. -**Adventist Home, 390.1, E. G. White**

Mothers should guard against training their children to be dependent and self-absorbed. Never lead them to think that they are the center, and that everything must revolve around them. Some parents give much time and attention to amusing their children, but children should be trained to amuse themselves, to exercise their own ingenuity and skill. Thus, they will learn to be content with very simple pleasures. They should be taught to bear bravely their little disappointments and trials... Study to suggest ways by which the children may learn to be thoughtful for others. -**My Life Today 197.6, E. G. White**

Offer hospitality to one another without grumbling. **1 Peter 4:9**

The cities are to be worked from outposts... 'Shall not the cities be warned? Yes, not by God's people living in them, but by their visiting them, to warn them of what is coming upon the earth. **Evangelism p 7 by E. G. White**

In India, China, Russia, and the cities of America, thousands of men and women are dying of starvation. The monied men, because they have the power, control the market. They purchase at low rates all they can obtain, and then sell at greatly increased prices. This means starvation to the poorer classes, and will result in a civil war. There will be a time of trouble such as never was since there was a nation. "And at that time shall Michael stand up, the great prince which standeth for the children of thy people: and there shall be a time of trouble such as never was since there was a nation, even to that same time; and at that time thy people shall be delivered, everyone that shall be found written in the book... Many shall be purified, and made white, and tried; but the wicked shall do wickedly, and none of the wicked shall understand but the wise shall understand." **Manuscript 114, 1899, E. G. White**

On one occasion, when in New York City, I was in the night season called upon to behold buildings rising story after story toward heaven. These buildings were warranted to be fireproof, and they were erected to glorify their owners and builders. Higher and still higher these buildings rose, and in them, the most costly material was used. Those to whom these buildings belonged were not asking themselves: "How can we best glorify God?" The Lord was not in their thoughts. I thought: "Oh, that those who are thus investing their means could see their course as God sees it! They are piling up magnificent buildings, but how foolish in the sight of the Ruler of the universe is their planning and devising. They area not studying with all the powers of the heart and mind how they may glorify God. They have lost sight of this, the first duty of man. As these lofty buildings went up, the owners rejected with ambitious pride that they had money to use in gratifying self and provoking the envy of their neighbors. Much of the money they thus invested had been obtained through exaction through grinding down the poor. They forgot that in heaven an account of every business transaction is kept; every unjust deal, every fraudulent act, is there recorded. The time is coming when in their fraud and insolence men will reach a point that the Lord will not permit them to pass, and they will learn that there is a limit to the forbearance of Jehovah.

The scene that next passed before me was an alarm of fire. Men looked at the lofty and supposedly fire-proof buildings and said: "They are perfectly safe." But these buildings were consumed as if made of pitch. The fire engines could do nothing to stay the destruction. The firemen were unable to operate the engines.

... when the Lord's time comes, should no change have taken place in the hearts of proud, ambitious human beings, men will find that the hand that has been strong to save will be strong to destroy. No earthly power can stay the hand of God. No material can be used in the erection of buildings that will preserve them from destruction when God's appointed time comes...

There are not many, even among educators and statesmen, who comprehend the causes that underlie the present state of society. Those who hold the reins of government are not able to solve the problem or moral corruption, poverty, pauperism, and increasing crime. They are struggling in vain to place business operations on a more secure basis. If men would give more heed to the teaching of God's word, they would find a solution of the problems that perplex them.

The scriptures describe the condition of the world just before Christ's second coming. Of men who by robbery and extortion are amassing great riches, it is written: "Ye have heaped treasure together for the last days. Behold the hire of the laborers who have reaped down your fields, which is of you kept back by fraud, crieth: and the cries of them whicih have reaped aer entered into the ears of the Lord of Sabaoth. Ye have lived in pleasure on the earth, and been wanton; ye have nourished your hearts, as in a day of slaughter. Ye have condemned and killed the just; and he doth not resist you."

But who reads the warnings given by the fast-fulfilling signs of the times? What impression is made upon worldings? What change is seen in their attitude? No more than was seen in the attitude of the inhabitants of the Noachian world. Absorbed in worldly business and pleasure, the antediluvians "knew not until the Flood came, and took them all away." Matt 24:39. They had heaven-sent warnings, but they refused to listen. And today the world, utterly regardless of the warning voice of God, is hurrying on to eternal ruin. The world is stirred with the spirit of war. The prophecy of the eleventh chapter of Daniel has nearly reached its complete fulfillment. Soon the scenes of trouble spoken of in the prophecies will take place. **Testimonies Vol 9 11.4, 12.1, 12.2, 12.3, 13.1, 13.2, 13.3, 13.4, 14.1, E. G. White**

Discussion questions

1. Can you think of other Bible stories which shed light on moving to the country?
2. In the context of country living, define and describe the word "country."
3. Study the story of the Israelites as they planned to cross over to the Jordan on their journey from slavery to freedom.
a. What does the Jordan river signify?
b. How long did it take?
c. What was the significance of the 12 stones?
d. What is significance of the Jordan river for us today (i.e., Israel crossed over Jordan, Jesus baptized in Jordan, Naaman dipped 7 times in Jordan), Elisha recovered axe head in Jordan
4. On a scale of 1 to 10, 1 = least and 10 = most important, how critical is a move to the country?
5. What are your top reasons for considering a move to the country?
6. How will you know the will of God for your family and in choosing where to live?
7. What additional written or video resources could be useful?

Chapter 3
Special equations

Equation writers rule the world. They are the people who codify natural and physical phenomena into mathematical equations. This allows engineers to calculate the trajectory of a moving target. It allows the physician to determine the correct therapies specific to a person's weight and other factors. Which happily married lover never gets tired of writing the "school girl's" equation?

Wesley + Evelyn = ♥

Here is a famous equation representing Einstein's theory of special relativity:

Energy = Mass x Speed of Light^2 OR $E=mc^2$

This is just a half-page chapter encouraging you to think about spiritual, health and other country living equations. How can we express our love for Christ as an equation? How did He express his love for us? Here is God's love equation:

Jesus' ♥ for us = †

Other equations:

Faith = (Promises X Prayer)^{Praise}

Love = (time spent with others x listening to others x sacrificing for others)$^{Praising\ God}$

Write your famous equation(s):

Chapter 4
Simplicity principle

Keep it simple (KIS). The KIS principle is almost always the best option for succeeding in life. Nineteenth century author and poet, Henry David Thoreau, took a time out from city living to spend two years living on a lake called Walden Pond. His writings describe the wildlife living on or near the pond. In his book, Walden, he strongly encourages his readers to "simplify, simplify!" We rush through life earning a living, keeping up with the neighbors and staying so busy we forget how to think and even how to relax. We need stimulants to wake up and pills to go to sleep. This chapter is about simplifying your life in a way that gives you the most freedom.

A number of theories directly or tangentially support the simplicity philosophy. One theory includes Occam's Razor. This states a possible criterium for evaluating or choosing between two differing theories or opinions, is, "What is the simplest explanation?" Usually the simplest theory consistent with the data is the best option. Einstein is noted to have said, "everything should be made as simple as possible, but no simpler." Another modern-day philosopher frequently says, "Fish the near water first." And if you haven't heard this acronym yet, I grew up hearing it from my parents. It is useful when discussing the simplicity principle, DIN or "do it now." If you wait to do things, they tend to accumulate and become bigger tasks. The DIN philosophy is another hallmark of a successful person.

Elaborate plans are oftentimes difficult to implement because they depend on many variables (some out of our control) aligning together in a timely manner. This does not mean elaborate plans should be avoided, they are absolutely essential, but it is advisable to condense planning into discrete units, without having to define every single aspect of a plan. Sometimes fluidity within a plan allows for a better outcome as long as there are none to only a few 'major' surprises. This book is a great example of simple planning without going too far into detailing each aspect of designing a garden, determining what to keep in your food storage plan, etc. If you spend hours and days planning everything down to the exact amount of salt you may need, you may miss opportunities to do other more meaningful things (i.e., there are only 24 hours in a day and of course you always stock more salt than you think you may need). For some activities, you may sacrifice a small degree of accuracy for speed and efficiency without negatively affecting your goal. It is important to find a balance between spending your time in productive ways as well as planning for specific goals. When it comes to effective teams, usually someone is better at anticipating details and another person sees the big picture. This combination is useful.

Not every area of our life can benefit from the simplicity principle. For example, we may enjoy a simple life without excessive obligations, but we might have a complex mind. We might enjoy a simple walk through the park on most nights but make a detailed plan for month long vacation to build a missionary hospital. We enjoy a simple meal while having a highly technical conversation about the best classical guitarist (it is going to be Segovia), but the debate about who takes second, third, fourth, etc., places is fierce and nuanced, requiring hours of discussion and listening time.

Simplicity does not imply ignorance. In fact, it may take complex life decisions to arrive at a place of stark simplicity. You may have a closet full of clothes but after moving several times, you learn the value of having fewer more functional clothing over having lots of clothes. This reminds me of my friend, Barbara. She owns 10 outfits, and no more. We were eating dinner at her place one weekend when this came up during the course of conversation. I didn't believe her so she invited me to her room and opened her closet. She had exactly 10 outfits hanging in her closet plus a few pairs of scrub pants and tops in drawers. This represented a turning point for me. I hope to one day attain this level of simplicity.

As Christians we look to Jesus to set an example. Jesus grew up in a carpenter's home with brothers and sisters. He studied the scriptures and learned his father's trade. In the early morning hours, Jesus could be found in seclusion searching the scriptures and in prayer. Even as a young child he knew and increasingly began to understand the scriptures and his role in the events foretold in scripture. He was familiar with every word of the scriptures. Jesus didn't need artificial excitement and meaningless activity in his life. He looked to his Father for comfort and inspiration. His choices in life reflected the will of his Father. He understood this because he connected to his Father at the beginning of every day. This gave meaning and direction to the rest of his day. Our lives may also be this simple if we follow His example by starting each day in prayer and meditation with our Saviour, Jesus.

In the book, The Pursuit of God, A. W. Tozer, warns Christians to simplify their lives. He cites examples of how Christians must deal with a constant intrusion of distractions. He states, "One way the civilized world destroys men is by preventing them from thinking their own thoughts." This occurs when we care more about what strangers think than we care about what our loved ones think. It happens when we spend our time watching TV, working, playing computer games, hanging out at the local bar, caring more about an agenda formulated in local and national newsrooms than about the agenda of our own household. Some of us live our lives as a disconnected observer. Instead of living every single moment and welcoming the pain as much as the joy, we take every opportunity to escape from our reality. We join a vicarious disconnected life of endless work, we jump in and out of disconnected and ultimately unsatisfying social interactions almost as frequently as we change marriage partners, etc. We care more about our social networking accounts than our children's report cards. We learn to express outrage at the drop of a hat in response to insignificant and personally irrelevant issues, while millions of third world children go hungry, suffer from malnutrition, and many are children and young women are forced into prostitution and slavery.

Now is the time to be cutting back our possessions and not increasing them.

We are good at faking just about everything, except what matters the most, Love. Love cannot be faked or imitated. A friend loves at all times, even during rough patches. If you haven't read 1 Corinthians 13 recently, read it again. Love can only be expressed as consistent actions which reflect the love of God toward us. Love = Christ.

In a sermon titled, "The Simplicity and Sublimity of Salvation," Charles Spurgeon (sermon # 2259), states, "To receive Christ, a man must be born of God. It is the simplest thing in all the world, one would think, to open the door of the heart, and let him in; but no man lets Christ into his heart till first God has made him to be born again, born from above… To believe is to trust. Prove that you believe in Christ by risking everything upon him. 'Upon a life I did not live, upon a death I did not die, I risk my whole eternity.'

On his who lived for me, and died for me, and rose again for me, and has gone into heaven for me; on him I throw the whole weight of past, present, and future, and every interest that belongs to my soul, for time and for eternity. This is a very simple matter, and I have noticed a great many sneers at this simple faith, and a great many deprecatory remarks concerning it; but, let me tell you, there is nothing like it under heaven. Possessing this faith will prove you to be a son of God; nothing short of it ever will. 'To as many as received him, to them gave he power to become sons of God;' and he has given that power to nobody else. This will prove you to be absolved, forgiven. 'There is, therefore, now no condemnation to them which are in Christ Jesus;' ... One grain of faith is worth more than a diamond the size of the world; yea, though thou shouldst thread such jewels together, as many as the stars of heaven for number, they would be worth nothing compared with the smallest atom of faith in Jesus Christ, the eternal Son of God."

By faith in God we move forward and make decisions. Achieving simplicity requires complex and often difficult decisions. Alfred North Whitehead, an English mathematician and philosopher, had many things to say about humanistic thinking. He argues life is a series of processes and not just material objects. Serial processes interact and make up the complexity of life. He writes, "The aim of science is to seek the simplest explanations of complex facts." One of my favorite Whitehead quotes, "It requires a very unusual mind to undertake the analysis of the obvious." Another quote, "Not ignorance, but ignorance of ignorance is the death of knowledge." Important concepts to contemplate.

We need to realize when we could benefit from outside input. It's OK to be ignorant about a certain issue as long as we seek God's guidance and then once we feel we understand God's direction, we take steps to augment or supplement this area with expert opinions and knowledge. In this case, use this book as a starting point and supplement areas of weakness. It is ideal to interact with this material in small groups or a classroom setting. This allows each person to stand on the shoulders of those who have gone before us. We don't have to make the same mistakes as others if we can learn from their mistakes. Associate with people who complement your weaknesses. When others need your help, freely share your areas of expertise with them.

Now is the time to cut back our possessions and not increase them. It is time to see our greatest treasures as human currency and a humble character and not materialistic, inanimate objects as our life's goals. Removing the focus on materialism helps to sharpen Biblical truths. As long as we are surrounded by every comfort, every possible convenience and luxury, we may not feel the pull of the Holy Spirit on our lives. We may miss the calling to minister to our local community or to an even greater audience. Possessions have a way of blinding us to spiritual truths. We trade money for things which have no bearing on our spiritual health or the ultimate spiritual goal, to spread the Gospel to the world and ensure as many people as possible have the opportunity to choose eternal life over eternal death. By stepping out in faith your witness in doing so may encourage others to follow your example. Never underestimate the power of your actions on your friends and family.

The Bible addresses simplicity as a virtue in **Psalm 116:6** (KJV), The Lord preserveth the simple; I was brought low, and He helped me. **Psalm 19:7** (KJV), "The law of the Lord is perfect, converting the soul: the testimony of the Lord is sure, making wise the simple." Micah 6:8 (KJV), He hath shewed thee, O man, what is good; and what doth the Lord require of thee, but to do justly, and to love mercy, and to walk humbly with thy God? Paul gives us this perspective in **1 Corinthians 14:33**, "For God is not a God of confusion, but of peace."

"Each soul may reach heights, depths, and breadths of knowledge in spiritual things, and be fitted for the higher life. When parents take the first steps, making their own habits and practices in eating, dressing, and living, as simple and natural as possible, with an eye single to the glory of God, there will be order in the home, and the children will not be neglected; but time will be devoted to their instruction and development." - **Counsels on Sabbath School work, page 5**.

Change your family's destiny by moving from the overcrowded and polluted city to the country. Children are not be exposed to worldly influences. They learn to perform useful tasks, care for and show kindnesses to animals, connect with the earth through gardening and other agricultural experiences. They reap the health benefits of direct contact with the ground and outdoor living. Ultimately, country living puts us in touch with family values and spiritual pursuits. I hope you enjoy your journey through this small but information-packed book about country living.

Reading books is critical for developing most types of intelligence. Most toys do not stimulate a child's intellectual development, in fact, most toys keep children from using their imagination. Reading, playing, making music, learning language, using their hands, interacting with others, solving problems are some of the best ways to promote brain development.

Children from the age of five and beyond, should be reading one age-appropriate book per day. This requires weekly trips to the library to keep hundreds of books from cluttering your space. Play is another critical activity. Children should learn the art of playing and not always just random, pointless activities. More often, play should be directed such as cleaning off the patio, organizing and cleaning garden tools, doing stretching activities, cleaning their rooms, preparing food, mowing a neighbor's lawn, helping organize for a garage sale, counting money, etc. Various types of play are important. Sometimes play can be fun and random, but it is more functional in brain development when it associated with a purpose.

Discussion questions

What areas of life benefit from the simplicity principle? Below is a list of areas where simplicity is a virtue.

1. When Christ was incarnated as a human, he lived as a human on earth for around 30 years. His return to heaven indicated he had finished his Father's work. Jeremiah 15:16, states, "Thy words were found, and I did eat them; and thy word was unto me the joy and rejoicing of mine heart: for I am called by thy name, O Lord God of hosts." How would moving to the country simplify my life and what example did Jesus give us while he lived as a human on the earth?

2. What virtues might contribute to successful country living?

3. Simplicity is a virtue. Each statement is a conversation starter and may be used to stimulate sharing between small groups. Read through this list and add your own ideas and share them with others.

    A. Meals: I have a menu cycle and recipes that are nourishing and my family loves them.

    B. Pantry: I have an organized and streamlined pantry which also includes emergency supplies.

    C. Laundry: I have a system for streamlining laundry chores.

    D. Laundry supplies: I like bleach, borax, lemon, salt, washing soda, Fels Naptha soap and sunlight.

    E. Cleaning supplies: better to have a few standard supplies than to have a different cleaning solution for every household surface. I like Bar Keeper's Friend, dish soap, vinegar, bleach, borax, orange oil, peroxide, and UV light.

    F. Garage and sheds: My garage is clean and organized by function using dedicated spaces, wall hanging units, tool boxes, and shelving. Describe an organizational system that may work for you.

    G. Automobiles: I have a yearly, monthly, weekly and daily system to monitor my family's cars. I keep my cars gas tank at least half full.

    H. Home maintenance: I have a yearly, monthly, weekly and daily system to monitor my family's home maintenance needs, etc. I write out on a calendar, all home maintenance needs and upkeep activities which need to be done on a regular basis.

    I. Finances: I have a personal financial system which works well.

    J. Bills: Most of my bills are on autopay or pain in advance.

    K. Cars: I like cars that do not break down so I buy a _____, model.

    L. Clothing: I like white cotton or linen shirts because when they get a stain, I can bleach them. I like black pants and jackets because when they get a stain, it won't show.

    M. Gardening: I have a monthly schedule that keeps my gardening tasks streamlined and efficient. Using the provided 12 Months of Gardening Tasks, place an "X" in the months which apply to your specific situation. The green shaded areas are general guidance but may not be specific to your area. Add additional tasks if necessary. This may help keep you on track and make your gardening experience more enjoyable and successful.

    N. I address weeds in the garden: I like using mulch on the garden so I don't have to weed as much.

    O. Greenhouse: I like a greenhouse because it can extend the growing season.

P. Simplify your social calendar: I like simple get-togethers where most of the cooking happens as people are arriving and everyone chips in and helps.

Q. Personal time: I prefer to primarily read documentaries, biographies and religious material which allows me more time to do other things with my family.

R. Mealtime: I prefer to eat two meals a day as opposed to three meals a day. This frees up about an hour or more of time every day to do other things I enjoy.

S. Priorities: I prefer to get the most difficult things done first thing in the morning so I can enjoy the rest of my day.

T. My philosophy about possessions: I prefer a simple home without a lot of nick knacks to collect dust and require frequent cleaning. This leaves time for family mission, and God.

U. The kids' toys: My children have a few simple toys (less than 10) and prefer to spend time outdoors.

V. Clutter: Toys and stuff does not clog up spaces in my home. I am clutter-free because of monthly vigilance.

W. Others:

4. Do I have too much stuff (i.e., am I a hoarder)?
5. How functional and useful is my stuff?
6. Why am I attached to material things?
7. When was the last time I used everything in my home?
8. Is it a good idea to get rid of things you have not used in the past year? If your answer is yes, are there exceptions?
9. Could someone else benefit from my excess stuff?
10. Does the excess stuff in my house make it difficult to keep clean, hygienic and tidy?
11. Is it possible the excess stuff in my house is making me sick?
12. How many toys does a child need?
13. What would happen if children were just provided with 10 or fewer toys, including but not limited to, building blocks, Legos, a chemistry set, an electronic circuit board, bikes, a drone, etc.

Chapter 5
Downsizing for country living

As a kid, I never enjoyed being on the receiving end of discipline. From time to time I required a whack or two on the backside, but as a general rule, I preferred to modify my behavior before I knew it would require Mother to get involved. This ability to think ahead and anticipate possible future events is an important skill and when combined with good frontal lobe function, is one characteristic out of many, of a Christ follower.

If we knew in advance a tornado would level our home or an earthquake would take out the bridge we were driving on, we would take corrective actions in advance. **As Christians who read and study the Bible, we are given advance warning about the future.** We can see the writing on the wall, in fact, as Christians, we can see and understand the writing on the wall. But do we warn others or keep this information in the family? Maybe we don't even see an ongoing and real time existential threat. We are hypnotized by convenience. We are lukewarm because we have never been hot or cold. We are legalistic because we do not understand the depth of God's love for us. We are oblivious to the danger of flirting with sin because in God's mercy we are shielded from the full consequences of sin.

In Old Testament times, God sent prophets to warn His people. Daniel was one of God's greatest prophets. **Daniel 5**, describes the fateful night a disembodied hand wrote the four words, "mene, mene, tekel, upharsin." The archaic words (either written in the local unvocalized Aramaic in cursive script or written as ideographs in Neo-Babylonian cuneiform script according to The Encyclopedia of the Bible) are translated – *numbered, numbered, weighed, divided*. Daniel is called to the king's side and immediately understands the words and their meaning. He translates and then eloquently interprets the words for the Babylonian king as, **"God has numbered the days of your kingdom and brought it to an end; you have been weighed and found wanting; your kingdom is divided and given to the Medes and Persians."** This is the terrifying message given to the heretofore indestructible Babylonian kingdom as Belshazzar is in the midst of a grand feast, drinking from cups stolen from Solomon's temple in Jerusalem (c. 1,000 – 586 BC). That very night, Darius conquered Babylon and killed Belshazzar. The Babylonian empire, corresponding to the head of gold (see Nebuchadnezzar's dream and Daniel's interpretation in **Daniel 2**), came to an end and the Medo-Persian empire, corresponding to the breast and arms of silver, began. Isaiah and Jeremiah each prophesied the Medes and Persians would overtake the Babylonian empire (**Isaiah 13, Jeremiah 25 and 51**). Additional prophecies by Ezra, foretold during the reign of Medo-Persia, the Jews would return to Judah; these experiences are recorded in the books of **Esther**, **Nehemiah** and **Ezra**. Greece, the brazen portion of the image, succeeded the Medo-Persia empire as the dominant world power, just as foretold in Nebuchadnezzar's dream. Greece fell to the Romans, just as predicted by Daniel's interpretation of

Nebuchadnezzar's dream. The Roman empire divided into smaller powers which make up Europe. By interpretation, they never mix together, just as the dream foretold. We now await the remainder of the **Daniel 2** prophecy to be fulfilled. Verses 34 and 35 have not yet occurred. Their fulfillment is described in verse 44, "And in the days of these kings shall the God of heaven set up a kingdom, which shall never be destroyed: and the kingdom shall not be left to other people, but it shall break in pieces and consume all of these kingdoms, and it shall stand forever." If the Bible is accurate and predictive. Christians should learn to trust the scriptures and build their life in accordance with them. We are on the verge of the most incredible unfolding prophecy yet to come. We should be thrilled as well as humbled to be alive during this time.

Just as Christ called the Rich Young Ruler to give up his lifestyle and follow Him, Christ calls us to sacrificially live for Him. To take up our cross and follow Him (**Matthew 19:16-22**). What does it mean, to bear the cross of Christ? How does the story of the Rich Young Ruler relate to downsizing, the topic of this chapter? What can we learn from this story as it relates to downsizing? It is one of many stories in Scripture which describe a lack of insight and understanding of where we are on God's historical timeline. If the Rich Young Ruler knew he was speaking with the God of the universe, would he have behaved differently? In **Matthew 25**, the 10 virgins waiting for the Bridegroom are depicted as sleeping when the Bridegroom shows up. However, only five had enough oil in their lamps to join the wedding party. All 10 virgins knew the Bridegroom was coming but only five prepared for him. Christ's three disciples, with him in the Garden of Gethsemane, are unable to stay awake, falling asleep twice, even as Christ asks them to pray for him (**Luke 22:39-46**). If we are awake and watching what is happening in the world, it's clear we're living at the end of prophetic visions and events right before Christ's 2nd coming.

As Christians, we anticipate Christ's second coming. We hope to be alive when it happens. But do we really believe it will happen during our lifetime (**Luke 21:34-36**)? The partying Babylonians never imagined the end to their existence was threatened that evening. The 10 virgins all planned to go to the wedding. Cognitive bias oftentimes distorts reality. We twist our conception of current events to minimize their significance and downplay how prophecy may play out. We do not know the hour or day of Christ's coming but it is sooner than ever before. Downsizing and moving to the country is one aspect of keeping your lamp full of oil. If you are prepared for what is coming, your preparations are not in vain. Christ honors our actions.

By downsizing and moving to the country, we do so in faith. We also reap the benefits of country living, simple living, working the land, and carving out more time for God and family. If there are things we can do right now to prepare for the time immediately preceding Christ's second coming, why would we hesitate? The Bible recommends we study to show ourselves approved. For those who study the Bible and are convicted Christ is returning soon and are convinced it is time to move out of the big cities, downsizing is a great first step.

Downsizing accomplishes several goals every Christian should desire. It removes the need to tend and care for material possessions, thus freeing up time and capital to dedicate to the Lord, "And he said unto them, Go ye into the world, and preach the gospel to every creature." **Mark 16:15**. Downsizing is compatible with caring for the environment and protecting against needless appropriation and mis-use of precious resources, "And God blessed them, and God said unto them, Be fruitful and multiply, and replenish the earth, and subdue it: and have dominion over the fish of the sea, and over the fowl of the air, and over every living thing that moveth upon the earth." **Genesis 1:28**.

Luke 9 (RSV) provides some insight into simple living. Beginning with verse 3, "Take nothing for your journey, no staff, nor bag, nor bread, nor money; and do not have two tunics. And whatever house you enter, stay there, and from there depart. And wherever they do not receive you, when you leave that town shake off the dust from your feet as a testimony against them." In verse 12 and onward, Luke describes how the crowd had gone to a desolate place to hear Jesus and be healed. Most had nothing to eat. Jesus commanded the disciples to give the crowd something to eat – 5,000 men plus women and children. Christ used a small boy's lunch of five loaves and two fishes, to feed thousands of people, a testament to the miracle of Christ's creative powers of adding new carbon sources to the planet when the need arose. They even had leftovers.

In Luke 9:23, Christ admonishes the crowd, "If any man would come after me, let him deny himself and take up his cross daily and follow me. For whoever would save his life will lose it; and whoever loses his life for my sake, he will save it. For what does it profit a man if he gains the whole world and loses or forfeits himself? For whoever is ashamed of me and of my words, of him will the Son of man be ashamed when he comes in his glory and the glory of the Father and of the holy angels. But I tell you truly, there are some standing here who will not taste death before they see the kingdom of God."

The last verses of **Luke 9**, are possibly the most provocative. As they were going along the road, a man said to him, "I will follow you wherever you go." And Jesus said to him, "Foxes have holes, and birds of the air have nests; but the Son of man has nowhere to lay his head." To another he said, "Follow me." But he said, "Lord, let me first go and bury my father." But Jesus said to him, "Leave the dead to bury their own dead; but as for you, go and proclaim the kingdom of God." Another said, "I will follow you, Lord; but let me first say farewell to those at my home." Jesus said to him, "No one who puts his hand to the plow and looks back is fit for the kingdom of God."

It sounds like Jesus was the ultimate minimalist. He knew all of heaven could be mobilized to meet the needs of his children. "I have been young, and now am old; yet have I not seen the righteous forsaken, nor his seed begging bread." **Proverbs 37:25**. There is power behind every promise in the Bible. What price is too high for Christ? How often do we say, I will do ABC when I retire, or I will spend more time in prayer and reading scripture when I get done with XYZ? Christ dealt in real time, not future time, not down-the-road time, but in the moment. He never missed an opportunity to ask people to follow Him. Possessions, family, obligations, even death were not good enough reasons to postpone following Christ. As we fix our gaze on the One who conquered death we become less tied to our material possessions and more in tune with God. The purpose of this chapter is to learn to shift our gaze from things of this world to Christ, like the words from the hymn, Turn Your Eyes Upon Jesus describes. … And the things of earth will grow strangely dim, in the light of His glory and grace (Helen Howarth Lemmel, 1863-1961).

We know Christ is coming soon. We know tumultuous times are on the horizon for Christians. We see how the world is turning against Christians. Christians are rapidly losing their majority status in the USA, while Europe and other traditionally Christian regions have all but lost their Christian identity. Strong political and psychological forces are garnered against Christians and those upholding Christian values. Maybe you have not personally experienced your faith on trial, but if you choose to remain in the city, it is likely you may experience passive or even aggressive discrimination because of your Christianity.

Downsizing is about taking baby steps to achieve your goals. However, if you are an over-achiever, you may choose to take giant leaps out of the city! Either way, it is a journey which begins with lightening the load. As we give up material possessions, we are more likely to have time and energy to study God's word. Some of us have minimalistic tendencies while others of us are pack rats. Taken to the extreme, are the hoarders (we will not go there). Downsizing accomplishes several difficult personal sacrifices. The first sacrifice is related to materialism. As we are able to downsize, we give up our material possessions. Sometimes these material possessions include family heirlooms such as boxes and boxes of photos, picture albums, family videos, fine china, a beautiful hutch, etc. Other times, the heirlooms are books, a Chinese vase received from a dear friend, a stunning cut crystal vase received as a wedding gift, a 1965 Mustang which occasionally runs, etc. Once gone, these sacrifices seem insignificant and pale in comparison to the trade off – more quality time with God and family.

When it comes to downsizing, devise a plan which includes a logical and sequential process. You may find it easier to start with each room of your home. Children should be allowed to do their rooms. Do an inventory and evaluate each item.

Eliminate duplicates when possible. Sometimes you may need more than one similar type item. For example, owning several pairs of black pants might be useful. However, 10 pairs of black pants might be excessive. Evaluate the frequency each item is used and then sort each item by its frequency related usefulness. Suggested frequency categories include: daily, weekly, monthly, seasonal, holiday, yearly, less than yearly, never – it still has the tag on it.

Additional considerations for clothing include: does it fit, is it functional, is it stylish, is it in good shape, does it require dry cleaning or can it be laundered at home, does it have sentimental value, does it make me feel happy / good, is the color great for me, is it versatile or limited, etc.? For men, evaluate clothing by color, fit, frequency of use, care required, condition, sentimental value, etc.

Many Christians make it a point to be fashion-forward, which is diametrically opposed to what is found in the Bible. **1 Peter 3:3-4** (NIV) reads, "Your beauty should not come from outward adornment, such as elaborate hairstyles and the wearing of gold jewelry or fine clothes. Rather, it should be that of your inner self, the unfading beauty of a gentle and quiet spirit, which is of great worth in God's sight." And, **1 Timothy 6:17-19** (NIV), "Command those who are rich in this present world not to be arrogant nor to put their hope in wealth, which is so uncertain, but to put their hope in God, who richly provides us with everything for our enjoyment. **Command them to do good, to be rich in good deeds, and to be generous and willing to share.** In this way they will lay up treasure for themselves as a firm foundation for the coming age, so they may take hold of the life that is truly life."

Sometimes it seems as if church is more of a fashion show than a place of worship. On the drive home after church, we make comments about what so-and-so wore and did you see what this person was wearing? Before anyone gets defensive about what kids wear to church (which I believe we should never criticize what young people wear to church and be 100% happy they are at church), we need to ask the question, "Why do kids feel compelled to focus on their outward appearance when their character is the critical element of their personhood?"

This is an interesting quote from E. G. White regarding criticism of others: "I saw that some are withering spiritually. They have lived some time watching to keep their brethren straight – watching for every fault to make trouble with them. And while doing this, their minds are not on God, nor on heaven, nor on the truth; but just where Satan wants them – on someone else." Testimonies for the Church, Vol 1, 145 (1885) (go to www.whiteestate.org and search for the whole excellent quote)..

Why do young girls focus on their physical attributes and feel insecure if they do not measure up to worldly standards? Why do young people across all walks of life feel compelled to mutilate and drastically change their physical appearance? Where did they learn to focus on fashion and outward appearances? Did they learn this at home or somewhere else? **If parents are superficially focused, their children learn the same values.** What is the real message they are sending to others by their actions, their dress, modifications to their physical body, etc.? **Is their cup empty or full? Are they broken or whole?** How can the corporate church family contribute to their spiritual growth without over-emphasizing the superficial things? Should we accept their choices or point them in a better direction? What are the risks of doing this? There are many more questions to ask and contemplate as we discuss this topic, but we need to stay focused on downsizing and not get too distracted.

The concept of country living and downsizing might actually help us better address the fashion forward issue from a practical perspective. Country living is likely to resolve this problem without making it a big issue by shifting the focus from minor issues to the larger picture of knowing God, companionship with like believers, and outreach in the community. **Most of the time, we leave church and even the adults cannot remember the pastor's message. Maybe city life really is the issue.** Maybe there are too many distractions in the city to stay focused on spiritual matters for more than a few minutes.

If the fashion show doesn't happen at church, maybe school is where students make a fashion statement. This used to be limited to just females, but over the past several decades, guys have joined the fashion forward crowd as well. This means they must own the latest fashions, shoes, accessories, look like a magazine model, etc. Guys must have the perfect sag in their pants, the right underwear band which peeks out at the top of their jeans or pants, the T-shirt with a cultural appropriation message, etc. Instead of clothes being just functional they now make a statement or send a cryptic message, colors and patterns may even indicate gang affiliation, etc.

This topic reminds me of my dad. One day I overheard Mother on the telephone explaining to one of her friends why her husband still wore an old brown polyester suit to church every week. She waxed on about the time she tried to replace his suit with a new one, but he made her return it. **She explained to her friend he didn't want to be better dressed than the poorest person who attended church. He wanted to express a quiet solidarity for those with whom he shared a similar past.** Maybe in a similar sense, Paul in the book of Acts records the believers were of "one accord." This level of community described by Paul throughout the New Testament is unprecedented in modern times. Take the time to study how the early believers came together in agreement about the Good News Gospel!

Moving to the country removes the need for fashion forward purchases (saving money and helping improve the budget). This might be one of many valuable reasons to move your family to the country. **Cows and chickens do not care what you think about polar bears at the North Pole or your favorite band.** Good luck rototilling in a pink and white tutu while wearing ballet shoes. In fact, you may find that children who move to the country and participate in country living chores and tasks, find fashion-forward statements are unnecessary and even wasteful. Princess and ninja turtle outfits become silly and superficial. **This revelation can only come about when their values are realigned.** This may not happen until their environment changes, family tasks are reoriented, their social environment is family and country living focused, and they become responsible for earning their own spending money. This transition from fashion forward to functional fashion may happen overnight or it may take time. The less parental involvement in making this happen, is better. It may be a good idea to allow kids to keep a certain amount of their fashionable clothing. This keeps them in the decision loop and makes it more likely they may ultimately make improved future decisions.

Downsizing is painful, especially if you have a lot of stuff. On a scale of 1, being least and 10, being most, make determinations of the usefulness of each possession. If you are working in the garage and sorting through tools and equipment, you could set up a form which might include category of tool (e.g., car repair, wood working, lawn, home repair), frequency of use, is it essential, how many similar tools are there, is the size of the tool critical, etc. Tools, unlike many other household items, are inherently valuable. It is good to keep what is necessary or even potentially necessary, but eliminating duplicates of non-essentials can be helpful when downsizing. Also, when possible, pass extra tools on to your children, relatives and friends.

The kitchen is the hub of the home.

It is where family and friends gather to prepare and share food; bake cookies; smear creamy butter and raspberry freezer jam on warm oven-fresh bread; harvest, preserve, and store food for the winter, etc. A farm kitchen is usually larger, with lots of counter and table top space, a few more burners, extra oven space, oversized pots and pans, a large apron sink, a working island, and lots of storage, etc. Many have an extra freezer and refrigerator and it may include an indoor and / or an outdoor root cellar. A farm kitchen usually has different types of kitchen equipment such as several large speckled enamel canning stock pots, a canner pressure cooker, a multi-pot juicer steamer, and other oversized kitchen equipment.

As we give up material possessions, we are more likely to have time and energy to study God's word.
Photo credit: Orlova Maria Tblisi Georgia, from Unsplash.com

Farm kitchens usually come with an outside door leading to an herb garden and sometimes a chicken coop. While there are unlimited versions of farm kitchens, just about any kitchen size and shape is acceptable as long as it is functional for your family. Some kitchens with minimal appliances can be highly functional. This makes me think of rustic kitchens with just a large fireplace and an oversized wood burning cook stove and ovens. Regardless of whether or not you have a farm kitchen, if you are moving to the country, you need to think about how you plan to use your kitchen. Maybe you are planning to grow microgreens or make designer pesto to sell at the local market (check with local health department requirements). Do you have an apple or peach orchard? Do you plan to preserve some or most of the harvest? Will it be used to can and process hundreds of quarts of produce? Do you need a significant amount of pantry storage? Where will you store large pots and pans. Is one oven enough? Are four burners enough? Planning to feed 4 people is different than needing to feed 20 people. Think about how the kitchen may be used. Do you need expanded pantry storage? A large dining table? A root cellar?

While you may need either a small, medium or large country kitchen, it may be a good idea to downsize what goes in the kitchen. Downsizing is an important issue. Simplicity and downsizing are intimately related. For example, you may be able to substitute a stick blender for a larger size blender. Another level of thinking is how would you blend food if you didn't have electricity? These are the types of things to consider as you downsize and move to the country. It is ok to have electronic equipment but there may be a time where electricity is a limited commodity. Best to have a back-up plan for this contingency.

Instead of accumulating material things, learn how to think about maximizing the use of fewer tools and equipment. For example, a bread machine is unnecessary if you know how to make bread without one. Teach every family member how to make bread. This makes a bread machine unnecessary. If you love pasta, invest in a manual pasta machine. If you like to dehydrate your excess produce, build a solar or electric dehydrator. For that matter, you can even build a solar oven. A crock pot is a nice way to prepare a meal without spending a lot of time in the kitchen, but you can also cook in a Dutch oven on top of the stove. Invest in quality equipment which is durable and sturdy. Flimsy wooden spoons may not last but ones made with hard wood and thick handles endure for decades.

Electronic equipment should be NSF certified, usually indicating a safer and higher quality product. Commercial kitchen equipment may make certain tasks simpler. For example, a 20- or 30-quart floor or table top commercial mixer will make quantity bread making much easier and require less time. If you are making large batches of bread, you may need an outdoor oven to accommodate multiple loaves. With commercial kitchen equipment, you have the potential to make and sell food products such as bakery items, sweet breads, muffins, cookies, casseroles, etc.

If you are planning a move to the country, downsize before you go. This gives you more time when you arrive in the country to accomplish your priorities as you begin a new life. As you downsize your possessions, prioritize what you use on a regular basis, maybe even daily or weekly. Label what you use once per month or less and then another category of things you use once per year or less.

As you go through each room in your home, identify the contents and give each item a mental frequency-of-use label. For infrequently used items, determine if they are really necessary or could another item work just as well. You may go room by room or you may go by categories such as: food, kitchen appliances, pots and pans, canning, entertaining, dishes, party wares, glasses, electronic equipment, small wares, clothing, shoes, king / queen / twin bedding, pillows, cleaning supplies, toys, paperwork, kids clothing, pet stuff, paperwork, family pictures, wall hangings, mirrors, tables and chairs, lounging furniture, display furniture, laundry room items, books and bookshelves, music and instruments, sports equipment, tools, collections, camping equipment, backpacking equipment, travel stuff, birthday and other gifts (not yet given), coats and outerwear, pool supplies, lawn care, gardening and seeds, pharmacy stuff, essential oils, crafts, hobbies, work-related, computers, home school, lighting, clocks, nick knacks, wedding gifts, writing materials, first aid supplies, legal and other important documents, telephone and communication equipment, artwork, curtains and window treatments, bathroom supplies, baskets, quilts, sewing supplies, health equipment, etc. To organize, choose a category and place everything in that specific category in one place to assess what is essential.

As you organize, go through each item and eliminate duplicates, damaged or in-operable units, out-of-date items, items you never use, etc. Maybe invite one of your minimalist and brutally honest friends to help you. Make sure you can handle their constructive comments and criticisms. **If you are unsure about whether or not you can live without an item, pack it up, put it in long-term storage and re-evaluate in one year. Sometimes, the passing of time allows our mind to disconnect from material things and put them in the right perspective.**

When it comes to downsizing, make sure your priorities are in the right place. **Coach Tom Landry of the Dallas Cowboys (1960 – 1988), never hesitated to define his priorities. It was the first thing he stated at the beginning of every season as he welcomed the new recruits and the returning players to spring training. His priorities were in this order: Faith (God), Family and Football.** By his excellent example he inspired hundreds of young football players to follow in his steps. He also inadvertently inspired millions of his fans in a similar fashion. Tom Landry was a man of few words. His players knew better than to try to talk over him or disrespect him. He was the consummate football coach and Texan. Some of my favorite quotes attributed to him include:

- Being the best at whatever talent you have, this is what stimulates life.

- Coaching is simple. It's about getting players to play better than they think they can.

- Take away winning, and you take away everything that is strong about America.

- Life is really about finding the right relationship between yourself and God.

- My hats gave me an identity. In fact, if I had a dollar for every time someone has seen me bareheaded and said, 'I almost didn't recognize you without a hat on,' I could have bought the Cowboys myself.

"Achievement builds character."
-Tom Landry

- As a Christian, I know my life is in God's hands. He has a plan for me. Therefore, I never worry about winning or losing football games. This knowledge gives me composure in tough situations.

- I've learned that something constructive comes from every defeat.

Think about your priorities and organize your life in a way that matters and positively reflects Christ. To keep important relationships in the right dimensions, avoid spending time on divisive conspiracy theories; even if they are true. Even when true, conspiracies are widely mocked and any association with political conspiracies should be avoided. In addition, consider avoiding most types of political activities, including demonstrations, in some cases even voting or supporting a candidate can lead to hyper-polarization, internet diatribes, etc. Prioritize your life in such a way that gives you the greatest assurance of making good decisions. Putting God first, your relatives second, and everything else in an order you designate.

Resources

- The life-changing magic of tidying up by Marie Kondo (book)
- Tidying up with Marie Kondo (Netflix)
- The home edit series
- Organized simplicity by Tsh Oxenreider (book)
- Daily docket by Tsh Oxenreider (daily planning checklist) – See God given tasks in the appendix
- https://www.youtube.com/watch?v=jTX02y0nJBw

Discussion Questions

1. Do Christians have an advantage over others when it comes to understanding what will happen in the future?
2. How should Christians relate to political debate?
3. How should Christians view prophetic proclamations in the Bible, especially ones which are cloaked in symbolism?
4. Is it possible for Christians to miss the full meaning of prophecies?
5. What gives one the ability to understand Biblical prophecies?
6. Can you describe several reasons downsizing might benefit Christians living today?
7. How should Christians view their material possessions?
8. What is your greatest possession?
9. What would you not be willing to give up amongst your material possessions?
10. List 3 benefits of downsizing and reducing your material possessions.
11. What are your top 3 priorities and would your family and friends list the same 3 that you would?
12. What was Christ's most important material possession while living on earth?

Chapter 6
Character development

What makes a person interesting? I find the most interesting people are those who know the Lord and endure hardship and come out on the other end as positive and optimistic people who know how to lift up the Lord to others. They don't have all the answers. They are humble and exhibit a servant mentality and not a know-it-all, the-world-owes-me obnoxiousness. **Christians do not expect other people to give them things, to respect them, or even to be kind to them.** We have learned to rise above societal norms and demands and live in a way that reflects Christ's love for others. In every single case, I find true Christians to have a strong personal relationship with the Lord. They don't stop searching and studying the deep truths in the Scriptures. When a Christian goes through a rough patch, they don't blame others or exhibit caustic behaviors, they learn to rely on the Lord for their strength. Being a Christian doesn't mean one has a simple or even ignorant mind, but it means we rely on a higher power for our strength. This actually increases our influence in the world.

Many Christians flirt with sin. This is because we do not fully understand sin. If we did, we would do everything possible to avoid it. What does it mean to flirt with sin? It means we continue in our sinful ways to the point we don't recognize it as sin. We deny the power of the Gospel, we begin to believe more in our own ways than in the calling to bear the cross of Christ.

Sin always has consequences. The story of Samson (found in **Judges 13 - 16**), is about one of the most unorthodox judges of Israel (1154 – 1124 BC) and a member of the tribe of Dan. Samson took a Nazarite vow (see **Numbers 6**) to separate himself from wine and similar drink; he shall drink neither vinegar made from wine nor vinegar made from similar drink; neither shall he drink any grape juice, nor eat fresh grapes or raisins. All the days of his separation he shall eat nothing produced by the grapevine, from seed to skin. All the days of the vow of his separation no razor shall come upon his head; until the days are fulfilled for which he separated himself to the Lord, he shall be holy and shall let the locks of his hair grow. He should separate himself from dead bodies. All the days of his separation he is holy unto the Lord...

After years of successfully following the Nazarite vow, Samson gives it up in a spectacular fashion. Even though it appears Samson failed as a judge, Paul mentions Samson in **Hebrews 11:32**, the faith chapter. He refers to Samson as a man of great faith. Three times the "Spirit of the Lord" came upon Samson **(Judges 13:25; 14:6, 19; 15:14)**. What makes Samson a man of great faith? If we carefully read the story of Samson's life, we see how at the beginning and at the end of his life, Samson understood his role and he cooperated with God, ultimately bringing destruction to 3,000 Philistines, even at the cost of his own life. This act ultimately weakened the Philistine nation and led to delivering the Israelites from the hands of the Philistines.

In his last act, Samson, in his weakened and blind condition was chained and taken to a Philistine celebration that included worship to the Philistine god of fertility, Dagon. Samson fully understood the depravity of the Philistine nation and knew his role would be, just as it was written in **Judges 13:5**, "It is he who shall begin to deliver Israel from the hand of the Philistines." After his death, this epic struggle against the Philistines was continued by subsequent judges and kings, including Samuel, Saul and David. God's view encompasses the entire timeline of the world and not just the lifetime of a few people. He uses one generation after another to accomplish his goals.

As our character becomes more Christ-like, we begin to see our role as cooperating with God in standing against evil. When we lift up the Standard of Christ against Satan and his evil angels, evil is cast down. The work is not complete until Jesus comes again and takes us to Heaven. All was won at the Cross, but for each person and each generation since Adam and Eve, the stakes are equally high. Character is the only thing we take to heaven. We all make mistakes and sin against God, but in the end and hopefully over our lifetime, we always seek to cooperate with God while fighting against evil.

The great stories in the Bible about those who cooperate with God should give everyone hope. We have so much to be thankful for, but some Christians are tone deaf and attempt to impose a legalistic and even hypocritical view of God on others. Other Christians ignore or minimize certain aspects of scripture to neuter or place God in a certain box. In some cases, Christians interpret the Bible from deep-seated emotional issues such as abandonment, abuse, a violent past, peer pressure or poor self-esteem. Some Christians prefer their "designer" interpretation of scripture over a "thus saith the Lord…." Some are so stuck on their own paradigm of the Gospel they must write their own bible, leaving out verses which conflict with their version of the Gospel, and modifying other verses to glorify their pathological cognitive biases. If we stay on track and see God as using us to accomplish His purposes, whether or not we understand every detail of His plan, we may be known as a person who cooperated with God. Our sphere of influence may be small or large. We may win our entire family to Christ or we may win an entire platoon to Christ. We are only limited by our vision. **The fight against evil forces seeking to degrade and dehumanize us does not end until we are redeemed.**

Biblical truths build and amplify the Bible and do not change it. Certainly, new light through reading the scriptures is revealed to us every single day, but the new light never conflicts with present truth. Changing and slightly twisting the truth is Satan's tactic. God doesn't need a human PR firm to cast Him in a human-perceived "acceptable" light. **God needs Christians to point people to Christ – He must be lifted up! Christ and Christ alone must be lifted up, not our favorite pastor or speaker, not our spouse, not our parents, not our children, not our co-workers, not our boss.** Only Christ should be lifted up as worthy of complete devotion. Do not fear, God is bigger than the most destructive forces on earth. He has many ways to reach all of humanity with the Gospel – God is Love!

Love is the most powerful force in the universe. Christians should be known as people who love others. They are not infallible, but people who are continually deepening their understanding of a loving Saviour and exhibiting their love for others by actual outreach and interventions on behalf of those who are less fortunate. **If a Christian always has their hand out for this and that, if they insist on playing the victim role, they are missing**

out in understanding the deep and enduring love our Father has for his children and the many ways God is capable of caring for us. **Matthew 20:16** (as well as **Mark 10:31** and **Luke 13:30**) states, So the last shall be first, and the first last: for many be called, but few chosen." Jesus makes it clear, it is more difficult for a wealthy person to enter heaven. The Jews of that time believed only wealthy people could attain God's favor by giving offerings and doing good works. Jesus was speaking to the Jewish rabbis who believed they would enter the kingdom of heaven first because of their standing in the church. Jesus' words contradicted their dearly held belief. It does not matter who you are, what you have done, or how much money is in your bank account, but if you believe on Him, if you repent of your sins, if you have faith in His words, if you learn to depend on Him for everything, your reward is in heaven. If you want to change your life, sacrificially serve others in ministry and outreach, and see how the Lord rewards you!

Love is not the only virtue a Christian exhibits. "But the fruit of the Spirit is love, joy, peace, forbearance, kindness, goodness faithfulness, gentleness and self-control. Against such things there is no law." **Galatians 5:22-23**.

Ways to strengthen our Christian walk include scripture reading and memorization, prayer for our loved ones as well as prayer for others (i.e., stranger prayers), praising God at every opportunity (as opposed to taking God's name in vain and complaining about our condition), claiming Bible promises and fellowship with others. Take every opportunity to know the Lord. Tell others what He has done for you. Expound on His virtues. As Christ increases in our life, our needs, desires and wants begin to fade. We learn to live sacrificially for others.

When it comes to prayer, God works on our behalf in ways we do not comprehend. When a child dies prematurely, a drunk driver kills your wife and three children, or when your spouse gets a chronic degenerative diagnosis, we either turn to God for comfort or we blame God. God did not invent sin but He allows it to operate for now. He set up the standard in the Garden of Eden but as humans, we regularly fail to reject sin.

This quote sums up how we should approach our prayer life. "We all desire immediate and direct answers to our prayers, and we are tempted to become discouraged when the answer is delayed or comes in an unexpected way. But God is too wise and good to answer our prayers always at just the time and in just the manner we desire. He will do more and better for us than to accomplish all our wishes. And because we can trust His wisdom and love, we should not ask Him to concede to our will, but we should seek to enter into His will and accomplish His purpose."-**Ministry of Healing, p 230-1**.

Character is the only thing we take to Heaven. When we die, our bodies break down and turn into minerals and decomposed organic matter, with a value of about $1, unless you have gold fillings, which would boost your value. When Christ returns and the dead in Christ are raised up, their bodies are reconstituted and given immortality. The only thing which remains intact is the character we possess when we die. The following in an excerpt from **Counsels for the Church, pages 98-99** (E. G. White), about the importance of developing our character.

God has given parents their work, to form the characters of their children after the divine Pattern. By His grace they can accomplish the task; but it will require patient, painstaking effort, no less than firmness and decision, to guide the will and restrain the passions. "And they shall teach my people the

difference between the holy and profane, and cause them to discern between the unclean and the clean." Ezekiel 44:23. Old Testament priests were given the task of discernment, a difficult task. Parents should also pray for discernment. A field left to itself produces only thorns and briers. He who would secure a harvest for usefulness or beauty must first prepare the soil and sow the seed, then dig about the young shoots, removing the weeds and softening the earth, and the precious plants will flourish and richly repay his care and labor. Character building is the most important work ever entrusted to human beings, and never before was its diligent study so important as now. Never was any previous generation called to meet issues so momentous; never before were young men and young women confronted by perils so great as confront them today.
-Child Guidance, p. 169

Strength of character consists of two things — power of will and power of self-control. Many youth mistake strong, uncontrolled passion for strength of character; but the truth is that he who is mastered by his passions is a weak man. The real greatness and nobility of the man is measured by the power of the feelings that he subdues, not by the power of the feelings that subdue him. The strongest man is he, who, while sensitive to abuse, will yet restrain passion and forgive his enemies. Such men are true heroes. **Maranatha, p. 223.**

Many have such meager ideas of what they may become that they remain dwarfed and narrow, when, if they would improve the powers which God has given them, they might develop a noble character and exert an influence that would win souls to Christ. Knowledge is power; but intellectual ability, without goodness of heart, is a power for evil. **Counsels for the Church, 198.6**

God has given us our intellectual and moral powers, but to a great extent every person is the architect of his own character. Every day the structure is going up. The word of God warns us to take heed how we build, to see that our building is founded upon the eternal Rock. The time is coming when our work will stand revealed just as it is. Now is the time for all to cultivate the talents which God has given them, that they may form characters for usefulness here and for a higher life hereafter. **Counsels for the Church, 198.7**

Discussion questions

1. Every Christian is called to bear the cross of Christ. What is your cross to bear and what things can we do to successfully bear the cross of Christ?
2. How can we best sear the Word of God into our hearts and mind?
3. What can we do to minimize bearing a false witness as a Christ follower?
4. What role does prayer play in Christian growth, Christian service and Christian fellowship?
5. What characteristics do Christ, Mahatma Gandhi and Mother Theresa have in common?
6. What makes up our character?
7. How difficult is it to develop a character formed after what Christ modeled for us?
8. What characteristics, if any, are universal to Christians?
9. How can we as Christians, improve our influence in the world?

Chapter 7
Your brain, what it means to be human, and the frontal lobes

There are 5 important take home messages in this chapter related to the brain, what it means to be human, and the importance of good frontal lobe function. An infinitely complex and loving God created us. He wants to be in constant fellowship with us. Each person's brain is uniquely designed to communicate and fellowship with God. Someday soon, we expect to be in fellowship with all of Heaven, but for now, our lifeline to God and the only way to Heaven, is through our brain and how we choose to relate to Christ and the plan of salvation, initiated to save the fallen and lost human race. God draws us to Him through His word, through Jesus' love for humanity as shown by his role in the plan of redemption, the beauty and majesty of nature, and through interactions with those around us including our family and friends and even the animals. The Holy Spirit continuously reminds us of the beauty of the Plan of Salvation and how great was the sacrifice for our redemption. This is why it is imperative we keep our brain healthy and open to hearing God's voice and seeing His sovereign work in us and through us.

There are many aspects to understanding what it means to be human. Examining what makes us uniquely human requires we explore the brain's frontal lobes. I should make it clear, animals also have frontal lobes. Some animals have more complex and larger frontal lobes relative to humans, including dolphins, elephants, whales, etc. **But there is something unique about human frontal lobes and spirituality and how this connection is primed by making choices such as caring for our body, resting, worshipping, daily exposure to sunlight and fresh air, regular physical activity, hard work, fellowship with others, loving relationships, etc.**

Frontal lobes are infinitely complex. It seems simplistic to limit the discussion to just 5 aspects, but this chapter is not intended to be an exhaustive treatise on frontal lobes. It is just enough to provide a grid for you to do your own research and make your own relevant observations. Hopefully you will share your experiences with others as new insights arise.

The 5 messages are as follows:

1. **The science of salvation encompasses every aspect of our existence, whether it is genetics, molecular biology, medicine, nutrition, language, music, art, etc.**

2. **We connect with heaven through our frontal lobes**, the control panel of our humanity. Our frontal lobes may be compromised by many things including chronic unrelenting stress, a poor diet, inverted circadian rhythm, behaviors, music, computer games, TV, accidents, toxins, chronic degenerative disease, etc.

3. **The Bible identifies those who are Christians as sealed in their foreheads (frontal lobe area considered to be the seat of spirituality) and their hands (illustrative of helping others).**

4. **The brain is the most highly metabolic region of the body and needs a constant supply of oxygen, nutrients, and voltage.** Oxygen is essential to the health of the brain and the optimal functioning of cranial nerves and sensory inputs. Complex neural cells are voltage driven using ions found in the brain and the body. Nutrients supply essential metabolic components giving life to complex brain cells and tissues.

5. **Good brain functions translate into health, equanimity, gratitude, good choices (expression of free will), spirituality, vitality, a servant mentality, and many others, all traits and characteristics of Christ's followers.**

In 1961, Stanley Milgram, a psychologist at Yale University conducted one of the most controversial experiments of modern times, examining the link between following one's conscience vs. taking orders from a person in "authority." He designed his experiment to investigate communist Germany and the Nazi atrocities of World War 2, where thousands of German Nazis housed, tortured and murdered millions of Christians and Jews, living in Germany and neighboring countries. Their methods of neutralizing (i.e., dehumanizing, canceling) their fellow human beings, even including the elderly and young children and then murdering them, have been studied for more than half a century. A decade or so after WW2 ended, Stanley Milgram designed a study to determine the ability of the average person to resist authority when an "authority" figure was asking them to do something morally reprehensible.

Participants in the Milgram experiments were <u>told to obey all instructions</u>. Subsequently, they were told to deliver gradually increasing electric shocks to a subject who was in a different room, when the subject gave a wrong answer to a question. Unbeknownst to the participants, the subject "receiving" the gradually increasing shocks for wrong answers, was an actor. As the experiment commenced, the participants were able to watch the subject (i.e., the actor) through a one-way window as they received shocks but the subject was not able to see the participant. The subject (i.e., the "actor") was strapped into an electric chair and then the researcher (wearing a white coat), in charge of the experiment provided instructions to the experiments' participants who were recruited to deliver the shocks to the subject (i.e., the "actor") when they gave a wrong answer. The voltage of each shock increased for each wrong answer. As the voltage increased, the subject (i.e., the 'actor') would make increasingly audible and aggravated protests. As the shocking voltage increased with each wrong answer, the subject (i.e., the "actor") began to beg and plead for mercy, sometimes even banging their fists and crying. **Not all participants complied as the researcher prodded them to continue the electric shocks.** A few of them would stand up and argue with the researcher while saying things like, "keep your money, I'm not doing this," as they walked out… The participants were reimbursed $4 for their time and participation in the experiment, the equivalent of $34 in today's value.

Let's fast forward to the results. **In the first set of experiments, 65% of participants in the study delivered the equivalent of a "lethal" shock to the subject (i.e., the actor).** In some cases, the participant wanted to stop, but the researcher prodded them on and they reluctantly complied. **In Stanley Milgram's follow-up experiments, the percentage of participants willing to give the equivalent of a lethal shock, ranged from 28% all the way up to 91%.** (Also read about the Stanford Prison experiment.)

What do the Milgram experiments say about frontal lobe function? Which participant would you be? Would you refuse to obey a "self-proclaimed" authority (i.e., the researcher wearing a white coat), or would you be one who would deliver the equivalent of a lethal shock? Statistically speaking, most people fall into the latter category. Does being a Christian matter? As Christians, are we willing to cede our frontal lobe functions to a person in "authority?" What if the person in "authority" is our pastor, spouse, parent, child, president, etc.? What if the subject (i.e., the person needing "correction") is a different color, religion or nationality? Are we willing to watch as our fellow humans suffer and die? **Who is our authority?** How are we allowed to exercise our God-given free will? Is every person's free will of equal value? Does anyone else have the right to over-ride our free will? **How do our frontal lobes protect us against the perils of the society in which we live?** Are we willing to be part of the lawless mob or do we stand up and guard each person's humanity and dignity?

Our frontal lobes provide a line of communication with Heaven. When we make choices to protect our frontal lobes, we participate in a wonderful experiment, known as life with God. We choose an abundant life of knowing and following Christ. This life is not guaranteed to be perfect. Read the books of Job and Ecclesiastes if you doubt this. Each of the Gospel writers describe the crucifixion of Jesus. Paul also describes Christ's crucifixation. "For ye, brethren, became followers of the churches of God which in Judea are in Christ Jesus: for ye also have suffered like things of your own countrymen, even as they have of the Jews: Who both killed the Lord Jesus, and their own prophets, and have persecuted us; and they please not God, and are contrary to all men: Forbidding us to speak to the Gentiles that they might be saved, to fill up their sins always: for the wrath is come upon them to the uttermost" **1 Thessalonians 2:14-16.** In these verses, Paul speaks about how his fellow "countrymen" were willing to torture and kill for their beliefs. When our beliefs become so powerful they cause one group to single out another group and ridicule, torture and kill them, we have descended into an evil Satanic tyranny. **Are you willing to ruin another person's life because you believe differently?** Where do you get your authority? Is your moral code better than someone else's?

What if someone commits a moral slip or makes a spectacular moral fall? Are you willing to discredit and dehumanize them? I'm guessing Jesus might start writing your sins in the sand for you to contemplate. When you are tempted to virtue signal your "goodness" (which is like filthy rags) and gaslight another person, remember the verse **Romans 3:23**, "For all have sinned and come short of the glory of God." In a short verse in **Jude**, we are given the perfect response to any temptation to gossip or degrade another human being. "Yet Michael the archangel, when contending with the devil he disputed about the body of Moses, durst [past tense of dare] not bring against him a railing accusation, but said, the Lord rebuke thee." Even Christ would not directly rebuke the devil when contending for Moses' body. This is how serious it is to avoid the temptation to judge and criticize others. Think about Christ and the woman caught in adultery. Christ chose the spiritual solution over moralizing with the woman. I believe a person with good frontal lobes will see the spiritual aspect of the situation, even when it may contradict a societal norm or "moral."

Recently I had an insightful conversation with some dear friends, Dr's Norman and Leona Gulley. Norman said something profound. **He said everything we know, experience, and understand, is about the plan of salvation.** It didn't fully register with me until I settled into bed that evening. I recalled their comments and began to process them. I thought certainly I could find an exception to this statement, but after going through as many examples as my tired brain could imagine, I came to the realization his statement was correct.

When every aspect of our life is viewed through the lens of the plan of salvation, we perfectly see how God created the world not only for our pleasure and enjoyment, but for His as well. He made us and all living things to be in communion with him. We are meant for Him. It is when we view ourselves through his lens, all the pieces of this puzzle known as planet earth, make perfect sense. God created each and every living thing with the innate ability to connect with Him through our infinitely complex brain. Think about it. **We would only need an infinitely complex brain to connect with the infinite God of the universe. Anything less would fail to reflect His majesty and glory.** It is through creation, we see the Creator in every aspect of our planet. We also see how sin has marred what was once perfect. **Luke 19:40** provides insight into this concept.

As Jesus entered Jerusalem a week before his death on the cross, he rode in on a borrowed donkey. The people lined the streets to praise Him as "the king who comes in the name of the Lord" (**Luke 19:38**). When the Pharisees heard the crowd cheering Him, they called upon Jesus to rebuke the crowd, but Jesus boldly answered, **"I tell you, if these should hold their peace, the stones would immediately cry out." Colossians 1:16** states "For by him were all things created, that are in heaven, and that are in earth, visible and invisible, whether they be thrones, or dominions, or principalities, or powers: all things were created by him and for him."

Psalm 148 declares, **"Praise ye the Lord,** Praise ye the Lord from the heavens: Praise ye him, all his angels: Praise ye him, all his hosts. Praise ye him, sun and moon: Praise him, all ye stars of light. Praise him, ye heavens of heavens, and ye waters that be above the heavens. Let them praise the name of the Lord: for he commanded, and they were created. He hath also stablished them for ever and ever: He hath made a decree which shall not pass. Praise the Lord from the earth, ye dragons, and all deeps: fire, and hail; snow, and vapor; stormy wind fulfilling his word: mountains, and all hills; fruitful trees, and all cedars: beasts, and all cattle; creeping things, and flying fowl: kings of the earth, and all people; princes, and all judges of the earth: both young men and maidens; old men and children: let them praise the name of the Lord: **for his name alone is excellent**; His glory is above the earth and heaven. He also exalteth the horn of his people, the praise of all his saints; even of the children of Israel, a people near unto him. Praise ye the Lord."

Many Bible verses attest to the glory and majesty of the Creator. One of my favorite quotes about salvation is one of the most profound I have ever read outside of the Scriptures. I hope you enjoy reading it as much as I do, even after having read it hundreds of times. Here it is:

> There the redeemed shall know, even as also they are known. The loves and sympathies which God Himself has planted in the soul shall there find truest and sweetest exercise. The pure communion with holy beings, the harmonious social life with the blessed angels and with the faithful ones of all ages who have washed their robes and made them white in the blood of the lamb, the sacred ties that bind together "the whole family in heaven and earth'" (**Ephesians 3:15**) – these help to constitute the happiness of the redeemed.
>
> ## There, immortal minds will contemplate with never-failing delight the wonders of creative power, the mysteries of redeeming love. There
> will be no cruel, deceiving foe to tempt to forgetfulness of God. Every faculty will be developed, every capacity increased. The acquirement of knowledge will not weary the mind or exhaust the energies. There the grandest enterprises may be carried forward, the loftiest aspirations reached, the highest ambitions realized; and still there will arise new heights to surmount, new wonders to admire, new truths to comprehend, fresh objects to call for the powers of mind and soul and body.
>
> ## All the treasures of the universe will be open to the study of God's redeemed. Unfettered by mortality, they wing their tireless flight to worlds afar – worlds
> that thrilled with sorrow at the spectacle of human woe and rang with songs of gladness at the tidings of a ransomed soul. With unutterable delight the children of earth enter into the joy and the wisdom of unfallen beings. They share the treasures of knowledge and understanding gained through ages upon ages in contemplation of God's handiwork. With undimmed vision they gaze upon the glory of creation – suns and stars and systems, all in their appointed order circling the throne of Diety. Upon all things, from the least to the greatest, the Creator's name is written, and in all are the riches of His power displayed.
>
> And the years of eternity, as they roll, will bring richer and still more glorious revelations of God and of Christ. As knowledge is progressive, so will love, reverence, and happiness increase. The more men learn of God, the greater will be their admiration of His character. As Jesus opens before them the riches of redemption and the amazing achievements in the great controversy with Satan, the hearts of the ransomed will thrill with more fervent devotion, and with more rapturous joy they sweep the harps of gold; and ten thousand times ten thousand and thousands of thousands of voices will unite to swell the mighty chorus of praise.
>
> And every creature which is in heaven, and on earth, and under the earth, and such as are in the sea, and all that are in them, heard I saying, Blessing, and honor, and glory, and power, be unto Him that sitteth upon the throne, and unto the Lamb for ever and ever. **Revelation 5:13**.

The great controversy [between Christ and Satan] is ended. Sin and sinners are no more. The entire universe is clean. One pulse of harmony and gladness beats through the vast creation. From Him who created all, flow life and light and gladness, throughout the realms of illimitable space. From the minutest atom to the grandest world, all things, animate and inanimate, in their un-shadowed beauty and perfect joy, declare that God is love." -**Great Controversy, p 677-8**

Let's go back to Jesus' triumphal entry into Jerusalem. Luke, the physician and only non-Jew apostle (not one of the original disciples), tells us, had not the crowd cheered for Jesus, the inanimate rocks would have cried out! The entire creation is endeared to Christ, the Creator. We are as well, to the extent we accept Christ and commit to follow Him. **Truly, everything we know, experience and understand is about the plan of salvation.**

We connect to God through our frontal lobes. If you take the palm of your hand and place it just above your eyebrows and then move back one more hand width, you are touching the area known as your frontal lobes. This region of the brain is responsible for emotions such as empathy, gratitude, love, generosity, reasoning, patience, spirituality, spiritual discernment, morality, communication, self-organization, planning, long-term memory, impulse control, problem solving, judgment, initiation, sexual behaviors, social interactions, recognition, speech patterns, and others. When we pray, our frontal lobes are involved. **In fact, lack of empathy, prayer avoidance, and lack of spiritual discernment, are several of the most accurate signs one's frontal lobes are compromised.**

Moses describes how empathy combined with gratitude, as manifested in kind and loving actions, are connected with frontal lobes. **Deuteronomy 11:18-19** reads, "So commit yourselves wholeheartedly to these words of mine [10 commandments]. **Tie them to your hands and wear them on your forehead as reminders. Teach them to your children. Talk about them when you are at home and when you are on the road, when you are going to bed and when you are getting up.**" In addition, the Bible connects our hands, a symbol of how we serve and help others, to our forehead, a symbol of being connected to Christ. **When we are**

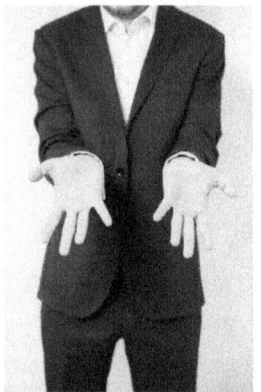

connected to Christ through our frontal lobes, our hands seek to help and serve others, thereby vicariously acting as God's hands. This biological phenomenon is reflected in theology, we are justified in Christ through our conception – we become part of God's family at this precise point in time. We go through birth, growth, a number of birthdays, until we reach the time where we feel God's calling on our life. At this point, most people opt for baptism or a public acknowledgement of their personal conviction. It is at this time the process of sanctification begins.

Sanctification is when we "marry" our frontal lobes with our hands. It is how we act out of love for Christ by serving others. We stop counting our favors for others and we see our work as pointing souls to Christ. Our good works never serve to save us but they serve to seal us as His chosen children.

We experience His presence, we discern His will, we see His sovereignty in our lives when our frontal lobes are healthy and connected. The converse is also true. When our frontal lobes are damaged or not functional, we lack spiritual insight, we view others as less than human, we throw away lifelong friendships as if they mean nothing, we rationalize away our humanity, we divorce our best friend and the mother/father of our children, we can't stand to spend time with our parents, we refuse to lend a helping hand to others, we undermine other's legitimate efforts, etc. **When our frontal lobes are damaged we mock spirituality in others, we don't want to pray and fellowship with believers, we dehumanize all aspects of God's created beings, we destroy His creation, we accept and promote violence as a means to an end, we fail to see our value in society, we fail to see the value of others, we seek to damage and destroy our lives and the lives of others.** We resort to lower brain functions of survival not controlled by reason, we sacrifice equanimity for a cheap "thrill," we worship information while sacrificing our God-given intelligence, we mock the God who made us, while we deny the Creator's existence. We fail to see the beauty and grandeur of each precious life, we become friends with sickness and infirmity, we lose our ability to have meaningful interactions with others, we become rude and crude, etc.

There are many reasons to be thankful, even when we face life's darkest moments, such as an unprecedented pandemic, financial collapse, social unrest, death of a loved one, disability, etc. **Gratitude is a gift and is abundantly evident to those around us as we experience life's exciting and thrilling moments, as well as life's low moments. Both highs and lows are critical to developing good frontal lobe function.** This allows us to experience the entire range of human emotions and still maintain equanimity. Good frontal lobe function allows us to experience empathy and treat all of God's creatures with dignity and respect. There is almost never a point of "no return" when it comes to frontal lobes. Even the vilest of humans can experience the miracle of restored frontal lobe function. One of the best examples is the thief on the cross. As he hung next to Christ on a cross, he recognized the God of the universe. He cooperated with God and gave his heart to Jesus. He believed. At that moment, his sins were forgiven and wiped clean. Praise God for His never-ending mercies toward us earth-bound sinners.

From the beginning of time and the times of the Israelites and prophets, let's go to the last book of the Bible, where a series of visions make up the book of Revelation. John, the last of the living disciples, is living on the rocky volcanic island of Patmos in the Mediterranean Sea. Today, Patmos is a Greek island located off the western shores of Turkey. It is a beautiful and tranquil place, but 2,000 years ago, John is not there by choice. He has been taken as a prisoner and slave, by order of the Roman emperor, Domitian, who persecuted and murdered Christians. John, an old man, is made to work long hours doing hard labor in the local mines.

While on the Isle of Patmos, John in **Revelation 7**, writes about the sealing of the 144,000. In verse 3, the Angel of God commands the four angels holding back the power to harm the earth, "Hurt not the earth, neither the sea nor the trees, till we have sealed the servants of God in their foreheads." Later in Revelation, speaking metaphorically, John connects our forehead to our hands, how we help others. **Revelation 14:9–11** (KJV) reads: "And the third angel followed them saying with a loud voice, If any man worship the beast and his image and receive his mark in his forehead, or in his hand, the, same shall drink of the wine of the wrath of God, which is been poured out without mixture into the cup of his indignation; and he shall be tormented with fire and brimstone in the presence of the holy angels, and in the presence of the Lamb." Everyone receives a mark on their forehead and hands. The mark of a Christian is love and gratitude, which is manifest as a spiritual connection, spending time in prayer, and being the hands of Christ by helping others.

Loss of frontal lobe functions (i.e., empathy) is one of the greatest tragedies of human existence. It leads to war, divorce, addictions, disease, self-adulation, suicide, and every imaginable and even the unimaginable evils. Loss of frontal lobes leads to self-worship and having no need of a Saviour. It mocks the complete reliance on an unseen God, while paradoxically, worshipping our self (created by our Saviour). It detaches spiritual connection with God and functionally makes one vulnerable to the influences of Satan and his evil angels.

A long list of symptoms may indicate our frontal lobes are not optimally functioning. This does not necessarily affect the intellect. One or two symptoms may not indicate frontal lobe impairment, especially if temporary. However, the more symptoms you have and the longer they persist, the more likely you are to have frontal lobe issues. Some signs of frontal lobe issues include: loss of empathy, change in warmth for others, emotional blindness, distorting the truth (aka, lying), inability or refusal to engage in usual communication patterns, poor insight, the inability to recalibrate ineffective relational skills, poor judgment, increase in sweet and carbohydrate cravings, dramatic changes in personality, loss of social graces, decline in personal hygiene and grooming, mental rigidity, inflexibility, distractibility, hyper-orality (talking too much), frequent risk-taking behaviors, lack of behavioral restraint, compulsive behaviors, ritualistic behaviors, loss of emotional recognition, inappropriate sexual behaviors, confabulation, apathy, loss of motivation, changes in moral beliefs, perseveration (inability to end task), loss of interest in helping others, frequently yelling and screaming at

family and friends, lack of sensitivity to other people's feelings, the inability to sustain meaningful relationships, loss of spontaneity, lack of situational appropriate concerns, addictions, disorganization, inability to properly use language, dementia, chaotic thinking, and deception, to name a few.

Maybe you have caught up with a friend you knew before he or she was married. At the time you thought he (or she) was perfectly matched and had a great future as a family man (or woman), ahead of him (or her). You meet up with him 15 to 20 years later. After a long and possibly semi-honest discussion, you find out he has had multiple affairs, claimed bankruptcy, travels for his employer at least 50% of the time, and appears to be addicted to alcohol. He cannot concentrate, cannot complete a sentence without one or more curse words, suffers with impulse control, and may or may not have seen or spoken with his children within the last week or even month or so. You notice his phone keeps ringing and a picture of a young woman shows up on the screen. As your conversation ends and he walks away, you see him get into a corvette and call someone before he takes off. He immediately begins an animated conversation with the person on the other end… "What just happened," you ask? Where did this relationship go off the rails?

One sure sign of frontal lobe dysfunction is the refusal to pray or engage in activities which support a healthy spiritual life. Frontal lobes are how we connect with God. If at one time you were engaged in prayer, reading the Bible, attending church and Bible study and now you have no interest in these activities, it is possible your frontal lobes are not engaged. Satan, the original court jester, has you firmly in his control. If you have lost important relationships and have started using curse words, please consider taking steps to turn this around. "Keep a cool head. Stay alert, the devil is poised to pounce, and would like nothing better than to catch you napping. Keep your guard up. You're not the only ones plunged into these hard times. It's the same with Christians all over the world. So, keep a firm grip on the faith. The suffering won't last forever. It won't be long before this generous God who has great plans for us in Christ – eternal and glorious plans they are – will have you put together and on your feet for good. He gets the last word; yes, he does." 1 Peter 5:8-11 (The Message).

"Finally, my brethren, be strong in the Lord, and in the power of his might. Put on the whole armor of God, that ye may be able to stand against the wiles of the devil. For we wrestle not against flesh and blood, but against principalities, against powers, against the rulers of the darkness of this world, against spiritual wickedness in high places. Wherefore take unto you the whole armor of God, that ye may be able to withstand in the evil day, and having done all to stand. Stand therefore, having your loins girt about with truth, and having on the breastplate of righteousness; and your feet shod with the preparation of the gospel of peace; above all, taking the shield of faith, wherewith ye shall be able to quench all the fiery darts of the wicked. <u>And take the helmet of salvation, and the sword of the Spirit, which is the word of God: praying always with all prayer and supplication in the Spirit and watching thereunto with all perseverance and supplication for all saints</u>; and for me, that utterance may be given unto me, that I may open my mouth boldly, to make known the mystery of the gospel, for which I am an ambassador in bonds: that therein I may speak boldly, as I ought to speak." **Ephesians 12:10-20**. Sounds like Paul understands how to fortify and strengthen the frontal lobes. It would be hard to explain it better than Paul does in this passage.

The average brain consists of 120 billion neurons and at least that many if not more, of supporting glial cells and astrocytes. Each neuron is capable of communicating with its environment. One communication mode uses electrical activity in the presynaptic neuron and converts this via voltage-gated channels (like opening up the car pool lanes during traffic hour to alleviate a traffic jam), to a release of one or more of 40 plus neuro-transmitter chemicals, including serotonin (5HT), dopamine (DA), acetylcholine (ACH), GABA, norepinephrine (NE), glutamate (Glu), thyroid hormones, histamine (HA), etc. The average neuron contains a resting voltage of approximately -70 millivolts (mV), similar in one sense to a car being in park or neutral. Charge is created (your foot presses the car's gas pedal) and travels along the neuron's axon, by the movement of positively charged ions into the cell. This creates an electrical charge and a release of neurotransmitters. Electrical current results in a chemical signal (the car moves). The chemical interacts with the cellular environment and the functional location to elicit a response, a thought, or some kind of action, even if it is no action (i.e., restraint, inhibition). Transporters pick up neurotransmitters and move them along functional pathways. Every single process in the brain can be influenced or affected by our thoughts, actions, what we hear, what we see, etc. With every thought and action, we reinforce or establish a brain or neural pathway. We either reinforce that pathway or we weaken it based on our thoughts and actions.

The neurotransmitter serotonin is synthesized from tryptophan, the rarest essential amino acid found in protein rich foods as well as found in smaller amounts in most plant-based foods. Experimentally, when tryptophan is blocked from entering the brain (blocked at the blood brain barrier), within 6 minutes, subjects began to feel less equanimity and a dip in their mood. When one of the brain's serotonin transporters (VMAT2) is blocked, it causes depression. In experimental animals, mice born without a serotonin transporter die within several days of being born. In adult humans, blocking this transporter results in anxiety and increased reactivity to aversive situations (i.e., coping mechanisms are blunted). The reason for this discussion in a book about Country Living is, modern scientists have tagged the serotonin transporter, VMAT2, as the "God" gene. Serotonin is what supports empathy, spirituality, and equanimity. It drives Christians to serve others as the hands of Christ. It drives us to spend our vacation time building an orphanage or providing medical care to starving children in Yemen. Serotonin is what floods the frontal lobes (via the raphae nuclei). When serotonin is available to the brain, a person is more likely to have congenial relationships, an avid prayer life, and a spiritual connection to God. There is a level of "friendship" with God which gives one complete equanimity in life, even when the world is in turmoil.

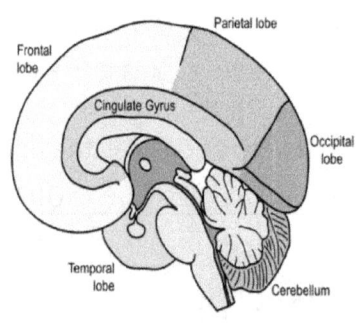

Mid saggittal left view
By NEUROtiker - Own work, CC BY-SA 3.0,
https://commons.wikimedia.org/w/index.ph

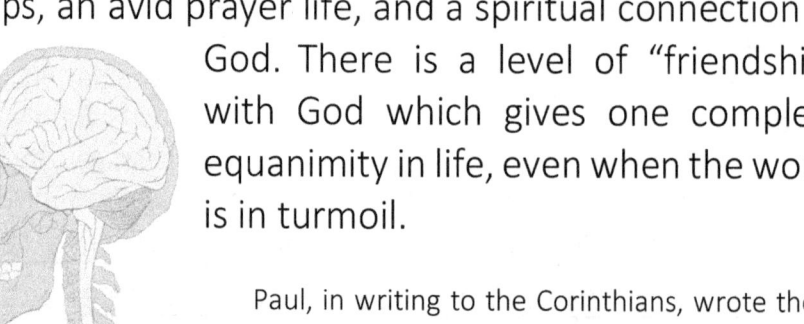

Paul, in writing to the Corinthians, wrote these inspiring words, "By the humility and gentleness of Christ, I appeal to you – I, Paul, who am "timid" when face to face with you, but "bold" toward you when away! I beg you that when I come I may not have to be as bold as I expect toward some people who think that we live by the standards of the world. For though we live in the world, we do not wage war as the world does. The weapons we fight with are not the weapons of the world. On the contrary, they have divine power to demolish strongholds. We demolish arguments and every pretension that sets itself up against the knowledge of God, and <u>we take captive every thought to make it obedient to Christ</u>." 2 Corinthians 10:1-5 (NIV).

Neuroplasticity or the ability to rewire your brain is critical to restoring frontal lobe functions related to spirituality, spiritual discernment, and morality. Our altered behaviors and thoughts are not our destiny if we, by exercising our free will, choose differently. We can experience neuroplasticity at any age, in other words, God created us to connect with Him and in the process of doing so, our brain is restored through regular communication with Him as well as time spent in nature. **"Trust in the Lord with all thine heart; and lean not unto thine own understanding. In all thy ways acknowledge him and he shall direct thy paths." Proverbs 3:5-6.** Trust the Lord to do His good work in you. This involves taking control of our thoughts and motives by submitting them to scrutiny. Pray over every decision. Nothing is too trivial for the Father. The admonition to "take every thought captive," should give us great hope that we can be restored to His likeness and demonstrate His character of love. **This is the final message to the world – God is love.** It is the righteousness of Christ that stands in our stead as we stand before God.

In addition to the infinite complexity of the brain, it is the most highly metabolic region of the body and needs a constant supply of oxygen, nutrients, and voltage. Metabolic activity requires a master blueprint involving genes and epigenetic influences, directing nutrients, oxygen, and voltage. Oxygen is essential to brain health and the optimal functioning of cranial nerves and sensory inputs. Nutrients supply essential metabolic components. Combinations of neurotransmitters and hormones are respon-sible for almost every aspect of human life. Even sub-threshold events are significant as are inhibited synapses. There is an entire brain alphabet and language of synaptic and non-synaptic events, yet to be decoded. Experimentally, we can view the brain in digital code but it is the analog data that provides more interesting insights. It's the same in our lives. We can live a digital version of a materialistic life, attached to spiritually meaningless activities and possessions, or we can live an analog life full of Christ-centered interactions and outreach.

This highlights the need for a healthy lifestyle including daily activity, nutrient rich food, meaningful relationships, a spiritual connection with God, etc. **Good frontal lobe functions allow for spiritual discernment and the ability to reason from cause to effect. We take the time to know Jesus and understand the Heavenly economy is 100% devoted to our salvation.** We avoid mistakes which would harm others. We learn from our past mistakes and avoid repeating them.

If you ignore the laws of health and frequently justify poor decisions – these choices may make it more difficult to experience the fullness of God's blessings. We should not be discouraged though. God has already made a way for us to return to Him. To regain what has been lost. Christ is not only our Saviour, but he is the Great Physician. He died not only for our sins but for our infirmities. He wants to restore our health and give us a life full of meaning and ever-increasing faith. Only you can choose to let go and give everything to Christ. Give up your memories of abuse and abandonment, give up your resentment, give up your pride, your greed, your uncharitable ways, your criticism of others. Give up relying on yourself. You have the most incredible brain, capable of being re-programmed for salvation! No sin or infirmity is too severe for God to forgive. Don't let the opposition win!

If you are needy and wanting others to serve you and give you "free" things, you may not be able to experience the beauty of good frontal lobe function. It is easy to identify Christians with good frontal lobes. They don't complain about social, societal or economic inequities, but they show gratitude to their Saviour in countless ways. They are a pleasure to know and bless everyone around them. They uplift Christ and not the shortcomings and sins of others. They expose Christ's good works toward us.

Christians should experience gratitude toward God and their fellow men on a regular basis. When you finish drinking the last drop of freshly squeezed grapefruit juice, you offer words of gratitude to the Creator for all the juicy, delicious grapefruits He has provided. As you load your vehicle with bags of groceries you thank God for the groceries, the means to purchase food, and the vehicle which transported you to the store. As you prepare to eat a meal you prepared for your family, you stop and offer thanks for the store that sold you the food, the truckers who transported the food, the pipeline workers who laid the pipeline for the fuel the truckers needed to transport the food, the day-workers who harvested the food, the farmer who planted and tended the crops, for the rain and sunshine which coaxed the seeds to grow, and for the Creator who made and designed the food which delivers essential nutrients in an infinite combination of tasty and delicious packages. This ongoing conversation of gratitude with our Creator sets the stage not only for health and wellness, but it opens the door for spiritual insights and a more meaningful walk with God, maybe similar to how Enoch walked with God. Gratitude is an essential component of good frontal lobe functions.

How do we "lose" our frontal lobe functions? Chronic, unrelenting stress builds and multiplies if not checked by a healthy lifestyle, adequate intake of protein and B vitamins, good thyroid functions, and a meaningful devotional life. Chronic stress, as well as other conditions, alter frontal lobes. If as a Christian you find yourself yelling at your family, focusing on negative and not positive events, "living on the edge," finding faults with everyone, unable to disconnect from the stresses of life, etc., you may have compromised frontal lobe functions. If you distort your earthly relationships, your heavenly relationship is also distorted (and vice versa).

The law of reaping what one sows is not karma, but it is built into life; it is a part of every created aspect of planet earth. It is physiological, psychological, spiritual, relational, and even social. When we virtue signal our goodness, gaslight others, sow discord, gossip, promote or participate in violence, act with jealousy, speak harsh words, lust after what belongs to someone else, etc., we are not elevated, we are degraded. **When we choose to mock and degrade others, we end up degrading ourselves.**

John 8 describes the incredible moment when the Pharisees brought before Jesus a woman brazenly caught in the act of adultery. They challenged Jesus to condemn her based on the Mosaic laws (a moralistic perspective of religion). Virtue signaling at its best! But instead of condemning her, Jesus bent over the ground and silently spelled out their sins in the sand. As the Pharisees saw their sins written in the sand, one by one, they silently fled out of the room. Jesus chooses the salvational solution to the woman's sin. Now, it is just Jesus and the woman in the same room together. Jesus knows the Pharisees are hypocrites. Why was her male lover not singled out for condemnation? But regardless, she has just experienced the most incredible moment of God's grace. His next words to her are golden, "When Jesus had lifted himself, and saw none but the woman, he said unto her, 'Woman, where are your accusers? Hath no man condemned thee?' She said, No man, Lord. And Jesus said unto her, 'neither do I condemn thee: go and sin no more.'" **This perfectly illustrates the law of sowing and reaping. Jesus does not want us to continue in our sin. It is too dangerous. Sin has terrible consequences.**

Many people, including pastors and Bible scholars, believe it is impossible to quit sinning. They believe we will be sinning right up and until the day of Jesus' return. However, it is entirely possible to be a sinner but not sin. This is an important distinction. We can only gain power over sin when we plug into an endless source of Free Power – available to all. Someday, every sin we have committed and not confessed will return to our account. Right now, we may be living large on sinful credit, when in reality, sin has an expiration date. The ultimate "bill" for sin comes at our death. It is not a vengeful act but a necessary act to purge the universe of evil. The universe must be clean for God's kingdom to be restored on earth. All artifacts of sin are eradicated with one exception – the Everlasting Gospel of Christ's death and resurrection – the scars on his hands, feet and side. Those scars will always be evident and serve to remind the universe of the great price of redemption.

God cannot be in the presence of sin. It is antithetical to his glory. We should pray to always reflect and deflect any praise and honor which comes our way to the only person who deserves praise and honor, God. **Sin only harms the sinner.** When we choose to follow and abide by God's laws, we reap the benefits of peace, love, patience, and the rest of the fruits of the Spirit. This does not mean we escape suffering but it does mean our suffering has spiritual meaning and contributes to shaping a character fit for Heaven.

The sowing and reaping principle is Biblical. God's "wrath" is not about whether or not God "kills." Sin has a built-in lifespan. It does not infect the universe forever. The clock is ticking. In the end, sin only harms the sinner. **The saints are forgiven (Hebrews 10:14-18) and their sins**

are "washed white as snow," "as far as the east is from the west (Psalm 103:12)," our sins are "covered" by God, atoned by Jesus on the cross (Colossians 2:14), He does not charge us with iniquity (Psalm 32:2; Romans 4:8), He washes away our sins (Psalm 51:2), He puts our sins behind his back (Isaiah 38:17), and He forgets them (Hebrews 8:12).

If we murder, harm others, commit adultery, lust after things which belong to others, if pride directs our actions, if narcissism dominates our relationships, if we lie to the boss, cheat on an exam, fail to support our children, live a greed-fueled life, gossip about friends, virtue signal our good works to others, expose other's shortcomings, fudge on taxes, cheat our employer, gaslight and demean others, etc., these types of actions follow the principle of sowing and reaping. It is easy to sow the seeds of sin without thinking about reaping the harvest of sin. Whether it occurs immediately, two decades later, or on the judgment day; unless we repent and restore, the result is inevitable. **Tolerating evil numbs us to its true nature. By accepting hundreds of small moral compromises / decrements over a lifetime, our earthly and heavenly relationships become distorted; this is just one possible result of frontal lobe dysfunction.**

A loving God has already programmed sin for eradication. When Lucifer sinned, God mobilized every resource in heaven to redeem the fallen angels. A majority of angels remained true to God, but one third of the angels followed Lucifer into a sin-driven state. **God programmed our free will to either secure our salvation or be forever gone.** It is elegant and simple, Jesus = life (accepting Jesus leads to life) or sin = death. There are only two choices, but both are not equal. One choice leads to complete eradication. The other choice results in eternal life with God, the ability to study creation, to more fully understand the mysteries of redemption, etc. The best choice leads to the fellowship and beauty of associating with other humans who experienced sin but accepted Christ's robes of righteousness to completely cover our sin and secure a future in heaven. **Our Saviour hopes we choose to be with him.**

For some, loss of frontal lobe functions is not a descent into an overtly sinful lifestyle but simply failing to understand God's character, failure to rely on Him for our daily sustenance, and failure to relate to Him as our Heavenly Father in a holy, joyous and reverent manner. **When we fail to understand God's character, how his actions have always lifted up humanity, and how all of Heaven is working to redeem as many humans as possible, we distort our relationship with Him. Until we take steps to restore our frontal lobes we may live with a distorted view of God.** Others completely deny His existence.

For some, moving from the city to the country is an isolating experience. If you are used to an extensive support system at church and within the community, country living can be a big change. Leaving behind family, life-long friends, and the conveniences of city living is so traumatic for some, it may lead to may lead to depression if it is not recognized early and prevented. If depression becomes entrenched, the risk of frontal lobe related issues increases. If you and your family move to the country and one spouse is busy and thriving while the other spouse is isolated and sad, you take the risk one spouse will resent the move. This is never an ideal situation. **Discuss this in advance and set up regular activities and check-points to counter any negative emotions associated with making a major life change such as moving to the country.**

In 1967, the Journal of Psychosomatic Research, published the Holmes-Rahe Life Stress Inventory (found in the appendix). It is a Social Readjustment Rating Scale, designed to quantify various life events. It is based on a scale of 1 to 100, with 100 being the most stressful event. Retirement from work, major business readjustment, change in finances, changing to a different line of work, change in responsibilities, a major change in living conditions, change in social activities, etc., all add up to a level of stress associated with changes in mental and physical status. Do not underestimate the significance of leaving behind family and friends as you move to the country. Instead, use a move to the country to cement your relationship with God. **Spend an hour with the Lord in the morning on your home's deck while enjoying a chorus of songbirds.** Start a home-based Bible study group. Support small local churches. The Lord blesses those who walk with Him in faith.

You can change the health and functions of your body by making positive lifestyle choices including: daily exposure to sunlight, nightly refreshing sleep, prayer, highly nutritious and electron-rich foods, optimal hydration, avoiding toxins, avoiding overconsumption, regular contact with nature including the ground, satisfying relationships, tenderly caring for others (including animals), forming strong bonds of friendship, water therapies, ensuring a hygienic living environment, etc.

If we focus this complex organ, known as our brain, on Christ and the good news of the Gospel, it is impossible to uncouple our love for Him with our good works on His behalf. This wonderful interplay of form and function makes up each person's unique contribution to society. We can be intellectually thankful for a loving God who cares for every aspect of our life; however, gratitude toward a loving God manifests as individual actions, such as feeding the hungry, sheltering the needy, paying an unpaid bill for a friend, passing along your old washing machine to someone who needs one, etc. **Gratitude cannot be legislated nor required. It spills over from having more than enough, even if you are money-poor.** Shower your friends and family with the most beautiful version of love, agape love.

Habits which may improve your mood / serotonin: exercise, sauna, "clean" eating, eating enough protein, ingesting optimal amounts of vitamins and minerals, gardening, hiking, helping others, prayer, raw food, juicing, coffee enema (infrequently), meditation on heavenly matters, green smoothies, sun bathing, vacations, drinking adequate amounts of water, mission work, daily walk, regular refreshing sleep, bike rides, niacin / sauna detox, standing under a waterfall, clean living environment, feeling productive, team-work, fasting, Bible time, company of stimulating people, chiropractic care, Epsom salt bath, micro-frequency sessions, earthing, intermittent fasting, devotional time, reading, peroxide baths, self-help, self-care, parasite cleansing, balanced lifestyle, challenges, caring and loving relationships, eating fresh fruit, anonymous acts of kindness (both giving and receiving), being REAL with people, high dose B vitamins, orthomolecular interventions, detoxing, novel environments, fresh air, springtime, swimming, being at a healthy weight, mental health, curiosity, learning, etc.

Bible verses: Genesis 1:26; Exodus 13:16; 28:36–38; Leviticus 13:41–43; Numbers 24:17; Deuteronomy 6:8; 11:18, 19; Job 31:35-40; Psalm 7:17, 19:1, 148, 150; Isaiah 43:21, 55:12; 1 Samuel 17:49; 2 Chronicles 26:19, 20; Jeremiah 48:45; Ezekiel 3:8, 9; 9:4; Zechariah 9:9; Habakkuk 2:11; Matthew 3:9; Luke 19:40; Revelation 4:11; 5:13; 7:3; 9:4; 13:6; 14:1; 14:9; 17:53; 20:4, 22:4

References and sources

Neuropsychopharmacology volume 36, pages 2538–2550 (2011)

Thanks to **Robert P. Iacono,** MD, FACS, (1952 – 2007) for his mentorship on this topic (and others) and for inviting me to join his neurosurgery practice in Southern California and learn and experience incredible insights from hundreds and hundreds of his neurology / neurosurgery patients. For many years my mother claimed we never had a conversation which did not include the topics of serotonin and frontal lobes. Even today, this topic is prescient to what lies ahead and critical to the optimal functioning of our spiritual compass and our relationship with God and others. I feel this is possibly the most important chapter in this book and I am glad you have taken the time to read it. It is my prayer this information will serve to enrich your spiritual life.

Discussion questions

1. Write out ways you can show gratitude to God and others.

   Examples include:
   - When your parents or spouse works late, show gratitude by doing extra chores around the house.
   - When your friends go on vacation, offer to keep their pets, keep up their yard, pick up newspapers, etc.
   - Care for the children of friends while they welcome a new baby or require a hospital stay.
   - Keep your corner of the environment clean and tidy.
   - Care for the beautiful animals God has given us to protect.
   - Provide beautiful music for others to enjoy.
   - Participate in sacrificial relationships.
   - Exercise fruits of the Spirit, such as joy, patience, longsuffering, peace, kindness, forbearance, gentleness, faith, modesty, self-control, speaking words of wisdom and knowledge, etc.
   - Choose peaceful thoughts over fear.
   - Serve others.

2. Give one or more examples of how to effectively reason from cause to effect to prevent making the same mistake over and over.

3. Describe how to disavow hateful thoughts and attitudes.

4. Describe how to disavow destructive types of conflict and maintain positive relationships.

5. Describe a situation where someone you know may have compromised frontal lobes and what may have contributed to damaging their frontal lobes.

6. Listen to others.

7. Visit the elderly, prisoners, lonely people, etc.

8. Learn how to say "thank you" when someone does something for you, no matter how small. Respect other people's time (i.e., avoid wasting their time).

9. Respect other people's accomplishments and views.

Section 2

Country Living

Health and Lifestyle

Introduction

There are many possible health-restoring techniques ranging from simple to sophisticated. Simple methods are usually preferred for less cost and usually less risks associated with treatments. Simple techniques range from stretching and deep breathing to herbals to lifestyle modifications such as exercise and active hobbies.

For millennia, ancient to modern societies have included a variety of "health" practitioners. Modern society has produced more types of specialized "health" care providers than any previous society. We have more health practitioners and less health to boast about than ever before. In other words, most of us are struggling with one or more bothersome symptoms, we are sick, or we are almost dead. Very few societies boast of robust health and low health care costs. When it comes to spending on healthcare, the USA is #1. As an example, in January 2020, Investopedia compared MRI costs between several modern countries (www.shorturl.at/cGIS8). An MRI exam in Spain costs $181. If you hop a plane and fly to Australia, you may pay about $215. The same MRI costs $811 in New Zealand and an MRI scan in the USA may cost anywhere between $1,119 and $3,031. It may actually cost less to fly to Spain, spend several nights there, get an MRI and return back to the USA than to get an MRI in the USA. As many of us know, money spent on healthcare does not always translate into better health.

In an 18 March 2019 article by Tanza Loudenback, and published by Business Insider, records reveal the average employee pays $4500 to $8,300 for supplemental healthcare. Between individual and government spending, per capita health care costs are around $10,500 in the USA, $4,826 in Canada, and $4,246 in the UK.

Instead of focusing on costs, let's focus on wellness and prevention. This topic is not widely discussed because it is almost impossible to prove a "pertinent negative." A pertinent negative may be defined as, a positive outcome as a result of a preventive action. This means if you maintain your weight, eat healthy, never take up smoking, and lead a reasonably active life, you are unlikely to develop type 2 diabetes, heart disease, arthritis, COPD, metabolic syndrome, stroke, etc. When it comes to healthcare, if you maintain a healthy weight and lifestyle in combination with good genetics, you may never need to be hospitalized for a knee replacement, cardiac bypass or cancer surgery. You have effectively prevented one or more disease-related hospitalizations but common statistics are not designed to capture these outcomes; they show morbidity (disease) and mortality (death) incidents.

The techniques in this section are widely known, most of their mechanisms are understood, and they are available to everyone! I hope you find something "new" that speaks to your situation and gets you excited about restoring optimal health to you and your family. Remember, Christ is the Great Physician and Healer. The Bible provides ample examples of how He provides for our healing. One of the most pertinent questions is, "Do you want to be healed?" Take the time to ponder this question.

If you have an entrepreneurial spirit, choose one or more items in this section and start a business. You may want to help others clean up their living spaces. You may want to start a hydrotherapy spa or day retreat. Start a restaurant or food truck that makes high antioxidant smoothies or lunches. The possibilities are endless.

Chapter 8

Clean up your living environment

Cleanliness is next to Godliness

A friend's husband had been admitted to the hospital for observation and diagnosis. He suffered from general malaise, struggled with psychological issues, and only seemed to get worse. Every test his physicians ordered, came back negative. On the 9th day of his ~~incarceration~~ hospitalization he asked his wife to push him in a wheelchair outside of the hospital. After quite a bit of dialogue between hospital personnel and his wife, he and his wife finally took off for the great outdoors. They spent almost two hours navigating the hospital grounds before they returned to his room. He felt better. He had also not showered or bathed since the day of his hospital admission. He asked his wife for one more favor – to help him shower. Without asking permission, she took him to his room and showered him, IV poles notwithstanding. After emerging from his shower, he felt so much better he asked to go home, however, his physicians wanted to keep him. Within one hour, he had checked out and was headed home. Whatever combination of sunlight, vitamin nature, serotonergic waterfalls (i.e., a shower, spray electrification or the waterfall effect), quality time with his wife, etc., this man felt like a new person and has since remained in relatively good health.

Being clean involves many targets, including our physical body, a sound mind, pure and joyful thoughts, healthy blood, a hygienic living environment, meaningful relationships, and avoidance of unnecessary stuff which depletes our bank account while accumulating in our homes and closets. **Moses, in the book of Leviticus, expounds on living a holy and clean life. The Israelites were admonished to leave their old Egyptian ways of doing things and embrace a new way of living.** God constantly reminded them to avoid adopting the customs and habits of the Canaanites and other cultures of their time. Many stories in the Bible center around going from being unclean to being clean (e.g., Israelites, Naaman, Miriam, the priests).

Being clean could be compared to living a holy life.

The ultimate result of cleanliness is health, wellness, and maybe even a touch of godliness. A fresh smelling home with clean and sparse furnishings is a sharp contrast to a home which is filled to the max with furniture, toys, knick knacks, boxes of excess things, clothes and things which have no permanent storage location. This reminds me of when I was in grad school and renting a house with one of my college friends. My only furniture was a bed and a dining room table. My housemate had recently moved in and because she had a job and I was still in grad school, she bought some nice furniture including two white couches. A mutual friend of ours from church had asked her out on a date. The only catch was he was large and odiferous. I was left home on a Saturday night with a dilemma. I knew they would be home soon and would probably want to sit on one of the new white sofas for a few minutes before he left. In my mind, I didn't want him to sit on the sofa because it might get dirty and smell bad. At the last minute a brilliant idea popped into my head – I removed all the sofa cushions and put them in my room. When they got home, from the privacy of my room, I could hear the surprise in her voice about the condition of the sofas. Fortunately, my strategy worked and they ended up sitting at the dining room table for a few minutes before he left. After he left, we had a great laugh over my strategy, a strategy which I would not repeat as a more mature Christian, but the point remains valid. As Christians, we should make every effort to stay clean and remove every barrier to witnessing and associating with others. If we are dirty, smell bad, have bad breath, garlic breath, messy cars, homes that reek of animal smells or artificial scents, messy yards, etc., how can we witness to others about Christ? Cleanliness affects almost every aspect of our life whether we understand it or not. Learn to live a clean life and your actions may be a positive witness to others.

Clean teeth, a clean mouth, and healthy gums are critical to good health.
A dentist friend, Dr. Heather Martinson, has spent many years studying the connection between oral and physical health. The links are indisputable. She describes many cases where the first signs of early disease show up in the mouth. Some experts suggest up to 90% of all systemic diseases manifest in the mouth as dry mouth, gum disease, red and bleeding gums, dry socket, cavities, swollen gums, excessively red areas, thrush, etc. Some of these early manifestations may be a harbinger of more serious conditions such as oral cancer, leukemia, diabetes, pancreatic cancer, heart disease, kidney disease, etc.

Daily oral care should take a total of about 5 to 15 minutes. This includes: brushing, flossing, water blasting (i.e., water irrigation), pulling, and gargling. Before going to bed, gargle with colloidal silver. This takes out the bad microorganisms which would otherwise be left unchecked for up to 8 to 10 hours. If your mouth is in bad shape, brush before and after eating. This minimizes your exposure to pathogenic microorganisms. The health of your gums is a window to the health of your body. Nutrition experts can also detect vitamin and mineral deficiencies by examining the mouth.

The skin is the body's largest detox organ. The skin's pores are large enough to allow water, minerals and even toxins to escape. It also allows chemicals and even toxins to enter as well as leave. If you don't regularly bathe, toxins your body releases through the skin may remain on the skin and possibly be reabsorbed. Daily showers wash away dirt, sweat and other unwanted compounds eliminated by your skin. Bathing also allows those around you to better enjoy your excellent company without the whiffs of various body odors and disturbing visuals unique to unbathed individuals.

Daily showers or baths with alternating hot and cold water promote circulation, improved immunity, better respiratory functions, detoxification, and overall improved health and wellness.
In general, showers are considered a better option than baths, but both have their benefits, especially therapeutic baths, hydrotherapy-based baths, etc. If you participate in hard manual labor and profusely sweat throughout the day, daily bathing should be considered essential. Even for the sedentary, bathing (i.e., a shower or bath) should be part of one's daily routine. Bathing opens up the pores, removes dirt and toxins, and returns robust normal functions to the organs of the body.

Showers are amazing. In addition to cleaning us, they wake us up, charge us up, and boost serotonin levels. How many parents think their kids spend too much time in the shower? This could be due to its serotonin-boosting effects. As children transition into the teen years, their serotonin goes from a relatively high level down to adult levels, however, this is neither a linear nor smooth process. Sometimes their serotonin levels may go way below what is considered a normal adult level. It is at this point, they become susceptible to questionable friend-related influences. **You may have the best kid in the world, but as they go through puberty and head into the middle and late teens, if their serotonin is unstable, they are susceptible to bad influences.** This is why it is critical for parents to spend a lot of time with their teens. It is also a time when teens prefer to spend less and less time with their parents. This means you must find creative solutions to keeping your teens close. Country living is a great way to raise children and teenagers. It provides a backdrop and multiple functions for learning responsibility, hard work habits, learning how to reason from cause to effect, caring for and a beautiful dominion over the animals, earning money, and developing critical life skills.

Christians should be known as squeaky clean people, in both our external and internal body habitus, our living environment, working environment, cars, homes, and our mind. There are many reasons to maintain a clean environment, some of which have been addressed in previous sections. Why are showers important? Most people shower out of convenience. It is easier to run some water over the top of our body, do a quick scrub, shave, wash and condition hair, and be done. Now you are ready to take on the day. Baths tend to be a more leisurely way to clean up, but they are not as serotonergic as taking a shower (i.e., a waterfall type of experience). Baths can be used when time allows to soak up minerals and ease sore muscles. Baths are great for relaxing and enjoying some down time. Both baths and showers are used therapeutically, but for a daily routine, most people shower. This is why it is critical to maximize your time in the shower.

How frequently should we shower? Well, this depends on several factors. Some prefer to shower in the evening and some in the morning. Some do both. Out of courtesy, most people shower before they enter a public pool or jacuzzi. Keep in mind the skin is the body's first line of defense against all types of bad microorganisms. Take advantage of shower time to gain the maximum benefits. Start with warm water and end with cool or even cold water. This invigorates the body and energizes mitochondria, the body's power generating system. **Add some sinus opening herbs and oils to the shower.** Use this time to stimulate the surface of the skin with a friction mitt. **Light scrubbing in combination with contrast showers, demarginates (releases) white blood cells, a part of the body's immune system, boosting them into the circulation and improving related immune functions.** The following are suggestions for how to take a shower. Most suggestions are grounded in a principle or a known mechanism. Adopt what makes sense for you.

A good shower routine may include:
- Put on some beautiful music while you are in the shower or bath. Music sets the tone for the day.
- If you are taking a morning shower, take all your B vitamins and supplements before your shower. One exception to this is vitamin B3 or niacin. High dose niacin may cause some to flush. Typically, if you are on a detox program, ask your provider about how to incorporate high dose flushing niacin with warm or hot water showers. Typically, a niacin flush should not coincide with a warm or hot shower unless advised otherwise by your healthcare provider. The niacin flush targets circulatory vessels as well as the temperature receptors in the skin. Temperature receptors may flip from cold to hot, depending on the most recent exposure. This means the flush represents the areas of your skin exposed to warm or hot temperatures. If you have splashed warm or hot water on your face and neck,

a niacin flush targets the areas of skin exposed to the hot water. **Hot water and niacin cause vasodilation and if you take niacin right before a shower or shortly after a shower, the flush may be more intense than usual. Actually, for some people, this is a desirable outcome.**

- Drink at least 16 to 24 ounces of room temperature water before a shower or bath.
- Do not eat right before taking a shower.
- **If you can, spend at least 5 minutes with some part of your body touching the moist earth. Ideally, do this both before and right after a shower. Even better, set up an outdoor shower.**
- Your shower should have a non-slip base preferably with a handle somewhere built into the shower wall. Anyone of any age can slip and fall in the shower. It is best to have some way to pull yourself up if needed.
- If you are older, movement impaired, or frequently inebriated, eliminate glass shower doors and switch to shower curtains. A fall can put you in the middle of a thousand pieces of broken glass. This happened to my mother who had Parkinson's disease and lost her balance in the shower.
- If you live alone, designate a place to put your cell phone near the shower where it does not get wet but is available in case of an emergency. Be sure to place a cloth over the phone during your disrobing, showering and dressing times.
- When you disrobe, place dirty clothes directly into dirty clothes hamper and not on the floor, this way you only touch them once before you shower.
- If you have a eucalyptus tree, rosemary bush or other fragrant herbs in your yard, hang a small branch or bunch of herbs on the shower head to scent the area while you are showering.
- Make sure your bathing area has plenty of light and circulating fresh air.
- If you have space in your bathing area, keep orchids and / or other humidity-loving plants.
- Make sure you keep the shower floor and walls free from soap, shampoo and conditioner buildup.
- Make sure your soap holder is sturdy and the soap is not able to easily slide off.
- Shower accoutrements may include: razor, shaving cream, pumice stone or other "sanding" device for feet, friction mitts, mirror, brush, comb, body and facial scrub, lotions, shampoo, conditioner (washout), conditioner (leave-in), magnesium spray, baking soda exfoliating body scrub, etc.
- As you get into the hot shower, take about 30 seconds to lean against the wall under the shower head and let the hot water hit the back of your head and run down the rest of your body. If you are fortunate you may have a vertical shower head that targets most of your body with jets of hot water. This promotes parasympathetic tone, the rest and digest mode. It is amazing what this simple maneuver does for your stress.
- As you wash your hair, use downward strokes. This preserves the overlapping cuticles of each hair shaft and promotes healthy, shiny hair.
- Shower cleaning tools to use while you are showering or after taking a shower may include: toothbrush to clean grout lines, vinegar in a spray bottle, Bar Keepers Friend, etc. Several times per week, spend a few minutes cleaning a section of your shower.
- You may choose to clear your sinuses in the shower. Eucalyptus hanging in the shower may help.
- A good natural soap is best. Stay away from chemical-laden soaps which along with friction and warm water make the chemicals more easily absorbed by porous skin.
- Using a friction mitt, gently scrub your body, being extra careful with delicate, thin skin areas. The order of showering should be something like this: hair, face (shave and use a friction mitt to lightly

scrub), ears, neck, underarms, arms, chest, man/lady parts, scrub and shave your legs, feet, between your toes (scrub with friction mitt and then use the pumice stone if necessary on heels and feet areas). Sometimes conditioner may find its way into your ears, be sure to clean out your ears, both inside and behind. As you are washing and conditioning your hair, be sure to do some gentle but semi-firm scrubbing with the ends of your fingers. While you are washing your face and hair, take each hand and do some light lymphatic massage on your face. Using each hand, place two fingers behind your ears and the remaining fingers in front of your ears. Gently stroke downward. Now take four fingers and beginning at the middle of your forehead, lightly stroke downward along the sides of your face all the way to your neck. Do the same downward stroke beginning at the upper bridge of your nose. This moves lymphatic fluid which tends to build up in the face, towards the heart so lymphatic fluid can join the regular circulation.

- It may be beneficial to focus a hot water stream on your lower back area, where a bundle of nerves known as the cauda equina, carry nerve messages back and forth from your brain to your muscles and soft tissues. It is also important to keep this area constantly warm and not allow it to get cold. Keep this in mind as you choose what to wear.
- **At the end of your shower, alternate between hot and cold water at least once if not several times. Hot water for about 10 to 15 seconds and alternate with cold. Always end with cold water.**
- As you wrap up your shower, wrap up your body with a towel that has a Velcro or button fastener so your towel will not fall off. Now you can run around without worrying your towel will fall off. Believe me, your kids do not want to see your naked body.
- After showering, push back your cuticles and trim your nails. Apply deodorant. Dry and style hair.
- If you put on body lotions or creams, ensure they contain only natural ingredients. A light sesame oil, coconut or olive oil are good ways to moisturize skin.

While not every aspect of an "ideal" shower is going to be possible for everyone, adopt the reasonable components. Maximize your time in the shower with the right tools, shampoos and conditioners which are not full of harsh chemicals, but are natural.

A unique property of skin is its low pH of 3.5 to 5.5. A low pH allows the skin to fend off invading bacteria, viruses, and other pathogenic microorganisms. When we wash our hands, faces and body with soap, the pH barrier is disturbed for around 90 minutes. During this 90-minute period our body's skin defense is lowered. While you may feel like you have removed germs, you have also removed the skins protective acid mantle. Hand washing is good but it is better to learn to avoid touching your face all the time and potentially transferring pathogenic bacteria from your hands to your face. Wear gloves if you are going to be in a situation where you need to constantly wash your hands.

Drink water! Water drinkers can boast of younger looking skin, improved energy, better brain function, improved detoxification functions, better blood pressure and many other benefits. Recently recommendations for water have increased from 64 ounces to 92 ounces for women and 125 ounces for men. This translates into 11 ½, 8-ounce glasses for women and 15 ½, 8-ounce glasses of water for men. Upon waking up in the morning, drink 2 to 3, 8-ounce glasses of water. This is a good start to the day and promotes good kidney functions.

In addition to keeping our body clean, we should strive to keep our mind clean. "Do not wear yourself out to get rich; do not trust your own cleverness. Cast but a glance at riches, and they are gone, for they will surely sprout wings and fly off to the sky like an eagle. Do not eat the food of a begrudging host, do not crave his delicacies; for he is the kind of person who is always thinking about the cost. "Eat and drink," he says to you, but his heart is not with you. You will vomit up the little you have eaten and will have wasted your compliments. **Do not speak to fools, for they will scorn your prudent words. Do not move an ancient boundary stone or encroach on the fields of the fatherless, for their Defender is strong; he will take up their case against you.** Apply your heart to instruction and your ears to words of knowledge." **Proverbs 23:4-12** (NIV)

Banish negative thoughts. If your mind begins to repeat a stressful scenario or you are tempted to re-live an agonizing experience, or you cannot seem to work through grief, abandonment, dealing with a narcissist, abuse or any other emotional trauma, learn to control your thoughts. The Bible actually commands us to take captive every thought. **2 Corinthians 10:3-6** reads,

"For though we walk in the flesh, we do not war after the flesh: (for the weapons of our warfare are not carnal, but mighty through God to the pulling down of strong holds;) casting down imaginations, and every high thing that exalteth itself against the knowledge of God, and **bringing into captivity every thought to the obedience of Christ**; and having readiness to revenge all disobedience, when your obedience is fulfilled."

These verses give us the assurance of victory over our negative thoughts and meanderings. If you are divorced, do not retell the stories of your past. This keeps you in the past and not moving forward, and if you are remarried, it is an affront to your current spouse to keep reliving those details. **Do not let your thoughts and words drift into areas where negativity can take over.** This places you on dangerous ground, where Satan can wear down your mind to the point of biochemically and physically altering your physiology and your body. **Make it a point each day to begin with the most important thing – time with God in prayer and Bible study and to end each day with time with God in prayer and meditation. Finish each day with praise and gratitude toward God. Reflect on your blessings.** If applicable, ask for forgiveness of any sins. Take the time to review the day, consider how you could have behaved differently, and think about how you would behave in the future given a similar situation; then accept the day and be done with it. You don't have to like the events of the day but the sooner you accept them and move on, the better your life can be. Tomorrow is a new day and you can take steps to make it better!

In addition to cleaning up your body and your mind, take time to streamline your environment including your home, car, office, boat, RV, garage, shed, barn, chicken coop, etc. Some people would rather schedule a root canal than clean up their environment and get rid of excess and unnecessary stuff. Some families collect things like electronics, toys, hobby related tools, clothes, decorative items, etc. Most of the time these items are non-essential. If your living spaces are crowded, there's no space under the bed, you cannot park in the garage, you may have too much stuff.

Too much stuff (i.e., hoarding) eventually leads to health and mental issues. You may have two people the exact same age, even in the same family, with similar socio-economic status, but the one person who lives in a messy and contaminated environment ages faster and looks older. Too much stuff may even hold you back from moving to the country. Some of the freest people have minimal material possessions. While there is nothing wrong with possessions, it can lead to restricted thinking and even restricted life options.

Mold in homes is a major issue when the humidity hovers or goes above 55%. This tends to be an issue in the south where many homes must install humidity remediation systems for thousands of dollars. Even in drier climates, homes kept moist and warm may have mold issues. If mold has invaded your home, it has also invaded your lungs and your bloodstream. If dust and the waste products of mites are flying through the air in your home, you are breathing this into your lungs. When inhaled, your immune system kicks in, and you may develop symptoms such as frequent sneezing, non-productive cough, watery eyes, and a runny nose. A physician friend shared how when cats clean themselves, they leave behind saliva on their fur. When the fur falls off and we breathe in the fur or it gets into food, we develop allergies to their saliva and not necessarily their fur. **The more knick knacks in your home, the more surface area for dust and other microscopic particles to collect on.**

Mites can be a big issue for people living in unhygienic environments. Common signs of mite infection include: red rash-like marks, small red bumps which can become hard and inflamed, itching, swollen and blistery skin near the bite, etc. There are different types of mites. Dust mites are found indoors while chiggers and bird mites find a host roaming outdoors. They attach themselves to humans and then burrow under the skin. If you do not wash your hair every day, mites may find their way into your hair follicles. Some researchers suggest links between mite infestations and thinning hair, acne, skin disorders, etc. Domesticated birds in the home may cause lung problems (aka, bird fancier's lung). This causes inflammation in the lungs and may lead to irreversible lung damage. Mites can also take up residence in plants. It is important to make sure your indoor plants are healthy, have adequate nutrients and do not have mites, which eventually become visible after damaging the plant's leaves. A few diseases transmitted by mites (the vector) include: scabies, ear problems (some mites inhabit the ear canal), allergic reactions, asthma, typhus (potentially transmitted by chiggers), encephalitis, tularemia, dermatitis, filariasis, etc. *(Diseases transmitted by blood sucking mites and integrated mite management for their prevention, published in the American Journal of Food Science and Health, 2016).*

When overwhelmed and stressed, the ability to reason from cause to effect is short-circuited. It may go something like this, "I need to go through my electronic equipment, but I just don't have the energy right now." Or it might sound like this, "Someday I may find a use for 10 different types of kitchen whisks." Here's another one, "I love this shirt but I never wear it." When we fail to see how our actions result in a certain outcome, we are doomed to repeat the same scenario. Learn to reason from cause to effect or learn to accept defeat and failure as a normal part of your life.

The justifications for clinging to stuff may interfere with more useful thoughts of how to minister in the community or being able to spend more time with family and friends. Instead of requiring a child's brain to focus on cleaning up hundreds of toys in their room all the time (i.e., developing a chaotic thinking pattern), it would be better to use this time to read and accomplish other tasks.

If you can learn to live with less, you may find more time for meaningful activities. If your home is sparse and clean, it takes much less time (as well as money and effort) to clean than a home with lots of furniture and nick knacks, etc. Whittle down to the necessities of life.

In addition to streamlining your cleaning routine, getting rid of unnecessary items benefits your health and mind. When Jesus chose his disciples, he didn't give them a rule book to read, he just asked them to "follow me." There are really no rules to being a Christ follower, except to follow and to be like Him. When we make Christ the center of our vision, of our life, of our actions toward others, our family, our friendships, there is no need for elaborate rules and regulations. Sure, the 10 commandments are still binding but so is love, so are the fruits of the Spirit, so is respect and clear communication with others. When others know we value them, their opinion and want to hear their story, we may effectively have a preview of heaven on earth. **This means your agenda, your wants, your desires, your needs are subject to God's desire to use you to reach others. Cooperation with God is essential if we want to live with Him in heaven. If you are inwardly focused, you may never have spiritual eyes to see the needs and poverty of spirit in people all around you.** One of the first steps to being useful for God is to strip off whatever might be holding you back from serving God. Back to the original point, clean up your environment and streamline your life and see if God doesn't take you places you have never been! "Even the youths grow tired and weary, and young men stumble and fall; but those who hope in the Lord will renew their strength. They will soar on wings like eagles; they will run and not grow weary, they will walk and not be faint." Isaiah 40:30-31 (NIV). "He maketh my feet like hinds' feet, and setteth me upon high places." Psalm 18:33.

Everyone suffers from one or more cognitive biases. Cognitive biases keep psychologists in business. It is the basis for funny sitcoms, family vacation stories, and even the inability to ask for directions when hopelessly lost. Take the time to research cognitive biases described in the appendix. The more we understand our biases, the better quality of life we can make for ourselves and our family. Children have a way of pointing out our most egregious cognitive biases. This is because they are young enough to be mostly free of significant and complex cognitive biases. However, this rapidly changes depending on the degree of cognitive biases in people they interact with on a regular basis. Ultimately, when two people marry, they largely accept each other's cognitive biases (at least in the beginning) and oftentimes their children learn to accept their parents' cognitive biases. Bias can be implied in one's tone of voice, in casual conversation, body language, etc.

Cognitive bias splits families, friends, marriages, businesses, etc. It is critical to take an inventory of one's possible cognitive biases, especially the ones which might be most problematic. Awareness is the first step to addressing cognitive bias and improving your life. For example, a common cognitive bias is confirmation bias. We all use this bias to affirm what we believe and reject what we do not believe. This occurs when there is conflicting information on both sides of an issue. For example, when it comes to vaccines, medical doctors can be found on both sides of the debate: from the belief that no vaccines are the safest practice all the way to dozens, almost up to 100 or more vaccines over one's lifetime is the best practice. Each physician easily accepts facts which support their position while they are be quick to dismiss facts which do not support their position. When in fact, the issue is nuanced and complex and varies from one individual to the next. Cognitive bias blinds one to the possibility of a different truth. Keep in mind facts do not always represent the truth. Each perspective has its own set of facts. Truth takes into consideration many factors including historical precedents, Biblical principles, context, motivation, etc. See the appendix, section 1, for a list with explanations of almost 200 cognitive biases.

Cognitive biases may limit your ability to live a full, satisfying life. Satan knows how to use cognitive bias to limit our options, make poor decisions, cling to a belief system which separates us from a relationship with God, etc. Oftentimes, when two people marry, they end up adopting each other's biases. For example, it is usually a good idea for the woman to adopt her husband's favorite hockey team. This usually makes for smoother sailing. It is also a good idea for the man to learn to enjoy his wife's cooking. Maybe he hates onions but his wife loves them. He's probably going to eat onions at home but not when he goes out to eat and chooses his meal off of a menu. These are simplistic examples and reading about the different cognitive biases briefly described in the appendix could be a beneficial use of your time.

For some, marriage is a battle. Each person clings to their "beliefs" about the other, both good and bad, real and imagined. Hard feelings become entrenched. Daily interactions and emotions end up as bloodied casualties on a battlefield of cruel words and alienating behaviors. **If each person chooses to maintain their cognitive biases, the relationship becomes less and less functional.** Some may stay in the relationship but choose to make the other miserable, constantly stealing joy from each other. For other families, the parents or children choose to alienate each other by adopting the worst possible beliefs about the other. I see parents of small children limiting the interaction of their children with their parents (the children's grandparents) because the grandparents have a different political affiliation or the parents of the children cannot get over an event that happened in the far past. This does not negate the facts that some people are unsafe and their interactions should be supervised and limited. Those situations excluded, **learn to manage and minimize your cognitive biases. This makes you a more effective emissary for Christ, especially among your family and close friends.**

Procedural drift occurs without strict controls in place. During my doctoral research in a neuro-toxicology lab, we had an elaborate set-up procedure to start our neuronal recording experiments. It involved about 40 steps. If we tried to take a short-cut, we eventually had to face the professor and try to explain why our results were inadequate. He called this lab-related phenomenon, "procedural drift." It happens to a degree in every person's life. We hold one standard and then over time, we gradually drift away from that standard. Let's take body weight for example. Most of us do not gain 25 to 50 pounds in one year. We gain one or two pounds every year and after 20 or so years, we now weigh more than we ever imagined we would weigh. A friend's granddaughter recently got married. When her daughter (the mother of the bride) got married 30 years before, she told all her bridesmaids to lose weight if they needed to or they would not be in the wedding. Fast forward 30 years and this same person now carries about an extra 35 pounds. I jokingly suggested my friend remind her daughter of what she said to her bridesmaids 30 years ago, which of course would be a terrible thing to actually do, but this illustrates the phenomenon of procedural drift. Take some time to think back to your youthful ideals. Are they the same today as they were 5, 10 or even 20 years ago? Have you compromised? What effect does this have on your quality of life? What effect(s) has it had on your spiritual life?

Another common example of procedural drift is going-along-to-get-along. At age 25 we may believe it is "wrong" to smoke pot, binge drink, stay out all night, go to rave parties, cut and mutilate ourselves, get tattoos, etc. However, as we marry and have children and our children grow up to be young adults and they may adopt one or more "harmful" habits. Do we accept these behaviors as the new "normal or do we uphold our principles?" It is usually easier to adapt to new cultural and societal norms.

Everything depends on the right action of the will.

When it comes to living by Biblical principles, we should never apologize for our beliefs. By upholding these principles, we point others to Christ. As He is lifted up, all men are be drawn to Him! When we take our eyes off of Christ, we drift into dangerous waters. When we allow our thoughts and actions to be less than 100% pure, we are in dangerous territory. When we live unhygienically, we open the door to disease. It is critical to take inventory of everything that may be hindering our progress toward a relationship with Christ. Do we harbor unclean thoughts? Have we relaxed our standards? How does our example affect others? Take the time to learn about best cleanliness practices. See how a 3-day water-only fast may improve your life. God rewards those who follow in His footsteps. This is not legalistic. It is not about "working" our way into heaven. It is about developing a character which is fit for heaven. If by our example of permissiveness or acceptance we lead others to believe Biblically incorrect things, we are held accountable for what we know and how we failed to present the light of the truth to others.

Bible verses: Genesis 2:15; Numbers 35:33-34; Deuteronomy 20:19; Job 12:7-10; Psalm 24:1; Psalm 89:11; Proverbs 12:10; Ezekiel 34:18; Jeremiah 2:7; Matthew 6:26, 16:24; Mark 10:21; Luke 5:27, 18:22; John 8:12, 21:19; Romans 13:13; Hebrews 12:1-29; Rev 4:11; Rev 11:18; Rev 13:8

Discussion questions

1. How important is a clean body?
2. Do your hygiene habits aid in detoxification or hinder the body's detoxification efforts?
3. How important is a clean mind and what does it mean to have a clean mind?
4. On a scale of 1 to 10, with 1 being least and 10 being most, how much stuff do you have that is not used on a regular basis?
5. Is there a certain category of "stuff" you tend to accumulate?
6. What can we learn from Jesus' example of owning things?
7. How does your "stuff" either enhance or interfere with living a productive and holy life?
8. What does the term "Cleanliness is next to Godliness" mean to you? How do we achieve this?
9. How many toys do kids really need? How many clothes do we really wear? Is it an ethical issue to buy so many toys for your child when most kids around the world do not have enough food to eat? What about spending hundreds of dollars on a pair of shoes or a dress?
10. Does excessive spending and accumulation of things contribute to global inequities? If you answered yes, how would Jesus want us to remedy this?
11. What would it mean to live with less? How would you spend the extra time, money?
12. How much money do you spend buying "stuff" you rarely if ever use?
13. Using the Cognitive Biases table in the appendix, describe one cognitive bias' you may suffer from.
14. Do you see procedural drift in any area of your life?

Chapter 9
Time spent outdoors

Healthy, active lifestyles include contact with the earth and being outdoors

A country setting provides a perfect backdrop to work outdoors and enjoy the many benefits which accrue over time. Benefits including fresh air (oxygen therapy), forest bathing (phytotherapy - exposure to beneficial plant compounds from trees), sunlight (photon and vitamin D therapy, improved sleep therapy), contact with the earth (electron transfer therapy), exposure to the earth's magnetic field (magnetic therapy), growing flowers for bouquets (scent and visual therapy, stimulating the olfactory nerve), growing food (nutrient therapy; epigenetic enhancements; meaningful activity), eating fresh food (taste and pleasure therapy), touching and feeling natural elements (kinesthetic therapy), inspiration (clear-your-thoughts therapy), time to contemplate nature (God's creation and his second Bible), observation of the incredible array of textures and colors (vision and depth of field therapy), lovingly caring for the animals within your charge (the ability to demonstrate a lovely dominion over animals – one aspect of being human), working with others (teamwork), and the ability to complete meaningful tasks (work therapy).

The human body is wired for action.
It needs to move to recharge and remain vital.

When the body fails to move, its composition is altered (body weight changes) and voltage is lowered enough to allow infirmity and disease to become established. Before the arrival of the combustion engine, our ancestors walked or rode horses or chariots to move around the country while benefitting from fresh air, sunlight, companionship of others, extended contact with the earth and many other benefits afforded in nature. In Bible times, it was common to walk 5 to 10 or even 20 miles a day. Today, we are lucky to get in 5,000 to 10,000 steps (about 2 to 4+ miles). There are good reasons for this. We travel to work in a car, we park within a few feet of the entrance, we sit at a desk only moving to take a short break to eat a donut and drink coffee, and then we eat lunch and return to a desk and go home. When our 9 or 10 hours are up, we return home via a car and proceed to eat another meal, watch TV and go to bed, only to repeat a similar sequence the next day.

In Genesis 1, we read about Creation. It is a highly simplified account. God spoke and what he spoke came into existence. As God spoke Adam and Eve into existence, God gave them a special greeting. "And God blessed them, and God said unto them, 'be <u>fruitful</u>, and <u>multiply</u>, and <u>replenish the earth</u>, and <u>subdue</u> it: and have <u>dominion</u> over the fish of the sea, and over the fowl of the air, and over every living thing that moveth upon the earth.'" Their humanity was never explicitly explained but their activities were proscribed and their humanity was inferred by God's proscriptions. "And God said, Behold, I have given you every herb bearing seed, which is upon the face of the earth, and every tree, in the which is the fruit of a tree yielding seed; <u>to you it shall be for meat</u>. And to every beast of the earth, and to every fowl of the air, and to every thing that creepeth upon the earth, where there is life, I have given every green herb for meat: and it was so." Gen 1:28-31.

The word "fruitful" means, abundantly productive. In Hebrew, the word is para (pronounced paw-RAW). It is used literally and figuratively to mean grow, increase, cause to be, bring forth fruit, and bear. The second message the Creator gives to Adam and Eve is to multiply. The Hebrew word for "multiply," is raba, another verb. This word means: be in authority, bring up, enlarge, excel, be full of, grow up, heap, be long, give, have, make, be, gather, over, take, nourish, store, thoroughly, to increase, bring in, abundance, etc. Keep in mind, the Creator had just made a new habitable world, an effort of unbelievable imagination, creative thinking, and an incalculable energy. Of course, the Creator desires his created animals and humans to be active, creative and energetic. Subdue means to bring under control, to persuade or overcome. When your small child throws a temper tantrum, you work quickly to subdue their out-of-control conduct. You understand this type of behavior does not work to their advantage. You understand the more times they are allowed to be out-of-control, this may develop into a neural pathway of "acceptable" behavior; but this out-of-control child will struggle more throughout their life because their parents failed to subdue unfruitful behaviors. **To subdue something means to care enough to train it or make it into something better. To have dominion over something is a beautiful thing.** If you own land, you have dominion over the land, you want to make it beautiful and functional. If you are a leader, you may have dominion over the people within your jurisdiction. This should be a lovely type of dominion, not a demanding, exacting, controlling type of dominion. **When the command was given for man to have dominion over the animal kingdom, it was not a murderous, violent type of dominion. Nothing died in the garden of Eden until sin entered.** Dominion included naming the animals, caring for their needs, spending time with the animals, appreciating their beauty and various attributes. Dominion could even be used to describe "studying" the animals. Observing them for spiritual insights. In Proverbs 6:6-8, we read about ants: "Go to the ant, thou sluggard; consider her ways, and be wise. Which having no guide, overseer or ruler, provideth her meat in the summer, and gathereth her food in the harvest."

The Creator is a Life Force. Using this amazing Life Force endowed to us at the time of Creation is possibly the greatest testament to the Creator. Live your life by getting to know Him. Introduce others to Him. Help others. Explore the beautiful world he created. Learn how to protect and respect all life including the animals. Take care of the environment. Use the energy and life force the Creator endowed to us for the betterment of all of Creation. God transferred part of his Life Force to us and all living creatures during Creation week. This Life Force keeps us going until we die. When Christ returns, he restores his Life Force to the dead in Christ and they arise. 1 Thessalonians 4, paints a picture of the second coming. "But I would not have you to be ignorant, brethren, concerning them which are asleep, that ye sorrow not, even as others which have hope. For this we tell you by the word of the Lord, that we who are alive, who are left to the coming of the Lord, will in no way precede those who have fallen asleep. For the Lord himself will descend from heaven with a shout, with the voice of the archangel, and with God's trumpet sounding. First the dead in Christ will rise, then we who still remain alive will be caught up together with them in the clouds, to meet the Lord in the air. **So we will be with the Lord forever**. Therefore comfort one another with these words." Wow, what a message! **We may die, but if we "fall asleep" in the Lord, at the second coming we are raised up! Just as Jesus conquered death, we also conquer death through the power of the Creator, at the resurrection.**

God created everything on earth for one or more aspects of our pleasure, for developing our minds and bodies, for extending kindness and compassion, etc. **We are to worship God and God alone.** When we honor his commands and desires for us, we also care deeply for each other, the animals and the environment. Caring translates into verbs, which are action words. Christ-like actions are essential to identify Christ's followers. We are to be <u>fruitful</u> and <u>productive</u>. God wants us to <u>multiply</u> our efforts to reach the lost. We <u>care</u> for our family. We <u>subdue</u> the earth and ourselves. We provide for a lovely <u>dominion</u> with the animals, etc. As we learn more about the Creator, we desire a close relationship with him. **He is the Way, the Truth, and the Light.** Only through Him, do we have access to Heaven. Worshipping an animal, a rock or even the planet does not save mankind. Only Jesus saves.

The most useful form of exercise is physical work! God honors our physical labor. **2 Kings 6:1-7** describes a group of young men studying with the prophet, Elisha. The young men had requested to build living quarters and Elisha approved their request. As one of the young prophets was chopping down a tree, the borrowed axe head flew off the handle and landed in the Jordan river. He immediately ran to Elisha and described what had happened. Realizing the hard work of the young man and the implications of losing the borrowed axe head, Elisha immediately cut off a piece of wood from a tree and threw it in the river. The axe head floated to the top of the water and Elisha instructed the young man to retrieve it. **This miracle demonstrated to the young prophets that God is in control. His work is not stopped.** Had the axe head not been retrieved, the borrower might have had to sell himself into slavery to pay the debt.

Elisha's faith was developed in his father's household. His father was a wealthy farmer. **His household was one of the few which had not bowed the knee to Baal.** His simple country upbringing prepared him to be one of God's greatest and most colorful prophets. When Elijah saw Elisha toiling in his father's fields, he recognized God's calling on Elisha's life. **Luke 9:62** refers to this event, **"No man, having put his hand to the plough, and looking back is fit for the kingdom of God."** As Elijah passed his mantle to Elisha as he was carried up to heaven, he gained a double blessing of God's power. It was Elisha's upbringing that allowed him to cooperate with God and to be a faithful instrument in leading Israel in the fight against evil.

Water played a large role in Elisha's recorded life. Shortly after Elijah was taken to heaven, Elisha parted the waters on his way to Jericho. He cast salt into the bitter spring water, turning it into pure sweet water. Elisha advised Naaman to wash seven times in the muddy Jordan, healing his leprosy. Water miracles were nothing new to Elisha. The story of the axe head represents a beautiful expression of God's love for Elisha and the young prophets. This event must have shored up their faith and increased their desire to serve God. What a beautiful ending to a potentially tragic story. **God can snatch anyone from the jaws of slavery and defeat.**

In the next few verses in **2 Kings 6**, we read about another remarkable experience of Elisha and his servant. The account is about the army surrounding Elisha in the darkness of night and his servant's fearful report. Elisha's predictions had been irritating the King to the point the King wanted to eliminate him. One morning after the King had ordered his army to find and capture Elisha, the army surrounded the city where Elisha was staying. In the morning, the servant looked out the window and saw the vast army surrounding the city. Knowing Elisha was the object of their forces, he fearfully reported this to Elisha. Elisha prayed to the Lord to open the eyes of his servant. After the prayer the servant looked out the window again and saw the hillside covered with heavenly horses and chariots of fire. The story takes an unexpected twist when Elisha asks the Lord to strike blind the Syrian army. God's methods are not our methods. His ways are not our ways and his thoughts are not our thoughts. It is stories like this which increase our faith and give us hope in Christ. For as sure as He cared for the young prophet and his servant, He cares for us and wants us to better understand his care and protection for us.

When we live where we have elbow room to move, plant a small garden, hike the trails, explore the creeks, grow some beautiful flowers, cut trees to build a home – we learn the lessons hard work teaches. Just as in the Garden of Eden, God designed the land to supply our needs. Just as working on a farm prepared Elisha for his work as a prophet, we daily prepare ourselves to cooperate with God when he makes a calling on our life.

Physical labor allows children and adults to learn valuable skills. **Physical labor requires eye – hand – and foot coordination, it strengthens the frontal lobes, improves intelligence, and promotes character development.** Physical work also accomplishes a number of essential tasks such as mowing, cutting hay, trimming bushes, planting and weeding a garden, building a greenhouse, painting a shed, repairing the roof, etc. In the country there seems to be an infinite number of tasks to accomplish. Plan your days around at least 1 to 2 hours of physical labor.

Living in the country is useful for refining and shaping one's character. Both men and women should learn useful outdoor tasks such as gardening, landscaping, mowing, edging, planting and transplanting, equipment and small house repairs, painting, etc. This increases your value improves your ability to make meaningful contributions in group projects, mission outreach and even in training others for country living. If children have been allowed to watch TV and spend time on the internet, they must un-learn sedentary and lazy habits.

Oftentimes, people claim to have a certain skill set or ability, but in reality, their personal assessment is overly optimistic and claimed skills and talents are theoretical and not actual. Unfortunately, this frequently occurs. If someone claims they can repair a tractor or plant a 45,000 square foot (1 acre = 43,560 square feet; 4,840 square yards; 660 X 66 feet; 75% of an American football field) orchard or vegetable field, you should always ask for their references, pictures of their work, and confirm their skills by checking with their references and working with them until you have confidence in their abilities. **Always get everything in writing.** Contracts keep business interactions clean and straightforward. There can be no doubt of expectations when everything is spelled out in a legal contract. Once you have a contract, monitor to make sure it is kept. I have heard stories of people claiming to have specific skills and promising to complete this and that project but, when given the opportunity and means to do so, they end up failing or worse yet, destroying and devaluing the property they had promised to improve. If you are providing housing in return for physical labor, always make a contract which spells out daily, weekly, monthly and yearly tasks and projects which are required in return for housing and other considerations. In the Appendix, Section 1, you find the Country Living Personal Skills Inventory (PSI). This may form the basis for interviewing people whom you might want to work or partner with. It may also be used to assess skills for communal or group projects. Check it out and see how you fare as well. Monetize the contract. This means, even if you are trading housing for labor, the value of the housing and the value of the labor should be spelled out. If you are providing someone with a small home in return for labor, put a value on the home, say $750 to $1,000 per month and then assign an hourly value to their labor. Start with $15 / hour unless they have specialized skills such as nursing, electrician, plumber, etc. This translates into roughly 70 hours / month or 18 to 20 hours per week of labor dedicated to activities and projects you define. Children's labor does not count unless they are old enough and have the necessary skills and a reasonable work ethic. Also define what behaviors lead to termination of the contract. Contracts keep everyone honest and allow each party flexibility to fulfill the terms of the agreement or terminate the relationship.

In addition to accomplishing valuable work, physical labor done outdoors carries with it many additional benefits. Earthing, direct physical contact of the human body with the surface of the earth, provides powerful effects on human biochemistry and physiology. Grounding is making an indirect contact with the surface of the skin to the surface of the earth. An example of grounding is using sheets embedded with conductive material and attached to a ground wire which is inserted into the ground about a foot or so using a metal peg. This allows for the flow of electrons from the earth along the wire and throughout the conductive sheet to the human body.

Earthing places the body in direct contact with the earth; where the conductive surface of the skin touches the ground, sand, water, or other conductive earth surfaces.

When two conductive objects (e.g., humans and the earth) touch each other, there is simultaneous transfer of charge so that two objects equilibrate to the same electrical potential. When any part of the body touches the earth, there is rapid transfer and equalization of the electrical potential of the body with the potential of the earth. For example, after a thunderstorm (i.e., where the lightning injects gazillions of electrons into the surface of the earth), you may see cows and other farm animals lying on the ground. In part, they are experiencing the transfer of electrons from the earth to their body and utilizing them for physiological purposes. We too can benefit from earthing right after a thunderstorm.

Free electrons found in the earth, trees, plants, animals, etc., act as antioxidants, neutralizing inflammatory free radicals.

When we are disconnected from the earth due to unnatural living and working conditions, the body has reduced availability of free electron transfer into biological tissues. This paucity of electron transfer from the environment may result in chronic pain, stiffness, and other degenerative issues. The earth is a source of electrons. When we connect with the earth, the earth's electrons (i.e., antioxidants) are transferred to our body and equilibrate into the body and stabilize the internal electrical environment.

Transfer of electrons from the earth to the body occurs rapidly. Skin conductance is altered within two seconds of grounding (PMID: 31831261, 28987038, 22757749; Med Hypotheses 77(2011)824-6; https://doi.org/10.1016/j.mehy.2011.07.046). Polish Physicians Karol Sokal (son) and Pawel Sokal (father), (2012, PMID: 24066011, 22420736, 22291721, 21856083, 21469913), measured electrical potential in earthed and unearthed subjects. The electrical potential of an unearthed person, standing or lying down, is around 0 mV. A grounded / earthed person shows a rapid decrease of electrostatic potential to -200 mV (this is good). When standing on the earth but wearing rubber-soled shoes, the body is covered with positive charges and a voltage of +200 mV. When voltage drops, current flows. If you live in a multi-story building, you need to add +457 mV for every floor above the second floor. This makes it critical to spend time outdoors soaking up negative charges.

The earth's negative potential and regular, frequent contact with the earth, creates the opportunity for the human body to maintain a stable internal environment for the body to do work, as indicated by a decrease in electrostatic potential. The transfer of electrons from the earth's surface sets biological clocks, regulates physiological rhythms, provides an endless supply of antioxidant electrons to combat inflammation and oxidative stress, shifts the body into parasympathetic mode, improves sleep, thins the blood, improves pain perception, and many other benefits.

Below is a partial list of benefits related to earthing and grounding:

- **Improved facial blood circulation** (restores blood flow regulation to the face suggesting enhanced skin tissue repair, movement of lymphatic fluid, and improved facial appearance) (2010, PMID: 20064020, 22757749, 20192911, 26443876, 26665041, 22291721, 26665039, 30448083, 25748085, 25848315).

- **Improved protein balance** (i.e., positive nitrogen balance possibly reflecting decreased breakdown of muscle creatine, a potential increase in muscle mass, and increased protein synthesis) while grounded and exercising (cycling) and extending to the post-recovery phase. The mechanism may relate to "changes in the electrical, aqueous environment in humans who are earthed (2013, PMID: 24066011).

- Earthing reduces indicators of ongoing osteoporosis including statistically significant changes in mineral and electrolyte concentrations in blood serum for iron, ionized calcium, inorganic phosphorus, sodium, potassium and magnesium. Renal excretion of both calcium and phosphorus was significantly reduced, indicating a role for earthing in osteoporosis.

- Earthing affects thyroid functions. A single night of grounding was associated with a significant decrease of free T3 and an increase of free T4 and TSH. Individual reports of people on thyroid meds and initiating earthing as a lifestyle therapy may lead to symptoms of hyperthyroidism including heart palpitations, tachycardia, etc. Symptoms usually resolve when thyroid meds are reduced or stopped. This may be a supportive therapy before advancing to hypothyroid meds.

- ## Reduces inflammation.

- While sleeping grounded, study participants experienced a more predictable and normal trend of 24-hour cortisol secretion (PMID: 22291721).

- Reduces / eliminates chronic pain.

- Earthing has a direct and statistically significant positive effect on uncontrolled blood glucose levels in NIDDM subjects. Using only earthing as the intervention, Sokal's Polish study showed a decrease in fasting glucose concentrations from 10.6 +/- 1.2 to 7.4 +/- 0.8 mmol/L, $p < 0.05$.

- Improves the healing response.

- ## Normalizes biological rhythms.

- Reduces stress hormones.

- Sympathetic activity in the CNS is associated with "fight and flight" behaviors. Para-sympathetic activity in the CNS is associated with "rest and digest" types of activities. Each system is necessary and essential. It is the overall balance between these two systems that determines whether or not one is more likely to suffer from overactivation of the stress response.

Over-activation of the sympathetic system is associated with heart disease, stroke, inflammation, hypertension, sleep dysfunction, stress, pain, depression. Grounding increases para-sympathetic activity.

- **Earthing and grounding reduces blood viscosity.** This leads to reduced cardiovascular risk. "Grounding increases the surface charge on RBCs and thereby reduces blood viscosity and clumping. Grounding appears to be one of the simplest and yet most profound interventions for helping reduce cardiovascular risk and cardiovascular events."
- The strong electrical net charge (electrophoretic mobility) of RBCs is known as the zeta potential (a way to measure blood viscosity), ensuring a minimum of approximately 18 nm of spacing between two RBCs. Earthing increases the zeta potential of red blood cells (RBCs) making them less likely to stick together. Reductions in pain perception and inflammation are associated with higher zeta potentials (PMID: 22291721).
- Earthing for just 15 minutes after a long flight shifts one's biological clock to the new location.
- Grounding while sleeping improves sleep quality.
- Earthed and grounded subjects experience improved sleep apnea compared to non-earthed and non-grounded individuals. Other sleep-related factors showing significant improvement include falling asleep more quickly, fewer sleep interruptions, improved morning fatigue level, improved daytime energy levels and improved nighttime pain scores (PMID: 22291721).
- Earthing also protects against external electric fields. During earthing, the earth's negative potential creates an ideal internal bioelectrical environment. Linking the human body to the earth by walking barefoot on moist ground may also provide chronobiological cues for setting internal rhythms. When the earth's electrical potential is linked to the human body, the body is protected from "ambient voltages induced on the body from common electricity power sources." Parameters that may improve include: time to fall asleep, quality of sleep, feeling rested, muscle stiffness and pain, chronic back and / or joint pain, and general well-being. (PMID: 22291721).
- Spending time outdoors around waterfalls and flowing water magnifies the other beneficial effects of being outdoors. Inhaling negative ions from waterfall spray (aka, electrified air) appears to have a direct effect on human physiology via improved mood and a greater ability for relaxation. If trees surround the waterfall, the overall health benefits are greater.

For the record, not everyone experiences the same benefits when changing their diet and lifestyle. Just because someone else experienced a benefit does not mean you will experience the same benefit. A person may try something like earthing or grounding and if it doesn't work after one or two sessions, they give up and claim it didn't work. However, biological resets while sometimes dramatic and immediate, tend to work more gradually and with less immediate dramatic results. Dramatic results should leave no doubt as to the effect(s) but oftentimes this is seen as unrelated! Also, biological resets usually tend to require upkeep of reset type behaviors for a certain amount of time, although this varies with the type and duration of the reset period. Even you may not experience the same results at different times. We are never the same organism. There are synergistic influences which we often fail to recognize. We also frequently fail to recognize a "healing response" also known as a "Herxheimer" reaction, which in the process of healing we actually feel worse before we get better. This occurs when the normal routes of toxin elimination are overwhelmed (i.e., the bladder and colon) and secondary eliminative organs are recruited (i.e., sinuses, lungs, skin). This reaction has likely discouraged and prevented thousands if not millions of people from realizing some pretty awesome results. As a practitioner, I have seen this first hand in myself as well as in my clients. Ask your provider to devise a gentle detox if you want to avoid a Herxheimer reaction.

The placebo effect is evidence of a powerful non-pharmacological mechanism in play for treating bothersome symptoms. The mind is powerful enough to effect a positive resolution and sometimes even a cure (i.e., a biological correction). It may seem like a placebo effect, however, maybe the placebo effect, in part, provides encouragement, gives hope, reinforces positive self-care habits, etc. When one begins to take control of their health and their life, they may get outdoors more frequently, go for walks or hikes in nature, kayak around a lake or down a stream, etc. These interactions with nature provide the opportunity to restore health and eliminate bothersome symptoms. As you learn about novel methods to regain what you have lost, it becomes clear, most of us could benefit from more time outdoors, more time working outside, more time to spend in prayer and communion with God. Country living provides the perfect backdrop for more time outdoors, more meaningful tasks and labor and more time to spend in nature, God's second Bible.

Discussion Questions

1. How much time do you normally spend outdoors?

2. With slight modifications, are you willing to take steps to earth / ground?

3. Are you willing to take advantage of "free" antioxidants that flow directly from the ground and do not have to be "eaten?"

4. When you spend time outdoors, how do you feel at the end of the day?

5. What are implications for living in multi-story buildings such as apartment housing, high-rise condominiums, penthouses, etc.?

Chapter 10
Chronobiology and country living

Chronobiology is a branch of biology concerned with natural physiological rhythms and other cyclical phenomena. Chrono- is a prefix relating to time. Biology is the study of life, living organisms and the processes which support life and living organisms. Chronobiology is a subset of biological studies examining the presence and functions of time-related physical phenomena. For example, circadian rhythms are biological cycles occurring about every 24 hours. Sleep is a circadian rhythm. **About every 16 hours the human organism requires around 7.5 to 8 hours of sleep.** This cycle repeats over the course of our entire life. It is also known as the sleep-wake cycle. The Germans have a word for the external phenomena controlling internal cyclic rhythms, zeitgebers (time-givers). Examples of zeitgebers include light (or the absence of light), temperature, and mealtimes.

Internal biological rhythms are classified by their periodicity, or the time it takes for one cycle to begin and end before starting another cycle. Biological rhythms with more than a 24-hour period are known as infradian rhythms (i.e., biological cycles greater than 24 hours). A good example of this is a woman's menstrual cycle, controlled by the rising and falling of the hormones, estrogen and progesterone. This repeats every 28 days until menopause. Pituitary and ovarian hormones prime the ovarian follicle and the endometrium to receive a fertilized egg. Body temperature rises at ovulation. When no fertilized egg implants into the uterine wall, the cycle completes and begins again.

The Bible mentions a 7-year cycle known as the Jewish Jubilee. At the end of every 7 years, slaves and prisoners were freed and debts were forgiven. At the end of 7 cycles of Jubilees (the 49th year) and beginning with the 50th year, people returned to their land, property and family. There was no sowing and reaping the land for food, but only what grew from the ground from seeds left behind the previous year. If you and your family had been sold into slavery to pay off debts, everything was reversed during the month of Atonement during the Jubilee year. A new cycle began and what had been lost was restored.

Ultradian rhythms are biological cycles occurring more than once per day, or 24-hour period. A circannual cycle is a biological process covering a year (i.e., 365 days) before beginning a new cycle. Circaseptan rhythms cover a 7-day cycle or a physiological phenomenon occurring every 7 days. These include 7-day rhythms for heart rate, immune responses and blood pressure. Lunar rhythms follow the lunar month (29.5 days). Ocean-based tidal rhythms impact marine shore-based creatures which experience altered biorhythms between high and low tide, occurring every 12.4 hours.

For millennia, human rhythms were closely coupled to nature. Before Thomas Edison introduced electricity in 1879 and modernized life as we know it today, humans relied on external cues for sleeping, rising and eating. External cues, or zeitgebers, synchronize with internal clocks to produce a pattern of human behaviors. Sleep is one of those human behaviors strongly influenced by external and internal cues. While most people sleep during night time hours, some are night time workers, others are night owls and feel more productive at night time, and yet most of us could not stay up all night if our life depended on it.

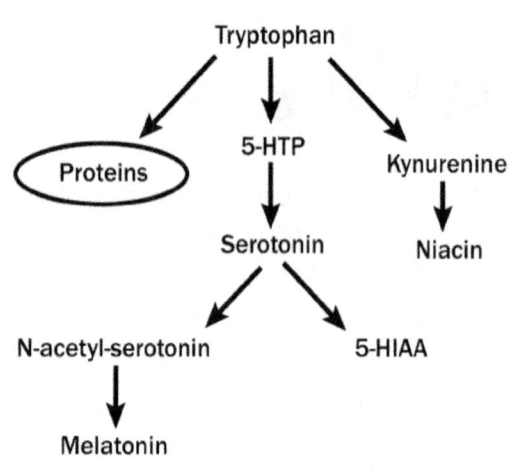

Chronobiology and country living, Figure 1, Tryptophan pathways. Greenleaf Executive Nutrition and ...
http://greenleafexecutive.blogspot.com/

Uncoupling the body's internal natural rhythms from external cues is almost never healthy; it is rarely recommended. It is out of necessity we shift our circadian rhythms. For example, nurses working the night shift have greater risk of certain types of cancer, obesity, diabetes, gut issues, and even heart disease. Some may experience anxiety, chest pains, exhaustion, altered epigenetics, poor concentration, weight gain and much more. In these cases, one's circadian rhythm is inverted, sometimes resulting in altered thinking patterns, mental dullness, impulsivity, depression, and lowered immunity, etc. Shift work throws off the body's circadian rhythm, altering the body's internal clocks and repair and restore mechanisms.

If you recall the discussion about frontal lobes, you may remember the rarest essential amino acid, tryptophan, is the precursor to making serotonin, the neurotransmitter associated with spirituality and equanimity (see Figure 1). Serotonin follows a daily circadian rhythm. Researchers have found serotonin peaks at different times throughout the brain. Some areas of the brain peak right before sunset at dusk and others areas are not as affected by circadian rhythms. The relevant point to make about serotonin is that it is the precursor to making melatonin, the body's premier antioxidant. **Melatonin doesn't make you sleep, it makes it safe for you to fall asleep.**

Normal circadian rhythms are also associated with less depression, anxiety and addictions. Low melatonin levels have been found to occur more frequently in certain types of cancer, which may or may not cause the cancer but might be related. A possible explanation for why low melatonin might be associated with hormone dependent cancers is its association with luteinizing hormone.

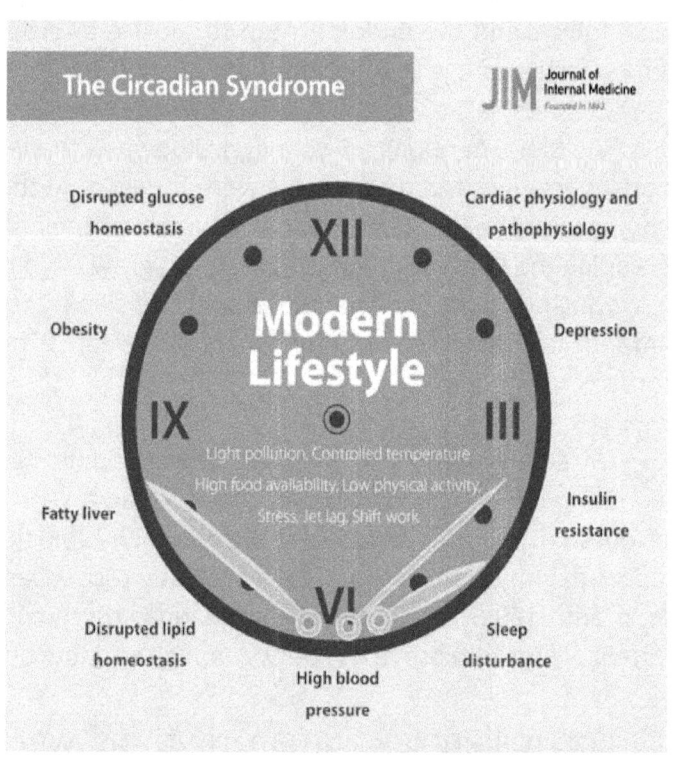

Figure 2. Chronobiology and country living, The circadian syndrome: is metabolic syndrome and much more! By P. Zimmet, K. Alberti, N. Stern, C. Bilu, et al.

As melatonin increases, it suppresses luteinizing hormone, thereby protecting hormone sensitive tissues such as the ovaries and gonads from estrogen and testosterone stimulation during periods of elevated melatonin. This is also consistent with melatonin's effect on telomeres. Telomeres are caps found at the end of a chromosome. They are a measure of gene health. **Melatonin is critical to good health. It slows down the aging process and gives us the opportunity to enjoy getting older.**

Increasing latitude is associated with depression, mental fatigue, obsessive compulsive disorder (OCD), low physical activity, multiple sclerosis, and other conditions. This cluster of symptoms is known as seasonal affect disorder (SAD). In addition to seasonal affect disorder (SAD), mainstream researchers have observed a cluster of symptoms they have termed, "Circadian Syndrome." This syndrome includes: disrupted glucose homeostasis, cardiac physiology and pathophysiology, depression, insulin resistance, sleep disturbances, high blood pressure, disrupted lipid transport and homeostasis, fatty liver, and obesity. This syndrome is directly attributed to a modern lifestyle which readily accepts light and noise pollution, controlled temperature thermostats, high food availability, low physical activity, stress, frequent jet lag, and shift work as part of a normal lifestyle. It is this uncoupling of natural physiological processes to our modern lifestyle which may continue to lessen our ability to live free from infirmities and bothersome symptoms.

Some gene expression is rhythmic and may follow a circadian, infradian, ultradian, circaseptan or for some, even lunar expression pattern. Clock type genes show greater expression during certain times of the day or week or even year. The brain houses the master clock, controlling the release of melatonin and other chemicals associated with periodicity, but there are other clocks. These peripheral clocks are found in digestive tract cells, the heart, the endocrine and immune systems, the reproductive organs, and the thyroid gland. Detoxification-related genes may be cyclic and their expression related to the sleep-wake circadian cycle. When rhythmic cycles are altered, detoxification processes are negatively impacted. **Data also reveal human longevity is associated with regular sleep patterns and early risers appear to have an advantage over those sleeping in.**

A recent interesting development is the use of exogenous melatonin to tamp down cytokine storms, seen in Covid-19 infections. It's role as a premier antioxidant now includes the potential to suppress widespread inflammation seen in advanced Covid-19 cases. Melatonin works with other hormones such as vitamin D to ensure a healthy circadian rhythm. These observations have expanded and included as part of the therapy for advanced Covid-19 cases (see Figure 3). Studies are ongoing but because of its rapid response, melatonin should be considered as one armament in treating Covid-19.

The biochemistry behind circadian rhythms involves tryptophan and serotonin. Tryptophan, the rarest essential amino acid, is the precursor to serotonin. Most of the body's serotonin is made in the gut and circulates in platelets (involved in blood clotting) with about 5% synthesized in the brain. In the brain, the amino acid tryptophan prefers to make the water-soluble vitamin niacin but if there is enough niacin available to the brain, tryptophan makes serotonin. Serotonin is a neurotransmitter associated with mood regulation, happiness, social behavior, appetite, digestion, sleep, memory, sexual arousal, body temperature, etc. Serotonin also ensures frontal lobes are functional. The pineal gland secretes melatonin (under influence of suprachiasmatic nucleus (SCN) of the hypothalamus). The SCN is regulated by light and correspondingly influences body temperature. When evening hours approach and the sun goes down, darkness comes, serotonin decreases, and melatonin increases.

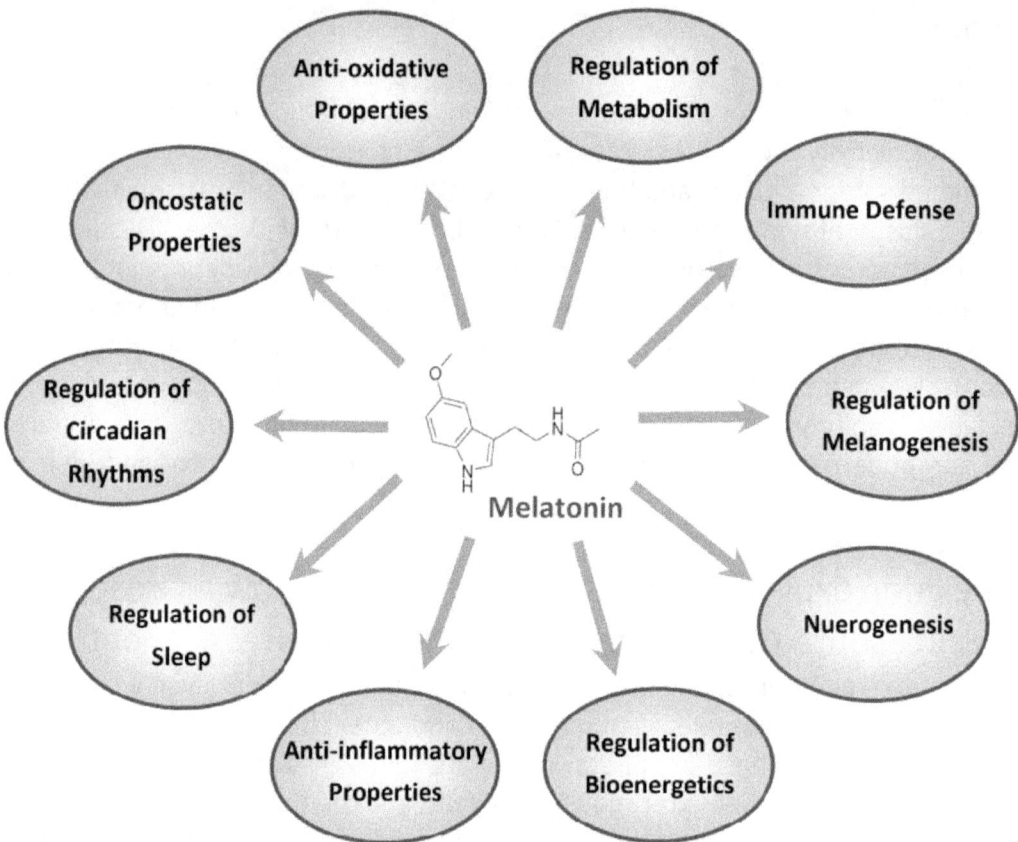

Figure 3. Chronobiology and country living. Important functions of melatonin in normal physiology and in the treatment of viral conditions such as C19, in Clinical Trials for the Use of Melatonin to Fight against Covid-19 are Urgently Needed, by Kleszczynski K, et al., in Nutrients, 24 August 2020. doi:10.3390/nu12092561

To put it another way, melatonin is the chemical expression of darkness. Melatonin doesn't make you go to sleep, it makes it safe for you to go to sleep. Serotonin is the precursor needed to synthesize melatonin in the pineal gland. Circulating melatonin during nighttime hours is an order of magnitude higher than during the daytime.

As you can see from Figure 3, melatonin has many physiological and biochemical functions in the body. As previously mentioned, melatonin is also a premier antioxidant, penetrating both the water- and fat-soluble cellular compartments. Melatonin, once secreted and circulating in the blood, has far-reaching effects in the body. It is thought to organize both short and long-term memory. Night time melatonin secretion promotes physiological processes thought to increase longevity such as increasing telomere length and promoting a youthful appearance. Telomeres are the caps found on the end of chromosomes (humans have 46 chromosomes which store DNA – the blueprint for life). Telomeres are thought to protect chromosomes from damaging influences such as oxidative stress. Every time a cell reproduces, the telomeres may slightly shorten. Increasingly shortened telomeres are thought to serve as an aging signal in the body's cells. Shortened telomeres are associated with an increased pace of aging and chronic diseases of aging. Melatonin enhances DNAs repair capacity by directly influencing DNA repair genes, limiting oxidative stress, and helping to maintain healthy telomeres.

Humans are primed to fall asleep from about an hour after the sun goes down until midnight. If you go to bed too much after midnight, your natural rhythms may be altered making it more difficult to fall asleep. The strongest drive to sleep occurs between 1 am and 4 am. The best time period to sleep is between 9 pm and 6 am. **Sleep before midnight is more refreshing and physiologically beneficial than sleep initiated after midnight.** Going to bed around 9 pm is ideal, but not always practical. During sleep, the body goes through four sleep stages every 90 minutes. Most people require five to six 90-minute cycles (i.e., 7.5 to 9 hours of sleep per night) to feel rested and primed for a productive day. This time does not include time spent falling asleep or time spent waking up and falling back to sleep. Sleeping less than six hours per night (less than four 90-minute cycles) is associated with disruption of hundreds of genes responsible for the immune system, fighting inflammation, metabolism, and maintaining a natural sleep-wake cycle.

Sleeping too many hours – hypersomnia or sleeping for 9 or more hours – is also associated with symptoms such as poor mental health, persistent depression, increased chronic pain, cognitive impairment, inflammation, obesity, diabetes, heart disease and stroke.

There are favorable and unfavorable factors related to whether or not you achieve a refreshing nights sleep. Bright lights, eating late, stressful situations, computer time, loud noises, ambient city noises, train whistles, all interfere with reaching peak melatonin levels. Rest is a critical component to good health. It is also important to learn how to relax as a precursor to sleep. People who are able to ease into the evening hours without thinking and participating in stressful experiences usually experience more refreshing nighttime rest. **Spending time in prayer and meditation is an excellent way to prepare for refreshing rest.**

There are several ways to reset your circadian rhythm. **Getting early morning exposure to sunlight results in a higher melatonin peak later that same evening.** Spend early morning hours in the garden, walking, canoeing, yard maintenance, etc.

Fasting for 1 to 3 or even up to 5 days and then re-introducing whole, unprocessed foods, resets one's internal clock, restores robust immune function, and reverses factors which lead to more rapid aging. If you have certain conditions such as diabetes, if you are pregnant or lactating, if you are frail and elderly, if you are sarcopenic (severe muscle loss), if you have liver or kidney dysfunction, hyperthyroidism, dementia, or if you have an eating disorder, fasting may not be recommended.

Depending on the length of a fast and the degree of ketosis, the body goes through various stages of fasting. Within 12 hours of eating no food or beverages except water, insulin begins to drop and your body <u>gently</u> goes into ketosis (it may occur sooner if you are active). This occurs as your body's supply of glucose begins to wane. The body shifts to partially using ketone bodies which are 2 to 4 carbon by-products of fat breakdown. Your entire body benefits from the presence of ketones (excluding diabetic keto-acidosis, a complication where the lack of insulin leads to excess ketones). After 24 hours of no food or beverages except water, your body begins to "clean out" old proteins and defective cells as well as cellular debris. This process is known as autophagy (self-eating). This process is rejuvenating to cells and tissues. It is like cleaning out old accumulating junk from your home.

At 48 hours of fasting, your body begins to make more growth hormone. This preserves your muscle mass and promotes fat loss. **As day 3 of fasting arrives, your body's immune cells begin a renewal process and you begin to make new stem cells.** You may wrap up your fast or you may choose to go another 2 days. If you fast longer than 3 days, it is best to do so under the care of a physician.

Fasting beyond 3 days puts you into robust ketosis and accelerates fat loss. It is usually better to do more frequent fasting than to do one long fast (a long fast being 5 to 10 days or more). For example, a 3-day fast every 6 months has the potential to reduce your risk of diabetes, cancer and other neurodegenerative diseases.

As your fast wraps up, it is best to gradually add back nutritious foods such as fruits, vegetables, whole grains, nuts and seeds. Avoid sugar and processed foods. **Eating a lot of processed and high sugar foods accelerates the aging process.** Avoid foods which may lead to rapidly raising your blood sugar such as sweets and fast food.

There are evidences two meals per day benefits melatonin physiology. If you want to reset your circadian rhythm, go to bed and rise around the same time every day, avoid computer time right before bedtime, and avoid bright lights and stimulating inputs several hours before going to bed. Naps may benefit some people. People who respond positively to increasing melatonin levels during naptime may benefit from greater learning and memory consolidation with afternoon naps but not everyone taking a nap sees an increase in nighttime melatonin.

Interestingly, melatonin has been found in all plants which have been tested, and paradoxically it is found in stimulating plant-based beverages such as coffee and tea. The plant kingdom perfectly balances phyto-melatonin (i.e., plant-based melatonin) with other beneficial compounds to confer health benefits. Some plants have enough melatonin to raise the blood level of melatonin upon consuming. Those plants include coffee, tea, corn, rice, wheat, barley, oats, and walnuts. Other foods with significant amounts of melatonin include tart cherries, pistachios, bananas, grapes, herbs, plums, olive oil, pineapple, oranges, tomatoes, etc. (see Wikipedia under the term, "melatonin; PMID: 12074994, 17167296, 31284489; 11570431).

Ecclesiastes 5:12 gives us insight into restful sleep, "**The sleep of a laborer is sweet, whether they eat little or much, but as for the rich, their abundance permits them no sleep.**" Restorative sleep is a gift from God. It is tied to our labor. Country living more closely couples hard work and rest. In addition to more physical labor the country provides a symphonic backdrop of animal and insect sounds which gently lull the mind into restful sleep. The night sky provides the moon and stars as well as clouds to keep our minds open to the ways of the Lord. **Genesis 1:16**, "God made the two great lights, the greater light to govern the day, and the lesser light to govern the night; he made the stars also." **Amos 5:8** describes the day-night cycle, "He who made the Pleiades and Orion and changes deep darkness into morning, who also darkens day into night, who calls for the waters of the sea and pours them out on the surface of the earth, the Lord is his name." **In Job 38:31-32**, God asks of Job, "Canst thou bind the sweet influences of Pleiades, or loose the bands of Orion? Canst thou bring forth Mazzaroth in his season? Or canst thou guide Arcturus with his sons?" The movement of the planets and stars serves to remind us the Creator has perfectly made everything to reveal His glory and character. **Even the night sky reminds us to rest in Jesus and to trust in Him to wake us up in the morning.**

Modern humans have figuratively and literally short-circuited their circadian rhythms by the use of all-night lights, artificially changing the ambient temperature, staying up late, drinking alcohol, frequent jet travel (without time to adjust to changing external stimuli), daily use of stimulants such as coffee, erratic eating patterns, long periods of digestion due to eating significant amounts of meat, variable activity patterns, frequent infections, parasites, inflammation, low oxygen, low nutrients, etc. We expect our physiology to keep up with our lifestyle, but unless we are willing to honestly and brutally reason from cause to effect, we may never see how modern conveniences have limited our ability to thrive and survive. In fact, modern living disconnects us from God and from being intimately coupled to His creation. Instead of believing in Him, we believe in our own intelligence and ability to invent, create, and to elaborate on what He has already created.

Country living places humans amongst trees, plants, and animals which are intricately tied to chronobiological cycles. If we choose country living and purposefully live in a way that honors our physiology, we may experience amazing blessings including improved health, a vibrant prayer life, improved familial relations, and less dissonance induced by city living.

Bible verses: Job 14:12, 33:15; Proverbs 3:24, 6:9, 20:13; Psalm 3:5, 4:8, 23, 91, 127:2; Isaiah 35:3-6; Ecclesiastes 5:12; Matthew 8:24, 11:28-30; John 11:12; 1 Thessalonians 4:13-18; Revelation 21:4, 23-25, 22:5.

References and sources
https://doi.org/10.1152/ajpendo.1993.265.5.E801
https://doi.org/10.1210/jcem.74.4.1548337
https://doi.org/10.4161/auto.6.6.12376

Discussion Questions

1. Describe your circadian rhythm and on a scale of 1 (being least) to 10 (being best), how strong is your circadian system?

2. What has served to strengthen your sleep cycle?

3. What has served to weaken your sleep cycle?

4. What other activities are on a periodic cycle?

5. What are you willing to do to improve your circadian rhythm?

6. Why do you think God created the nighttime?

Chapter 11
5G – Electromagnetic pollution and country living

What is 5G? 5G is a new system for the transfer of information over higher frequency waves, hugely expanding the capability of sharing information in real time without lags or streaming issues. The information on 5G expands daily and there is even the promise of 6G, soon to arrive through our front door, the walls, etc. Obviously, some of what is written today may be obsolete by tomorrow.

The reason for including a short chapter, really more of an informational section, is that 5G may impact your quality of life. **Living in the country may or may not protect you against 5G, but living in the country may give you more options for minimizing exposure to 5G and other frequencies such as microwave frequencies.** For some who may be sensitive to electromagnetic pollution, country living is the best option. Below is a compiled list of statements pertaining to 5G. To the best of my knowledge the accuracy of each statement is good. **This chapter has been reviewed by a mechanical engineer** (i.e., Wesley Whitten, PE, my father) and is to the best of his knowledge, is accurate.

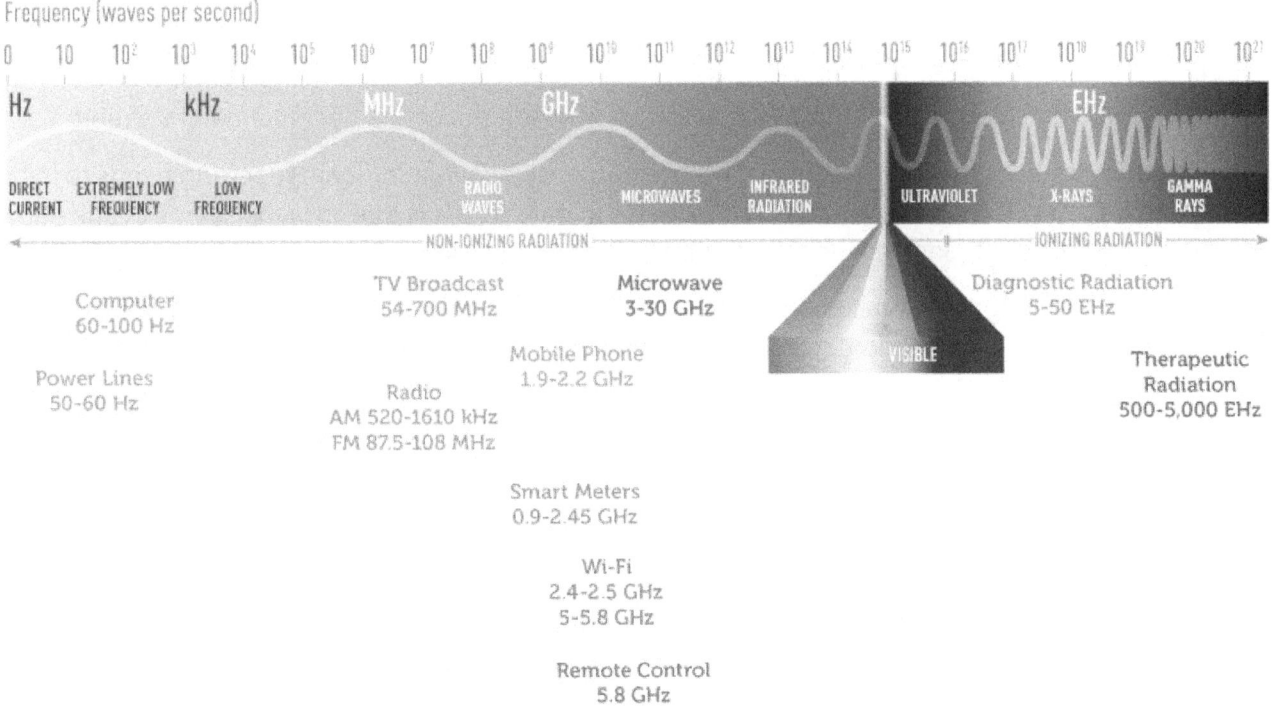

Figure 1. 5G – Electromagnetic pollution and country living. Source: American Cancer Society, https://www.cancer.org/cancer/cancer-causes/radiation-exposure/cellular-phone-towers.html

What are electromagnetic fields (EMFs)? They are invisible energy fields from electromagnetic radiation, which is a type of electricity. Magnetic fields are created when electric currents flow (e.g., powerlines, appliances, lighting, wiring, automobiles, power tools, motors). Electric fields include breaker boxes, wiring, outlets, lighting, switches, extension cords, monitors, etc. Typical sources of dirty electricity include smart meters, dimmer switches, power adapters, wiring, plasma TVs, fluorescent lights, motors, etc. Electromagnetic radiation is a range of wavelengths and frequencies measured in hertz (Hz) or cycles per second. (https://www.medicalnewstoday.com/articles/326141#What-is-electromagnetic-radiation?) Radio frequency EMFs include wavelengths from 30 KHz to 300 GHz. Figure 1, is a graphic depiction of the various frequency waves (e.g., wi-fi, mobile phones, cordless phones, baby monitors, cell towers, microwave ovens, RFID).

Non-ionizing refers to electromagnetic radiation which may generate heat but is not strong enough to remove electrons from atoms. Sources of non-ionizing radiation include: microwave ovens, computers, house energy meters, cell phones, wireless routers (WiFi), Bluetooth devices, high voltage power lines, MRIs, electrical wiring, extremely low frequency induction furnaces, radio waves, etc. How do you know if you are exposed to EMFs? If you have contact or proximity to cell phones, tablets, phone base stations, certain medical applications, WiFi, TV antennas, etc., you are exposed to non-ionizing radio frequencies.

What is 5G and should we be concerned?

- Microwaves are used for 2G to 4G technology; 5G uses millimeter waves for the first time in addition to microwaves. Low band range: 600 MHz, 800 MHz, and 900 MHz. Mid band range: 2.5 GHz, 3.5 GHz, 3.7 – 4.2 GHz. Millimeter wave (high band from around 1 to 10 millimeters) range: 24 GHz, 28 GHz, 37 GHz, 39 GHz, and 47 GHz. Radio spectrum (mobile devices, broadcast TV, HAM radio, and aircraft communication): 30 Hertz to 300 GHz. 5G operates across several frequency bands (30 to 300 GHz). One GHz = 1 billion hertz.
- 5G allows for greater bandwidth, faster downloads, no lagging while streaming, and more towers.
- 5G is expensive because it requires more towers and additional engineers to maintain them.
- The drive for 5G is the rapid rise in global data traffic. 5G allows additional spectrum bands to handle more data traffic than 4G. A significant increase in data traffic is due to viewing videos and games. The goal for 5G is to increase speeds by up to 20 times over 4G.
- 5G is necessary for the widespread use of smart appliances, smart homes, self-driving cars, remote surgery, industry automation, cloud storage, 3D video, voice over IP, etc.
- 5G is used alongside with 4G – unfortunately, there are no data showing the combined effect.
- For those living in densely populated urban areas and cities, there is no escape from radio waves permeating the air around us.
- The wattage of 5G is 30,000 watts per 100 MHz of spectrum.
- 20,000 low earth orbiting satellites beaming 5G onto planet earth are being placed in space.
- Transceivers are mounted on utility poles as well as other locations.
- 5G antennas are usually needed every 100 to 200 meters. This dramatically increases exposure.

- 5G employs new technologies: beam-forming antennas, multiple combinations of inputs and outputs, and phased arrays. This means there is pulsing and modulation of the carrier signals. None of which has been studied for adverse effects in humans.
- Pulsed EMFs are much more biologically active than non-pulsed.
- Countries / large metroplexes who have banned 5G (subject to change): Australia, Switzerland, New Zealand, Japan, Taiwan. Some cities ban 5G from residential areas; others place limitations.
- Uses a shorter wavelength, high frequency signal, which helps avoid interference, but has a much shorter range.
- Requires more transmitters and towers because the waves don't travel as far and nodes need to be closer to the ground.
- Millimeter waves are absorbed within a few millimeters of the skin and other superficial layers including the eyes and testes.
- Not everything labeled 5G is the same.
- 5G uses military grade millimeter wave technology (which can be used to disperse crowds).
- There are no data on how 5G affects biodiverse systems, ecosystems, marine systems, pollinators – all living beings.
- The American Cancer Society, as of 2020, has not categorized 5G as a carcinogen. In part because 5G is below the ionizing radiation range, which directly damages DNA. Check here for their latest report: https://www.cancer.org/cancer/cancer-causes/radiation-exposure/cellular-phone-towers.html
- The National Toxicology Program has not included radio frequencies as a carcinogen in their Report on Carcinogens.
- Many experts, not paid for by industry, believe 5G may cause adverse systemic effects as well as skin and other superficial effects.
- We have minimal data proving safety in free living people exposed to millimeter wave lengths for 24/7 for continuous exposure over consecutive years.
- There are no data establishing safety in pregnancy, infancy, periods of rapid growth, illness, etc.
- The FDA and the FCC do not see a problem with 5G.

Adverse Health Effects of Wireless Radiation on Humans				
Metabolic Disturbance	Reactive Oxygen Species Generation	Genotoxicity and Carcinogenicity	Immunotoxicity and Inflammation	Apoptosis and Necrosis
Discomfort Symptoms	Sensory Disorders	Sleep Disorders	Congenital Abnormalities	Precancerous Conditions
CANCER	**NEURODEGENERATION**	**INFERTILITY**	**NEUROBEHAVIORAL**	**CARDIOVASCULAR**

Figure 2. 5G – Electromagnetic pollution and country living. Source: Adverse health effects of 5G mobile networking technology under real-life conditions by Kostoff R.N., Heroux P., Aschner M, and Tsatakis A. in Toxicology Letters, Vol 323, 1 May 2020, p 35-40.

- In 1996, President Clinton signed the Telecommunications Act into law. Section 704 of the TCA states that no health or environmental concern can interfere with the placement of telecom equipment. Our rights in regard to wireless technology and health were taken away. This law took power from states to regulate location of cell towers based on health.

What are the potential and proven health effects of 5G?

Many of the effects of electromagnetic frequencies (EMFs) have been shown with current cell phone technology in the 2G to 4G range. **The most well-established biological effect of EMFs is the thermal effect of heating up.** If your skin heats up, it may lead to cellular and tissue changes, burns and other types of damage. In addition to heating up tissue, risks of EMFs may include increased oxidative stress, altered immunity, skin effects, altered gene expression possibly leading to brain tumors (PMID: 24192496; 18941554), thyroid cancers (PMID: 29285437), reduced sperm quality and count (PMID 24982785), and possibly salivary gland tumors. The location of these cancers indicates a possible association with cell phone usage and transportation.

The following information is presented for your analysis. Standards may change over time so these numbers may not always reflect the most recent standards. These numbers are associated with the electric and magnetic fields (also referred to as radiation) required for wireless operations (see this site: https://mdsafetech.files.wordpress.com/2018/09/conversion-chart-microwave-electromagnetic-radiation-pdf.pdf).

- Cell phone minimum required to operate is (www.powerwatch.org): 0.0000000002 µw/cm^2
- Premature aging of pine needles occurs here (Selga T, Selga M, 1998): 0.000027 µw/cm^2
- Short term exposures for children which cause headaches, irritation, and concentration difficulties, behavioral issues, etc. (ages 8 to 17; Heinrich, 2010; Thomas, 2010): 0.05 µw/cm^2
- **Wireless exposure limits in various countries:** 300 MHz – 300 GHz in microwatts/cm^2

USA standard:	200 – 1,000 µw/cm^2
Canada:	1,000 µw/cm^2
China, Russia, Italy, France, Poland, Hungary:	10 µw/cm^2
Switzerland:	9.5 µw/cm^2
Swiss schools, hospitals:	4.25 µw/cm^2
Belgium, Bulgaria, Luxembourg, Ukraine:	2.4 µw/cm^2
Lichtenstein:	0.1 µw/cm^2
Austria outdoors:	0.001 µw/cm^2
Austria indoors:	0.0001 µw/cm^2

- Building biology guideline (what is considered safe for homes) – level for extreme concern / very far above normal (German standard) = 0.1 µw/cm^2
- Laptop Wi-Fi: sperm DNA fragmentation, decreased sperm viability (Avendano, 2012) = 1.0 µw/cm^2
- Headache, dizziness, irritability, fatigue, weakness, insomnia, chest pain, difficulty breathing, indigestion (Simonenko V. B., et al. 1998) = 1.0 µw/cm^2
- Altered calcium metabolism in heart muscle cells (Wolke (1996); Schwartz (1990)) = 2.5 µw/cm^2

- Changes in the hippocampus affecting memory and learning (Tattersall, 2001) = 4.0 µw/cm²
- DNA damage in cells (Phillips, 1998) = 6.0 µw/cm²
- Single smart meter (Electrical Power Research Institute) = 7.93 µw/cm² (at 1 foot distance)
- Safety standard for Switzerland, Liechtenstein, Luxembourg = 9.5 µw/cm²
- Safety standard for China, Poland, Russia = 10.0 µw/cm²
- Changes in behavior; avoidance (after 30-minute exposure; Navakatikian, 1994) = 10.0 µw/cm²
- Apartment complex with multiple smart meters = 19.8 µw/cm²
- Safety standard for Canada, USA = 200 – 1,000 µw/cm²

Potential health effects of smart meters, 5G

- 5G not only affects humans. "Numerous recent scientific publications have shown that RF-EMF affects living organisms at levels well below most international and national guidelines. Effects include increased cancer risk, cellular stress, increase in harmful free radicals, genetic damages, structural and functional changes of the reproductive system, learning and memory deficits, neurological disorders, and negative impacts on general well-being in humans Damage goes beyond the human race, as there is growing evidence of harmful effects to both plant and animal life." EMF Scientist at, EMFscientist.org.
- Smart meters (emitting radio frequency radiation) at a distance of 1 foot for 2 minutes: see degradation of RBCs, cells wall breaks, cell mutations.
- Smart meter at 1 foot for 2 minutes: RBCs corrugation / bottle cap (due to oxidation or exposure to free radicals) – alters the shape and therefore the function of RBCs.
- Smart meter at 1 foot for 2 minutes: headache. Rouleaux is a condition where red blood cells aggregate or stack up making it difficult for blood to deliver oxygen to tissues via capillaries.
- WiFi = 2.4 giga hertz (in same range as microwave).
- 5G = 60 giga hertz, burns skin, could impair oxygen absorption rates in body.
- Radio frequencies used for crowd control.
- Biotoxins develop within the body's microbiome.
- Interferes with DNA signaling.
- May see an increase in autism spectrum disorders.
- Infertility.
- Alzheimer's disease.
- Decreased sperm count.
- Effects on pregnancy.
- Sterility in men and women.
- Dead birds and animals.
- Dead pollinators.

- Dead plants.
- Damage to mitochondrial DNA (organelle of the cell involved in bioenergetics); long-term effects are possible.

5G alternatives (According to author, Lloyd Burrell)

- Fiber optic (buried in the ground) is a safer alternative to 5G. It uses light to transmit data instead of current.
- EMF blocking house shielding paint and building foil.
- 3G and 4G constantly transmit signals, but 5G only activates when you initiate a connection.
- The beam from 4G is always on and covers about 120 degrees compared to 5G which is much more focused between 2 and 15 degrees wide.
- Turn off WiFi at night time.

5G Quotes by Expert Scientists

"Putting in tens of millions of 5G antennae without a single biological test of safety has to be about the stupidest idea anyone has had in the history of the world." -Martin L. Pal, PhD, Professor Emeritus of Biochemistry and Medical Sciences at Washington State University

In a letter written on 7 January 2020 to Mrs. Simonetta Sommaruga, President of the Swiss Confederation, and signed by 22 physicians and scientists appointed to study 5G and EMF effects on humans. The letter asks the Swiss president to declare a moratorium on 5G until independent research performed by scientists WITHOUT ties to industry confirm the safety of 5G. The scientists also pointed out that 3G, 4G and WiFi are also not safe. https://www.spandidos-publications.com/10.3892/mco.2020.1984

"Over 230 scientists from > 40 countries have expressed serious concerns regarding the ubiquitous and increasing exposure to EMFs generated by electric and wireless devices already before the additional 5G rollout. They refer to the fact that numerous recent scientific publications have shown that EMFs affect living organisms at levels well below most international and national guidelines. Effects include increased cancer risk, cellular stress, increase in harmful free radicals, genetic damages, structural and functional changes of the reproductive system, learning and memory deficits, neurological disorders, and negative impacts on general well-being in humans." https://www.spandidos-publications.com/10.3892/mco.2020.1984

"The world's largest study, National Toxicology Program, shows statistically significant increase in the incidence of brain and heart cancer in animals exposed to EMF [intensities] below the International Commission on Non-ionizing Radiation Protection guidelines followed by most countries." https://www.spandidos-publications.com/10.3892/mco.2020.1984

"An increasing part of the European population is affected by ill health symptoms that have for many years been linked to exposure to EMF and wireless radiation in the scientific literature. The International Scientific Declaration on electromagnetic sensitivity and multiple chemical sensitivity, Brussels, declares that: 'In view of our present scientific knowledge, we thereby stress all national and international bodies and institutions… to recognize EHS and MCS as true medical conditions which acting as sentinel disease may create a major public health concern in years to come worldwide (i.e., in all the countries implementing unrestricted use of electromagnetic field-based wireless technologies and

marketed chemical substances... Inaction is a cost to society and is not an option anymore... we unanimously acknowledge this serious hazard to public health... that major primary prevention measures are adopted and prioritized, to face this worldwide pan-epidemic in perspective."
https://www.spandidos-publications.com/10.3892/mco.2020.1984

"Evidences about the biological properties of RF-EMF are progressively accumulating and, although they are in some cases still preliminary or controversial, clearly point to the existence of multilevel interactions between high-frequency EMF and biological systems and to the possibility of oncologic and non-oncologic (mainly reproductive, metabolic, neurologic, microbiologic) effects." -Dr. Agostino Di Ciaula, Division Internal Medicine Hospital of Bisceglie, Italy (International Journal of Hygiene and Environmental Health)

"Cell towers should be distanced from homes, daycare centers, schools, and places frequented by pregnant women, men who wish to father healthy children, and the young." -Dr. Lennart Hardell (Frontiers in Public Health)

In a review of the literature on this subject published in 2019, Swedish authors, M Simkó and Mats-Olof Mattsson, read and analyzed 94 relevant publications studying millimeter waves, and concluded there is inadequate information to conclude this technology is safe. They make the point, there is a need for a safety assessment regarding local heat developments on surfaces such as skin and the eye, as well as the need for comprehensive studies on the environmental impact of 5G. "In summary, the majority of studies with millimeter wave exposures show biological responses. From this observation, however, no in-depth conclusions can be drawn regarding the biological and health effects of millimeter wave exposures in the 6 – 100 GHz frequency range. The studies are very different and the total number of studies is surprisingly low. The reactions occur both in vivo and in vitro and affect all biological endpoints studied." (PMID: 31540320)

For several years during my doctoral program, I participated in rounds with Dr. William Rea, MD. He trained as a cardio-thoracic surgeon but ended up founding environmental medicine in the USA in 1978 and shifted from being a surgeon to starting the Environmental Health Center in Dallas. People from all over the world, with acute sensitivity to electromagnetic fields, came to seek treatment and learn from Dr. Rea and his staff. Dr. Rea called electromagnetic pollution an epidemic of the 21st century. Every cell in the body is electric. Wireless technologies impact almost every aspect of our physiology but because it is difficult to measure and thus document, oftentimes even highly educated people scoff at the prospect of electromagnetic fields negatively impacting health (https://manhattanneighbors.org/rea/). Some people are so exquisitely sensitive to electromagnetic fields they cannot be in the same room as an electronic device such as an electric wall clock.

Environmental medicine seeks to lower electrosensitivity and minimize exposures. In a letter dated 19 March 2013, from the Academy of Environmental Medicine to the Los Angeles Unified School District, statements like this describe the concern environmental medicine physicians have for increasing exposure to wireless radiation and the effects on children and learning. Here are a few statements from the letter: "There is consistent emerging science that shows people, especially children are affected by the increasing exposure to wireless radiation... Adverse health effects from wireless radio frequency fields, such as learning disabilities, altered immune responses, and headaches, clearly exist and are well documented in the scientific literature. Safer technology, such as the use of hard-wiring is strongly recommended in schools... WiFi systems in schools are typically hundreds of times more powerful than the home consumer systems... They are also dozens of times more powerful than the café and restaurant systems... The WiFi systems in schools are necessarily more powerful than any microwave communication systems in any other setting because they are required to run hundreds of computers simultaneously. They are also exposing children – the most vulnerable to microwave radiation – to extended periods all day, for their entire childhood. This is an unprecedented exposure with unknown outcome on the health and reproductive potential of a generation…"

The letter continues, "It is unlikely there are currently enough doctors in Los Angeles County familiar with the biological effects of microwave radiation to diagnose and treat the numbers of children who will potentially become symptomatic from exposure to your wireless system should you elect to install it. Statistics show that you can expect an immediate reaction in 3% of your students and time-delayed reactions in 30% of them. This will also include teachers… Children who are required by law to attend school also require a higher level of protection than the general public. You may be directed by technology proponents that the science on the human health effects of WiFi is not yet certain. This uncertainty is not a reason to subject a generation of children to such extreme exposure. Rather, it is the foundation upon which caution must be exercised to prevent a potential public health disaster… While technicians and sales staff argue about the validity of the dangers posed by cell towers, cell phones, WiFi and other forms of wireless radiation, it is the doctors who must deal with the fallout. Until we, as doctors, can determine why some of our patients become debilitatingly sick from WiFi and other microwave communications, while others do not, we implore you not to take such a known risk with the health of so many children who have entrusted you to keep them safe while at school."

How does country living reduce the effects of EMFs?

- Country living returns the human to nature where each component of nature has the potential to provide healthy influences on human physiology and biochemistry.
- Country living reduces exposure to 5G and other types of electromagnetic pollution.
- Country living almost always translates into less interactions with multiple sources of electromagnetic pollution.
- Many others!

Sources:
https://www.medicalnewstoday.com/articles/326141#What-is-electromagnetic-radiation?
https://www.thelancet.com/journals/lanonc/article/PIIS1470-2045(11)70147-4/fulltext
https://lennarthardellenglish.wordpress.com/
https://www.environmentandcancer.com/letter-to-simonetta-sommaruga-07-01-2020-english/
https://www.emfscientist.org/index.php/emf-scientist-appeal
https://www.spandidos-publications.com/10.3892/mco.2020.1984
https://www.sciencedirect.com/science/article/abs/pii/S1438463917308143?via=ihub
https://www.frontiersin.org/articles/10.3389/fpubh.2019.00223/full

Check your app store for apps that detect EMF (limited usefulness but can be helpful).
https://www.amazon.com/Meterk-Electromagnetic-Radiation-Detector-Dosimeter/dp/B0754VVW4W
EMF blocking paint, EMF blocking fabrics, EMF blocking clothing

Discussion Questions

1. What are some ways to protect yourself from excessive exposure to electromagnetic fields?

Chapter 12
Take down inflammation

Inflammation is a normal defensive response to injury or a breach in the body's immune system. Typically, the body uses inflammation to accelerate healing, but occasionally, there are not enough trophic factors present to move the process forward and the body gets stuck in a chronic inflammatory state. The inflammatory process may be visually observed or perceived as redness, heat, swelling, pain, and sometimes loss of function. Inflammation can also be detected by sampling the blood for inflammatory markers such as homocysteine, C-reactive protein, erythrocyte sedimentation rate (ESR), plasma viscosity, oxidized LDL, low HDL, and procalcitonin (PCT). But, these tests are just the tip of the iceberg when it comes to defining and addressing systemic inflammation.

A number of conditions indicate the presence of inflammation. Some of those conditions include: infections, chronic pain, soreness, obesity, gum disease, Alzheimer's disease, Parkinson's disease, heart disease, cancer, asthma, type 2 diabetes, inflammatory bowel disease, autoimmune diseases, sympathetic overdrive, excess catecholamines, excess cortisol, oxidative stress, thyroid imbalances, insomnia, chronically inflamed arteries, clots and platelet aggregation, thick sticky blood (Rouleux effect), mineral imbalances (excess calcium, magnesium deficiency), vasoconstriction / spasms, etc.

The immune system is activated as a result of an infection (i.e., pathogens), injury, toxins, low oxygen (ischemia) and allergic reactions. The activated immune system triggers the release of chemicals meant to support healing and restoration. However, if the immune system is overactivated or continuously activated, the chemicals used to support healing and restoration may negatively impact a local area or the entire organism.

A number of conditions, both physical and psychological, trigger inflammation or indicate the presence of widespread inflammation including: excessive intake of toxins, acute and chronic stress, infection, injury, trauma, radiation, allergic reactions, high arachidonic acid diet (i.e., high meat intake and intake of processed vegetable oils), chronic pain, atherosclerosis, thrombosis, autoimmunity, cancer, insulin resistance, neurodegeneration, inflammatory bowel disease, metabolic syndrome, etc. Inflammation causes the release of immune and blood factors, including cytokines, bradykinin, thromboxanes, histamine, oxidants and others. If inflammation lingers, it begins to weaken the circulatory system and even the organs. Eventually you may show signs and symptoms of chronic inflammation mentioned above. Elevated histamine and inflammatory factors may interfere with getting refreshing sleep (this is why taking aspirin or Benadryl, may help with getting to sleep and staying asleep), mobility, and even clear thought processes.

Ideally, when the body encounters inflammation, its duration is short. However, if you introduce inflammation-causing triggers on a regular basis, the body remains in a pro-inflammatory condition without the ability to recover and restore a healthy constitution. Stress, diet and hygiene are critical factors.

Chronic, unrelenting stress is devastating to the body's immune system. Stressors may include: loneliness, job, family, friends, social unrest, political uncertainty, divorce, poor diet, etc. These are just a few stressors responsible for causing inflammation.

If you do not take good care of your mouth, gums and teeth, bacteria and other pathogens have an open door to invade your body leading to inflammation. Poor hygiene factors such as regular bathing, a clean living and working environment, clean fresh air and water, are just a few critical factors in keeping the body healthy and free from inflammation. It is impossible to control all inflammatory triggers but the more pro-inflammatory factors you minimize the healthier you may be.

Sometimes a person heals rapidly while other wounds languish and fail to resolve. Orthopedic surgeon, Dr. Robert Becker, author of The Body Electric, describes a phenomenon essential for healing and recovery. Through research and clinical practice, he was able to show relatively weak electrical currents flow through our body and charge each cell. Currents are responsible for healing and regeneration of damaged cells. A cell with a low charge is less likely to heal. If a cell's charge is high enough, healing is rapid and complete. Slow and incomplete healing indicates inadequate cell charge to support the healing process.

If you have a wound or condition which has not successfully resolved, consider earthing and grounding as one possible treatment option. There are very few drawbacks to contact with the earth other than ants and a few other small, almost microscopic pests. As discussed in the previous section, earthing is an excellent mode for reversing inflammation and restoring balance to pro-oxidative conditions. It is free and available to all. Country living puts you in a perfect setting to take advantage of the earth's benefits!

The human body is not designed to endure long-term exposure to pro-inflammatory conditions. Because this topic is so broad, so this discussion is limited to just a few dietary, lifestyle and psychological factors known to cause inflammation as well as dietary and lifestyle factors known to resolve inflammation.

Diet. Include: foods high in antioxidants such as fruit, vegetables, seeds, whole grains, legumes, fresh herbs and spices, leafy greens, etc. A low histamine diet may be beneficial for some (see appendix). Avoid: processed foods, processed meat, animal products, greasy or fried foods, sugar, food with trans fats, gluten in processed foods, processed oils, margarine, soda pop, smoking, over-eating, alcohol, etc.

Lifestyle. Ensure adequate rest, activity, time outdoors, active lifestyle, fresh air, sunlight, etc. Avoid stress, smoking, toxins, limit alcohol, lose weight if necessary, etc.

Mental. Strive for an enriched and stimulating environment, read, write letters, perform simple calculations, engage in meaningful conversation, etc.

Hygiene. Keep a clean body, clean thoughts, clean living environment, clean short nails, excellent oral hygiene, clean sheets, clean air, clean car, etc.

Social. Connect with friends and family, group prayer, group gatherings, helping others, etc.

Spiritual. Fellowship with like believers, read the Bible, pray, praise God, claim God's promises, be kind and tactful, longsuffering, etc.

Others. Smile, sing, whistle, hum, skip, dance, vigorous walking, high intensity intermittent exercises, swim, pay attention to your grooming, etc.

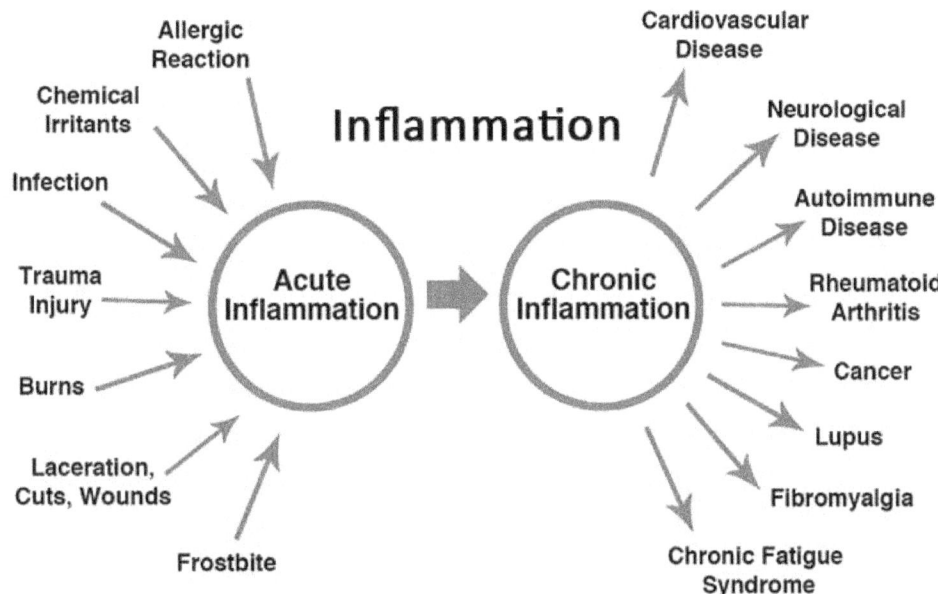

Figure 1. Conditions Associated with Acute and Chronic Inflammation.
Graphic may be found at www.vistasolmedicalgroup.com/everything-you-need-to-know-about-inflammation

Bible verses: Jeremiah 17:8; 2 Kings 20:7; Acts 28:4-6; John 9:1-41; James 5:14

Discussion Questions

1. How might inflammation be affecting your health?
2. What types of changes are you willing to make to minimize pro-inflammatory factors?

Chapter 13

Hydrotherapy

Contrast (hot and cold) hydrotherapy. Water, when mentioned in the Bible, oftentimes represents life. Many stories are illustrated using water such as Jesus walking on water, Jesus turning the water into wine, John the Baptist baptizing Jesus in the Jordan River, Naaman washing seven times in the Jordan River, Moses striking the rock for water, Jesus healing the man beside the pool, Jesus' conversation with the woman at the well, and the ultimate river of the water of life, as clear as crystal and flowing from the throne of God – promised to those redeemed from earth.

Lotus flower, Singapore.
Photo credit: Matthew Tan

Forward thinking health practitioners understand the current paradigm of detached office-based medical care supplemented with extremely distressful and invasive hospital stays to 'stabilize' the body's attempts to return to homeostatis via the production of extreme symptoms, is missing the mark. The Germans and others have pioneered holistic integrative approaches to chronic degenerative conditions and bothersome symptoms for centuries. Their state-of-the-art hospitals look and operate more like an exclusive spa resort than a cold and sterile institution which requires colossal amounts of capital to operate, frequently trading a temporary minimization of symptoms via pharmaceuticals, procedures, and invasive therapies for poverty and years of payments for medical interventions that are not always effective, and in some cases, cause more damage. As cynical as our current situation may sound, there are other options! Restoring the body's natural functions while minimizing exposure to toxins and negative stressors ideally occurs in nature's settings. Outdoor time, direct contact with the moist surface of the earth, sunlight exposure, fresh air, positive connections with others, prayer and meditation, beautiful music, mentally stimulating conversations and activities, hydration, and even hydrotherapy are all aspects of holistic and integrative approaches to restoring health. A wide range of health practitioners who specialize in cleaning the blood and organs, upregulating immune systems, oxygenating the body, building muscle tone, eliminating excessive fat and stored toxins, restoring balance to the gut's microbiome via consumption of prebiotic foods and a range of dietary fibers, nourishing the body by using fresh fruits / vegetables / nuts / seeds, determining adequate but not excessive amounts of protein, implementing hyperthermia and hypothermia options, a hygienic living environmentment, etc.,all work together to restore the body's immune and regulatory systems – making the body so healthy it cannot harbor disease.

This chapter is on hydrotherapy. The Natural Remedies Encyclopedia (7th ed.), categorizes hydrotherapy into the following functional categories (see the list on the next page). These categories are useful for discussing various therapy approaches. If you are interested in learning hydrotherapy techniques, obtain a copy of the Natural Remedies Encyclopedia. This is a good resource as well as watching teaching videos, learning from others, and studying the various types of techniques of interest to you. The categories below briefly describe how to use water as an adjunct therapy for many issues including but not limited to depression, congestion, chronic pain, rehabilitation, neurodegenerative disorders, immune compromise, circulation, and lymphatic drainage.

- The application of **local cold packs** (cloth and blanket applications) – cold compress, ice pack, ice cravat, ice bag, proximal compress.
- **Cold to hot** (apply to area of concern to bring circulation to the area) – throat compress, joint compress, abdominal bandage, wet girdle, heating chest pack, trunk pack, etc.).
- **Larger cold to hot** – wet sheet packs.
- **Local hot and cold** – alternate compress, revulsive compress, hot and cold to the head, simultaneous hot and cold to the head, alternating hot and cold to spine.
- **Local hot** – fomentations, hot gauze compress, hot water bottle, local hot paraffin bath, kidney stone pack, sinus pack, heat lamp.
- **Poultices** – charcoal and flaxseed, clay and glycerin, ginger and arrowroot, clay, flaxseed, garlic, mustard (sinapism), cabbage, etc.
- **Local and larger hot** – full body hot blanket pack, hot trunk pack, hot hip / leg pack, etc.
- **Tonic frictions** – wet hand rub, cold mitten friction, wet sheet rub, dripping sheet rub, ice rub, salt glow, etc.
- **Hydro-massage** – uses hand massage as well as pressure jets.
- **Sponging** – fever sponges, hot sponge, cold sponge, tepid sponge, neutral sponge.
- **Pail pours** (aka, affusions) – general pail pour, local pail pours.
- **Partial baths** – half bath, contrast baths, contrast bath to hand or arm, contrast bath to the feet, contrast bath to the legs, hot foot bath, cold foot bath, sitz bath.
- **Full baths** – hot tub bath, neutral bath, cold tub bath, cold shallow bath, plunge bath, graduated bath.
- **Shower baths** – hot shower, continuous hot shower, neutral shower, cold or cool shower, graduated shower, revulsive shower, alternate hot and cold shower.
- **Spas** – involves pools, showers, whirlpools, baths which are usually unsupervised.
- **Mustard bath** – involves adding 3 to 4 tablespoons of mustard powder to warm water, either a bath or foot soak, along with ½ cup baking soda and several drops of essential oils such as rosemary, thyme, eucalyptus, etc. Other compounds are often added including ginger, chamomile, lavender.
- **Miscellaneous baths** – steam baths, Russian bath and sauna, steam chair (steam sweat), vapor inhalation, radiant heat bath, oatmeal bath, soda alkaline bath, starch alkaline bath, sunbath, sea bathing, sun / air / water bath, wet grass bath, mineral bath, herbal bath, summer spray.
- **Steam inhalation therapy** – opens up congested lung passages.
- **Irrigations** (administered by professionals) – ear, nasal passages, eye, throat, rectum, colon.
- **Douches** (hand held sprays administered by professionals).

For video examples showing how to apply many of the above mentioned videos plus many more hydrotherapy techniques, please visit this YouTube channel: Preparing for the Time of Trouble videos – **hydrotherapy and other helpful videos here: www.youtube.com/@preparingforthetimeoftroub8279/videos**

Application of hot and cold treatments is the basis of most water-based therapies. There are a few therapies which use body neutral water temperatures, but many therapeutic applications require the alternating application of hot and cold to achieve powerful effects. Therapies such as the half-bath, the plunge, the cold wet sheet pack, compresses and fomentations target specific conditions. Hydrotherapy, with or without massage, stimulates circulation, relieves fatigue, relieves congestion, improves digestion and absorption functions, and stimulates internal organs including the lungs. Almost all hydrotherapy sessions end with a cold application. This stimulates circulation and improves alertness. A number of conditions positively respond to the combination of hydrotherapy and massage.

A rudimentary knowledge of hydrotherapy principles may be helpful in understanding the therapeutic aspects. Working out in water allows several principles to combine. These principles may include buoyancy, capillary action, conduction, density, hydrostatic pressure, resistance, solutions, surface tension and viscosity. The physical principles in support of water therapy are listed below with a brief description of each principle.

Buoyancy. Buoyancy is based on Archimede's Principle of Buoyancy. It describes how a boat floats in water. This principle allows a ship weighing thousands of tons to float and not sink in the water. It is the parallel of the "lift" principle accomplished by long extended wings on the side of a tubular cabin, allowing airplanes to take off and "lift" up into the air. This principle states when a body is partially or totally immersed in water, (or other liquid) it is buoyed up by a force equal to the weight (volume) of the fluid which is displaced by the body. An object whose density is less than the density of water, floats. However, if the density of an object is greater than water's density, the object will tend to sink. An aspect of this principle is also at work in sensory deprivation tanks (also known as flotation tanks). Up to 1,000 or more pounds of Epsom salts are added to a large tank, super saturating the water with magnesium and sulfur (changing the density). Floating is rapidly becoming an option for relaxation, pain relief, anxiety, sleep disorders, and cardiovascular health. In general, buoyancy is a counterbalance to gravity and is useful when working with patients who have movement disorders, joint problems, and chronic pain. It is also beneficial for those with lymphatic issues.

Capillary action. Capillary action was first described by Leonardo da Vinci. In 1660, Irish chemist, Robert Boyle, also discussed this phenomenon. However, it was not until the 1805, when Thomas Young and Pierre-Simon Laplace submitted an equation describing capillary action. Carl Friedrich Gauss described conditions at the liquid-solid interface. William Thomson, 1st Baron Kelvin, described the effect of the meniscus on a liquid's vapor pressure (i.e., the Kelvin equation). Franz Ernst Neumann described the interaction between two immiscible liquids, and Albert Einstein also studied and wrote about capillary action (Wiki, 2020). This is a phenomenon describing how water bonds together and also adheres to other substances as it moves through a narrow space, against the force of gravity. This explains why dipping a towel in water draws the water up along the cotton fibers. Plants and trees also use capillary action to transport water upward from soil up through the roots and then up through the trunk of the tree. Capillary action also occurs is various body tissues including the eyes' tear ducts. When a tear duct gets plugged, it is not able to bring tears to the eye and the result is a dry eye. Capillary action is partially responsible for the movement of tears into the eye, which keeps the eye clean. Applying a warm or hot water pack to the eye may relieve the blockage.

Conductivity. Thermal conductivity of water depends on temperature and pressure. Metals, air and land are better thermal conductors compared to water. However, when water is uniformly heated and used in hydrotherapy applications, it works well to distribute heat to a large surface area, such as the skin. Water has a high heat capacity. Heat capacity is the amount of heat needed to add to a material to raise its temperature by a given amount. Water, while not a great conductor of heat (thermal conductivity), remains a good medium for therapies targeting pain and mobility. Applying heat through warm or hot water increases body temperature facilitating many aspects of heat-related effects such as vasodilation. Slight increases in body temperature also promote improved enzyme functions.

Density (D). Density is the ratio between the mass of a substance (kg) and the space it occupies (m^3). Due to water's density, it is a counterbalance to the effects of gravity; if the object weighs less than the amount of water displaced, it floats. The density of fresh water at 1 atmosphere of pressure and 39.2 °F (4 °C) is 1,000 kg / m^3 and for saltwater it is 1,027 kg / m^3. The density of the human body is

950 kg / m³, and usually floats in water. However, a highly muscular body may have a body density (specific gravity) greater than 1, making their body less likely to float in freshwater.

Hydrostatic pressure. This is represented by a chemical equation including the variables pressure, depth, force, area, density, volume, mass, etc. If you are submerged in 1 cubic meter of water, the pressure is 1.4 psi or 72.4 mmHg. The deeper your body is submerged, the greater the hydrostatic pressure. This facilitates several physiological changes in the body such as requiring more breathing capacity, reduced swelling, increased circulation, reduced pain, improved venous return, and improved elimination of lactic acid. These factors combine to help oxygenate the body and aid the body in mild detoxing.

Resistance. The viscosity of water provides resistance and buoyance supports the weight of the person. Basic stretching and water exercises produce impressive results when done on a regular basis. Other factors such as hydrostatic pressure improve lymphatic and venous return. Water aerobics is a great way to strengthen muscles and improve aerobic capacity.

Solutions. Water provides a medium for dissolving therapeutic substances such as salts, clay, plant-based compounds, scents, etc. Many solid substances dissolve in water. Clay packs combine water and clay powder to make a poultice or skin treatment. Fats do not dissolve but float in water, this provides a way to apply a fat-soluble compound to the skin. Water is a relatively poor conductor of electricity but when ions are in water (a solution), the water becomes more conductive.

Sulphurous warm or hot water (i.e., from dissolving Epsom salts in water) has been linked to healing and curative effects.

Surface tension. Water has almost the highest surface tension for all liquids. This means water molecules attract each other. At the air-water surface, water molecules "pull" down the molecules at the top, making the surface shrink. This is known as the meniscus. A meniscus is a concave curve occurring when water molecules have a stronger attraction to each other than to container.

Temperature. Water temperature confers a wide range of therapeutic interventions ranging from ice pack therapy, liquid-based therapies to steam and vapor therapies. Contrast hydrotherapy techniques utilize temperature extremes to control blood flow. The coldest temperature to use is around 60 °F (13 °C) and the hot water temperature range is 95 °F – 113 °F (35 °F – 45 °C). Colder water temperatures may be used to instigate shivering which when done consistently for around 11 minutes a week, may lead to improved metabolism.

Viscosity. The viscosity of water is ideal for its use as a solvent. It is considered relatively thin compared to other liquids. Water therapy takes advantage of the unique properties of water to provide a solution for therapeutic minerals and other compounds, buoyancy, and resistance. Variations in water temperature are used to apply immune boosting temperature sensitive therapies.

We have yet to tap into the powerful and extensive benefits of hydrotherapy. American households with a pool and jacuzzi are on the right track, but there are so many more techniques available to treat anything from a mild cough to serious lung infections. I am not claiming hydrotherapy cures or heals anything, but it certainly stimulates the body to make some beneficial adjustments.

Perfect circulation is necessary for perfect health. Circulation is improved with various types of hydrotherapies. A recent study, The thermal effects of water immersion on health outcomes: an integrative review, by J. An, I. Lee, and Y. Yi, and published in the International Journal of Research Public Health (2019; PMID 30974799), summarized some of the scientific findings of water-based therapy including: hot water immersion results in potential protective effects against ischemia and reperfusion-induced vascular dysfunction (Brunt, 2016); hormone levels including leptin and insulin levels increased after warm water immersion (Shimodozono, 2012); red blood cells, hemoglobin, hematocrit, and white blood cells increased after warm water immersion (Shimodozono, 2012); total cholesterol increased after warm water immersion (Shimodozono, 2012); exercise training improved after warm water immersion (Bailey, 2016); cold water immersion is the most effective modality for changing nerve conduction (Herrera, 2012); warm water immersion results in a transient improvement in systemic arterial stiffness and repeated sessions can promote vascular health (Hu, 2012); improvesskin blood flow (Wakabayashi, 2012); repeated cold water immersion produces cold adaptation (Wakabayashi, 2012); cold water immersion increases pain threshold while hot water immersion produced a slightly higher subjective pain experience and the toleration period was shortened (Streff, 2015); hot water immersion transiently increased BDNF and lowered cortisol (Kojima, 2014); and a warm foot bath before bedtime improves several aspects of sleep (Valizadeh, 1995).

> **The 1918 Spanish Flu**
>
> In 1918, the Spanish flu devastated the world. Approximately 1/3rd of the world's population at that time contracted the virus. 50 million died, including 675,000 in the USA. Make-shift hospitals popped up everywhere to take care of the sick. The mortality rate was 10% to 20%. About 10 small church-affiliated sanitariums treated 670 out-patients and 450 inpatients. The mortality rate of the outpatient group was 4% and the mortality rate of the inpatient group was 1%.
>
> What made the difference? Hydrotherapy and other natural remedies were used to save lives during the worst pandemic known to humankind.

Below is a list of therapies. Many of these therapies can be done at home, while others require specialized equipment and trained therapists. Read through the list and if any of the options are of interest, explore them further and watch your health improve. The point of this exhaustive list is to demonstrate there are many ways to use water in establishing and even recovering health. Keep in mind, most nationalities have a rich heritage of hydrotherapy including the Romans, Koreans, Japanese, Russians, Greeks, Egyptians, Persians, Germans, Swedes, and many others. Explore these options for greater health!

Not all of the therapies are simple. Some require training, specific techniques, and even medical adjuncts and equipment. However, there is something for almost everyone on this list. Focus on the therapies easily available to you.

An excellent resource is found in the Natural Remedies Encyclopedia, 7th ed, in the chapter on Basic Hydrotherapy. A good review of this topic is found in the North American Journal of Medical Science, 2014 May 6(5): 199-209, by Mooventhan and Nivethitha. (https://www.ncbi.nlm.nih.gov/pmc/articles/PMC4049052/). Professionals need to read this article before administering therapeutic hydrotherapy interventions. Information from this article is cited in this chapter, to the benefits and cautions section and to related information in the appendix. A recent book on this topic is The Science of Hormesis in Health and Longevity, by Davinelli and Scapagnini, the chapter on Thermal Waters and the Hormetic Effects of Hydrogen Sulfide on Inflammatory Arthritis and Wound Healing, 2019.

Dedicate a room or an outdoor area to hydrotherapy sessions. This could include a far infrared sauna, jacuzzi, pool, float tank, table with jets, small bedroom for cold sheet therapies, fomentation pads and towels, friction mitts, fragrant and therapeutic oils, salt / sugar scrubs, minerals, massage table, lift or ramp into the pool, etc. If water is expensive, explore digging a well to minimize water costs.

Hydrotherapy is useful for:

- Water buoyancy lends a feeling of weightlessness, taking pressure off painful joints.
- Assists in venous return.
- Assists lymphatic functions.
- Surface tension provides for greater work and resistance.
- **Brief periods of face immersion in cold water can shift a person from sympathetic drive to parasympathetic drive. This serves to lower blood pressure, heart rate, and release of certain hormones.**
- Longer periods of cold-water immersion may lead to increased heart rate, blood pressure, and a decrease in cerebral blood flow, etc.
- Hot water therapy may shift a person from parasympathetic drive to sympathetic drive, increasing vessel dilation, hormones, enzyme activity, etc.
- Alternating between hot and cold restores the body's natural temperature-driven functions.
- Improved lung functions including increased tidal volume.
- Improved quality of life in those with chronic obstructive lung disease.
- **Improves circulation via stimulating nitric oxide.**
- Foot baths may relieve pain, treat migraine headaches, and lower blood pressure.
- Improves cardiac functions such as increasing left ventricular ejection fraction.
- During water exercise, heart patients may experience lower cardiovascular stress.
- Improves blood lipid transport proteins such as LDL and HDL.
- Improves peripheral circulation in cerebral palsy and multiple sclerosis.
- Chronic pain: increases opioid tone and receptors thereby lessening pain.
- Relieves arthritis pain.
- Increases immunity.
- **Reduces inflammation.**
- Restores muscle and joint functions such as flexibility.
- Improve strength via water-based resistance training.
- Excellent for fighting fatigue.
- **Aids in relaxation and lowering stress.**
- Improves gastrointestinal functions.
- Great for those with Parkinson's disease (removes disinhibition of inhibitory center).
- Improves muscle mass and therefore metabolic rate.
- Reduces muscle spasms.
- May activate the hypothalamic-pituitary-adrenal (HPA) and hypothalamic-pituitary-thyroid axis.
- Reduces anxiety; antidepressant.
- Activates components of the reticular activating system such as the locus coeruleus and raphae nuclei – improves overall capacity of the central nervous system.
- May induce an antipsychotic effect similar to electro-shock therapy (ECT).

- Improves range of motion in conjunction with appropriate physical therapy maneuvers.
- May improve certain types of headaches.
- Benefits those with fibromyalgia.
- Cold water stress reduces level of serotonin in most regions of the brain except the brainstem.
- Warm moist air may improve tear stability, ocular fatigue, Meibomian gland dysfunction, etc.

Contraindications and Cautions

- **Avoid temperature extremes for high risk patients – may cause blood vessel spasms and plaque rupture or thrombosis of heart vessel. Rapid cooling after sauna is a real risk for someone with coronary risk factors. Regular radiant heat or far infrared units appear to be safer.**
- Avoid contrast hydrotherapy if you have diabetes, if you do not have good sensation in your extremities, peripheral vascular disease, if you easily bruise and bleed, etc.
- Vital capacity less than 1 liter.
- May cause transient arrhythmias in patients with heart problems.
- May inhibit humoral immunity in some.
- Sudden ice-cold water immersion may produce transient pulmonary edema and increase blood brain barrier permeability.
- Those with open wounds and lines should avoid hydrotherapy, especially in communal settings.
- A colostomy is not compatible with using jacuzzis, pools, and community shared water features.
- Skin infections such as tinea pedis and ringworm.
- Water and airborne infections such as influenza, GI infections, typhoid, cholera, poliomyelitis, etc.
- Bowel or bladder. Bowel accidents require pool evacuation, chemical treatment, and drainage.
- Seizures may be a contraindication.
- Those with active infection should avoid hydrotherapy in communal settings.
- Those with altered skin sensations should avoid hydrotherapy using extreme temperatures.
- Those with hydrophobia should avoid hydrotherapy.
- Those with heat or cold intolerance.
- Those with poor balance should be closely monitored in deep water treatments.
- Pregnant women should avoid using sauna therapies.

One potential issue related to hydrotherapy in pools is their chlorine content. Chlorine is used to make pool water safe. In the right concentration and pH, it kills almost all pathogenic microorganisms. Chemically speaking, chlorine is one of five halogens: fluorine, bromine, astatine (the rarest earth element) and iodine. Iodine is critical for thyroid function. In fact, thyroid hormones are basically a molecule of tyrosine with one, two, three (tri-iodothyronine) or four (thyroxine) attached molecules of iodine. The thyroid gland takes up iodine and processes it into thyroid hormones. Every 17 minutes the body's blood supply goes through the thyroid gland, cleaning and picking up thyroid hormone for distribution. Thyroid hormones affect almost every cell in the body. The thyroid hormone receptor (TR), is a nuclear receptor. It is activated when thyroid binds to it. TRs affect gene regulation, transcription (copying a segment of DNA into RNA), translation (synthesis of proteins), second messenger activation (signaling molecules in the body), metabolic balance, responsible for fine tuning physiologic actions, and many other cell responses. Some of their actions include regulating metabolism, heart rate, growth, the functions of the nervous system, etc. These actions are the "big hitters" in the body. (PMID: 10878749, 9430643).

Not all exposure to water is positive. According to Amy Myers, MD, it is possible if you spend enough time in a strongly chlorinated pool, to absorb enough chlorine through your skin which could interfere with the assembly of thyroid hormone, especially if your intake of iodine is low or deficient. If you spend a lot of time in chlorinated pools, this may be something to consider. A salt-water, mineral, or ionizer system are several alternatives but they are not chlorine free. They just have significantly less chlorine. A natural pool using a biological ecosystem to filter the water is another better option. A recent method of cleaning pools is 35% hydrogen peroxide which uses concentrated oxygen to keep pools clean.

In 2001, I spent two months teaching at a small medical missionary college in Romania. A large section of the campus was dedicated to delivering in-house spa services for clients as well as providing nutritious meals and classes on preparing those meals. Their clients came from all over Europe. Hydrotherapy is a significant component used to restore health and wellness. Clients received several different types of hydrotherapy every day. They all went home feeling rejuvenated! For years, I have been interested in starting a hydrotherapy spa, one that would offer full hydrotherapy services, but this dream has yet to materialize. It would be best to work in a location where water cost and quality are not major issues. If you have the opportunity and desire, specialize in various hydrotherapy treatments. These methods may become more and more important in the prevention and treatment of various conditions. The appendix contains a list of hydrotherapies compiled several years ago with brief explanations of each.

Bible verses
2 Chronicles 4:4-5; Psalm 23:2; Proverbs 5:15; Isaiah 12:3; Isaiah 43:2; Isaiah 44:3; Isaiah 49:10; Ezekiel 36:25; Ezekiel 47:1-5; Matthew 10:42; John 4:14; John 7:38; Revelation 22:1,17.

References and Resources
- https://en.wikipedia.org/wiki/Capillary_action
- http://preparingforthetimeoftrouble.com
- https://en.wikipedia.org/w/index.php?search=water+conductivity&title=Special%3ASearch&go=Go&ns0=1

Discussion Questions

1. Do you see a role for hydrotherapy in your household?

2. What is the benefit of alternating hot and cold therapies?

3. What specific type of hydrotherapy technique have you tried? Did it work?

Chapter 14

Lymphatics

The immune system is composed of lymphocytes, T cells, B cells, plasma cells, bone marrow, the thymus, lymph nodes, mucosa associated lymphoid tissue (MALT; found in the throat, wall of the small intestine, walls of the colon, and walls of the appendix) and the spleen. **Blood carries nutrients and oxygen; lymphatic fluid carries infection fighting cells.** The lymph system is a critical aspect of the body's immune system. It closely follows the circulatory system, always ready to remove toxins and metabolic waste. It collects fluids forced out of the capillary beds, cleans them and returns them to the circulation. Lymph nodes filter and purify lymph fluid before it moves back into the venous system. This keeps the blood clean and free from pathogens. A swollen lymph node may indicate an active infection and activation of the immune system. The lymphatic system works closely with the kidneys, liver, circulatory system, musculoskeletal system, diaphragm, etc. If these systems are not working efficiently the lymphatic system may be negatively affected.

Unlike the body's circulatory system, the lymph vessels do not have the pumping action of the heart to pump blood through one-way valves. **Lymph fluid moves when the body moves.** It moves as a result of surrounding muscles, the diaphragm, and organs "squeezing" the fluid up and down the body. These actions move lymph fluid toward the heart where it rejoins the circulatory system. As much as 3 liters of lymph fluid may be found in the lymphatic system. Most of it however, is reabsorbed into the circulatory system and circulates as part of the blood.

When the body is stressed or damaged (as in trauma, surgery, sports injury, physical abuse, etc.) it may affect the lymphatics and impair the usual flow of immune-supporting lymph fluid. **Obesity also stresses the lymphatic system by increased weight and pressure which block the flow of lymph fluid.** Some parasites are known to infect the lymph system, impairing the smooth flow of lymph fluids. When lymph flow is impaired, the fluid may back up causing lymph edema. This leads to swelling in the legs and arms. It is usually progressive and has the quality of "pitting." This means when you take your finger and press into the swollen extremity, the indentation remains for up to one minute or longer. If the swelling does not go away, it can develop into cellulitis or fibrosis. **Sluggish lymph flow is also seen in hypothyroidism.** It can be tested by pressing on the flat side of the tibia leg bone. If the tissue above the bone is indented, it is known as pre-tibial myxedema, a strong sign the body is getting inadequate thyroid hormones.

Lymph edema can be seen in the face. Dysfunction this area may lead to headaches, TMJ, vision problems, twitching, etc. Many small lymph nodes line the head and neck. Head and facial massage can restore lymph flow. Up to 450 lymph nodes are found in the body including in the head and neck, armpits, chest area, surrounding the digestive tract, groin, behind the knees, and around the trachea (airway to the lungs) and bronchi (airways from trachea into the lungs). **Lymph dysfunction in the chest area may lead to chest pain, spasms, difficulty breathing, etc.** A poor diet and lifestyle may negatively impact the lymphatic system, leading to specific complaints as well as non-specific complaints such as stubborn weight loss, headaches, brain fog, lack of energy, recurrent sore throat, excess mucous in the morning, mucous drainage, ear popping and ringing, frequent colds, sluggish bowels, morning stiffness, heaviness in the extremities, arms or hands fall asleep at while sleeping at night, sore breasts, itchy skin, acne, dry skin and other skin issues.

Any person of any weight or size is susceptible to lymphatic issues. It is better to prevent an issue than to treat it. Several diet and lifestyle factors help to prevent lymphatic issues. If you make it a habit to do two or three of these practices on a daily basis, your chances of having lymphatic issues decreases. This list is a combination of preventive and therapeutic measures. If you tend to suffer from lymphatic issues, it is helpful to adopt as many as possible of the following therapies for the lymph system. The lymphatic system matters: Take your pick of preventive and / or therapeutic measures.

Here is the list:

- **Body wraps**
  When you experience lymph edema, target the affected area using a charcoal, clay or castor oil wrap or poultice. This is not necessarily preventive.

- **Chiropractic adjustment**
  A chiropractor does treatments targeting the lymph system and restoring lymph flow. Check around for a chiropractor who specializes in lymph treatments. Treatments produce a para-sympathetic effect, relaxing the body, restoring normal flow and increasing the body's ability to fight off infections.

- **Clothing matters**
  Avoid tight fitting undergarments and clothing which cuts off circulation without providing targeted compression. Compression socks may be indicated when edema is in the lower extremities and compression gloves or arm socks may be indicated when edema is in the hands and arms.

- **Deep breathing / diaphragmatic breathing**
  Purposeful deep breathing oxygenates the blood better than shallow breathing. Physical exercise illustrates this point very well. You don't have to briskly walk or vigorously swim laps to induce deep breathing. It can be done consciously and purposefully. If you tend to have a sedentary lifestyle, make it a practice to get up, walk around and stretch for several minutes of each hour. While you are walking or stretching, do 10 to 20 purposeful deep breaths. **Breathe in through your nose for 7 seconds, hold your breath for 4 seconds and exhale through your mouth (pursed lips) for 8 seconds.** The nose is a good filter and nose breathing is good for body voltage. Do 10 – 20 repetitions. When we consciously practice deep breathing we are lifting and exercising the muscles which facilitate oxygen exchange in the lungs. This also pumps the lymphatic system. Deep breathing pushes lymphatic fluids into the systemic circulation. This prevents lymph fluid from accumulating in the extremities. Some signs your lymphatic system might

be congested include: swollen fingers, swollen extremities, breast soreness, skin rashes, itchiness, cold extremities, headaches, stiffness, fatigue, brain fog, lowered immunity (e.g., frequent colds), bloating, weight gain, etc.

- **Detoxification (lymphatic)**
 The main function of the lymphatic system is detoxification. Immune cells in lymph fluid fight off invading pathogens and neutralize toxins. The lymph system also aids in eliminating the waste and debris generated from invading pathogens. Detoxing the lymphatic system involves many aspects. Exercise, sauna time, contrast showers, deep breathing, rebounding, targeted herbs, two meals per day, optimal water intake, lymphatic massage, dry brushing, herbs, nitric oxide boosting foods, etc. If you tend to have lymphatic issues, your lifestyle should include many possible target therapies.

- **Diet**
 Ensure you consume an adequate diet including some of the following as often as possible: leafy greens, apple, fresh herbs, fresh spices, herbal teas, lots of water, citrus fruits, berries, tropical fruits, carrots, beets, melons, cruciferous vegetables, omega 3 sources, A poor diet, including the pattern of eating, is oftentimes at the root of lymphatic issues.

 Constantly activated lymph nodes along the gastrointestinal tract affect absorption and may lead to multiple sensitivities and even allergies. Dietary toxins, chemicals, the constant flow of food into the system, all lead to irritation, congestion and sometimes blockage of lymph flow. This directly compromises immunity and the body's ability to fend off invading pathogens. It leads to frequent illnesses, fatigue, brain fog, and weight gain.

 Eating excessive amounts of dry food also internally dehydrates the body and stresses lymphatic functions. Dry foods include crackers, chips, pastry products, etc. It is also a good idea to avoid caffeine and alcohol intake. Three day and longer fasting leads to restoring normal gut and lymph functions. The immune system is basically rebuilt and recharged after a three day fast. Eliminate as many diet-related toxins and processed foods as possible to ensure smooth operation of the lymphatic system.

- **Dry skin brushing**
 Dry brushing removes dead cells and toxins and stimulates circulation. Use a soft short bristle. Brush 3 to 5 times in each area, stroking the skin from the most distant part of the extremity toward the heart. Pay particular attention to lymph node rich areas such as the head and neck, arm pits, mid chest, groin and back of the knee areas. Brush in one direction, toward the heart. This stimulates the skin and aids the lymphatic system in moving fluids out of the lymphatics into the circulation.

- **Essential oils**
 A number of oils are used to stimulate the lymphatic system. Some of these oils include: black pepper cypress, fennel, frankincense, geranium, ginger, grapefruit, juniper berry, lavender, lemon, lemon grass, mandarin, orange, peppermint, rosemary, thyme, etc.

- **Exercise**
 Exercise acts in several ways to stimulate the lymphatic system. It promotes circulation and improves delivery of oxygen and nutrients. It builds the large muscles which when contracted and used, act to move the lymph fluid. In addition to aerobic exercises such as walking, running, biking, swimming, etc., some work with weights is also recommended. For most people, high repetitions with small hand weights is adequate. To work the lower body, use static weights and resistance using rubber bands.

- **Fasting (water only)**
A three day fast rebuilds and recharges the immune system oftentimes restoring normal lymphatic functions.

- **Fasting (fresh juices only)**
Juice fasting is a great way to consume a lot of nutrients while giving the gastrointestinal tract a brief reprieve from processing fibrous fruits, vegetables, legumes, nuts and seeds. It also gives the gut a reprieve from breaking down animal-based foods.

- **Green smoothie**
The green smoothie provides large amounts of B vitamins including folate, fiber, water, chlorophyll, magnesium, and many other plant-based compounds. Greens are also alkalizing.

- **Herbal teas**
Some herbal teas known to support a healthy lymphatic system include: ashwagandha, burdock, cleavers, dandelion, echinacea, ginger, red clover, etc.

- **Herbs**
Herbs associated with improving the lymphatics include: astragalus, burdock, calendula, chicory, cilantro, cleavers, dandelion, echinacea, fenugreek, fennel, garlic, ginger, ginseng, milk thistle, oregano, parsley, pine bark, poke root, red clover, red root, rosemary, violet, etc. Herbs contain terpenoids, saponins, hormones, flavonoids, coumarins, mucilage, polysaccharides, volatile oils, xanthophylls, carotenoids, sterols, acids, tannins, lectins, etc. Herbal mechanisms of action include: anti-inflammatory, antimicrobial, antispasmodic, immune-stimulant, emollient, adaptogenic, lymphatic tonic and cleanser, anti-tumor, detoxifier, diuretic, etc.

- **Hydrotherapy**
Contrast hydrotherapy is a tried and proven method for stimulating lymphatic and systemic circulation. This includes contrast baths, alternating hot and cold showers, immersion, mineral baths, salt / mineral scrubs, etc.

- **Hypothyroidism**
Lymph nodes drain the thyroid gland, ensuring optimal function. When the lymph nodes are sluggish, the thyroid gland may be affected. Ensure you are consuming iodine and selenium rich foods or supplements as well as adequate protein.

- **Inversion table**
This uses gravity to move lymph fluid, which has settled in the feet and ankles, toward the heart. It involves getting strapped to a long table and then tipping backwards so your feet are above your head.

- **Liver detox (also see page 162)**
Liver health very important for ensuring optimal lymphatic functions. A liver detox is nothing more complicated than consuming foods and herbs known to stimulate the detox enzymes in the liver. This includes cruciferous vegetables, leafy greens, carrot juice, beet juice, and cranberries. Supplements include dandelion root, milk thistle, silmarin, licorice root, N-acetyl cysteine, vitamin D, B6, tyrosine, and ashwagandha root. Start with one or two supplements for a couple of weeks. If you feel better, maintain the supplements for as long as you desire.

- **Low fat, low sugar diet**
  A little-known function of the lymphatic system is the absorption of fat and fat-soluble vitamins. High fat meals flood the lymphatics with fat which must be rapidly processed and transferred to the general circulation and liver for additional processing. During the time the lymphatics are dealing with fat, they can become backed up. **A high fat diet interferes with real time immune functions in the lymphatic system.** Sugar alters the gut's microbiome. If enough bad bacteria multiply in the gut, some may enter the blood stream only to be removed by B cells and T-cells in the lymphatic circulation. Too much sugar overwhelms the body with bad bacteria and wide spread inflammation and backs up the lymphatic system.

- **Massage (lymphatic) with essential oils**
  Lymphatic massage is different from basic massage. Lymphatic massage uses steady pressure and long strokes to target circulation and movement of lymphatic fluid from the hands and feet toward the heart. As oxygen and nutrients are brought to the area of soreness, tissue regeneration proceeds. Massage may also reduce stress and promote relaxation. Ask the massage therapist to use thyme, citrus, peppermint, ginger, or rosemary oils to stimulate the lymphatic system. Drink adequate water before and after lymphatic massage. Facials also target lymphatic drainage.

- **Move your body every hour (vigorous walking, calisthenics, etc.)**
  Daily exercise is great, but it is important to move your body throughout the day. If you are sedentary, do not sit for longer than one hour without getting up and moving around. Take 3 to 5 minutes of every hour to walk, stretch, do calisthenics, or plank. This keeps your lymphatic fluid moving and able to fend off most of the terrible pathogens in the environment.

- **Planking**
  Planking facilitates parasympathetic tone, relaxing the body and stimulating lymphatic flow. Planking strengthens core muscles which also contributes to improved lymphatic functions. As few as 1 to 2 minutes of planking per day can be highly beneficial.

- **Plant-based diets**
  A plant-based diet is a great way to stimulate lymphatic functions and move lymph fluids. Citrus, beets, greens, berries, fresh herbs and spices, and seeds all contribute to improved blood flow and lymphatic functions. A plant-based diet may help lower kcalorie intake and facilitate weight loss. This usually improves lymphatic functions.

- **Posture**
  Good posture is an incredible defense against poor health. When your spine is aligned with your neck and head, nerves and lymphatics work better and receive nutrients and oxygen. Poor posture causes a strain at almost every point along the spine. This interferes with nerve signals and lymphatic functions. Poor posture ultimately causes difficult-to-treat issues. Try wearing posture support clothing, bras, shorts, and other corrective gear. Good posture improves voltage. If low oxygen, in a supine position, lift the head and stretch it back.

- **Poultices**
  Herbal, clay and castor oil poultices may be used to promote lymphatic drainage.

- **Psyllium husks** (high fiber)
  Add 1 to 2 tablespoons of psyllium husks to your morning water. This improves digestion, absorption and elimination. Drink 24 to 32 ounces of water with psyllium to ensure maximal effect.

- **Raw food diet**
  Raw foods are less inflammatory than processed and cooked foods. Some raw foods known to stimulate the lymphatic system include: apples, beets, cherries, cranberries, leafy greens, pomegranate, etc.

- **Rebounding**
  Jumping in place on a small trampoline moves congested lymphatic fluid. You may achieve a similar effect using an exercise ball.

- **Sauna**
  Far infrared sauna therapy jump starts the body's enzymatic machinery and stimulates circulation of both blood and lymph fluids. This brings healing nutrients and oxygen to the body. Start with a 10 to 15-minute sauna followed by a cold shower.

- **Spices**
  Spices associated with improving the lymphatics include: cayenne, cinnamon, cloves, ginger, turmeric, etc.

- **Stretching**
  A number of stretches and poses aid in moving lymph fluid. Be sure to combine stretching with deep breathing to get the maximum benefit.

- **Sunlight**
  Vitamin D generated by exposure of skin to sunlight is sulfated. This form of vitamin D is more effective compared to supplemental vitamin D. Vitamin D directly affects the immune system but until it is absorbed and hydroxylated in the liver and kidneys, it is not biologically active. However, when it is activated, it is responsible for wide ranging epigenetic effects throughout the body. This directly and indirectly improves lymphatic functions.

- **Vitamins, minerals, supplements**
  Ascorbic acid (5 – 20 grams), B vitamins, chromium, CoQ10, iodine, pycnogenol, selenium, etc.

- **Water (aim for 95 to 125 ounces)**
  When you are dehydrated, the lymph fluid gets congested and clogged. Adequate water intake works well to keep lymph fluids moving and improves the detoxification functions of not only the immune and lymphatic systems but also the liver, kidneys, skin, lungs, etc. When you are fighting off an infection, drinking water is essential for assisting lymphatic functions.

Discussion Questions

1. Do you have any symptoms of impaired lymphatic flow?
2. What are two or three habits you could adopt to improve the function of your lymphatic system?

Section 3

Country Living Nutrition

Chapter 15
Restore normal gut functions

The gut is critical for establishing and maintaining good health. It is a long tube, going from the top to the bottom of the torso. Food goes in, it is mechanically and then chemically broken down and the nutrients and water are removed with the remaining material prepared for elimination. This tells us digestion is efficient. The process of digestion, absorption and elimination occurs via the digestive tract and the kidneys and urinary tract. It is a remarkable process. The gut never quits processing what we eat unless we go on an extended fast, which for some can be remarkably successful method for restoring normal gut functions.

While fasting for several days is an excellent health strategy, unfortunately, it is something most people will not do. Non-fasting avenues exist for restoring normal gut function as well. Each person is unique; what may work for one person may not work for another. It is a good idea to get professional help when your gut is not working well. Signs your gut might be losing some function(s) include constipation, diarrhea, excess bloating, gas, pain, reflux, bad breath, smelly stools, messy stools, etc.

Most people believe their gut is working well, but upon questioning, we find out it is not optimized. First, let's describe normal gut functions. The gut, stretching from the mouth to the anus, is made up of various cells such as enterocytes, goblet cells, stem cells, and even lymph cells, known as Peyer's patches.

When we eat, the first physical contact we have with food occurs in the mouth. We chew and combine food with saliva and enzymes and then swallow it via the tube going from the esophagus to the stomach. This first contact we have with food in the mouth signals the brain about what to expect as far as nutrients. It also signals other organs such as the pancreas to start making insulin, which is necessary for transporting glucose from the blood into the cells.

For some, the number of bites we take per meal determines our satisfaction. We associate a certain number of bites with satiety, even though we are not consciously counting our bites. Some have suggested about 50 to 100 bites per meal is ideal, but this varies.

Thoroughly chewing food is good for digestion. When we eat and swallow, the stomach fills up with chewed (or unchewed) food. Chewing food combines saliva with food. Saliva contains enzymes which begin to break down carbohydrates (salivary amylase) and proteins (salivary kallikreins), antibacterial substances, electrolytes, and others. This begins the mechanical and chemical processes of digestion which continues in the stomach, small intestine and the large intestine. To aid salivary gland functions, include moist food, broths, soups, sauces, dressings, dips, gravy, salad, fruit, and vegetables with your meals.

If you do not eat all your food, give the leftovers to your animals. This is an incredibly humane and excellent way to get the most value from your food. I frequently refer to the fridge as the "storage bin for the trash can or compost bin." If you find yourself frequently tossing out leftovers, consider how your animals, even wild animals, or the neighbors' chickens, might appreciate having leftovers.

Eat slowly. Some might call this "mindful" eating, but it is really about taking charge of your health. Eat at a table with others when possible. Eliminate competing activities such as the TV, computer, phone, all social media, etc. Avoid stressful topics while eating. Learn to laugh and enjoy mealtimes. Eating slowly allows your brain's satiety signaling to catch up with your mouth. If you eat fast, you are more likely to overeat because it takes 20 minutes or more for your brain to realize you are getting full and eating should slow down and end. Take a page from the Europeans, who eat in courses, beginning with hors d'oeuvres, soup a main course and salad, and ends with a small sweet dessert.

Swallowing food involves bypassing the epiglottis, which is found at the back of the throat, and then it goes down the esophagus through the cardiac sphincter, found on the top of the stomach. This occurs even if you are horizontal or upside down. The esophagus is a muscular tube about eight inches in length. It goes behind the windpipe and the heart but in front of the spine. Food spends only several seconds in the esophagus before it reaches the stomach. No absorption occurs in the esophagus.

When the stomach is empty, its volume is just under 2 ounces, the equivalent of about 4 tablespoons. Before you chow down a huge meal, keep in mind the stomach is a potential space, meaning it can expand by up to 74 times its resting size to hold about a gallon of food. Practically speaking, the stomach can expand to hold up to 16 or more cups of food. However, if you regularly eat even half this much food, you may become overweight and eventually obese.

Resist the urge to eat more than 2 to 4 cups of food at any given meal. Of course, the type of food also matters. For example, if you plan to eat spaghetti, you could have 1 cup of spaghetti, ½ cup of sauce, vegetables, a salad and a breadstick. This would be a hefty 2 to 3 cups of food. Learning to limit food intake and not exceed a reasonable amount of food at mealtimes is maybe one of the greatest habits you can adopt for good health. The sooner you learn to eat this way, the better.

When food reaches the stomach, it is held there until it is thoroughly blended by actions of the triple layer of muscles which make up the stomach. Each layer works to ensure a smooth and seamless mixing of foodstuffs into a mixture known as chyme. The stomach secretes several substances known to aid in digestion and absorption of nutrients. Several nutrients are also absorbed into the body from the stomach (see Figure 1).

The small intestine is a diverse organ, capable of performing hundreds of chemical reactions and doing complex chemistry. It is lined with receptors for absorbing nutrients (see Figure 1).

Once food is homogenized in the stomach, about 2 to 5 milliliters of chyme is released into the duodenum about every 20 seconds until the stomach is emptied. Chyme enters the first section of the small intestine, the duodenum, where substances are released by the pancreas to neutralize the acidic chyme mixture. As the chyme moves through the duodenum through the jejunum and ileum, vitamins, minerals, amino acids, sugars, fatty acids and other substances are absorbed. Each section of the small intestine is highly specialized for transport, extraction of nutrients, and absorption of nutrients across the small intestine wall. In the large intestine, a five-foot long section of the gut, water, sodium, chloride and potassium are absorbed as well as short chain fatty acids. There is some evidence vitamin K and biotin are absorbed from the large intestine.

Nutrients are absorbed and then transported to the liver for use and distribution. Fatty acids and fat-soluble vitamins are absorbed and transported to the lymphatic system where they are cleaned up and then transported via the blood stream to the liver for use and re-distribution.

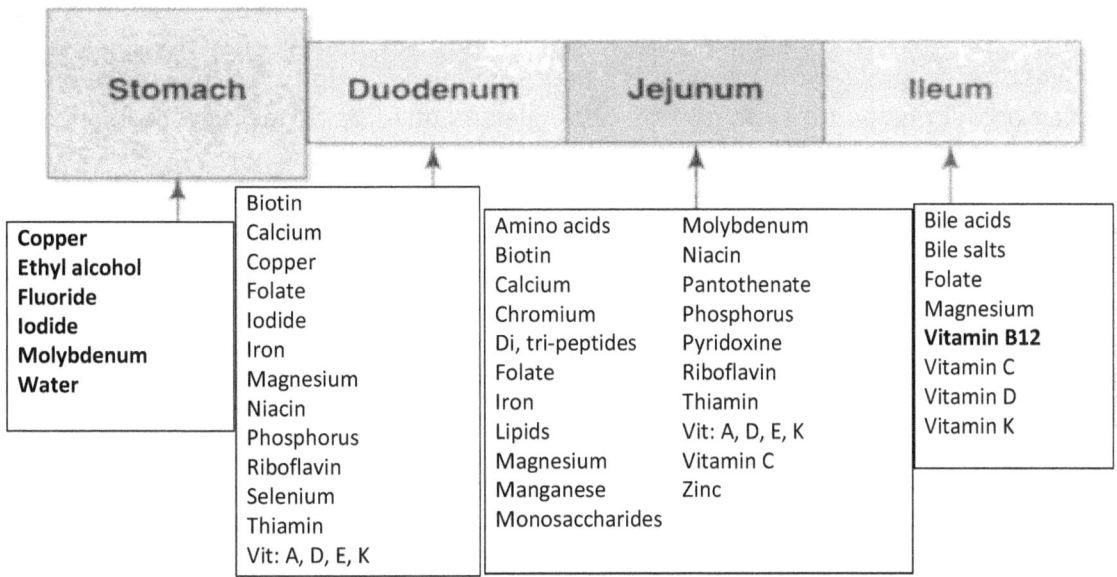

Restore normal gut functions, Figure 1.
Sites of absorption of vitamins, minerals and nutrients,
in Epomedicine, Gastrointestinal System, Physiology. March 2018

The gut-brain axis (GBA) is critical for good health. The GBA is a link between the digestive tract, also known as the enteric nervous system (ENS) and the central nervous system (CNS). These two systems are in constant communication, each influencing the other through various channels. Overeating, frequent eating, poor quality food, chemicals, pesticides, and GMO foods may negatively affect the GBA.

About 95% of serotonin produced in the body is made in the gut. Other neurotransmitters produced in the gut include dopamine, GABA, norepinephrine, and epinephrine. Pathologic changes to the gut may influence the development of chronic depression, autism, and schizophrenia. Histamine, another neurotransmitter consumed in food as histidine, is also produced in the gut. Histamine intolerance and related symptoms are gaining in recognition and may be responsible for a number of gut issues. A low histamine diet has helped some (see the Appendix).

When you hear a rumbling noise coming from your abdominal area, it is usually air or fluid moving in the intestines. The sounds are known as borborygmus (singular) and borborygmi (plural). This movement indicates your gut is in good working order. Most of the time you never hear this movement, but if you have a stethoscope, you can place it over your lower abdomen and hear the sounds. However, too much air moving through the stomach, small and large intestines causes belching, bloating, and gas.

As food transitions from the small intestine into the large intestine, it passes by the appendix and through the ileocecal valve. The large intestine houses the body's diverse microbiome, a collection of microorganisms, by some estimates, weighing about 5 pounds. The microbiome is made up of hundreds of different types of healthy bacteria. Each person's microbiome is unique. These bacteria are responsible for digesting certain types of fibers, discouraging pathogenic invaders, lessening allergic potential, and many other functions. When good bacteria are present, the gut functions well. However, when bad bacteria take over the gut microbiome, various gut issues surface and may cause concern. Disruptions to the microbiome are associated with allergies, autoimmune conditions, metabolic disorders, and even neuro-psychiatric disorders.

"Clean" eating is associated with fewer non-pathogenic gut microorganisms. Recently, the NIH studied human microbiomes and found almost all healthy people carry pathogenic bacteria but based on their healthy diet, these pathogenic microorganisms are kept in check. However, in some people, these pathogenic microorganisms can turn into disease causing elements. Tipping the balance in favor of non-pathogenic gut microorganisms is the goal.

It is critical to maintain a balance of good bacteria in the gut. Healthy foods support good bacteria compared to processed and sugary foods which feed the bad microorganisms. Foods which support the gut microbiome include high fiber foods, cabbage, beans, onions, garlic, greens, fresh herbs, fermented foods, etc.

When the chyme mixture reaches the large intestine, it combines with the microbiome and water and sodium are removed and re-absorbed into the body. Bacteria may synthesize vitamin K in the large intestine but it is not absorbed into the body from the large intestine; it is destined for excretion. However, the presence of vitamin K in the gut may improve the profile of good bacteria. Some dietary fibers are digested in the large intestine and yield short chain fatty acids (SCFA), a great fuel for the gut. The mixture moves along the large intestine until it reaches the rectum. When the rectum fills up, it triggers a reflex to empty. The process of digestion and absorption has completed a cycle. This cycle repeats for every meal.

Two meals per day is probably ideal for most sedentary adults.

This gives the digestive tract and associated organs the ability to completely digest each meal and even "rest" before the next meal is initiated. Ideally, this means your large intestine is only processing one (this is ideal) or two meals at a time. If you want to determine how many meals are being processed in your body, eat something like beets or take 10 charcoal tablets. Now count how many bowel movements you have before one is either red (reflecting the presence of beets) or black (reflecting the presence of charcoal). If you are interested in losing weight, consider consuming two meals within a 6 to 8-hour window of time. This not only allows the body to thoroughly digest food and rest between meals, but it makes it more likely your body may go into slight ketosis between the last meal of the day and the first meal of the next day. Eating one or less meals per day may actually prompt the body to go into an energy conserving mode. This is not recommended unless there is significant justification for this level of food restriction. A water-only fast one day per week is a good strategy for weight loss. Add a second day of fasting per week and weight loss may accelerate after the first week or two.

What happens when food (i.e., chyme) doesn't efficiently move through the gastrointestinal tract? Constipation occurs. It can even be mathematically defined. For every meal you consume, a bowel movement is generated or if you prefer an equation: 1 meal = 1 bowel movement. This means, if you eat 3 meals a day you should have 3 bowel movements per day. Anything less than this equation is constipation. I guarantee if you were to present this information to your physician, s/he would get a good belly laugh! The medical establishment has not yet accepted this definition. If you go to the commonly used medical reference text, Harrison's Principles of Internal Medicine, the definition of constipation is having fewer than 3 bowel movements per week. If we were to go by this definition, a person eating 3 meals per day could be missing 18 bowel movements and not be (medically) considered constipated. So where do all the "missing" bowel movements go? Well, let's just say they don't magically disappear. This is less than ideal and leads to many issues from minor to serious.

The easiest way to reverse constipation is to start taking magnesium citrate (aka, colon dynamite or colon blow (SNL skit from the 1980s or 1990s)). I recommend starting with 250 mg in the morning, the second day, 500 mg, the third day take 750 mg, the fourth day take 1,000 mg and keep increasing until you achieve "loose" stools. The highest I have had to go with my patients has been almost 7,000 mg. Now go back to the last dose which did not cause "loose" stools and stay on that dose until you get "loose" stools at some point in the future. Each time this occurs, keep backing down until you reach a dose which gives you equilibrium. If you want to immediately reverse constipation, take a handful of magnesium citrate at one time and stay home and within a few feet of a toilet!

I cannot help but insert a brief spelling lesson here. **The words "lose" and "loose" mean two different things (look them up if you doubt it).** I may "lose" my driver's license but I do not "loose" it. My linen pants become "loose" after wearing them for a few minutes but hopefully I do not "lose" them. When you eat less food and exercise more, you "lose" weight. You can only "loose" weight (fat) if you can somehow mechanically detach and remove the fat from its internal locations scattered throughout the body.

Fortunately, when it comes to the gut, we can use both "lose" and "loose" to describe what goes on in the gastrointestinal tract. We can "lose" our lunch, meaning we experienced reverse peristalsis or nausea and vomiting. We may also experience "loose" stools when we take loads of magnesium or vitamin C. Both functions are 100% proper and normal and constitute the body's protective mechanisms.

One more clarification. There are 26 letters and 10 numbers. Letters are not numbers. Look at your keyboard. There is a zero and there is also the letter "O." An O (the letter O) is not a 0 (the number zero). The phenomenon of calling the number zero by an alphabet letter, "O" primarily occurs in the USA. Scientists oftentimes put a slash through the a zero to further distinguish it as a number. For years I have distinguished between the two and it is still easy to catch myself in conversation saying the letter "O" in place of "zero."

Back to the gut. Symptoms of a poorly functioning gut include but are not limited to: constipation, nausea, diarrhea, heartburn, reflux, lower back pain, bloating, chronic bad breath, foul smelling bowel movements, etc. If these early symptoms are ignored they may transition into more severe conditions such as malnutrition, toxemia, etc.

Inflammation, due to excess body fat, is linked to poor gut function. **As few as 5 to 10 pounds of weight loss may improve gut functions.** An increase in physical activity is also helpful. Keep in mind, certain foods, supplements and medications may promote constipation while other foods promote regularity. Avoid constipating foods when inflammation or constipation is present (e.g., cheese, alcohol, white flour products, milk, high meat intake, fried foods). Some may find taking a "bread" or "wheat" holiday may improve gut functions. This does not mean you will never again, eat a slice of fresh, warm bread with melting butter and topped with strawberry freezer jam. It may mean one or more components of a food such as wheat may be causing symptoms and when the offending substance is removed, the gut will heal and the symptoms will go away, eventually allowing for the consumption of the previously offending food.

Inflammation may be linked to one or more foods or it may be due to contamination with the common toxins such as the herbicide glyphosate. Once gut issues are addressed and inflammation is tamed, occasionally consuming organic wheat may not be problematic. A water-only fast one day a week may also be helpful and provide the bowels a brief respite from digestion. Abdominal massage, vibration / frequency therapies, saunas, castor oil packs, etc., are just a few more targeted therapies to restore gut functions.

Strategies for improving gut function include but are not limited to the following:

- One tablespoon of psyllium husks in 15 – 20 ounces of water every morning.
- Consume 25 – 50 grams of fiber / day.
- Magnesium!
- Vitamin C to bowel tolerance.
- Avoid consuming beverages with meals.
- Avoid drinking cold beverages w/ a meal.
- Avoid highly processed foods.
- Avoid gluten / wheat if you have a sensitive gut.
- Avoid eating highly allergenic foods such as seafood, milk, peanuts, etc., if you have gut problems.
- Avoid foods with added chemicals.
- Avoid pork products.
- Avoid raw fish and meat products.
- Thoroughly chew your food.
- Take at least 20 minutes to eat a meal, preferably take 30 to 60 minutes.
- Avoid > 3 meals/day including snacks.
- Space meals at least 4 to 5 hours apart.
- Space your last meal of the day at least 12 hours before next meal the next day.
- Make mealtimes enjoyable.
- Get one to two hours of daily activity.
- Lose weight if overweight or obese.
- Avoid stressful situations around meal times and in general.
- Eat less sugar.
- Get an adequate amount of rest / sleep.
- Avoid taking antibiotics if possible.
- Avoid alcoholic beverages.
- Avoid caffeinated beverages.
- Avoid soda.
- Incorporate prebiotic foods into diet.
- Occasionally consume unprocessed naturally fermented foods.
- Ensure adequate daily sunlight.
- Incorporate as many raw foods and vegetables as possible.
- Be sure to include food sources of omega-3 fatty acids every day.
- Keep your gums and teeth healthy!
- Freely add fresh herbs and spices to your meals.
- Take a 5 to 15-minute walk after eating.

Estimates suggest up to 85% of Americans are infested with parasites. This is an unpleasant thought, especially if you google and view all the possible types of parasites known to infest the human body. There are many types of parasites. Some parasites primarily inhabit the intestine, while others are absorbed into the bloodstream and may eventually lodge in organs and tissues. Parasites may be found in just about every single body compartment including the brain. This reminds me of the second person I detoxed; she had ALS. I put her on a specialized brain detox and when we met for our first follow-up session, she told me that twice, as she was putting on her make-up in the morning, a worm crawled out of her eye. This is one of several proofs the detox was working.

Detoxes are meant to make a parasite's living environment intolerable. Parasite detox substances usually cause the parasites to leave the newly volatile environment and seek a different host. Parasites exit through the gastrointestinal tract, the urinary tract, the skin or any nearby orifice. While parasites live in a host, they consume nutrients and oxygen and release metabolic by-products. These by-products may cause a wide range of non-specific complaints such as pain which tends to move around, rashes, bumps, redness, strange skin sensations, etc. I have detoxed people who can see the parasites moving around just beneath their skin. This is heightened around the time of a full moon. It is possible, parasites are the primary cause of issues such as malnutrition (which often occurs in the obese), anemia, body aches and pains, skin irritation, abdominal pain and bloating, immune disorders, etc. Common parasites include: skin mites (scabies), thread or pin worm (causes anal itching), roundworms, hookworm, trichinosis, tapeworm, lice, Chagas disease, and others. Take for example Chagas disease. From the time of infection to when symptoms first appear may take several months. Initial symptoms may be mild such as slight fever, body aches and pains but then the symptoms usually worsen and may include an irregular heartbeat, congestive heart failure, difficulty swallowing, etc. If it is not successfully treated, Chagas disease may cause death from cardiac arrest.

If you suspect you have parasites, schedule an appointment with your physician for testing. Testing involves either bloodwork and / or a stool sample. Your physician may treat parasites with prescription medications. However, if you prefer to use more natural means, you can purchase over-the-counter treatments which include tablets, drops, tinctures, teas and targeted foods. Most people benefit from a minimum of a simple four-month parasite detox program. Why four months? The life cycle of gut parasites is four months. From the time a parasite lays its larvae until the larvae hatch and die, is four months. Anything less than a four-month commitment may not yield the desired results.

You can do a rigorous detox or a mild one. Either way, consult a physician, functional nutritionist or a naturopath for expert guidance. Otherwise you may not optimize your time and efforts. Never trust an inexperienced person in matters such as this, if you are interested in the optimum outcome. If you want to proceed on your own, purchase supplements or tinctures containing the following elements: black walnut hulls, wormwood, astragalus, mimosa pudica, papaya seed, cloves, garlic, ginger, etc. The timing and use of binders is recommended. Use as instructed continuously for four months. Follow the directions on the package. At a minimum, this accomplishes a mild detox.

If you have blood-borne parasites, you may experience a Herxheimer reaction. This is caused by the parasites dying off, leading to an immediate immune response which makes you feel sick. This resulting sickness may be mild and feel like a cold or it may be more severe. It usually passes after a day or two. You may go through several Herxheimer reactions before your body expels the parasites.

In summary, gut issues are critical. Problems must be solved or they can lead to more issues which can become increasingly difficult to resolve. Once you address your gut issues and your gut is properly functioning, many of your other "non-gut" issues may resolve. I have seen this happen many times. Digestion, absorption and utilization of nutrients appears to be a seamless process, one that we oftentimes take for granted until we begin to experience symptoms such as constipation, indigestion, bloating, back pain, blood in the stools, brain fog, etc. Never underestimate the power of improving gut functions. This involves learning about normal gut functions and taking appropriate steps to restore those functions. Oftentimes this requires major adjustments to your diet, lifestyle and how you deal with stress. Take one step at a time. As you experience relief from your worst symptoms, it may motivate you to keep making progress in your diet and lifestyle changes.

Bible verses: Genesis 43:11; Exodus 15:26; Exodus 30:23; Leviticus 11:1-47; Numbers 11:5; Numbers 13:23; Deut7:12-15; Deuteronomy 14:1-29; 1 Samuel 30:11-12; 2 Samuel 17:28; Proverbs 4:20-22.

Chapter 16

Top off vitamins, minerals and antioxidants

As a nutritionist, I could post the top 10 food list for each vitamin and mineral. In fact, I had started this list and then deleted it and decided to go with supplemental forms of the vitamins and minerals.

Most people do not want to significantly modify their diet. This applies to extremely healthy dietary patterns all the way to dangerous unhealthy dietary patterns. Most people would rather change their religion than change the way they eat (yes, this was an actual patient comment). A plant-based diet may include up to 15% of kcalories from animal products. A 100% plant-based diet is somewhat similar to a vegan diet, includes honey, but without the militant attitude often seen in vegans. In fact, it is probably ideal to consume a diet that sometimes may be vegan and on occasion may include animal products such as cheese, yogurt, butter, etc. Instead of being black and white, be temperate and use reason and intelligence guided by Biblical and other inspired writings. Even Proverbs 27:27 describes the inclusion of goats' milk in the diet: "And thou shalt have goats' milk enough for thy food, for the food of thy household, and the maintenance for thy maidens." When good habits begin to gain a foothold in your lifestyle, the bad habits will eventually be crowded out. This is the basis of the new food guidance system outlined in the next chapter.

It usually takes a major health event such as a stroke, heart attack, cancer or other scary diagnoses and conditions before most people agree to make significant, positive dietary and lifestyle changes. **Because most people will take a supplement, I decided to start with this approach.** Here are my top 10 + 1 vitamin, mineral, fiber and fatty acid supplement recommendations. Keep in mind, this top 10 list slightly changes over time. In reality, each nutrient needs to be individualized to your health history and your current condition. **There is no one-size-fits-all solution.**

In general, only educated, experienced and licensed health professionals are qualified to guide you when it comes to your restoring your health. If you rely on untrained, uneducated people with no experience who may have a financial stake in selling you products, what they do not know may hurt you. Respect yourself enough to get expert advice which may lead you in the right direction and keep you from wasting time, money and efforts on the low-return and even the wasteful opinions of others and the random use health products. If a person has an established medical condition such as obesity, diabetes, heart disease, cancer, neurological conditions, gut issues, growth and development issues, depression, eating disorders, malnutrition, deficiencies, toxicities, etc., you must be a registered or licensed dietitian to provide counseling (i.e., otherwise known as medical nutrition therapy). If a person is pregnant or lactating, they need to seek professional advice. Providing nutritional information, including the use of supplements and herbals, may expose the untrained and uneducated people to legal liability.

I have seen hundreds of untrained and uneducated people try to guide their friends, customers and others in making good health-related choices. Unfortunately, most novices and untrained people do not have a well-thought out approach (because they are not educated and experienced). **They take a shot-gun approach of try this or try that without laying the groundwork and methodically addressing issues in a logical and sequential way.** Avoid taking advice from people who have a financial stake in providing advice to you! This oftentimes taints their objectivity. You end up spending money on unnecessary products and before you know it, confusion sets in and nothing seems to work for long. I have seen people come into a health food store looking for a quick fix. Someone tells them about the latest and greatest supplement which will take care of their issue(s). **Oftentimes, a placebo effect occurs, and the patient feels better, but this usually a temporary fix. In a week or month or so, the customer is back with another issue.** If your finances are limited, continue reading this chapter to see which supplements pack the most bang for your bucks! One item on the list is even free!

Another area of caution is the use of naturopaths. I am a huge supporter of naturopathy and actually have co-opted many naturopathic principles into my practice, however, naturopathy is not uniformly regulated in the USA. Each state defines who may and may not use the title of "naturopath." **This has opened the door for <u>formally uneducated</u> naturopaths to claim this title. If you choose to use a naturopath, ask them where they trained, the year they graduated, where they completed a residency, and ask to see their degree certificate at the time of your visit.** If in doubt of their qualifications, contact the institution they claim issued their degree to confirm their assertion. Every single profession has their fair share of copycats and imitators. A legitimate practitioner has no qualms about confirming their qualifications. If they squawk about this, there is a good possibility they are an interloper.

There are 5 accredited naturopathic schools in the USA (Bastyr University has two campuses, one in Washington state and one in California) and 2 in Canada (Vancouver BC and Toronto ON). USA schools are in Seattle, San Diego, Portland (Oregon), Chicago and Phoenix. According to the American Association of Naturopathic Physicians website, as of the year 2020, 21 states, Washington DC, Puerto Rico and the US Virgin Islands have strict laws requiring state-issued licenses to practice naturopathy. Each state with laws in place may have slightly different regulations and requirements for practicing naturopathy. Those states are: Alaska, Arizona, California, Colorado, Connecticut, Hawaii, Idaho, Kansas, Maine, Maryland, Massachusetts, Minnesota, Montana, New Hampshire, North Dakota, Oregon, Utah, Vermont, Washington. California, Colorado, Idaho, Minnesota, Montana, New Hampshire, New Mexico, North Dakota, Oregon, Pennsylvania, Rhode Island, Utah, Vermont and Washington have state-specific restrictions on the use of the titles, "Naturopath," "Naturopathic Doctor," and "Naturopathic Physician." In some states not listed above, the title, "Complementary & Alternative Health Care Practitioner" is allowed.

In South Carolina and Tennessee (at this time), it is unlawful to practice naturopathy. If you did not see your state listed in the above paragraph, your state does not regulate who may use the title of "Naturopath." In other words, if you live in one of the following states, any person, whether formally trained or not, can claim to be a naturopath: Alabama, Arkansas, Delaware, Georgia, Indiana, Iowa, Kentucky, Louisiana, Mississippi, Missouri, Nebraska, Nevada, New Jersey, Ohio, South Dakota, Texas and

West Virginia. States with pending naturopath regulations include: Illinois, Michigan, New York, North Carolina, Oklahoma, Virginia, Wisconsin, and Wyoming. Keep this in mind as you allocate your health care dollars and choose your health care providers.

Another profession with a state-variable scope of practice is chiropractors. For the most part, I have been fortunate to know many excellent chiropractors! However, there are a small minority who may cross the line from legitimate procedures and scope of practice into areas of unproven efficacy. Chiropractors attending accredited universities are taught to perform 97 diagnostic, management and evaluative services (I suppose this could vary a bit). According a recent survey of state practices, the number of services a chiropractor can perform ranges from 33 services in Texas to 92 services in Missouri. The 97 services include: diagnostic and examination certifications (full spine, soft tissue, barium studies, surface EMG, vascular analysis, throat swab, blood / urine analysis, pre-employment physical, DOT physical), physical exams, gender-specific services, physio therapeutics, specialty adjusting techniques), adjunctive and specialty services (diet formulation, botanical therapy, ear and colonic irrigation, obstetrics, vitamin injection, oxygen therapy, electro-acupuncture, electrolysis, etc.). I am a huge fan of chiropractors and fully advocate for the use of legitimately educated and trained chiropractors. In fact, I believe many people can benefit from seeing a chiropractor. Just keep in mind, depending on your state, they may or may not have the full range of practice available to them.

For the most part, supplements are not going to make up for a poor diet, a toxin-laced diet and lifestyle, a lazy lifestyle, excessive stress, excess fat consumption, under-used muscles, and established chronic disease. Keep in mind, it is best to eat a healthy diet, maintain a healthy lifestyle and avoid obvious and even the less obvious toxins in food, water and the environment.

If you want to establish a healthy baseline and your diet is not perfect, you may consider adding the following supplements. These supplements are not expensive and they provide long-term benefits. When available, I usually recommend tablets and not capsules. Liquid forms may help those with swallowing issues. You may always take these supplements and blend in a coffee grinder and add to applesauce or consume in a smoothie. <u>This does not constitute medical advice</u>, but serves mainly to reinforce the concept of getting enough of the following nutrients may not regularly occur or possibly these nutrients might be subject to decreased availability in the body due to common diet and lifestyle choices. If you have the MTHFR genetic mutation, you may need to use the methylated forms of the B vitamins. I always recommend getting folate from food and not supplements, but B complex 50 does contain folic acid, the synthetic form of naturally occurring food-based folate (see recommendation #7).

1. B complex 50 or 100
    a. The B vitamins are critical co-factors for almost every metabolic pathway in the body.
    b. Recommend taking in the morning.
    c. May split tablet and take ½ in the am and ½ at noontime; avoid taking before bedtime.
    d. Some may benefit from taking additional thiamin (B1), riboflavin (B2), niacin (B3) and folate (B9).
    e. Biotin (vitamin B7) is important for skin, nails, hair, salivary gland functions, etc.
    f. Specific groups benefit from additional B6 (in addition to what is found in B complex 50).
    g. Most people get enough pantothenate (B5).

h. Other compounds (some controversial) considered to be in the water-soluble category but are not necessarily considered vitamins because most are made by the body include: choline, inositol, adenine (B4), carnitine, (B_T), salicylic acid, adenylic acid (B8), laetrile (B17), etc.
2. 200 – 1,000+ mg magnesium
   a. Magnesium is involved in over 300 metabolic interactions.
   b. Start out using magnesium citrate and maybe adding magnesium threonate which is able to cross the blood brain barrier.
   c. Titrate the level of magnesium to avoid loose stools or diarrhea. Some people may need more than 1,000 mg of magnesium.
3. 100 – 200+ mcg selenium or 2 Brazil nuts
   a. If you are a small person, take the lower dose.
   b. It is important to take selenium if you also take iodine.
   c. Selenium is part of antioxidant and thyroid enzymes.
4. 500 – 1,000+ mcg iodine
   a. Most people benefit from adding an iodine supplement.
   b. An excellent book on the topic of iodine is: Iodine: Why you need it and why you cannot live without it, by David Brownstein, MD. (ISBN13: 978-0966088236)
   c. The amount of iodine required needs to be assessed and individualized by a nutrition or medical professional.
   d. Some people may benefit from supraphysiological doses of iodine in the 10 – 50 mg range.
   e. Significantly more than this recommended amount may also be desirable.
5. 3 – 20+ grams vitamin C (ascorbic acid)
   a. Everyone could benefit by taking additional vitamin C.
   b. Helps maintain the body's immune system.
   c. Essential for recovering from an infection.
6. 100 – 500 mcg vitamin B12 (methyl cobalamin)
   a. Most people either don't consume enough vitamin B12 or they don't absorb enough vit B12.
   b. There is no toxicity level to methyl cobalamin.
   c. It is advisable to take additional vitamin B12 to prevent an insidious, slowly progressive deficiency which is oftentimes attributed to "normal" aging.
7. Green leafy foods (chlorophyll) or a daily green smoothie or supplement green powder (folate)
   a. One of the most important dietary changes you can make is to consume more greens which provide a source of natural folate as opposed to the synthetic form, folic acid.
   b. Keep in mind, spinach is super high in oxalates so if you are sensitive to oxalates, choose a different type of leafy green.
   c. Consuming a green smoothie on a regular basis is a great habit to adopt!
8. Psyllium husks
   a. Take 1 – 2 tablespoons of psyllium husks in 18 – 24 ounces of water in the morning before you eat breakfast.
   b. Psyllium is a type of fiber which encourages your gut's goblet cells to produce mucous. This protects the gut.
   c. One tablespoon (18 g) of psyllium husks provides 68 kcalories, ~165 mg potassium, 13.5 g fiber, 0.4 mg iron, 60 mg calcium.

9. Plant-based omega-3 fatty acids (plant-based food sources are best)
    a. Includes foods such as chia seeds, hemp seeds, flax seeds, walnuts, etc.
    b. Add a teaspoon or two of chia seeds to water along with a squeeze of fresh lemon and ice for a refreshing chia fresca.
10. Chia seeds
11. Sunlight (vitamin D) – it's FREE!
    a. Aim to get 15 to 30 minutes of sunlight on sunny days.
    b. Early morning sunlight exposure is best.
    c. Expose as much skin as possible.
12. 5 – 20 mg copper
13. 100 mg zinc (at bedtime)
14. Minerals and ultra-trace minerals
    a. Consider adding liquid minerals to your water or other beverages.

Physician Steven Haltiwanger, in his monograph, <u>The Electrical Properties of Cancer Cells</u>, describes the electrical properties of the body (http://www.royalrife.com/haltiwanger1.pdf). He states, "cells of the body are composed of matter made up of atoms, which are mixtures of negative charged electrons, positively charged protons and electrically neutral neutrons. When an electron is forced out of its orbit around the nucleus of an atom, the electron's action is known as electricity. Electrical potentials are created in biological cells when charges are separated. Biological material with an electrical potential possesses the capacity to do work. 'An electric field forms around any electric charge (Becker, 1985).' Haltiwanger continues, electricity is the flow of mobile charge carriers in a conductor or a semiconductor from areas of high charge to areas of low charge driven by electrical force. Again, this allows biological tissue to harness this electrical force to do work. When two areas of unequal charge are connected, current flows in a way to equalize the charge difference. The difference in potential between two points gives rise to a voltage, which causes charge carriers to move and current to flow when the points are connected. This force causes motion and causes work to be done. Current is the rate of flow of charge carriers in a substance past a point, measured in amperes. In biological tissues, both mobile ions and electrons carry current. When current flows, an expanding magnetic field is created." This gives each animate and inanimate object it's unique charge and frequency.

In 1985, Dr. Haltiwanger proposed "multiple structures in the cell act as electronic components. Cells receive, transduce and transmit electric, acoustic, magnetic, mechanical and thermal vibrations." He further states, what are generally considered to be "thermally weak or non-ionizing" electric fields may contain rich biological informational content. The "weak" biological electromagnetic fields, sometimes seen as "noise," may exert frequency-specific effects and exhibit a non-linear dose response curve. For many without formal training in electronics and circuits, this information may seem confusing and misplaced. However, it is important to understand the electric nature of the body and why nutrients are critical. Nutrients such as carbohydrates, amino acids, lipids, sterols, minerals and other elements, vitamins, phytochemicals, hydrogen, oxygen, photons, and their quantum effects in the human body, support every single function related to life. Nutrients support the brain, DNA functions, they are essential for bioenergetics of all life, all movement, and all thoughts are functions of nutrients and their electrons and ions interacting in biological systems.

Healing requires electric currents. Every cell in the body is electrical. In inorganic systems such as the electrical wiring in your home, electrons carry the current. In biological systems, ions and electrons carry current. Each cell requires a certain level of electron flow to maintain function. When the charge drops, even briefly, symptoms appear. If the charge remains low eventually a "disease" appears and progresses unless corrected. What we eat, the composition of our body, our lifestyle habits, and even our thoughts impact the healing potential of the body.

Conductors are material which allows the flow of electrons. In biological tissue, there are several barriers to the flow of current such as fat. Fat acts as an insulator, unable to carry current. Other biologicals form resistance to current flow and the electric charge dissipates as heat. Impedance opposes flow of a current through a conductor. Capacitors store a charge and return it at a later time.

Relatively speaking, the nervous system including the 12 cranial nerves, uses a lot of relatively small voltages: the nerves including olfactory, optic, oculomotor, trochlear, trigeminal, abducens, facial, vestibulocochlear, glosso-pharyngeal, vagus, spinal accessory, and hypoglossal. When the nerves are exposed to toxins or low oxygen, they weaken leading to issues such as loss of smell, ringing in the ears, taste changes, gut issues, abnormal muscle movements and twitching, altered touch perception (e.g. paresthesias), etc. I have found in the case of tinnitus or ear buzzing / ringing, if you do several deep breaths, the ringing may go away. The ringing may signal the auditory nerves are affected, possibly by low oxygen. Deep breathing immediately oxygenates the body and the ringing usually stops. Nutrients and oxygen are critical to brain health. **Adaptations to low oxygen occur in the body, but if maintained over long periods, may lead to symptoms and ultimately to pathological changes.** Dysfunction in face area is significant because of the convergence of the nerves in the brain. Nose breathing is good for the body because it improves voltage and is more efficient. The nose is also a good filter. Good posture is another way to improve voltage (Haltiwanger).

When we begin to see the human body as an electrical field with vibrational energy, we may better understand how important it is to be connected to natural phenomena such as the ground, nature, freshly harvested foods, pure water, sunlight, meaningful relationships, etc. (think of the Beach Boys song, Good Vibrations). All animals vibrate at slightly different frequencies. In fact, different organs and tissues each have a specific frequency. As disease gets established in the body, the frequency is altered. Normal frequencies must be restored before health returns. This is not witchcraft or worshiping gaia. Vibrational frequencies are part of every aspect of creation. As a new seedling bursts forth out of the dirt and into the light, it vibrates at a specific frequency. Newborn babies vibrate at a specific frequency. It is possible the frequency of all living things is how we are programmed (created) to praise God! It is possible that when sin is cleansed from the earth, all of creation will share one pulse of harmony and gladness. One heavenly frequency will infuse everything.

Many factors converge to ensure optimal health. The condition of the liver is also critical for every body system and every aspect of life. Clean eating helps promote liver health. This involves avoiding foods which tax the liver such as sugar, processed foods, alcohol, heavy high kcalorie meals, frequent eating, toxin-laced foods, etc. If you want to maintain excellent liver functions, ensure you consume cruciferous vegetables, berries, bitter greens and herbs, citrus, garlic, onions, high fiber foods, nuts, seeds, whole grains, milk thistle (as a supple-ment), ashwagandha root (as a supplement), the B vitamins, vitamin A (beta-carotene), and an adequate amount of natural fats in the diet (also see page 144).

Raw plants are a primary source of high energy electrons as well as vibrational frequencies (i.e., check out "plant bioacoustics" at wikipedia). Every plant contains antioxidants or plant chemicals which help fight off disease-causing radicals. Fresh plants have more power than cooked plants. Natural foods have more power than processed foods. Sugar, while providing glucose and kcalories, provides no support nutrients needed to process glucose. Eating animal-based food provides minimal electrons with low vibrational frequency.

For those who have never heard about vibrational frequencies and may have some doubt about the validity of such claims, there are numerous scientific publications on this topic at pubmed. For example, the article, Electronic and vibrational properties of carotenoids: from in vitro to in vivo, by MJ Llansola-Portoles, AA Pascal and B. Robert and published in J R Soc Interface (PMID: 29021162), describes over 700 carotenoid compounds exhibiting vibrational properties. Each carotenoid's frequency is specific to its function as an antioxidant and for protecting the structures in which it resides. Additional studies show all biological molecules studied thus far, exhibit electrical and vibrational activity. **Vibrational activity correlates with their function(s).** Because the magnitude of vibrational activity is low, measuring it requires highly specialized equipment. Keep in mind, each cell in our body is electrically and vibrationally sensitive. As our living environment continues to house more high frequency, high energy waves generated by communication towers, satellites (invisible to the human eye) and their receivers, it is inevitable the stronger electromagnetic fields interact with the much smaller signals, potentially exerting difficult to detect negative influences on human physiology.

Another example includes honeybees. In an article titled, "The recruiter's excitement – features of thoracic vibrations during the honey bee's waggle dance related to food source profitability," by M. Hrncir, et al, and published in the Journal of Experimental Biology, researchers detail how the vibrational frequency of a honey bee's chest cavity transfers information about the location, distance, and quality of a foraging site. Interruption of this communication mode may interfere with their activity. This is one of the concerns regarding 5G technology as well as their exposure to agricultural toxins.

Let's get back to supplements and health. **It appears eating fresh plants is the best strategy to ensure health and even to restore health.** It is an excellent strategy if perfectly executed. If a person can figure out how to eat the perfect diet, live the perfect lifestyle, stay forever young, perfectly handle stress, and avoid all toxins and reverse all degenerate codes in their body, I would heartily agree with them. However, we never come close to this level of perfection. We can only perceive it from a human perspective of where we are in time. This does not allow us to fully understand the human body as it was originally designed, perfect and defect free. We can only overlay our idea of perfection on top of thousands if not millions of altered epigenetic changes. Absolutely eat more fresh plants!. This is imperative. A daily green smoothie is one of the single best habits for achieving excellent health. It allows for consuming natural folate in the form of fresh greens. Other beneficial foods such as nuts and seeds can be added. However, it is almost impossible to execute a perfect diet because the perfect diet is not just about the food we eat but how our lifestyle, mental health, social connections, stress, toxins and things we cannot see or detect, interact with what we eat to impact our health.

As we go forward in time, I would caution against expecting the environment in which we live, to improve. This is why supplements, while not perfect, are important. Much more could be written about this philosophy, but in brief, supplements allow us to boost our intake of nutrients which otherwise would be impossible to ingest given what most of us are used to consuming. Because most supplement critics, as well as their proponents, do not have advanced degrees in nutrition, molecular biology, chemistry, physics, and biochemistry, their voices, while important, do not carry the weight of those who have comprehensively studied this issue for decades and are not genuflecting along with societal trends or closely held biases. **The orthomolecular approach, as advocated by twice Nobel Prize winner Linus Pauling, as early as 1968, is timely and ideal for addressing many modern-day symptoms and disease states.** It is crucial to find a competent practitioner (whether a physician or nutritionist), who uses orthomolecular principles as one arrow in the quiver of their patient care approach.

If you had to choose one antioxidant to supplement, consider vitamin C (i.e., ascorbic acid). Powdered ascorbic acid is functionally equivalent to natural vitamin C. One teaspoon of pure powdered ascorbic acid contains approximately 4,000 mg of vitamin C (see Table 1). Each molecule of vitamin C donates either one or two electrons. **Almost everyone can benefit by taking 3 to 5 grams of ascorbic acid per day.** This helps your body fight off oxidative stressors encountered in everyday life. It may seem like a big jump going from the RDA of 90 mg to 4,000 mg for vitamin C. However, getting enough vitamin C is a huge blessing we gain from eating delicious foods as well as supplements.

Some fruits and vegetables are good sources of vitamin C, but probably the highest source is rose hips. Rose hips are the fruit portion of the rose flower. They contain the seeds of the rose plant and make a great jelly, jam, tea or dessert. Dried rose hips may also be ground into a flour and added to baked goods. Whether you consume citrus, fresh fruits and vegetables, rose hips or even ascorbic acid powder, vitamin C is essential for good health. **Healthy eating is the best way to get nutrients.** Guava is another vitamin C superstar. Guava can be added to smoothies and fruit salads. It can be juiced along with other tropical fruits such as pineapple. One kiwi is an excellent source of vitamin C. Combine kiwi with lychees and strawberry slices for a high vitamin C fruit salad. There are many ways to incorporate more high vitamin C foods into your diet. See Table 1 for the vitamin C content of selected foods. The information in this table should provide you with enough particulars to choose high vitamin C foods every day.

God designed plants to deliver nutrients.

Plants are excellent sources of antioxidants and many nutrients. It is only with sin that plants began to accumulate toxic chemicals, grow thorns, and taste bitter. If you eat less than a perfectly healthy diet, you may benefit in the antioxidant category from supplementation with ascorbic acid. What a blessing it is to have knowledge of and be able to take advantage of ascorbic acid when in times of need such as rampant chronic disease, infection, and immune compromise.

Top off vitamins, minerals and antioxidants

Table 1. Vitamin C in Selected Fruits and Vegetables
(DRI for Vitamin C is 90 mg)

Vitamin C Carrier / Food	Amount, mg	% DRI
1 tsp (4 g) Ascorbic acid	~4,000	4,444
~ 3 oz (100 g) Rose hips	426	473
1 cup Guava	377	419
1 lg Bell pepper (yellow)	341	378
1 cup Kiwi	167	185
1 cup Bell Pepper (red)	152	169
1 cup Lychees	136	151
1 cup Strawberries	98	108
1 cup Brussels sprouts, cooked	97	107
1 cup Orange	96	106
1 cup Papaya	88	98
1 cup Broccoli, fresh	81	90
1 cup Parsley, fresh	80	89
1 cup Cabbage, cooked	56	63
1 cup Tomato, cooked	55	61
1 cup Cauliflower, cooked	55	61
1 cup Sweet potatoes, cooked	42	47
1 cup Snow peas	38	42
1 cup Beet greens, cooked	36	40
1 cup Watercress	35	38
1 cup Butternut squash, cooked	31	34
1 cup Crookneck squash	25	27
1 cup Zucchini, cooked	23	26
1 cup Green peas	23	25
1 cup Kale, cooked	21	23
2 x 5 inch Baked potato	20	22
1 cup Dandelion greens	19	21

Top off vitamins, minerals and antioxidants			
Table 2. Plants High in Antioxidants			
Acai berry	Carob	Grape juice	Peaches
Agave	Cherries	Hazelnuts	Peanuts
Alfalfa sprouts	Chia seeds	Kale	Pears
Almonds	Chili powder*	Kiwi	Pecans
Apples	Chokeberry	Legumes	Pepper, black*
Apricots	Cinnamon*	Lemons	Peppermint
Artichokes	Cloves*	Lemon balm	Pistachios
Avocados	Cranberries	Lentils	Plums
Avocado seed	Cumin seeds	Lettuce, red	Raisins
Basil	Dark chocolate	Mangosteen	Raspberries
Beet greens	Dates	Maqui berry	Rice bran
Bell peppers	Dill	Marjoram	Sorghum
Blackberries	Elderberries	Molasses (blackstrap)	Spinach
Blueberries	Figs	Mustard seeds	Strawberries
Bran cereal	Flax seeds	Onions	Thyme
Broccoli	Garlic	Oranges	Turmeric
Cabbage, red	Ginger	Oregano, fresh	Walnuts
Cantaloupe	Goji berries	Paprika	Whole grains
Cardamom	Grapefruit	Parsley	
Use small amounts if you are sensitive or avoid.			

Bible verses: Psalm 119:103; Deuteronomy 8:8; Deuteronomy 26:9; Ezekiel 4:9; Mark 1:6; Luke 10:34

Discussion questions

1. On a scale of 1 (being least) and 10 (being best), how would you rate your diet and the diet of each family member?

2. Which of the supplements would benefit your family the most?

3. Are you for or against using supplements, explain your position.

4. Circle the foods above that you could include more frequently in your daily diet.

Chapter 17

Plant-based food guidance and lifestyle graphics

Meals matter: Take your pick©

Take your pick: Sample Breakfast, Lunch and Dinner Menus ©

Make each lifestyle habit count: Take your pick©

Food preferences are deeply personal. Food not only has nutritional value but carries emotional currency, meaning we eat for many reasons besides survival. We eat because we are happy, sad, hungry, need energy, etc. **Some people eat only to live but most of us, live to eat.** Over the past 4 to 5 decades, we have seen the role of food in society dramatically change from eating primarily for nourishment to eating as a social statement or even as a status symbol (i.e., think about all those beautiful plates of food and fancy coffee we see posted on social media).

This chapter and the accompanying graphics take us on a journey, selectively covering about 200+ years of American food-related history. It is in no way comprehensive, but it highlights selected aspects of our history which have shaped policy and contributed to the American view of diet and lifestyle. **Instead of government guidance shaping diet and lifestyle habits for health and wellness, their increasingly reductionistic guidance has inadvertently led to unprecedented increases in chronic debilitating and life-robbing conditions.** This can be reverse engineered if enough people are willing to invest their time and energy into the process. These graphics included at the end of this chapter are a good start to reversing the tragic aspects of modern life such as consuming a majority of one's diet as processed food, consuming acid-based soda pop and other types of beverages instead of pure water, adding hundreds and thousands of chemicals to food and water, etc. **Many people, instead of enjoying good health from their childhood into their late 70s and 80s, struggle with their health in almost every decade of their life.** Instead of accepting this as the norm, we need to take back control over our diet and lifestyle. Epigenetically speaking, every meal matters and every lifestyle habit counts either in a "win" or "loss" category. Change starts with the individual and spreads to communities and beyond.

Unlike most countries which are smaller and less diverse, the USA has a wide range of dietary patterns and lifestyle habits which reflect its population. For example, it is fundamentally different than the country of India, where even with significant variations between the north and south, most residents have a similar heritage, lifestyle and food intake. Even though Russia is geographically almost twice the size of the USA, it is also more homogenous with similar nutrition and lifestyle habits among their civilian population (more than 80% of the country is ethnic Russians). In contrast, the USA is an amalgam of widely diverse beliefs and practices. It is a large conglomerate of states, territories and Native American tribes, covering a relatively large land mass and including numerous islands. It includes a variety of climates, terrain and natural resources. Some areas are mountainous and other areas are low-lying coastal regions. Some areas are fertile while others areas are largely infertile, made up of sand and cacti. To some degree, the local population must adapt to its immediate climate and terrain. Each American's dietary pattern is influenced by local geographic factors. For example, if you live in on the west coast, you have abundant access to fresh produce from thousands of small farms. It is similar on the east coast. Many small farmers sell their produce either at local farmer's markets or through community-supported agriculture (CSAs) programs where local families proactively support their local farmers. This symbiotic relationship between small farmers and local consumers provides an ongoing abundance and variety of fresh produce during the growing seasons. However, if you live in North Texas, there are relatively few agricultural farms and most fresh produce is shipped in from South Texas, California and Florida. Cattle is the mainstay "crop" in North Texas. Good luck trying to find a produce-focused CSA group. Even with a global transportation network available to transport food anywhere in the world, this system remains vulnerable to disruption and stoppage, potentially affecting the delivery of fresh agricultural products.

California, with its diverse terrain and climate is considered to be the "bread basket" of the USA. California is home to more than 70,000 commercial farms (not including thousands of small non-commercial farms), 400 different commodities, with annual sales exceeding 45 billion dollars. It accounts for over 13% of the nation's agricultural endeavors. Iowa, Nebraska, Texas, Minnesota, Illinois, Kansas, Wisconsin, North Carolina, Indiana and Florida also boast of robust agricultural farms and related industries. What does not grow in the USA is readily imported from other countries. Our neighbor to the south, Mexico, produces tropical fruits such as bananas and pineapples, cacao, beans, tomatoes, corn, avocados, vanilla, spices, etc. Coffee beans, a widely consumed commodity in the USA and around the world, are not widely grown in the USA due to climate requirements. Coffee must be imported from Mexico and other countries.

Because of great diversity in climate, location, traditions, economic status, etc., dietary patterns in the USA are almost impossible to characterize. Almost every nationality is represented in the USA along with its unique food pattern. Each family member brings their values to the table. At this time, food availability in the USA is good and what is not grown in the USA is easily imported or sometimes grown on small farms. It was only a few years ago, several of my Filipino friends introduced the moringa tree and its nourishing leaves. They gave away small moringa trees as gifts for their friends and moringa leaves began showing up in their soups, salads and vegetable dishes. I am sure Moringa has been around for a long time, but it has only recently entered the American lexicon. Same with "bubble" or "boba" tea. Americans have eaten cassava-based tapioca pudding for hundreds of years, but only recently have we come to love the large pearl-sized black tapioca balls that grace the bottom of creamy sweet "bubble" tea and require large girth straws.

As a nutritionist, every time a new food emerges in American markets, I research and learn about it while determining its nutrient profile and possible benefits and concerns. Upon checking with WebMD, I found moringa leaves are considered to be safe but the moringa roots contain spirochin, a nerve-paralyzing toxin. When moringa leaves are eaten in small amounts, there is no problem. However, if moringa roots are consumed, the chances of negative consequences, even though relatively small, increases. When it comes to bubble tea, large tapioca balls found in boba tea have been known to accumulate in the stomach. A recent case of constipation in a young Chinese girl was caused by the accumulation of over 100 boba balls in her stomach and small intestine. This appears to be an isolated case, but it does underscore the need for public education and caution as new food trends emerge.

Early research into essential compounds found in foods today and known as vitamins, began in scientific pockets around the world, including the USA, Japan, Holland, Poland, Indonesia, Denmark, and Great Britain in the late 1800s. Before the first vitamins were discovered, food guidance in the USA began in 1894, when Dr. Wilbur Olin Atwater advocated for variety, proportionality and moderation in eating. He also recommended focusing on nutrient dense foods and measuring kcalories; he warned against consuming too much fat, sugar and starch. His recommendations surprisingly sound familiar to current dietary guidance (see Figure 1, The 5 Dietary Guidelines for Americans).

Figure 1. The 5 Dietary Guidelines for Americans:
1. Follow a healthy eating pattern across the lifespan;
2. Focus on variety, nutrient density and amount;
3. Limit calories from added sugars and saturated fats and reduce sodium intake;
4. Shift to healthier food and beverage choices; and,
5. Support healthy eating patterns for all.

Healthy eating in modern America is not as simple as it sounds. Much of our food is processed, contaminated with herbicides, fungicides, pesticides, genetically modified organisms, perfumed to smell good, colored to look good, chemicals added, flavor enhanced, and in some cases the food is unrecognizable from its original form. Instead of a dietary pattern primarily inclusive of native whole foods, the USA dietary pattern (and likely Canada's dietary pattern) is one of the only dietary patterns in the world established in the modern era to include highly refined plants with the bulk of kilocalories coming from animal products and refined starches. Almost every other dietary pattern around the world is based on a rich tradition of whole foods as opposed to processed foods. For example, when French fries and catsup were included in the vegetable food group during the 1980s, and the starch group included highly processed, sugar- and chemical-laden white flour hamburger buns, cheese was a dairy serving, and meat was a protein, and a vanilla milkshake was several dairy servings, you could easily eat a "balanced" happy meal at McDonald's. **Today, we understand foods within the same food group are not all equivalent in nutrients and health contributions. However, the construct of grouping food has been a difficult concept to erase. We don't consume food groups, we consume food, which just happens to have a combination of 3 macronutrients (i.e., protein, carbohydrate and fat) and an infinite combination of essential and non-essential nutrients.** Instead of artificially categorizing foods into 5 or 6 food groups, health professionals should acknowledge individual foods and dietary patterns as the predominant educational targets and not food groups.

In the late 1950s when the USA started publicizing their dietary guidance, it was seen as modern and superior. However, by the late 1960s and since, as the American populace began to experience increasing rates of degenerative conditions such as obesity, diabetes, heart disease, cancer and neurological conditions, some health experts began to see weaknesses in the USA approach to nutritional guidance. Instead of teaching Americans about healthy foods we grouped every single food into one of 5 or 6 food categories based on its composition of the macronutrients: protein, carbohydrate and fat. Whether it was intended or not, this equated white bread to whole grain bread, it equated beans with fried chicken, etc. This was a huge mistake. Special interest groups have also contributed to popularizing some foods over others. These special interest groups include but are not limited to the Dairy Council, The Cattlemen's Association, Livestock Marketing (lobbyists), the fast food industry, food manufacturers (e.g., Coca Cola), etc. (always follow the money). **In the attempt to simplify the educational approach, we lost the granularity of understanding the special attributes of each plant / food.** The same confusing approach of using food groups has been used to teach diabetic diets. In the end, the American approach was too clever by half. We are now digging out of this paradigm and beginning to appreciate other long-standing dietary patterns. Compare the USA with the Middle East, Mediterranean or Asian countries, which can boast of several millennia of relatively stable dietary patterns associated with well documented health benefits. Much more could be said here, but this chapter is not intended to be a review of the topic, only a brief introduction to a new system providing basic dietary guidance.

Many significant events have impacted dietary guidance. **As the scientific era dawned in the USA, allopathic medicine (i.e., Western medicine) began to establish deep roots within the scientific and medical community.** Another widely practiced form of medicine is osteopathy. Osteopathic medicine is closely associated with allopathic medicine but at its core, it seeks to identify causes of infirmity and address the causes and not just the symptoms. Osteopathic medicine utilizes the same pharmaceuticals as allopathic medical practitioners, but there is usually more reticence to start out with pharmacotherapy and the emphasis is on utilizing naturopathic methods when appropriate. Both allopathic and osteopathic practitioners pass the same medical boards and are considered physicians. **Naturopathic practitioners also go through a four year post graduate education and training and a hospital-based residency. They are equipped to treat most conditions physicians treat, but usually without the pharmaceuticals used in allopathic and osteopathic practices.** Naturopaths utilize a variety of procedures such as hydrotherapy, herbs, homeopathic substances, vitamins, minerals, specific foods with therapeutic potential, etc. **As allopathic medicine overtook naturopathic methods, many of the natural approaches to achieving health and wellness were abandoned for more "modern" methods. This paradigm shift left behind many broadly effective therapies for targeted pharmaceuticals.**

Another area of medical practice is orthomolecular medicine. Any health professional, within their scope of practice and with appropriate training and experience, can study and adapt orthomolecular principles to their practice. Nutritionists, physicians, and naturopaths all use orthomolecular approaches to treat qualifying conditions. According to Orthomolecular.org, the term "ortho" is a Greek term referring to "correct" or "right" and "molecule." Linus Pauling coined the term "orthomolecular" in 1968. He advocated for the therapeutic use of vitamin C (i.e., ascorbic acid), in the treatment of a number of conditions. Subsequently, a number of physicians (including Dr. Klenner, Dr. Cathcart, Dr. Abram Hoffer, Dr. Thomas Levy, etc.) have used "orthomolecular" doses of vitamin C (and other vitamins and minerals) to successfully treat a number of conditions. The amount of vitamin C used is in the gram range and not even close to the RDA for vitamin C of 90 mg. Some conditions aretreated with up to 150 grams of IV vitamin C and some physicians have suggested a total dose of 750 grams of vitamin C be used to resolve the deadly, rapidly progressing hemorrhagic disease, Ebola and its close relative, Marburg disease, both of which destroy by way of free radicals and both of which can be "neutralized by massive doses of IV sodium ascorbate." https://vitamincfoundation.org/www.orthomed.com/ebola.htm

In the early 1900s, about the same time allopathic medicine began to gain a foothold, Americans saw pharmaceutical prescription drugs displace folk and natural remedies (i.e., more closely associated with naturopathic medicine than allopathic medicine). But even before this occurred in the early 1900s, medical professionals observed widespread malnutrition among younger people who should have been healthier and better nourished. This could have been the result of a series of events beginning with the Civil War in 1861. This war robbed the USA of up to 750,000 young men (not counting civilian losses) and an additional 400,000 seriously injured and ill (approximately 1/30th of the population at that time). Our country never recovered from this event (i.e., the loss of young males and a significant proportion of the male gene pool) and the significant loss of young male lives. The losses in World War I, were followed by the Great Depression and widespread deprivation, followed by World War 2, the Korean War and Vietnam.

As a relatively new country without a long time period to adjust to climate patterns, develop community systems, and establish agriculture and trade patterns, the USA did not have the benefit of a long-established healthy dietary pattern. In fact, I would say it has never had a healthy multi-generational dietary pattern, except for maybe small coastal communities with access to both agricultural land and ocean or lake-based access to food and possibly several Blue Zones where life spans are significantly longer compared to their surrounding communities. **One Blue Zone in the USA is found in Loma Linda, California where a disproportionate number of Seventh-day Adventists live.** Many in this community are almost life-long vegetarians and pay special attention to their health and lifestyle. Both men and women in Loma Linda live almost a decade longer than their neighboring cohorts.

In the 1800s and early 1900s, communities established in land-locked states relied heavily on corn and grain agriculture in addition to cattle (i.e., beef). Communities along the coasts and large lakes, had greater diversity of food available and could take advantage of maritime-based trade and commerce. Communities in the southern part of the USA with longer growing seasons, relied more on summer crops such as greens, beans, carrots, tomatoes, eggplant, etc. Even in the south, poverty and poor nutritional habits continue to prevail. Today, significant pockets of poverty exist and to some degree, negatively impact the health and wellness of those communities. It was different among northern land-locked states and inland areas. These regions experienced shorter growing seasons, less food diversity, greater reliance on animal-based food and less availability of plant-based foods during cold months.

The industrial revolution aided by the agricultural revolution beginning in the late 1800s rapidly advanced modern agricultural methods of crop rotation, new crops, and the use of modern farm equipment. This revolution was augmented by mechanization in the 1920s and the green revolution in the 1960s and 1970s, which pushed crop production to its current highs. Today we live in the age of the digital revolution, which has transformed the planning and distribution aspects of agriculture. However, mechanization and modernization of agriculture has failed to boost most Americans' health. In fact, country-based small farmers all across Europe and the rest of the world surprisingly may fare better than most modern Americans.

Small farmers who actively grow their food, preserve their harvest, raise their own chickens (and therefore have farm fresh eggs), shop primarily to supplement their harvests, prepare most of the meals from scratch, and physically labor in the field and / or kitchen to bring food to the table, may experience better health and wellness compared to most Americans.

Rapid industrialization occurring over a relatively short period of time resulted in most Americans being completely detached from the origins of their food. We eat processed food for breakfast, fast food for lunch and packaged food for dinner. The occasional "health nut" may buy a "fruit" smoothie made from syrup, powders, supplementals, maybe a few pieces of fruit, and fluoride- and / or chloride-containing water and ice. In the end, excess sugar and processed food robbed of nutrients, only serves to jeopardize our health. Most people have never planted a garden, purchased seeds, planted seeds, watered and tended to their garden's needs, dealt with large and small pests attacking their crops, dealt with various plant diseases, dealt with weather extremes both positively and negatively impacting their crops, harvested a crop, found a buyer and contracted with a trucker to transport their crop, and then dealt with the buyer on issues with their produce at the marketplace. Farmers must purchase expensive equipment, seeds, pesticides, and other equipment. They must locate personnel to help harvest their crops. They deal with complex issues on a daily, if not hourly basis. Once fresh produce reaches the market, it is a race against time to showcase and sell the produce before it degrades and loses appeal. There is always an element of food waste which is factored into food prices. This chain of events is rarely considered by the average market buyer who is primarily concerned with convenience and not health.

Farmers specialize in producing living raw foods! Small farmers grow what they enjoy eating and usually the entire family participates in one or more aspects of agriculture. Growing your own corn means you can choose one or more of your favorite varieties. You can grow several different types of tomatoes. You can experiment with unusual vegetables such as cardoon, salsify, kohlrabi, etc. If you grow enough, you can sell what is not needed at local farmer's markets or to local restaurants. Over time, small farmers may expand and specialize, providing a reasonable income as well as supplying food for their family. This type of paradigm is the exception and not the norm in the USA and many other developed nations. However, going forward, small farms may form the basis for achieving a significant measure of health and wellness.

Apple pie, potatoes, okra, corn, and wheat are traditional American foods. Historically speaking, corn, potatoes and wheat have shaped much of America's food history. However, food processing of these foods and others has significantly impacted the quality of food consumed in the USA. In 1870, with the introduction of the modern steel roller mill, the nutritious components of wheat – the bran and the germ – were processed out, removing important nutrients and fatty acids. White bread became widely available and not just to the upper class. This was hailed as great progress. Another processing modification made to wheat flour is bleaching. To make white flour whiter and less yellow (due to the presence of small amounts of carotenoids), the "bleaching" process produces small amounts of a byproduct known as alloxan. Alloxan is a chemical associated with the des-truction of body's pancreatic beta cells. It is used to chemically induce diabetes in lab animals. Does the possible contamination of nutrient-depleted bleached white flour with a small amount of alloxan cause type 1 diabetes in humans? The answer is, "we don't know." Remember, it's the dose that makes the "poison." There are protective factors and exacerbating factors in both diet and life-style. If you consume a pro-inflammatory diet, it may exacerbate the effects of small amounts of alloxan. However, if you consume a minimally processed diet with a combination of raw and cooked fruits, vegetables, legumes, nuts and seeds, your chances of being negatively impacted by small amounts of alloxan are minimal. This illustrates the potential of an unintended consequence or collateral damage related to food processing. The potential contamination of bleached flour with alloxan is just one example. It is best to purchase organic whole grains and make your own flour. Different types of flours are now available including minimally processed: acorn, almond, buckwheat, chestnut, chickpea, coconut, corn, fava bean, gram, green pea, millet, potato, quinoa, rice, sorghum, soy, spelt, and teff flours. Many of these are good substitutes for wheat flour.

Corn has hugely impacted American diets. Most everyone loves sweet corn on the cob, smothered in butter and sprinkled with salt and pepper. This is one of summer's simple luxuries. However, in the early 20th century, the poverty-stricken south, heavily relied on corn for a large percentage of their calories. Some people experienced a debilitating disease, known as pellagra. It impacted more than 3 million people and killed 100,000 Americans between the years 1900 to 1940. Initially the disease perplexed the medical community. Dr. Goldberger, a Hungarian born physician, demonstrated pellagra was a vitamin deficiency, commonly seen in Southerners who consumed a diet largely composed of meat, corn and molasses. After extensive studies and a large skeptical community, Dr. Goldberger honed in on the missing factor – vitamin B3 also known today as niacin!

When corn is consumed as a large percentage of daily calories, it may lead to malnutrition due to its low tryptophan (i.e., rarest essential amino acid) and niacin content. In addition to being associated with malnutrition, studies show chronic corn consumption is associated with a marked reduction in brain serotonin. Several decades ago, this was more problematic, but today, it is not a widespread issue due to consuming a wider variety of foods. **Most of these issues with corn and wheat have been addressed as public health issues, but new concerns have surfaced including the widespread use of glyphosate, a chemical used to harvest both corn and wheat.**

Glyphosate is the primary chemical in Roundup, a Monsanto-Bayer product which has come under heavy criticism for causing harm. Glyphosate is used on both wheat and corn crops right before the harvest. Here is a link to a Glyphosate Fact Sheet: https://usrtk.org/pesticides/glyphosate-health-concerns/ . Glyphosate, classified as a "possible human carcinogen," is a dangerous chemical associated with damaging lymphocytes, a type of immune cell in the blood. **Glyphosate is also associated with depleting serotonin and causing widespread inflammation.** Many health professionals believe there is a link between the use of glyphosate on wheat and gut sensitivity to wheat and wheat products. The greater the exposure, the more problematic glyphosate may be. Monsanto, recently acquired by Bayer Company, also widely promotes genetically modified crops. The USA has been the primary user of their products until the past several decades. Countries which were once clean and free of Monsanto's chemical and biological reaches, are now choosing to use glyphosate and GMO products. However, as of the end of 2020, 21 countries have either restricted or banned the use of glyphosate. It is ideal to buy organic wheat and corn products when possible. These products should not be contaminated with glyphosate.

Other issues with corn include processing and refining corn. It has been refined and fractionated to the extent it is unrecognizable. It is now processed into corn starch, corn syrup, high fructose corn syrup, corn oil, dextrins, maltodextrins, dextrose (glucose produced from corn), fructose and even a gasoline additive. When you drink a soda, you are likely drinking corn-sweetened phosphoric or citric acid with a proprietary blend of flavors. Table sugar, a disaccharide, is half glucose and half fructose. Table sugar is a fractionated product refined from sugar beets or sugar cane. Corn sugar is composed of the monosaccharide, glucose with no natural fructose. Regular corn syrup is commonly used to make pecan pies. High fructose corn syrup (HFCS) is slightly sweeter than corn syrup, because more than half of the glucose is converted to fructose. HFCS is used to sweeten sodas, candies, sweets, yogurt, juices, salad dressings, etc.

HFCS is an ultra-processed form of sugar extracted from corn starch. It begins as glucose and is enzymatically converted (sometimes in the presence of mercury) to a majority (55%) of fructose. Fructose is known as "fruit sugar." Fructose, when consumed as a whole fruit, is attached to fiber, water, minerals, vitamins, and tens if not hundreds of plant chemicals, making whole fruit taste uniquely sweet and delicious. HFCS, a highly processed form of corn, is found in many processed foods. It has no accompanying fiber or nutrients; it is just glucose and fructose. There are significant health consequences to consuming too much HFCS. As of this writing (i.e., July 2022), 678 Pubmed articles come up when using the search terms, "high fructose corn syrup humans." Results of HFCS consumption include: obesity, mineral imbalances, altered hormones (e.g., insulin, ghrelin, leptin, cortisol), fatty liver, altered fat accumulation / storage, inflammation, tumor growth, cardiovascular risk, cancer, diabetes, etc.

In the course of a few short paragraphs, several major issues have been described regarding two staple American foods. Many more issues exist. If just these two foods, corn and wheat, have been so highly processed, refined, modified and contaminated, what could we expect to discover about other foods? The point is the American diet is largely composed of convenience and fast foods which are refined and highly processed. These factors and others contribute to inadequate intake of essential nutrients and excessive intake of fat, sugar, preservatives, food additives, etc. In these ways and others, the American dietary pattern significantly differs from other regions such as the Mediterranean and Middle East, some northern African countries, and some Asian countries.

Food preferences are strongly influenced by the addition of sugar and fat. Sugar lends an addictive property and fat increases the enjoyment of food, especially cooked foods. Food preferences and habits start early. Children do not consciously choose their dietary pattern. It evolves over time and changes with experience. **Two children from the same parents may have widely varying food preferences and dietary intake.**

Adults are more likely to consciously choose their dietary pattern while children are usually at the mercy of their parent's preferences. Sometimes dietary patterns change for the better and sometimes they change for the worse. These changes occur at various times and critical periods throughout the life cycle such as starting school, when parent's divorce and remarry, going away to college, getting married, moving to a new city or state or even to a different country, during frequent travel, a change in income and / or employment status, manifestation of health issues, pregnancy and lactation, adopting a diet-sensitive social issue or religion, playing specific sports / competitions, etc. As children grow older, their dietary pattern is the result of how permissive their parents are with processed foods, how the parents eat, socioeconomic status, geographic location, etc.

As people reach older age, their appetites may wane and they may lose muscle mass (leading to sarcopenia – low muscle mass and decreased strength). This predisposes one to malnutrition and altered immunity. **Most people are not going to make huge changes in their dietary pattern without the presence of powerful motivators.** In fact, most people would rather change their religion than change their dietary pattern. This is why education is critical. Information and life experiences, provided in the correct context, can be a valuable motivator for change.

From 1992 to 2011, the USDA used the Food Guide Pyramid to depict dietary recommendations based on six food groups: 1. bread, cereal, rice and pasta; 2. vegetables; 3. fruit; 4. meat, poultry, fish, dry beans, eggs and nuts; 5. milk, yogurt and cheese; and 6. fats, oils and sweets. In 2011, the USDA shifted to a plate graphic which eliminated the fats, oils and sweets categories (see Tables 1 and 2). As a nutrition professional, I have never observed the USDA approach to food guidance to be highly effective. In fact, if you study the basis of USDA nutrition guidance, you will soon understand it is based on data targeting primarily the prevention of deficiencies and not promoting health and wellness.

To my knowledge, the US government has yet to successfully define a healthy American dietary pattern which includes data describing pockets of healthy, long-lived Americans and making recommendations specific to geographic location and culture. **At present, powerful PACS and corporate interests have unduly influenced dietary and food guidance strategies.** Instead of examining healthy dietary patterns (including supplementation strategies), governmental agencies have defaulted to the Dietary Reference Intakes (DRIs). The USA adopted DRIs including the following specific recommendations related to macronutrients, vitamins and minerals: Recommended Dietary Allowances (RDAs), Adequate Intake (AIs), and Tolerable Upper Intake Level (ULs). The USDA view of nutritional requirements is based on normal distribution (i.e., the bell curve). Some of the younger age categories are extrapolations of adult data and not based on any studies. Every single American is assigned a Recommended Dietary Allowance (RDA) category based solely on their age and gender. A small 5-foot Asian woman weighing 95 pounds hypothetically has the same nutritional requirements as a six foot black or white woman weighing 210 pounds because they are both in the same age and gender category. It is little more than a semi-sophisticated construct. Food manufacturers have learned to either fortify foods (i.e., add vitamins and minerals to foods) or enrich foods (i.e., add back some nutrients lost during processing) to meet DRI standards and "health claims" labeling requirements. These processed foods are usually devoid of critical "support" nutrients removed during processing, but they have added back the exact amount of 3 or 4 specific essential nutrients recommended in the DRIs.

Overall, the DRIs quantify the amount of each essential vitamin and mineral required to prevent a deficiency. The first RDAs were published in 1943, with numerous ongoing modifications. Each RDA, AI, and UL is formulated to prevent overt deficiencies of vitamins and minerals. It is understandable that over the past 80 years, information has emerged to justify expanding the reach of the RDAs, not only to prevent deficiencies but to promote wellness and optimum health. A possible "unspoken" bias of DRI authors is that the RDAs should be achievable by diet alone. This has precluded consideration that a number of scientific studies show nutrient amounts far in excess of some of the RDAs, are ideal. For example, the USRDA for vitamin B12 is 2.6 micrograms (µg). This is the lowest of all the RDAs including the ultratrace minerals, some of which are just given the designation, "Estimated Safe and Adequate Daily Intakes (ESADDI)." The ultratrace minerals, those minerals "required" in the microgram range, include iodine, selenium, molybdenum, copper and chromium. Admittedly, the intake data on chromium may be inadequate to make an accurate assessment. Most of these minerals, with the exception of iodine and possibly selenium and copper, may be consumed by a reasonable, varied diet.

Vitamins required in the microgram range include vitamin A, vitamin D, vitamin K, biotin, folate and cobalt (vitamin B12). Maybe half of these vitamins are consumed by a reasonable, varied diet with several exceptions including vitamin A, vitamin D, folate (not folic acid) and vitamin B12. Vitamin D is only found in several foods including: fatty fish, beef liver, cheese, egg yolks mushrooms, fortified milk, and fortified cereals. If you do not consume these foods, you may be getting inadequate vitamin D. The good news is if you expose your skin to sunlight, your body makes the sulfated form of vitamin D. This may be useful during the summertime, **but during fall and winter months, vitamin D supplementation is advised**. Vitamin D is considered to be a hormone, critical to establishing a robust immune system. The top sources of vitamin A include beef liver, cheese, Atlantic herring and fortified cow's milk. Foods high in beta carotene also contribute to vitamin A and include sweet potatoes, spinach, pumpkin, carrots, spinach, cantaloupe, romaine lettuce, red bell peppers, apricots, broccoli and podded peas. Natural folate is found in green leafy vegetables, lentils, asparagus, broccoli, avocados, mangos, and oranges. Sources of vitamin B12 include only animal-based products and fortified plant-based products. In summary, fortified and enriched foods (i.e., usually processed foods) may help Americans consume adequate amounts of specific essential vitamins and minerals, but other healthy components are frequently removed, modified, or destroyed during food processing procedures. While fortification and enrichment of processed foods may seem like an acceptable practice, it has had the opposite effect on health and wellness, causing widespread overweight, obesity and chronic disease (i.e., whether or not it is a direct or indirect effect).

The requirement for vitamin B12 illustrates one weakness of the RDAs. A significant number of Americans are likely to consume an inadequate amount of vitamin B12 if they avoid animal products and fortified foods. Even those consuming "adequate" amounts of B12 often gradually and insidiously develop a deficiency. The requirement for vitamin B12 is the lowest of all of the essential nutrients (and ironically, vitamin B12 is arguably the largest and most complex of the essential nutrients). It is needed continuously for several critical pathways. Unfortunately, vitamin B12 is poorly understood and rarely considered when unusual neurological symptoms arise. Lamentably in older adults, healthcare providers oftentimes attribute vitamin B12 deficiency symptoms to normal "aging" and not to a vitamin deficiency. **This allows a B12 deficiency to progress and cause issues such as balance problems, paresthesias, neuropathies, increased susceptibility to tripping and falling, reversible dementia, etc., <u>even when vitamin B12 blood tests show adequate levels of vitamin B12.</u>**

Vitamin B12 is heavily utilized in both the central and peripheral nervous systems. It is an essential component of myelin, the nerve sheath surrounding peripheral nerve fibers. The nerves may show depleted vitamin B12 before blood levels are affected, but there is no way to test for this other than testing 128 Hz vibration sense at the ankles and knees. In some cases, the blood compartment is the last "tissue" to show vitamin B12 depletion. In this sense, the RDA for vitamin B12 is inadequate to prevent gradual depletion. **In reality, it may take significantly more vitamin B12 to prevent a deficiency, in which case, supplementation becomes necessary, beginning** sometime during the 4th decade of life (i.e., beginning in one's 30s), if not sooner for vegetarians and vegans.

Dietary guidance partially targets the macronutrients by categorizing protein-based food groups together, predominantly carbohydrate-based foods are grouped together and fats and oils are grouped together. This places avocado in the same category as margarine – one is healthy and the other is an artificial food. Two categories are grouped based on common culinary definitions and not macronutrient groupings. This includes the fruit and vegetable categories. As of 2011, food guidance transitioned from the Food Guide Pyramid (see Table 1) to Choose My Plate (see Table 2). **Fats, oils and sweets, formerly found on the Food Guide Pyramid, must be completely banned because they do not appear on the newest graphic, Choose My Plate.** Government experts must believe by removing fats, oils and sweets from the graphic, Americans will just eliminate them from their diets! In effect, the graphic alone gives no guidance on fats, oils, sweets, beverages, fresh herbs or spices. It makes no distinction between high quality food and highly processed foods.

In reality, healthy food can be delicious and healthy. Ingredients such as oats, dried fruit, dates, maple syrup, seeds, coconut, raw cacao, and many plant-based foods, can be combined to make fantastic desserts which contain no chemicals, no preservatives, and nothing is commercially processed. Other examples include fruit-based sorbets and ice creams, fruit-based pies and pastries, fruit-based beverages such as smoothies, healthy cookies, even healthy fudge. Healthy unprocessed fats may include avocado, coconut, olives, nuts and seeds. Fresh herbs and spices are not depicted on any food guidance graphic even though they provide significant amounts of flavor and nutrition without providing many kcalories.

Fresh spices and herbs are known as flavor profile components which are oftentimes specific to a culture's dietary pattern and commonly consumed dishes and meals. Each culture has a unique flavor profile of commonly used herbs, spices, foods and beverages broadly characteristic of their country of region. A popular flavor profile is Italian. Let's compare a possible Italian flavor profile to a possible American flavor profile. An Italian flavor profile is composed more of single foods, unprocessed foods and not food combinations. It includes herbs, spices and foods such as: basil, oregano, thyme, sage, rosemary, fennel, parsley, garlic, white beans, red pepper, olives, olive oil, capers, balsamic vinegar, tomatoes, eggplant, lemons, buffalo mozzarella, parmesan cheese, fish, shellfish, pasta, gnocchi, coffee, wine, mineral water, etc. **The USA flavor profile might look something like this: McDonald's hamburger / fries / shake, Taco Bell burritos and tacos, Hooter's chicken wings, steak and potatoes, apple pie, chocolate chip cookies, fried chicken, mashed potatoes, hot dogs, baked beans, potato salad, pizza, cheddar cheese, bread, head lettuce salads, salt, pepper, sugar, soda, beer, s'mores, ice cream, jello, and candy bars.** The average American, regardless of being overweight or even obese, having a chronic disease or sickness, usually defends their choices and jokingly mocks healthier dietary patterns.

Another issue is individual foods within a food group may not equally promote health and wellness. Plants and their nutritional components are infinitely complex unless they undergo processing to standardize their appearance, nutrient composition and taste. Food processing almost always strips plants of their valuable components. For example, carrots with a deeper orange coloration usually contain more beta carotene. Purple carrots contain more anthocyanins than orange carrots. In fact, foods within the same food group may widely vary in their nutrient content and how well they contribute to meeting the DRIs.

The bottom line is, government food guidance has failed to address food-related health conditions such as obesity, diabetes, hypertension, heart disease, cancer and other conditions in ways which are substantive, meaningful, sensible, effective, and positive. In fact, it cannot address these issues under the current system. This does not preclude individuals and various organizations which have devised their own dietary guidelines. In fact, several organizations promote more aggressive and potentially useful dietary guidance than the government (e.g., Oldways, the Loma Linda University Vegetarian Diet Pyramid, Physicians Committee for Responsible Medicine), although most of these groups continue to promote the outdated concept of food groupings.

Education is one of the keys to improving nutritional status. For example, nutritional guidance for those living in Arizona may be drastically different for those living in Pennsylvania. Guidance for those living in Mississippi may be different for those living in Washington state. Even within a state, widely variable economic and income status may account for completely different nutritional intakes. This means everyone has a different starting point. **People often discount nutrition education because on many levels, it deals with food, something everyone must deal with on a daily basis.** Most people believe they are "nutrition experts" because they look good, or they are skinny, or they are muscular, or they can do 10 pull ups. This is not necessarily true. Most people don't immediately suffer from their poor food and beverage choices (at least in ways they recognize). **People can make poor food choices for decades before they have a medical event, but they have literally suffered for decades with small almost imperceptible decrements in their health such as short attention span, negativity, brain fog, lack of mental acuity, low job satisfaction, stressful relationships, unable to achieve one's optimal potential, poor digestive functions, inability to participate in normal activities due to obesity, shortness of breath on exertion, bad moods, etc.** This list is almost endless. Once a person begins to pay attention to their diet and improve their nutritional intake, they almost immediately begin to feel better, sleep better, etc. **This places nutrition at the forefront of self-care.** When we learn to adopt good habits, they hopefully begin to crowd out the poor habits to the point the poor habits are replaced. **The new food guidance system introduced in this chapter is based on adopting new, healthy habits. On the next page, you see the current guidance brought to you by the USA government. I think when you see the new system, you will appreciate the new approach.**

Why should most of us change our dietary pattern? **One of the greatest arguments for a good diet and lifestyle is a strong immune system.** Hopefully, Covid-19 has taught us the importance of minimizing underlying conditions such as overweight and obesity, type 2 diabetes, smoker's lungs, gastro-intestinal dysfunction, consumption of dietary and environmental toxins, etc. Many diet and lifestyle-related conditions weaken immunity and lead to the accumulation of new symptoms. Symptoms, if not quickly reverse engineered, may develop into conditions, which develop into diseases, which lead to greater susceptibility to opportunistic pathogens and even premature death. **Disease does not usually appear overnight.** It progresses incrementally over varying periods of time. If caught early in its sequence, it can be reverse engineered. If bad habits continue unabated, you may eventually reap what you have sown, especially if combined with unrelenting stress and lack of protective lifestyle factors.

Another motivating factor to consider when making dietary and lifestyle changes is epigenetics. **Epigenetics is the study of how external factors and lifestyle habits influence our genes.** There are epigenetic aspects related to your dietary pattern and lifestyle habits. Everything we do has the potential to either protect us from bad influences or increase the risk of experiencing a negative outcome. Positive epigenetic

Table 1. Food guidance graphic. USA Previous Food Guidance Graphic: Food Guide Pyramid

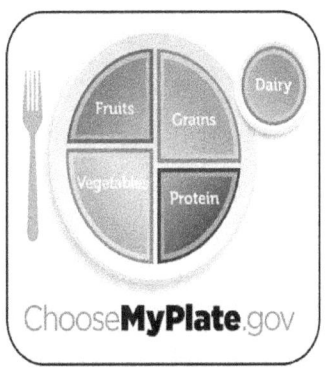

Table 2. Food guidance graphic. USA Current Food Guidance Graphic: Choose My Plate

factors turn off genes responsible for things such as cancer, accelerated aging, heart disease, etc. Other factors such as a poor diet, stress, and lack of protective lifestyle factors may lead to turning off protective genes or activating disease pathways. For example, if you take a 2-hour bike ride on a beautiful sunny day, your body may make the sulfated form of vitamin D, increase your blood and tissue oxygenation, improve your mood, and impact many additional beneficial aspects of your physiology. The simple act of taking a bike ride on a sunny day may turn off up to 80 cancer genes while turning on protective factors. Some cancer-related genes may be turned off for as little as 2 hours while others may be turned off for as long as 2 months. This is an epigenetic effect of many complex biochemical and physiological interactions. Epigenetic influences in our parent's lives may have impacted our health and well-being beginning with the time period right before our conception, during and after our conception, and during our fetal development (time in the womb). At all times throughout our lifespan, we are influenced by epigenetics.

The concept behind the plant-based food guidance system, "Meals matter: Take your pick!" presented in this chapter, is a system for adding healthy foods to your current dietary pattern while addressing potentially harmful habits. At some point after adopting enough healthy habits, hopefully the new habits eventually crowd out the less healthy habits. This food guidance is directed to both the 5% of the population who are highly motivated and readily adopt positive habits without complaining and the 95% who are more resistant to making changes. The first group is an elite group known as the "5% club." The remaining 95% of the population often prefers to cling to their poor habits for a variety of reasons. This group usually requires a major motivating event at which point, they may proceed with small baby steps to make changes which may or may not make much of a difference in their long-term health outcomes. **Regardless of which group you are in, as positive internal and external health**

changes occur, motivation to continue making changes, improves. Drastic changes begat drastic results but small steps also move you forward and are sometimes easier on you and your family.

Another reason this book on Country Living includes this chapter on dietary guidance is the aspect of growing one's food. Every person living in the country or planning a move to the country could benefit from starting a small garden. Even if you are a novice, you may find small scale farming to be healthy and rewarding. This may lead to expanding your garden and even helping others learn useful techniques. Study each plant and determine which ones are your favorites. Then plan to grow some of your favorite plants.

This new system of diet modification primarily targets individual foods and small groups of foods with similar positive properties and a proven track record.
There are still food groups but they are smaller and primarily used to educate the lay public about specific healthy food choices. Each of the groups is associated with a frequency only (not amounts). Instead of copiously counting kcalories every day, the emphasis is on small targeted food groups and frequency of consumption. In most cases frequency is used to improve dietary intake of essential nutrients, fiber and phytochemicals. In some cases, frequency is limiting habits that may be unhealthy such as eating fast food, fatty foods, etc. There are 6 frequency categories and 46 recommendations. The 6 frequency categories are: 1. changes you make at every meal; 2. changes you make once or twice every day; 3. changes you make 4 to 6 times per week; 4. changes you make 2 to 3 times per week; 5. changes you make 1 time per week; and 6. changes you make 0 to 3 times per month. For example, a highly motivated person could choose to eat raw food at every meal or add leafy greens or even brown rice to every meal and it would provide almost immediate and positive benefits. A busy, motivated person could choose to add one or more plant-based sources of omega-3 fatty acids on a daily basis such as eating a handful of walnuts once a day or adding flax or chia seeds to their morning bowl of oatmeal. **Eating an apple a day is another great daily habit!** One benefit of eating an apple is they contain pectin, a type of soluble fiber. Pectin is not absorbed in the small intestine but when it reaches the large intestine, one or more of 500 healthy bacteria present in the large intestine, break down pectin turning it into a fuel for energy production within the colon. Adding a handful of Brazil nuts once per week is associated with positive heart and thyroid benefits.

Keep your current dietary pattern but adopt one or more healthy habits or limit some of your bad habits. Choose a frequency and from that category, add one or more healthy options to your current dietary pattern. This system takes away the frustration of food categories, counting calories, and deciphering the appropriate amounts, and transfers the focus to healthy foods. The ultimate goal is to shift some good choices into your current dietary pattern. As you choose more positive habits, some of the less healthy food choices should decrease in frequency and a new, healthier dietary pattern may emerge. This takes time, but it is more likely to be a permanent change if you see and feel the benefits of your new habits.

Some of the recommended changes are tangential and provide value in various ways. For example, learning how to identify and consume edible wild plants may not have a scientifically "proven" basis but it may be a valuable acquired skill. Just the time it takes to research, forage and learn about edible wild plants may introduce you to a new group of friends, an outdoor hobby, and a "survival" skill if it is ever needed. It feels good to know you will not die because you thought you were eating wild carrots and it was poisonous hemlock. Learning how to incorporate edible flowers into your diet may lead to planting a flower garden and spending more time outdoors. Maybe you want to grow your own apples. After reading the chapter on Orchards, you decide to plant 10 or more apple trees. Leverage one good habit with another one which becomes your passion.

Several options are not strictly food-related. Two categories are water and supplements. Fasting is the third non-food category; they are all health related. One of the weekly to monthly or even yearly options is a water-only 24-72 hour fast. Some promote eating a regular diet for 5 days and fasting or limiting food intake to 25% or less of regular food intake two days per week. Regular and intermittent fasting (e.g., limiting food intake to an 8-hour window, allows the body to go into a mild ketosis) forcing a **powerful biological reset**. This allows the microvilli and villi of the small intestine to return to their "functional" size as well as promoting weight loss and fewer food sensitivities (i.e., gluten).

A near continuously utilized (i.e., frequent meals and snacks) gut may eventually become swollen and edematous. When this occurs, the gut loses its absorptive capacity, especially at the microvilli level. The microvilli are small "fingers" of the gut wall that cover larger villi or "fingers" of the small intestine. The microvilli and villi increase the absorptive capacity of the small intestine to about the size of a tennis court. This allows the gut to extract most of the nutrients from consumed food. When the microvilli and villi become swollen and edematous, the absorptive capacity is compromised. This allows for the absorption of larger compounds which are normally not absorbed until they are more completely broken down. This contributes to food sensitivities, allergies and other complaints.

Another fasting-related benefit is weight loss. **There are 3 ways to lose fat: 1. breathe it out (via vigorous exercise and kcalorie restriction), 2. pee it out (via ketosis), or 3. cut it out (via plastic surgeon).** Breathing out fat breathes it out 1 carbon at a time in the form of CO_2. However, fasting, the most rapid way to achieve ketosis, allows one to pee out fat in 2, 3 and even 4 carbon fragments, known as "ketones." Fasting one day per week or even intermittent fasting on two or three non-consecutive days per week allows one to restore normal gut functions and achieve rapid weight loss. Not everyone can fast for 24-72 hours on a weekly or even monthly basis, but for those who can, there are significant benefits. Check with your physician before beginning a fasting routine.

Reverse engineering the USDAs dietary guidance for the last 80 years and landing on new territory may be necessary to achieve true health and wellness. **It is critical we begin to understand we have been deceived, probably not intentionally, but as a type of collateral damage on our way to modernity.** If you are 80 to 100 years old, you have lived through several significant time periods. You have seen the victory farms of the WW2 era to swanky backyard gardens with their designer raised beds, fancy greenhouses, and chicken coops built for a king. We have also gone from small corner markets to grocery stores with thousands of highly processed, modified, chemical-laden products available, full of sugar, added fat, and other additives to meet the most discriminating tastes. How do we return to a simpler era of whole foods, prepared using healthful methods? How do we get back to the basics after we have eaten like royalty and we are addicted to convenience and highly processed foods? If we stay on this trajectory, where does it lead us? Can we afford to get fatter, accumulate more blockages in our arteries? How long can we afford to pop a pill to treat our type 2 diabetes? Does it bother you when your young children are obese and diagnosed with type 2 diabetes? What does it matter if we walk around with a few extra pounds?

You may be surprised by how much better you feel as you begin to make meaningful changes to your current dietary pattern. For example, in my opinion, the single best thing a person can do for their health is to consume a green smoothie every day (see chapter 21). This accomplishes complex biochemistry with far reaching effects. It is a great way to add important ingredients such as walnuts, yogurt, fresh greens, herbs, spices, enzyme-containing fresh pineapple, vitamin E sources, supplements, etc. If you have the time, go to YouTube and watch Sergei Boutenko's video on the 30-day Green Smoothie Challenge. It provides recipes and good information to motivate your choices.

Use the opportunity of each meal to maximize your health. Every time you eat a healthy meal you are placing your health in the positive column. Every time you implement one or more aspects of a healthy lifestyle, you are placing your health in the positive column. Every meal matters and every lifestyle habit, counts. Learn about the best choices available to you. As you add the good stuff, hopefully it begins to crowd out the bad stuff and the bad habits which have held you hostage for years. I hope this new system is not as overwhelming as it may initially appear. Once you understand the variable is one "new" food or one new habit in a proscribed frequency, you can choose one or more categories and add that positive habit to your current dietary and lifestyle patterns or if indicated, some habits on the graphic should be limited and appear in the lower frequency categories (e.g., limiting meat consumption to 2 to 3 times per week). Each person will choose a different option. It is all about establishing a healthy dietary pattern for you and your family. This does not negate your current dietary pattern or lifestyle but it allows you to move forward with one or more positive changes. Make each meal matter: Take your pick, is designed with you in mind. You are the target and hopefully you are ready to make your meals matter. Hopefully you are ready to restore your health and to wildly pursue the best person you can be. Build a better you, whether you are age 1 to 92! It's never too late to change direction and choose life!

The epigenetics of our lifestyle, how we choose to think, the level of happiness we grasp, the level of frontal lobe function we exhibit (i.e., empathy), the level of cognitive biases we tolerate, the distortions we accept, the degree to which we align our beliefs to Scripture (the highest level of scientific philosophy), the approach we take to relating to our best friend, Jesus, etc. – all of these and more matter. But for now, this chapter is about a new approach to dietary guidance as well as graphics devoted to lifestyle and epigenetic factors. It is about having choices – lots of choices.

Just one bad meal combined with multiple toxic exposures, including psychological distress, may potentially be problematic. One bad lifestyle habit may be dooming your long-term health. Make each meal and lifestyle habit matter. Make them work to your advantage. Tackle the toxic elements of your lifestyle by adopting positive elements to eventually crowd out the bad ones. Start today. Walk with God down this pathway to maximize and energize your positive choices. Don't worry if something healthy and positive is not on the following graphics. You can add it! This system is flexible.

Plant-based Food Guidance — Every Meal Matters: Take Your Pick! ©

Pick a category and serving recommendation below and follow for 30 days to establish a new healthy habit!

Water, 95 – 125 oz/day: alkalized, club soda, deionized, distilled, filtered, lemon, mineral, spring, tap, well, etc.

Could Eat at Every Meal

Leafy Greens, 1 – 3 x/day: arugula, beet greens, bok choy, chard, kale, lettuces, romaine, sorrel, spinach, etc.	
Natural Fats, 1 – 3 x/day: avocado, coconut, olives, nuts, seeds, etc.	**Raw food at every meal**
Rice, 0 – 3 x/day: black, brown, purple, red, wild	**Grains, 0 – 3 x/day:** barley, buckwheat, oats, quinoa, wheat

Servings per day — Could Eat One or More Times per Day (Ideally two to three meals a day)

Alliums, 0 – 3 x/day: chives, garlic, leeks, onions, shallots	**One or two apples a day**
American & Asian Vegetables, 5 – 14 x/week: Beet, bitter melon, cabbage, carrot, celery, gourd, green beans, long bean, pea, pumpkin, radishes, squash, tomato, etc.	
American & Tropical Fruits, 3 – 7 x/day: Apples, apricots, bananas, blueberries, cherries, citrus, coconut, dragon fruit, grapes, grapefruit, guava, kiwi, lemon, lime, mandarins, mangoes, melon, oranges, papaya, passionfruit, peaches, pears, persimmons, pineapple, plum, raspberries, star fruit, strawberries, tangelos, etc.	
Anti-inflammatory Beverages, 0 – 2 x/d: beet, celery, ginger, greens, licorice roots*, pineapple, pomegranate	
Beans / Legumes, 0 – 2 x/day: Black, black eyed peas, cannellini, garbanzo, kidney, pinto, etc.	
Fresh Juices / Green Juice, 0 – 1 x/day: apple, beet, carrot, celery, cucumber, ginger, pineapple, pomegranate	
Fresh Herbs, 1 – 2 x/day: Basil, cilantro, parsley	**Spices, 0 – 2 x/day:** cayenne, cinnamon, ginger, turmeric
Functional Foods & Compounds, 0 – 3 x/day: coconut oil, high antioxidant foods, high fiber, psyllium, etc.	
Herb Teas, 0 – 3 x/day: chamomile, ginger, green tea, hibiscus, lemon balm, mint, peppermint, rooibos, sage, etc.	
Nuts, 1 x/day: Almond, cashew, pecan, peanut, walnut	**Seeds, 1 x/day:** chia, flax, hemp, pumpkin, sunflower
Oils, 1 x/day: avocado, coconut, olive, olive oil mayo	**Omega 3 Foods, 1 x/day:** chia, flax, hemp, walnuts
Prebiotic Foods, 1 – 2 x/day: asparagus, avocado, bananas, barley, chicory, oats, onions, pumpkin seeds, etc.	
Sprouted Grains, Legumes, Seeds, 1 – 2 x/day: bean sprouts, bread (sprouted), microgreens, sprouts, etc.	
Starchy / Root Vegetables, 0 – 3 x/day: cassava, corn, parsnips, plantains, potatoes, sweet potatoes, yams	
Supplements, Dietary Adjuncts, daily: compounds, elements, herbals, minerals, vitamins, B12/cobalamin, etc.	

4 – 5 times a week

Natural Sweeteners, 4 – 5 x / week: Agave, coconut sugar, dates, dried fruits, honey, lucuma, maca powder, maple syrup, monk fruit, molasses (black strap), palm sugar, rapadura, stevia, yacon, etc.

Servings per week 2-3 X /Week

Dairy, 0 – 3 x/wk: cheese, milk, yogurt	**Eggs, 0 – 3 x/wk**	**Lean Clean Meat, 0 – 3 x/wk:** beef, chicken, fish
Desserts, Sweets & Candy, 0 – 2 x/week: cake, cookies, pies, etc.		
Natural Sweeteners, 0 – 5 x/wk: blackstrap molasses, coconut sugar, dates, honey, maple syrup, sorghum, stevia		
Omega-3 Rich Fish, 0 – 2 x/week: tuna, trout, wild salmon, etc.		**Probiotics, 0 – 1 x/week**
Soy*, 0 – 3 x/week: edamame, miso, flour, oil, milk, nuts, protein, protein isolates, soy sauce, tofu, etc.		
White Bread / Refined Grains / White Rice, 0 – 5 x/wk: bread, pasta rice, etc.		

One Serving a Week

Brazil Nuts, 1+ x/wk	**Edible Flowers, 0 – 1 x/wk**	**Refined Sweeteners, 0 – 1 x/wk:** Brown / white sugar
Sea Vegetables, 0 – 1 x/week	**Fermented Food, 0 – 1 x/wk**	**WATER ONLY FAST Day(s), 1 – 2 x/week**

0 – 3 Times a Month

Fast Food, 0 – 2 x/month	**Fried Food, 0 – 2 x/month**
Processed Food, 0 – 3 x/month	**Margarine, refined fats and oils, 0 – 1 x/month**

*Limit / avoid soy if you have thyroid issues.

95 – 125 oz Water Every Day

Eat at Every Meal
Eat these foods at every meal and watch your health improve!

Leafy greens (lightly steamed or raw): Arugula, beet greens, bok choy, chard, collards, endive, greens, kale, lettuce, romaine, sorrel, spinach, w-cress
Natural fats: Avocado, coconut, flax seed, olives, etc.
Raw food at every meal (fruit, vegetables, etc.)
Rice – unrefined (for Asian cultures)
Whole unprocessed grains

Eat One or More Times a Day
Adopt one or more habits from this group.

American fruits (2 – 4+ fruits/day): Apple, apricot, banana, cherry, grapes, kiwi, melons, peaches, pears, persimmons, plums
American & Asian vegetables (eat freely): Asparagus, beets, broccoli, carrots, cabbage, cucumber, eggplant, green bean, jicama, mushroom, pea, potatoes, pumpkin, squash, sweet potatoes, tomatoes, yams, etc.
Apple – an apple a day keeps the doctor away…
Avocado / olive oils (substitute for highly processed unhealthy oils such as rapeseed/canola oil, corn oil, etc.)
Beans / legumes & sprouted seeds (eat a cup or more of beans per day and learn how to prepare broccoli sprouts for a nutritious boost to your sandwich or salad)
Berries (many health benefits for daily consumption): Blueberries, raspberries, strawberries, etc.
Chives, garlic, leeks, onions, shallots
Citrus fruit: Grapefruit, lemon, lime, mandarin, orange, tangelo
Fresh juices / green juice – a top notch habit!
Herbal teas – consume teas to enhance your mood
Hibiscus flower beverages – lower blood pressure
Nuts and Seeds (a handful/day): Almonds, Brazil nuts, chestnuts, chia, flax seeds, hazelnuts, hemp, macadamias, peanuts, pecans, pine nuts, walnuts
Omega-3 rich foods (daily intake important): Chia seeds, flax seeds, hemp seeds, walnuts
Prebiotic foods (helps your gut): Apples, asparagus, bananas, barley, chicory root, chocolate, cacao, dandelion greens, flax seed, garlic, Jerusalem artichoke, leeks, oats, onions, quick ferments (< 1 hour)
Spices: Cardamom, cayenne, cinnamon, ginger, turmeric
Supplements, dietary adjuncts, nutraceuticals
Therapeutic fresh herbs and spices: Basil, cayenne, cilantro, cloves, curcumin, ginger, nutmeg, parsley, sage, thyme, turmeric, etc.
Tropical fruit: Guava, mango, papaya, pineapple

Use Natural Sweeteners 4 to 5 Times a Week
Use sweeteners in limited amounts.
Natural sweeteners: Agave nectar (use sparingly), coconut sugar, dates, dried fruits, honey, lucuma, maca powder, maple syrup, monk fruit, molasses (black strap), palm sugar, rapadura, stevia, yacon, etc.

Eat 2 to 3 Times a Week
Some people do better when limiting these foods to several times per week.

Dairy (small amounts of cow's milk and products): Butter, buttermilk, cheese, cottage cheese, cream, crème fraiche, ice cream, milk, yogurt
Edamame / soybeans / tofu – may negatively impact thyroid and other hormones, best to limit
Eggs (free range)
Lean clean meat (small amounts): Beef, fish, poultry
Pasta / noodles (refined) – concentrated carbs
Pro-biotic foods: Kefir, kimchi, miso, sauerkraut, yogurt
Refined fats: non-hydrogenated margarine, oils
White / refined grains and rice
Whole grain pasta – whole grain pasta packs a lot of carbs

Eat Once a Week
Try something new and healthy while limiting refined and sugary foods to once per week.

Brazil nuts – 2 to 4 Brazil nuts / week for thyroid and heart
Edible flowers: Borage, calendula, hibiscus, lavender, nasturtium, pansy, rose, sage, squash blossoms, violets, etc.
Exotic fruits and vegetables – try something different and more is just as good: Celeriac, dragon, jack fruit, Kohlrabi, parsnips, passion fruit, star fruit, etc.
Fermented foods – use at least several times a month to improve gut microbiome (quick ferments are also beneficial): injera, kefir, kimchi, miso, pickled foods, sauerkraut, sourdough bread, tempeh, etc.
Refined sweeteners / brown or white sugar – limit
Sea vegetables – try something novel: Agar, arame, carrageenan, dulse, kombu, nori, wakame
Water only fasting day(s) – up to 2 day per week for weight control and disease prevention
Wild grasses / wild rice / wild edible plants – try something novel

Limit to Several Times a Month if at All
Alcohol – Eliminate for best health!
Fast food – Limit to several times a month
Fried food – limit to several times a month for optimum health!
Margarine and processed oils (best to avoid): canola, soy, vegetable oils, hydrogenated margarines, etc.
Processed food – limit for optimum health!

Category	Every Meal	1+ x Day	4 – 5 x Week	2 – 3 x Week	1 x Week	1 – 3 x Month	0 – 6 x Year*
Raw Food/ Salad	X	X					
Leafy Greens	X	X	X				
Garlic, Onions, Shallots	X	X	X	X			
Natural Fats	X	X	X	X			
Berries	X	X	X	X	X		
Rice, Unrefined	X	X	X	X	X		
Therapeutic Herbs and Spices	X	X	X	X	X		
Herbal Teas	X	X	X	X	X	X	
Supplements / Adjuncts / Nutraceuticals	X	X	X	X	X	X	
95 – 125 oz Water / day		X					
American Fruit		X	X				
American & Asian Vegetables		X	X				
Citrus Fruit		X	X				
Omega 3 Rich Foods		X	X				
Apples, one to two apples a day		X	X	X			
Beans / Legumes		X	X	X			
Fresh / Green Juice		X	X	X	X		
Nuts / Seeds		X	X	X	X		
Root Vegetables		X	X	X	X		
Avocado / Olive / Nut Oils		X	X	X	X	X	
Hibiscus Flower Beverages		X	X	X	X	X	
Sprouted Seeds / Grains		X	X	X	X	X	
Tropical Fruit		X	X	X	X		
Brazil Nuts			X	X	X		
Natural Sweeteners			X	X	X		
Exotic Fruits and Vegetables			X	X	X	X	
Pre-biotic Foods			X	X	X	X	
Pro-biotic Foods			X	X	X		
Edible Flowers, Wild Plants, Grasses			X	X	X	X	X
Sea Vegetables			X	X	X	X	X
Eggs (Free Range)				X	X	X	
Fermented Foods				X	X	X	
Pasta / Noodles				X	X	X	
Rice, White				X	X	X	
White / Refined Grains				X	X	X	
Dairy: cheese, yogurt, ricotta, ice cream				X	X	X	X
Lean Clean Meat				X	X	X	X
Refined Fats				X	X	X	X
Soybeans / Tofu				X	X	X	X
Refined Sweeteners					X	X	X
Water Only Fasting Day					X	X	X
Fast Food						X	X
Fried and Processed Foods						X	X
Alcohol (best to eliminate)							X

*Not part of the graphic representations and considered non-essential
To download a color copy of this guide, go to www.buildabetteryou.us

Take Your Pick! Sample Plant-based Breakfast Menus ©

1 – Oatmeal		Oatmeal w/ grated apple, cinnamon, blond raisins, walnuts, sweetener, green smoothie with pineapple, cucumber, greens, ginger, mint, protein powder
2 – Waffles		Whole grain waffles w/ nut butter, syrup, applesauce, cinnamon, blueberry smoothie w/ protein powder and a few fresh basil leaves
3 – Asian		Short grain brown rice w/steamed vegetables and marinated tofu / protein w/ fresh parsley, apple slices, and herbal tea
4 – Omelette		Vegetable omelette w/ black rice, feta, avocado, spinach, jalapeno, and tomatoes, served with hibiscus tea w/ lemon and chia seeds
5 – Roasted veg		Scrambled tofu (or eggs) and quinoa served in roasted poblano pepper, roasted fingerling potatoes, roasted cherry tomatoes served with greens in light vinaigrette alongside fresh apple or orange or tangelo juice
6 – Burritos		Whole grain tortilla, pinto beans, scrambled eggs or tofu, avocado, spinach or other greens, black rice, cheese (optional), chipotle sauce, salsa, apple slices, fresh squeezed grapefruit juice
7 – Smoothie bowl		Blackberry smoothie w/ cantaloupe, honeydew, kiwi, banana, raspberries, sunflower seeds, chia seeds, mint, served w/ breakfast cookie, banana bread, muffin or granola bar
8 – Cornbread		Corn bread or sweet polenta (grits) with plant-based butter, honey, fruit and yogurt parfait with strawberries, blueberries, kiwi, coconut yogurt or whipped cream, mint, walnuts, pumpkin seeds, fresh juice
9 – Root hash		Carrots, potatoes, sweet potatoes, onion, parsnips, celeriac, turnip and tofu hash browns served w/ avocado, tomato, onion, basil, white beans, lemon, garlic, olive oil and salt, apple slices and fresh carrot juice
10 – Crepes		Buckwheat crepes with fresh fruit, poppy seeds, coconut whipped cream, walnuts, Brazil nuts, piña colada smoothie made with some fresh greens
11 – Fritatta		Vegetable frittata, hummus, Greek yogurt, olives, cherry tomatoes, cucumber, pita, red onion, baked potato wedges, grapes, figs, apple slices, nuts, hibiscus tea
12 – Pancakes		Blueberry corn cakes with blueberry sauce, syrup, fruit salad, nuts, coconut whipped topping and green or herbal tea
13 – Pudding		Coconut milk, chia seeds, apricot jam, fresh fruit, pepitos, blueberry muffin, fresh juice
14 – Potato dish		Potato casserole, plant-based sausage patty, parsley sauce, tomato slices, avocado slices, cucumber slices, apple slices, kale-celery-apple juice
15 – Sweet rolls		Apple & nut sweet rolls, bowl of fresh berries, vanilla protein shake
16 – Avocado toast		Bread, avocado, scrambled eggs / tofu, tomato, jalapeno, feta, red onion, basil, fresh OJ
17 – Toast		Whole grain seeded bread, peanut butter, applesauce, orange, hot chocolate (or carob)
18 – Coffeecake		Blueberry poppy seed coffee cake, fruit kabob, nuts, hot beverage
19 – Fritters		Zucchini fritters, black beans, chipotle sauce, greens, sliced citrus fruit, lime chia water
20 – Strudel		Apple / fruit / nut filled puff pastry strudel, coconut chia pudding, fresh fruit, hot drink
21 – French		French toast with fresh fruit, maple syrup, whipped topping, nuts, high protein smoothie

Take Your Pick! Sample Plant-based Lunch Menus ©

1 – Lentils & potatoes		Roasted new potatoes, onion, red pepper, zucchini w/ lentils, parsley and plant-based sour cream, apple slices, hibiscus / lemon / mint iced tea
2 – Soup & salad		Vegetable quinoa soup, croutons with kale cranberry salad, licorice root iced tea
3 – Baked potato		Baked potato, sour cream, cheese, Greek salad w/ garbanzos, cranberry lemonade
4 – Nachos		Black corn chips, pinto beans, cheese, red pepper, onions, fresh greens in light vinaigrette, jalapeno, salsa, plant-based sour cream, mineral water
5 – Asian bowl		Edamame, black rice, kimchi (or shredded cabbage), carrots, green onion, tofu, bok choy or other greens, avocado, black seeds, ginger peanut or teriyaki sauce, tea
6 – Pasta salad		Pasta salad with cherry tomatoes, broccoli, red pepper, red onion, feta, carrots, olives, walnuts, golden raisins, cucumbers, jalapenos, white beans, sauce (pesto, ranch or chipotle, etc.), apple slices, carrot juice
7 – Sandwich / wrap		Roasted vegetable sandwich with hummus, feta, coleslaw, apple, fresh juice
8 – Tomato soup		Roasted red pepper and tomato soup with pesto or avocado toast, garbanzo bean salad, apple slices, tea or fresh carrot juice
9 – Pizza		Pizza with tomato sauce, roasted vegetables, garlic sautéed spinach, cheese, pesto, fresh basil with arugula and spinach salad, apple, lemonade
10 – Veggie burger		Whole grain roll w/ veggie burger patty, arugula in vinaigrette, chipotle sauce, fresh beefsteak tomato slices, roasted vegetables, jalapeno, red onion, steak fries, apple, hibiscus iced tea
11 – Ancient grains bowl		Quinoa, hemp, bulgur, sweet potato, roasted onions, portobello mushroom, zucchini, avocado, hemp seed pesto, greens in vinaigrette, pineapple, ginger apple & kale juice
12 – Southern sides		Black-eyed peas, corn on the cob, coleslaw, mashed potatoes with gravy, squash and cheese casserole, fried or baked okra, apple pie, hibiscus iced tea
13 – Haystacks / tacos		Black corn chips, pinto beans, shredded lettuce / cabbage / carrots, tomatoes, onions, jalapenos, cilantro, cheese, salsa, hot sauce, sour cream, guacamole, hibiscus lemonade
14 – Spaghetti		Spaghetti, roasted tomato sauce, garlic, zucchini, mushrooms, parmesan, spinach salad, pecan balls, apple, limeade
15 – Gnocchi		Gnocchi, roasted red pepper tomato sauce, onion, basil, white bean salad, steamed broccoli, garlic bread, kale lemonade, kiwi / strawberry / lychee fruit salad
16 – Braised garbanzos		Garbanzos, eggplant, okra, harissa tomato sauce, parsley, pecan balls, rice, mango lassie
17 – Ramen bowl		Ramen noodles, vegetables, gluten, coconut tomato broth, sesame seeds, green tea
18 – Pizza		Pizza w/ pesto, sautéed mushrooms, caramelized onions, cheese, salad, apple, lemonade
19 – Pad Thai		Pad Thai with tofu or lean meat, spring rolls, miso soup, green salad
20 – Quesadilla		Quesadilla with black beans or lean meat, avocado, roasted red peppers and red onion, plant protein, salsa, green onions, apple slices, strawberry chia mint lemonade
21 – Cobb salad		Brown rice, fresh cut corn, red pepper, red onion, white beans, asparagus, avocado, romaine lettuce, jalapeno, plant protein, dressing, limeade, nut brownie

Take Your Pick! Sample Plant-based Dinner Menus ©

1 – Pot pie	Pot pie w/ vegetables, protein, puff pastry, mashed potatoes, green salad, pumpkin bread, tea
2 – Risotto	Wild mushroom risotto, roasted asparagus, kale salad with garbanzo beans, garlic croutons, lime-aid with mineral water, apple slices, date bar
3 – Nut loaf	Nut, legume and grain-based loaf with herb topping, mashed potatoes, gravy, green beans, salad, pear and beet juice beverage, raspberry pie with coconut ice cream
4 – Stew	Vegetable lentil stew, scalloped potatoes, watercress salad, pear, peach and hibiscus tea
5 – Stir fry	Vegetable stir fry with tofu or other protein, vegetables, spring rolls w/ peanut sauce, miso soup, matcha coconut ice cream, tea
6 – Panang curry	Curry with broccoli, red peppers, protein / tofu, fresh basil, brown basmati or jasmine rice, garlic naan, mango lassi
7 – Chili	Bean-vegetable chili, baked potato, beet and goat cheese salad, piña colada fresh juice
8 – Fajitas	Fajitas w/ roasted red pepper, poblanos, onions, green onions, portobello mushrooms, tofu or meat substitute, Spanish rice, chips, salsa, chipotle sauce, guacamole, lime wedges, apple slices, cantaloupe slush
9 – Mezza	Lebanese rice, vegetable shish kabobs, falafel balls, hummus, tabouleh, baba ghanoush, tzatziki, olives, cherry tomatoes, stuffed grape leaves, pita bread, grapes, pomegranate, apricots, hibiscus iced tea, vanilla pudding
10 – Fettuccini	Fettuccine alfredo using cashew-based sauce, roasted asparagus and cherry tomato halves, steamed broccoli, fava bean mash, romaine and avocado salad with balsamic Dijon mustard dressing, melon fizz
11 – Crepes	Wild rice and plant-based chicken crepes, pan roasted potatoes with rosemary, watercress salad with feta, pear, candied walnuts, mineral water with citrus, flan
12 – Enchiladas	Black bean, corn, quinoa enchiladas, kale salad, chips, guacamole, salsa, sweet potato fries with chipotle sauce, apple, honeydew limeade, cinnamon rolls
13 – Glorioso	Mushrooms, sautéed in plant-based butter with lots of garlic and parsley, over pasta, Parmesan, white bean puttanesca salad, garlic bread, pear, grape juice, Italian cookie
14 – Fried rice	Fried rice with plant-based chicken, egg, carrots, green peas, green onion, broccoli, sesame seeds, garlic, jalapeno, miso soup, blueberry and basil coconut ice cream w/blueberry sauce
15 – Green curry	Green curry w/ protein, broccoli, green peas, red pepper, basil, basmati rice, mango lassie
16 – Macaroni	Mac & cheese, roasted vegetables, sofrito, salad, pumpkin seeds, pear, ice cream w fruit sauce
17 – Lentils	Lentils, roasted cauliflower, tahini sauce, pine nuts, hummus, pita, apple slices, green mint coconut smoothie
18 – Lasagna	Lasagna roll-ups with spinach, sautéed zucchini, salad w/ garbanzos, sorbet, fruit, lemonade
19 – Veg steak	Gluten steaks (or other protein) with mushroom gravy, twice baked potatoes, salad, steamed broccoli, apple, cranberry juice, strawberry pie with coconut strawberry basil ice cream
20 – Red lentils	Red lentil dahl, basmati rice, onion or spinach fritters, cilantro chutney, tamarind chutney, garlic naan, fresh cucumbers and tomatoes, mango ice cream
21 – Portobello	Portobello mushroom steak with creamy sauce, lentils, roasted vegetables, steak fries, melon slush, apple pie with vanilla ice cream and cinnamon sauce

Plant-based Shopping Guide

Beans / legumes
Beans, assorted
Black
Fava
Garbanzos
Giant
Lentils, brown / green / red
Pinto
White

Beverages
Barley, roasted
Chicory
Cranberry juice
Grape juice
Hibiscus
Mineral water
Pomegranate juice
Tea, assorted

Dairy / eggs
Butter (Plant-based)
Coconut yogurt
Cottage cheese (Plant-based)
Cream cheese (Plant-based)
Eggs
Feta cheese (goat cheese)
Greek yogurt
Mizithra (sheep/goat cheese)
Mozzarella, fresh
Parmesan
Ricotta cheese
Sour cream

Fats
Avocado, avocado oil
Flax seed oil
Nut / seed butters
Olives, black
Olives, green
Olives, Kalamata
Olives, other
Olive oil, other oils

Fruit
Apples
Apricots
Bananas
Berries, assorted
Cantaloupe
Cherries
Cranberries
Dried, assorted
Figs
Grapefruit
Grapes
Honeydew
Kiwi
Lemons / limes
Mandarin
Mango
Oranges
Papaya
Passion fruit
Peaches
Pears
Persimmon
Pineapple
Pomegranate
Tangelo
Watermelon

Grains (reg / sprouted)
Bread, assorted
Bulgur
Cereals, assorted
Chips, assorted
Couscous
Croissants
Pasta, assorted
Popcorn
Puff pastry dough
Quinoa
Rice, assorted

Herbs, fresh
Basil
Cilantro
Dill
Mint
Oregano
Parsley
Rosemary
Sage
Thyme

Herbs/spices, dried
Cinnamon, Ceylon
Cloves
Cumin
Nutmeg

Nuts / seeds (and butters)
Almonds
Cashews
Flax seeds
Macadamia
Pecans
Pine nuts
Pistachios
Seeds, assorted
Walnuts

Pantry items
Balsamic vinegar
Canned goods
Capers
Chocolate
Coconut milk, canned
Condiments
Flour, assorted
Honey
Miso, assorted
Sun dried tomatoes
Sweeteners
Tomato paste
Vinegars, others

Protein foods
Analogs
Assorted
Lean meats
Tofu

Vegetables
Choose seasonal and fresh
Asparagus
Beets
Bitter melon
Broccoli
Butternut squash
Cabbage (red, green)
Carrots
Cauliflower
Celery
Cucumbers
Eggplant
Garlic
Green beans, long beans
Greens, assorted
Lettuce, assorted
Mushrooms
Okra
Onions, assorted
Peas
Peppers, bell
Peppers, hot
Potatoes
Pumpkin
Squash
Sweet potatoes
Tomato
Zucchini

Miscellaneous

Lifestyle Guidance – Make Each Lifestyle Habit Count: Take Your Pick! ©
Pick a recommendation below and follow for 30 days to establish a new healthy habit!

Could do 1 – 2 or more times a day
Meditate on God's Word: Pray, claim God's promises, read/listen to Scripture, read inspiring books, etc.
5,000 – 20,000 steps (or more) / day (3 – 10 miles): walking, jogging, running, daily activity
20 – 40 minutes of sunlight: avoid peak sun, expose as much skin as possible
Fresh outside air: forest bathing, hiking, trail biking, gardening, farming, outdoor life, etc.
A lovely dominion over animals: walking the dog, brushing your animals, companionship with animals, caring for your animal's needs, feeding them, caring for their health, talking with them, etc.
7.5 hours of refreshing sleep (nightly): need five 90-minute sleep cycles (preferably consecutive), good ventilation, fresh air, minimize disturbing noises, clean sleeping environment, etc.
Daily shower: shower/bathe daily to remove toxins, keep hair clean, showers are serotonergic
Avoid known toxins: alcohol, sugar, chemical-laden foods, tobacco, air fresheners, drugs, etc.
Earthing / grounding: barefoot contact with the earth, ground your bed, spend time in nature, etc.
Drink a total of 95 – 125 ounces fresh pure water per day: includes high water fruits and vegetables
Companionship and fellowship with others, active social network: talk with others, stay in touch, keep communication open with family and friends, etc.
Keep your mind active: reading, puzzles, math problems, avoid TV, avoid video games, etc.
Demonstrate gratitude, positivity and thankfulness toward God, faith in the human experience, etc.
Improve core strength and do resistance exercises: plank, pilates, squats, sit-ups, pull-ups, bands, etc.
Active hobbies: gardening, cleaning, mowing, walking, swimming, tennis, dancing, soccer, ultimate, etc.
Be a positive voice seeking solutions: gratitude, thankfulness, humility, patience, are virtues to seek
Avoid gossip at all costs: lift up people, avoid highlighting the plight of others unless you are a positive part of solution, guard each man's dignity
Spend 15 – 30 minutes cleaning your living environment: including your car, office, home, yard, etc.
Deep breathing: deep breathing improves blood oxygenation and stimulates the lymphatic system, make sure to do 3 – 5 deep purposeful breaths every hour you are awake (mouth closed)
Make every meal matter: Eat meals that matter and improve your health
Listen to or play beautiful music: Keeps your brain active, helps make memories, etc.
Speak words of affirmation to your loved ones
Sacrificial acts for others: Take time to witness to others as Christ does for us
Acts of kindness: Kindness goes a long way when directed toward those who are suffering or angry
Avoid debt like the plague, pay your bills 2 to 3 months ahead, financially help others when possible.
Others:

Lifestyle Guidance – Make Each Lifestyle Habit Count: Take Your Pick! ©
Pick a recommendation below and follow for 30 days to establish a new healthy habit!

Could do 2 – 6 Times per Week

Check in with elderly relative, friend or neighbor: stay in touch with those who are not highly mobile.

Set aside time to clean house, make repairs, work on projects

Personal ministry and outreach: pray for others, deliver food to shut-ins, chores for others, prison ministry, feed the homeless, etc.

Write a letter, keep a journal: write thank you notes, letters to your relatives and friends, stay in touch the old-fashioned way, keeping a journal is a good way to jog your memory about events in the past

Read a book: reading expands your world and broadens your perspective on life, keeps you from being boring, improves your vocabulary, and gives you things to discuss with others

Go to the gym, on a hike, long walk, bike ride, rock climb, ski, etc.

Stay in touch with your grandparents, parents, adult children, aunts, uncles, cousins, etc.

The Bible advises working 6 days a week and resting on one day, the Sabbath day! Work provides a means to maintain financial independence and accountability to society.

Minimize toxins in your environment: clean water, fresh air, natural cleaning products, organic food

Other:

Could do Once a Week

Go to church and Bible study: fellowship with others at church and with your Bible study group

Take one day of rest per week: Remember the Sabbath day to keep it holy, our body's follow a circaseptan cycle of needing 1 day of every 7 days to rest, reset and refresh

Trim & care for your nails & skin: keep nails trimmed and healthy, free from fungus and infections,

Other:

Could do 1 – 2 Times per Month

Hydrotherapy, epsom salt soak, massage, float tank, etc.: relaxing and promotes circulation, etc.

Other:

Could do 1 – 10 Times per Year

Learn a new skill: learn how to bake bread, change car's oil, power wash your home, etc.

Volunteer your services: work at a free medical clinic, food distribution to elderly and poor

Mission or service type vacations: plant trees, build a church or school, etc.

Active vacations: canoe, kayak, ski, construction, etc.

Deep clean your living areas: Pass on your used items to those in need, donate your unused clothes, furniture, appliances, etc. Give canned food to the needy.

Other:

References and resources

- Marion Nestle and Ted Wilson (2012) in Chapter 22 Food Industry and Political Influences on American Nutrition, in Nutritional Health: Strategies for Disease Prevention, N.J. Temple et al, (eds.). Springer Science+Business Media, LLC.
- https://www.youtube.com/watch?v=JXKuWcB0cl0&t=35s – Lecture by Thomas Levy, MD, JD at Silicon Valley (this is an important lecture to hear).
- https://en.wikipedia.org/wiki/History_of_USDA_nutrition_guides#:~:text=The%20USDA's%20first%20nutrition%20guidelines,Atwater%20as%20a%20farmers'%20bulletin.
- https://shorturl.at/axMNW

Discussion Questions

1. Which 3 or 4 picks would you make on the Plant-based food guide graphic, Every Meal Matters, Take Your Pick!?

2. What meal would you add to the Plant-based Breakfast, Lunch or Dinner menus?

3. What lifestyle factor would you be most willing to add?

Chapter 18

Vaccine detoxification: before and after

There is no intent to convince you to vaccinate or not vaccinate yourself and / or your children. You need to have this conversation with your family and with your trusted experts. Spend time in prayer and do extensive research and due diligence before deciding whether or not you are willing to vaccinate your family and if you decide to vaccinate, which vaccines you are willing to receive. This chapter is intended to assist you if you do decide to get a vaccine. Detoxing does not change the primary function of the vaccine, but it may minimize the effects of the other ingredients. When you bump up your health and immunity, a vaccine may not have the same side effects. This is a good example of a pertinent negative. A pertinent negative is taking pro-active steps to PREVENT a negative outcome or consequence of a planned action. For example, if you keep vitamin D levels high, you are going to be more immune to ingested and even directly injected toxins than a person with a lower vitamin D level. If you choose to get a vaccine, intense and deliberate preparation in advance of receiving a vaccine is wise.

Not all vaccines are equal. The antigenic material, used to prime the immune system to make a defensive response to a specific pathogenic microorganism, varies. Some are attenuated (weakened) and some are inactivated. Some are recombinant material and others contain an inactivated toxin. With the emergence of Covid-19, mRNA and DNA-based vaccines are being rapidly developed and distributed. Pfizer and Moderna use new technology which injects modified mRNA into your body, programmed to direct cells to make specific proteins. Johnson & Johnson use DNA and a modified cold virus (i.e., a type of corona virus) to get into the cell's nucleus and using mRNA, make spike proteins which are recognized as "foreign" and activate the immune system. In the future when exposed to a spike protein, the immune system fights off the more dangerous corona virus, SARS-CoV-2, and allegedly you won't get sick or you will have a mild case. Pfizer and Moderna vaccines require two doses and the Johnson & Johnson vaccine requires one dose. Other vaccines such as Sputnik V is made in Russia and has been widely distributed around the world. It claims a 91.6% efficiency and 100% efficiency against severe cases. It is based on two human adenovirus viral vectors, a long-known and well-tested vaccine technology. It contains a gene which encodes the full spike protein and requires two doses. Other companies have similar type vaccines in various stages of development and approval. The recently approved Novavax covid vaccine is a traditional purified protein of the Covid-19 virus and is mixed with adjuvants to stimulate the body's immune response.

Another option besides a vaccine is to shore up and rely 100% on your immune system in combination with a hygienic lifestyle in combination with the option to use medications such as ivermectin and hydroxychloroquine (HCQ), and their vitamin and mineral adjuncts. The recovery rate from covid is high; for ages 0 to 19 years – 99.997%; for 20 to 49 years – 99.98%; for 50 to 69 years – 99.5%; 70+ years – 94.6% (Covid-19 survival rates cited by CDC although the CDC may not be the source of these numbers; source: Austin American Statesman, 23 Dec 2020). Even if these survival rates change over time or marginally adjust, survival at this time is high. If your vitamin D is high, you take in a diet rich in vitamins and minerals, you avoid sugar and processed foods, and to the degree possible, you avoid a diet and lifestyle which exposes you and your family to agricultural and manufacturing toxins, you will likely fare well. Unfortunately, none of us are "bullet proof" when it comes to illness. Each illness comes with its own unique parameters in combination with our current condition.

In the case of vaccines, children are not small adults. **A child's immune system is not fully developed and functional until sometime in their mid to late 20s.** This means for every vaccine received, they must rely on a relatively immature immune system to deal with directly injected vaccine ingredients. Children's health at the time they reach puberty and throughout puberty sets the stage for the quality of health for the rest of their lives.

Vaccines contain antigenic material, cell culture ingredients used to nourish the antigen, adjuvants (chemicals used to enhance the immune response and stimulate it to recognize and then make antibodies against the pathogenic microorganism), stabilizers, preservatives, inactivating ingredients such as formaldehyde, and antibiotics such as neomycin. Adjuvants may include aluminum, designer lipids and oils, and a synthetic form of DNA. All vaccine ingredients are referred to as excipients.

If you have genetic or metabolic issues, it may be a good idea to get genetic testing to determine the robustness of your methylation pathways. If you have a defect in these pathways, you may have weak endogenous detoxification pathways and may need to take additional measures to detox. The test is known as a MTHFR test. Some have proposed, weak methylation pathways might be related to a riboflavin deficiency as well as deficiencies of niacin, pyridoxine, folate and cobalamin. Other deficiencies may also be involved. Take a B-complex "50" once or twice a day if you suspect you might be susceptible to one or more B vitamin deficiencies.

It may be preferable to receive vaccinations during warm but not hot months, for those living in the northern hemisphere, this is April through June. Always get a copy of the administering nurse, supervising physician, vaccination insert, amount given, lot number, and route of administration for your records. Take a before and after picture and / or video of the vaccine site and a whole-body picture (wearing only undies) if possible, to document your baseline physical condition.

The human body is capable of incredible detoxification processes. Most toxins enter through the lungs, skin, and mouth and are eliminated through the lungs, skin, kidneys, gut / intestine, and a variety of body fluids, including breast milk, tears, semen, menses, sputum, etc. Toxins are not physiological to the body. The body will seek to eliminate toxins when possible through every possible route out of the body (i.e., any opening in the body will serve as an elimination route for toxins).

The gut is one of the primary gate-keepers against toxins. A healthy gut will pass along common toxins for rapid elimination. However, if the gut is not healthy, toxins are more likely to cause problems. The body's organs detoxify as does most cells. Once a toxin enters the body, the lungs, lymphatic system and the liver are one of many hubs of detoxification activities as well as the kidneys, skin, and the gut. There are at least two phases of liver detoxification. Phase one involves cytochrome p450 enzymes which transform fat-soluble toxins and prepares them for the next phase of detoxification. **B vitamins, vitamin A, vitamin E, vitamin D, glutathione and the many various plant chemicals known as flavonoids are needed in this phase.** Phase two takes the by-products of phase one and prepares them for elimination by making them water-soluble. **Nutrients needed for phase two include B vitamins, amino acids, glutathione, and water.** Toxins not eliminated reside within the body, usually in fat depots, bones, the liver (causing liver "congestion"), joints, tissues, and muscles.

J. H. Tilden (1851 – 1940), a physician known as the **Father of Natural Hygiene**, wrote much about the theory of toxemia. **He recognized the role of stress in causing disease.** He wrote extensively about the causes of disease. Here are a few of his quotes:

> "There is no disease per se. What is called disease is impaired health, and is brought on from retention of waste products in the blood. These waste products are called toxins, and in normal and limited amounts, are natural and give a needed stimulation. But, like all stimulants, when an excessive amount is retained in the system, they create over-stimulation, resulting in enervation – or toxemia.
>
> Every so-called disease is a crisis of toxemia; which means toxins have accumulated in the blood above the toleration point, and the crisis, the so-called disease – call it cold, "flu" pneumonia, headache – is a vicarious elimination. Nature is endeavoring to rid the body of toxins."

There are many more excellent quotes. I recommend you download and read his free book, "Impaired Health: It's Cause and Cure." http://whale.to/a/tildencomp.html See Figure 1., below.

Figure 1. Screenshot of web page to download J. H. Tilden's book, Impaired Health: It's Cause and

It may be worth your time to consult with an experienced and successful naturopath or another professional about your current condition before you to choose to receive a vaccine. There are many reasons people negatively react to a vaccine. First, there is the composition of the vaccine, the condition of the person at the time of the vaccine, the patency of the immune system, the toxin load / status, the stress level at the time of the vaccine, etc. **At this time, there is no study which defines risk factors for a negative vaccine outcome.** Such a study would help to provide guidance for avoiding adverse effects of a vaccine. In the absence of this information, if you choose to receive a vaccine, at a minimum, you may want to read through the following suggestions:

1. Pray about making the right decision.
2. Give this decision adequate due diligence and get to the point where you feel 100% comfortable with receiving a specific vaccine.
3. Schedule your vaccine on a day off or on a day where you are not overly stressed out.
4. Be positive and affirming during your vaccine appointment.
5. Schedule your vaccine during morning hours. A recent study showed elderly patients receiving the flu vaccine developed significantly larger increases in antibody concentration (this is considered good) when receiving the flu shot in the morning versus the afternoon. This may or may not translate to other types of vaccines.
6. The time of the year may also matter. You want to get a vaccine as close to the time of highest transmission as possible. This means, if you are getting a flu vaccine, do it just before the flu season begins, not 2 or 3 months before the flu season begins. Again, this may not apply to all types of vaccines. Just an aside, because it is impossible to predict which strain of the flu will be prevalent, I think this increases the risk of the flu vaccine, possibly to the point of avoiding it. I have personally observed numerous cases where elderly persons have had serious cognitive decrements for months after the flu shot. Again, you must decide for yourself and in consultation with trusted medical professionals which vaccine(s) you are willing to receive.
7. Make sure you are well hydrated for several days before receiving a vaccine. Avoid all artificial beverages. Avoid caffeinated beverages.
8. Avoid sugar and processed foods for 1 month before receiving a vaccine.
9. Avoid as many other environmental, food and water toxins at least 1 month before receiving a vaccine (see paragraph below).
10. Make sure you are consuming adequate amounts of protein for several weeks before the vaccination. This allows your body to produce antibodies to the vaccine's antigen(s).
11. Make sure you are well-nourished for at least a month if not several months before a vaccine.
12. Make sure you take generous amounts of vitamins and minerals for at least a month before.
13. Ensure your immune and detoxification systems are working well for several months before receiving a vaccine. For example, if you are sick, constipated, have a rash of unknown origin, have chest or sinus congestion, if you have a breakout on your face, if you feel weak and constantly fatigued, if you have brain fog, if your joints ache a lot, if your muscles easily tire and become sore, if you are unable to get a refreshing night of rest, etc., you may not be in a condition to easily detox vaccine adjuvant ingredients, aimed at stimulating your body's antibody response. It may be a good idea to see a functional physician, naturopath, or a highly experienced nutritionist to explore detoxification options before and after receiving a vaccine.
14. I strongly recommend following a detox protocol described later in this chapter as well as the protocol for before and after a vaccine. The detox protocol involves at least one month of taking high dose niacin in combination with at least 2 saunas per week. This initiates a powerful combination of detoxification methods aimed at enhancing the body's natural detox systems, while restoring balance to natural routes of toxin elimination.
15. If possible, right before and right after receiving a vaccination, spend time earthing or in direct contact with the ground. This could be at a park, on a walk, or playing with your dog.

Vaccines are actually a minor source of toxins (although vaccines are delivered directly into the body without going through the stomach and small intestines and with the opportunity for transformation and fecal elimination). This in no way minimizes their significance. Common sources of toxins include (see www.immune-health-solutions-for-you.com): <u>cigarette smoke</u> (benzene, lead, arsenic, acetone), <u>auto exhaust</u> (benzene, carbon monoxide, formaldehyde), <u>volatile organic compounds or VOCs</u> (paint, paint strippers, adhesives, cleaning products), <u>mercury</u> (fish, some vaccines, pesticides, emissions), <u>cadmium</u> (batteries, plastics, insecticides), <u>glyphosate</u> (systemic herbicide, soy and most soy products, some wheat, testosterone preparations, 750+ products in USA contain glyphosate), <u>aluminum</u> (some cookware, antacids, skin creams, dandruff shampoo, antiperspirants), <u>excitotoxins</u> (food additives, hydrolyzed protein in processed food, MSG), <u>pesticides and herbicides</u>, <u>carcinogens</u> (dioxin, radiation, asbestos, vinyl chloride used to make plastics), <u>formaldehyde</u> (preservative, printer toners, building materials, body preservative, air-fresheners), <u>naphthalene</u> (air fresheners), <u>phthalates</u> (dryer sheets, flexible plastics, solvents, vinyl flooring, adhesives, detergents, lubricating oils, automotive plastics, nail polishes, hair spray), <u>chlorine and chloroform</u> (bleach, pools, released from chlorine containing water in a hot shower), <u>fluorine / fluoride</u> (toothpaste, water), <u>bromine</u> (pool water, flame retardants, BVO found in some sodas, brominated white flour, plastics, dye, prescription drugs), <u>acetaminophen</u> (reduces level of glutathione), <u>lead</u> (paint, equipment, ammunition, polluted soil and water), <u>polychlorinated biphenyls</u> (lubricants, electrical equipment), <u>household cleaners</u> (acetone, benzenes), <u>radiation</u> (microwaves, X-rays, UV from sunlight), <u>electromagnetic fields or EMFs</u> (cell phones, electric blankets, computers, TV screens, cell phone towers), <u>Perc</u> (used as a solvent in dry cleaning), <u>acetone</u> (automobile exhaust, industrial emissions), <u>aflatoxin</u> (moldy nuts such as peanuts / peanut butter), <u>aromatic hydrocarbons</u> (fuel, solvents), <u>nitrosamines</u> (smoked and cured foods, hot dogs, bologna, etc.), <u>benzopyrenes</u> (fuel exhaust, BBQ foods), <u>per-fluorinated chemicals</u> (non-stick cookware, non-stain carpets, etc.). **This is a small subset of many toxins which could have be on this list.**

The previous paragraph describing toxins and their potential sources is included primarily to put into perspective the average human's exposure to undisclosed and unknown toxins in our immediate environment. Even ethanol is a toxin most adults willingly imbibe.

Toxins affect almost every aspect of human physiology. They impact genes, epigenetics, DNA, immunity, growth, mental functions, psychological fitness, etc. In my experience, a more toxin-naïve person experiences greater effects from even small amounts of a toxin compared to a person who has a higher overall toxin exposure, but this likely does not apply to everyone. In reality, it is impossible to predict how a person may respond to toxin exposures. Accumulation of toxins affects almost every aspect of your life. This is why it is important to minimize known toxin exposures.

If you choose to get a vaccine, get one vaccine at a time, not multiples.

Before you choose to receive a vaccine, do some research. Look up the vaccine's ingredients. Research each ingredient. Research information available about the vaccine. Look into vaccine support groups. Each bit of information will help you make an informed decision. Keep in mind, the decision to receive a vaccine is an individual one.

Those choosing not to receive a vaccine should be considered the norm, also known as the control group. Those choosing not to receive the vaccine should also be encouraged to maintain healthy lifestyle choices to ensure strong immunity and resistance to dangerous pathogens. If you choose to rely solely on your immune system, keep in mind habits such as smoking, drinking, drugs, processed food, irregular sleeping habits, etc., may make it more difficult to resist the effects of toxins and pathogens. It is only modern society which has formulated and made a place for a heavy schedule of vaccines as part of common medical practice.

Not all vaccines are equivalent in their actions and coverage. This is why research is important. Some people choosing to receive vaccines may choose a modified schedule, spacing vaccines at later ages and further apart and may they may choose not to receive some. **The choice to vaccinate should be respected as should the choice to refrain from vaccination.** Make sure each and every day you place your choices in the positive column of habits. Epigenetic factors play an important role and make every meal, every lifestyle habit, every thought, every action matter! **A strong immune system combined with a hygienic environment offers the greatest opportunity to support the body's natural detoxification systems and maintain resistance to opportunistic pathogens.**

Below, is a suggested vaccine detoxification regimen beginning one month before the scheduled vaccination and ending about six months after vaccination. You may choose one or two items from each list or you may adopt a significant amount of the program. Adopting more items on the list will improve your body's ability and efficiency in neutralizing, detoxing and removing harmful vaccine ingredients. Russel Blaylock, MD (neurosurgeon) recommends taking a cold pack with you to the vaccine appointment and immediately after and for the rest of the day, keep a cold pack over the injection site. This may lessen the local immune reaction. He recommends continued use of the cold pack along with cold showers and baths if there is any type of immediate local or even systemic reaction. Vaccine toxins may include: thimerosal, aluminum, formaldehyde, egg protein, gelatin, MSG, squalene, polyethylated glycol, polysorbate 80, aborted human fetal tissue (genetically either male or female), lipid nanoparticles, N-methyl-pseudo-uridine, etc. The recommendations below are for adults.

One month before vaccination
- Optimize your sleep time. If needed, take additional melatonin.
- Optimize physical activity and active hobbies.
- <u>Ensure adequate water intake of 3 to 4 quarts of water / fluids per day.</u>
- Avoid swimming in chlorine-containing swimming pools.
- Optimize gut functions by taking 1 tablespoon psyllium husks in 15 – 20 ounces every morning.
- 1 – 2 Tbsp colloidal silver (on empty stomach) every morning.
- Take ½ B-complex 50 in the morning and ½ B-complex 50 around noontime
- 50 – 1,000 mg niacin (1 – 3 X / day) – over 100 mg you may flush
- 9 – 18 grams vitamin C (ascorbic acid) – break into 3 – 6 doses (more if tolerable)
- 2,000 – 5,000 IUs vitamin D3 with K2
- 200 mcg selenium, 1 – 12 mg iodine, 30 mg zinc
- 1,000 – 3,000 mg NAC and 300 – 600 mg alpha lipoic acid
- Fulvic and humic acid supplements every day (could include shilajit)
- Take compounds which enhance liver functions such as: broccoli and other crucifers, beets, garlic, milk thistle, silymarin, raw foods and juices, greens, dandelion root, grapefruit, etc.
- Protease enzymes (anti-biofilm): fresh ginger, amylase, pectinase, amylase, serrapeptase, serrazimes, lipase, galactosidase, invertase, beta-glucanase, etc.
- Pre-biotic foods such as onions, garlic, bananas, asparagus, etc.
- Epsom salt and / or fulvic acid baths
- Start on a low histamine diet, eliminating foods which are strongly histaminergic (see appendix)
- Avoid the common allergens: peanuts, milk, eggs, fish, shellfish, soybeans, etc.
- Optimize your diet to include up to 80% fresh and raw foods
- Green smoothie every morning

- Sauna 2X/week (Sauna is an effective detox and when combined with niacin, is even more efficient at "rebound lipolysis," which liberates toxins from fat stores and the sauna allows the toxins to escape the dermis layer (skin) and be eliminated via sebaceous sweat).
- Weekly lymphatic massage
- 1 – 10 deep breaths every waking hour
- Daily flushing amounts of niacin (you may initially flush when taking niacin but this will subside over time). Start with 100 mg and work up to 1,000 to 3,000 mg / day.
- Daily contrast shower
- Daily sunlight
- Broccoli every other day

One week before vaccination (add to above and continue for several months after vaccination)
- High sulfur foods (if no sulfur allergy), such as onions, garlic, eggs, nuts, seeds, lentils, cruciferous, leafy greens, nuts, legumes, whole grains, etc.
- Add 100 – 150 mg pycnogenol –once per day; add 100 mg liposomal CoQ10 (ubiquinol) 2 x/day w/ food.
- Add 3 – 5 mg boron.
- 50 mg zinc.
- Milk thistle supplement.
- Chiropractic adjustments for liver, gut, etc. (once or twice).
- Sauna every day if possible.
- Add fresh parsley and cilantro to meals.
- Daily earthing.
- Daily 1-ounce 10 ppm colloidal silver.
- Avoid wheat and nuts except for almonds.
- Beet extract supplements.
- Take an Epsom salt soak – preferably the day before the vaccination.
- Zeolites.
- Diatomaceous earth (silica), 1 – 2 teaspoons in water every day or every other day.
- Homeopathic preparations – discuss with homeopath when possible.

Day of vaccination
- Breakfast: oatmeal w/ grated apple/cinnamon/ginger/maple syrup, green smoothie w/ parsley.
- 1 tablespoon of psyllium fiber in 24 ounces of water in the morning.
- Up to 1,800 mg NAC (2 – 3 divided doses).
- 1,000 IU vitamin E.
- 10,000 mg vitamin C before vaccination and 10,000 mg after vaccination (divided into 3 doses each, 90 minutes apart).
- MSM (methyl sulfonyl methane).
- EDTA or serrapeptase.

Right after mRNA type vaccination
- Charcoal poultice at vax site, apply moist hot heating pad for 10 minutes then ice x 2 hours.
- Drink ½ tsp bentonite clay in 10 oz water.
- 2000 FA Nattokinase twice a day (for up to 6 months).
- 500 mg bromelain once a day for up to 6 months.
- 100 mg liposomal CoQ10 (ubiquinol) twice a day with food.
- Castor oil pack at site of vaccine for several days in a row.

After vaccination
- 12 mg ivermectin daily for 4 to 8 weeks.
- 3,000 mg ascorbic acid every 3 hours.
- 2 – 4 charcoal tablets in the evening (offset from the other supplements mentioned below).
- Alternating hot and cold showers, at least once per day; always end with cold.
- EDTA.
- 2 ounces 10 ppm colloidal silver by mouth for 2 weeks.
- 10 chlorophyll tablets right before bedtime for 3 weeks.
- 1 oz fresh squeezed ginger juice.
- 1 tsp bentonite clay in 8 ounces of water – drink.
- Cilantro tablets or capsules or cilantro tincture.
- Zeolites (powdered, tablet, capsule).
- Coffee enema – dilates liver vessels (hemorrhoidal, mesenteric, bile ducts) and releases toxins.
- Ozone insufflation as directed by your MD. Ozonides bind with the toxins and eliminates them.
- 1 – 2 teaspoons up to 3 tablespoons of diatomaceous earth in water.
- Low dose naltrexone, begin at 1 mg/day and increase to 4.5 mg/day for 2 to 3 months (mRNA).
- 81 mg aspirin/day (mRNA) if not taking cayenne pepper which also contains salicylates.
- Mono meal of only watermelon (yes, this may cause you to pee all night long, but this is good).
- Take a detox bath before bedtime containing 1 cup Epsom salts, ¼ cup baking soda, ¼ cup borax, 2 Tbsp bentonite clay and a few drops of your favorite essential oils.
- Discuss possible short-term use of phentermine with your physician to reset dopaminergic, serotonergic and adrenergic activity.

Within a week of vaccination
- 2 saunas coinciding with high dose niacin (50 – 1,000 mg – enough to flush – confirm this is safe with your physician), consume 2 cups water for every 15 minutes in sauna. For each sauna, spend 15 to 30 minutes in sauna, 5 minutes swimming in a cool pool then repeat two more times.

Continue above detox program for at least two weeks and up to 6 months after vaccination.

Discussion Questions

1. What are your pros and cons for receiving vaccines? mRNA vaccines?
2. Are you for or against all vaccines or only selected vaccines?
3. What happens if you cannot enroll your children in school unless they are vaccinated?
4. What happens if your employer requires you get one or more vaccines?
5. Have you spoken with your healthcare provider about any concerns you may have?
6. Do you have reasons to avoid taking vaccines?
7. What if you could not enter a country without taking a vaccine?
8. Do you feel a healthy lifestyle imparts adequate immunity against most pathogenic microorganisms?

Chapter 19

Immunity and Covid-19

This section is dedicated to potential adjunctive (mostly non-prescriptive) Covid-19 therapies. <u>The therapies listed here do not usurp what your physician has outlined for your care, but they serve to enhance the effect of most medical modalities.</u> They may or may not be directly related to Covid-19. For example, a plant-based diet does not prevent, treat or cure Covid-19. However, those following a plant-based diet may have a healthier immune system and they may fare better than someone who consumes the Standard American Diet (SAD) who may have a weaker immune system.

Risk factors for more serious complications related to SARS-Cov-2 are: older age, male sex, smoking, smoking, diabetes, hypertension, heart disease, kidney disease, respiratory disease, etc. It is critical to <u>seek medical attention</u> if you suspect you are infected with SARS-Cov-2. While your case may be mild, it may also become worse and rapidly progress towards acute respiratory (i.e., lung and upper airways) complications and even multiple organ dysfunction syndrome (MODS). <u>Seek medical attention right away if you begin to exhibit symptoms. This should be done immediately and not after a long course of self-treatment.</u> As always and throughout this text, <u>I recommend you consult with your physician before starting a new program or adopting a new habit whether the new habit is herbal, supplemental, or lifestyle oriented</u>. This chapter has been reviewed by a physician for accuracy.

The first section is broken down into 5 categories which generally define the 5 stages of Covid-19: 1. Prevention; 2. Mild Symptoms (early viral stage); 3. Major Symptoms (late viral stage); 4. Major Symptoms – Host Inflammatory Response Stage with MODS; and 5. Recovery (uncomplicated to "long haulers").

Both my dad and I came down with Covid-19 on the same day in late 2020. I had a short, mild case while Dad had a longer, more complex case. We likely had the same strain but with different symptoms. One positive aspect of having survived and recovered from Covid-19 is an extended, and possible multi-year period of immunity against SARS-Cov-2. Most people who have had Covid-19 exhibit some degree of immunity (at a minimum for their specific strain) for at least 3 to 6 months, if not much longer (PMID: 33594378). The second section in this chapter lists <u>potential adjunctive therapies for those with Covid-19</u>. Again, <u>no claims of efficacy are made</u>. <u>No claims of preventing, treating or curing are implied or otherwise made.</u>

The initial viral response stage occurs when the virus enters the body and multiplies. This stage is variable and may last for 2 to 3 (or more) days. During this stage you can transmit the live virus – your body is full of it. You may be either an asymptomatic carrier (i.e., a person who is infected but never develops symptoms; Dad and I got the virus from an asymptomatic relative) or a pre-symptomatic carrier (no symptoms but very soon will develop symptoms). Early clinical symptoms may start out mild such as a slight fever, dry cough, diarrhea, headache, loss of taste and smell, fatigue, and mild hypoxemia. This is the stage where inexpensive anti-viral agents are most effectively used (e.g., hydroxychloroquine with a Z-pack and zinc in combination with quercetin, ivermectin, monoclonal antibodies). Over time, other symptoms may show up such as difficulty breathing, moderate hypoxemia as measured by pulse oximeter placed on the tip of your index finger (O2 sat = 85% - 90%), etc. This happens as the virus multiplies to the point where the host begins to react in part with an inflammatory response by producing substances known as cytokines, chemokines and other proteins.

This stage overlaps with the viral stage, but eventually the virus is killed and the remaining dead virus in the body continues to activate the host's immune system (a dead virus cannot transmit the virus to another person). If the pro-inflammatory cytokine response is overwhelming and not kept in check, excess cytokines may damage the lungs, heart, brain, circulatory system and other organs (aka, multi-organ dysfunction syndrome or MODS). The resulting cytokine storm is oftentimes the primary cause of severe symptoms and death in Covid-19.

When the host's immune system kicks in and begins producing pro-inflammatory cytokines, chemokines, and proteins such as IL-8 (IL = interleukin), IL-7, IL-6, IL-2, NF-kB, TNF, C-reactive protein, ferritin, D-dimer, troponin, etc., the results can be devastating. For example, IL-8 participates in the recruitment and activation of neutrophils, a type of white blood cell. It's counterpart in the lymph tissue are the lymphocytes. In severe Covid-19, the white blood cells (i.e., lymphocytes and neutrophils) are impacted and many may be destroyed. One function of neutrophils is to deliver vitamin C to the infection site. This is why vitamin C is important for the resolution of Covid-19. If you are ill and do not have access to a physician who will provide intravenous (IV) vitamin C, you should make sure you are taking the maximum amount of vitamin C by mouth.

Once the body mounts a defense against the presence of the virus (i.e., toxin) and the virus begins to die off, the host-inflammatory response emerges. This is a pivotal stage. If you had a huge viral load, when the virus dies off, cytokines are activated to eliminate the viral load. There may also be a huge release of pro-oxidants including iron. Ferritin, an iron storage compound, may be significantly elevated in Covid-19 patients. Those with severe disease have higher ferritin compared to those with mild disease. Excess iron can be damaging to every tissue in the body as it produces the highly reactive and destructive Fenton reaction. It will also consume and deplete vitamin C unless vitamin C is continuously replaced.

In one sense the reaction to dying and dead viruses is a huge Herxheimer reaction (i.e., a reaction potentially involving headache, body aches, rapid heartbeat, hyper-ventilation, etc.), which sometimes occurs during aggressive detoxification or while treating parasitic infections. Symptoms result from mobilization of stored toxins and / or the die off of parasites as the body eliminates them. An article published in Immunology, 26 Feb 2021, states intestinal parasites are known to aid other infectious agents such as a virus. Whether or not you have intestinal parasites, a viral-induced inflammatory response can be dangerous. It is at this stage one may experience more severe symptoms such as lung issues (e.g., dry cough, sore throat, pneumonia, runny nose, acute respiratory distress syndrome, hypoxemia, difficulty breathing), heart / cardiac issues (e.g., chest pain, arrhythmia, rapid heart rate, cardiac inflammation, cardiomyopathy, acute heart failure), kidney / renal issues (e.g., renal failure, acute renal injury, protein in the urine, blood in urine), brain / neurological issues (e.g., fever, chills, seizures, headache, nausea, vomiting, anorexia, dizziness, severe body pain, loss of smell, loss of taste, visual disturbances, fatigue, Bell's palsy, shock, strokes, coma, Guillain Barre, neuropathy), gastrointestinal (GI) issues (e.g., nausea, vomiting, diarrhea, heartburn, loss of appetite, abdominal pain / bloating, GI bleeding), vascular issues (e.g., blood clots, occlusions, cytokine storm, pulmonary embolism, DIC), immune issues (e.g., rash, cytokine storm, destruction of WBCs and resulting leukopenia), and endocrine issues (e.g., diabetics have more severe disease, difficult glucose control, higher cytokines, higher inflammatory factors, hydroxychloroquine is hypoglycemic agent so to watch glucose if using, lower NK (immune) cells in adrenal insufficiency, acute thyroiditis, thyrotoxicosis), etc. The final stage is either recovery or death. For some, recovery takes months, possibly longer. Many experience lingering effects such as fatigue, loss of smell, lung scarring, etc. Autopsies on those who have died from / with Covid-19 have found viral particles in almost every tissue in the body including the GI tract, heart, kidneys, liver, fluid in the brain, tears, semen, etc. Some experts believe the SARS virus is not cleared from the body but lies dormant with the possibility of re-emergence, similar to the chicken pox virus (not a corona virus but varicella zoster virus). There is no evidence this occurs (i.e., by examining the course of other corona viruses such as MERS and basic cold viruses) but it remains a remote possibility. PMID: 32696264 https://doi.org/10.1210/jendso/bvaa144

Prevention efforts do not always keep you from getting Covid-19, although if your vitamin D and C levels are high enough, you have a MUCH lower risk. However, prevention efforts may make the disease less lethal and decrease recovery time and the number of severe symptoms. Some suggest as the disease progresses efforts aimed at enhancing the immune system should be tamped down. This coincides with the emergence of the host's (i.e., your body's) immune response. These are issues to discuss with your physician as well as with a naturopathic doctor (when possible). Timing may be a critical component to a successful recovery from Covid-19. The longer the disease ravages your body, the more likely you will experience long-term effects. It is a good idea to engage an experienced and savvy physician, one willing to use known and effective therapies, to help you navigate the twisted and sometimes convoluted course of this viral infection. In addition to standard treatment protocols, the physician and naturopathic doctor should be willing to address all of your symptoms with a combination of off-label use meds, ortho-molecular, nutritional, lifestyle, alternative therapies, supplements, herbals, and public health approaches.

Sometimes those with the viral infection do not know they are infected with SARS-Cov-2. Some with asymptomatic Covid-19 may experience exacerbations of their current disease symptoms. For example, a type 1 diabetic may experience loss of blood sugar control. Someone with skin issues may experience a difficult-to-treat-rash. Another person with gut issues may experience more severe GI symptoms. Some may only experience loss of smell and /or taste. Much remains unknown about the mRNA and DNA vaccines, which remain under "experimental" designation at the time of this publication. New drugs in development show promise of "curing" the viral infection. Many countries have successfully distributed inexpensive prophylactic anti-virals such as ivermectin and hydroxychloroquine along with support vitamins and minerals. Many avenues for addressing covid concerns, including non-traditional and natural approaches, should be considered.

Poor prognosticators include: age > 65, comorbidities (diabetes, chronic obstructive pulmonary disease, cardiovascular disease, hypertension, cancer), respiratory failure requiring intubation, going on a ventilator, neutrophil to lymphocyte ratio < 3.13, LDH > 245 u/L, ferritin > 300 ug/L, CRP > 100 mg / L, D-dimer > 1,000 ng/mL and IL-6 < 80 pg / mL.

There is not a standard Covid-19 experience. Each person responds differently to SARS-Cov-2 infection. One person has a mild course and another person visits the ER several times before going through a slow recovery process (aka, "long haulers"). Unfortunately, many people have lost their lives due to Covid-19. This, in part, may be attributed to politics gone gravely awry and an early misunderstanding of the nature and the course of the disease. **For example, we have meta analyses and data showing the early use of ivermectin (0.2 mg/kg) and / or hydroxy-chloroquine (HCQ) is an effective treatment and relatively safe. This drug was withheld from hundreds of thousands of people with Covid-19 based on political machinations, primarily in the USA.** An example of "long haulers" may be seen in a small subset of people who develop neurological conditions such as paresthesias (numbness and tingling in hands and feet), nerve damage affecting the myelin sheath (i.e., the protective covering for peripheral nerves), Guillain-Barré, foot drop, Bell's palsy, sleeping sickness, brain inflammation, fainting spells, delirium, and / or a stroke. Most people recover but some may experience residual neurologic as well as other types of symptoms.

"Long haulers" are those experiencing extended covid-19 symptoms for more than 2 weeks. Long covid is symptoms lasting more than 12 weeks post infection. Some experience complications for months and even years. As many as 10% of those who have had covid-19 are "long haulers." Their symptoms often include cognitive issues, muscle and joint pain, fatigue, lethargy, post-exertional fatigue, GI issues, erratic heartbeat, dizziness, hair loss, loss of smell, loss of taste, etc. Their symptoms and treatment options will likely get better over time. As more data emerge there are more options for targeting the virus and limiting the cytokine storm. Most who have had Covid-19 develop immunity to their specific strain of corona. The short-term effects of various Covid-19 viruses are known but the long-term effects are just becoming clear. Hopefully these effects are negligible and reversible.

Because the brain is affected by many things including viruses and inflammatory factors in the blood, it is important to address the issue of **neuroplasticity**, especially for those who have suffered with Covid-19 and especially the older folks who have had Covid-19. During or even after Covid-19 some experience emergent anxiety and depression. Others experience post-exertional fatigue and long-term chronic fatigue. Others experience brain swelling (i.e., encephalitis). Worst case scenario is damaged or destroyed brain cells leading to cognitive changes and even disability. To preventively address the issue of Covid's impact on the brain, it is important early in the course of the infection, to do purposeful eye-hand coordination exercises such as sewing, knitting, using hand weights, playing an instrument, painting a picture, working on your car / truck, etc. It is also ideal to stimulate various cognitive functions which is done by doing crossword puzzles, reading out loud, memorizing Bible verses, etc. Challenging and repetitive activities are best. Ensure you use as many aspects of your brain function as possible including verbal, mental, physical, etc. All of these activities as well as others promote neuroplasticity and are superior to passively watching TV or worse yet, doing nothing. You don't have to spend a lot of time on these activities, but it is important to engage in purposeful activities throughout the day to preserve cognitive functions and promote neuroplasticity.

In addition to addressing neuroplasticity, it is a good idea to learn about **nootropics** (pronounced: Noah-TROPE-iks). Nootropics are substances used to enhance and optimize cognitive functions. **The most well-known nootropic is caffeine** (PMID: 22841916). Sixty-four percent of Americans consume coffee and worldwide, about half of all adults regularly consume coffee. The caffeine in coffee stimulates the brain by blocking adenosine receptors, making you more alert. When adenosine binds to its receptor, neural activity slows down and you begin to feel sleepy; caffeine counters this effect. Instead of waking up and feeling tired and lethargic because you didn't sleep well, drinking a cup of coffee stimulates your brain and temporarily gives you an energy boost. However, caffeine has several downsides which make it a less than perfect nootropic including its addictive properties, and variable effects over time on cognitive performance. A recent study at the University of Basel, and published in Cerebral Cortex, showed **caffeine consumption is associated with a reduction in the brain's gray matter.** After just 10 days of caffeine vs placebo intake, the placebo group (i.e., the group not receiving caffeine), had greater gray volume. It was most pronounced in the hippocampus area of the temporal lobe, an area of the brain used for memory consolidation (https://doi.org/10.1093/cercor/bhab005). Caffeine-withdrawal may also result in debilitating headaches. Acute caffeine use may temporarily increase attention and awareness, however, chronic caffeine use may lead to dependence and increasing usage needed to obtain its stimulating effects.

Ginkgo biloba is a nootropic shown to boost memory and decrease levels of cortisol, a stress hormone. Exercise is an excellent nootropic. If done regularly, it increases the production of a highly beneficial substance known as BDNF (brain derived neurotrophic factor). Other factors considered to be nootropics and associated with increasing BDNF and neurogenesis are niacin (PMID: 20671245), omega-3 fatty acids (PMID: 30264663), resveratrol (PMID: 26706021), prebiotic foods (PMID: 27793220, 27560964), magnesium (PMID: 23541145), lithium orotate (PMID: 19523343, 32428928), dark chocolate (PMID: 31744119), N-acetyl cysteine (NAC; PMID: 28942748, 26891662), ginseng (PMID: 29464125), matcha green tea (PMID: 29464125), ashwagandha (PMID: 29464125, 22096544), zinc (PMID: 30352697, 28215299), and sunlight (PMID: 23133609, 25206384). There are hundreds of nootropics on the market used to stimulate and preserve a range of brain functions.

Vitamin C is critical for immune function and for restoring balance to oxidative influences. In addition to immune functions, vitamin C is a cofactor ensuring collagen integrity, needed for carnitine metabolism, for catecholamine production (hormonal regulation), for gene transcription, epigenetic regulation, DNA methylation, as well as other critical functions. Various immune cells have the highest content of vitamin C in the body. This is because white blood cells (WBCs) immediately respond to an infection by delivering vitamin C to the site of the infection. For example, the concentration of vitamin C in the immune cells (white blood cells) and other types of cells is: 1,350 µM in neutrophils (WBC), 3,100 µM in monocytes (WBC), 3,800 µM in lymphocytes (WBC), 2,790 µM in platelets (involved in blood clotting) and 45 µM in red blood cells (RBCs). Vitamin C is also concentrated in many organs of the body. The concentration of vitamin C in the brain is 800 – 900 µM, 200 µM in CSF, 2,300 to 2,800 µM in pituitary gland (in brain), 600 – 900 µM in spleen, 100 µM in thyroid, 400 µM in lungs, 600 – 900 µM in liver, 600 to 900 µM in pancreas, 1,700 to 2,300 µM in adrenals, 1,400 – 1,800 µM in eye lens, 136 µM in gastric juice, 200 µM in urine, etc., (PMID: 26808119). As you can see, the body's immune system as well as most of the body's organs are highly dependent on electrons from vitamin C. When enough vitamin C is available, the infection is more easily controlled and the body quickly returns to normal functions. If enough vitamin C is not delivered to the infection, oxidative stress may overwhelm and the infection may expand, leading to secondary issues. As vitamin C and glutathione are depleted, an infection becomes difficult to control.

Vitamin C is not only critical to preventing infections but also for recovery from infection. Getting enough vitamin C can be a difficult barrier to overcome. It may take hundreds of GRAMS of vitamin C to quench the toxicity of a severe and / or prolonged infection. Small amounts of vitamin C, such as the RDA of 90 mg (1,000 mg = 1 gram), is inadequate to address infection and restore healing to the body. Ideally, in extreme cases, vitamin C may be given via an IV by a trained and specialized physician (or an infusion clinic). In this case, more can be given in a shorter period of time. You will need to find an MD familiar with this technique and the possible complications such as hypoglycemia. If possible, you can take ortho-molecular doses of vitamin C by mouth. Your tolerance level to vitamin C is dependent on your condition (i.e., the sicker you are the more vit C you tolerate – meaning it does not cause loose stools or diarrhea).

Most people tolerate taking up to 3 grams of vitamin C orally every 90 to 120 minutes. This allows for receiving up to 24 to 30 grams per day by mouth during waking hours. One way to determine vitamin C needs is to do a bowel tolerance study. It's fairly straight forward but usually takes a couple of hours if not a half a day. Of course, you can do other things while the study is in progress. Designate a day to fast and stay near a bathroom. Start by taking 1000 – 2000 mg of vitamin C every 15 to 20 minutes. At some point in the near future, you will reach what is known as, "bowel tolerance." This means you will either have loose stools or diarrhea. At this point you know your body has been saturated and instead of the vitamin C being absorbed into your body, it is rapidly moving through the large intestine and wreaking osmotic havoc with the contents. Take the amount you needed to get to this point and multiply by 80%. For example, if it takes 20,000 mg of vitamin C to cause loose stools, you should now supplement at 20,000 mg X 0.80 = 16,000 mg of vitamin C. Because most people cannot tolerate taking more than 3,000 mg of vitamin C at one time, you will need to divide 16,000 mg of vitamin C by 3,000 mg of vitamin C per dose. This equals 5.3 doses (round this number either up or down to a whole number). In this case, round down to 5 daily doses. So, you take a total of 16,000 mg of vitamin C and divide by 5 doses/day = 3200 mg of vitamin C, 5 times/day. I recommend rounding down to 3,000 mg five times/day. You could also take 2,000 mg every 2 hours for a total of 8 doses or 3,000 mg every 2 hours for a total of 5 or 6 doses. If at any point in the future you experience loose stools or diarrhea, cut down the dose or cut down the number of doses per day. If you get sick or ill in the future, your requirement for vitamin C may increase. Be aware of the dynamic nature of vitamin C requirements and make appropriate adjustments.

A good choice for increasing your intake of vitamin C is taking lyospheric vitamin C. A 1,000 mg dose of lyospheric vitamin C is claimed to be equivalent to taking 5,000 to 10,000 mg of ascorbic acid (vitamin C). A combination of lyospheric and regular ascorbic acid can be used to optimize delivery of vitamin C to cells and other body compartments. I recommend watching this video on the medical uses of vitamin C, by physician and author, Thomas Levy, MD, JD. https://www.youtube.com/watch?v=JXKuWcB0cI0

Vitamin D, also known as a hormone, is critical to defending against corona and other types of viruses. The vitamin D receptor is on the cell's nucleus, maintaining its ability to regulate a large number of genes. It is important for favorably shifting epigenetic factors to protect against viruses, some types of cancers, and for making up a healthy immune system. Those who are likely to be vitamin D deficient include: overweight / obese, nursing home patients, 70 to 80% of all Americans, 80% of African Americans, 70% of Hispanic and Native Americans 47% of Caucasian Americans, 80% of hospitalized patients, 90% of ICU patients, and those who have a suppressed or impaired immune system. Vitamin D also regulates the cytokine response to inflammation triggers. For more than half the year, most Americans are unable to synthesize adequate amounts of vitamin D. The presence of adequate levels of vitamin D decreases risk of testing positive for corona virus (PMID: https://doi.org/10.1371/journal.pone.0239252; R. Cole, MD). More is not always better. Vitamin D is fat-soluble and too much can have negative effects.

Melatonin is another interesting compound the body synthesizes at night time (i.e., melatonin is the chemical expression of darkness). The body also effectively uses exogenous sources. Melatonin is a remarkable compound. It functions as an antioxidant, but also exerts metabolic effects on mitochondria, the body's energy producing sub-cellular compartment. This effect makes it a potentially beneficial compound in the adjunctive treatment of Covid-19. Melatonin is part of the recommended protocol for prevention, treatment and recovery from Covid-19. Even though your body synthesizes melatonin, taking supplemental melatonin may provide additional benefits. PMID: 32621295, DOI: https://doi.org/https://doi.org/10.32794/mr11250068 , https://doi.org/https://doi.org/10.32794/mr11250033 , https://doi.org/10.3390/ijms22020764

Quercetin is a yellow-colored, water-insoluble plant-based antioxidant found primarily in plants, including: almonds, pistachios, apples, berries, cherries, citrus fruits, tomatoes, green tea, bell peppers, kale, broccoli, Brussels sprouts, cabbage, red onions, green onions, capers, buckwheat, black tea, cilantro, dill and lovage. Capers have the highest amount of quercetin.

Quercetin supports immune functions. It is a potent inhibitor of SARS-Cov-2, interfering with its ability to replicate and with its ability to dock with ACE2 receptors, the main target of SARS-Cov-2. Quercetin enhances the effect of zinc, shuttling zinc into the cells where it fights against viral infections. Foods with quercetin promote gut health and enhance the microbiome. You may increase your intake of foods containing quercetin or you may take quercetin as a supplement.

SARS-Cov-2 is heat sensitive and can be destroyed by temperatures tolerable to humans. Heat-based therapies include hot springs, saunas, Turkish steam bath/hammams, steam rooms, sweat lodges, steam inhalations, hot mud, heat-applied poultices, etc. Heat treatments may be combined with inhalation of steam-containing essential oils (PMID 32742639). These therapies are targeted to adults and not young children. Consult your health care provider before starting a heat-based therapy regimen.

The protocols contain 5 different stages for addressing the concerns related to Covid-19.

1. Prevention Protocol
2. Mild Symptoms, Early Viral Stage Protocol (no hospitalization required)
3. Major Symptoms, Late Viral Stage, Early Host Immune Response Stage with Cytokine Storm and Oxidative Stress Protocol (usually avoid hospitalization but not always; under MD/DO/ND supervision)
4. Major Symptoms, Ongoing Host Inflammatory Response Stage with Cytokine Storm, Oxidative Stress and Multi-system Organ Dysfunction Syndrome (MODS) Protocol (usually hospitalized)
5. Recovery Protocols (quick recovery and long hauler's)

Each of the 12 categories and their sub-categories listed below contain relevant recommendations. Read through the recommendations and discuss them with your regular healthcare provider. Use the recommendations which best match your unique set of circumstances and clinical symptoms.

- Diet and nutrition Rx
- Gut functions
- Immune Rx
- Lungs / cardiac / endocrine
- Supplements
- Herbals
- Essential oils
- Lifestyle factors
- Alternative therapies
- Oral care
- Public health
- Your physician

<u>**When it comes to the recommendations for each of the categories, use what makes sense for your situation. Obviously, the more recommendations you adopt the better chance you have to defend against the virus and optimize your body's natural healing and recovery processes.**</u> When essential nutrients are marginal and rapidly used up by the infectious process, you are more susceptible to experiencing severe symptoms. To maximize your chances of a successful recovery, consider high doses of essential nutrients suggested in the protocols. The supplement category is not necessarily comprehensive. This list could drastically expand so it is truncated at some of the most essential supplements, acknowledging there are others which could also be on this list. In fact, none of the categories provide comprehensive recommendations. Each category provides enough guidance to possibly mount a defense and make a difference in length and severity of the infection, especially for those living in the country, without immediate access to a wide variety of practitioners. Prescription meds change so check with a Covid-treating qualified physician to supplement this section.

After the protocols is a section on **Potential Adjunctive Covid-19 Therapies**. This section provides ideas for either preventively or therapeutically addressing the various complications of Covid-19. The therapies listed fit into the category of alternative therapies, diet (positive and negative), herbals / oil / supplements, and lifestyle interventions. <u>Read and discuss the options with your MD/DO/ND.</u>

DISCLAIMER: Information provided does not represent a "service." Data discussed and presented here, understood mechanisms of action, use of various and diverse substances are to be only under the care and supervision of your physician. Nothing within this book should be construed or considered as providing medical care, a service, sale or advertisement of a product or medical advice. **Any care or treatment provided to you is the responsibility of your personal physician, as well as yourself, and should follow informed consent.** There is no expressed U.S. Constitutional authority under Article I or II, for the Federal Government to direct, govern, or otherwise be involved in your personal health care. https://constitutioncenter.org/interactiveconstitution/full-text 1

Addendum for medical professionals only: In an article titled, Epigenetics in cancer therapy and nanomedicine, published in Clinical Epigenetics, on 16 May 2019, by Authors A. Roberti, A Valdes, et al., (**doi: 10.1186/s13148-019-0675-4; PMID: 31097014**), the article describes the use of nano-sized particles used to target solid tumors. This discussion, occurring at the end of the article is worth reading if you have a medical background. These are a few of the messages I derived from the article and how this might relate to the current Covid-19 crisis. Again, it must be emphasized there are very few experts in nano-medicine because this is an emerging specialty. There is much we do not know about how nano-sized particles behave in humans. Most nano-type medical research is done using animals, which does not always translate to humans. Here are a few of the comments from the article. Keep in mind this article is describing the use of NPs in treating solid tumor cancers by delivering an anti-cancer drug(s) to the solid tumor where the drug is released and serves to disable the viable mass of cancer cells including their recently developed tumor vasculature. Naturally occurring nano-particles are generated by erosion and volcanic eruptions, dust storms (aluminum, calcium silicon, iron,) bacteria, fungi and even some plants produce nano-particle sized minerals (source: https://www.azonano.com/article.aspx?ArticleID=4837).

- "When a nano-particle (NP) enters a biological environment, several proteins bind to its surface, leading to the formation of a "corona." These interactions can modify the physiochemical properties of NPs and in turn, determine the physiological response they elicit, such as cellular uptake, distribution, bioavailability, and toxicity, and thus effectively generating a particle with a "new biological identity."
- To keep the NPs from being recognized by the body's immune system and keep them in circulation for longer, their surface is coated with polyethylene glycol chains and other markers such as CD47 or sometimes the NPs are camouflaged with cellular membranes purified from white blood cells (leukocytes), red blood cells, and cells responsible for blood clotting (thrombocytes).
- NPs are sometimes combined (conjugated) with attachments (ligands) that recognize specific cellular targets. The NP circulates until it finds its target and then docks to the target and delivers it's "payload drug." Various attachments or ligands used include antibodies, polysaccharides (carbohydrates), peptides (proteins), transferrins (iron), folates (vitamin B9), and other small molecules.
- NPs are able to travel across the vasculature endothelium (internal artery walls).
- NPs can be designed to target specific cells and / or tissue.
- "Both internal and external stimuli can trigger release of drugs by generating a change in the structure of the nanocarrier."
- Hypoxia (the condition of low oxygen), pH, temperature, magnetic and even ultrasound-sensitive are all conditions by which NPs can be programmed to release their payload.
- Combination NP therapies may be conceptually used to synchronize delivery of 2+ NP-type drugs.
- NPs are used to "co-deliver a therapeutic agent alongside a diagnostic or tracking agent provide a great platform for integrating diagnostics, therapy, and follow-up data."
- "Despite their obvious clinical potential, the accumulation of NPs in the body still raises concerns about their safety for human health. NPs can induce genotoxicity, directly by their interaction with genetic material or indirectly via intermediate biomolecules that cause DNA injury or chromosomal abnormalities. Indirect genotoxicity is principally due to oxidative stress induced by the induction of reactive oxygen species by NPs and is strongly linked to inflammatory cell response and immunotoxicity. Moreoever, numerous studies have demonstrated the possible epigenetic toxicity of NPs.

Country Living Prevention Protocol for Covid-19
By Crystal Whitten, Ph.D.

Diet and Nutrition
- Diet: At least 50% raw, plant-based diet, include foods high in vitamin C and beta carotene.
- Meals: 2 – 3 meals, no snacks.
- Fiber: 1 – 2 Tbsp psyllium husks and / or chia seeds in 24 ounces of water first thing in morning.
- Foods high in omega 3: walnuts, flax / hemp / chia seeds, black seed oil, flaxseed oil, cold water fish.
- Baking soda protocol: ½ tsp in ½ cup water, 6 doses/day (q 2 hours) for 3 days, tapering off 3rd day.
- Evaluate for depletion of nutrients and potential for increased requirement for essential nutrients.
- Foods high in omega 6: avoid red meat, fried foods, refined vegetable oils, margarine, etc.
- Sugar / sweets: limit / avoid.
- Water / fluids: 95 – 125 fluid ounces of alkaline or spring water (avoid tap/city water), hibiscus tea.
- Alcohol: limit use, avoiding alcohol is ideal.
- Functional foods: pineapple (bromelain, comasain, ananain; stem high in bromelain), apple (pectin), papaya (papain), ginger root (gingerol), turmeric root (curcurmin), greens (chlorella), beets (nitrates and betalain) and beet greens (carotenoids), fresh herbs (myristicin, limonene, eugenol, alpha-thujene, apignin, linalool, estragole, gamma-caryophyllene, ursolic acid, etc.), garlic (alliin, diallyl trisulfide), leeks (kaempferol), honey (gluconic, acetic, butyric, lactic acids), lemon (terpenes, citric acid), grapefruit (flavones, furanocoumarins, anthocyanidin, naringin, quercetin), tonic water (quinine), fermented foods (probiotics), cultured yogurt (probiotics), capers (quercetin), legumes (phenolic acids, flavonoids, tannins, enzyme inhibitors, saponins), nuts (linolenic acid, vitamin E), seeds (phytosterols), black seed oil (thymoquinone, alkaloids, saponins), etc.
- Functional & therapeutic beverages: black tea (catechins, quinic acid, etc.); matcha green tea (catechins); elderberry (anthocyanins, catechins, tannins, alpha and beta-amyrin, ursolic acid, oleanic acid, betulin, betulic acid); pine needle tea (suramin); ginger shots (terpineol, linalool); carrot juice (beta carotene, carotenoids); wheat grass shots (chlorophyll, bioflavonoids, alkaloids, saponins, gum, mucilages, indole); green smoothie containing pineapple, greens, ginger (chlorophyll, bromelain, etc.); tonic water containing quinine (be sure to take 50 mg zinc); honey / lemon / ginger oxymel; fresh beet juice (combine with apple or pear juice); watermelon juice (lycopene, citrulline, carotenoids); ginger shots (anti-syncytial); fresh papaya / pineapple / guava / ginger (anti-syncytial actions) / passionfruit beverage (polyphenols, harman, piceatannol); raw cacao (epicatechin, theobromine, resveratrol, polyphenols, esters) with ginger / cinnamon (cinnamaldehyde, cinnamic acid, eugenol, coumarins) / cloves (eugenol, beta caryophyllene, alpha humulene, cinnamic acids) / cardamom (cineole, limonene, terpinyl acetates) / nutmeg (myristicin, terpenes, pinene, sabinene, cymene, thujene, terpinine, safrole, elemicin, ferulic acid) / star anise (suramin); hibiscus tea (anthocyanins); fresh pineapple juice (enzymes); licorice root tea (glycyrrhizin, flavonoids, triterpenoids, coumarins, stilbenoids; avoid if you have high blood pressure); chia seed water (essential fatty acids), dandelion tea (suramin), fennel tea (suramin), raspberry (quercetin); mint, etc.

Gut Functions
- Gut function: 1 bowel movement per meal eaten is essential for gut health.
- Prebiotic foods: avocado, garlic, onions, leeks, asparagus, bananas, capers, chicory root, dandelion greens, Jerusalem artichokes, spinach, lentils, oats, feta cheese, carrot juice, naturally fermented cabbage, kimchi, cherries, dark chocolate, carob, cooked beans, etc.
- Aim for 35+ grams of dietary fiber.
- One tablespoon of psyllium husks has 165 mg potassium, 30 mg calcium, 0.9 mg iron, and 3.5 grams fiber. Add 1 tsp to 1 Tbsp psyllium husks to water, stir and rapidly drink. May need to limit to one time a day; decrease to 1 to 3 times per week if GI issues arise. Not pleasant but effective.
- 1 tsp to 2 Tbsp food grade diatomaceous earth in 12 oz water (could combine with psyllium)
- Mix 1 Tbsp chia seeds in water and drink before and after meals and during day if hungry.

Prevention Protocol for Covid-19, continued

Immune
- 12 mg ivermectin twice per week, 150 mg ashwaghanda daily or prn.
- White blood cell health: Eat foods high in vitamin C (to keep immune cells competent).
- Lymphatic system: Keep lymph fluid moving by walking, rebounding, deep breathing, etc.
- Regular activity: Stay active for at least 2 hours every day or 5,000 – 20,000 steps / day.
- Nasal irrigation: 1X / day w normal saline or Vit C water (1 tsp ascorbic acid: 1 cup distilled water).
- 3-day water-only fast may rebuild and revitalize the immune system.
- If exposed to covid: 12 mg ivermectin, 100 mg zinc, 500 mg quercetin, 1,000 mg cysteine.
- Nicotine patches on a daily basis when you anticipate potential exposure.

Supplements, Vitamins and Minerals
- Vitamins & minerals (avoid taking iron).
- B-complex 50 or 100 (am).
- Vitamin B12 lozenge (100 – 1,000 mcg methylcobalamin).
- 100 – 200 mg niacin, 1 – 3 x / day (maintain higher doses for those who regularly use niacin).
- 250 – 1,000 mg magnesium (citrate or combination of threonate).
- 2 – 12.5 mg iodine / iodide (200 - 500 mcg if you have thyroid issues) – take separately from vitamin C. One drop of 2% Lugol's = 1 mg elemental iodine and 1.5 mg potassium iodide.
- 100 – 200 mcg selenium (may substitute 2 – 4 Brazil nuts/day).
- 3,000 – 20,000 mg vitamin C (divided doses) – consider higher orthomolecular amounts.
- 1,000 – 10,000 IU vitamin D.
- 45 – 50 mg zinc and 6 mg copper.
- Probiotic: *bacillus subtilus* should be included.
- 500 mg to 6 g fulvic acid.
- Drives Zn into Cells: 250 – 500 mg Quercetin, 40 mg/kg black seed oil, or wormwood (check w/ MD).
- 0.3 – 30 mg melatonin, 45 minutes before bedtime.
- Andrographis (may lower furin cleavage), ashwagandha (adaptogenic), mucuna pruriens, lobelia extract.
- Chlorella tablets at bedtime.
- Colloidal silver, 10-20 ppm.

Herbals / Herbal Teas (ensure you are using high quality herbs and herbal teas)
- Ashwagandha, basil, black tea, cloves, echinacea, fennel, eucalyptus, ginger, hibiscus, holy basil, lemon balm, licorice root, matcha green tea, mint, mullein, oregano, raspberry, reishi, rhodiola, rose hips, rosemary, sage, thyme, turmeric, white tea, mucuna pruriens herb, lobelia extract, etc.

Essential Oils (aroma or other therapy)
- Essential oils: thieves, hyssop, lavender, lemongrass, ylang ylang, bergamot, sweet orange, or citrus oil, etc., for aroma therapy. Eucalyptus oil (1,8 epoxy-p-menthane or 1,8-cineol) for keeping immediate environment clean and hygienic.

Lifestyle Factors
- Lifestyle: Spend time outdoors, forest bathing, fresh air, 20 – 60 min sun exposure (early morning is best), far infrared sauna 1X/week, adequate sleep time, social contacts, etc.
- Steps: 3,000 – 20,000+.
- Spritz: Spritz colloidal silver on face before and after wearing a mask.
- Practice excellent hygiene habits such as a daily shower / bathing, oral care such as brushing and cleaning teeth 2 to 3 times per day, avoid touching public surfaces with bare hands, etc.

Prevention Protocol for Covid-19, continued

Alternative Therapies
- Alternative: music, negative ion generator, UV light sterilizer, blood electrification, sauna or sauna blanket (far infrared), thermography to detect any thermatomes abnormalities (if indicated), etc.
- Anti-covid frequency generators. Earthing.

Oral Care (PMID: 35260129)
- Oral care: brush 3 X / day, water pick, floss, etc. At least once per day, end brushing with dipping a clean toothbrush in 3% hydrogen peroxide and brushing again. Leave on for 30 seconds and rinse.
- Gargle: evening with colloidal silver (swallow after gargling) or gargle with a dilute iodine solution.
- Painful oral adverse reactions may occur after Covid 19 vaccination (e.g., ulcerations, stomatitis, petechiae, white oral mucosal lesions, swelling, local pain, candidiasis, necrotizing gingivitis). Meds may be prescribed by your MD/DDS or you may use natural approaches outlined in chapter 47.

Lungs / Cardiac / Endocrine
- Deep breathing: 1 – 2 X / hour.
- Nebulize: nebulize colloidal silver or 1% to 3% food grade hydrogen peroxide, etc.
- Over-the-counter: 81 – 325 mg aspirin (anti-platelet) or use cayenne (see below; contains salicylates).
- Cool Cayenne pepper, 100,000 heat units (anti-coagulant, vasodilator – take separately from aspirin).
- Avoid: smoking (tobacco), vaping, mold, breathing dangerous fumes, etc.
- Pre-existing endocrine conditions may be worsened by Covid-19.

Neuro
- 120 – 600 mg total ginkgo biloba (may divide into 3 doses taken 3X/day).
- Other nootropics of your choice such as methylene blue.
- Stay mentally and physically active, take supplements, keep up with social contacts, etc.

Public Health
- Maintain good hygiene, masks if necessary, social distance, as required by your location, etc.
- Purchase pulse oximeter to monitor oxygen saturation once or twice a week and if early symptoms appear. To maximize use of pulse oximeters, use a validated device, take multiple readings every day, use only the index or middle fingers, only use values that are associated with a strong pulse signal, remove nail polish on test finger, test fingers on both hands, warm up cold fingers first.
- Guidance from federal health agencies should be weighed against other organizations (e.g., "go home, check your pulse oximeter, and go to the hospital when your sats are < 88% or your lips turn blue", may not be in your best interests. Start preventive therapies to stay low risk.

Your Physician
- **Discuss with physician the possible use of Ivermectin as a prophylactic**, especially if you have had a potential exposure. Rx (preventive): 150 – 200 μg / kg Ivermectin on exposure day, day 3 and then once per month indefinitely (10 – 15 mg for the average weight adult of 55 to 65 kg).
- Discuss potential preventive strategies with physician including the ones listed in this protocol. For example, some herbs upregulate the immune system and if used in high amounts, could "over-activate" the immune system, potentially triggering widespread inflammation. This has not actually been documented, but remains a theoretical possibility. Also, some herbs may interact with prescription meds by either decreasing or increasing the effectiveness of prescription meds. St. John's Wort and its active ingredient 5-HTP (not included on any of the Covid-19 protocols) widely interact with many prescription medications. In this case, it is always wise to discuss the use of St. John's Wort and 5-HTP with your physician. Discuss using aspirin or cayenne prophylactically.

Notes

Country Living Protocol for Covid-19 for Mild Symptoms and Early Viral Stage
By Crystal Whitten, Ph.D.

Diet and Nutrition
- Diet: fresh juices, green smoothie fast, juices keep electrolytes in check, low histamine diet, etc.
- Meals: no meals, primarily fresh juices and smoothies.
- Fiber: 1 – 2 Tbsp psyllium husks and / or chia seeds in 24 ounces of water first thing in morning.
- Foods high in omega 3: walnuts, flax / hemp / chia seeds, black seed oil, flaxseed oil, cold water fish.
- Foods high in omega 6: Avoid red meat, fried foods, refined vegetable oils, margarine, etc.
- Sugar / sweets / alcohol: Avoid.
- Push water / fluids: 95 – 125 fluid oz of alkaline or spring water (avoid tap/city water), hibiscus tea
- Functional foods: pineapple, papaya, ginger, turmeric, greens, beets / greens, fresh herbs, garlic, leeks, honey, lemon, grapefruit, tonic water, fermented food, nigella sativa, chlorella, turmeric, etc.
- Fluids: keep fluids high, at least 8 – 12 oz water every hour, 95 – 125 total ounces / day
- Therapeutic beverages: tonic water containing quinine (take w zinc); matcha green tea; honey / lemon / ginger oxymel; elderberry syrup elixir; pine needle tea; fresh beet juice (combine w apple or pear juice); watermelon juice; ginger shots (anti-syncytial) or home-made ginger ale; carrot juice; fresh papaya / pineapple / guava / ginger (anti-syncytial) / passionfruit beverage; raw cacao w ginger / cinnamon / cloves / cardamom / nutmeg; hibiscus tea; fresh pineapple juice; chia fresca; licorice root tea (avoid if high BP); ingredient in licorice root can activate hormone caused fluid retention and raise blood pressure; may benefit those with low BP; check w/ MD, etc.
- Bitters: Once or twice per week

Gut Functions
- Gut function: 1 bowel movement per "meal" eaten
- Prebiotic foods: bananas, chicory root, dandelion greens, fresh carrot juice, chia seed gel, etc.
- Aim for 35+ grams of dietary fiber. <u>One tablespoon psyllium husks (9 grams) has 14 mg potassium, 30 mg calcium, 0.2 mg iron, and 3.5 g fiber.</u> One tablespoon of chia seeds has 1.4 g of protein, 4 g fiber, 2.8 g of fat (1.6 g omega 3), 30 mg calcium.
- Coffee enema (using 3 Tbsp organic coffee boiled in 1 liter distilled water and 1 Tbsp blackstrap molasses, lay on right side to insert, hold for 15 to 20 minutes) – 1 to 3 times per week until well.

Immune
- If only early symptoms are present take: 12 mg ivermectin, 150 mg ashwaghanda, 100 mg zinc, 300 mg quercetin, 1,000 mg cysteine, 10,000 vitamin C (divided into 3 doses), 600 – 1200 mg NAC until symptoms gone
- Nasal washes and gargle at least 2 to 5 times with H2O2, iodine, vitamin C, colloidal silver, etc.
- White blood cell health: Eat foods high in vitamin C (to keep immune cells competent)
- Lymphatic system: Keep lymph fluid moving by walking, deep breathing, etc.
- This may be a good time for a 3-day water only fast to rebuild the immune system. In the acute phase of Covid-19, many lose their appetite making a 3-day fast much easier.

Supplements, Vitamins and Minerals
- Vitamins & minerals:
- B-complex 50 or 100 – take ½ in the morning and ½ at noon.
- Vitamin B12 lozenge(s) (100 – 1,000 mcg cyano- or methylcobalamin).
- 200 mg thiamin (divided into 2 doses or IV if hospitalized) – may go up to 1,500 mg/day.
- 200 – 1,000 mg niacin 3 X / day

Protocol for Covid-19 for Mild Symptoms and Early Viral Stage, continued

Supplements, Vitamins and Minerals, continued
- 250 – 1,000 mg magnesium (additional amounts may be indicated for some).
- 2 – 12.5 mg iodine / iodide (200 – 500 mcg if you have thyroid issues) – take separately from vit C. One drop 2% Lugol's = 1 mg elemental iodine and 1.5 mg potassium iodide.
- 200 – 400 mcg selenium.
- Vitamin C to bowel tolerance (some as lyospheric vitamin C) – at least 10,000 mg.
- If hospitalized, consider providing up to 3 grams by mouth and up to 150-grams via IV / day.
- <u>50,000 to 100,000 IU vitamin D</u> (Vit D hammer) – take up to 5 consecutive days; 2,000 – 10,000 IUs for maint during winter and summer months if you get minimal sun exposure.
- 75 – 100 mg zinc for 5 to 20 days; take 6 – 9 mg copper.
- 6+ mg boron.
- 0.5 g to 6 g fulvic acid.
- 100 – 1,000 IU vitamin E (mixed tocopherols / tocotrienols).
- Vitamin A hammer: 50,000 IU/d x 4 d (adults); 25,000 IU/d x 4 d (child 50 to 100 lb); 10,000 IU/d (child 25 – 50 lb). Daily: 1,000 – 3,000 mcg RAE (3,333 – 33,333 IU) vitamin A. 10,000 mcg RAE vitamin A is a one-time mega dose; (1 IU vitamin A=0.3 mcg retinol or 0.6 beta-carotene.)
- 100 – 300 mg Coenzyme Q10 (100 mg with meal) – may go up to 1200 mg (work up slowly).
- 200 – 300 mg alpha lipoic acid, 2 X / day.
- 600 mg N-acetyl-cysteine (NAC), 2 – 3X/day (if taking cysteine, then you don't need NAC).
- 5,000 mcg biotin (for dry mouth).
- Drives Zn into Cells: 500 mg Quercetin (2 or 3 X / day for 5 – 7 days), 400 mg epigallocatechin-gallate (1 X / day for 7 days) and 400 mg 2 X / day for 5 – 10 days, black seed oil, 30 mg niacin, or wormwood (check w MD). (https://doi.org/10.1016/j.bbamcr.2006.03.005 PMID: 25050823, 33520683).
- 6 – 50 mg melatonin, 5 mg during the day; up to 45 mg 45 minutes before bedtime.
- Andrographis, ashwagandha, marshmallow root, milk thistle, shilajit, slippery elm, etc.
- Chlorella tablets at bedtime, charcoal tablets as needed, colloidal silver, 10-20 ppm.
- 120,000 SPU serrapeptase (5 mg serrapeptase equivalent to 10,000 SPU).

Herbals / Herbal Teas (ensure you are using high quality herbs and herbal teas)
- Herbs / herbal teas: Hot beverages such as herbal teas, rosemary, basil, oregano, turmeric, ginger, cloves, sage, mullein, oregano, thyme, mint, lemon balm, green tea, fennel, holy basil, rose hips, white tea, licorice root (if not hypertensive), hibiscus tea, pine needle tea, etc.
- A "tea" of ½ tsp baking soda in 4 oz water, 3 – 4 times a day to alkalize and improve oxygenation.

Essential Oils
- 1 – 3 drops frankincense in water, 1 – 3 drops helichrysum in water
- Aroma therapy: thieves, hyssop, lavender, lemongrass, ylang ylang, sweet orange, citrus oils, rosemary, ravensara, tea tree, bergamot, eucalyptus, lemon balm, thyme, oregano, fennel, peppermint, cinnamon, clove, *Laurus nobilis*, cade (*Juniperus oxycedrus*), thuja, hyacinth may be effective against Covid-19 (PMID: 18357554, ISSN: 2249-4626).
- Eucalyptus oil (1,8 epoxy-p-menthane or 1,8-cineol) for keeping immediate environment hygienic.
- Thyme, sage and Dittany of Crete, as a combination, have been shown to inhibit SARS-Cov-2 proliferation. doi: https://doi.org/10.1101/2021.01.11.20248947

Protocol for Covid-19 for Mild Symptoms and Early Viral Stage, continued

Lifestyle Factors
- Lifestyle: Spend time outdoors (wear a hat to prevent heat loss during cold weather), fresh air, 20 min sun exposure, adequate sleep time, social contacts, etc.
- Steps: 1,000 to 5,000 steps.
- Spritz: spritz colloidal silver on face before and after wearing a mask.
- Bath: Epsom salt and mineral bath, 20 – 40 minutes, several times per week; warm 10-minute shower, sauna or sauna blanket.
- Thermophore heating pad: Keep extremities, chest and head warm (front and back).

Alternative Therapies
- Alternative: Hyperbaric oxygen therapy (HBOT), sauna or sauna blanket (far infrared), music, negative ion generator, UV light sterilizer, proning for increasing oxygen, Epsom salt soaks.
- Thermography to detect any thermatome abnormalities (if indicated), etc.
- Anti-covid frequency generators.

Oral Care
- Oral care: Brush 3 X / day, water pick, floss, etc. At least once per day, end brushing with dipping a clean toothbrush in hydrogen peroxide and brushing again. Leave on for 30 seconds and rinse.
- Gargle before bedtime with colloidal silver (swallow after gargling).

Lungs / Cardiac / Endocrine
- Deep breathing: 1 – 2 X / hour, cough and huff, watch video: youtube.com/watch?v=m_4CGZzTTCo.
- Nebulize (also good for gargling): Nebulize therapies (Rx): look into nebulizing colloidal silver, 3% food grade hydrogen peroxide (1 – 2 drops), iodine (1 – 2 drops).
- Hot and cold fomentations to the chest and affected areas.
- Over-the-counter: 325 mg aspirin (anti-platelet).
- Cool Cayenne pepper, 100,000 heat units (anti-coagulant – take separate from aspirin).
- 8 mg Bromexine, three times per day to clear mucus and chest congestion.
- Avoid: Smoking (tobacco), vaping, breathing dangerous fumes, mold exposure, etc.
- Hyperbaric oxygen therapy (HBOT).
- Pre-existing endocrine conditions may be worsened by Covid-19.
- Discuss anti-infective agents w/MD: 200 mg HCQ bid, 12 – 24 mg IVM x 5 doses, 250 AZM or 100 DOXY bid, monoclonal, Paxlovid bid, etc.

Neuro
- 120 – 600 mg total ginkgo biloba (may divide into 3 doses taken 3X/day).
- Other nootropics of your choice such as methylene blue.
- Stay mentally and physically active, take supplements, keep up with social contacts via phone, etc.
- Issues to address: lack of smell and taste if affecting food intake (if underwt, consider appetite stim).
- Discuss early use of prescription SSRI, fluvoxamine if significant neurological symptoms present.

Public Health
- Maintain good personal and living hygiene, masks, social distance, as required by your location, etc.
- Use a pulse oximeter to monitor oxygen saturation once or twice per day and more frequently if symptoms appear. If oxygen saturation percentage drops below 94% (considered hypoxia I), should be reported to your physician or health care provider.

Protocol for Covid-19 for Mild Symptoms and Early Viral Stage, continued

Public Health, continued
- Self quarantine at home for up to 3 days or longer if necessary.
- To maximize use of pulse oximeters, use a validated device, take multiple readings every day, use only the index or middle fingers, only use values that are associated with a strong pulse signal, remove nail polish on test finger, test fingers on both hands, warm up cold fingers first.

Your Physician
- Avoid acetaminophen (Tylenol), depletes glutathione.
- Initiating a successful medical protocol early is critical. Do not wait and get worse, treat immediately with over-the-counter supplements described here as well as contact your physician about initiating medical protocols such as the Fleming Protocol and others. Early treatment may also lessen the risk of "long haulers" syndrome. If you cannot get a prescription for hydroxychloroquine (200 mg 1 / week for 8 to 12 weeks) or other anti-viral, start drinking tonic water containing lesser amounts of hydroxychloroquine, which is better than none at all. Request prescription for 500 mg azithromycin 1 x / day for 6 to 10 days or 100 mg doxycycline twice / day for 6 to 10 days. Additional treatment could include 12 to 24 mg Ivermectin per day for 5 days then 1 to 2 times a week for up to 2 months, 1 mg / 2cc solution budesonide via nebulizer for 7 days, 6 mg dexamethasone once per day for up to 7 days, aspirin, oxygen and IV fluids (Zelenko pre-hospital protocol). If possible, start early treatments and avoid hospital. Work closely with a physician who is willing to maximize use of ivermectin, hydroxychloroquine, etc.
- Iron chelation may positively modify blood cell dynamics.
- Ask your physician about the use of synthetic monoclonal antibody therapy. This therapy is for those in the early days of infection (within the first 7 to 10 days of infection) and for those with one or more risk factors (as determined by your physician or health care provider).
- Pulse Ox: If less than 90% contact your physician.
- Discuss options for addressing the viral stage, including outpatient vitamin C IVs (4.5 g – 17 g IV vitamin C every 2 to 4 hours or 17 g – 210 g/d) and / or glutathione IV.
- Anti-viral Rx: Discuss with physician the possible use of Ivermectin and hydroxychloroquine.
- The protocol linked below was recently developed by Richard Fleming, PhD, MD, JD (it is not in earlier publications of this book because it is only recently published). I highly recommend going to his website and printing out his protocol for the medical management of C19. Here is the link to his site and the second link is to the protocol booklet.
    - https://www.flemingmethod.com/best-available-published-evidence
    - https://21a86421-c3e0-461b-83c2-cfe4628dfadc.filesusr.com/ugd/659775_409b4bb7107f4320be075ce1404b048d.pdf
- Discuss with your physician the possible use of Hydroxychloroquine or methylene blue.
- Wormwood is a possibility; it is not regulated by the FDA. There is some evidence it may have a similar action to hydroxychloroquine. This needs to be confirmed (similar mechanism as HCQ but without the concerns for cardiac liability; modification of RBC surface immunology). Thujone content should be < 35 mg/kg or thujone free. If using wormwood, consult a physician familiar with its safe use. Comes as an oil, tincture, tablet. Not safe for pregnant or lactating women.
- Andrograhpis may lower furin cleavage.
- Discuss possibility of niacin and serotonin depletion and possible repletion and treatment options (e.g., Fluvoxamine, Fluoxetine).
- Identify co-infections (e.g., herpes, Epstein Barr Virus, Lyme, etc.).

Notes

Country Living Covid-19 Protocol for Late Viral Stage, Early Host Immune Response Stage with Cytokine Storm and Oxidative Stress

by Crystal Whitten, Ph.D.

Diet and Nutrition

- Diet: Fresh juices, green smoothie with protein powder, juices keep electrolytes in check, low histamine diet, etc.
- Meals: If appetite present, give high protein soups.
- Fiber: 1 – 2 Tbsp psyllium husks and / or chia seeds in 24 ounces of water first thing in morning.
- Foods high in omega 3: walnuts, flax seed, hemp seed, chia seeds, flaxseed oil, cold water fish.
- Foods high in omega 6: Avoid red meat, fried foods, refined vegetable oils, margarine, etc.
- Sugar / sweets: Avoid.
- Water / fluids: 95 – 125 fluid ounces of alkaline or spring water, hibiscus tea.
- Alcohol: Avoid.
- Functional foods: Pineapple, papaya, ginger root, turmeric root, greens, beets and beet greens, fresh herbs, garlic, leeks, honey, lemon, grapefruit, tonic water, fermented foods, cultured yogurt, licorice root (if hypertension not an issue), etc.
- Fluids: Keep fluids high, at least 8 – 12 oz water every hour, 95 – 125 total ounces per day.
- Therapeutic Beverages: Tonic water containing quinine (be sure to take zinc); matcha green tea; honey / lemon / ginger oxymel; pine needle tea, elderberry syrup elixir; fresh beet juice (combine with apple or pear juice); watermelon juice; ginger shots (anti-syncytial) or home-made ginger ale; carrot juice; fresh papaya / pineapple / guava / ginger (anti-syncytial) / passionfruit beverage; raw cacao with ginger / cinnamon / cloves / cardamom / nutmeg; hibiscus tea; fresh pineapple juice; chia fresca; licorice root tea (avoid if you have high blood pressure; an ingredient in licorice root can activate a hormone in the body which causes fluid retention and raises blood pressure; may be beneficial for those with low blood pressure but first check with physician), etc.
- Bitters: Once or twice per week.

Gut Functions

- Gut function: 1 bowel movement per "meal" eaten.
- Prebiotic foods: Bananas, chicory root, dandelion greens, chia seed gel (1 Tbsp chia seeds in water).
- Aim for 35+ grams of dietary fiber. One Tbsp of psyllium husks has 165 mg potassium, 30 mg calcium, 0.9 mg iron, and 3.5 grams fiber.
- 1 – 3 tsp diatomaceous earth in large glass ice water.

Immune

- White blood cell health: Eat foods high in vitamin C (to keep immune cells competent), 150 mg ashwaghanda
- Lymphatic system: Keep lymph fluid moving by walking, deep breathing, massage, etc.
- Nasal irrigation: 1 – 2 X / day w/ normal saline or vit C water (1 tsp ascorbic acid:1 cup distilled water).
- May be a good time for a 3-day water only fast to rebuild the immune system. In the acute phase of Covid-19, many lose their appetite making a 3-day fast easier.

Supplements, Vitamins and Minerals

- B-complex 50 or 100 – take ½ in the morning and at noon.
- 200 mg – 1,500 mg thiamin (divided into 2 doses or IV if hospitalized).
- 200 – 3,000 mg niacin, divide into 2 doses for under 1,000 mg and 3 doses for 1,000 mg each.
- 250 mg – 1,000 mg magnesium.

Covid-19 Protocol for Late Viral Stage,
Early Host Immune Response Stage with Cytokine Storm and Oxidative Stress, continued

Supplements, Vitamins and Minerals, continued
- 2 – 12.5 mg iodine / iodide (200 - 500 mcg if you have thyroid issues) – take separately from vit C. One drop of 2% Lugol's = 1 mg elemental iodine + 1.5 mg potassium iodide. Avoid if MTHFR +.
- 400 – 800 mcg selenium.
- Vitamin C to bowel tolerance (some as lypospheric vitamin C) – at least 20,000 mg. If pneumonia suspected, take a 1,000 mg dose vit C every 6 minutes for up to 8 hours or until loose stools.
- If hospitalized, consider providing up to 3 grams by mouth and up to 150-grams via IV / day
- 100,000 IU vit D (Vit D hammer) – up to 5 days in a row; 2,000 to 10,000 IUs for maintenance dose during winter months and for those with minimal sun exposure during the summer.
- 75 – 100 mg zinc (up to 100 mg if recommended by your healthcare provider; ratio of zinc to copper of 15:1 is conservative)
- 6 – 10 mg boron.
- 20 mg copper.
- 500 mg to 6 g fulvic acid.
- 1,000 IU vitamin E (mixed tocopherols / tocotrienols).
- 1,000 – 3,000 mcg RAE (3,333 – 33,333 IU) vitamin A (10,000 mcg RAE of vitamin A is a one-time mega dose; beta carotene is not included in this number).
- 100 – 1,200 mg Coenzyme Q10 (100 - 400 mg with meals – divide into 3 doses).
- 500 mg alpha lipoic acid, 2 – 3 X / day.
- 600 mg NAC, 3X/day.
- 5,000 mcg biotin (for dry mouth).
- Drives Zn into Cells: 250 - 500 mg Quercetin, black seed oil, or wormwood (check w MD).
- 6 – 60 mg melatonin, 5 mg during the day and up to 55 mg 45 minutes before bedtime.
- Andrographis, ashwagandha, milk thistle, shilajit, slippery elm, marshmallow root, etc.
- Chlorella tablets at bedtime, charcoal tablets as needed, colloidal silver at 10-20 ppm.
- 120,000 SPU serrapeptase.

Herbals / Herbal Teas (ensure you are using high quality herbs and herbal teas; drink and / or gargle with)
- Herbs / herbal teas: Hot beverages such as herbal teas, pine needle tea, rosemary, basil, black tea, oregano, turmeric, ginger, cloves, sage, mullein, oregano, thyme, mint, lemon balm, green tea, fennel, holy basil, rose hips, raspberry, white tea, licorice root, hibiscus tea, eucalyptus, etc.
- A "tea" of ½ tsp baking soda in 4 oz water, 3 - 4 times per day to alkalize and improve oxygenation.

Essential Oils
- Essential oils: 1 – 3 drops frankincense in water, 3 – 5 drops helichrysum in water 2X/day
- Aroma therapy: thieves, hyssop, lavender, lemongrass, ylang ylang, sweet orange, citrus oils, rosemary, ravensara, tea tree, bergamot, eucalyptus, lemon balm, thyme, oregano, fennel, peppermint, cinnamon, clove, Laurus nobilis, cade (*Juniperus oxycedrus*), thuja, hyacinth may be effective against Covid-19 (PMID: 18357554, ISSN: 2249-4626).
- Eucalyptus oil (1,8 epoxy-p-menthane or 1,8-cineol) for keeping immediate environment clean and hygienic.
- Thyme, sage and Dittany of Crete, as a combination, have been shown to inhibit SARS-Cov-2 proliferation. doi: https://doi.org/10.1101/2021.01.11.20248947

Covid-19 Protocol for Late Viral Stage, Early Host Immune Response Stage with Cytokine Storm and Oxidative Stress, continued

Lifestyle Factors
- Lifestyle: Spend time outdoors (wear a hat to prevent heat loss during cold weather), fresh air, 20 min sun exposure, adequate sleep time, social contacts, etc.
- Steps: 500+.
- Spritz: Spritz colloidal silver on face before and after wearing a mask.
- Bath: Epsom salt and mineral bath, 20 – 40 minutes, warm 10-minute shower.
- Thermophore: Keep extremities, chest and head warm (front and back).
- Massage: Legs, arms, chest, back, neck..

Alternative Therapies
- Alternative: Hyperbaric oxygen therapy (HBOT), sauna or sauna blanket (far infrared), ozone insufflation, music, negative ion generator, UV light sterilizer, thermography to detect any thermatome abnormalities (if indicated), iron chelation therapy, etc.
- Anti-covid frequency generators.

Oral Care
- Oral care: Brush 3 X / day, water pick, floss, etc. At least once per day, end brushing with dipping a clean toothbrush in 3% hydrogen peroxide and brushing again. Leave on for 30 seconds and rinse.
- Gargle: Evening with colloidal silver (swallow after gargling).

Lungs / Cardiac / Endocrine
- Deep breathing: 1 – 2 X / hour, cough and huff, watch this video: youtube.com/watch?v=m_4CGZzTTCo
- Nebulize: Nebulize therapies (Rx): look into nebulizing 10 ppm colloidal silver, 1% to 3% food grade hydrogen peroxide, iodine, etc.
- Poultice / pack: Castor oil or mustard pack to chest.
- Fomentations: Hot and cold chest fomentations.
- Over-the-counter.
  - 325 mg aspirin (anti-platelet).
  - Cool Cayenne pepper, 100,000 heat units (anti-coagulant – take separately from aspirin).
- Hyperbaric oxygen therapy.
- Pre-existing endocrine conditions may be worsened by Covid-19.

Neuro
- 120 – 600 mg total ginkgo biloba (may divide into 3 doses taken 3X/day).
- Other nootropics of your choice such as methylene blue.
- Stay mentally and physically active, take supplements, keep up with social contacts, etc.
- If neuro symptoms & decreased 128 Hz sensation at ankle, give SQ 500-1,000 mcg methyl B12.
- Issues to address: Lack of smell and taste if affecting food intake (may need appetite stimulant).
- Discuss use of prescription SSRI, fluvoxamine if significant neurological symptoms present.

Public Health
- Maintain good hygiene, masks, social distance, as required by your location, etc.
- Use a pulse oximeter to monitor oxygen saturation 3 - 4 times/d. If oxygen saturation percentage drops < 94% (considered hypoxia I), report it to your physician or health care provider.

Covid-19 Protocol for Late Viral Stage,
Early Host Immune Response Stage with Cytokine Storm and Oxidative Stress, continued

Public Health, continued
- To maximize use of pulse oximeters, use a validated device, take multiple readings every day, use only the index or middle fingers, only use values that are associated with a strong pulse signal, remove nail polish on test finger, test fingers on both hands, warm up cold fingers first.

Your Physician
- Pulse Ox: If less than 94% contact your physician.
- Discuss options for addressing the viral stage, including vitamin C (4.5 g – 17 g IV vitamin C every 2 to 4 hours or 17 g – 210 g/d) and / or glutathione IV.
- Your physician: Discuss options for addressing late viral stage and early host inflammatory responses, including use of ivermectin, hydroxychloroquine, methylene blue, IV vit C and/or glutathione. Address chronic fatigue syndrome if present. Discuss strategy for each symptom as well as preventive measures. Discuss meds used to lessen viral load, inflammation, etc.
- Prescriptive measures may include (some may require hospitalization for monitoring responses, etc.): methyl-prednisolone, heparin, ivermectin, hydroxychloroquine, primaquine, nitazoxanide, dual anti-androgen therapy, fluvoxamine, cyproheptadine, famotidine, statins, therapeutic plasma exchange, budes-onide, antibiotics, interferon-alpha2B, Losartan, convalescent serum, tocilizumad (IL-6 inhibitor), aman-tadine, stem cells, dexamethasone, ruxolitinib, baricitinib, ARBs, etc.
- Gustavo Aguirre Chang, MD, has suggested the viral stage persists even in the advanced stages of the disease, "intracellularly and in a disseminated way in the cells of the walls of the blood vessels (endothelial cells and pericytes) and inside part of the blood cells." *(Aguirre-Chang, G. Persistent Symptoms of COVID-19: molecular tests by nasal and pharyngeal swabs do not detect the presence of the virus in intestines, heart and other organs and systems. Preprinter available in ResearchGate. August 22, 2020. DOI: http://dx.doi.org/10.13140/RG.2.2.30458.31688/2)* . In addition to infecting blood vessel cells, the virus is found in macrophages, monocytes, infiltrates (pulmonary alveoli, spleen, lymph nodes, kidneys).
- Discuss use of Ivermectin, Hydroxychloroquine or methylene blue (if in viral stage).
- <u>The protocol linked below, was developed by Richard Fleming, PhD, MD, JD.</u> I recommend going to his website and printing out his protocol for C19. Here is the link to his site and the link is to the protocol booklet.
    - https://www.flemingmethod.com/best-available-published-evidence
    - https://21a86421-c3e0-461b-83c2-cfe4628dfadc.filesusr.com/ugd/659775_409b4bb7107f4320be075ce1404b048d.pdf
- Canadian Covid Care Alliance protocols are here: https://www.canadiancovidcarealliance.org/treatment-protocols/
- Anti-viral, other: Wormwood is not regulated by the FDA; some evidence it may have a similar action to hydroxychloroquine. This needs to be confirmed (similar mechanism as HCQ but without cardiac liability; modification of RBC surface immunology). Thujone content should be < 35 mg/kg or thujone free. If using wormwood, consult a medical professional **familiar with its safe use**. Comes as an oil, tincture, tablet. Not safe for pregnant or lactating.
- Anti-inflammatory Rx: Check with your physician about the best approach (licorice root tea may be useful but may raise blood pressure).
- Identify co-infections or potential dormant viruses (e.g., herpes, Epstein Barr, Lyme, etc.).
- Discuss use of niacin, serotonin depletion and possible repletion (e.g., Fluvoxamine, Fluoexitine).

Notes

Country Living Covid-19 Protocol for Major Symptoms, Ongoing Host Inflammatory Response Stage with Cytokine Storm, Oxidative Stress and Multi-system Organ Dysfunction Syndrome (MODS) – Usually in the hospital

by Crystal Whitten, Ph.D.

Diet and Nutrition

- Diet: Fresh juices, green smoothie with protein powder, juices keep electrolytes in check, minimize dietary histamine.
- Meals: Maintain a minimum of 35 – 50 grams of protein intake / day.
- Avoid all added sources of iron, including fortified foods.
- Fiber: 1 – 2 Tbsp psyllium husks and / or chia seeds in 24 ounces of water first thing in morning.
- Foods high in omega 3: walnuts, flax seed, hemp seed, chia seeds, flaxseed oil, cold water fish.
- Foods high in omega 6: Avoid red meat, fried foods, refined vegetable oils, margarine, etc.
- Sugar / sweets: Avoid, compromises immune system for up to 12 hours or more.
- Water / fluids: 95 – 125 fluid ounces of alkaline or spring water, hibiscus tea.
- Alcohol and sodas: Avoid at all costs.
- Functional foods: Pineapple (highest bromelain in central core – good to juice), papaya, ginger root, turmeric root, greens, beets and beet greens, fresh herbs, garlic, leeks, honey, lemon, grapefruit, tonic water, fermented foods, cultured yogurt, etc.
- Fluids: Keep fluids high, at least 8 – 12 oz water every hour, 95 – 125 total ounces per day.
- Functional and therapeutic beverages: Honey / lemon / ginger oxymel, elderberry syrup elixir, pine needle tea, licorice root tea (avoid if you have high blood pressure), fresh beet juice (combine with apple or pear juice), watermelon juice, ginger shots (anti-syncytial), carrot juice, fresh papaya / pineapple / guava / ginger (anti-syncytial) / passionfruit beverage, raw cacao with ginger / cinnamon / cloves / cardamom / nutmeg, hibiscus tea, fresh pineapple juice, chia fresca, etc.
- Bitters: Once per day.

Gut Functions

- Gut function: 1 bowel movement per "meal" eaten is essential for optimal gut and physical health.
- Prebiotic foods: Banana, chicory root, dandelion greens, chia seed gel (1 Tbsp chia seeds in water).
- Aim for 35+ g of dietary fiber. One tablespoon of psyllium husks has 165 mg potassium, 30 mg calcium, 0.9 mg iron, and 3.5 grams fiber. One tablespoon of chia seeds: 1.4 grams of protein, 4.1 grams carbohydrate, 4 grams fiber, 2.8 grams of fat (1.6 grams omega 3), 39 mg calcium.

Immune

- White blood cell health: Eat foods high in vitamin C (to keep immune cells competent), 150 mg ashwaghanda.
- Lymphatic system: Keep lymph fluid moving by walking, deep breathing, etc.
- Nasal irrigation: 1 – 2 X / day with ascorbic acid water (1 tsp ascorbic acid: 1 cup distilled water).
- This may be a good time for a 3-day water only fast to rebuild the immune system. In the acute phase of Covid-19, many lose their appetite making a 3-day fast much easier.

Supplements, Vitamins and Minerals

- B-complex 50 or 100 – take ½ in the morning and at noon.
- 400 – 1,500 mg thiamin (divided into 2 or 3 doses of 500 mg or via IV if hospitalized).
- 300 – 3,000 mg niacin (100 – 1,000 mg X 3 times per day).
- 250 – 1,000 mg magnesium.

Covid-19 Protocol for Major Symptoms, Ongoing Host Inflammatory Response Stage with Cytokine Storm, Oxidative Stress and Multi-system Organ Dysfunction Syndrome (MODS), continued

Supplements, Vitamins and Minerals, continued
- Iodine hammer: 2 - 12.5 mg iodine / iodide (200 - 500 mcg if thyroid issues) – take separately from vit C. 1 drop of 2% Lugol's = 1 mg elemental iodine and 1.5 mg potassium iodide.
- 600 – 1,000 mcg selenium (divided into two doses) – tamps down cytokine storm.
- Vitamin C to bowel tolerance (some as lypospheric vitamin C) – at least 10,000 mg. If in hospital, consider providing up to 3 grams PO every 2 hours and up to 200 grams via IV / day. Need IV vitamin C within 6 hours of hospital admission. Waiting longer may compromise efficacy.
- 100,000 IU vit D (Vit D hammer) – take up to 5 days in a row; 2,000 to 10,000 IUs for maintenance dose during winter and for those with minimal sun exposure during summer.
- 50 – 150 mg zinc (up to 150 mg if recommended by HCP; ratio of zinc:copper of 15: 1 is usual).
- 6 - 10 mg boron.
- 20 mg copper.
- 500 mg to 6 g fulvic acid.
- 1,000 IU vitamin E (mixed tocopherols / tocotrienols) divided into 2 doses.
- 3,000 mcg RAE (10,000 IU) vitamin A.
- 100 – 1,200 mg Coenzyme Q10 (100 – 400 mg with meal).
- 500 mg alpha lipoic acid, 2 – 3 X / day (some don't tolerate well).
- 600 mg NAC, 3X/day.
- 5,000 mcg biotin (for dry mouth).
- Drives Zn into Cells: 250 - 500 mg Quercetin, black seed oil, or wormwood (check w MD).
- 15 – 80 mg melatonin, up to 20 mg during the day; up to 60 mg 45 minutes before bedtime.
- EDTA chelation if excess iron / ferritin is in play (3X/day) or discuss a Rx for deferasirox with MD. Also discuss how to replete essential minerals using a liquid mineral supplement.
- Andrographis, 150 mg ashwagandha (adaptogen), milk thistle, shilajit, slippery elm, marshmallow root, etc.
- Chlorella tablets at bedtime, charcoal tablets as needed, colloidal gold or silver at 10-20 ppm.
- 120,000 SPU Serrapeptase.

Herbals / Herbal Teas (ensure you are using high quality herbs and herbal teas; drink or gargle)
- Herbs / herbal teas: rosemary, basil, oregano, turmeric, ginger, clove, pine needle tea, sage, black tea, raspberry, mullein, oregano, thyme, mint, lemon balm, green tea, fennel, holy basil, rose hips, white tea, licorice root (avoid if high blood pressure), hibiscus, slippery elm, eucalyptus, wormwood, etc.

Essential Oils
- 1 – 3 drops frankincense in water, 3 – 5 drops helichrysum in water 2 – 3X/day.
- Aroma therapy: thieves, grapefruit seed extract, hyssop, lavender, lemongrass, ylang ylang, sweet orange, citrus oils, rosemary, ravensara, tea tree, bergamot, eucalyptus, lemon balm, thyme, oregano, fennel, peppermint, cinnamon, clove, Laurus nobilis, cade (Juniperus oxycedrus), thuja, hyacinth may be effective against Covid-19 (PMID: 18357554, ISSN: 2249-4626).
- Eucalyptus oil (1,8 epoxy-p-menthane or 1,8-cineol) for keeping environment clean and hygienic.
- Thyme, sage and Dittany of Crete, as a combination, have been shown to inhibit SARS-Cov-2 proliferation. doi: https://doi.org/10.1101/2021.01.11.20248947

Covid-19 Protocol for Major Symptoms, Ongoing Host Inflammatory Response Stage with Cytokine Storm, Oxidative Stress and Multi-system Organ Dysfunction Syndrome (MODS), continued

Lifestyle Factors

- Lifestyle: Spend time outdoors (use hat to prevent heat loss during cold weather), fresh air, 20 min sun exposure, social contact (if possible), far infrared sauna 1 – 3 X / week, adequate sleep time, etc.
- Steps: 500+.
- Spritz: Spritz colloidal silver on face before and after wearing a mask.
- Bath: Epsom salt and mineral bath, 20 – 40 minutes, warm 10-minute shower.
- Thermophore: Keep extremities, chest and head warm (front and back).
- Massage: Legs, arms, chest, back, neck.

Alternative Therapies

- Alternative: Hyperbaric oxygen therapy (HBOT), sauna or sauna blanket (far infrared), ozone insufflation (O3 delivered via hemorrhoidal artery to liver), music, negative ion generator to clean air and home environment, UV light sterilizer, thermography to detect thermatomes abnormalities (if indicated), UV blood irradiation with ozone, iron chelation.
- Anti-covid frequency generators.

Oral Care

- Oral care: Brush 3 X / day, water pick, floss, etc. At least once per day, end brushing with dipping a clean toothbrush in 3% hydrogen peroxide and brushing again. Leave on for 30 seconds and rinse.
- Gargle in the evening with colloidal silver (swallow after gargling).

Lungs / Cardiac / Endocrine

- Deep breathing: 1 – 2 X / hour, cough and huff, watch this video: youtube.com/watch?v=m_4CGZzTTCo
- Nebulize: Nebulize therapies (Rx): look into nebulizing colloidal silver, 1% to 3% food grade hydrogen peroxide, iodine, ascorbic acid / sodium ascorbate, etc.
- Poultice / pack: Castor oil or mustard pack to chest.
- Fomentations: Hot and cold chest fomentations.
- Over-the-counter:
  - 325 mg aspirin (anti-platelet) or Cool Cayenne (see below; also contains salicylates).
  - Cool Cayenne pepper, 100,000 heat units (anti-coagulant – take separately from aspirin).
  - Hyperbaric oxygen therapy (HBOT).
  - Pre-existing endocrine conditions may be worsened by Covid-19.
  - If thick mucus: hot chest fomentations, hot steamy shower, gentle chest massage, gentle back percussion, exercise, hum, sing, inhale steam / vapors, hot lemon / ginger / honey tea, etc.

Neuro

- 120 – 600 mg total gingko biloba (may divide into 3 doses taken 3X/day).
- Other nootropics of your choice such as methylene blue, gingko, NAC, etc.
- Stay mentally and physically active, take supplements, keep up with social contacts, etc.
- If neuro symptoms present & decreased ankle 128 Hz, need 500 mcg methylcobalamin SQ, weekly.
- Address: lack of smell and taste if affecting food intake (may need appetite stimulant).
- Discuss use of prescription SSRI, fluvoxamine if significant neurological symptoms continue.

Covid-19 Protocol for Major Symptoms, Ongoing Host Inflammatory Response Stage with Cytokine Storm, Oxidative Stress and Multi-system Organ Dysfunction Syndrome (MODS), continued

Public Health

- Maintain good hygiene, masks, social distance, as required by your location, etc.
- If you are at home, use a pulse oximeter once every hour or two. If oxygen saturation percentage drops below 94% (considered hypoxia I), should be reported to your physician or health care provider. If you are in the hospital, this parameter will be continuously monitored.
- To maximize use of pulse oximeters, use a validated device, take multiple readings every day, use only the index or middle fingers, only use values that are associated with a strong pulse signal, remove nail polish on test finger, test fingers on both hands, warm up cold fingers first.

Your Physician

- During this stage, you may need frequent contact with your physician or even hospitalization.
- Pulse Ox: If less than 94% contact your physician
- Discuss options for addressing the critical viral stage, including vitamin C (4.5 g – 17 g IV vitamin C every 2 to 4 hours or 17 g – 210 g/d) and / or glutathione IV, wormwood cocktail.
- Anti-inflammatory Rx: Check with your physician about the best natural approaches.
- Your physician: Discuss with physician your options for addressing the host inflammatory responses including IV vitamin C (up to 50 – 100 grams every 8 hours) and / or glutathione. If ferritin is high, discuss iron chelation therapies such as deferasirox. Also discuss how to replete essential minerals which may be chelated and eliminated with the use of deferasirox.
- Your physician: Address persistent and ongoing viral infection. Gustavo Aguirre Chang, MD, has suggested the viral stage persists even in the advanced stages of the disease, "intracellularly and in a disseminated way in the cells of the walls of the blood vessels (endothelial cells and pericytes) and inside part of the blood cells." *(Aguirre-Chang, G. Persistent Symptoms of COVID-19: molecular tests by nasal and pharyngeal swabs do not detect the presence of the virus in intestines, heart and other organs and systems. Preprint available in ResearchGate. August 22, 2020. DOI:* http://dx.doi.org/10.13140/RG.2.2.30458.31688/2 . In addition to infecting blood vessel cells, virus is found in macrophages, monocytes, infiltrates (pulmonary alveoli, spleen, lymph nodes, kidneys).
- FLCCC Prevention and Treatment Protocols for Covid 19, MATH+ Hospital Treatment Protocol for Covid 19 is here: https://covid19criticalcare.com/covid-19-protocols/math-plus-protocol/
- Your physician: Discuss with your physician their strategy for each of your symptoms.
- The protocol linked below was recently developed by Richard Fleming, PhD, MD, JD (it is not in earlier publications of this book because it is only recently published). I highly recommend going to his website and printing out his protocol for the medical management of C19. Here is the link to his site and the second link is to the protocol booklet.
    - https://www.flemingmethod.com/best-available-published-evidence
    - https://21a86421-c3e0-461b-83c2-fe4628dfadc.filesusr.com/ugd/659775_409b4bb7107f4320be075ce1404b048d.pdf
- Canadian Covid Care Alliance protocols are here: https://www.canadiancovidcarealliance.org/treatment-protocols/
- Discuss possibility of niacin and serotonin depletion and possible repletion options.
- Identify co-infections (e.g., herpes, Epstein Barr Virus, Lyme, etc.).
- Address chronic fatigue syndrome when present.

Notes

Country Living Covid-19 Recovery Protocol (Simple Recovery to Long Haulers)
By Crystal Whitten, Ph.D.

Diet and Nutrition

- Diet: At least 50% raw, plant-based diet, choose foods high in vitamin C, low histamine diet, may need to limit gluten, shellfish, dairy, etc. Combat against weight gain and obesity by limiting meals to twice a day, avoiding highly processed and artificial foods, and possibly limiting food intake to an 8 to 10 hour window of time (intermittent fasting). Another successful strategy for some is to avoid food intake after 4 pm and front load carbs to breakfast. Ensure adequate intake of protein, vitamins and minerals.
- Meals: 2 – 3 meals, no snacks.
- Fiber: 1 – 2 Tbsp psyllium husks and / or chia seeds in 24 ounces of water first thing in morning.
- Foods high in omega 3: walnuts, flax seed, hemp seed, chia seeds, flaxseed oil, cold water fish.
- Avoid foods high in omega 6: red meat, fried foods, refined vegetable oils, margarine, etc.
- Alcohol: limit / avoid.
- Sugar / sweets: limit / avoid, sodas.
- Functional foods: Pineapple, papaya, ginger root, turmeric root, greens, beets, beet greens, fresh herbs, garlic, leeks, honey, lemon, grapefruit, tonic water, fermented foods, cultured yogurt, etc.
- Fluids: 95 – 125 fluid ounces of alkaline or spring water.
- Therapeutic Bev: celery juice, honey / lemon / ginger oxymel, matcha green tea, elderberry syrup elixir, pine needle tea, licorice root tea (avoid if high blood pressure), fresh beet juice (combine with apple or pear juice), watermelon juice, ginger shots (anti-syncytial), carrot juice, fresh papaya / pineapple / guava / ginger (anti-syncytial) / passionfruit beverage, raw cacao with ginger / cinnamon / cloves / cardamom / nutmeg, hibiscus tea, fresh pineapple juice, chia fresca, etc.
- Bitters: Once or twice per week.

Gut Functions

- Gut function: 1 bowel movement per meal eaten.
- Prebiotic foods: Garlic, onions, leeks, asparagus, bananas, chicory root, dandelion greens, Jerusalem artichokes, capers, avocado, spinach, lentils oats, feta cheese, fresh carrot juice, tapioca, naturally fermented cabbage, kimchi, cherries, dark chocolate, carob, cooked beans, chia seed gel, etc.
- Aim for 35+ grams of dietary fiber. One tablespoon of psyllium husks has 165 mg potassium, 30 mg calcium, 0.9 mg iron, and 3.5 grams fiber. One tablespoon of chia seeds contains 1.4 grams of protein, 4.1 grams CHO, 4 grams fiber, 2.8 grams of fat (1.6 grams omega 3), 39 mg calcium.

Immune

- 12 mg ivermectin daily for 1 month; 150 mg ashwaghanda.
- White blood cell health: Eat foods high in vitamin C (to keep immune cells competent).
- Lymphatic system: Keep lymph fluid moving by walking, deep breathing, etc.
- Regular activity: Stay active for at least 2 hours every day.
- Nasal irrigation: 1–2 X/d w/ normal saline or vit C water (1 tsp ascorbic acid:1 cup distilled water).

Supplements, Vitamins and Minerals

- B-complex 50 or 100 (am), additional 500 to 1,000 mg Thiamin (vitamin B1).
- 100 mg niacin / nicotinic acid (may want to stay on higher doses, up to 1,000 mg three times per day, to enjoy the benefits of flushing, especially w/ residual covid symptoms).
- 250 – 1,000 mg magnesium (citrate or combination of threonate), Epsom salt baths 1 – 2x/wk.

Recovery Protocol (Simple Recovery to Long Haulers), continued

Supplements, Vitamins and Minerals continued

- 2 – 12.5 mg iodine / iodide (200 - 500 mcg if you have thyroid issues) – take separately from vitamin C. One drop of 2% Lugol's = 1 mg elemental iodine and 1.5 mg potassium iodide.
- 200 – 400 mcg selenium.
- 3,000 – 20,000 mg vitamin C (divided doses) – more than 20,000 mg may be necessary (macrophage / monocyte repolarization therapy).
- 1,000 – 2,000 – 5,000 IU vitamin D for maintenance dose during winter months and for those with minimal sun exposure during the summer.
- 500 – 1,000 mcg RAE vitamin A.
- 45 – 100 mg zinc and 6 – 20 mg copper.
- 500 mg to 6 g fulvic acid.
- 500 – 1,000 mcg methylcobalamin.
- 100 – 300 mg Coenzyme Q10 (100 mg with meals).
- 200 – 300 mg alpha lipoic acid, 1 – 2 X / day (if tolerated).
- 600 mg NAC, 1 – 3 X / day.
- 5,000 mcg biotin, 1 – 3 X / week (or as needed for dry mouth).
- Drives Zn into Cells: 250 – 500 mg Quercetin, black seed oil, or wormwood – for "long haulers."
- Single amino acid supplements: 1000 mg lysine up to 2x/d (start with low dose, may raise Zn and Ca levels, may increase cardiac output); nuts and seeds are good sources of arginine.
- 0.3 – 30+ mg melatonin, 5 mg during the day and 15 – 25 mg 45 minutes before bedtime.
- Andrographis, ashwagandha (adaptogenic), shilajit, slippery elm, marshmallow root, etc.
- Chlorella tablets at bedtime, charcoal tablets as needed, colloidal silver, 10–20 ppm.
- 120,000 SPU Serrapeptase.
- Wormwood.

Herbals / Herbal Teas (ensure you are using high quality herbs and herbal teas)

- Herbs / herbal teas: black tea, herbal teas, raspberry, rosemary, basil, oregano, turmeric, ginger, cloves, sage, mullein, oregano, thyme, mint, lemon balm, matcha green tea, fennel, holy basil, rose hips, white tea, pine needle tea, licorice root, hibiscus tea, eucalyptus, etc.
- A "tea" of ½ tsp baking soda in 4 oz water, 3 to 4 times per day to alkalize and improve oxygenation for long-haulers (if no positive response after 3 or 4 days, discontinue use).

Essential Oils (for a variety of uses including aromatherapy)

- Essential oils: Thieves, grapefruit seed extract, hyssop, lavender, lemongrass, ylang ylang, bergamot, sweet orange, or citrus oil, etc., for aroma therapy. Eucalyptus oil (1,8 epoxy-p-menthane or 1,8-cineol) for keeping immediate environment clean and hygienic.

Lifestyle Factors

- Lifestyle: Spend time outdoors, forest bathing, earthing, fresh air, 20 – 60 min sun exposure (early morning is best), far infrared sauna 1X/week, adequate sleep time, social contacts, etc.
- Steps: up to 3,000 (vigorous exercise may lead to relapse or worsening of symptoms). If you are improving, aim for up to 10,000 steps a day and 5 to 30 minutes of vigorous activity if tolerated.
- Spritz: Spritz colloidal silver on face before and after wearing a mask.
- Bath: Epsom salt and mineral bath, 20 – 40 minutes (1 – 2 X / week), warm 10-minute shower.

Recovery Protocol (Simple Recovery to Long Haulers), continued

Alternative Therapies

- Alternative: Hyperbaric oxygen therapy, sauna or sauna blanket (far infrared), music, negative ion generator, UV light sterilizer, transcranial direct current stimulation (tDCS), thermography to detect any thermatome abnormalities (if indicated), 528 Hz music therapy, etc.
- 2 mg Nicotine gum (chew 1 to 2 pieces a day for 5 days in a row).

Hair Loss (aka telogen effluvium) – addressing general inflammation is important

- This is a difficult symptom to treat. Not a lot of solid data exist to make scientifically sound recommendations. Other factors may be involved such as hormone imbalances, etc. This means that oftentimes anecdotal information is promoted until solid data become available.
- Ensure adequate protein intake, between 55 to 85 grams per day (higher amounts for men).
- Ensure adequate intake of natural folate from fresh and raw green leafy vegetables.
- Ensure adequate oxygenation (i.e., activity, exercise) and time spent outdoors (i.e., exposure to sun and conversion to vitamin D).
- Topical prescriptions: minoxidil, nanoxidil, aminexil.
- Ensure strong, healthy circulation: arginine, ginseng, cayenne pepper, copper, boron, adenosine
- 5,000 mcg biotin several times per week.
- 1 – 2 Tbsp diatomaceous earth daily; drink in cold water.
- Red light therapy in 630 nm to 660 nm range (aka, photobiomodulation, low level laser therapy, low power laser therapy).
- Castor oil may increase PGE2 in the scalp, a prostaglandin that is low in people with hair loss. 1 Tbsp castor oil + 1 Tbsp coconut, jojoba or almond oil + ½ tsp vitamin E oil and rub on scalp, let sit for 1 hour, shampoo twice to remove.
- Other herbals and supplements: saw palmetto, lysine, stinging nettle tea, low dose PABA, etc.

Oral Care

- Oral care: Brush 3 X / day, water pick, floss, etc. Once per day, end brushing with dipping a clean toothbrush in 3% hydrogen peroxide and brushing again. Leave for 30 seconds and rinse.
- Gargle: Evening with colloidal silver (swallow after gargling).
- Avoid using fluoride-containing dental products.

Lungs / Cardiac / Endocrine

- Deep breathing: 1 – 2 X / hour, watch this video if breathing difficulties persist: youtube.com/watch?v=m_4CGZzTTCo
- Nebulize: Nebulize lung therapies – 10 ppm colloidal silver, 1% to 3% food grade hydrogen peroxide.
- Over-the-counter
  - 81 – 325 mg aspirin (anti-platelet) – use as needed
  - Cool Cayenne pepper, 100,000 heat units (anti-coagulant – take separately from aspirin).
- Hyperbaric oxygen therapy (HBOT).
- Pre-existing endocrine conditions may be worsened by Covid-19. Take steps to minimize worsening of endocrine issues by maintaining a healthy weight, eating 2 to 3 meals per day (eliminate snacks unless otherwise advised by your healthcare provider), etc.

Neuro

- 120 – 600 mg total ginkgo biloba (may divide into 3 doses taken 3X/day).
- Other nootropics of choice including methylene blue, lion's mane extract for stimulating NGFs.
- Stay mentally and physically active, take supplements, keep up with social contacts, etc.

Recovery Protocol (Simple Recovery to Long Haulers), Neuro continued

Neuro, continued

- If neurological symptoms are present and decreased 128 Hz sensation at ankle, give PO or SQ 500 to 1,000 mcg methylcobalamin.
- Address: lack of smell and taste if affecting food intake (may need appetite stimulant)
- Discuss use of short-term prescription SSRI, fluvoxamine if significant neurological symptoms continue. Only recommend short term use. Does contain fluorine which should be avoided but may provide a benefit even when used briefly.
- Address the issue of NAD+ depletion and serotonin dysfunction oftentimes seen in "long haulers." Read this article if link is still available: https://nkalex.medium.com/the-team-of-front-line-doctors-and-biohackers-who-seem-to-have-solved-long-covid-5f9852f1101d

Public Health

- Maintain good hygiene, masks, social distance, as required by your location, etc.
- As long as you have long-haul covid symptoms, use a pulse oximeter once per day to confirm oxygen levels are within a normal range.

Your Physician

- Common Covid-19 "long haul" symptoms may include: cognitive issues, depression, anxiety, sleep disorder, stroke, skin problems, renal failure, diabetes, arrhythmias, heart inflammation, hair loss, palpitations, increased resting heart rate, chest pain, joint pain, red eyes, limb edema, anosmia, chills, pain, weight loss, hair loss, hearing loss, tinnitus, reduced lung capacity, chest discomfort, cough, red eyes, new hypertension, attention disorder, fatigue, low grade fever, hallucinations, impaired memory, short-term memory loss, delirium, intolerance to physical or mental activity, inability to concentrate, erratic heartbeat, GI issues, muscle and joint pain, proprioception issues (touching things and feeling vibrations), etc. Your physician: Discuss an effective strategy for complete recovery including the residual presence of symptoms affecting different systems of the body: immunological, neurological, gastrointestinal, psychological, cardiac / circulatory, respiratory, endocrine, dermatological, bioenergetics, latent viral infections (e.g., Epstein Barr), etc.
- Low dose naltrexone: 1 mg daily increasing to 4.5 mg daily for 2 to 3 months.
- Discuss options for addressing long-haul recovery, including outpatient vitamin C IVs (4.5 g – 17 g IV vitamin C every 2 to 4 hours) and / or glutathione IV.
- Discuss possibility of niacin and serotonin depletion and possible repletion options.
- Discuss possible off label short-term use of phentermine with your physician to reset dopaminergic, serotonergic and adrenergic activity.
- Gustavo Aguirre Chang, MD, has suggested the viral stage persists even in the advanced stages of the disease, "intracellularly and in a disseminated way in the cells of the walls of the blood vessels (endothelial cells and pericytes) and inside part of the blood cells." *(Aguirre-Chang, G. Persistent Symptoms of COVID-19: molecular tests by nasal and pharyngeal swabs do not detect the presence of the virus in intestines, heart and other organs and systems. Preprint available in ResearchGate. August 22, 2020. DOI: http://dx.doi.org/10.13140/RG.2.2.30458.31688/2 .*
- In addition to infecting blood vessel cells, the virus is found in endothelial cells, macrophages, monocytes, infiltrates (heart pericytes, pulmonary alveoli, spleen, lymph nodes and kidneys). Check out his publication, Management of the Patient with Persistent Symptoms.

Notes

Selected Potential Adjunctive Covid-19 / Influenza Therapies

<u>To be perfectly clear, none of the information presented in this book and specifically the chapter on Covid 19 is promoted as a preventive, treatment, or cure for SARS-Cov2 (or any other disease)</u>. I am not promoting any specific treatment or therapy. It is certain new critical information will emerge after the publication of this book. It is important to keep up-to-date on all aspects of health, including ways to enhance the immune system. **Each element of this chapter is meant to support the philosophy of health – to make the body so healthy it cannot harbor disease.** This does not mean healthy people do not get sick from a virus or other pathogen. It does mean they are better equipped to fend off pathogenic microorganisms. Vitamin C does not cure a cold, but it makes it much more likely the duration of the cold is shorter and the bothersome symptoms are lessened (although to be fair, supra-physiological doses of vitamin C have not been tested). The same is true of almost any infection. Vitamin C may not prevent the infection (although some would say this is debatable), but it may be used in large quantities (along with primary therapies) to quickly resolve an infection which is capable of rapidly depleting the ability of immune cells to deliver vitamin C to the site of the infection.

An important factor to consider is that some physicians and healthcare practitioners may hold one belief or standard to be true, but in their practice, they apply a different standard, one that is supported by scientific studies and data. <u>This does not preclude the fact that their personal beliefs may also correct</u>, but it may mean they are unable to back-up their closely held personal beliefs with widely acceptable scientific studies and data. Their personal beliefs may be based more on anecdotal evidence (i.e., casual observations in their clinical practice and not necessarily scientific analysis) and the study of mechanisms and molecular biology, human biochemistry, and physiology. For many, these casual observations are just as valid as scientific observations, but they lack acceptance by the broader scientific community. To keep their license, they must stay within acceptable practice standards. If possible, during your conversation with your healthcare practitioner, you may be able to ascertain their personal viewpoints without expecting them to practice outside of their comfort zone and what are considered to be standard-of-care guidelines.

Alternative and complementary therapies, foods, nutraceuticals, herbals / supplements, and lifestyle factors, also significantly contribute to overall health. Making a few positive changes almost always leads to better health. Under each listed therapy or health factor on this list, is one or more references supporting the information provided here. These claims are not mine but are made by others considered experts in their field. <u>None of the therapies listed here are intended to be a primary treatment for Covid-19 or any other medical condition</u>. **One or two articles supporting the same claim are usually not enough to support strong claims of efficacy but may be considered early evidence.** A possible mechanism should be proposed and generally accepted or at least recognized. Much of the research on Covid-19 is preliminary and needs several years of multiple investigations to fully understand the evolving nature of this pathogen and formulate effective treatment protocols.

Other countries besides the USA have different regulatory procedures for approving pharmaceuticals as well as natural approaches for treating various conditions. Many countries are more open to using natural therapies such as functional foods, herbals, hydrotherapy, alternative and complementary approaches, homeopathy, supplements, etc., as first line therapies.

For example, a research article coming out of the UK claims functional foods protect against Covid-19. Here is the title of the article: "Functional foods prevention of non-communicable disease can be translated into protecting against respiratory viral infections and Covid-19". Functional foods and nutraceuticals within popular diets contain immune-boosting nutraceuticals, polyphenols, terpenoids, flavonoids, alkaloids, sterols, pigments, unsaturated fatty acids, micronutrient vitamins and minerals (including vitamin A, B1, B2, B3, B5, B6, B7, B9, B12, C, D, E and K), and trace elements (including zinc, iron, selenium, magnesium and copper). Foods with antiviral properties include fruits, vegetables, fermented foods and probiotics, olive oil, fish, nuts and seeds, herbs, roots, fungi, amino acids, peptides and cyclotides (small disulfide rich peptides from plants). Regular moderate exercise may contribute to reduce viral risk and enhance sleep quality during quarantine, in combination with appropriate dietary habits and functional foods. Lifestyle and appropriate nutrition with functional compounds may offer further antiviral approaches for public health." By Alkhatib A. in Nutrients 2020, 12(9), 2633. https://doi.org/10.3390/nu12092633

An Austrian research group led by Alexander G. Haslberger, published a paper in 2020 claiming bioactive, food-based plant compounds and their unique form and function operate against the attachment and replication of the SARS-Cov-2 in humans. It is suggested the SARS receptors, ACE-2 and CD26, "show associations with mechanisms that regulate human senescence." Senescence is also known as growing old or aging. **Beyond the obvious observation, this implies specific foods act in ways to counter inflammation, alter epigenetic influences, and even alter the ability to fight an infection.** Researchers have also observed that, "Viral infections were seen to accelerate human aging… Infections also trigger a DNA damage response." (Haslberger A., et al. Mechanisms of selected functional foods against viral infections with a view on COVID-19: Mini review, in Functional Foods in Health and Disease 2020; 10(5):195-209.)

One of the items on the following list is curcumin, a compound found in turmeric, a commonly used ingredient in curries. This might lead you to believe that continental Indians (i.e., from the country, India) would experience less Covid-19. For comparison sake, the number of confirmed Covid-19 cases in the USA (in Jan 2021) was 25,050,308 compared to India's confirmed cases of 10,689,527. Using early data, covid-19 deaths in 2021 for the USA were 417,889 compared to India's deaths of 153,724. The population of the USA is 339,996,563 and the population of India is 1,326,093,184 (WHO Coronavirus Disease Dashboard). India's population is roughly four times more than the USA's population, but they had only 43% of covid cases and only 37% of covid deaths. These numbers alone are inadequate to fully understand the differences between the USA and India but they are interesting and more recently, India is comparable to the USA. Does the widespread and daily use of curcumin (and perhaps other plant-based foods and herbs) in India have an impact? It is possible a research protocol could be developed to address this question?

Figure 1. Covid-19 comparison between India and the USA
Using current Worldometers.info – covid data no longer collected as of 4/2024

Country	Covid Cases	Covid Deaths	Population
India (Jan 2021)	10,689,527	153,724	1,326,093,184
India (Feb 2022)	42,905,844	513,512	1,402,383,889
India (Oct 2023)	44,999,765	531,930	1,432,685,440
USA (Jan 2021)	25,050,308	417,889	332,639,104
USA (Feb 2022)	80,532,307	972,200	334,204,743
USA (Oct 2023)	109,003,518	1,179,690	339,996,563

We know curcumin is a protective factor against inflammation, in cardiovascular diseases, and possibly in some forms of cancer. If Americans thought consuming curcumin would protect them from Covid-19, how many Americans would consume as much curcumin as is consumed in Indian diets? Without examining more detailed epidemiological data and only considering the numbers in Figure 1, I would like to suggest this difference in Covid-19 susceptibility is related to many factors, possibly including dietary pattern. As previously discussed in chapter 17, the USA has never had a widespread healthy dietary pattern which provides protection from dietary and lifestyle related degenerative conditions such as heart disease, cancer, obesity, diabetes, neurodegenerative conditions, etc. Again, I am not suggesting the Indian dietary pattern is the reason for their lower early Covid-19 death rates. Their death rate might dramatically increase at any time. Most experts would claim this to be comparing apples and oranges. My only reason for pointing out this difference is because I believe their dietary pattern has more protective elements than most Americans' dietary patterns. In addition to dietary pattern, there are other confounding issues such as socioeconomic factors, access to health care, hygienic factors, geographic factors, family structures, prophylactic use of hydroxychloroquine and ivermectin, etc.

In support of curcumin protecting against Covid-19 is an article published in the Indian Journal of Clinical Biochemistry (PMID: 32641876) suggests curcumin is a "wonder drug and a preventive measure for Covid-19 management." The Indian authors go on to say they have noticed natural immunity against Covid-19 infections in many hospitalized patients in Indian settings, which is only now being more widely acknowledged. They propose a hypothetical treatment strategy using curcumin as a potential inhibitory agent for the initial infection, use of curcumin to modulate the inflammatory effects of SARS-Cov2, and they also suggest curcumin regulates the renin-angiotensin-aldosterone system (RAAS) – a system involved in regulating blood pressure. The biological properties and the protective aspects of curcumin could be considered by Americans when choosing a healthy dietary pattern. For example, adding turmeric in the form of one or two curry meals per week, warm turmeric and black pepper milk before bedtime, adding turmeric to smoothies and fresh juices, adding to bakery products, adding to scrambled tofu, etc., are reasonable dietary changes. Eating curry / turmeric occasionally may not have the same impact as eating turmeric at almost every meal. But adding enough protective and functional foods may, at some point, begin to lower your level of chronic inflammation or it may gradually lower your blood pressure – all excellent outcomes of making many small changes. Again, we are just beginning to put the pieces of the Covid-19 puzzle together. Does curcumin play a minor or significant role? It is likely one of many factors which in combination with other protective factors, may tip the balance of susceptibility in a protective direction. Of course, there are many other factors to consider and there may be other substances with similar or greater efficacy.

Suggested "therapies" in this chapter are adjunctive, meaning they should be used with the knowledge of your physician, as secondary therapies and not as primary therapies in the treatment of serious infections such as Covid-19 and influenza.

Alternative and complementary techniques which may be useful as adjunctive therapies

1. **Electromagnetic frequencies**: one or more manufacturers have Covid-19 specific frequencies.
   - Rife frequencies operate on the assumption that healthy cells and organs have specific frequencies which are different from diseased cells and organs.
   - Specific frequencies are used to either boost healthy cells or to target unhealthy cells. This is thought to reinforce and/or restore normal functions.
   - Some rife machines are programmed with up to 57 "anti-covid-19" frequencies. These frequencies could be run in doctor's offices, hospitals, nursing homes, public places, homes, etc.
   - Rife's light frequencies target hundreds of conditions and may be found at this website as a downloadable 171-page pdf: www.sppky2rife.com .
   - Non-Rife frequency generators use radio frequencies and some include audio.
   - Bemer therapy uses electromagnetic waves to stimulate activity in cells and improve circulation. There may be significant differences between various electromagnetic frequency generators on the market. Do your research and discuss your options with each company expert before you decide to purchase a unit.
   - Personally speaking, I have seen this technology used by an MD who has continued to see patients and frequent visitors in his home during 2020 and into 2021, without any transmission of SARS-CoV-2. They keep the frequencies running almost continuously and have not contracted Covid-19.
   - Check out units which have anti-covid frequencies.
   - Corona virus frequencies (ETDFL 2020 update) https://rifedigital.com/
     - Coronaviridae Infections: 0.04,0.24,9.68,42.85,172.5,203,412.5,592.5,775.29,819.34
     - Coronavirus (Human 1) 229E (HCoV-229E, OC43) : 0.04,0.24,33.4,72.54,305.37,443.5,512.5,621.73,775,900.4
     - Coronavirus (Human 2) NL63 (HCoV-NL63, HKU1): 0.05,0.2,33.4,72.54,305.37,443.22,507,621.73,735,900.4
     - Coronavirus (Middle East RS) (MERS-CoV): 0.05,0.2,33.4,75.5,308.5,441.5,507,621.73,735,900.4
     - Coronavirus (Novel) (2019-nCoV) : 0.05,0.2,33.4,72.54,305.37,452.55,509.75,621.73,738.5,900.4
     - Coronavirus (SARS) NL63 (HCoV-NL63, HKU1): 0.05,0.2,33.4,72.54,305.37,443.22,507,621.73,735,900.4
     - Coronavirus (Wuhan) (2019-nCoV): 0.05,0.2,33.4,72.54,305.37,452.55,509.75,621.73,738.5,900.4
   - PMID: 24206915, 31488097, 22843038, 24416255, 21829195, 31160272.

2. **Hyperbaric oxygen**: supports oxygenation and attenuates pulmonary inflammation. This potential therapy for Covid-19 has several ongoing clinical trials. <u>Initial results look very good</u>.
   - Route of administration: oxygen entry via lungs and possibly skin.
   - One or more treatments has potential to reduce inflammation and restore immune functions.
   - HBOT (hyperbaric oxygen therapy), may lead to immediate improvement in C-19 symptoms.
   - Caution: keep eyes closed to prevent oxidation of delicate lens which could cause cataracts.
   - PMID: 32574446.

3. **Magnetic fields**, pulsed electromagnetic fields (PEMF, transcranial magnetic stimulation): wide range of applications, restores circulation, promotes movement of lymphatic fluid, etc.
   - Used to treat non-union bone fractures. FDA cleared for pain therapy. Route of administration: apply to problematic area, may heat up over time. Monitor for excessive heat, usually after 40+ minutes of treatment.
   - Caution: Restoring circulation may promote detoxification of local tissues and in some cases, this may cause transient increased pain; this is usually temporary. Discontinue use and restart in a day or two at shorter treatment times.
   - Static magnetic field therapies are widely used and accepted for conditions such as pain, edema, fibromyalgia, sleep disorders, etc.
   - PMID: 4821958, 598067, 380258, 15180031, 11512529, 26665041; ISBN: 0-9664227-0-8.

4. **Microcurrent therapy**
   - Route of administration: skin contact using various attachments.
   - When to use: use over and around areas of pain (acute and chronic).

- Delivers a microcurrent that targets C-fibers (responsible for pain).
- Features an interactive response which constantly adjusts to changes in tissue characteristics (the body does not "habituate" or "accommodate" the signal).
- Avazzia Pro Sport ™ is an electronic microcurrent device approved by the FDA and cleared for the symptomatic relief and management of chronic, intractable pain and adjunctive treatment in the management of post-surgical and post-traumatic pain.
- Cautions: Do not use directly over heart or thyroid gland, do not use if you have metal implants, stimulator, pacemaker, etc. (https://www.avazzia.com/). You need a physician's prescription to obtain this product for personal use.
- PMID: 21496375, 27168571, 11022637, 6854110.

5. **Music therapy** (e.g., 528 Hz): Bach, hymns, singing, etc., increases the body's production of immune cells and lowers cortisol. Humming and whistling are also beneficial. PMID: 17400143, 27170831.

6. **Negative ion generator**: high voltage used to generate negative ions, some air purifiers are equipped with negative ion generators. Used to clean the air from airborne pathogens.
    - Set negative ion generator in home or office areas, hospital rooms, extended care rooms, etc.
    - Caution: A slight amount of ozone is produced during the process of generating negative ions. Take appropriate precautions.
    - Used to inactivate viruses.

7. **Ozone Treatments** (e.g., Ten Pass – done ten times): small amount of blood is withdrawn via a needle, heparinized to prevent clotting, combined with an equal volume of ozone at high concentration, and infused back into the patient under hyperbaric pressure. Each treatment takes about 40 minutes to 2 hours and is done by a qualified physician in the physician's office. Other ozone treatments may include ozone insufflation – also done under the supervision of a physician.
    - Improves blood oxygenation.
    - Ozone oxidizes glycoproteins and lipoprotein enveloped viruses (although this effect is questioned by some when the virus is in the body as opposed to in a lab setting).
    - Activates several biochemical and immunological pathways which send several viruses into retreat.
    - Powerful, safe treatment for conditions such as infections (e.g., influenza and pneumonia).
    - Must super-hydrate at least a day before the treatment.
    - Cost per treatment is around $500 to $1,000; Non-USA based treatments may be significantly less but you may also take increased safety risks.
    - Anecdotal success; not documented in the medical literature.
    - Used by some to treat Lyme disease.
    - Cautions: a physician will evaluate you and inform you of risk / benefit.
    - PMCID: PMC7498916.

8. **Red light therapy**: as of this writing, a clinical trial using red light therapy to treat acute lung inflammation has begun (NCT 04524715). It is red or near-infrared light which penetrates the body and stimulates mitochondria. Used as recommended, it does not burn your body and does not expose you to UV rays. Too much exposure may damage skin.
    - Light therapy (aka known as phototherapy) in combination with frequencies stimulates potentially sluggish metabolic processes.
    - Promotes tissue repair and used for wound healing.
    - May benefit psoriasis lesions.
    - May help with pain relief.
    - Many additional potential applications.

9. **Sauna bathing therapy:** sauna therapy is used to enhance the body's ability to detox and release fat-soluble toxins. Seek advice from people familiar with the different types of saunas and their best uses. Studies have shown sauna bathing is associated with cardiac, lung, neurological, cognitive, inflammatory, and skin benefits. (PMID: 32742639, 33197669, 21432093, 21951023, 11165553, 18525205, 30561752)
    - Time in the sauna should be titrated to your tolerance.
    - Different types of saunas and / or therapeutic bathing may include: infrared (near and far), near infrared lamp saunas (under supervision of a trained person), traditional saunas such as a wet sauna, wood burning or Finnish sauna, electric sauna, dry heat sauna, smoke sauna, sweat lodge, Russian Banya, sauna blanket, steam shower, hot springs, deep sea water bathing, steam inhalations, hot mud, poultices, etc.
    - Near infrared saunas activate cells and support metabolic processes.
    - Studies show sauna therapy may destroy enveloped viruses such as SARS-Cov-2, which is sensitive to heat and destroyed at temperatures tolerable to humans.
    - Studies show regular use of saunas decreases risk of dementia and Alzheimer's disease.
    - Near infrared saunas are used to stimulate circulation and "decongest" the body's organs.
    - Fever therapy via saunas is used to treat infections and kill of bacteria, viruses and fungi.
    - Sauna-induced hyperthermia is used to treat damaged and mutated cells and restore normal functions.
    - Sauna therapy combined with flushing-niacin is a powerful detox using the phenomenon of "rebound lipolysis" to release toxins typically found in fat stores. Before beginning sauna therapy, check with your physician about any potential negative side effects. Many people do not recommend combining flushing niacin and saunas. Before combining these two therapies see how you tolerate each therapy (i.e., flushing niacin and saunas) used individually. If you are uncomfortable with one of the therapies, combining them may be uncomfortable. Only combine if you are a seasoned sauna user and a seasoned niacin user.
    - Ensure you are well hydrated before using a sauna and drink water during the sauna session.
    - Frequent use of saunas may deplete minerals. To replace minerals, take liquid mineral drops on a regular basis. A significant amount of sodium is lost during sauna bathing. Repleting mineral losses for regular sauna bathers is important.
    - Be sure to wipe off sweat every few minutes.
    - Symptoms you need to immediately leave the sauna include: red face, racing heart, dizziness, feeling faint, feeling weak, overheating, feeling nauseated, etc.
    - Saunas are considered relaxing and typically activate the parasympathetic nervous system. For some, sauna bathing improves sleep quality.
    - You may lose up to 1 pint of sweat (about 1 pound) during the average sauna session.
- **You may have a "healing" reaction also known as a Herxheimer reaction when first beginning to use a sauna. You are not getting sick, but you are releasing internally stored toxins. This is a sign you may need to spend less time in the sauna and instead, gradually work up to longer times.**
    - As a practitioner, I have recommended saunas for my patients with difficult to treat / cure body rashes. This works about 50% of the time. Saunas may improve skin health.
    - Pregnant women and children should avoid saunas unless otherwise recommended by their healthcare provider. Other contraindications for sauna bathing include: unstable angina, <u>recent</u> heart attack, aortic stenosis, etc.
    - Do not combine saunas with consuming alcoholic beverages.

- Check with your physician to make sure any medications you are taking do not adversely affect using regular saunas.
- Never use a sauna without an easy-to-exit door.

10. **Scenar** (electrical pulses): Uses computer modulated electrical impulses to stimulate the brain, and then in return the brain's signals are received by the scenar device and this goes on until a healthy "equilibrium" is achieved.
    - Stimulates production of brain neuropeptides.
    - Used to restore healthy neural communication patterns, without permanently entraining (allows for restoring healthy neural responses.
    - Provides real-time feedback and constantly adjusts to the body's local energy.
    - Stimulates blood vessels and skin.
    - Influences nervous, endocrine and immune systems (www.backtohealthphysio.com.au/scenar-therapy)
    - PMID: 20879466, 16924799; NCT03755817.

11. **Thermography**: the human body is mostly thermally symmetrical. Comparative views of left and right sides may detect early abnormalities. Thermatomes relate to sympathetic control of blood flow.
    - Used for early diagnosis, narrows down and directs additional diagnostic measures. May be used to detect areas of concern in Covid-19 patients as well as detect surface skin temp.
    - Detects presence of inflammation where blood flow is either increased or decreased.
    - Used to diagnose 77+ conditions including early diagnosis of breast cancer, arthritic joints tend to have higher temperatures and this shows up on thermography, vascular abnormalities, hypo-perfusion, fibromyalgia, etc.
    - Views skin thermatomes, which are dependent on sympathetic nerve control of blood flow. The sympathetic system, including blood flow, reacts to pathology anywhere in the body. It is controlled by the CNS and may be observed using medical grade thermography – see video referenced below.
    - Thermatomes: Cranio-cervical (T1-T2); Upper limbs (T2-T7); Thorax (T1-T4); Abdomen (T1-L2); Lower extremities (T11-L2) (see book below, page 17).
    - PMID: 12144858; ISBN: 0-8493-8667-5 (Chronic pain: RSD Prevention & Management, p 17).
    - Video: https://www.youtube.com/watch?v=8Oz8WAnMKW8 – The clinical applications of digital thermal imaging.

12. **Transcranial direct current stimulation** (tDCS): this is a device providing an electrical current. It claims to increase, repair or otherwise improve brain functions. Used in conjunction with nootropics or substances known to enhance and optimize brain functions.

13. **Ultrasound**: high-frequency sound waves, considered safe and may have fewer side effects compared to medications.
    - May reduce inflammation.
    - https://cse.umn.edu/college/feature-stories/ultrasound-may-prove-be-effective-noninvasive-treatment-covid-19
    - https://cse.umn.edu/college/news/ultrasound-stimulation-spleen-could-lead-new-treatments-inflammatory-arthritis

14. **Vitamin C.** vitamin C supports immune functions. When it runs low, the infection becomes more difficult to control. For out-of-control hemorrhagic conditions, vitamin C is administered in gram ranges, preferably using IV vitamin C and under physician's supervision (but oral will work as well) up to 700 grams over a period of 5 to 7 days (Thomas Levy, MD on Ebola).

Diet (positive)

1. **Algae** (carrageenan, red algae such as dulse, laver, agar), high in lectins, recognizes the SARS-CoV spike protein, exhibits anti-viral properties. Could be due to high content of sulfur found in algae. PMID: 33041391.
2. **Antioxidant foods**: fruits, vegetables, herbs, spices, nuts, seeds, whole grains, legumes. Antioxidants interfere with increased oxidative stress seen in infections. May be protective against corona-induced encephalitis. PMID: 3173281
3. **Carrageenan:** There are 3 forms of carrageenans (repeating galactose units) based on their sulfate content with varying properties and functions: kappa, iota and lambda. Kappa has one sulfate per disaccharide, iota has two sulfates, and lambda has three sulfates per disaccharide. It is not proven to be an unsafe ingredient. As of 2018, carrageenan is deemed non-toxic (at 75 mg/kg body weight / day). Irish moss is a source of gelling carrageenan (Wiki, accessed Nov 2020).
4. **Cranberry**: compounds in cranberries inhibit bacterial-based biofilm. Anti-inflammatory. Targets pathogens responsible for gingivitis, yeast infections, urinary tract infections, etc.
5. **Fasting, 1 day** (water only fast): promotes mild ketosis. A 1 day fast is good and possibly desirable.
6. **Fasting, 3 days** (3-day water only fast): rebuilds immune system, promotes biological reset, weight loss, improves brain functions, etc.
7. **Fermented food** (non-pasteurized): jalapenos, sauerkraut, hot sauce, pickles, etc. Epidemiological data show countries consuming fermented foods may have less Covid-19 due to potential changes in the gut microbiome. DOI: https://doi.org/10/1101/2020.07.06.2014725
8. **Fresh herbs:** alpha pinene is the most commonly occurring terpene in nature and is produced by many herbs including basil, dill, parsley, etc. It is anti-inflammatory and exerts anti-pain properties (PMID: 30497379, 23607933)
9. **Garlic**: compounds in garlic (e.g., ajoene, allicin) are known to be anti-viral and may decrease elevated cytokines seen in in Covid-19. Garlic does not cure Covid-19 but may play a role in preventing Covid-19 if regularly consumed. Helps prevent depletion of endogenous antioxidant enzymes such as glutathione and catalase. Decreases cytokines. Anti-bacterial biofilms. PMID: 32512493, 31151279, 32803479.
10. **Grapefruit**: A compound in grapefruit juice can block the action of a liver enzyme, CYP3A4. This results in some medications remaining active in the circulation for longer than usual. This may lead to having too much of a drug in the circulation. This effect may last for up to 3 days. If you consume grapefruit juice, be sure to inform your physician before starting a new prescription. In reality, if you like to regularly consume grapefruit juice and take a medication which is affected by it, discuss taking a lower dose of the medication with your physician. Citrus fruits boost the immune system due to bioflavonoid, vitamin C and other beneficial compounds. Grapefruit seed extract-based nasal spray can kill corona virus (must come into direct contact with the virus). Grapefruit seed extract is effective against some pathogenic biofilms. PMID: 31136636
11. **Ginger (fresh):** antiviral. Syncytial cells fuse together with neighboring cells when invaded by a virus. Both the influenza virus and herpes virus form syncytial cells. This usually leads to the degeneration and destruction of good cells. Fresh ginger blocks the virus from attaching to healthy cells and forming syncytia. PMID: 2312394
12. **Greens every day** (raw is best). Greens are rich in natural folate and minerals. They boost the immune system and keep viruses away. Always wash fresh greens to ensure they are clean and safe to eat.
13. **Honey/lemon cocktail**: Additional ingredients could include fresh ginger juice, cayenne pepper, etc.
14. **Leeks**: high in lectins, recognizes the SARS-CoV spike protein. Plant lectins are potent inhibitors of coronaviruses by interfering with two targets in the viral replication cycle (PMID: 17428553).

15. **Mediterranean diet**: assoc with reduced risk for underlying inflammatory conditions and respiratory disease. Mediterranean diet includes foods with powerful bioactive compounds which protect against a wide array of modern lifestyle and epigenetic induced degenerative conditions. PMID: 32995043.
16. **Omega-3 fatty acids**: consume adequate amounts of omega-3 fatty acids found in plant sources such as Brussels sprouts, chia seeds, edamame, flax seed, hemp seed, perilla oil, walnuts, fish oil, etc. Omega-3 fatty acids and their long chain derivatives are more anti-inflammatory than their omega-6 fatty acid counterpart. Two to four servings of omega-3 containing foods per week is recommended. PMID: 32471251, 32438620.
17. **Plant-based diet**: Focus on a plant-based dietary pattern which may include up to 15 to 20% of calories from animal products but may also be 100% plant-based.
18. **Prebiotic foods**: asparagus, banana, garlic, Jerusalem artichokes, leeks, onions, seaweed, etc.
19. **Protein**: Low protein may increase risk of infection. (PMID: 32471251)
20. **Stinging nettle**: high in lectins, recognizes the SARS-CoV-2 spike protein (PMID: 33041391)
21. **Tonic water**: contains a small amount of quinine, but has not yet been shown to positively impact Covid-19.
22. **Water**: 95 – 125 oz water. Even though water has zero calories, it is critical to consume adequate water to promote regular detox functions. Optimal hydration helps regulate body temperature, eliminate metabolic waste products, maintain good blood pressure, promotes optimal bowel functions, and many more. The minimum amount of water necessary for health is 64 ounces per day. However, this may be inadequate for optimizing the immune system. Drink at least 4 8-oz glasses in the morning upon waking. Schedule your water intake throughout the day to ensure you meet the newest recommendations. It is best to avoid consuming water with meals. Drink 30 minutes before a meal and then wait to drink large quantities of water for at least 90 minutes after a meal.

Diet (negative)

1. **Alcohol**: limit alcohol to 1 drink / day. None is best when fighting off an infection. (PMID: 17726308).
2. **Arachidonic acid** (avoid consuming excessive amounts of foods high in omega-6 fatty acids): cows, dairy, fish, organ meats poultry, seafood, etc. As the covid-19 virus attacks the body, it stimulates the release of large amounts of pro-inflammatory cytokines. These cytokines interfere with the immune system and damage lung and other cells. This may ultimately lead to death. PMID: 32281329.
3. **Inflammatory foods**: avoid margarine, fractionated oils, red meat, allergenic foods, etc.
4. **Sugar** (avoid): sugar negatively affects the immune system, causing a reduction in white blood cells for up to 5 hours after consumption. White blood cells are targeted in Covid-19. Autopsies of those who died from Covid-19 shows widespread destruction of the immune system and destruction of white blood cells. PMID: 32281329.
5. **Avoid wheat** and wheat products due to gluten content and possible contamination with glyphosate, which may worsen the effects of Covid-19. Corn, soybean, alfalfa, cotton, sorghum and oat products may also be contaminated with glyphosate. The EPA continues to find no risks to public health when glyphosate is used in accordance with its current label. One international regulatory agency (the International Agency for Research on Cancer) has concluded glyphosate may be a carcinogen, while other international agencies have determined it to be an unlikely carcinogen. Glyphosate is thought to negatively alter the gut's microbiome possibly making one more susceptible to Covid-19 and altering the body's immune response to SARS-Cov-2 infection.
https://www.gmoscience.org/covid19thegutmicrobiotaandglyphosate/ , https://doi.org/10.1111/jgh.15047 , https://www.gmoscience.org/glyphosate-and-roundup-disrupt-the-gut-microbiome-by-inhibiting-the-shikimate-pathway/

Herbals, Oils and Supplements

1. **Ashwagandha**: molecular docking study showed six probable inhibitors against SARS-CoV-2 and ashwagandha is one of the six, along with tulsi, giloy, ursolic acid, etc. May bind to the spike protein of SARS-CoV-2. PMID: 32851919, 32684166.
2. **Berberine**: in barberry & turmeric; reduces viral titers. Suppresses some cytokines. (ISSN: 2160-3855).
3. **Bismuth** (found in Peptobismol): anti-biofilm. May suppress SARS-CoV-2 replication leading to decreased viral loads in upper and lower respiratory tracts. Bismuth thiols potent combination against antibiotic resistant bacteria. PMID: 32500504, 33028965.
4. **Black seed oil** (*nigella sativa*): If no HCQ, use black seed oil to drive zinc into the cell. Considered to be an ivermectin alternative at 40 mg/kg per day (1 – 2 tsp/d). Anti-viral, anti-oxidant, anti-inflammatory, immune modulator. May be a novel preventive and therapeutic strategy against SARS-Cov-2. Natural antiviral against SARS-Cov-2. PMID: 33047412, 32462996.
5. **Bromelain**: bromelain is a component of pineapple and the central pineapple core. It has been shown to inhibit SARS-CoV2 S-proteins. It is anti-viral, anti-inflammatory, anti-pain, anti-coagulant and fibrinolytic. It also inhibits proliferation of pro-inflammatory cytokines. Bromelain may work synergistically with turmeric. PMID: 33205039, 33084621, 32995771.
6. **Cat's claw**: Contains isoteropodine, an immunologically active alkaloid, antioxidant (20 – 60 mg / day) – avoid if you have had a transplant.
7. **Cayenne pepper**: improves cough. Acts as an anti-coagulant and vasodilator. PMID: 33432283.
8. **Charcoal**: charcoal works to clean the gut and bind some toxins. There is some evidence charcoal can bind certain chemicals in the gut which are associated with worsening symptoms of Covid-19, specifically worsening of lung symptoms.
9. **Chelation therapies**: Chelation therapies are important. They remove toxic heavy metals, iron, excess calcium, treat lead poisoning, improve circulation, etc. A high toxic load may worsen outcome of Covid-19. Chelation therapy may be a reasonable preventive measure if you are at higher risk for contracting the virus. Chelation agents / therapies include: penicillamine (used for copper toxicity; require prescription), EDTA (ethelene-diamine-tetra-acetic acid; oral or IV; approved for removal of lead), DMSA (dimercapto-succinic acid; approved for removal of lead; requires prescription), DMPS (2,3-dimercapto-propane-sulfonic acid; not FDA approved), TTFD (thiamin tetra-hydrofurfuryl disulfide; not FDA approved), desferasirox (iron toxicity; prescription), etc. Chelating also removes some nutrients including vitamins C and E. Natural, mild chelators include milk thistle (silymarin), cilantro, parsley, chlorella, chlorella-cilantro, alpha lipoic acid, food grade clays, far infrared sauna, Epsom salt baths, charcoal, liposomal glutathione, NAC, dandelion root, etc. Before beginning chelation therapy, seek medical guidance from a physician, naturopath and / or an experienced nutritionist. Ideally, a nutritionist works with your physician. Chelation therapy is short-term and not intended for long periods of time. It must be based on your specific condition and the type of chelating agent(s) used. Seek professional medical advice before beginning chelation.
10. **Coenzyme Q10**: If electron transport system (bioenergetics) is crippled by viral infections, you can support with supplemental CoQ10. CoQ10 is used to provide metabolic support for heart failure, exercise performance, diabetes, Parkinsons disease, protects the lungs, etc.
11. **Colloidal silver**: Drink up to 2 ounces daily of 10 ppm. May also use as a gargle, for nasal lavage, throat spray, face spray, etc.
12. **Copper**: Copper kills most germs. Copper in combination with NAC, colchicine and nitric oxide are used together as an experimental treatment for SARS-Cov-2. PMID: 32503814.
13. **Curcumin**: Binds to three protein receptors including ACE2 and SARS-CoV2 protease. Active against influenza virus, hep C virus, Zika virus, HIV, herpes 2, HPV, and CHIKV. Dose in the range of 3 mg / kg body weight. See turmeric. ISSN: 2160-3855.

14. **Elderberries**: Elderberry extracts may decrease the ability of a virus to infect a cell.
15. **Epigallocatechin gallate (EGCG) / ellagic acid**: Found in green tea. EGCG interacts with the ACE2, a target of SARS. Drink 2 – 3 cups/d or take 200 mg/d.
16. **Frankincense** (boswellia): Frankincense is anti-inflammatory, it may improve lung functions, and it inhibits inflammatory cytokines. Anti-biofilm properties. Strongly anti-bacterial against gram positive.
17. **Fulvic acid:** product of decomposition. Potential benefits include reduced inflammation, enhanced immune functions, may protect against specific types of brain diseases, may boost cellular functions, enhance gut health, boost testosterone, etc. May take food grade fulvic acid internally, use for foot baths, half body baths, face masks, etc.
18. **Ginkgo**: Ginkgo compounds (e.g., ginkgolic acids) have shown in vitro effects of anti-tumor, inhibits lipogenesis, decreased AMPK activation, potentially rescues amyloid-beta related synaptic impairment, anti-viral, etc. Studies show ginkgo compounds inhibit virus entry into cell by blocking the initial fusion event of enveloped viruses. PMID: 32179788, 32606248.
19. **Ginseng**: Modulates the immune system and may possess both preventive and supportive mechanisms for SARS-Cov-2. PMID: 33159391, 33013395, 33100613.
20. **Grapefruit seed extract**: Nasal spray containing grapefruit seed extract and xylitol may prevent colonization of nasal passages with SARS-Cov-2. PMID: 33173650.
21. **Helichrysum**: anti-inflammatory, anti-viral, anti-coagulant. PMID: 20933508.
22. **Hyssop**: Anti-viral. PMID: 21513560.
23. **Iron chelation**: EDTA may help with iron chelation / binding; could be beneficial in addressing cytokine storm symptoms related to high iron. PMID: 32681497, 32418885, 32318324, 33381464. EDTA also binds calcium, cadmium, and strongly binds zinc. Other heavy metal chelating agents include: DMSA (dimercaptosuccinic acid) and DMPS (2,3-dimercapto-1-propanesulfonic acid) for chelating potentially toxic metals antimony (Sb), arsenic (As), cadmium (Cd), lead (Pb) and mercury (Hg). DMPS is best for multiple metal overexposures. DMPS strongly binds copper.
24. **Licorice root**: Glycyrrhizic acid (licorice root), found to be best suited for preventing entry of SARS-CoV-2 into the cell. Strongly anti-inflammatory. May protect against viral infections. PMID: 32552462, 33159391.
25. **Methylene blue**: One of oldest synthetic treatments for malaria. Rapidly cures malaria and prevents re-infection. Thought to abort effects of bradykinin by inhibition of nitric oxide synthase inhibitor and **promotes oxygen saturation**. **Converts ferric iron to ferrous iron.** It is a MAOI, which means it can raise risk of serotonin syndrome when used concomitantly with SSRIs. It is inexpensive but widely available. Limit dose to 2 mg / kg (half this dose if using SSRIs – check with your healthcare provider first). **Avoid if G6PD deficient, on SSRI or pregnant**. A strong antioxidant, good against brain inflammation. Effective in reduced or oxidized form. Accesses and targets CNS. Methemoglobinemia. Infections. Good for mitochondria. ARDS. Septic shock. Currently in phase 2 clinical trial for treatment of SARS-CoV2. NCT04635605, PMID: 33254484.
26. **Mullein**: targets lymphatic and respiratory problems. Recommended for cough, common cold, bronchitis, COPD, asthma, and viral infections. Use as tea or tincture.
27. **N-acetyl cysteine (NAC)**: precursor to the endogenous antioxidant, glutathione. Used to loosen thick mucus in the lungs. Used to treat Tylenol overdose. Boosts the immune system. Metal chelator. Suppresses viral replication, Reduces inflammation. Improves cell mediated immunity. Decreases the frequency of the flu as well as the severity and duration of the flu. Suppresses cytokines such NF-kB, IL-8, IL-6, etc. May be a direct inhibitor of SARS-Cov2. PMID: 33177829, 32503814.
28. **Nattokinase (soy product)**: produced by *bacillus subtillus*. May prevent SARS-CoV-2 infection via spike protein degradation. May prevent clot formation. PMID: 36080170, DOI: 10.3390/molecules27175405

29. **Nicotinic acid**: SARS-CoV-2 attaches not only to ACE2 receptors but nicotinic acetylcholine receptors (nAChRs). As described by Marco Leitzke (PMID: 36650574), nAChRs are the principle structure of cholinergic neuromodulation (major neurotransmitter involved in higher brain functions). Viral attachment to nAChRs, as in the case of SARS-CoV-2, the virus substantially compromises neuronal communication, leading to cognitive, neuromuscular, mood impairment, and in rare cases, vegetative states. The presence of nicotine is thought to displace the virus and promote cholinergic transmission, leading to complete remission. Nicotine patches are good for preventing covid infections.
30. **Oregano oil**: antiviral, antibacterial. 1 – 2 drops/d. Also, food grade neem oil at ¼ - ½ tsp/d.
31. **Papain**: A papain-like protease shows promise of anti-viral activity against C-19. PMID: 32845033.
32. **Phloretin**: Found in apples, pears, strawberries. Influences charge, fluidity and permeability of cells. Regulates cytokines via epigenetic mechanisms. Negatively impacts virus reproducibility. ISSN: 2160-3855.
33. **Polyphenols**: Found in sage. Targets herpes simplex 1 virus, HIV & SARS-CoV. ISSN: 2160-3855.
34. **Quercetin** (and luteolin): Anti-inflammatory. Zinc ionophore (other zinc ionophores include: ECGC, pomegranate and citrus peel, HCQ, olive leaf extract (1 tsp, 1 – 3x/d), oregano, black walnut husks, etc.). Found in onions, capers, chives, Gingko biloba, St. John's Wort, and elderberry. Used to inhibit entry and docking of virus in early stage of influenza. Inhibits docking station ACE. **Rec dose: 50 – 800 mg / day**. May improve mental performance, anti-carcinogenic, anti-inflammatory, anti-viral, antioxidant, etc. ISSN: 2160-3855.
35. **Rosemary**: known to have epigenetic action, anti-cancer actions such as causing apoptosis of tumor cells, PMID: 32532056, 27869665, 32362243.
36. **Serrapeptase**: anti-biofilm, anti-inflammatory, infections, wound healing, carpal tunnel, mucolytic. Alternative to NSAIDS. Reduces swelling. Recommend 120,000 to 240,000 spu serrapeptase.
37. **Shilajit**: substance secreted by rocks in some mountain ranges, particularly high in fulvic acid.
38. **St. John's Wort**: May have beneficial effects on SARS-CoV-2 induced cytokine storm. PMID: 32501634.
39. **Sulforaphane**: Found in broccoli. Targets influenza and Epstein Barr viruses (EBV). Upregulates immunesystem. Induces DNA methylation. ISSN: 2160-3855.
40. **Suramin**: effective for inhibiting a wide range of viruses, including enteroviruses, Zika virus, Chikungunya and Ebola viruses via inhibition of viral attachment, viral entry into the cell, etc. (Yin, Luan, Zhou, Xu, et al., Nature Structural & Molecular Biology 28, 319-325 (2021).
41. **Thieves oil**: Blend of clove, lemon, cinnamon, eucalyptus and rosemary oils. PMID: 32803479.
42. **Thymoquinone**: Found in nigella sativa (black seeds) and black seed oil. Targets avian influenza virus (H9N2). Reduces pathogenicity of virus. Modifies epigenetic machinery such as DNA methylation / demethylation. ISSN: 2160-3855.
43. **Turmeric**: Turmeric in combination with black pepper show potential to minimize the cytokine storm related to SARS-CoV-2 infection. The combination of turmeric and bromelain have been shown to interfere with SARS-CoV-2 infection. PMID: 33206688, 33205039.
44. **Wormwood (artemisinin)**: Has been shown to attenuate inflammation and cytokine storms. Similar mechanism as HCQ without cardiac liability; modification of RBC surface immunology. PMID: 32405226.

Lifestyle

1. **Air filtration**: HEPA filter, ozone function, negative ions, UV, etc.
2. **Colloidal silver**: Silver nanoparticles, around 10 nm are effective in inhibiting extracellular SARS-CoV-2 at concentrations ranging between 1 and 10 ppm; cytotoxic effects are observed at 20+ ppm. PMID: 32958250. Generally anything above 30 ppm is unnecessary and 10 ppm is ideal.
3. **Earthing / grounding / forest bathing**: get outside and make direct contact with moist earth.

4. **Exercise**: activates BDNF. If possible, stay active, getting 3,000 to 20,000 steps per day. If ill and weak, aim for 500+ steps per day.
5. **Gargle / oral rinses**: avoid alcohol-based gargles; use colloidal silver, iodine water, ascorbic acid water, diluted hydrogen peroxide water, etc.
6. **Hydrogen peroxide**: Use 3% food grade hydrogen peroxide to gargle and brush teeth after regular brushing routine. Rinse with water. Also good for immediate treatment of bites, cuts, scrapes, etc.
7. **Hydrotherapy**: This is an important adjunctive therapy with several possibilities. Hot and cold fomentations, half baths, therapeutic showers, pail pours, etc. See appendix on hydrotherapy.
8. **Iron toxicity**: Terminate ferritin toxicity / cytokine storm possibly by using EDTA or a physician prescription for using deferasirox 20 mg / kg / day, treat anaerobic bacterial integration and blood attack using: prescription for Metronidazole 15 mg / kg / day with potential adjunct therapy using broad spectrum antibiotics (prescription). Be sure to discuss methods of repleting essential minerals lost during iron chelation therapy with deferasirox and other methods.
9. **Nasal lavage**: one route of entry for viruses is the nose. Keep your nose and nasal passages clean, especially if you are routinely exposed to the virus.
10. **Nebulize:** Pulmicort, albuterol – both prescriptions, discuss with your physician. Non-prescription options include colloidal silver, highly diluted iodine, 1% to 3% food grade hydrogen peroxide, etc. look into Dr. Shallenberger's hydrogen peroxide nebulizer treatment for early onset colds. Dilute 5 ml of 3% food grade hydrogen peroxide in 100 mL of saline solution. Store in a dark sealed glass container. Use 3 mL (3 cc) of the solution for each treatment. Repeat this treatment hourly for 1 day and then 4 – 6 times per day until condition resolved. Dr. Jocker's protocol is: add 2 tsp of 3% food grade hydrogen peroxide to 8 oz saline water to make a 0.1% solution. Use 2 – 3 ml or ½ tsp of this mixture for each nebulizing session. Keep refrigerated. Dr. Brownstein's protocol just takes the hydrogen peroxide recipe above and adds 2 drops of 2% nascent iodine. You can go up to 5 to 6 drops after adjusting to 2 drops. You can also nebulize 10 ppm nano silver (not home-made colloidal silver bc the particles are too large). For acute infection, nebulize 6 to 7 minutes 3 to 5 times a day. For prevention, nebulize up to twice a day. For lung regeneration, nebulize starting at once a day. www.georgekramermd.com/hydrogenperoxide/
11. **Obesity**: lose weight if necessary; avoid weight gain. Obesity exacerbates inflammation and increases risk of hyper-coagulopathy. PMID 32849309. Obese people have triple risk of hospitalization due to Covid-19. Obesity also decreases lung capacity and reserve making Covid-19 more lethal.
12. **Sauna (infrared)**: Enveloped viruses are sensitive to heat. Heat can assist in clearing the upper airways, deactivating and dislodging viruses. PMID: 32742639.
13. **Thermophore**: Thermophore heating pads provide moist heat. They can be used as a type of hot fomentation. May be used for pneumonia, bronchitis, coughs, arthritis, colitis, peptic ulcer, influenza (but not for tuberculosis or heart attacks). https://www.ucheepines.org/fomentations/
14. **Vitamin C IV**: A physician may administer vitamin C via a butterfly IV, a pH-balanced, isotonic solution including vitamin C. Usually sodium ascorbate is used. Depending on the amount in the IV solution, the infusion may last 5 to 30 minutes. You need to eat something before receiving the IV vitamin C push (may lower blood glucose). Cost may range from $50+ depending on the amount given. You may need to supplement the IV with oral vitamin C. Take oral vitamin C to bowel tolerance.

Chapter 20

Health parties

Maybe you are excited about your excellent health and want to share your enthusiasm and experience with others. If this is the case, consider planning a health party. You can design a health party, but instead of calling it a "health" party, make up a more exciting name which would work with your friends. This chapter is short and more about providing you with ideas to further develop.

Think about your goals for the party. Is it an icebreaker or is it to model or teach a new healthy behavior or demonstrate a skill? Maybe you want to introduce a group of friends to a new health concept. A party is a great way to have fun and learn something new.

Potential activities for a "health party"
- Think about your goals for the party such as having fun, education, model a behavior, teach a new skill, etc.
- What does it take to implement a fun and successful party?
- Think about the mixture of attendees and how they may affect the success of the party.
- Always invite a couple of people with sanguine temperament and at least one "heckler," this is a good combination.
- How many people can you accommodate?
- What ages are you targeting or does age matter?
- Contact any professionals or experts you may want to have at the party to determine their availability to attend and participate.
- Always do a disclaimer at the beginning of each party and make sure everyone knows you are not practicing medicine, etc. Make sure everyone realizes there is no liability for participating in any activities. Either get in writing or on video.
- Always make sure everyone knows there are going to be differing opinions; no one is the repository of everything correct and true all the time.
- Emphasize there is room for competing and differing opinions.
- **Never single out a person or embarrass them without getting their permission in advance if you are going to use them as an example. Keep in mind, medical information is privileged. Just because you know something about someone's health does not make it ethical to discuss it with others without their explicit permission and the exact scope of what may be divulged.**
- Choose from one or more activities on the next page or make up your own games.
- Do one or more food demos of healthy snacks, beverages, etc.
- Demonstrate culinary techniques such as opening a coconut, knife skills, etc.
- Mystery ingredient – identify based on description, taste, etc.
- Make a "medicine cabinet" item such as a lip or skin balm, soap, salve, tincture, etc.
- Outdoor physical activity, partner a low activity person with a high activity person
- Indoor physical activities

Potential activities for a "health party" continued

- Competition: outdoor activity which is healthy and competitive (e.g., who lowers their BP the most, who has the highest O2 sat, who has the highest skin conductivity, etc.
- Test the new health "device" such as a 1 to 4 lead EKG, thermographic camera, pulse oximeter, stethoscope, otoscope, 128 Hz tuning fork for vibration sense, etc.
- The doctor-is-in game – 10 hints to describe the condition from hardest to easiest.
- Group games
- Group song – completely made up on the spot and recorded and posted on social media.
- Guess this condition game.
- Exercise your senses!
- The professor-is-in session: short lecture or illustration (not more than 5 minutes) then let every attendee add their "content" for 30 seconds.
- College bowl: teams compete to answer health questions correctly.
- New research findings corner.
- Keep a diary of each health party and what was taught and learned.
- Who can scavenge the most different wild edible plants and correctly ID.
- Who makes the best wild edible salad?
- Greatest lecture ever given – go! Watch out TED!
- Watch short health videos.
- Plant seeds, seed exchange, plant exchange, etc.
- Building project demonstration (teach a specific skill or build something) such as a sauna, strawberry tower, solar oven, etc.
- Color-based potluck (e.g., green, red, purple, etc.) – describe the benefits of your potluck dish ingredients.
- Vitamin D party: do something outdoors on a sunny day and expose your skin (just not all of it).
- The healthy mentor the unhealthy: every healthy person adopts an unhealthy person and teaches them healthy habits, activities, etc. Advertise in the church bulletin for healthy members who would like to occasionally mentor people desiring to improve their health. This could involve introducing them to new activities, sharing recipes, encouraging them to make positive changes, etc.
- The periodic table game – buy or check out a book about the periodic table and come up with questions about each element.
- Chemistry is destiny game – choose a common or even a rare chemical and describe how it is important in human life (e.g., calcium signaling, voltage gated calcium channels in neurons, sodium potassium pumps in neurons, tyrosine and thyroid hormone, dopamine and movement, fatty acids and inflammation, melatonin makes it safe for you to sleep (premier antioxidant), dancing and dopamine, nitric oxide, etc.
- Health intervention in the community such make smoothies or fresh juices for those in nursing homes, make them healthy teas, give out nice soaps, bathe feet, cut nails, etc.
- What does the Bible say (about a specific health issue)?

Section 4

Country Living Plant-based Culinary Arts

Chapter 21
The green smoothie

Chlorophyll is a family of green pigments found in all plants and algae. Chlorophyll is a complex compound with a ring structure and a molecule of magnesium in the center. Structurally, it resembles hemoglobin which is found in human blood and has a ring structure with iron in the center. The chloroplast is the basic functional unit in plants. Each chloroplast absorbs sunlight and carries out the chemical process known as photosynthesis. Photosynthesis is how plants synthesize carbohydrates using sunlight, CO_2 and water. Green smoothies are rich in chlorophyll. For example, spinach is 1% chlorophyll by dry weight. It can be beneficial to eat ½ to 1 pound of greens per day – the green smoothie is the best way to do this!

Some health benefits of green smoothies may include:

1. Green plants such as spinach, kale, Swiss chard, watercress, beet greens, Romaine, etc., are nutrient superstars!
2. You can eat more greens in a smoothie than most people would eat in one week.
3. Greens are excellent sources of magnesium.
4. When greens are blended and consumed, the color-giving chlorophyll molecules are so high in phytonutrients they provide healing as well as health-promoting properties.
5. Chlorophyll possesses antioxidant properties and protects against specific toxins.
6. Chlorophyll is associated with reduced risks of certain types of cancers.
7. Regular and generous consumption of chlorophyll is associated with delayed onset of age-related diseases, oftentimes associated with excess free radicals.
8. Chlorophyll has been reported to inhibit radiation-induced mitochondrial and DNA damage.
9. Chlorophyll is associated with a healthy body composition.
10. Chlorophyll is anti-inflammatory.
11. Chlorophyll promotes wound healing.
12. Chlorophyll has been shown to induce beneficial effects in those receiving chemotherapy and it may minimize chemotherapy-related side effects.
13. Chlorophyll may benefit rheumatoid arthritis.
14. Chlorophyll induces healthy changes in the gut microbiome.

15. Chlorophyll produces positive changes in ulcerative colitis.
16. Chlorophyll is beneficial in hematological conditions.
17. Green smoothies are rich in calcium, vitamin K, magnesium and other bone healthy nutrients.
18. Green smoothies are known to improve seasonal allergies.
19. Green smoothies promote an alkalizing metabolism.
20. Green smoothies promote mental clarity.

Details about green smoothies

1. Fresh green smoothies are type of fruit- and vegetable-based beverage. They include leafy greens, fruit, some type of liquid, maybe a sweetener and any other flavors you may want to add. Smoothies retain all the ingredients of whatever you add to the blender. In fact, high-speed blending may break open cell walls which even digestive processes may not access. Blending is a great way to consume a lot of healthy nutrients and fiber. This means you must peel, core, de-seed (some seeds are not as bitter as others), and remove anything from the fruit you do not want to drink. Smoothies also retain both the soluble and insoluble fibers of the original food. They promote a wide range of gastrointestinal (GI) health. One caution regarding spinach is its high oxalate content. If you regularly consume spinach be sure to drink plenty of water.

2. Common smoothie ingredients are frozen fruit (bananas, pineapple, mango, berries), melons, avocado, greens, cucumbers, nuts and seeds. Smoothie liquids include water, ice, nut and grain-based milks, fruit juice and tea. Other ingredients include coconut milk or water, coconut meat, seeds, oats, vanilla, protein powders, herbs, spices, vanilla extract and / or chocolate.

3. If you are 100% plant based, you are not consuming any animal products. This puts you at significant risk for a number of vitamin and mineral deficiencies as well as a deficiency of omega-3 fatty acids. However, if you are not 100% plant based, a smoothie is a good way to incorporate animal products such as milk and yogurt. If you are 100% plant-based, adding coconut milk or other plant-based products such as cashews, walnuts, flaxseeds, plant-based yogurt or plant-based cream cheese may be good options. Some processed plant-based products may have added vitamin B12 which would be a bonus.

4. **If you regularly consume liquid meals, you may be bypassing a significant aspect of the digestive process, chewing and mixing food with saliva.**

5. Smooth, creamy and ice-cold smoothies require a high-speed blender.

6. A word about sweeteners. Many have concerns about the increasing use of honey, especially when harvested by large scale honey farmers. It is not because honey is a bad sweetener, it is because of the effects on the honey bee population. For this reason, sparingly use honey. Fortunately, there are other great sweeteners. Here is my top 14 list of sweeteners (not in any order): Blackstrap molasses, maple syrup, dates / date paste, coconut or palm sugar, brown rice syrup, licorice root- / stem-derived sweet liquid, fruit, yacon syrup, Lacuma, xylitol, barley malt syrup, rapadura, monkfruit with erythritol, and brown sugar.

7. Another concern about bee products is pollen. Pollen is collected by sticky mats as the bees fly into their colony to deliver the pollen. It is not uncommon for the sticky pollen collection mats to also remove the bee's legs / feet. It is for this reason, **I never recommend the use of bee-collected pollen**.

Green smoothie ingredients

- Add four or five handfuls of fresh greens including spinach, kale, beet greens, Swiss chard, small head of lettuce, etc. Greens are rich in nutrients. Be sure to drink at least 95 to 125 ounces of water every day to ensure optimal absorption and digestion. If using kale, add to hot water for 1 to 2 minutes to soften the cell walls, then add the wilted kale to a high-speed blender with remaining ingredients.

- Add 2 cups frozen or fresh pineapple (frozen makes it really cold and tasty). Adding fruits such as pineapple makes green smoothies easy to digest, improves immunity and improves blood functions. If you use fresh pineapple instead of frozen pineapple, you may want to add about a cup or so of ice. This may slightly dilute the flavor. The pineapple stem and fresh unpastuerized pineapple juice is rich in bromelain.

- Ginger root is strongly anti-inflammatory. Add about a one-inch knob of fresh ginger. Peel and thinly slice it unless you plan to juice it first.

- Cucumbers are low in calories, high in water, and nutrient rich.

- Adding green coconut water and the coconut meat takes a fantastic green smoothie and makes it extra delicious! The coconut water adds a unique depth of flavor and makes the green smoothie a true superstar of functional foods.

- Vanilla flavored protein powder gives the green smoothie a rich, sweet taste.

- To add omega-3 fatty acids to your green smoothie routine, add four to six walnuts or a teaspoon or two of flax, hemp or chia seeds and blend. It makes your smoothie thicker and adds valuable nutrients.

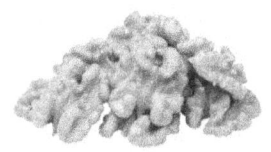

- Lemons brighten up a green smoothie and add additional nutrients. Squeeze a wedge or use the whole lemon. If you add a lemon, be sure to drink it right away or it may develop bitter flavonoids. May reduce the taste of sweet ingredients.

- Add fresh mint for an extra refreshing smoothie.

- If you want more protein, add protein powder, yogurt, or milk instead of water.

Equipment

I use a Professional Waring blender (I get no financial compensation for this endorsement). It has more horsepower than either a Vitamix or Blendtec. Both of these are good blenders. The Blendtec does better in several categories. It blends up small strawberry and raspberry seeds better than any other blender I have ever used, and I have experimented with most of them. It also processes ice into an icee really well, better than any other blender. The Waring (commercial blender with 3.5 hp), Vitamix (2.5 hp), Blendtec (2.5 hp), NutriBullet (0.8 hp) and Magic Bullet (0.34 hp), are all good options. The Bullet blenders are not considered high-speed but do a decent job with smoothies for around a quarter of the cost.

The waring blender is found in almost every restaurant and bar in the world. It is the food service industry standard and is NSF certified. The best part of a professional Waring blender may even beat the price of both Vitamix and Blendtec. I also like the Waring blender because of its ½ gallon blending container which exceeds both commonly available Vitamix and Blendtec models.

A simple and inexpensive electric citrus juicer costing around $10 to $15, works well. It is great for juicing grapefruit, oranges, tangelos, lemons and limes. If you juice a lot of citrus and / or you enjoy fresh pomegranate juice, a heavy-duty commercial grade citrus press works well for both.

Juicers include a wide range of juice extraction technology. Juicers range in price from $35 to $1,000+. You may choose from single auger to double auger (twin gear) juicers. The centrifugal force juicer is a fast juicer. I like the centrifugal juicers, especially if you are juicing for a crowd. The masticating slow juicers are a newer addition to juicers. They slowly grind the juice without heating up from the high kinetic type centrifugal juicers. This is thought to better preserve nutrients. The two-stage hydraulic press-type juicers are another good choice but take considerable time and effort and they tend to be extremely heavy, bulky and difficult to clean, making it less likely to use. I have been happy with the lower end cost centrifugal juicers. I look for juicers which take large pieces of fruits and vegetables, making the prep a little easier. One way to test the efficiency of a juicer is the pulp should be relatively dry and not dripping with juice. Either compost the pulp or give to your farm animals. If you are using lemon, ginger, hot peppers, etc., be sure to remove their pulp before giving to an animal. I have been the fortunate recipient of several excellent juicers and each time I use these juicers, I feel a debt of gratitude to each of the people who gifted them.

Wheatgrass juicers are relatively inexpensive. If you frequently drink wheat grass, you should be able to find a juicer for under $40.

Ginger juicers are ceramic with small sharp points across the top. Ginger is rubbed across the top and the juice is separated from the fibrous hairs in the ginger rhizome and flows into the small collecting moat around the perimeter. Sometimes I add fresh ginger juice to a smoothie instead of putting in the peeled rhizome to lessen the fibers in a smoothie. You can address this by peeling and then slicing into thin rounds and then blending. Juicing vs. blending removes almost all of the ginger fibers.

Prep all the fruits and vegetables before you start blending. When I juice, I prep all the fruits and vegetables and place the prepped fruit and vegetables in bowls. This allows you to alternate hard and soft fruits and vegetables when juicing. For making a smoothie, add the leafy greens first followed by fruits and vegetables on the top. Add the liquid and turn on the blender. I like to add some ice cubes to make sure the smoothie is cold.

Smoothie combinations

- 2 – 3 oranges, orange zest, 2 cups frozen berries, ½ cup pomegranate juice, 1 vanilla yogurt, 1 tsp beet powder
- 1 frozen banana, 2 Tbsp almond butter, 1 Tbsp carob powder, 2 Tbsp Roma powder, 3 cups plant milk, 2 medjool dates, 1 tsp vanilla extract
- 3 cups frozen strawberries, 1 cup frozen pineapple, 1 Tbsp beet powder (or small piece of beet), 2 Tbsp protein powder, 3 cups plant milk.
- 2 cups frozen pineapple, 2 cups frozen mango, 3 cups coconut water, ½ cup passionfruit nectar, 1 tsp vanilla extract, 4 – 6 oz vanilla yogurt.
- 4 cups cantaloupe, 1 cup fresh orange juice, 2 Tbsp fresh mint, juice of 1 lime, lime zest.
- ½ cup almond butter, ¼ cup walnuts, ¼ cup pecans, 1 frozen banana, 4 cups plant milk, ¼ cup chocolate sauce or hazelnut spread, ¼ cup Roma powder, 2 tsp vanilla extract, pinch salt.
- 4 cups frozen mango, 12 ounces vanilla yogurt, 1 cup mango nectar, ¼ cup plant whipped cream.

Fun smoothie additives: cooked tapioca balls (add after blending), coconut water, coconut flakes, fruit powders, fruit nectars, nuts, seeds, spinach, lettuces, frozen fruit concentrate cubes, spices, parsley, granola, applesauce, fresh juices, etc.

Resources

https://www.youtube.com/watch?v=flwkhuLdjas - Sergei Boutenko
https://www.youtube.com/watch?v=2HTT37VdE-8&feature=emb_rel_end 30 day green smoothie challenge

Discussion questions

1. How does the quality of each individual ingredient affect the taste and character of the final product?
2. Would you be willing to try the 30-day green smoothie challenge by Sergei Boutenko?
3. What types of health benefits would you expect to experience at the end of a 30-day green smoothie challenge?

Chapter 22

Fresh juices as a part of a healthy lifestyle

There is a certain simplicity to juices and smoothies. Usually the ingredients are fresh, sweet, easy to consume, requires only a glass and straw, and the only equipment needed is a juicer or high-speed blender. What could be easier?

Fresh juices are a great way to consume amazing amounts of nutrients. For example, you may not eat 10 pounds of carrots in one week, but juicing 10 pounds yields a lovely half gallon or so of sweet, health-promoting, life-giving carrot juice. You may not like spinach, but you may love drinking a "green smoothie" full of spinach, pineapple, cucumber and fresh ginger. Both fresh juices and smoothies contain lots of nutrients, but during the process of juicing, much of the fiber is removed. This is not the case for smoothies, where all the fiber is retained and consumed. However, this should not detract from juicing. There are times and conditions where low fiber juices are preferred over fiber-containing smoothies. Consuming juices and smoothies provide raw factors such as enzymes, heat sensitive vitamins, the natural form of folate, etc.

Fresh juices are meant to be slowly sipped and savored, not gulped. While there are huge benefits to both juices and smoothies, there are a few drawbacks as well. One drawback is we do not have to chew the fruits and vegetables. We basically swallow them. Potentially you could drink 16 or more ounces of juice or a smoothie within a few seconds, which would be impossible to do if you were eating the equivalent amount of whole fruits and vegetables. This uncouples the stomach from signaling the brain about fullness and satiety, which takes around 20 minutes from the first bite. Without chewing, the brain does not have enough time to adequately anticipate the arrival of food in the stomach and send critical messages to the brain regarding food composition. Also, because the food is already blended, it may not spend as much time mixing with saliva, stomach acid, and possibly intrinsic factor (needed for vitamin B12 absorption).

Another issue with liquids and juices relates to the salivary glands. The actions and movements of chewing stimulate secretion of saliva into the mouth. Saliva is necessary for beginning the processes of digestion. Juicing is a great lifestyle but it is critical to combine great habits with sustainable habits such as chewing something at every meal (the more you chew the greater the saliva output; thoroughly chewing each bite is important – 25 to 30 chews per bite is recommended), consuming optimal amounts of vitamins and minerals, getting enough fiber, drinking enough water, etc.

The long-term health effects of under-utilizing two critical proteins required for absorbing food-based vitamin B12, haptocorrin and intrinsic factor, are unknown. Vitamin B12 has the lowest requirement of all the vitamins and minerals. The absorption of the most complex of all the vitamins, vitamin B12, is also complicated. It resembles a track relay race. First, the salivary glands produce and secrete a protein in response to the ingestion of food, known as haptocorrin. If you consume food-based vitamin B12 (e.g., meat, fish, poultry, dairy, eggs) with a meal, it quickly binds with salivary-based haptocorrin in the stomach. After the haptocorrin-vitamin B12 complex moves from the stomach into the small intestine, haptocorrin hands off vitamin B12 to another carrier, a stomach-made protein known as intrinsic factor.

Intrinsic factor carries vitamin B12 for the entire length of the small intestine before it reaches the vitamin B12 receptors in the terminal ileum. The terminal ileum is the last bit of real estate before the small intestine becomes the large intestine. Vitamin B12 is handed off to the vitamin B12 receptors in the terminal ileum which facilitate the absorption of vitamin B12 into the bloodstream. Here it catches a ride with a plasma protein, transcobalamin II for distribution to the body's organs and tissues. Any glitch in this sequence of events means vitamin B12 goes into the large intestine for elimination and it is not absorbed into the bloodstream.

The use of stomach-targeting drugs such as H2 blockers or proton-pump inhibitor drugs prevent both acid and intrinsic factor secretion into the stomach. Metformin, a diabetic medication, phenobarbital, an antiseizure drug and others are associated with decreased vitamin b12 absorption. People taking these drugs may more rapidly develop a vitamin B12 deficiency.

The number of receptors available to absorb vitamin B12 is another limiting factor. As described above, vitamin B12 absorption is complex. It begins in the mouth and ends in the terminal ileum, before it is handed off to a receptor and absorbed into the body. As previously stated, the terminal ileum is the last stop before food passes by the appendix and transitions into the large intestine, also known as the colon. It is possible to interfere with this complex chain of events and end up with minimal to no absorption of vitamin B12. This eventually leads to a vitamin B12 deficiency, even while consuming vitamin B12. We spent some time on vitamin B12 to illustrate the complex nature of essential nutrients. We have barely touched the surface, only covering a few highlights. This vitamin, with the smallest requirement, is found in almost every cell in the body. However, it is probably the most difficult to absorb and ultimately utilize. This is why supplementation is important. In the case of vitamin B12, supplementation should begin sometime in your 30s and continue for the rest of your life. You may take a large supplemental dose 2 or 3 times per week or you may take smaller doses daily, but it should be supplemented, especially those excluding all sources of animal products from their diet. Please note, the injectable form of vitamin B12 (i.e., cyanocobalamin) contains aluminum and at this time I cannot recommend it (it is not found in the ingredient list but is mentioned in the warning section of the package insert for those requiring dialysis).

We have covered a few of the potential drawbacks of drinking fresh juices so let's examine some positive aspects. If you are aware of the potential drawbacks, there are a few steps you can take to minimize the potential downsides to juices and smoothies. **For example, if you are going to juice or make a smoothie, eat some of the fruit or vegetables you are using to make the juice or smoothie before blending or juicing them.** Also drink the juice or smoothie slowly, savoring each sip before swallowing. This ensures you have food in the stomach to utilize intrinsic factor. If you are 100% plant-based, take vitamin B12 to supplement your juice routine.

It is difficult to beat sweet, smooth, pure carrot juice! For many, carrot juice is the king of all the juices. It contains beta-carotene, vitamins, minerals, phytochemicals, carbohydrates and even amino acids. It combines well as a juice co-ingredient with most fruits and vegetables. In about 10 minutes, 5 to 10 pounds of carrots become about a half to one gallon of a rich, smooth, perfectly sweet juice.

In the process of juicing, carrots release their tightly held beneficial compounds. Beta-carotene, a phytochemical found only in plants, is converted to retinal, a form of vitamin A. The other form of vitamin A is retinol, obtained from animal sources. Retinol and retinal readily convert to each other, allowing retinal to replete retinol stores in the liver (for the chemists, retinal performs both oxidation to retinoic acid and reduction to retinol). Retinal is involved in bodily functions such as vision, response to dim light, and the production of melatonin by the pineal gland. However, retinal is the only form used to make retinoic acid, another type of vitamin A required for growth, reproduction and for melatonin synthesis. This latter process requires thyroid hormone. If one's thyroid hormones are low, there may be inadequate conversion of retinal to retinoic acid. Inadequate intake of protein, iodine, selenium and other essential nutrients may negatively impact thyroid hormones. This has a downstream effect of not making enough retinoic acid. WHAT THIS MEANS, is that carrot juice, a great source of beta carotene, is excellent for keeping oxidation in check and for keeping the liver stores of vitamin A in good shape. It also helps with vision, sleep, reproduction, growth etc. It would be almost impossible to eat enough carrots to provide what a fresh pint of carrot juice provides in the form of vitamin A. Carrot juice is also a part of Gerson Therapy, a program designed by physician, Dr. Max Gerson in the early 1900s, in the treatment and reversal of various types of cancer. Even decades after his death, this form of medical nutrition therapy remains popular, mostly in clinics outside of the USA due to FDA regulatory issues and the various claims of "curing" cancer. Carrots are just one of dozens, if not hundreds, of fruits and vegetables with incredible therapeutic value when juiced. According to Livestrong.com, one cup of carrot juice contains 45,133 IUs of vitamin A (beta-carotene, vitamin A precursor), more than 1,000% of the RDA while 1 large carrot contains about 400% of the RDA for vitamin A. It becomes easy to see why carrot juice is the king of juices!

If you juice a lot, you are removing most, but not all of a plant's fiber. This may make it more difficult to achieve the daily fiber recommendation, 25 to 35 grams of fiber. Juicing makes this slightly more challenging. However, people following a plant-based diet are likely to consume amounts above the recommended levels. Some even consume double to triple the recommended amounts of fiber. If you believe your juicing routine is affecting your fiber intake, consider taking one or more tablespoons of psyllium husks or acacia fiber in 24 ounces of water in the morning. Each heaping tablespoon of psyllium provides about 5 grams of fiber. This is a nice balance to boost fiber intake which is missing from juices if you are a daily juicer. If you would rather not take psyllium, be sure to consume other high fiber foods throughout the rest of the day, including unprocessed fruits, vegetables, whole grains, legumes, nuts and seeds. Apples, pears, bananas and oranges have 3 to 5 grams of fiber. One cup of raspberries has 8 grams of fiber. A medium baked potato has 3 grams of fiber if you eat the skin. Even avocado has fiber, around 10 grams per 1 cup. One cup of broccoli has 2.5 grams of fiber. One cup of lentils has 13 grams of fiber and 1 cup of beans has 7 to 13 grams of fiber. Nuts and seeds also contribute fiber. Oats are also a great source of fiber. Even dark chocolate has a little fiber 😊.

Here are some benefits of juicing

1. Juicing fruits and vegetables concentrates the nutrients and removes most of the insoluble fibers. This may seem counterintuitive, as most people want to increase their fiber. However, juicing does offer the option of delivering concentrated nutrients which otherwise might not be possible to consume in the same quantity, as a whole food. For example, one could easily juice and drink five pounds of carrots but it would be difficult to eat five pounds of carrots at one sitting. Don't get me wrong, if you want to eat five pounds of carrots, I am going to support you in your effort. However, most people are not going to sit down and eat five pounds of raw carrots.

2. Juices are not completely devoid of fiber. Some of the soluble fraction of fiber is usually retained when juicing. Soluble fiber is partially water soluble and tends to form an undigestible gel. This eases elimination and helps form a protective barrier between the contents of the large intestine and the intestinal wall. Another important role of soluble fiber is to facilitate the removal of cholesterol from the body via the entero (gut)-hepatic (liver) circulation (i.e., a circulation loop which goes from the liver to the upper small intestine and then travels through the intestine to the lower small intestine and then is absorbed and goes back to the liver). This is the only mechanism we have to naturally eliminate cholesterol from the body. Bile is made in the liver, using cholesterol as a building block. Bile is then stored in the gall bladder and secreted into the small intestine to aid in the digestion of fats. Soluble fibers in the gut bind to bile and instead of bile being reabsorbed back into the body via the enterohepatic circulation, it remains in the gastrointestinal tract bound up to soluble fiber and is eliminated. Removing bile from the enterohepatic circulation effectively lowers serum cholesterol because it requires more cholesterol to make new bile. Soluble fibers also help regulate the absorption of glucose, thereby helping diabetics more easily control their blood sugar. Some soluble fibers ferment in the large intestine and provide fuel sources to keep the gut healthy. Soluble and insoluble fibers both promote a healthy gut microbiome. It is critical to meet daily fiber goals.

3. Juicing is an art. You may start out with juicing carrots or apples but for some, juicing evolves into a means of consuming more greens, herbs, roots and other novel ingredients. Usually the more novel the ingredient the more caution must be used to determine if you might experience negative side effects. For example, not everyone tolerates pure ginger shots, but if you are inclined, adding ginger to your juices helps reduce inflammation. Check with your physician or nutritionist if you have a question about juicing an unfamiliar plant. In all cases, it is best for pregnant women to avoid novel herbs and foods.

4. Juicing involves various types of equipment intended to optimize each type of juicing ingredient. For example, if you want to juice wheat grass, you may want a wheat grass juicer for the most effective way to extract juice from grass. A slow masticating juicer may work well, but may not be as efficient at extracting juice from harder fruits and vegetables. Centrifugal juicers are fast and can take soft to hard fruits and vegetables. Other juicing methods include triturating (double auger juicers which crush and grind), and juice presses.

5. Good greens to juice are: spinach, lettuce, chard, collards, kale, parsley, beet greens, dandelion greens, wheat grass, cabbage, bok choy, etc. Remove the tough, bitter stems before adding to your smoothie. Rotate the types of greens you use in a green smoothie.

6. Some unique ingredients to add to your juices include but are not limited to: fennel root, turmeric root, potato, sweet potato, celeriac, red cabbage, etc. Start by adding a small amount of a new food and then add more if you like the flavor.

7. Benefits of juicing include but are not limited to: providing a concentrated source of essential nutrients and antioxidants, provides the body with a rapidly digestible form of nutrition, juicing provides lots of antioxidant capability in the form of free electrons, juicing effectively releases tens if not hundreds of phytochemicals from their storage vesicles in plant walls. Juicing may improve the skin's appearance. It allows the body's immune system to rally against uncontrolled cancerous conditions. Adding beets to your juicing queue translates into more nitric oxide and better heart and artery health. There are many excellent health reasons to juice. The more you juice, the more benefits you are likely to experience.

8. Fresh juices promote a wide range of positive gastrointestinal (GI) health effects.

9. A word about sweeteners. Many have concerns about the increasing use of honey, especially when harvested by large scale honey farmers. The concerns are not because honey is a bad sweetener, it is because of the effects on the honey bee population. We should sparingly use honey. Fortunately, there are other great sweeteners. Here are some good sweeteners to use when needed (not in any order): xylitol, blackstrap molasses, maple syrup, dates / date paste, coconut or palm sugar, brown rice syrup, licorice roots / stems sweet liquid, fruit, yacon syrup, Lacuma, barley malt syrup, Monk fruit with erythritol, rapadura and brown sugar.

10. Another concern about bee products is the pollen. Pollen is collected by sticky mats as the bees fly into their colony to deliver the pollen. It is not uncommon for the sticky pollen collection mats to also remove the bee's legs / feet. It is for this reason, **I never recommend the use of bee-collected pollen.**

In summary, never underestimate the power of water, juices and smoothies. They are important components of a healthy dietary pattern and deliver a wide range of essential and non-essential nutrients. People choosing to juice or make smoothies on a regular basis need to consider the following organizational techniques. These techniques make juicing and blending a streamlined process, making it more likely to retain a great habit.

Plan a month in advance for juicing and smoothies. For example, when fresh pineapple is on sale, purchase 5 to 10 at a time and process for freezing or immediate juicing. When grapefruit is in season you may want to purchase cases of grapefruit and focus on drinking grapefruit juice for a time. Use the **Seasonal and Fresh Produce Calendar for Juicing, Smoothies, Salads, Canning and Food Preservation, etc.**, form found in the next chapter for aiding your planning, shopping and prepping schedule.

Designate a place in your kitchen to keep juicing equipment, a sort of juice and smoothie bar area. This could include a high-speed blender, centrifugal juicer, juice press, wheat grass juicer, single auger juicer, citrus juicer, ceramic ginger grater, etc. If your juicing and smoothie equipment is kept in a convenient and easily accessed area of the kitchen, you may be more likely to regularly use it.

Designate "produce" bowls. I like to use 3 to 5 four-quart wood, ceramic or metal bowls. If you are juicing, prep your fruits and vegetables and place in bowls. I like to separate juicing ingredients by hardness. Prep all your juicing and smoothie ingredients before you begin to process them. This way you do not have to stop to peel or cut additional ingredients. Keep your "produce" bowls in the same area as the juicing equipment. If you are using a juicer, cut your produce to easily fit in the juicer chute.

If you are juicing greens such as kale or swiss chard, you may want to remove the hard ribs, which tend to be slightly more bitter than the tender leaves. You may prefer to juice the stems. Experiment to determine your preferences. When juicing greens along with harder fruits and vegetables, alternate adding them to the juicer with the harder fruits and vegetables. **A good rule-of-thumb is one-part leafy greens to three parts fruits and vegetables.**

Keep in mind the sweetness, bitterness and sourness of fruits and vegetables may vary with the season. This may change the flavor of juices and smoothies. Make appropriate adjustments to increase or decrease sweetness. Juiced celery tastes sweet and different from eating raw celery. Carrot juice is almost always sweeter than eating a raw carrot. Juicing concentrates the carbohydrates while separating the fiber.

Adding pineapple, pears, apples and carrots improves palatability by increasing the sweetness.

The pulp by-products of juicing may be used to make crackers, desserts such as raw carrot cake, or composted and the nutrients returned to the earth. If you have farm animals, they love the fruit and vegetable pulp, especially horses! Be sure to remove sour and hot pulp (e.g., grapefruit, lemon, lime, ginger, hot peppers) before giving to animals.

Some tasty fruits and vegetables and various combinations. You may add ice and a small amount of club soda to the carrot + apple + beet + ginger juice and serve as a beautiful sparkling beverage.

- Green apples + cucumber + celery + ginger
- Carrots + apple + lemon (add 1: red beet, orange, sweet potato, tomato, red bell pepper)
- Carrot + apple or pear
- Carrot + apple or pear + beet + ginger
- Celery + spinach + kale + apple + lime + ginger
- Apples or pears + oranges + lemons + ginger + turmeric
- Pineapple + coconut water + passion fruit
- Pineapple + mango + parsley
- Grapefruit (I like to add salt and ice to grapefruit juice)
- Tangelo
- Orange + grapefruit + tangelo + lemon
- Green apples + sweet red apples + kale leaves + ginger
- Cranberries + pears + ginger
- Cantaloupe
- Honeydew
- Watermelon
- Cantaloupe + greens + cucumber
- Carrot + apple + orange
- Celery + mint
- Grapes
- Ginger shots
- Pineapple + mango + oranges
- Beets + carrots + kale leaves + celery + apples / pears + lemon + ginger
- Sweet potato (peeled) + apple + ginger
- Tomato + cucumber + celery + red pepper + basil
- Sweet potato (peeled) + carrots + orange
- Sweet potato (peeled) + pineapple + pear
- Pear + spinach + ginger
- Cucumber + celery + apples + lemon or lime (add 1: fresh mint, parsley, cilantro, greens)

Discussion Questions

1. Describe your ideal smoothie?
2. Describe your ideal juice combination?
3. Would your family benefit from consuming more fruits and vegetables as a smoothie or juice?
4. What equipment and steps could you take to incorporate more smoothies and juices into your lifestyle?

Chapter 23
Using and preserving the harvest

Use the chart, **Seasonal Fresh Produce Calendar for Juicing, Smoothies, Salads, Canning, Food Preservation**, to plan your garden, choose fresh ingredients for juicing and making smoothies, and to plan for canning and preserving your fresh produce. Each gardener varies in their preferences for consuming produce fresh straight from the garden or first canning and preserving the produce. If you enjoy fresh carrot juice, you may want to plant an extra-large section of carrots. Some gardeners prefer to consume freshly picked green beans as opposed to canned. Tomatoes are easily canned and preserved for later use, however, canning asparagus significantly changes its flavor and texture, making it unpalatable for some. Most gardeners do both. Ideally, consume produce right from the garden at peak nutrient content and plant enough to can and preserve for use over the winter and early spring. Canning, freezing, and most other storage methods results in moderate nutrient losses, but it is worth the effort to have flavorful tomatoes for winter stews and sauces.

In addition to canning, you may dehydrate / freeze dry, make powders, jams, jellies, curds, syrups, confits, chutneys, ferments, salsa, extracts, flavored vinegar, flavored or infused oils, flavored butter, chips, pesto, hot sauce, and many more methods for preserving summer's produce. Use each method to take advantage of each food. For example, when hot pepper plants are going gang busters, I pick as many peppers as I can find and dump them in a large stock pot, usually roasting some of them to bring out their smoky flavor, before adding to the pot. I cook them down to a paste, maybe throwing in some tomatoes, garlic and salt and a pinch or two of sugar. I can and freeze the hot sauce for use the rest of the year. I also dehydrate some of the peppers, make pepper infused olive oil, and freeze some whole. Invest in airlocks to use in making pepper ferments, a source of natural probiotic organisms.

There are many ways to preserve the harvest and process food. Listed below are some of the many ways to preserve the harvest. Each method deserves special attention and study. The method(s) you choose should reflect your lifestyle and taste. Check this website for state-specific produce calendars: https://www.farmflavor.com/lifestyle/season-produce-calendars-50-states/

Using and preserving the harvest	
Table 1. Ideas to Preserve the Harvest	
Alcohol, water, vinegar and honey infusions	Flavored butters, oils, salt, sugar, vinegar
Beverage bases (dehydrated, powered or syrups)	Freeze and freeze dry
Candied (orange peel, apricots, etc.)	Hot sauces
Chips (potato, zucchini, etc.)	Jams, freezer jam, jellies, marmalade
Chutney, dips, spreads	Juices
Concentrates	Leather (e.g., fruit leather)
Confit (vegetables & herbs, fruit, condiments, etc.)	Oxygen removal / absorbers and store
Curds	Pesto
Dehydrate, dry, freeze dry	Pie filling (e.g., apple pie filling)
Extracts (e.g., vanilla, lemon, mint, cinnamon, etc.)	Pickling, quick pickles
Ferments (e.g., sauerkraut, pickles)	Powders
Preserves	Salsas
Pressure canning	Syrups
Root cellar (storage)	Water bath canning

Seasonal Fresh Produce Calendar for Juicing, Smoothies, Salads, Canning, Food Preservation, etc.

January	February	March
Citrus: curd, sugar, marmalade	Avocado: freeze	Pineapple: preserves, jam, dry
Kale: chips, freeze	Citrus: syrup, extracts, vinegars, oils	Mango: dry, jam, curd, syrup
Fruit leather	Juices: apple, citrus, pear, greens	Juices: apple, citrus
Juices: apple, citrus, pears	Juices:	Juices: pineapple

April	May / early June	June
Mushrooms: dry, powder	Strawberries: freezer jam, syrup	Apricots: jam, jelly, chutney, juice
Eggs: dry, pulverize shells for garden	Mint: syrup, dry, powder	Blueberry: freeze, syrup, powder
Juices: apple, citrus, mango	Rhubarb: sauce, syrup, dry	Cherry: can, pie filling, dry, syrup, vinegar, powder
Juices: pineapple	Greens: freeze, dry, powder, etc.	Strawberries: jam, dry
	Beets: can, pickle, dry, powder, ferment	Shelling peas: dry, freeze
	Mango: dehydrate, jam, syrup, chutney	Snap peas: freeze
	Asparagus: pickles	Garlic scapes: pesto, freeze
	Peaches: preserves, jam, syrup	Cherry tomatoes: dry, freeze
	Juices: apple, citrus, mango	Juices: citrus, mango, tomato
	Juices: tomato, raspberry	Juices: berries, pineapple
	Juices: watermelon, cantaloupe	Juices: melons, beet, peaches
	Juices: pineapple	

July	August	September
Apricots: dried, curd, leather	Apples: sauce, butter, pie filling	Apples/pears: sauce, dry
Berries: freeze, sauce, jam, syrup	Blueberries: dry, powder, leather	Blueberries: freeze, syrup, curd
Cherries: freeze, dry, powder	Squash/zucchini: pickle, dry	Cucumber: pickle, kimchi
Strawberries/raspberries: freeze	Strawberries/raspberries: curd	Fresh herbs: dry, freeze, extract
Cabbage: sauerkraut, kimchi	Tomatoes: can, dry, freeze, salsa, confit	Basil: pesto, freeze, oil, vinegar syrups, etc.
Onions, leeks, chives: cure, dry	Hot peppers: hot sauce, pepper sauce, dry, freeze, oil seasoning, etc.	Carrots: pickles
Beets: can, dry, powder		Vegetable flavored salt
Green beans: pickle, dry, can freeze, etc.		Tomatillo: salsa
Grapes: butter, juice, dry	Corn: freeze, pickle, chutney	Elderberries: syrup, dry
Radishes: pickles, ferments	Figs: jam, dry	Ginger: pickle, dry, juice (freeze)
Juices: citrus, mango, tomato	Juices: citrus, mango, tomato	Juices: citrus, tomato, pomegranate
Juices: berries, grapes, melons	Juices: berries, grapes, melons	Juices: berries, grapes, melons
Juices: beet, peaches	Juices: beet, peaches, pears	Juices: beet, peach, apple, pear

Root cellar: sweet potatoes, potatoes, beets, carrots, onions, winter squash, parsnips, celeriac, etc.

October	November	December
Apples: pie filling, dry, sauce	Apples: pie filling, dry, sauce	Cranberries: freeze, syrup, dry
Juices: citrus, tomato, pomegranate	Cranberries: freeze, syrup, dry	Juices: citrus, pomegranate, beet
Juices: berries, grapes, melons	Pecans: forage, freeze	Juices: cranberries, grapes
Juices: beet, apple, pear	Persimmon: freeze, dry, chutney	Juices: apple, pear
	Pomegranate: jelly, syrup, curd	
	Cabbage/greens: ferment, pickle	
	Juices: citrus, pomegranate, beet	
	Juices: cranberries, grapes	
	Juices: apple, pear	

Root cellar: tomatoes, beets, Brussels sprouts, pumpkins, onions, cabbage, winter squash, parsnips, etc.

Chapter 24
Plant-based food for 4 for a year

Food and water are two of our most basic needs. Add to this list a hygienic and safe place to live, clothing, meaningful relationships, minimal drama and ongoing personal chaos, fellowship with others, love and a sense of belonging, connecting in the larger community, meaningful work, the ability to provide for the needs of our family, intellectual stimulation, satisfying work, financial stability, meaningful events to anticipate, and purpose in life. As Christians, we include our Biblical beliefs and a desire to spread the Gospel as part of our basic needs. All aforementioned needs aside, the most basic and primary need in life is to connect with God, accept Christ as our Saviour, and to cooperate with the work of the Holy Spirit in our lives.

When it comes to food, we assume there is an endless supply of food to purchase at the supermarket. Most of us were not alive during the great depression of 1929 which lasted until the late 1930s. This depression impacted the worldwide global economy. Food became scarce. Crop prices fell by 60%. The depression was worsened by natural disasters such as the drought which began in the early 1930s. The scarcity of food impacted the nation's health. People of all ages suffered from malnutrition. All around the world, children's growth was stunted and intellectual development impacted.

It is impossible to describe the true impact of this global depression. It took decades to recover and for the economy to revive. In fact, it took a world-wide war to end the depression and revitalize the economy. However, the price we paid in human capital has never been recovered. During the deadliest USA war, the civil war (1861 to 1965), our country lost around 750,000 lives, not to mention the maimed and wounded soldiers. We never recovered from this loss of human life. According to Wikipedia, it claimed 10% of all Northern men between the ages of 20 and 45 years and 30% of southern men, ages 18 to 40 years. Tragically, these young, energetic, vital men were taken out of the gene pool and their legacy, forever left only in the annals of the history books.

Human losses to the USA in World War I added up to 116,516 deaths and 320,000 sick and wounded. Total loss of human life in World War 2 was around 405,000 with 670,846 wounded. War is never a good solution to man's problems because of the human cost in lives as well as the subsequent loss of mental and physical functions. Unfortunately, the drive for power and wealth by nationalistic politicians, many world leaders, and super-power countries seems to ensure there are endless wars.

Because there are no guarantees in life, it is good to prepare for potential scenarios which may impact your family's ability to obtain food. **It may not be feasible to stock up on food for long periods of time, but it is useful to consider what a family of four might consume over the course of a year.** You may be able to store and cover part of a year's consumption. Whether or not you are planning for hard times, it's interesting to see how much food a family of 4 consumes in a year.

Those who live in the country and know how to plant a garden may have greater confidence in surviving an economic depression and food shortage. The recent pandemic of 2020 has served to reinforce the notion of self-sufficiency, not only in food security but in energy sufficiency. It is painfully obvious those living in the country have fared better as far as food security and safety. **There are many reasons to move to the country. Food security and putting distance from dangerous cities are just two good reasons to consider country living.**

For those who might be interested in how much food a family of four might consume, this is a rough guide. If you want to get together with others and expand on this list, the following are suggested activities to personalize this list to your family's needs. Use the worksheet provided below. Adjust the foods found on the list to fit your family's needs. You fill in the amount column based on the number of people in your family. Customize this amount to the best of your ability to fit your family's anticipated needs. You fill in the cost column based on local supermarket prices. Of course, it does not take into consideration eating out while traveling for business or pleasure.

This activity may or may not take into consideration the amount of food you grow. If you grow and can your own tomatoes, you should have a ready stock of freshly canned tomato sauce, salsa, tomato soup, juice, tomato paste, etc., available to you over the cold winter months. If you regularly can and preserve food, add these supplies to the worksheet in the appropriate section.

The storage form column is important. This is used to indicate whether or not the food item can be stored in its original container (OC) or does it need to be in glass jars (GJ) or another type of storage container. You should plan for space in your pantry, root cellar, freezer or refrigerator. Use the storage form location column to indicate where you plan to store the food items. The notes column is for adding additional information. Each section has several empty rows for you to add your own food items.

Here are some plant-based meal ideas corresponding to <u>*Table 1., Planning Worksheet:*</u>
- Mexican: haystacks, enchiladas, fajitas, beans and rice, burritos, tacos, 7-layer bean dip
- Rice: stir fry veg over rice, fried rice, broccoli rice casserole, side dishes, risotto, pudding, etc.
- Veggies: stir fry, roasted, soup / stew, side dishes, stuffed peppers, spaghetti squash, etc.
- Pasta: mac-N-cheese, fettuccini, spaghetti, pasta salad, stuffed shells, lasagna rolls, angel hair, pesto pasta, minestrone, butternut squash ravioli, etc.
- Potatoes: mashed, baked, gnocchi, roasted, twice baked, soup, etc.
- Indian: curry, mushroom masala, aloo gobi, biryani, chana masala, dahl, korma, dosa, etc.
- Thai: pad Thai, fried rice, green curry, panang curry, Tom yum soup, spring rolls, etc.
- Italian: ravioli, pizza, eggplant parmesan, rigatoni, fettuccini alfredo, frittata, calzone, etc.
- Mediterranean: falafel, mujadara, hummus wraps, tabouleh, spanakopita, stuffed cabbage, baba ghanoush, etc.

Plant-based food for 4 for a year
Table 1. Planning Worksheet

Food Category	Amount	Cost	Storage Form	Shelf Life	Notes
Legumes & Lentils					
Beans/lentils/split peas	200 – 300 lb		GJ, PB	1 year	1 lb beans ~ 6 cups cooked beans
Shelf-stable tofu	25 cartons		OP	1 year	Use within 3 – 4 days after opening
Falafel (boxed mixes)	10 – 20		OP	1 – 2 yr	10 – 20 falafel-based meals
Condiments, Oils, & Other					
Avocado oil	1 – 2 gallons		OP	1 – 2 years	
Baking powder	¼ lb		OP or GJ	18 months	
Baking soda	1 lb		OP or GJ	2 years	Purchase more for non-cooking needs
Balsamic vinegar	½ gallon		OP	indefinite	Salad dressing ingredient
Cacao butter, raw	5 lb		GJ	1 year	For sweets and savory sauce
Cacao, dark choc powder	5 lb		GJ	1 year	For sweets, baking and beverages
Chocolate, dark	15 lb		CE, SP	6 – 24 mo	For sweets, baking and beverages
Chocolate, white (sweet)	5 lb			6 – 24 mo	For sweets, baking and beverages
Coconut oil,	1 – 3 gallons		CE	3 years	Sweets and baking
Cream of tartar	¼ lb		OP	2 – 3 yr	
Curry / masala paste	10 – 20 tins		OP	2 – 3 yr	Panang, red, green, masaman, etc.
Extracts and flavorants			DP	1 – 3 yr	E.g., vanilla, almond, rum, etc.
Herbs, dehydrated			GJ	1 – 3 yr	E.g., oregano, dill, etc.
Ketchup	6 1-liters		OP	1 year	
Liquid Aminos	1 liter		OP	1 – 2 yr	
Mayonnaise	2 gallons		OP	3 – 4 mo	
Miso	1 – 5 lb		OP	6 months	
Mustard	2 1-liters		OP	2 years	
Nutritional Yeast	½ lb		GJ	1 – 2 yr	
Olive oil	2 gallons		OP, CE, DP	1 year	
Olives, assorted	5 – 10 lb		OP	1 year	
Roma beverage	8 jars		OP	1 – 3 yr	
SAF instant yeast (red label)	1 bag		R, GJ	Test viability	Baking
Salt	8 – 10 lb		GJ w/ PL	indefinite	
Seasonings			GJ or OP	1 – 3 yr	
Spices			GJ or OP	1 – 3 yr	
Tamari sauce	½ gallon		OP	1 – 3 yr	Stir-fry, dressings, sauces
Teas, assorted teas			GJ, OP, PB	1 – 3 yr	
Vanilla extract / gel	½ pint		GJ or OP	1 – 3 yr	
Vege bouillon powder	8 oz		GJ or OP	1 year	Soups, sauces, entrees, etc.
Vinegar, various flavors	2 – 3 liters		OP	1 – 3 yr	
Walnut oil	1 liter		OP, R	1 year	
Staples: dairy or plant-based products					
Butter	10 lb		OP	Freeze	
Cheese, hard	10 lb		OP	Freeze	
Cream cheese	2 lb		OP	2 – 4 wk	
Milk, powdered	2 #10 cans				

Food Category	Amount	Cost	Storage Form	Shelf Life	Notes
Staples: fruit					
Applesauce	10 #10 cans		GJ or OP	12 – 18 mo	Canning 1 bushel yields 18 quarts
Blueberries	2 #10 cans		GJ or OP	12 – 18 mo	
Cherries	2 #10 cans		GJ or OP	12 – 18 mo	
Cherries, maraschino	1 – 2 lb		GJ or OP	1 – 3 yr	
Coconut milk, full fat	50 – 100 cans		OP	2 – 5 yr	
Coconut milk, cartons	25		OP	6 – 12 mo	
Coconut powder	2 lb		GJ or OP	1 year	
Dehydrated fruit	10 – 20 lb		GJ, OP, PB	6 – 12 mo	
Lychees	2 #10 cans		OP	12 – 18 mo	
Mandarins	2 – 5 #10 cans		OP	12 – 18 mo	
Peaches	5 #10 cans		OP	12 – 18 mo	
Pears	5 #10 cans		OP	12 – 18 mo	
Pineapple	5 #10 cans		OP	12 – 18 mo	
Staples: grains**					
Arborio rice, sushi rice	3 – 10 lb each		GJ or PB	1 year	4 risotto meals, 4 sushi meals
Black rice	5 – 10 lb		GJ or PB	1 year	Omelette, side dish
Brown / White Rice	50 – 200 lb		GJ or PB	1 year	1 lb/2 meals, combo short/med grain
Bulgur	3 lb		GJ or PB	8 – 12 mo	12 tabouleh recipes
Corn, dry	50 – 100 lb		GJ or PB	1 year	Chips, tortillas, grits, polenta
Couscous, Israeli	5 lb		GJ or PB	2 years	10 – 15 dishes with couscous
Energy bars	200 bars		OP	6 – 12 mo	50 days of energy bars (1/person)
Flour, white	50 – 100 lb		GJ or PB	6 – 12 mo	Pies, sweets, bakery, pizza, etc.
Frito's corn chips	20 2-lb bags		OP or PB	2 years	60 haystack meals
Linguini, fettuccini	20 lb		OP or PB	2 years	40 linguini meals
Millet	3 – 10 lb		GJ or PB	8 – 12 mo	1 cup makes ½ gallon milk bev.
Oats, rolled / steel cut	50 – 100 lb		GJ or PB	1 year	½ lb = oatmeal
Pasta, various shapes	20 – 30 lb		OP or PB	2 years	½ lb / meal
Popcorn	10 - 15 lb		GJ, OP, PB	1 – 3 yr	2 oz / large bowl (80 bowls)
Quinoa	5 – 10 lb		GJ or PB	1 – 2 yr	
Red rice	5 lb		GJ or PB	1 year	1 lb / day (2 meals)
Spaghetti, vermicelli	20 lb		OP or PB	2 years	40 spaghetti dinners
Wheat /wheat berries	200 – 250 lb		GJ or PB	1 year	1 loaf bread = 1 – 2 lb
Wild rice	2 lb		GJ or PB	1 year	Add 1 – 2 Tbsp to soups
Ramen noodles	5 lb		OP		20 ramen noodle meals
Staples: grain and legume-based protein sources such as vegie meat, sea vegetables and animal products					
Asian gluten (cans)	25 cans		GJ, OP, PB	1 – 3 yr	12 – 25 stir fry / fajita meals
Vital wheat gluten flour	5 lb		GJ, OP, PB	1 – 2 yr	7–8 recipes for gluten steaks
Fruit/Veg powders	1 – 5 lb		GJ or PB	1 – 2 yr	Smoothies and beverages
Veggie hotdogs	8 – 10 cans		OP	1 – 2 yr	1 can / meal
Veggie meat / burger	25 cans		F, OP	1 – 2 yr	25 vege burger meals

Food Category	Amount	Cost	Storage Form	Shelf Life	Notes
Staples: nuts and seeds					
Black seeds	1 lb		GJ or PB	1 – 2 yr	
Broccoli seeds	2 – 3 lb		GJ or PB	1 – 2 yr	For sprouting
Butter, nut & seed spreads	20 lb		GJ or OP	1 – 2 yr	
Cashews	25 – 50 lb		F, GJ or OP	4 – 12 mo	
Chia seeds	5 – 10 lb		GJ or PB	1 – 2 yr	For sprouting, water, baking
Nuts, assorted	50 lb		F, GJ or PB	4 – 12 mo	
Poppy seeds	½ lb		GJ or PB	1 – 2 yr	
Pumpkin seeds	5 lb		GJ or PB	6 – 12 mo	
Sesame seeds	1 lb		GJ or PB	6 – 12 mo	
Sunflower seeds	5 lb		GJ or PB	6 – 12 mo	
Tahini	5 – 10 lb		GJ or OP	6 – 12 mo	
Staples: sweeteners					
Blackstrap molasses	1 gallon		GJ or OP	10 years	
Honey	2 lb		GJ or OP	indefinite	
Jams, assorted	15 – 20 lb		GJ or OP	1 year	
Maple syrup	2 – 5 gal		GJ or OP	6 – 24 mo	
Stevia			GJ or PB	indefinite	
Sugar	30 – 50 lb		GJ or OP	indefinite	
Sugar, brown	20 lb		GJ or OP	indefinite	
Sugar, powdered	4 lb		GJ or OP	indefinite	
Staples: vegetables					
Beets, dehydrated	5 lb		GJ or PB	1 – 2 yr	
Beets, powder	1 lb		GJ or PB	2 – 3 yr	
Corn, mini	2 #10 cans		OP	12 – 18 mo	
Corn	5 #10 cans		OP	1 – 2 years	
Cornstarch	1 lb		GJ or OP	18 months	
Green beans (canned)	50 quarts		GJ	1 year	
Green peas, dehydrated	10 lb		GJ or PB	1 – 2 yr	
Mushrooms, dehydrated	5 – 10 lb		GJ or PB	1 – 2 yr	
Pea protein powder	5 lb		GJ or PB	1 year	
Pickles, relish	3 – 5 lb		GJ or OP	1 – 2 yr	
Potatoes, dehydrated	25 – 50 lb		GJ or PB	1 – 2 yr	Hash browns, soups
Shiitake, dehydrated	1 lb		GJ or PB	1 – 2 yr	
Tapioca pearls	1 – 3 lb		JG or PB	1 – 2 yr	
Tomatoes, dehydrated	10 lb		GJ or PB	12 – 18 mo	
Tomatoes, diced	10 #10 cans		GJ	12 – 18 mo	
Tomato, sauce	10 #10 cans		GJ	12 – 18 mo	
Tomatoes (home canned)	10 – 100 qt				
Zucchini, dehydrated	5 lb		GJ	6 – 8 mo	

Food Category	Amount	Cost	Storage Form	Shelf Life	Notes
Fruits and Vegetables in the Root Cellar (32 – 40 °F, 90 to 95 % humidity)					
Apples	80 lb		RC, SL	2 – 7 mo	Applesauce, sweet breads, etc.
Beets	25 – 100 lb		RC, SL	3 – 5 mo	Soups, salads, etc.
Brussels sprouts	2 – 4 stalks		HUD, RC	3 – 5 wk	
Cabbage	10 heads		RC	3 – 4 mo	
Carrots	100 lb		RC	4 – 6 mo	Juice, soups, etc.
Celery	25 lb		RC	4 – 6 mo	Juice, soups, etc.
Citrus	50 – 100 lb		RC, SL	1 – 2 mo	
Garlic	5 – 10 lb		C, RC, SL	5 – 8 mo	Store 50 - 60 °F; 60 – 70% humidity
Grapefruit	100 – 200 ea		RC, SL	1 – 2 mo	
Leeks	10 – 20 lb		RC, SL	3 – 4 mo	
Lemons	100 – 200		RC, SL	1 – 2 mo	
Limes	200		RC, SL	1 – 2 mo	
Onions	50 – 60 lb		C, RC, SL	5 – 8 mo	Place on newspaper, screen, cloth
Parsnips	10 – 20 lb		RC, SL	1 – 2 mo	
Pears	40 – 80 lb		RC, SL, IW	2 – 3 mo	Ideal storage temp is 29-31 °F
Potatoes	100 – 200 lb		C, LWH, RC, SL	4 – 6 mo	Separate from ethylene releasing F/V. Store at 40 to 45 °F
Pumpkins	2 large		C, RC	5 – 6 mo	Store at 50 – 60 °F
Rutabagas	3 – 5		O, RC	2 – 4 mo	Releases unpleasant odor
Sauerkraut	10 lb		GJ, RC	4 – 6 wk	
Shallots	5 lb		C, RC	3 – 6 mo	
Squash, winter	2 – 4 large		RC	4 – 6 mo	
Sweet potatoes	20 – 50 lb		C, LWH, RC, SL	4 – 6 mo	Store at 55 – 60 °F
Tomatillos	3 – 5 lb		RC, IW, HUD	1 – 2 mo	
Tomatoes on the vine			HUD, RC	up to 4 mo	
Turnips	10 – 20 lb		RC, SL	4 – 6 mo	
Other					
Cookies	12 – 24 pkg		OP	1 – 2 mo	1 – 2 pkg / month
Crackers, assorted	20 – 40 pkg		OP	1 – 3 mo	
Jellybeans	3 – 5 lb		GJ or OP	indefinite	
Rice paper (spring rolls)	5 pkg		OP	1 – 3 yr	
Roasted seaweed	20 pkg		OP	1 – 3 yr	

*C = cure first; CP = cool place; DP = dark place; F = freezer; F/V = fruits and vegetables; GJ = glass jar; HUD = hang upside down; IW = individually wrapped; LWH = layered with straw; MB = mylar bag; OP = original packaging; OA = oxygen absorbers; O = outside; P = pantry; PB = plastic bag; PL = plastic lid; R = refrigerator; RC = root cellar; SE = sealed environment; SP = sealed packaging; S = shelf; SL = single layer

**Store whole grains in mylar bags and in plastic buckets with oxygen absorbing packets. Will last for 8 – 10 yrs.

Chapter 25

Learn how to cook: the choir of flavors

For many foodies, cooking and eating are two of the greatest joys in life! They are a creative undertaking involving every sensory aspect of the body. It is not just about the food, but about the setting, the company, the flowers, the table and service wares, the season, the quality of the ingredients, the ambient background sounds. **Cooking and eating are infinitely complex, but unfortunately, many people never get past the hamburger, fries and a shake mentality.** Tradition and habit rule the palate. On a scale of 1 to 10 with 1 being the least and 10 being the most, the culinary finesse of many Americans would not exceed a score of 5.

Many cultures have rich culinary traditions including Mediterranean countries, Asians, Africans, Eastern European countries, etc. These countries defy the basic 4 or 5 food groups Americans use to categorize food intake. Most culinary-rich cultures are not obsessed with defining food groups but they are committed to high amperage flavors and taste. Fresh herbs, wild spices, hundreds of sweet and hot pepper options, and bitter greens, are just a few ways flavor and taste define their food culture.

Some people fully embrace and learn to cook in a way which is not only flavorful but also deeply satisfying. We may be caught daydreaming about drinking a cool vanilla bean infused blended beverage, or eating a perfectly balanced green or Panang curry with fragrant jasmine rice. Who can resist the complex combination of spices that make up mushroom masala served with garlic naan and basmati rice to mop up the sauce? **We can't wait to tear apart pieces of sour, fermented Ethiopian bread known as injera, and use it to scoop up earthy, pungent spicy vegetables and savory stews.** When it comes to dessert time, simple and fresh or complex and rich contribute to the perfect ending, even if it means eating a bowl of fresh Ataulfo mango chunks with a few squeezes of fresh lime juice. **When it comes to desserts, our memory is short. The dessert we are eating is always the best.** Who can resist warm apple pie with freshly churned ice cream or a fresh fig tart with a flakey crust served with slightly sweetened whipped cream?

Simple spaghetti can go from coach class to first class with freshly roasted tomato and red pepper sauce spiked with a touch of cream (plant or dairy), jalapeno, fresh herbs and a few slivers of Parmesan cheese (or leave off if you are vegan). Serve spaghetti with roasted vegetables, freshly harvested from the garden and dressed up with a light olive oil and lemon juice vinaigrette with a hint of garlic and perfectly seasoned with salt and fresh herbs. If you are a raw foodist, substitute zucchini noodles (i.e., zoodles) and make a fresh tomato sauce and serve with a salad and a cool mint green pea soup.

Meal planning is critical. Consider using Pinterest and other internet platforms to guide your meal planning and provide visual cues for making each meal visually appealing as well as gastronomically pleasing. Food tastes better when you share it with family and loved ones. Learn to bring together groups of people who appreciate food and love to cook. You might even be surprised by your friend's hidden cooking talents.

Maybe you are not a seasoned home chef, but you enjoy eating. Learning how to combine different flavors can go a long way toward increasing your enjoyment of food. It definitely takes cooking to the next level. You begin to view food and your garden's yield as a valuable commodity, one worthy of dedication and hard work. Learning to cook increases the likelihood your health will improve. When you learn a few basics about how to correct common culinary mistakes, cooking becomes more satisfying.

The commonly accepted taste senses are sweet, salty, sour, bitter and umami; other flavors and mouth sensations are described below. Taste occurs at the interface of various food components coming in contact with receptors on the tongue. **A German publication, "How does our sense of taste work?" describes 5 tastes, 10 levels of intensity and up to 100,000 different flavors.** This provides for an infinite combination of food chemicals and receptors known to confer our sense of taste.

In reality, humans have more than 5 taste perceptions. Some have described up to seven additional taste mechanisms and likely there are more. Piquancy, also known as hot and spicy, is a function of capsaicin, a chemical found in chile peppers. Capsaicin activates pain receptors on the tongue and in the mouth to convey heat. The Scoville scale is used to measure spiciness or "heat." A bell pepper registers a "0" on the Scoville scale. The common jalapeno checks in between 2,500 to 8,000 Scoville units. The hottest pepper in the world, the Carolina Reaper, registers at 2,200,000 Scoville units, the highest known food-based score, yet quite a bit under pure capsaicin at 15,000,000 Scoville units. **If you can tolerate it, small, balanced amounts of capsaicin add flavor, drama, brilliance and intensity to food.** For the most part, we manage to perceive mild levels of capsaicin as a positive when combined with other taste senses. This is why some cultures add hot peppers to many dishes, including chocolate and other types of sweets. If you are a super-taster, highly flavored and spicy food may possibly overwhelm densely populated receptors causing extreme pain. Super tasters usually prefer more delicately seasoned foods.

Another high impact taste sensation is pungency. Some include pungent with spicy capsaicin-based foods, but pungency does not require capsaicin to be pungent. Some see them as separate categories. Pungency is attributed to various chemicals and volatile oils found in plants. Pungent foods include strong cheeses (e.g., limburger, muenster, Stinking Bishop, roquefort), horseradish, ginger, mustard, vinegar, sauerkraut, radish, natto, etc. In the case of mustard, it contains sinigrin, which when combined with the enzyme myrosinase (an enzyme found in broccoli, cauliflower, cabbage, kale, daikon radishes, etc.) and water, the combination turns up the heat. Myrosinase converts glucosinolates, compounds found in cruciferous vegetables, into isothiocyanates, thicyanates and nitriles; compounds potentially with cancer-protective functions in humans but may also prevent iodine uptake in the thyroid gland leading to goiters (i.e., goitrogenic). Ginger contains gingerol, a volatile oil, providing another type of spicy taste sensation. Piperine in black pepper is spicy. Allicin in fresh garlic is another example of a spicy food without necessarily containing capsaicin.

Cooking and drying alter volatile compounds found in plants, changing their strength. Pungency and umami are often paired together. Umami is what we taste when we eat certain types of foods such as tomatoes, mushrooms, asparagus, cheese, animal products, etc. The food additive, MSG, is responsible for umami flavor. Umami is perceived by glutamate receptors on the tongue.

Another taste sensation is astringency. Most people around the world drink tea and coffee, eat grapes and occasionally dream about dark chocolate desserts – all are foods known to contain tannins. The chemicals attributed to astringency are tannins. They lend a slight astringent taste but when balanced with other taste sensations, astringency is perceived as smooth and delicious. Most people do not consume unsweetened dark chocolate due to its high content of bitter and astringent compounds. This is why varying amounts of sugar and milk (milk chocolate) are added to improve the flavor of chocolate.

LiveScience has suggested several newcomers to taste science. These include the taste of calcium (a chalky taste which most people don't like), kokumi (the perception of "mouthfulness" and "heartiness"), coolness (the sensory perception of cool and minty fresh usually from peppermint or menthol compounds), and the highly novel taste sensation of "tingling" as carbon dioxide comes into direct contact with your tongue (CO_2 is dissolved in carbonated beverages).

A few other novel taste sensations include a taste found only in some Brazil nuts – kind of a "soapy" flavor. Another candidate is the sensory perception of mucilaginous foods such as okra, etc. If you have ever ground up vitamins and minerals and added to food, there are also different "flavors" of some of the B vitamins and minerals. When fats oxidize and turn rancid, this results in an "off" flavor, warning us to avoid this ingredient. There is also a unique compound in castor oil (most people do not voluntarily consume castor oil). Grass also has "grassy" qualities. Regardless of whether or not these novel flavors have distinct receptor mechanisms, food does have an infinite ability to stimulate the palate and provide pleasure and satisfaction.

It turns out, taste is complex and dynamic. Taste receptors and other components in the mouth perform amazing chemistry to give us pleasurable sensations. As molecular biology expands to include molecular gastronomy, we may expect more novel taste receptors to be identified.

Palate fatigue is a phenomenon of a food becoming less desirable as the number of bites goes up. It is common among chefs and those who prepare food. This may be a mechanism to limit food intake, which we oftentimes override. It is observed as the cook who has labored over a hot stove for several hours preparing a meal, who only eats a small plate of food at mealtime. **Sometimes, just one bite is enough, especially when it is rich foods and heavy desserts.** A well-trained cook / chef understands how to add various flavor components to rich food or traditional recipes to pique interest and to avoid palate fatigue. An example of this is adding a small amount of bitter greens or a sweet unexpected element to a typical salad. Try adding fresh basil, finishing salt or cayenne to jazz up a dessert recipe. Eating just one bite of a rich cheesecake can heighten the sense of taste and increase satisfaction and even lead to future anticipation of the next encounter with this same dish.

Cheesecake Factory capitalizes on avoiding palate fatigue. If they only offered two or three types of cheesecake, they would be just another high-end chain restaurant. However, they take cheesecake to the next level. People are willing to pay $10+ for one slice of cheesecake because they are tricked out with cookies, sauces, whipped cream, fruit, chocolate bars, ganache and more.

How does this topic relate to Country Living and culinary arts? The more knowledge we have about food and how we enjoy food helps us as we educate others about how to make healthy and flavorful dietary changes. Keep this in mind as you teach healthful cooking classes and you make a vegan, gluten-free, low-fat cheesecake which you want everyone to love and accept as an alternative to Cheesecake Factory type options. If you serve up a brownish cheesecake with a soggy crust, your audience will not be eager to adopt the healthier eating habits you are promoting. However, if you make something beautiful, delicious, and healthy, you may end up with a few healthy eating converts. Eating is not only about taste, but includes smell, visual cues, previous experiences with the food, who you share a meal with, mental associations with food, and the emotional satisfaction of what is being consumed. **Learning about taste receptors gives us insight into exercising temperance. More is not always better, healthy or temperate.**

Our intemperance sets the stage for abusing our sensory receptors and our nerves, possibly further setting the stage for chronic degenerative changes. One example of this is eating a high fat meal – which I will arbitrarily set at 50 or more grams of fat (e.g., big meat eaters, those consuming large amounts of rich food, those following a low carb high protein and fat diet). Fat in a meal is absorbed differently compared to protein and carbohydrates. In the stomach, fat may slightly separate from other components (depending on a number of variables). When fat enters the small intestine, it is emulsified by the presence of bile. As fat is absorbed in the small intestine, it goes into the lymphatic circulation (via the lacteals, a lymphatic capillary which absorbs fats). It is not immediately absorbed into the bloodstream. Absorbed fatty acids form a transport complex known as a chylomicron. This carries fat through the lymphatic system and ultimately into the circulatory system, where fat is taken to the liver and then repackaged for sending out to the body for various uses. **Keep in mind the lymphatic system is dependent on the action of muscles and body movement to keep lymphatic fluid moving and dynamic.** If you remain sedentary after eating a high fat meal, your body may experience negative consequences (although you may not be aware of them or notice them at the time). If you examine medical drawings of the body, you may notice the lymphatics travel along a similar route with the circulatory system and peripheral nerves. Chronic high fat consumption may cause sluggish movement through the lymph system as evidenced by feeling bloated, constant swelling, brain fog, frequent infections, headache, etc. When you consume a high fat meal, the lymphatics may take up to 6 or more hours to process the fat. During this time, the lymphatics may not be giving due diligence to other functions such as fighting pathogens, etc. **As fat enters into the circulatory system, depending on your metabolic condition, it may cause insulin resistance, vasoconstriction, hypoxia, and accelerated atherosclerosis as well as other metabolic issues.** It should be noted, not all fats are equal, but that goes beyond this discussion but is briefly addressed in Chapter 17. It is optimal to consume minimally processed fats such as avocado, olives, nuts, seeds, coconut, cold pressed nuts and seeds, etc.

Sometimes when we are ill, food leaves behind a metallic taste or it has no flavor, indicating our taste receptors and possibly the cranial nerves involved are being stressed (i.e., facial, glossopharyngeal, and vagus) and are under duress. Smoking dulls how we taste food. Some medications alter taste sensations. Smell is another sensory input known to enhance the perception of how food tastes.

The olfactory nerve carries impulses for how food smells. Nutritional deficiencies are another avenue impacting taste perception. The optic nerve carries impulses for how food looks. The limbic system connects our sensory inputs to how we act and feel about a certain food or meal. **Eating is a complex task which should be respected and not abused.** Poor habits, low quality food, foods containing chemicals and toxins, and stressful events associated with eating may all converge to impact overall health and wellness. Every food and every meal count for our benefit or to our detriment.

When the various taste sensations are out of balance, food does not taste right. A basic but good example is oatmeal. I make oatmeal with water, oats, brown sugar, blond raisins, cinnamon and ginger. It absolutely tastes better with a shake or two of salt added to the boiling water. Occasionally, I add nuts or a square of dark chocolate and leave out the raisins. **No matter the ingredients, a small amount of salt in the water is critical to making it palatable.**

When food doesn't taste right, adding a small amount of a balancing flavor usually makes it taste better. This is known as flavor balancing. It is a critical skill in learning to cook. The remainder of this chapter is a description of each flavor, followed by a chart which provides basic flavor balancing ideas.

Start with small amounts when you first learn to flavor balance. **A correction may only require a grew grains of sugar or salt or a few drops of acidic sour lemon or lime. Adding too much may defeat your purpose.** I have always been amazed how little sugar, salt or lemon juice (i.e., an acid) are needed to put the spotlight on an otherwise dull and boring dish. Sometimes when a recipe calls for a small amount of sugar, I may add several red grapes or a few yellow cherry tomatoes – both with naturally occurring sugars and unique flavor components. Of course, it depends on the recipe and the other ingredients. Super-tasters are more likely to identify small amounts of unknown ingredients and herbs in a dish, but they tend not to enjoy hot, spicy and pungent foods. However, their concentrated taste recpetors are invaluable for reverse engineering a complex recipe.

Roasting vegetables brings out their sweetness while adding an element of depth and complexity. However, sometimes, eating fresh asparagus straight from the garden may be preferable to roasting. Or when it is hot outside you may want a fresh, crisp pepper for your sandwich or for using with a dip or in a sauce.

One reason an omnivore may have a difficult time adopting a vegetarian diet, is the choir of flavors present in animal flesh, including in the raw state all the way to the well-done piece of meat. Raw meat has a certain flavor but cooking meat leads to the Maillard reaction, causing hundreds of different Maillard-reaction types of flavors and aromatic products to form when grilling meat.

The Maillard reaction occurs when food heats up to around 280°F to 330°F. This temperature ensures food will brown. It is an enzymatic chemical oxidation reaction between amino acids and reducing sugars (i.e., the monosaccharides: glucose, fructose and galactose and the disaccharides: maltose and lactose). A non-reducing sugar cannot be oxidized and includes starch, sucrose, inositol and trehalose (sounds like a lot of whole foods). The Maillard reaction gives us toasted marshmallows (S'mores), lightly browned biscuits, cookies, toast, etc. It gives food a different flavor compared to its raw state. The Maillard reaction is a chemical reaction and it differs from caramelization which occurs with sugars and is a non-enzymatic reaction. The type of browning that occurs when food is cooked depends on the various amino acids present. If you enjoy reading about food chemistry, you might enjoy a career as a food scientist.

Flavors present in food depend on factors including the season, method of preparation, and the age of the ingredients (fresh-picked vs. refrigerated), etc. For example, butter may be sweet or it may be slightly salty, depending on the time of the year. Butter added to a recipe carries other flavors and gives food a richness, known as "fatness." **Butter is also used to correct flavor imbalances. It coats the tongue and covers up strong flavors, taking down the heat or correcting for too much sour (acid) or salt.**

Learn to take a few risks and hopefully they pay off with improved cooking skills. I hope this chapter provides you with just enough information to launch you on an exciting journey of a lifetime, learning to cook with passion and skill. Below are the different taste sensations as well as a few novel ones.

Sweet (examples: dates, dried and fresh fruits, agave nectar, maple syrup, sun-dried tomatoes, etc.)
- The harmonious flavor, bringing balance to all others
- Even small amounts of sugar bring out and enhance other flavors. Adding a pinch of sugar to a homemade tomato sauce balances the acid and gives it a nice balanced flavor.
- Increases our pleasure quotient.
- The sweet taste from adding sugar may not be present until you reach 0.5% by weight.
- Sweet balances salty, sour, bitter, and piquancy.
- Cold foods may need additional sugar.

Salty (examples: solar-dried sea salt, tamari, miso, sea vegetables, celery, etc.)
- Universal flavor enhancer; enhances sweetness.
- Adds depth and roundness to other flavors.
- Saliva is 0.4% salt by weight. If the salt concentration in a food is less than 0.4% by weight it tastes bland. If the concentration of salt is greater than 0.4% by weight, it tastes just about right or maybe slightly salty. The target salt concentration for all foods is 0.5 to 1% by weight.
- Food temperature affects how taste buds perceive salt. If preparing cold foods that use salt, you may need to add additional salt.

Acid/Tart/Sour (examples: lemon, lime, tamarind, grapefruit, orange, vinegar, etc.)
- Enhances other flavors (in small amounts).
- Reduces the amount of salt required.
- Adds a high note/brilliance/liveliness to other flavors.
- Sour balances salty and sweet.
- Keeps greens from oxidizing.

Umami – "Pleasant Savory Taste" (examples: cheese, nuts, vegetables, meat, mushrooms, soy sauce, marmite, nutritional yeast, etc.)
- Umami is present in savory foods and contributes to high food satisfaction.
- A mild but lasting aftertaste.
- Corresponds to the flavor of free glutamates; glutamate receptors are responsible for tasting umami.
- Combining umami with salt intensifies umami taste.
- Umami complements all flavors and "completes" a dish which might be just shy of balanced.

Bitter (examples: Romaine lettuce, kale, arugula, dandelion, beet greens, chard, parsley, basil, nutmeg, cumin, aromatic herbs, cacao nibs, quinine, etc.)
- Sometimes bitter is a warning to avoid a certain food, but not always. Many foods contain bitter elements.
- Bitter is an important flavor element to include when preparing food – bitter flavors play a role in healthy digestion, a healthy appetite and in rounding out various flavors in a meal.
- Bitter tannins may be alkalizing, promote blood sugar balance, balance hormones, and promote the health of digestive organs and improve digestion.
- Bitter balances sweet and fatty flavors.

Astringent (examples: unripe fruit, coffee, black tea, pomegranates, quince, dark chocolate, etc.)
- Tannins are responsible for astringent taste. When tannins come in contact with mucous membranes in the mouth, they cause them to shrink, providing an astringent sensation.
- This flavor may make your mouth pucker and feel like it is "drying" out.
- Leaves the mouth feeling "rough and dry."
- Bitter and astringency taste perception are both related to the tannin content of food. They are perceived at the same time but bitter usually dominates over astringency.
- Some adjectives used to describe astringency include: fine grain, medium grain, coarse grain, chalk, dryness, fullness, adhesive, puckering, tightening, etc. (PMID: 32498458)

Hot and Spicy (examples: chiles, cayenne)
- The sensation of hot and spicy is technically the result of activating pain fibers. Capsaicin causes a sensation of pain and heat.
- If a food is too spicy, it may be balanced with sweet or fatty ingredients.

Pungency (examples include: horseradish, ginger, hot garlic, onion, etc.)
- Pungency may be detected downstream from oral taste receptors. (PMID: 24961971)
- Pungency of food is influenced by other factors such as temperature, acidity, and carbonation (when present).

Fatness (examples: cold pressed oils, avocado, coconut milk / cream, etc.)
- Fat carries and emulsifies the other flavors – bringing them together.
- Volatile oils embed in fat and are released upon eating, providing lingering taste sensations.
- Too much fat in a dish may blunt the other flavors.
- Adding hot and spicy usually balances the fat.
- Fat gives food a nice "mouth feel" and increases satiety.
- A small amount of fat is needed to optimally absorb and utilize fat soluble vitamins and provide for a healthy liver.

Low note foods: earthy, lingering flavors including beans, mushrooms, onions, protein foods, etc.

Mid note foods: subtle, brief flavors such as raw vegetables, grains, etc.

High note foods: citrus, fresh herbs, hot peppers, garlic, etc.

The information in the table below may be used to improve your cooking skills by honing your ability to positively flavor balance almost any recipe.

Learn how to cook: the choir of flavors*		
Table 1. Flavor Corrections		
The Problem	The Flavor Solution	Corrective Foods
Food tastes too bitter	Add salt	Celtic salt, Himalayan salt, tamari sauce, seaweed, miso, etc.
Food tastes too sour, bitter, or spicy	Add sweetness / fat	Sugar, maple syrup, honey, agave, jam, jelly, molasses, stevia, sweet potatoes, carrots, carrot juice, beets, beet juice, butternut squash, corn, sugar snap peas, sweet potato, fruits, fruit juices, avocado, butter, etc.
Food is too spicy, sweet, bitter, or salty	Add acid / sour / fat	Lemon juice, lime juice, grapefruit juice, orange juice, blood orange juice, vinegar, tomato, tomato paste, pickled vegetables, avocado, chips, butter, yogurt, sour cream, etc.
Food is too sweet or salty	Add bitterness	Cocoa, cacao, cacao nibs, roasted chicory, coffee, grapefruit, green leafy vegetables, dandelion greens, endive, okra, broccoli, radicchio, etc.
Food is too sweet	Add spicy / bitter / more liquid or other ingredients	Jalapeno, habanero, ancho chili, harissa, hot sauce, ginger, Dijon mustard, horseradish, wasabi, arugula, radishes, watercress.
Food is too fatty	Add acid, blend with fruit or vegetable, add spicy, emulsify with acid or lecithin	Lemon, lime, tamarind, spicy pepper, potato, soy sauce.
Food tastes too bland	Add salt, umami, acid, sour, sweet, spicy	Salt, cheese, soy sauce, miso, pickled vegetables, mushrooms, citrus, corn, tomatoes, jalapeno, etc.
*Adapted from Living Light, Fort Bragg CA, as part of my raw food chef training and curriculum.		

References and sources: PMID: 28740628, 31884092

Discussion Questions

1. On a scale of 1 (being worst) and 10 (being best), how good of a cook are you?
2. How will you use the information about flavor balancing?
3. What types of meals are more amenable to flavor balancing?
4. How comfortable are you combining sweet and salty flavors?
5. How could you incorporate more bitter elements into your cooking?

Section 5

The Country Living Medicine Cabinet and Essential Skills

Chapter 26

Country living medicine cabinet essentials

This section begins with a disclaimer. No word, thought, or projection of purpose in writing this book is intended to take the place of your regular health care practitioners. Always consult your healthcare provider before beginning a new health habit or natural therapy. Each of us is responsible for our health. I am responsible for my health. You bear responsibility for your health. Our physician and other health care practitioners are not planning to move in with us. They are not going to be with us to monitor our every bite, every activity (or lack thereof), every thought, every conversation we have with our friends and family, etc. Therefore, our health is what we make it. In fact, each one us must learn to be her/his own "physician," a type of "self-care" we do for our own good.

Now having put all the responsibility firmly on our shoulders, let's admit, there are factors impacting our health which are out of our control and probably not even a part of our awareness. In 2014, David Bellinger, in The Atlantic, describes a silent pandemic. He claims generations of Americans in modern times have collectively forfeited a whopping total of 41 million IQ points as a result of exposure to lead, mercury and organophosphate pesticides. Ouch, that hurts! Lead and mercury are the tip of the iceberg when it comes to toxins. Organophosphate pesticides are found in 50% of all pesticides sold in the USA. Many homes and farms use these products. Other toxins are found in the air we breathe. For some, a lack of hygienic factors at work may be damaging your health (e.g., asbestos in the walls and ceilings). Items such as clothing, furniture, and petroleum-based products come with many hidden chemicals. Sometimes the toxin is invisible, such as electro-magnetic pollution. We assume the water coming out of the tap is "safe" when in reality, most water treatment facilities add chemicals such as fluorine and chlorine to neutralize pathogens in the water. Chemicals are added to foods as preservatives and flavoring agents. Even ingredients such as sugar can be toxic in excess. You may move to a new home and find out it was built on a toxic dumping site, or the nearby river where toxic waste is dumped has contaminated the underground water table. Other types of toxins may be less obvious such as toxins to the mind such as TV, computer games, violence, and countless others. These toxins have an impact on our health and wellness. If you regularly work with chemicals, be sure you understand the associated risks of each compound and take every precaution to avoid direct contact with known toxic chemicals.

Healthcare is going to significantly change. It is like the person who could not quit eating pizza and ice cream and kept finding friends to bring them more and more food until they weighed 650 pounds. No matter what happens in the future, it is clear, healthcare needs a renaissance! It is not even healthcare, it is disease care. The disease establishment cartel runs the system. The disease establishment includes (but is not limited to): Wall Street Pharmaceuticals, equipment manufacturers, politicians, lobbyists, PACs, inter-locking boards of directors, professional organizations, etc. As healthcare executives and their Boards milk the system, their employees, the actual providers, work on razor thin margins and take most of the risk, while executives take home millions in benefits, stock shares, travel benefits, use of the corporate jet, and a handsome income. As previously mentioned, an MRI is an order of magnitude more expensive in the USA compared to most other countries where healthcare costs have not spiraled out of control. Healthcare is cumbersome; burdened by regulations; expensive; administrative heavy; it has excessive middlemen with no connection to actual patient care who demand a hefty share of profits; documentation is time-consuming; physicians are often micromanaged; most providers are heavily reliant on constantly-evolving technology; it is too political; and healthcare oftentimes lacks moral and ethical bounds. The physician and other direct-patient care providers cannot continue to carry the burden of supporting the middle-men cartels. **Costs continue to rise, making healthcare the single largest "tax" on an employee's pay check (this is calculated as a percentage of an employee's wage).** An independent contractor may make 35% to 50% more than a salaried worker accounting for a hefty benefit package including healthcare costs, vacation days, etc. Those who are healthy and infrequently utilize healthcare services subsidize those who heavily utilize healthcare services. It is not unusual for a family of 4 to pay $700 to $1,500 (or more) per month for healthcare coverage. This amount goes up every year. It is not sustainable.

With so much uncertainty surrounding the future of healthcare, it is prudent to take steps toward educating yourself about natural approaches to promoting health, maintaining health and restoring health. There are many positive steps you can take to ensure you have adequate information to make healthcare-related decisions in the comfort of your own home, without frequent and stressful trips to the doctor's office. <u>Not everyone can cut back on their physician visits</u>. If you have cancer or severe heart disease, <u>you need to be under a physician's care</u>. However, if you are relatively healthy but could do better in the area of self-care techniques, then why not take charge of your health? Self-care techniques, adopting good habits, and related natural therapies may be able to assume a substantial proportion of targeting bothersome symptoms, preventing the progression of mild symptoms to even addressing moderate or severe issues (<u>while under your physician's care</u>). Dedicate some of your budget to preventive, nutritional, and naturopathy services. Take the time to read and study about your condition. Join a self-help group, utilize free counseling services offered by your healthcare plan. **Understand, it has taken some time to get to where you are and it will take time and effort to begin to reverse engineer your present condition.** There are no guarantees, but as you begin to understand the importance of high-quality food, good nutrition, a reasonably healthy and active lifestyle, the significance of protecting your frontal lobes, ensuring good mental health, the importance of good posture and spinal alignment, the role relationships and community play in health, you may learn to rearrange your priorities to reflect to your increasing knowledge and awareness of preventive measures.

Before taking a new herbal remedy or new type of therapy, check with your physician to make sure the herbal formula or new habit does not negatively interact with any medications or exacerbate or complicate your medical condition(s). This is a good time to take advantage of telemedicine services, usually offered as a "free" service for those with healthcare coverage. Use common sense.

When you try any new supplement, start with a small dose and over the period of a week or two, increase the dose to see how you tolerate each level. Different forms of the same herb may have paradoxical effects. Chamomile tea may work better than a chamomile supplement to relax and induce sleep. One herb may not have a perceived benefit at one time but a week or month later, it may work to resolve an irritating symptom. Start with small doses and work up to larger doses if necessary. **Large amounts of even the safest drug / chemical may cause severe complications and even death.** In fact, in the USA, medical errors are the 3rd leading cause of death. In 2013, data showed that up to 440,000 Americans annually die from preventable hospital errors. Before going to the hospital for scheduled services you may want to check their Hospital Safety Score (if available). Here is the website: www.hospitalsafetyscore.org . In fact, let's superficially look at two different types of health care. Kaiser Permanente is a member-only system of hospitals and outpatient clinics. Companies may choose Kaiser health care and their employees are encouraged to participate in preventive care activities such as cholesterol screenings, weight loss classes, diabetes education, etc. Kaiser Permanente makes money by keeping you out of their hospitals. Most other health care systems operate under a different paradigm – they want you to utilize their services and they benefit from your frequent use of their services. You can see the difference between the two types of systems. In either paradigm, it is usually best to do everything possible to avoid being a hospital patient unless it is absolutely unavoidable or essential!

According to 19th century physician and prolific writer, J. H. Tilden (his book: <u>Impaired Health: It's cure and cause</u>), "The habitual use of alcohol or tobacco may show no apparent effect on a 100% efficient man; but if he loses his resistance, becomes enervated [weakened, loss of vitality / energy], his accustomed drink, cigar or cup of coffee strangely and powerfully affects him... Germs which are said to cause disease do so only when resistance is broken... When energy is gone, man becomes prey to any pathological influences; even health- and life-imparting influences become disease and death-imparting when enervation is great; it is then that food becomes bane. The first cause must be enervation, and that can be brought about in a thousand ways. **The man who has spent his resistance is the man who makes friends with germs.**"

This speaks to the importance of individualizing each person's approach to wellness and restoring health. We often speak about resistance in terms of immune functions. The immune system may be likened to the military. There are large numbers of basic immune factors, comparable to the army, but there are also specialized immune "teams" available to the body when needed, comparable to special forces. When resistance is strong, good health prevails. **When resistance is low, the weakest link is exploited, symptoms progress, and disease gains a foothold.**

We hear innumerable stories of healthy people getting a devastating diagnosis and prematurely dying. At the other end of the spectrum are reports of people smoking, eating a dozen eggs every day, and participating in all kinds of debauchery, and yet they live to be 105 years old. **Each person has a unique key to good health or a unique key to disease progression.** We all die, but how many of us really live a vibrant, energized life with little to no impairments?

It would be negligent to write a book about country living and not include a section on natural approaches to restoring and achieving health. This chapter is not comprehensive; there are numerous other resources for reading on this topic (see resource section at the end of this chapter). However, choosing country living over city dwelling is one of the strongest steps you can take to improve your health. Moving to the country has many potential health benefits including but not limited to: more contact with the ground (i.e., earthing transfers electrons from ground to body), fresh air, better hygienic factors, the ability to grow your own food, opportunity for vigorous and essential manual labor, less city influences, less fast food and more home grown food, rest and sleep free from ambient city noise and lights, and more time to commune with God in nature.

In the course of maintaining your health you may need to learn new skills such as making herbal teas, infusions, decoctions, poultices, salves, etc. Each skill is relatively simple and straight forward. Once you learn the skill, you can teach others. This book does not teach every single natural approach or medicinal technique or skill set. Once you learn a few skills outlined in this book, you can research others. Some of the techniques are very similar with only minor differences. When you learn something new, share your knowledge with others. This aspect of sharing your country living experiences is perhaps the most important. Most people's health improves when they leave the city and move to the country. It is important to get baseline health data before you move to the country such as weight, lipid levels, nutrient levels, thyroid panel, etc. For some, the differences in their health profile between living in the city and living in the country is remarkable. Country living may also shift your reliance on traditional medicine to alternative and complementary approaches to achieving health and wellness.

When possible grow herbs and medicinal plants. Most medicinal plants are attractive and enhance landscaping features. Plant a medicinal garden, focusing on both annual and perennial medicinal plants. Most medicinal plants possess multiple therapeutic targets. For example, licorice (*Glycrrhiza glabra*) and its 300 or so naturally occurring plant chemicals, fights inflammation but has also been used as an antibacterial and antiviral to successfully used to treat infections. It has strong antioxidant activity. It is used for heart burn, acid reflux, upset stomach, and ulcers. Licorice is 50 times sweeter than table sugar. Licorice root tea can be used to sweeten beverages and other recipes requiring a liquid sweetener. As always, consider the possible side effects of using each herb. Regular use of licorice root may slightly raise your blood pressure. If you suffer from hypertension, you may want to find a different alternative to licorice root. This is the beauty of the plant kingdom – there are many options, each with its own unique characteristics.

A recent movement toward using herbal antibiotics has emerged. They are mild, speed up healing, and may help you and your family decrease the number of times you must resort to more harsh prescription antibiotics. Whole herbals contain tens if not hundreds of plant-based chemicals, known as phyto (plant) chemicals. Each plant has a unique chemical signature which includes amino acids, carbohydrates, lipids, sometimes sulfur, and hundreds of others. Plants with some degree of antibiotic activity include but is not limited to: garlic, chives, onions, black pepper, citrus, aloe vera, ginger, honey, licorice root, acacia, alchornea, ashwagandha, astragalus, berberines, boneset, cryptolepsis, echinacea, eleuthero, eucalyptus, goldenseal, juniper, red root, reishi, rhodiola, sage, sida, usnea, and wormwood (aka, artemisia). Sometimes prescription antibiotics are necessary and save lives. When my dad had Covid-19 which progressed to left lung pneumonia, he would have likely died without taking a strong antibiotic, which worked rapidly to help him recover. When you do you strong antibiotics, take steps to subsequently detox and restore normal gut microflora.

If you have a passion for medicinal plants, grow your favorite ones and sell them. Lavender is an example of a high yield crop which also sells for a good price. *Helichrysum italicum* (the curry plant), is a highly valued medicinal plant. It is a small evergreen flowering bush in the daisy family, able to grow in USDA zones 7-10. Grow several acres of lavender or helichrysum and sell to commercial producers.

Start a small group dedicated to learning the natural remedies and how to prepare them. Use the remedies as needed, remembering to keep your natural remedy-approving physician in the loop. This allows each person to benefit from the knowledge and experience of others.

Use this chapter to launch your personal research into plants and techniques of interest to you. It is impossible to know everything about medicinal herbals. Collect resources and learn how to be a valuable asset to your local community. Give lectures and demonstrations in your community. **If you are not formally educated in medicine, nursing, allied health, relevant sciences, then join up with someone who can help educate you about molecular biology, neuroscience, anatomy, physiology, nutrition, biochemistry, medicine, etc.** It is never too late to learn valuable information to share with others including your close circle of family and friends.

Resources:

1. The Herbal Remedies & Natural Medicine Bible by Lena Farrow
2. Essential Oils: Ancient Medicine by Josh Axe and Jordan Rubin
3. The Natural Remedies Encyclopedia, 7th Edition by Vance Ferrell and Harold Cherne
4. The Encyclopedia of Natural Medicine, 3rd Ediction by Michael Murray and Joseph Pizzorno
5. Encyclopedia of Herbal Medicine (ISBN-13: 978-0241229446)

Discussion Questions

1. What herbs or supplements do you find yourself using most often?
2. Take an inventory of your supplements and keep records.
3. Which herbal and natural remedies may address one or more of your health issues?

Herbal Supplement Inventory

Herbal Name	Contents: Dose	Quantity	Frequency	Additional Information
1.				
2.				
3.				
4.				
5.				
6.				
7.				
8.				
9.				
10.				
11.				
12.				
13.				
14.				
15.				
16.				
17.				
18.				
19.				
20.				
21.				
22.				
23.				
24.				
25.				
26.				
27.				
28.				
29.				
30.				
31.				
32.				
33.				
34.				
35.				

Chapter 27

Make herbal teas, infusions and elixirs

Herbal teas (tisane). Herbal teas provide many health benefits, especially when they are combined with other therapeutic modalities such as tinctures, infusions, fruit juices, spices and various sweeteners. You may grow an herbal tea garden including plants such as various mints, lemon balm, sage, oregano, basil, rosemary, etc. You may start with fresh herbs or start with a pre-packaged herbal tea such as red raspberry tea, chai, etc.

You can make a tea out of many non-tea (tea plants are the species *Camilla sinesis*) plants. You may make a tea out of elderberries, cranberries, lemon rind, sage leaves, dandelion, etc. Add fresh berries, cooling cucumber slices, chamomile flowers, purple basil, a shot of ginger juice and any number of other plant components. You are only limited by your imagination.

If you are foraging for herbal tea ingredients, properly identify each plant. Also, if pregnant or lactating, be sure to check with your physician regarding safe herbal teas. Common herbs used externally, such as comfrey, may not be safe to use in making tea. In fact, avoid ingesting comfrey. Keep in mind plants may carry herbicides and other contaminants. Always prepare foraged plants by thoroughly washing and removing possible contaminants. Photo-type plant reference books are essential to confirm the safety of foraged wild plants.

An electric tea pot with variable temperature control is the ideal way to make tea. It heats the water to the exact temperature for each type of tea. For example, the water temperature for making matcha green tea should not exceed 175 °F (80 °C). This protects the delicate phytonutrients while allowing optimum steeping. If you do not have access to an electric tea pot, you can boil water and add an ounce or two of cold water to the boiling water before combining with the tea. If the water is too hot the bitter flavonoids may be activated and the tea may carry more bitter flavor notes. When it comes to matcha green tea, it is a fine art to make the perfect cup of green tea. You need a bamboo whisk and high quality matcha. If the water is too cool, the matcha may not froth when whisked and will be bitter if too hot.

To make a tea or tisane

1. Choose your base tea ingredient(s) such as herbal, green tea, white tea, etc. Place 1 to 3 teaspoons of loose-leaf herbs in a tea strainer.
2. Add fresh or dried herbs, flowers, spices and any other ingredient you desire.
3. Bring 8 ounces of pure water to boil in a kettle (or to the appropriate temperature), tea pot, or on the stovetop.
4. Pour hot water over the tea and herbs. Cover your tea cup with a saucer. Wait 3 to 10 minutes.
5. Remove loose tea ingredients with a strainer. Add sweetener and steamed milk if you desire.

Infusions. Infusions are sometimes needed to mobilize beneficial plant chemicals found in woody or tough plants. If you have a delicate leaf or flower, you may only need to make a tea. A good example of when an infusion is indicated is extracting compounds from licorice roots and stems. An infusion brings out the lovely sweetness of the licorice roots and stems, which is sweet and tastes nothing like commercial licorice candy (which comes from the anise plant, *Pimpinella anisum*).

Not all infusions use hot water. Some infusions may use cold water over a longer period of time. This method is used when the desired extract is heat sensitive such as with mucilaginous herbs (e.g., slippery elm, marshmallow root, horehound, bladderwrack, etc.). Mobilization of the desired compound from the plant may occur rapidly or it may need a more time. For longer infusions, proceed as follows but allow the herbs and hot water to infuse for 4 to 8 hours, similar to how you would make sun tea but not necessarily exposing to the sun.

Marshmallow root and slippery elm have mucilaginous properties. If you do a cold infusion, the solution usually remains thin and watery. However, if you heat the marshmallow root or slippery elm with a liquid, it may thicken. Both methods are valuable and are used for specific conditions. Marshmallow root and slippery elm can be used externally to soothe inflamed skin or internally for sore throats and to soothe an upset stomach. Marshmallow root is considered safe to use during pregnancy while slippery elm should not be used during pregnancy. Both may be added to lozenges, used as a tea, a supplement, or used as a drawing agent in an herbal poultice. If you intend to use marshmallow root and / or slippery elm, be sure to consult your physician as these herbs may affect medications taken by mouth. They may potentially decrease the amount of medicine your body absorbs, thereby decreasing the effectiveness of your medicine. One possible solution is to space your medications at least one hour before taking marshmallow root or slippery elm. This allows the medication to be absorbed and not bound up in the mucilaginous herbs and potentially eliminated from the body without exerting their intended use.

A peppermint or ginger infusion may be used to soothe an upset stomach. To make a peppermint infusion, you need several cups of fresh and clean peppermint leaves. Heat several cups of water just short of boiling; add sugar and cook for 10 – 15 minutes (you don't have to add sugar but it makes the infusion more flavorful). Transfer peppermint leaves to a glass quart jar. Pour the hot syrup over the peppermint leaves; seal jar and allow to sit for up to 1 day. To use, remove the peppermint leaves and use 1 or 2 tablespoons for treating an upset stomach. To make a ginger infusion, take a 4-inch length of fresh ginger, wash and peel. Cut into thin slices and transfer to a quart glass jar. Make the same syrup used in the peppermint infusion and add to the ginger root (a syrup is equal parts sugar and water, cooked until the solution is reduced and slightly thickened).

You may want to infuse an oil with an herb or another plant. To make an infused oil, begin with a high-quality oil such as avocado, apricot, almond, rice bran oil, sunflower or olive oil. Each oil has different qualities which may or may not be appropriate for the herb you choose to infuse. It is best to experiment to see which combinations work best for you. To infuse olive oil with rosemary and garlic, add olive oil to a sterile glass jar with a lid and add washed and gently crushed rosemary stems and halved garlic cloves to the oil. Close the lid and allow the oil and herb combination to infuse for at least several weeks if not longer. The longer the infusion the stronger the flavor. You may even add a drop or two of an essential oil to complement the fresh herb you are using. I frequently add hot chili peppers to olive oil for a spicy hot version of olive oil. This goes great in salads and other dishes.

To make an infusion

1. Bring 4 cups of pure water to a boil in a kettle or in a pan on the stovetop.
2. Place 1/4 cup of herbs (or 1 ounce by weight) in a quart mason jar.
3. Pour water over herbs, place lid on jar, and shake once to mix herbs and water well.
4. Let sit anywhere from 30 minutes to overnight.
5. Strain and compost the herbs. Sweeten infusion with maple syrup or raw honey if desired. Drink recommended dosage throughout the day.

Elixirs (sometimes known as "mocktails). Elixirs were a popular route of drug delivery in the early 20th century. In fact, in 1938, it was an elixir-related tragedy which sparked the passage of the Federal Food, Drug and Cosmetic Act establishing stricter standards for therapeutic and medical modalities by the Food and Drug Administration. In 1937, an elixir known as Sulfa-nilamide, the first sulfa-based antimicrobial drug, diluted with di-ethylene glycol (i.e., a colorless, odorless, slightly sweet poisonous compound aka, antifreeze). One hundred and five patients died from drinking this elixir. It was promoted without any prior safety testing, which now has become a highly regulated standard of practice in the USA. In this section you will not find any deadly elixirs, but some of you might find one or two which may make you think you are dying (e.g., ginger shots, turmeric elixir II, turmeric shots – all elixirs with a significant amount of fresh ginger and / or cayenne).

Today, elixirs are one of the hottest non-alcoholic beverages around. One example of a popular elixir combines fresh apple cider, fresh orange juice, honey, cinnamon and lemon juice; add ice, shake and consume. Another combination is fresh lime juice, fresh coconut water, fresh pineapple juice, a dash of ginger juice and garnish with an edible orchid. A warm fig, vanilla, cinnamon and coconut milk elixir is reminiscent of Zanzibar spice farms and street markets.

Elixirs are known for their botanical bona fides including sweet and bitter components. Botanicals in all forms are used in formulating basic to wild and exotic elixirs. The base of an elixir may include fresh juices, sodas, infusions, decoctions, teas, hibiscus tea, licorice root tea, syrups, etc. Elixirs are a sweet version of a tincture but without the alcohol. Any natural sweetener may be used to make an elixir. Traditionally, honey is used, but maple syrup, licorice root water, stevia, xylitol, etc., are all acceptable sweeteners for making elixirs. Bitters are sometimes added as are fresh herbs, spices, roots, bark, pine needles, edible flowers, etc. Even fresh fruits and vegetables sometimes make their way into an elixir. Add ice, shake, and serve cold.

Elixirs may be just a fabulous tasting beverage or they may be formulated to address issues such as nausea, pain, anxiety, etc., known as functional beverages. Ingredients in elixirs may target anxiety, stress, mood, and other states. They contain functional ingredients such as hibiscus, licorice, rosemary, thyme, holy basil, rhodiola, rose hips, ashwagandha, etc. If you have heard of nootropics, they are usually natural substances used to improve mental performance. They enhance mental acuity, creativity, focus, motivation, etc. Nootropics may be added to elixirs. Examples of nootropics that could be added to beverages include: aloe vera, kava kava, lemon balm, methylene blue, charcoal, cacao, cat's claw, CBD, coconut oil, turmeric, green tea, etc.

Some elixirs are made with alcohol, but non-alcoholic versions are just as effective and even better without the risks of consuming alcohol, making them kid-friendly. You don't have to be a trendy socialite to enjoy a good non-alcoholic nootropic elixir at the hottest clubhouse in Los Angeles. What could be better than making a non-alcoholic elixir from fruits and herbs grown on your land and enjoying it with your family as you sit outside at nighttime, counting shooting stars. It's as simple as growing an herb garden, stocking your herbal medicine cabinet, juicing fresh produce and combining it with herbs and other compounds to make a healthy beverage. You do not need to pay $25 for a bottle of herb-infused syrup. Make your own and begin drinking beverages with a purpose! To lower the kcalories from sugar, substitute small amounts of xylitol, which has about 40% fewer kcalories than sugar and does not raise your blood sugar (does not count as a net carb).

The following are several recipes for non-alcoholic elixirs! Next time you have a party or company, make several elixirs in advance. Make and enjoy today!

- **Watermelon Elixir:** 1 quart watermelon juice, 10 mint leaves (optional), 1 cup ice, salt. Blend chilled watermelon, mint and ice. Salt the glass rims and serve cold with a lime wedge. Add cayenne to the salt for a twist.
- **Cantaloupe Elixir:** Flesh from 1 large cantaloupe, rind and seeds removed, 2 4-inch sprigs mint (leaves only), 1 cup hibiscus tea, 1 tsp fresh ginger juice. Blend ingredients with some ice and serve cold.
- **Cranberry Elixir:** 1 cup fresh firm cranberries, ¼ cup fresh lime juice, ¼ cup vanilla syrup (more if needed), ¼ cup water, 5 fresh basil leaves, 1 quart club soda (carbonated). Blend cranberries, lime juice, vanilla syrup, water and fresh basil leaves. Strain the juice and add the cranberry mixture to the club soda water with ice cubes. Serve with mint or rosemary sprigs. (some may prefer more sweetener)
- **Elderberry Elixir:** ½ cup elderberry syrup, 2 tablespoons lemon juice, 1 tablespoon ginger juice, ½ cup grape juice concentrate, 1/8 teaspoon lemon zest, 2 tablespoons sweetener (optional), 4 rosemary or lavender stems about 3 – 4 inches, 2 – 3 cups small ice cubes, ½ to 1 quart club soda. Blend syrup, lemon juice, ginger juice, grape juice concentrate, zest, and sweetener in a high-speed blender. Add ice and pulse several times. Distribute between 4 to 6 glasses and pour mineral water over the ice. Garnish with rosemary, lavender stems, dark rose petals, nasturtium flower, or place a few clean pine needles in the beverage as a non-edible garnish.
- **Grapefruit Elixir:** 2 tablespoons of fresh lemon juice, 8 cups of fresh grapefruit juice, ½ - 1 tsp salt, 2 cups ice. Combine juices, salt and ice. Gently stir before serving. Serve with a straw.
- **Hibiscus Elixir:** 1 quart hibiscus tea made from ½ cup dried hibiscus and 1 quart water), ½ cup mint leaves, 1 – 2 tablespoons of beet powder (optional), 1 lb fresh strawberries, 1 cup fresh or frozen pineapple, 1 cup fresh orange juice, ¼ - ½ cup sweetener, 1 – 2 tablespoons of lemon or lime juice, 1 teaspoon of citrus

zest, 1 quart club soda, fresh mint sprigs for garnish. Combine hibiscus tea with the fresh mint leaves. Simmer over low heat for 10 – 15 minutes; remove from heat and cool. Remove mint leaves and transfer the tea and remaining ingredients to a high-speed blender; blend until smooth. Divide mixture between 8 chilled glasses with a few spoons of crushed ice in each glass. Add club soda and swirl a few times. Garnish with additional fresh mint sprigs.

- **Piña Colada Elixir:** 1 cup loosely packed beet greens (reserve 4 leaves with long stems for garnish), 2 cups coconut water, 1 cup full fat coconut milk, 2 cups pineapple chunks (frozen is good), 1 inch knob fresh ginger (peeled and thinly sliced), 10 – 20 mint leaves, 2 cups ice, 1 passion fruit pulp. Combine all ingredients except passion fruit pulp and garnish, in a high-speed blender. Pour into 4 glasses and garnish with beet green leaves and maybe a small spoon of full fat coconut milk and passionfruit pulp on the top of each glass.

- **Berry Elixir:** 1-2 cups fresh or frozen black berries, 1-2 cups frozen blueberries, 1-2 cups frozen raspberries, 1 cup full fat coconut milk (divided), 3 cups coconut water (divided), 3 cups ice, 3 tablespoons coconut syrup. Blend blackberries with 1/3 cup full fat coconut milk, 1 cup coconut water, 1 cup ice and 1 Tbsp coconut syrup; set aside. Repeat for the blueberries and raspberries. Distribute equal amounts of each berry mixture into 4 cups. Gently swirl and serve right away. Garnish with a fresh berry and mint.

- **Coffee Copycat Elixir:** ¼ cup raw cacao powder, ¼ cup roasted chicory powder (e.g., Roma), 2+ tablespoons blackstrap molasses, ¼ to ½ cup maple syrup, 1 teaspoon vanilla extract, few salt grains, ½ cup plant-based creamer or full fat coconut milk, 20 ounces of plant-based milk, 2 cups ice. Blend and serve cold. To make it extra creamy and rich, add ½ to 1 cup raw cashews or substitute the cashews for the plant-based creamer.

- **Butterfly Pea Flower Elixir**: 1 tablespoon butterfly pea flower powder (reserve a few pinches for a garnish), 3 cups plant-based milk, ½ cup full fat coconut milk, 2 cups ice, ¼ cup of sweet vanilla syrup, ¼ cup black boba tapioca balls (small or large; cooked and softened). Add all ingredients except boba tapioca balls to a high-speed blender and blend well. Place a heaping tablespoon of prepared boba balls in each of four glasses. Add the beverage and garnish with a few pinches of butterfly pea powder. This drink may also be made as a hot beverage. To prepare as a hot beverage, heat and then froth the plant-based milk with the full fat coconut milk. Add the pea powder, vanilla sweetener and vanilla; froth again. If using, add boba balls to mugs and pour liquid into mugs. Garnish with pea powder. Notes: Butterfly pea powder is blue at pH 4 to 8. As pH drops below 4, it turns pink. Adding acids such as citrus alters the blue color.

- **Dandelion Elixir:** 2 – 4 cups yellow dandelion petals only, 4 cups hot water (brought to a boil), ¾ cup sugar (or sweetener of your choice), 1 Tbsp minced ginger, 1 tsp lemon zest, 1 tsp matcha green tea, up to 1 quart of mineral water. Transfer dandelion petals in a half gallon sealable glass jar. Boil 4 cups of water and turn off heat for 1 minute. Pour hot water over dandelion petals and seal the jar for 24 hours. After 24 hours, strain the dandelion petals out of the water. Transfer the liquid to a medium saucepan, add the sugar, ginger and lemon zest and heat over low for 4 to 5 minutes or until the sugar is dissolved. Remove from heat after 1 – 2 minutes, add matcha green tea. Cool and use or store in an airtight glass jar or used right away. Add the syrup, ice and water or club soda to chilled glasses, stir and serve right away.

- **Peach Elixir**: 10 – 12 apricots or 6 peaches, peeled and pits removed, 2 tablespoons of honey, ½ cup water, ¼ cup fresh basil leaves, 1 tablespoon lemon juice, 1 teaspoon lemon zest, pinch salt, ½ cup full fat coconut milk, 2 cups peach syrup from canned peaches, 2 cups peach tea, fresh basil on stems. Transfer peaches or apricots, 2 sweet apricot seeds, sweetener, water and basil to a high-speed blender and blend until smooth. Transfer to a medium saucepan and cook over low heat for 4 to 5 minutes (do not boil). Add the lemon juice, lemon zest and salt while cooking on the stove. Transfer hot mixture to a quart or half gallon sealable glass jar and refrigerate for 1 – 2 days. After 1 – 2 days, remove and strain mixture (optional). To serve, transfer peach mixture and remaining ingredients to a high-speed blender. Blend until smooth. Divide between 6 to 8 chilled glass. Add crushed ice and fresh basil to each glass, pour in peach mixture and serve.
- **Cucumber Elixir**: 2 medium cucumbers, 10 – 20 basil or mint leaves, 2 limes quartered, 1 tablespoon lemongrass (may use 1-inch knob peeled ginger), ½ cup sweetener, 2 tablespoons honey, 2 cups water, 1 quart mineral water. Transfer all ingredients except club soda to a high-speed blender and blend. Pour the mixture through a sieve and divide between 4 to 6 chilled glasses. Add about ¼ cup crushed ice to each glass and then top off with mineral water.
- **Honeydew Elixir**: ½ large honeydew melon, 2 ½ cups coconut water, 1/3 cup fresh mint leaves, 2 Tbsp fresh lime juice, pinch salt, 2 cups ice. Combine all ingredients in a high-speed blender and blend until smooth. Divide between chilled glasses and garnish with fresh mint sprigs.
- **Mango Elixir**: 4 large mangoes (peeled and edible flesh), 1 cup fresh pineapple chunks, 2 ½ cups coconut water, 2 Tbsp lime juice, 2 cups ice. Blend all ingredients until smooth. Serve in chilled glasses.
- **Strawberry Elixir**: 1 ½ pounds strawberries, ¼ cup fresh blueberries, ¼ cup fresh mint leaves, 2 Tbsp fresh lime juice, 1 tsp lime zest, ¼ cup sweetener, 2 cups ice, ½ - 1 cup full fat coconut milk, and lime slices for garnish. Blend all ingredients except lime slices. Divide between 4 to 8 chilled glasses. Top off with club soda and garnish with lime slices.
- **Orange Iced Tea Elixir**: 8 cups of your favorite tea, ¼ cup sweetener, 2 cups fresh orange juice, 2 tsp orange flower water, mint springs. Make at least 8 cups of your favorite tea. Steep for 15 minutes. Remove tea bags and stir in sweetener, orange juice, orange flower water. Garnish with fresh mint springs.
- **Charcoal Lemonade Elixir**: 1 cup freshly squeezed lemon juice, ¼ cup freshly squeezed lime juice, 1 tsp citrus zest, 1 cup sweetener, 2 tsp charcoal powder, 1 cup water, 2 cups ice, 1 quart club soda. Transfer all ingredients except club soda to a high-speed blender. Blend until smooth. Divide between 6 to 8 chilled glasses and top off with club soda. Stir and serve ice cold.
- **Cat's Claw Tea Elixir**: 4 bags rooibos tea, 8 cups water, ¼ cup sweetener (or 2 Tbsp honey), 2 pieces cats claw bark, ¼ cup freshly squeezed lemon juice, fresh lemon balm leaves. Make tea using water and bark pieces. Steep for 15 minutes. Remove tea bags and bark. Add sweetener and lemon juice. Garnish with fresh lemon balm leaves. Serve over ice cubes.
- **Ginger Elixir**: 8 oz ginger (peeled and juiced), ½ cup freshly squeezed lemon juice, ½ cup sweetener, 1 quart club soda. Blend all ingredients except club soda. Divide between 8 chilled glasses with ice cubes. Add mineral water, stir and serve chilled.
- **Aloe Vera Jelly Elixir**: 8 ripe pears (peeled, de-cored & juiced), 50 green grapes (juiced), 2 cups water, 1/3 cup sugar, 2 cups ice, 2 large aloe vera leaves (remove outer layer and dice inner gel into ½ inch cubes), 1 quart chilled club soda, 8 stems of basil with 4 or 5 leaves on each stem. Juice the pears and green grapes; set aside. When you have cubed the aloe vera leaves, transfer the aloe vera cubes to a

medium mixing bowl and cover with cold water for 15 to 30 minutes. Transfer the aloe vera cubes along with the 2 cups of water and sugar to a medium sauce pan over medium heat. Bring to a simmer and cook for about 20 minutes. Refrigerate syrup and aloe vera cubes for up to 3 or 4 days in an airtight glass jar. To make the elixir, combine the juice and ice and blend. Distribute the aloe vera cubes in syrup between 6 to 8 chilled glasses. Pour equal amounts of juice in each glass. Top off with 1 to 2 ounces of club soda and garnish with a stem of basil leaves. Give one quick stir before serving.

- **Turmeric Elixir I**: 2 cups full fat coconut milk, 1 cup water, 1 Tbsp turmeric, 1 – 2 tsp Ceylon cinnamon, 1 tsp cloves, 2 – 3 cardamom pods, 1 tsp ginger or 1 Tbsp ginger juice, ¼ - ½ cup maple syrup. Transfer all ingredients to a medium sauce pan and heat over low heat until the mixture is hot. Divide between 4 to 6 heated mugs and use a frother to make it extra creamy. Strain out the cardamom pods and serve in warmed mugs.

- **Turmeric Elixir II**: 10 ripe pears, 1 peeled lemon, 3- to 4-inch section of turmeric, 2 carrots, 1 inch knob fresh ginger. Juice all the above ingredients and drink chilled or over ice.

- **Ginger shots**: 1 pound fresh ginger, 10 oranges (juiced), 2 Tbsp honey. Juice the ginger and oranges and then combine with honey. May substitute lemons for the oranges.

- **Turmeric shots**: 4 to 5 inches fresh turmeric, 2 inch knob fresh ginger, 7 – 8 ripe pears, few black peppercorns. Juice the turmeric, ginger and pears. Using a mortar and pestle, crack open the peppercorns and grind until they are almost powdery. Add a pinch of pepper to the juice.

- **Carrot Juice Elixir**. Juice from 10 lb of carrots, 1 lb ginger, 2 limes and 3 to 4 cayenne peppers. Serve over ice.

- **Beetroot Ginger Lime Elixir**. Juice of 3 medium to large beets (peeled), juice of 1 sweet apple, 1 lb ginger, juice of 1 lime. Serve over ice and add a few ounces of club soda if desired. If you want to give your leftover juice fiber to your farm animals, remove the ginger fibers first. Animals do not like ginger root.

- **Chamomile Elixir**. 1 quart chamomile tea using ¼ to ½ cup dried chamomile flowers, ¼ cup dried hibiscus flowers, 1 cup berries, ¼ cup sweetener / syrup. Transfer chamomile tea, hibiscus flowers and sweetener to a medium sauce pan. Heat on low for about 20 minutes. Turn off heat and allow to sit for several minutes. Strain out the chamomile and hibiscus flowers and add the berries. Transfer to a high-speed blender and blend until berries are are smooth. Strain the mixture to remove any berry fibers. Store and add to beverage of your choice.

PMID: 7856995 – Elixirs, diluents and the passage of the 1938 Federal Food, Drug and Cosmetic Act.

Chapter 28

Make oxymels, cordials, shrubs and electuaries

Oxymels

Oxymels are the ancient equivalent of modern day "cough syrups," but their potential to treat minor infirmities, is exciting. If you are self-care novice, study herbals and even essential oils and begin to incorporate them in a targeted way into your family's self-care routine. An oxymel is a simple technique to learn. It allows you to introduce bitter herbs and plants while balancing the difficult-to-swallow bitter flavonoids with sweet and acid flavors.

The word "oxymel" is derived from the Greek word, "oxymeli," which refers to a drink made with honey and an acid. The most common oxymel is honey with fresh lemon or lime juice, used to soothe sore throats. The base of honey and an acid is used to extract bioactive compounds from bitter herbs and other therapeutic plants (e.g., cayenne pepper, garlic, citrus peel, elderberry). Modern oxymels are a combination of sweetener with an acid such as lemon or lime juice and fresh or dried herbs. Apple cider vinegar is the traditional acid but lemon or lime juice work as well. Add citrus-related beneficial compounds such as citrus zest or peels or citrus juice. An oxymel uses a sweetener to make bitter-tasting herbs and nootropics more appetizing.

To make oxymels. Elderberry syrup is an example of an oxymel, using a 1:1:1 or 1:1:0.5 ratio of elderberry (or other juice / tea) juice, sweetener (honey) and lemon or lime juice (the acid). You may also add other fresh spices and / or herbs such as ginger juice, licorice tea, cardamom, cloves, fennel, cinnamon, etc. The ratio may change based on your taste. Some people prefer more sweetener or less acid such as lemon or lime juice. The 1:1:1 is a good starting point and from there, adjust according to your taste. Some oxymels are raw and some are cooked. Heating the oxymel may destroy heat labile vitamins and phytochemicals. Seal the oxymel in a glass jar and let it sit in the refrigerator for 2 to 6 weeks. Now it is ready to use.

Cough Syrup Oxymel
1 fresh pineapple, outer skin removed (may use the core)
Juice of 2 lemons
Juice of 4-inch ginger section
1 cayenne pepper or ½ tsp cayenne pepper
¼ cup honey
½ cup coconut water

Add all ingredients to a high-speed blender and blend until smooth. Add additional coconut water if you prefer a thinner cough syrup. This oxymel is ready right away. Sip ½ to 1 cup slowly over 20 to 30 minutes.

Cordials

To make cordials. The word "cordial," contains the Latin root, "cor" which means "harmony." Cordials may include alcoholic beverages, a type of candy with a liquid filling and a chocolate shell, and a medicinal beverage. For purposes of this section, a cordial is considered a non-alcoholic drink with medicinal properties. It is to be used as a delicious sweet drink or in some cases, a sweet medicinal tonic.

Cordials are made from syrups, decoctions, extracts, teas, etc., so they are not necessarily health-promoting. Cordials are slightly syrupy and usually sweet. They may contain novel ingredients such as ground nuts, herbs, spices, fruits, etc. Alcohol-based cordials include amaretto (almond flavor), chambord (raspberry flavor), Cointreau (orange flavor), fragelico (hazelnut), etc. All of these cordials and many others can be made without the alcohol for culinary enjoyment as well as therapeutic uses. Non-alcoholic cordials may be added to desserts, teas, and other beverages.

As a disclaimer, I have never had an alcoholic cordial so I am not able to compare the alcoholic version to the following non-alcoholic versions. What I have done is look at the alcoholic versions and then experimented to come up with a non-alcoholic version. Without adding the alcohol, it is impossible to perfectly replicate, but the following recipes may come close. You may experiment and come up with your own versions. If you own a high-speed blender, you may use cashews, macadamias, or pine nuts with a small amount of a liquid to make a creamy base. If you do not want to use nuts, add additional liquids such as plant-based coffee creamer and other ingredients to make a creamy type cordial. Keep in mind, you need to keep it refrigerated. Use the nut-based cordial within 3 to 4 days. Instead of using water, add your favorite tea or other beverage. I like to add the cordial to club soda and cold and hot drinks.

Creamy Non-alcoholic Frangelico Cordial (hazelnut flavor)
1 cup cashews, soaked for 10 minutes and rinsed (may substitute non-dairy creamer)
½ cup whole blanched hazelnuts, skins removed
2 Tbsp raw cacao powder
1 Tbsp Roma or Pero (roasted chicory root powder)
1 ½ – 2 cups water, divided
½ cup sugar or maple syrup
2 tsp vanilla extract
Pinch salt

Transfer cashews, almonds and 1 ¼ cup of water to a high-speed blender. Blend until smooth and creamy. Add remaining water, using more if necessary, to make a smooth and medium thick mixture. Using a nut bag, add the nut mixture and squeeze through, removing any nut solids present in the liquid. Reserve the nut solids for another culinary use. Return the nut milk to the blender and add the remaining ingredients. Blend again, transfer to an airtight container and keep in the refrigerator until needed. This lasts up to 1 week. If you want to keep longer, freeze small portions and use as needed. Add to chai tea, bakery products, hot chocolate, etc. If using non-dairy creamer, blend half the creamer with hazelnuts before adding remaining ingredients and blending again. Garnished with cacao nibs.

Creamy Non-alcoholic Cointreau (orange flavor)
2 cups fresh orange or tangelo juice
½ cup sugar or sweetener
½ tsp orange extract (optional)
½ cup plant-based plain coffee creamer

Transfer all ingredients to a small saucepan and heat over low for 8 to 10 minutes, just barely simmering until all ingredients are combined and somewhat thickened. Store in an airtight container in the refrigerator. Use within 3 to 4 days.

Non-alcoholic Gewurtzraminer (aromatic wine grape)
1 container of white grape juice concentrate
¼ cup lemon or lime juice, freshly squeezed

Combine and add several tablespoons to mineral water and a glass full of ice cubes.

"Grenadine" Cordial
2 cups pomegranate juice
½ cup sweetener such as sugar, erythritol, or xylitol

Transfer ingredients to a small saucepan and heat over low to medium heat. Simmer for 8 to 10 minutes or until it is syrupy and coats a spoon. Add one or two tablespoons to tea or club soda water with ice.

Peach Cordial
2 fresh peaches, peeled and pit removed and sliced
4 cups peach nectar
2 cups heavy syrup from canned peaches or 1 cup sugar + 1 cup water
2 cardamom pods
2 whole cloves
1 Tbsp lemon juice
½ tsp lemon zest

Transfer all ingredients to a small saucepan and heat over low to medium heat for 30 to 40 minutes. When cooled, transfer to blender and blend until smooth. Allow the mixture to sit for 10 minutes. Pour through a sieve to remove the solids. Store liquid in a fridge in an airtight container for up to 1 week.

Non-alcoholic Framboise (raspberry flavor)
20 oz fresh or frozen raspberries (may also use other berries)
5 cups water
1 ½ cups sugar or erythritol granules
¼ cup fresh lemon juice
½ cup fresh mint leaves
Several drops of raspberry extract or oil (optional)

Transfer all ingredients to a medium saucepan over low to medium heat. Simmer for 30 to 40 minutes or until it is syrupy and coats a spoon. Transfer to a high-speed blender and blend. Allow to sit for 10 minutes. Pour through a sieve to remove the solids. Store in an airtight container in the refrigerator.

Non-alcoholic Peppermint Schnapps

2 cups sugar
2 cups water
4 cups fresh peppermint leaves (no stems)
10 – 20 drops peppermint oil
10 red hots or several hard peppermint candies (optional) or a pinch of beet powder

Add sugar, water, and fresh peppermint to a high-speed blender and blend on high for about 20 seconds (avoid over blending and releasing bitter flavonoids); transfer to a medium saucepan and heat over medium to low heat. Add remaining ingredients and cook for 10 to 15 minutes or until it is syrupy and coats a spoon. Store in an airtight container in the refrigerator.

Warm Spicy Elderberry Cordial

4 cups hot water, just boiling and let sit for a minute or two before using
Several tea bags (your choice)
1 cinnamon stick
½ tsp cloves
1 tsp cardamom
1 – 2 cups dried elderberries
1 cup sweetener (up to 1 cup of sweetener such as honey)
1 Tbsp lemon juice
1 tsp lemon zest
Pinch salt

Add cinnamon stick and cloves to the water. Bring to a boil. Remove from heat and add the tea bags. Steep for 1 minute with lid on the pan. Add elderberries to hot tea (but not boiling water) water that has been removed from its heat source; cover and allow to sit for 30 to 60 minutes. Using a wooden spoon, press the elderberries to release as much of their juices as possible. Now it is time to strain the juice from the berries, cinnamon stick and cloves. Add the honey, lemon juice and lemon zest and mix. Keep refrigerated. Use 1-3 teaspoons per day. Three servings per day when feeling ill.

Cherry Cordial

4 cups fresh cherry juice (or commercial if fresh not available)
½ cup pomegranate juice
2 cups honey
2 inch knob fresh ginger, peeled and thinly sliced
Juice of 1 lemon or lime
2 Tbsp dried hibiscus flowers
2 tsp vanilla extract or ½ vanilla bean pod, split in half lengthwise

Transfer all ingredients to a heavy bottom pan with a lid and simmer for 20 minutes. Strain out solids and transfer to canning jars. Process for 15 minutes in pint or 20 minutes in quart jar. Chef notes: you may substitute hawthorne berry juice for the cherry juice. To serve, add an ounce or two to your favorite tea or club soda

Shrubs

Shrubs. A shrub is a medicinal drink made of lemon or lime juice (some people substitute vinegar for the lemon or lime juice; tamarind may also be substituted), fruit or fruit juice, herbs and spices, and even elderberries are sweetened with a syrup. Oftentimes a shrub is sweetened with honey. To make a shrub, take ripe fruit such as cherries, pears, peaches, apricots, elderberries and mash. Add a sweetener or flavored syrup and fresh herbs and / or spices. Macerate and refrigerate in a large airtight mason jar. When ready to assemble the shrub, press the fruit mixture through a fine gage sieve and add mineral water. Garnish with fresh herbs or edible flowers. The following is just one shrub recipe. You may use this as a guide and substitute different ingredients or you may make a completely different type of shrub. It's fun to experiment with various ingredients to come up with an original.

Cherry Shrub
3 – 4 ripe pears, peeled and stem and seeds removed
10 cherries, pitted
1 small piece of a red beet
Pinch cinnamon
Pinch nutmeg
2 – 4 basil leaves, thoroughly rinsed
2 rosemary sprigs, thoroughly rinsed
2 Tbsp vanilla syrup, chilled
1 liter club soda, chilled

Combine the fruit in a small bowl and gently mash together (or pulse several times in a food processor fitted with an "S" blade). Transfer to a quart mason jar along with the piece of a beet, cinnamon, nutmeg, and rosemary springs. Store in the refrigerator for 24 hours. When ready to assemble, remove the rosemary sprigs and beet and discard; mash the remainder through a fine sieve. Combine the juice with the vanilla syrup. Add ice to four chilled glasses and evening divide the juice between the four glasses. Fill glasses with club soda. Swirl once or twice before serving.

Electuaries

To make an electuary. An electuary is defined as a medicinal substance mixed with a sweetener to form a paste. The sweetener is added to make the medicinal paste more palatable. You can take a spoonful of electuary and put in hot tea, add to a beverage, or take as a candy type paste.

Orange Basil Electuary
½ cup fresh basil (or other herbs and spices of your choice)
½ cup fresh orange juice or other liquid (e.g., distilled water, rose water, lemon juice)
1 – 2 Tbsp maple syrup or honey
2 – 3 tsp chia seeds
½ tsp psyllium powder

Transfer basil, orange juice and sweetener to a high-speed blender and blend. Remove and add remaining ingredients and stir to combine; allow to sit for 15 minutes. Press between wax or parchment paper to about ¼ inch and then cut into squares or whatever shape you desire. Use as a moist throat lozenge or add to tea.

Chapter 29

Make electrolyte water

Knowing how to make electrolyte water could save someone's life. The human body is largely made up of water. Children have an even higher percentage of total body water compared to adults, making it critical for children to maintain proper hydration.

Adequate water consumption is critical to good health. The average American drinks less than 24 ounces of water per day. This falls far short of drinking 95 to 125 ounces of water per day (the recommendation for women and men). This translates to about 75% of Americans who are dehydrated. Dehydration affects the ability to think clearly and may even replicate slight dementia. Dehydration can also cause agitation, drowsiness and apathy. Dehydration is a worldwide problem. Every year, millions of infants and children die due to dehydration from diarrheal diseases. In some cases, a few pennies worth of salt and sugar reverse dehydration and save lives. Knowing how to make electrolyte water may improve your ability to work and even thrive in hot and humid climates. Frequent consumption of water and electrolytes is essential for construction workers, ranchers, and anyone who spends a significant amount of time working in hot weather.

Working in a hot, dry environment, exercising or competing in a hot and dry environment, excessive loss of fluids through vomiting or diarrhea may all lead to loss of electrolytes. Without adequate electrolytes in our blood, the body does not function properly and will ultimately die.

The following are several recipes for electrolyte water. If you don't happen to have all the ingredients to make **Vitamin, Mineral and Electrolyte Water**, you may want to use one of the **Basic Electrolyte Recipes**.

Basic Electrolyte Recipes

RECIPE 1:
The most basic recipe for oral rehydration therapy is six level teaspoons of sugar and ½ level teaspoon of salt, dissolved in four cups or a quart (or liter) of water. Mix well until sugar and salt dissolve.

RECIPE 2:
If you do not have sugar and salt but you have fruit juice, dilute the juice in a 1:1 ratio of juice to water.

RECIPE 3:
2 cups water (could use coconut water)
2 – 4 Tbsp citrus juice (could be orange, lemon, grapefruit)
¼ tsp salt
2 tsp sugar

RECIPE 4:
2 cups pomegranate juice
2 cups coconut water
2 cups cold spring or mineral water
¼ tsp salt
1 tsp Calm plus Calcium

Vitamin and Mineral Rich and Electrolyte Water

16 oz pure water or coconut water (coconut water is good, but it is optional, plain water is just fine)
16 oz freshly squeezed juice (e.g., orange, grapefruit, tangelo) or 16 oz blended fruit such as melons
¼ tsp salt
1/8 tsp Epsom salt (optional)
1 – 3 drops Lugol's iodine (optional)
1 – 2 tsp sweetener
1 – 2 drops frankincense oil, therapeutic grade (optional)
4 – 5 leaves fresh herb such as mint, lemon balm, basil, etc. (optional)
½ B complex 50 (ground into powder)
½ tsp ascorbic acid
1 tsp diatomaceous earth

Add all ingredients to a high-speed blender. Blend well. Transfer to a half gallon mason jar and store in the refrigerator until ready to use (stir before serving to evenly distribute the larger particles). Lasts for up to several days. Freeze in ½ cup portions or as a popsicle for later use.

Chapter 30

Make alkaline water and nebulizer solutions

Alkaline pH Water. Water flowing over rocks or bubbling up from under the ground tends to be alkaline and healthy. However, processing water, adding chemicals to water and chemically treating water tend to make it acidic. To make water more alkaline and similar to naturally sourced water, one can take several easy and inexpensive steps. The first method uses baking soda, the second method employs pH drops and the third method uses alkalizing lemons. Additional methods are also provided. Use the method which suits you best. Each line is a separate method.

1. Add 2 grams or 1/8th teaspoon of baking soda to eight ounces of distilled water.

2. Add pH drops to your water. You can purchase pH drops at your local health food store.

3. Cut one lemon into eighths and add to a pitcher of water. Cover and refrigerate overnight. Alternatively squeeze half a lemon into a large glass of water and drink.

4. Use an alkaline water pitcher.

5. Water filtration system for kitchen water or whole house.

6. Water ionizer / electrolyzer such as Kangen water.

7. Magnesium prills. These are small magnesium beads that sit in water and impart alkalizing magnesium into the water.

Make Nebulizer Solutions

Nebulizers are a type of medical equipment used to deliver moisture and medications to the lungs. The machine forms a mist from the liquid and you inhale the mist into your lungs. Your lungs are fairly large organs and the lower parts of the lungs are not as accessible as the upper portions because most of us do not practice deep breathing. Nebulizer treatments are usually done over weeks if not months to reach as much of the lungs as possible.

You cannot nebulize just any liquid into the lungs. The following recipes are for making liquids to add to your nebulizer. It is important to use sterile techniques when making the following recipes. Do NOT use tap water or even filtered water. Either use normal saline solution which you can purchase at the pharmacy, make your own saline solution or use distilled water. When starting a new program, always consult with your physician or a knowledgeable practitioner who is familiar with your condition. The following nebulizer solution recipes are attributed to Dr. Jockers, Dr. David Brownstein, Dr. Thomas Levy and Dr. Joe Mercola. You can check out this website for additional information. www.drjockers.com/nebulizing/

To Make Normal Saline – add following ingredients to glass jar and stir until salt dissolves.

- ½ tsp straight salt (sodium chloride and no other minerals)
- 8 oz distilled water

To Make 0.1 % Hydrogen Peroxide (H2O2) Nebulizing Forumula
(recommended by Dr. Joe Mercola, Dr. Thomas Levy, Dr. David Brownstein)

- 1 tsp 3% Food grade hydrogen peroxide + 4 oz (½ cup) saline water
  OR
- ¼ tsp 12% Food grade hydrogen peroxide + 4 oz saline water
  OR
- ¼ tsp 36% Food grade hydrogen peroxide + 12 oz saline water

To Make Dr. David Brownstein's Protocol for Nebulizing both Hydrogen peroxide and Iodine

1. Start with 4 oz of a 0.1% Hydrogen Peroxide Solution Recipe (see above) + 2 drops nascent iodine solution.
2. Use up this formula.
3. If tolerated, you can make the next batch using 5 to 6 drops of nascent liquid iodine (up from using 2 drops of nascent iodine).

To Use Dr. Jocker's Nano Particle Silver Formula for Nebulizing
(avoid using homemade colloidal silver because the particles may be too large)

1. Purchase nanosilver.
2. Fill the liquid container of the nebulizer with undiluted nanosilver solution up to the 2 ml mark.
3. Turn on nebulizer and deeply inhale, hold for a few seconds and then gently exhale.
4. For those with an acute infection, use the nebulizer 3 to 5 times a day for 6 to 7 minutes each session.
5. For preventing respiratory infections, use twice a day for 6 to 7 minutes each session.
6. For lung regeneration, start with using once per day for 6 to 7 minutes each session.

Other compounds which can be nebulized include: ascorbic acid, sodium ascorbate, glutathione, NAC, magnesium chloride, colloidal B vitamins, colloidal minerals, etc. The level of vitamin C in the lungs is 30 times higher than in plasma. Exposure to ozone significantly reduces vitamin C content in the lungs. Consult with your usual physician before beginning a new medical regimen.

Chapter 31
Make charcoal, clay, diatomaceous earth (DE) or zeolite water

From time to time, we may benefit by consuming a concentrated source of charcoal, clay or diatomaceous earth (DE). Charcoal is good for **ad**sorbing chemicals and heavy metals. It is commonly used for treating overdoses. It removes bacteria and is an inexpensive way to perform a mild detox when you are feeling slightly under the weather. The best way to ingest charcoal is to swallow a tablet. However, if you really want to get the maximum effect, drop a tablet in a glass of water and stir until dissolved. Drink over the course of about an hour.

Bentonite clay, a volcanic type of rock, is a great way to ingest minerals. Clay contains calcium, iron, magnesium, potassium, silica, sodium and others. It is not digested because there is no carbohydrate or protein, but it provides essential minerals. It has a strong negative charge, potentially attracting positively charged toxins and pathogens. Bentonite clay is trophic for the gut and is known to improve gut functions. To use bentonite clay, take one teaspoon of food grade bentonite clay and add to eight ounces of water. Add a few ice cubes and blend. Transfer to a glass jar and using a straw, stir the water first and then take a few sips. The clay may settle between sips so be sure to stir the water before each sip.

Several mechanisms in support of clay's actions in the body include its high alkalinity (pH is 8.7 – 9.8). Clay, similar to charcoal, has a strong negative charge which attracts compounds with strong positive charges (which tend to be toxins). It also has a large surface area to tension ratio. Clay can help stop bleeding (hemostatic). It promotes wound healing. For example, according to clay miner, Darryl Bosshardt, one gram of clay has a surface area of 800 square meters giving it strong drawing properties. Numerous scientific articles tout the 'healing' properties of clay (PMID: 34452078, 24831081, 20640226, 24895893).

Diatomaceous earth (DE) is a form of silicon dioxide and an excellent source of silica. DE is 80% to 94% silica, 2% to 4% alumina and clay minerals and 0.5% to 2% iron oxide. It is absorbed from the diet and excreted in the urine. DE not absorbed by the body is excreted via the digestive tract. Silica stimulates the production of collagen type 1, needed for healthy hair, nails and bones and it stimulates skin's fibroblasts improving skin tone. Silica is the fossilized remains of oceanic diatoms. The silica diatoms or DE is the hard exoskeletons. Each diatom is unique and has sharp edges.

DE is a powerful negatively charged compound. It absorbs up to 1.5 to 4 times its weight in water. Adding a teaspoon and even up to 2 tablespoons of DE to water makes DE water. It is known to help kill viruses and purify water. As negatively charged DE moves along the digestive tract, it sloughs away positively charged toxins, bacteria and even parasites. It powerfully chelates (binds) aluminum. DE is used externally to kill ants, bed bugs, cockroaches, fleas, mites, spiders, ticks, etc.

<u>**High amounts of silica are found in the heart (aorta), bone, skin and trachea.**</u> Because of its strong electrical charge, DE interacts in the body in ways that promote detoxification through several pathways. DE deficiency can contribute to abnormal growth, skull and peripheral bone deformities, joint pain, reduced levels of cartilage and collagen in joints, disruption of mineral balance, and damage to the femur

and vertebrae. It is used internally to treat parasites, lower cholesterol / LDL / triglycerides, reduce gas, boost liver functions, and absorb blood-borne toxins. DE is used externally as an exfoliator and skin scrub.

Silica-rich foods include: artichokes, asparagus, bananas, bell peppers, cabbage, cucumber, greens, melons, oats, onions, radish, rhubarb, rice, soy, spinach, tomatoes, etc.

Zeolites are a group of hydrated minerals containing alkaline earth metals. Zeolites contain alumina and silica in an open tetrahedral structure. There are 40 naturally occurring zeolites and many more synthetic zeolites. Zeolites trap targeted molecules and exchanges them for beneficial ones. Zeolites are used to remove mercury and other heavy metals.

One summer I was invited to spend time in a physician's office and help with detoxing their patients. One day the physician asked me to go in and see a patient who possibly had lupus and whose hemoglobin and hematocrit levels were dangerously low and dropping. The caveat, the patient didn't talk much. The patient was a young black mother with four children and she was completely shut down. I could tell she didn't feel well and didn't want to open up. Because of my nutrition background, I decided to ask about her usual diet, starting with breakfast. For breakfast she had ½ piece of toast with butter and ½ cup of clay. Not batting an eye, we went on to lunch where she had 1 piece of chicken and 1 cup of clay. Dinner was similar. I asked where she got the clay and she said a friend in east Texas would dig up a bunch of clay and bring it to her. My next question was, 'How long since you had a bowel movement?' Her answer, 'At least 30 days.' She was dying from anemia and other medical issues became blaringly apparent. Now we could help her. Her intestines were likely impacted and there was potential for mineral toxicities. I include this true story to illustrate that even good things can be harmful when in excess. Carefully use clay, zeolytes, silica, and charcoal! They are wonderful mediums for promoting healing in some cases and restoration of health. But use them in moderation!

When you use charcoal, clay, DE, and zeolites it is important to not use them within an hour or two of taking prescription meds. You do not want the charcoal to interfere with your prescription meds. <u>If you have any health issues or might be pregnant, consult your physician before starting a new routine.</u> Food grade clay may contain high amounts of essential minerals. Keep in mind, high amounts of some essential minerals such as iron are not always recommended. It may be best to limit clay water to no more than once or twice per week. <u>Check with your physician if you have any concerns.</u>

Making charcoal, clay and / or DE waters

1 tsp activated charcoal powder or several charcoal tablets
OR
1 tsp bentonite clay
OR
1 tsp diatomaceous earth powder
OR
1 tsp zeolites
PLUS
1 – 2 cups spring or distilled water or lemonade

Blend with water and ice and drink right away. Stir before each sip. Using a straw may be helpful to stir the contents as the solids tend to settle fast.

Chapter 32
When and how to make antibiotic type juices and syrups

An antibiotic either inhibits the growth of germs or improves the body's ability to find and attack germs. Most plant-based foods have natural antibiotic type activity and some have antiviral and antifungal properties. Plants are designed with internal defense mechanisms known as plant chemicals or phytochemicals. There are literally thousands of phytochemicals isolated from plants, many of which form the basis of modern pharmaceutical drugs. Regular and robust consumption of minimally processed plants ensures a near continuous supply of protective plant chemicals.

However, there are times when an infection invades the body, overwhelming its defenses. It is at times like these the body needs high octane defenses. Oftentimes, the most powerful plant defenses are found in combination with strong flavors, a pungent smell and even spiciness. When these plants are combined and prepared together they form a formidable pathogen foe capable of potentially interfering with invading and rapidly multiplying bacteria. This educational chapter provides several recipes for making your own antibiotic preparations. Each recipe combines powerful plants and various methods of preparing the plants to maximize their effectiveness. Using a plant-based antibiotic does not preclude taking pharmaceutical grade antibiotics. **Always consult your physician when indicated**.

In addition to antibiotic juice therapy, it is a good idea to stay well hydrated, gargle with salt water at the first sign of a sore throat every 30 minutes, take the hottest shower you can tolerate then go to bed, keep your head covered, keep your chest and neck and extremities warm, make sure you have fresh air circulating in your bedroom, get 15 – 20 minutes of sunshine, if you cannot exercise do some stretches, and rest until you are well. If you use supplements, focus on increasing vitamin C, taking at least 600 mg NAC, and 50 to 100 mg Zinc.

The last "recipe" is for an essential oil "antibiotic bomb." I have used various combinations of this list and found it to be helpful.

Foods with antibiotic, anti-viral and anti-fungal properties
- **Fruits**: coconut oil, coconut water, cranberries, elderberry, grapefruit, grapefruit rinds (contain quinine), lemons, limes, pineapple, etc.
- **Herbs**: astragalus root, burdock, calendula, echinacea, licorice root, neem, oregano, stinging nettle, turmeric, usnea, wormwood, etc.
- **Spices**: cayenne, cinnamon, ginger, galangal, horseradish, garlic, turmeric, etc.
- **Vegetables**: beet, Brussels sprouts, cabbage, cayenne pepper, fermented food, garlic, kale, onion, spinach, etc.
- **Other**: honey.
- 1 liter of tonic water contains 83 mg quinine.

Soothing Syrup

4 Tbsp honey
4 Tbsp lemon juice, freshly squeezed
1 tsp turmeric or ginger powder
1 grate black pepper (use only if using turmeric)
Pinch salt

Mix together and let sit overnight. Use 1 to 3 teaspoon every day. You may add to warm water, tea or use in a latte.

Antibiotic Juice

8 lemons or limes, peeled
4 oranges, peeled
1 grapefruit, peeled
1 apple
1 onion
1 cucumber, peeled
1 head Romaine lettuce or two cucumbers
1 beet with tops
2+ garlic heads
4 inches fresh ginger
1 – 2 inches fresh horseradish
4 cayenne peppers or jalapenos
½ cup fresh cilantro
2 inches fresh turmeric or 1 Tbsp turmeric powder
2 Tbsp honey
10 drops oregano oil
4 oz colloidal silver water (optional)
Pinch salt

1. Using a centrifugal juicer, juice all ingredients except honey, colloidal silver water, oregano oil and salt.
2. After juicing all the fruits and vegetables, add honey, colloidal silver water, oregano oil and a pinch of salt. Using a whisk, mix all ingredients until combined.
3. Transfer juice to a mason jar. Seal and gently shake. Store in refrigerator.
4. To use, remove one or two tablespoons and drink up to six times per day.
5. Children require less.
6. Keep stored in the refrigerator.

Elderberry Syrup

1 cup dried elderberries
1 cup water
1 inch knob ginger, peeled and sliced into ¼ inch rounds
2 Tbsp honey
2 Tbsp lemon juice, freshly squeezed
½ tsp lemon zest
Pinch salt

1. Transfer elderberries, ginger and water to a small sauce pan. Heat over medium heat until the mixture gently simmers. Simmer for five to ten minutes.
2. Remove from heat and strain out the ginger and elderberries, reserving the elderberries.
3. Add honey, lemon and salt to the elderberry juice.
4. Add to a mason jar, seal and store in the refrigerator.
5. If you want to store for longer periods, follow canning procedures to sterilize the jars and heat process the contents.

Nature's Penicillin and Anti-viral Cocktail

4 or 5 grapefruit, peeled and rough chop
1 orange, peeled and rough chop
2 lemons, peeled and rough chop
4 or 5 large garlic cloves
½ onion, rough chop
2 inch piece ginger, peeled and thinly sliced or grated
½ cayenne pepper (optional)
1 cup water
½ tsp salt

1. Using a citrus juicer, juice the grapefruit, orange and lemons; set the juice aside.
2. Take the roughly chopped peels and add to a medium sauce pan, adding just enough water to cover the peels by several inches. Cover the pot with a lid and simmer for 2 hours without removing the lid.
3. When the time is up, leave the lid on the pot until the pan is cool to touch.
4. When the mixture is cool, remove the rinds (discard) and strain the liquid.
5. Add all ingredients, including the fresh citrus juices and citrus rind liquid, to a highspeed blender and blend until smooth.
6. Transfer to an airtight glass jar and store in the refrigerator.
7. You may also add to ½ cup of freshly squeezed juice or water and drink one tablespoon every hour or so.

Essential Oil "Antibiotic Bomb" (see cautions listed below)

- 2 – 5 drops oregano oil
- 2 – 5 drops lemon grass oil (effectiveness not documented, therapeutic application(s) cannot be recommended)
- 2 – 5 drops grapefruit oil
- 2 – 5 drops clove oil (in concentrated form, may be irritating to mucosal tissues; antiseptic, antibacterial, antifungal, antiviral, antispasmodic, topical anesthetic – use with a carrier oil such as coconut)
- 1 – 2 drops cinnamon oil (0.05 – 0.2 g; check with your health care provider before using internally; antibacterial, fungistatic, promotes motility)
- 2 – 5 drops thyme oil
- 2 – 5 drops tea tree oil
- 2 – 5 drops eucalyptus oil
- 2 – 5 drops frankincense
- 2 – 5 drops helichrysum
- 2 – 5 drops CBD oil
- 2 – 5 drops peppermint oil
- 2 – 5 drops winter savory oil
- 2 – 5 drops grapefruit oil
- 2 – 5 drops orange oil
- V-caps (sizes 000 (1.37 ml), 00 (0.9 ml), 00E (1.0 ml), 0E (0.78 ml), or 0 (0.68 ml))

1. Open the V-caps and while holding half of the V-cap, add 2 or 3 or any combination of the suggested essential oils into the empty V-cap and then place on the top and seal according to instructions. Take an "Antibiotic Bomb" every 3 to 4 hours.
2. **CAUTION: If you are pregnant, lactating, taking prescription medications or have a chronic, degenerative disease, it is recommended you check with your physician before internally taking any essential oil.**
3. Vegetarian capsules come in several sizes. The "00" holds about .91 ml when full but it is advisable to fill it about 80% full, closer to 0.7 ml. The "0" size V-cap holds 0.68 ml when full or around 0.5 ml at 80% full. There are 20 drops per milliliter; 14 drops per "00" V-cap and 10 drops per "0" V-cap.
4. You may also add several drops of any of the above oils to warm water and gargle to relieve a sore throat.
5. Notes: 1 drop = 0.02 to 0.03 grams (20 – 30 milligrams; 60 drops in a teaspoon).

Chapter 33

Make natural quinine-containing syrup

Take 5 to 6 grapefruits and juice them. After juicing them, chop the rinds into small pieces and place in a heavy bottom saucepan. Cover with distilled water, adding enough to cover the rinds by at least 2 inches. Cover with a lid and place over a low medium stove. Cook for two hours on low. Do not remove the lid at any point. After the rinds have cooked for about 2 hours, remove from the heat source and allow to cool. Do not remove the lid until the contents are completely cooled. Strain out the rind, add a natural sweetener like 1 – 2 Tbsp of honey or maple syrup and store the liquid in an airtight glass jar in the refrigerator for up to 2 weeks.

You may also make quinine-containing tonic water using cinchona bark.

Tonic Water

4 cups water
¼ cup cinchona bark powder or ½ cup cut cinchona bark
1 tsp whole allspice berries
3 green cardamom pods
1 tsp lime zest
1 tsp orange zest
¼ cup citric acid
¼ tsp salt
1 ½ cups sugar

1. Combine water, bark, berries, cardamom pods and citrus zest in a medium saucepan and bring to a low simmer. Cover and cook for 20 minutes.
2. Remove from heat and strain out the solids using several coffee filters.
3. Return the liquid to the stovetop and combine with the citric acid, salt and sugar. Stir until combined. Cook until the sugar dissolves and the mixture coats a spoon.
4. Store in an airtight glass container in the refrigerator.
5. Optional ingredients could include: ¼ cup lemongrass or fresh basil, 1 Tbsp dried lavender buds, 1 Tbsp allspice powder, cardamom powder, cloves powder, juniper berries, 1 cinnamon stick, citrus zest, 1 small piece of beet (for coloring the syrup), etc.

Chapter 34

Make decoctions, tinctures, bitters and extracts

Decoctions. A decoction is the process of concentrating either a tea or a non-oil-based infusion. In this situation, we want to reduce the liquid by almost half. This requires simmering for long periods until the liquid has evaporated off and the resulting liquid is thick and syrupy. Decoctions usually keep quite well, especially if there is a small amount of a natural preservative such as ascorbic acid or citric acid in the syrup.

To make a decoction

1. Bring 4 cups of pure water to boil on the stovetop. Once water comes to a boil, turn the heat to low. You want the water to steam or lightly roll, not boil.
2. Place 1/4 cup of herbs (or 1 ounce or 30 grams by weight) in saucepan with water. Mix well with spoon.
3. Let this simmer for desired length of time or until water is reduced by half (2 cups).
4. Strain out the herbs. Add sweetener if desired. Drink recommended dosage throughout the day.

Tinctures. Tinctures are alcohol-based and decoctions are water-based. Both are made from herbs and other plants. Sometimes natural compounds in plants are poorly soluble in hot water and require a different liquid to draw out the beneficial compounds. Alcohol-based tinctures are not for everyone but for some, a tincture is an efficient way to extract poorly water-soluble plant chemicals. In the case of tinctures, several liquids are used including vodka; non-alcohol-based glycerin may be used instead of alcohol if desired. Glycerin is viscous, clear and similar to aloe vera gel. It can be used as a solvent and it can be used to apply therapeutic substances to the skin. It keeps compounds in suspension. To make a tincture using glycerin, use a ratio of approximately 1:6:10 of fresh or dried herb, distilled water and glycerin. Place the mixture in a sealed glass jar and gently agitate several times every day. After 2 weeks, strain out herbs and store in a cool dry place.

To make a tincture

1. Start by adding fresh (dried herbs are also acceptable) herbs to a sealable glass jar. The ratio is approximately 8 – 10 ounces of fresh herbs or 4 – 6 ounces of dried herbs to one quart of liquid (e.g., vodka or rum; a 1:2, 1:4 or even a 1:10 ratio depending on the specific herb and other ingredients). Add enough vodka or rum to cover the herbs by at least several inches. Add the lid and seal the jar. Place a label on the jar to identify the contents and start date.
2. Place the tightly sealed jar in a dark place.
3. Shake the jar several times every day, returning the jar to a dark place.
4. After several weeks the liquid should begin to change color to reflect the pigments present in the fresh herbs. Usually oxidation and the combination of different pigments results in a brown tincture.

5. If you prefer a non-alcoholic liquid, substitute glycerin, vinegar or distilled water for alcohol. If using glycerin, briefly heat the herbs with the glycerin, on a low heat setting. If the therapeutic components of the plants are heat sensitive you may need to use the alcohol-based method.
6. To finish making the tincture, strain the liquid using a fine sieve to remove the fresh or dried herbs. Place the strained liquid in a sealable glass jar and label with contents and date.
7. You may also use a wheat grass juicer to extract juice from fresh herbs for use in the tincture.
8. A tincture dose is 1 teaspoon for adults and ½ teaspoon for children. Frequency of dosing is 3 to 5 times a day. You may dose hourly for acute and severe sickness.
9. If you are making a tincture with an exact ratio of herbs to vodka, you might consider using a scale and a graduated cylinder to achieve a more precise dose. If using fresh herbs, use a ratio of herbs to liquid of 1:3 or 1:4. The ratios for dried herbs are 1:4 or 1:5. For example, if you are using a 1:3 ratio, you need 30 grams of echinacea to 90 milliliters of alcohol.

Bitters. Homemade herbal bitters are used therapeutically as well as ingredients in non-alcoholic beverages. Bitters may be simple and have only two or three ingredients such as dandelion tincture or they may be complex with multiple flavor layers such as forest notes or warm spicy undertones. Small amounts of tinctures may be used as a bittering agent or even used to make more complex bitters. Bitters are used to stimulate various aspects of the body's systems, primarily working on the digestive and support organs. They are also used for treating conditions such as acid reflux.

Bitters are an external method for targeting and stimulating various different organs and systems. You may not see this information in the scientific literature but these various plant elements have been used for millennia to target specific organs and systems. In general, bitters target the gastrointestinal tract and the secretory organs including the liver, gallbladder and pancreas.

To make bitters. It is important to understand solubility. Not all plant chemicals are soluble in water. Sometimes a different type of solution is needed to extract plant chemicals and place them in a solution. Ethanol is sometimes necessary, even though **I am in no way advocating for alcohol consumption**. In fact, if you have any concerns about buying alcohol to extract plant bitters, then you should absolutely pass on this and jump to the next section. Reasons to avoid using vodka, include an alcoholic in the family, children or teens who might be prone to experiment with alcohol, you prefer not to have alcohol in your home, etc. In the case of tinctures (glycerin may be substituted for vodka to make some tinctures) and bitters, vodka is used to extract important plant compounds and then once extracted, the **alcohol is simmered off, leaving behind the extract, water and only trace amounts of ethanol**. Vodka is a 40% ethanol mixture, meaning it is alcohol combined with water. Evaporating the ethanol is possible. However, it is not possible to evaporate off 100% of the ethanol. Small traces remain, but the amount is negligible. Alcohol evaporates at 172 °F (78 °C). After cooking for 10 minutes at 175 °F, 80 to 90% of the alcohol is cooked off (it may take longer if alcohol is added to a food where it combines with soluble fibers and other ingredients making it more difficult to remove). Heating for 30 minutes removes 95% or more of the alcohol. Some food scientists claim less than half of 1% of alcohol remains. Small amounts may remain, but considering the total amount of the final product, the alcohol content is negligible and certainly not as high as an over-the-counter cough syrup. It may be less than the amount of alcohol in warm fresh bread, about 1.9% according to a 1920s American Chemical Society report.

To make bitters, choose one or more bittering agents from the list below (making sure to confirm all ingredients are safe, edible and free from herbicides and pesticides) and using the recommended ratio for just the vodka (do not include the water amount), add vodka and your bittering agents (see Table 1). For example, if you are using 200 ml of vodka, you need 40 milliliters or grams of bittering agents for a 1:5 ratio of bitter elements to vodka. If you are using roots, cut them into small pieces. If you are using bark, break into smaller pieces. If you are using leaves or flowers, gently crush or muddle. If you are using citrus peel, be sure to avoid using the soft edible fruit parts. If you are using hard berries, lightly crush them, if you are using cinnamon or nutmeg, grate them. Seal ingredients in a glass jar and allow to sit for a day or two, shaking several times per day. When ready to make the bitters, add water to the vodka mixture (add at least the same amount or even double the amount of water as vodka). Place in a medium sauce pan and simmer on low, without a lid for 45 to 60 minutes or until the volume is reduced by at least half. During this time, most of the alcohol evaporates. The alcohol is used to pull the bittering agents from their original form (e.g., bark, berry, rind, root, etc.). Once the bittering agents are pulled from the plant, they are now in solution with only a small amount of residual alcohol but mainly water. Remove the solids by pouring the liquid through a fine sieve. Again, the alcohol content is negligible at this point.

Now it is time to add the botanicals, aromatics and / or flavoring agents to the bitter liquid. The ratio of botanicals to bitter solution is either 1:2 or 1:1. See Table 2.

Ratios
1:5 to 1:8 bitter elements to vodka
1:2 to 1:8 botanicals, aromatics and flavoring to bitters the above solution

Make decoctions, tinctures, bitters and extracts Table 1. Bittering Agents*		
All spice	Cinnamon	Juniper berries
Angelica root	Citrus peel	Nutmeg
Artichoke leaf	Cleavers	Pine bark
Arugula	Cloves	Pine needles
Barberry root	Coffee	Licorice root
Black walnut leaf	Coriander	Milk thistle
Burdock root (fresh/dried/tincture)	Dandelion leaves	Mugwort
Calamus root	Dandelion root (fresh/dried/tincture)	Oak bark
Cardamom	Fennel	Oregon grape root
Cascarilla	Gentian	Sarsaparilla
Chicory root	Ginger	Wormwood
Cinchona bark	Grapefruit rind	
*Always check with your physician before using a new herb or supplement such as the above bittering agents.		

Make decoctions, tinctures, bitters and extracts Table 2. Aromatic Elements*		
Anise	Lemongrass	Rose
Basil	Matcha green tea	Sage
Chamomile	Mild thistle	Sorrel
Hibiscus	Mint	Valerian
Holy basil	Passion flower	
Lavender	Peppermint	
*Always check with your physician before using a new herb or supplement such as the above aromatic elements.		

Additional elements may include: spices, fruit, nuts, floral essences, syrups, and cooling elements.

Spices: cinnamon, cassia, turmeric, cloves, cardamom, chiles, fennel, ginger, nutmeg, juniper berries, star anise, vanilla beans, peppercorns, saffron, etc. Use in a ratio of ¼ tsp to 3 tsp to 1 cup liquid.

Fruit: peels and dried fruit.

Nuts and beans: nuts, coffee beans, cacao beans, cacao nibs, etc.

Floral: rose, saffron, lavender, hibiscus, etc.

Fruit flavored syrups

Cooling elements: cucumber juice, coconut water, etc.

To make bitters with a negligible amount of alcohol does require an initial input of alcohol to extract the bitter components from the bark, root, berry, rind, etc. Much, but not all, of the alcohol is cooked off and the bittering elements remain. Keep in mind, young children and older folks do not usually like bitters. Bitters is a taste that develops in adulthood and tends to disappear in older adults.

Bitters have been used for millennia throughout European and other cultures to help with digestion, heartburn, to stimulate appetite, stimulate digestive secretions (mouth, stomach, pancreas, liver), support detoxification, improve respiratory functions, improve gut microbes, anti-inflammatory, etc. Bitters are used to stimulate various digestive and secretory organs. Use bitters when digestion is sluggish. Use ¼ – ½ teaspoon of concentrated bitters or use more of sweetened bitters, 30 minutes before a meal to address gastric issues.

Extracts. For decades, home cooks were satisfied with the basic extract offerings of vanilla, almond, rum, peppermint, and a few others. Today, extracts are made using many different bases including mint, chocolate mint, pine needles, stevia, lavender, cinnamon, licorice, chocolate, cherry, lemon, grapefruit, etc. Home-made extracts are trendy and fun to make. Use your creativity to come up with unique combinations. Start by examining your personal preferences. Do you like warm and spicy or cool and clean combinations?

To make an extract or glycerite
1. First choose the flavor you want to preserve as an extract: vanilla bean, coconut, ginger, cherry, etc.
2. Wash, chop, toast, cut, or sift the product. Place in a glass (non-reactive) jar or bowl.
3. Pour vodka over the product, completely covering it.
4. Muddle the flavoring element using a muddler, a pestle, or the backside of a wooden spoon. Muddling is done to cause the release of oils and juices trapped in stems, leaves and rinds.
5. Seal the jar with a lid and place in a cool, dark corner.
6. Once or twice a day, gently shake the jar.
7. Once the flavor is infused (which may take up to 2 or more months), strain out the flavoring products and store in a glass jar in a cupboard for using in cooking or as a health tonic.
8. Be sure no original product remains in extract. Strain out original elements using a coffee filter.
9. If you prefer not to use alcohol, substitute 3 parts glycerin and 1 part distilled water for the alcohol.
10. Glycerin extracts have a shelf life of 2 years compared to alcohol which has a shelf life of 4 to 6 years. Glycerin extracts taste better than alcohol extracts, making them a better choice for children.
11. Alcohol extracts last longer than glycerin extracts. Best to keep glycerin extracts refrigerated.
12. If on medication, under a physician's care, pregnant or lactating, consult with your MD/DO/naturopath before adding herbal products to your regimen.

Chapter 35
Make plant powders

Plant powders are used in a variety of ways. They are added to beverages, smoothies, added to home-made pasta dough for flavor and color, added to soups for improving texture and taste, and they can be added to vegetable capsules for solo consumption.

One of my favorite plant (it's really a fungus) powders is shiitake mushroom powder. You can buy dehydrated shiitakes at your local Asian market and place in a coffee grinder and it makes a lovely powder. It adds a subtle umami flavor to cream sauces, soups, and casseroles.

Another easy to prepare plant powder is beet root powder. This is the main ingredient for the popular red powder that is sold in most grocery and health food stores. You may want to add powders to vegetable V-caps and take internally. Be sure you are using safe, edible plants.

Plant Powder Recipe

1. To make a plant powder, the fruit or vegetable must be blended with just enough water to make a thick slurry. For example, if you want to make a hot pink dragon fruit powder, peel and add the fruit and just enough distilled water to blend the dragon fruit. If you want to make beet powder, you need to cook the beets before processing into a slurry.

2. Strain the fruit slurry through a sieve and then spread on unbleached parchment paper or teflex and place in a dehydrator or an oven set to 125 °F. This takes from 4 to 8 hours in a dehydrator or about 45 to 60 minutes in an oven at 200 °F.

3. When the slurry is completely dried out, remove and peel off the parchment paper (or teflex mat). Transfer to a coffee grinder and grind until you have a fine powder. Sift the powder through a sieve and transfer to an airtight glass jar. Seal and use as needed.

4. Here is a good video describing how to make herbal plant powders:
   https://www.youtube.com/watch?v=3547m47wC6A

Chapter 36

Make plasters, poultices, compresses and fomentations

There are many types of poultices (aka, cataplasms). One of the more famous, or maybe I should say, infamous poultice is brought to us via Hogan's Heroes. Maybe you remember the episode where the well-nourished, sympathetic German guard, Sergeant Shultz, upon getting sick, requested French prisoner and chef extraordinaire, Sergeant LeBeau, to make him a mustard plaster. Hogan's crew joked there was not enough mustard in Germany to make Shultz a mustard plaster. Actually, the technical name for a mustard poultice is sinapism, defined as plaster containing powdered mustard seed and applied to the chest. It is a powerful stimulant for healing. The mustard poultice should not touch the skin. Its unique properties contribute to rapidly bring circulation to the application area. It must be timed and monitored. Not all poultices are as stimulating as a mustard plaster, but all poultices, depending on their contents promote healing and are effective.

To make a mustard plaster. Mustard plasters are used to treat respiratory illnesses (e.g., pneumonia, lung infections, flu, colds), rheumatoid arthritis and joint pain. A mustard plaster can be caustic to the skin, causing heat, redness, burning and even blistering. The mustard compounds combine with the applied oil on the skin to attract circulation to the treatment area. If treating the lungs, it is used to treat congestion. It stimulates the immune system and the results are quick. **Exercise caution when using on children and those with sensitive skin.** It is important to follow a ratio of mustard powder to flour based on age and skin sensitivity. Always remove the mustard plaster when the skin begins to turn red. Unless you are using the "Weak" or "Mild" ratio, set a timer for every 1 to 2 minutes to check the skin under the area of the plaster for redness. You need the following items: mustard powder, flour, water, old tea towel, blanket, washing cloth, olive or coconut oil.

Here are the ratios of mustard powder to flour:

- 1:8 Weak but safe. For example, ½ teaspoon of mustard powder to 4 teaspoons of flour.
- 1:6 Mild, suitable for some children, safe for overnight for some adults with normal skin.
- 1:4 Strong, good for chest congestion, use for limited time, set a timer for no more than 20 to 30 minutes. Check every 1 – 2 minutes for redness.
- 1:2 Robust strength, use only on adults, check every minute for a maximum of 20 minutes.

1. To make the plaster, mix together mustard powder and flour. Add just enough warm water to make a thin paste.

2. Spread the paste onto a piece of cloth covering less than half of the cloth; flip the uncovered half over the mustard-covered half of the tea towel.
3. Rub a small amount of the oil onto the skin over the treatment area.
4. Place the tea towel on the treatment area with the mustard side closest to the skin but not directly touching the skin. The mustard is on the inside of the cloth. Immediately remove plaster if it begins to burn or sting. Cover the plaster with a heavy towel or blanket.
5. Check the skin under the mustard plaster every minute for redness. When the skin begins to turn red, remove the mustard plaster and thoroughly wash off the oil.
6. Follow up with a warm or hot shower and plan to rest for an hour or two after a mustard plaster. May be repeated once a day.

Resources:
https://www.youtube.com/watch?v=sZL2zf-CY8Q
https://www.youtube.com/watch?v=-bK8j-l4X0s
https://www.youtube.com/watch?v=m_4CGZzTTCo how to get rid of phlegm

To make a poultice. Poultices are a type of thick paste made from ingredients which draw out an infection or even venom from the body via the skin. Poultices can be effectively used on people of all ages to treat many conditions. The components of a poultice include: a plant and / or herb, thickener or paste as a base, liquid is usually water, a thin cloth to protect the skin, a way to heat up the poultice if necessary, and a method to apply and maintain the poultice at the application site. Heat may be needed if bringing circulation to the affected area is necessary. Poultices are used to relieve sunburn pain, treat insect and even venomous bites, fight infection, reduce inflammation, relieve aches and pains, relieve chest congestion, stimulate organs, treat poison ivy, remove splinters, treat boils, etc.

A poultice is moist and soft. It may include medicated compounds and is often gently heated to increase its therapeutic effects. If you have never used a poultice, start with simple poultices. Once you are comfortable making and using simple poultices, branch out into more complex ones. Information in this chapter may peak your interst and get you started; from there you can tailor a poultice to your specific needs. Poultices can readily resolve aches and pains, improve circulation, and even speed up wound healing.

Poultices are applied in a thick layer and held together by a binder. Some poultices are stimulating and others are made to draw infection out of the body. Usually a combination of fresh or dried herbs are added to a poultice. The following list contains poultice ingredients and how they are commonly used. This list is not comprehensive, but contains important elements of the most common poultices.

A castor oil poultice is used for a variety of purposes. It tends to be a stimulating treatment as well as an anti-inflammatory treatment. Castor oil has anti-microbial, anti-bacterial, anti-viral and anti-fungal properties. It is also used to stimulate movement of lymphatic fluids. To prepare a castor oil poultice, gently heat castor oil and dip several pieces of flannel fabric in the castor oil and then layer over the target area and cover with plastic wrap. Apply a hot water bottle or heating pad to the area for about an hour. Do this several times a day until resolution. Castor oil poultices should not be used to treat menstrual pain.

A common charcoal poultice can be made using: 1 Tbsp activated charcoal powder, 1 Tbsp binder such as psyllium powder, cornstarch or arrowroot powder, 1 Tbsp warm water, and several strips of thin fabric (4" x 6"). Combine charcoal, binder and water; let sit for 5 minutes. Spread out on the middle section of one of the strips of fabric (about a 2"x2" square or a 3"x3" square). Place the other cloth over the top of the charcoal and place the poultice over the treatment area. Using plastic, wrap the area so the poultice is secure and won't move. Leave on overnight. Allow 4 to 6 hours in between application of each poultice.

Below is a description of various potential components of poultices.

- **Powdered thickeners and binders:** acacia powder, chia seeds, psyllium husk powder, food grade clay, ground flax seed, powdered herbs such as slippery elm, marshmallow powder, Irish moss, organic corn meal (fine grind), organic cornstarch, arrowroot powder, flour, etc.

- **Drawing agents:** acacia powder, baking soda, *charcoal, Epsom salt, slippery elm, figs, plantain leaf, clays, marshmallow root, echinacea root powder, burdock root powder, licorice root powder, goldenseal powder, cabbage, potato, dandelion, calendula, onion, psyllium powder, slippery elm, etc.

- **Fresh herbs and spices for therapeutic effects:** arnica, burdock root, calendula, dandelion, elderflowers, frankincense, garlic, ginger, goldenrod, goldenseal, helichrysum, lavender, lemon balm, licorice root, marshmallow powder, oregano, plantain, St. John's wort, slippery elm, tea tree, thyme, yarrow, etc.

- **Stimulating agents:** castor oil, cayenne (capsicum), garlic, ginger, mustard, onion, tinctures, etc. Avoid placing directly on the skin (with the exception of castor oil, garlic and onion).

- **Anti-bacterial agents:** echinacea, frankincense, ginger, goldenseal, lavender, myrrh, oregano, tea tree, various tinctures, garlic, thyme, mullein, basil, clove, etc.

- **Moisture:** aloe vera, licorice water, rose water, water, etc.

- **Some type of oil to moisten the area before applying the poultice:** almond, apricot, castor, coconut, olive, walnut, etc.

- **Skin protection:** gauze, thin flannel cloth, etc.

- **Outer wrap material covering the poultice:** cheese cloth, gauze, nut milk bag, thin cloth, saran wrap, etc.

- **Heat source (if using; not appropriate for all poultices):** hot water bottle, heating pad, hot fomentation treatment, sunlight, heat lamp, etc.

- **Timing:** check every 2 hours to see if poultice has dried out. If it has dried out, replace and keep checking every 2 to 3 hours until issue resolves. Wash area in between each new poultice.

- **To keep the poultice in place:** ace bandage, gauze strips, saran wrap, bandage, etc.

- **Thickness of a poultice:** $1/8^{th}$ to $¼^{th}$ inch

- **Coverage area:** The circumference or area of treatment should be at least twice as large as the affected site. If applying to the lung area, place over the upper chest area, covering at least several inches beyond the lung area. If you are placing on a sunburn, cover as much of the area as possible. If you are drawing out venom from a spider bite, apply the poultice to an area that is twice as large as the reddened area.

- **Contraindications include but are not limited to:** sensitive skin, broken skin, medical instability, metabolic instability, loss of consciousness, allergy to poultice substances, severe dehydration.

    Be cautious directly applying charcoal on an open wound unless the charcoal is combined with psyllium or ground flaxseed. If it is not in a gel format, it may enter the open would and be difficult to remove, leaving behind what is known as a charcoal "tattoo."

To make a cool or warm, moist or dry compress. A warm compress is used to address pain and soreness where additional blood flow is needed to bring nutrients and oxygen to the area to speed up healing. This might be the easiest treatment to set up. For a warm moist compress, dip an appropriately sized face cloth or towel in hot water and wring out the water. If the water is too hot, place one or more clean dry towels between the moist towel and the skin. Avoid using boiling hot water. You may choose to heat the moist towel in the micro-wave. Always test the towel using a small patch of your skin before applying it to your body or to a child's body. The temperature may increase so be prepared to add additional towels in between the hot compress and your skin. A warm dry compress is a heated rice bag, water bottle or a dry heating pad.

A cool compress decreases swelling and numbs the area. This restricts circulation and helps stop bleeding. To make a cool compress, dip a towel in cool or ice water and apply directly to skin. A slightly more complicated version of a moist or dry cool compress is as simple as rounding up ice and placing in a large zip lock bag and placing a thin cloth between the ice bag and injured area. You may need to slightly moisten the thin cloth to enhance the coolness for a cool moist compress. If you do not have ice, substitute a frozen package of green peas or wrap towels or a cloth around a regular ice pack. For fresh injuries, avoid using a warm compress and use a cooling compress to reduce pain, bruising and inflammation.

To make a hot fomentation (hot compress or hot pack). A hot fomentation is a hot cloth or towel soaked in hot water which may or may not have fresh herbs as part of the hot water. Hot fomentations are kept hot by either refreshing the hot water or placing a heating pad over the moist hot towel. First make the fresh herb tea and when the water is hot, dip a towel in the herb tea, gathering up some of the fresh herbs in the water, and apply to sore joints, muscles, local pain, congestion, etc.

Thermophore moist heating pad. It is a good idea to own several thermophore heating pads. They come in different sizes. They heat up only when you depress the 'on/off' lever and when the lever is released, the heat stops. They are designed to deliver deep heat to joints, the back or chest, extremities and anywhere deep heat is needed. Website: https://www.thermophore.com/

Chapter 37

Make clay masks, add clay to soaps, shampoo bars, etc.

Various types of clay may be used to treat skin disorders, ameliorate oily skin, wash and add moisture to hair, and make lovely soaps. Clay comes in various colors from white (e.g., bentonite, kaolin, sea clays) to golden (e.g., Rhassoul) to brick red (e.g., kaolin rose, Moroccan) to green (e.g., French green). Kaolin clay is a mild type clay good for most skin types. French green clay and Bentonite clay have stronger properties making them good choices for oily skin. Some claim bentonite clay can be used to lighten skin and tattoos. The color of clay usually reflects the mineral content. For example, brick red clay contains iron oxides. Green clay is a combination of one or more of the following minerals or compounds: iron oxides, montmorillonite, dolomite, magnesium, calcium, potassium, manganese, phosphorus, aluminum, silicon, cobalt, copper, selenium, chlorophyll and / or algae. Anytime you apply pigments to your skin, you can potentially leave a temporary stain on the skin. If you are unsure how a certain clay or powder will affect your skin, practice on a small patch of skin such as on your belly or your upper leg area which is not usually visible when dressed. Typically, clay is mixed with just enough distilled water to make a paste, but other dry ingredients may be added including hemp, spirulina, chlorophyll, beet powder (will leave a temporary stain on your skin), butterfly pea powder, spinach powder, powdered riboflavin, niacinamide powder, powdered caffeine, diatomaceous earth, charcoal powder, oatmeal powder, willow herb powder, ascorbic acid powder, etc. Herbal teas such as chamomile, ginger juice, licorice root tea, goat's milk, aloe vera gel, rose water, orange blossom water, coconut oil, okra mucilage, and others may be used as the liquid. While the clay mask is on your face for up to 20 or 30 minutes, apply an ice-cold towel, separated by saran wrap. You may also use a warm towel, depending on your needs. Leaving a clay mask on too long may dry out your face. Test each type of clay to determine its effects on your skin type before applying to your entire face.

One mechanism of clay is its strong negative charge. This attracts positively charged toxins found on the surface of the skin, usually excreted from the body as part of the detoxification process. Clay masks improve the appearance of the skin by toning and firming. The pores visibly shrink and the skin is smooth and soft after a clay mask application. Clay may also inhibit growth of skin-based bacteria and other pathogenic microorganisms.

Do not consume clay unless it is "food grade" clay. Otherwise you may be consuming high levels of unknown and potentially unhealthy levels of minerals. <u>As always, check with your health care provider before consuming clay products.</u> While small amounts of minerals are essential, large quantities of even essential minerals are toxic and may cause neurodegenerative disorders, bone problems, etc.

To make clay-based shampoo bars, search these terms on the internet. I found one that looked good at naturallyhandcrafted.com. This recipe uses Rhassoul or Moroccan red clay but any clay would work. Use silicon kitchen molds to shape the soap. I use clay-based soaps using goat's milk as the base. They last a long time and leave the skin feeling smooth and silky.

Shampoo Bar (adapted from www.happy-mothering.com webpage)

1 Tbsp cocoa butter
2 tsp cetyl alcohol
1 Tbsp coconut oil
½ pound goats milk melt and pour soap base, cubed
1 tsp vitamin E oil
1 tsp argan oil
1 tsp apple cider vinegar
2 tsp baking soda
1 tsp sea salt
Up to 30 drops of essential oils (use a combination of lemon, grapefruit, orange, neroli, rosemary, lavender, peppermint, tea tree, etc.)
¼ cup dried lavender, crushed or ground (optional; may also use other ingredients such as lemon zest, chopped rosemary, etc.)
1 – 2 drops of natural colorant (optional)

1. Transfer cetyl alcohol, coconut oil and cocoa butter to a double boiler over medium heat. Stir until ingredients are melted. Add the melt-and-pour soap cubes and continue stirring until melted and smooth.
2. Add apple cider vinegar, salt, baking soda, vitamin E, and argan oil into the warm mixture. Stir and then add in the essential oils and colorant if using. Stir until combined. Stir in the crushed herb(s) and / or citrus zest, reserving some for adding later.
3. Sprinkle some of the reserved crushed herb into the soap mold, which could be muffin tins or a silicon mold.
4. Gently pour in the shampoo mixture. Spritz the top with rubbing alcohol to dissipate the bubbles. Allow the shampoo bars to harden at room temperature or in the frig for at least 2 hours. The longer you allow the bars to cure after cooling, the less soap will be used with each washing.

Clay Hair Mask

1 Tbsp Red Rhassoul (for red or dark hair), French Green, White Kaolin or Bentonnite clay powder
1 tsp water or orange water or chamomile tea

1. Combine clay and water and apply to damp hair.
2. Sweep up hair in a bun and wrap plastic wrap around it for 30 minutes. Remove, rinse out clay using plenty of water, and style as usual.

Clay Facial Mask

1 Tbsp French Green or Kaolin Clay powder
1 tsp diatomaceous earth powder
2 tsp water, orange water, rose water or chamomile tea

1. Combine ingredients and brush on face, neck and / or décolletage using a make-up brush or gently apply using your fingers moving in gentle concentric circles. Leave on for 20 to 30 minutes.
2. Rinse with cool water to remove the mask.
3. If you have leftover mask material, cover in a small airtight container and store in the fridge for up to 3 days.

Chapter 38
Make a face wash and hand sanitizer

*First Wash**
1 Tbsp ascorbic acid powder
½ tsp Epsom salts
½ tsp white or green clay
¼ cup distilled water

- *First wash:* Combine ingredients and gently apply to face; leave on for several minutes before rinsing off. Store in a dark bottle.

Second Wash
1 tsp niacinamide
3 Tbsp licorice tea water
¼ tsp hyaluronic acid

- *Second wash:* Combine ingredient and gently apply to face; leave on for several minutes before rinsing off.

Final Leave-on Wash
1 – 2 drops coffee oil
2 Tbsp jojoba oil
10 drops glycerin

- *Third wash:* Combine ingredients and gently apply a small amount. Leave on.

*If you have rosacea, substitute borax for ascorbic acid in the First Wash.

Mild Face Wash

1 ½ cups witch hazel
½ cup marshmallow root tea (4 Tbsp simmered in 1 cup water for 20 minutes and then strained)
½ cup orange blossom water or licorice root water

Face Moisturizer

Carrier Oil
½ cup liquid carrier oil such as almond, argan, coconut, grapeseed, hemp, jojoba, olive, primrose, etc.

Additives – Essential Oils (add to carrier oil first): choose 3 to 5 oils

3 – 5 drops carrot seed oil	1 – 3 drops copaiba	1 – 2 drops lemon oil
1 drop citronella oil (for outdoor days and insect repellent properties)	3 – 5 drops frankincense	3 – 5 drops myrrh
	1 – 2 drops grapefruit oil	1 – 3 drops rose / rosehips oil
	1 – 2 drops helichrysum	1 – 3 drops spikenard
1 drop coffee oil	3 – 5 drops lavender	3 – 5 drops ylang

Floral Waters or Hydrosols

To make a flower or herb-infused water (hydrosol), you will need a large wooden or ceramic mortar and pestle. Take about 2 or 3 cups of your favorite edible flowers or herbs and rinse them well. Place half the flowers / herbs in the mortar. Gently press the pestle on the flowers or herbs to release their fragrance. Add to 1 quart of distilled or spring water, cover and allow to rest for at least an hour in the fridge. To use, strain and either drink the hydrosol or put it in a spritzer to use on your face or spritz on your favorite cotton or linen clothing (do a test check to ensure it won't stain or damage clothing).

Charcoal Wash

2 Tbsp activated charcoal powder
½ - 1 tsp psyllium powder
½ cup water
1 – 2 tsp rose or orange blossom water
1 – 2 drops essential oil such as rose or orange blossom

Mix ingredients. You end up with a paste. Take a small pea size amount of the paste and rub on moist skin. Leave on for several minutes before rinsing off.

Aloe Vera Wash

¼ cup aloe vera gel
½ - 1 tsp psyllium powder

3 – 5 drops frankincense oil
3 – 5 drops carrot seed oil

Mix ingredients. You end up with a paste. Take a small pea size amount of the paste and rub on moist skin. Leave on for several minutes before rinsing off.

Hand Sanitizer

1 cup witch hazel
½ cup aloe vera gel
1 tsp vitamin E oil

30 drops Thieves oil*
20 drops oregano oil

Alternatives to using Thieves oil:
- Citrus blend: 10 drops lemon oil, 10 drops lemongrass oil, 5 drops grapefruit oil, 2 drops helichrysum
- Lavender: 20 drops lavender, 5 drops lemongrass oil
- Bible oils: 10 drops frankincense, 10 drops myrrh, 5 drops spikenard, 5 drops rosemary
- Strong: 20 drops bergamot, 5 drops ginger, 5 drops orange, 5 drops rosemary, 5 drops patchouli
- Spicy: 10 drops each of anise, orange, rose, cardamom, nutmeg
- Floral: 10 drops each of bergamot, jasmine, chamomile
- Therapeutic: 20 drops cajeput, 5 drops helichrysum, 10 drops chamomile, 10 drops rosemary, 5 drops frankincense
- Minty: 30 drops peppermint

Using a small blender, blend and transfer to a pump bottle. If you prefer to use as a spray, use half the aloe vera and leave out the vitamin E oil. Shake before each use.

Chapter 39

Make sterile sinus rinses and nasal sprays

Sinus rinses are used to keep first line immune barriers, such as the nose and sinuses, free from air-borne pathogens. You can use a neti pot to rinse sinuses and a nasal spray to spray sterile water with bioactive ingredients to protect yourself from invading pathogens. Ideally use preventively before going out in large groups, public travel, going to school, going to church, going out to dinner, etc. Use them when you are surrounded by sick people who are coughing and sneezing. Use them when you feel the very first signs of a cold such as a tickle in your throat or even in your nose. Just about everyone can use them.

When you make medical solutions at home it is always critical to keep everything sterile. These fluids are going into your nose and sinuses and therefore need to be sterile. Only use distilled water and sterilized glass storage containers, sterilized measuring utensils and washed and clean hands. Make in a super clean kitchen with no pets around, especially cats whose dander can float in the air for long periods of time.

Making these solutions at home may not be for everyone but if you are interested, you will save a lot of money not needing to buy pharmaceutical-grade solutions which are significantly marked up over the cost of materials, which are literally just pennies. The key is keeping the process as sterile as possible. One way to ensure this is to purchase a UV light to sterilize your surfaces and work area ahead of making these solutions. This is not necessary, but for those who need additional assurances of safety. Be sure to follow the guidelines for using UV lights, which is basically never directly look at them. I have a light that has a timer so I set it and leave the room and it lights up for 5, 10 or 30 minutes. They do produce ozone, so keep the room vented well, open the windows, etc.

The nasal sprays are similar to the sinus options but there are two differences. Xylitol alone or in combination with carrageenan reduces transmission of viruses. Xylitol and carageenan work in combination with your natural mucus secretions to block covid and other viruses by up to 80%.

Sinus rinses

Sinus rinse option 1 – 1% Baking soda solution

- 1 tsp baking soda in 12 oz distilled water

Sinus rinse option 2 – Baking soda and salt solution

- 1 quart distilled water + 1 tsp kosher salt + 1 tsp baking soda

Sinus rinse option 3 – Salt and baking soda combination for storing as a dry powder.

- ½ cup kosher salt + ½ cup baking soda.
- Use ¼ teaspoon of this mixture dissolved in enough distilled water per nasal rinse.

Sinus rinse or nasal spray option 4 – Normal saline solution

- normal saline solution purchased from pharmacy
- make at home: 4 cups distilled water + 2 tsp non-iodized salt (only NaCl and not additional minerals) + sterile glass jar with lid. Add ingredients and shake. Keep sterile.

Sinus rinse option 5 – Hypertonic (concentrated) saline solution

- 2 Tbsp kosher salt (non-iodized) + 4 cups distilled water

Sinus rinse option 6 – Vitamin C

- 1 tsp ascorbic acid + 1 cup distilled water (may use sodium ascorbate) – store in dark bottle.

Sinus rinse option 7 - Iodine

- 1 - 3 drops 2% Lugol's Iodine + 1 quart / liter distilled water or normal saline (1 vertical drop = 2.5 mg iodine + 3.75 mg potassium iodide).
- Avoid if you have an iodine allergy.
- **I would not use this continuously but on the occasion of early infection symptoms such as sore throat, sinus drainage, etc.**

Option 8 – Colloidal silver

- add 1 tablespoon 10 ppm colloidal silver water to your usual nasal wash solution.

Nasal sprays

Nasal spray option 1 – 1% Baking soda solution

- 1 tsp baking soda in 12 oz distilled water

Nasal spray option 2 – Baking soda and salt solution

- 1 quart distilled water + 1 tsp kosher salt + 1 tsp baking soda

Nasal spray option 3 – xylitol

- 1 quart distilled water + 1 tsp kosher salt + 1 tsp baking soda + ¼ tsp xylitol granules

Nasal spray option 4 – xylitol and iota or lambda carrageenan powder

- 1 quart distilled water + 1 tsp kosher salt + 1 tsp baking soda + ¼ tsp xylitol granules + ¼ tsp carrageenan powder

Chapter 40
Make natural gargling liquids, throat sprays and room sprays

Gargling and throat sprays

Option 1
- 1.5% hydrogen peroxide: 3% hydrogen peroxide and distilled water (1:1 ratio)

Option 2
- 1 tsp ascorbic acid + 1 cup distilled water – store in a dark bottle

Option 3
- 10 ppm colloidal silver (gargle and then swallow)

Option 4
- 1 – 3 drops 2% Lugol's iodine + 2 cups distilled water

Option 5
- 1 tablespoon of baking soda in ½ cup water

Room sprays

Option 1 – Hydrogen peroxide room spray
- Add to a spray bottle: 2 cups 3% hydrogen peroxide + 4 cups distilled water + 3 to 5 drops clove extract

Option 2 – Herbal scented room spray
- Add to a spray bottle: 1 cup distilled water + 1 cup witch hazel + 10 to 20 drops herbal oils (e.g., rosemary, sage, pine, spruce, etc.)
  Optional: add several sprigs of thoroughly rinsed fresh rosemary

Option 3 – Citrus or vanilla scented room spray
- Add to a spray bottle: 1 cup witch hazel + 1 cup distilled water + ½ cup chopped orange peels (just the orange part and not the white pith) + 10 – 20 drops citrus oil or 2 tsp vanilla

Option 4 – Lemon grass scented room spray – good for kitchens and keeping kitchen gnats away
- Add to a spray bottle: 1 cup unflavored vodka + 2 cups distilled water + 20 drops lemongrass oil + 20 drops lime essential oil (see www.ouroilyhouse.com)

Some ideas for when kids get sick with a mild cold

1. Make sure they are well-hydrated – see chart below. The daily intake of water for children depends on activity status, age, air temperature, caffeine intake, humidity, intervening medical factors, sex, and weight. Pure water is the optimal way to satisfy these requirements.
2. Gargle with salt water or baking soda water every hour or two for no less than 1 minute.
3. Give them an herbal soaking bath using Epsom salts or magnesium flakes, iodine, bentonite clay, peppermint oil, baking soda, etc.
4. Give them the hottest shower they can handle (not too hot though and not to the point they are uncomfortable) with steam and all. If you have natural eucalyptus branches, place them in shower to inhale some of the eucalyptus oils. Be sure they blow their noses and clear their sinuses while in the shower while their nasal mucus is solubilized.
5. Place them in direct sunlight for 30 to 45 minutes with as much skin exposed as possible while also based on outside temperature and conditions, etc.
6. Make sure their ears are clear of wax. You can add a few drops of hydrogen peroxide if indicated.
7. Encourage them to drink a ½ to 1 cup of warm lemon – honey water every hour.
8. Make sure their electrolytes are stable – give them small amounts of freshly squeezed fruit juices, coconut water, freshly squeezed vegetables juices, etc.
9. Give them 250 to 500 mg vitamin C every two hours. For children over the age of 12, they can take 3,000 mg vitamin C every 2 hours or to bowel tolerance.
10. Take zinc.
11. Gargle with baking soda.
12. Combine honey and lemon juice with a small amount of warm water and drink.
13. Using a thermophore heating pad on their chest may be beneficial.
14. Gently massage their arms and legs, shoulders and back.
15. Rub a little coconut oil along with a few drops of lavender oil on their chest.
16. Always consult your child's pediatrician when your child is sick.

Age / Wt	Feeding mode	Fluid, ounces	Fluid, milliliters	Number of 8 oz glasses of water
Birth to 1 yr	Breastfed*			
Birth to 1 yr	Bottle fed**			
7.5 – 22 lb 3.5 – 10 kg	Oral	3.5 oz/2.2 lb or 1 kg of wt	100 ml/2.2 lb or 1 kg	
23 – 45 lb 11 – 20 kg	Oral			
80 lb	Oral	40 – 60		8
100 lb	Oral	50 – 65		8
120 lb	Oral	60 – 85		10 – 12
140 lb	Oral	70 – 95		10 – 12
160 lb	Oral			10 – 12
180 lb	Oral			10 – 12
200 - 250 lb	Oral			10 – 14
250 – 300+ lb	Oral			10 – 14
*Breastfed babies do not necessarily need additional fluids unless there is excessive sweating or fluid loss. Check with your pediatrician for specific guidelines.				

Chapter 41
Make natural hair shampoo, rinse and detangler

Hair is frequently mentioned in the Bible. "But if a woman has long hair, it is her glory? For her hair is given to her for a covering. **1 Corinthians 11:15**. "Gray hair is a crown of glory; it is gained in a righteous life." **Proverbs 16:31**. "His head is the finest gold; his locks are wavy, black as a raven." **Song of Solomon 5:11**. "Mary therefore took a pound of expensive ointment made from pure nard, and anointed the feet of Jesus and wiped his feet with her hair. The house was filled with the fragrance of the perfume." **John 12:3**

Hair provides many clues about a person such as their level of hygiene, their attention to detail, how they want to be perceived, etc. Color, length, type of cut, etc., all give clues about a person. When it comes to hair, there are some things generally outside of our control such as going gray, hair color (although this can be changed), texture, degree of curliness, the absence of hair (i.e., being bald), etc. Regardless of what you cannot change, assuming you have hair, there are many aspects of your hair within your control. **Take the time to keep your hair clean and to ensure your haircut and style reflect your values and the value God places on you!**

Below are several all-natural hair care recipes. One is a natural shampoo, a natural hair rinse, and a hair detangler. Not everyone benefits from these recipes. Some people may need to use these recipes for up to a week or two before they begin to "work." This shift from chemicals to natural compounds may take a few days or even weeks to work. In fact, you may learn that the natural products work much better for you after you have adapted to their qualities.

Natural Substances to Use on Hair as Shampoo, Hair Mask, Conditioner, Natural Color, Hair Growth, etc.

Soapnut powder (aritha, reetha)	Indica Amla powder	Bhringraj leaf powder
Hibiscus powder	Henna natural black powder	Brahmi powder
Shikaki powder	Chebe powder	Aloe vera powder

Easy Shampoo: 1 tsp baking soda + 2 – 3 Tbsp vinegar, combine and use.

MSM Shampoo: 2 tsp MSM powder + 16 oz water, shake until dissolved. Use a small amount as a shampoo.

Hulda Clark's Natural Shampoo (adapted)

1/8 cup borax   1 gallon distilled water

1. Combine ingredients by shaking together (could use a ½ gallon mason jar and halve this recipe). Some borax will settle on the bottom of the container, this is ok.
2. Transfer to a pump dispenser and use in the shower or at the kitchen sink.
3. Notes: substitute chamomile tea, rose water, orange blossom water or any other water-based liquid for some of the water.

Peppermint Shampoo

2 cups distilled water   1 Tbsp jojoba oil
2 cups liquid Castile soap   1 tsp peppermint oil

Combine all ingredients and store in an appropriate container. Shake before each use.

Hulda Clark's Natural Hair Rinse (adapted)

1 Tbsp + 1 tsp citric acid powder (no subs)   1 tsp Epsom salt
1 Tbsp ascorbic acid   1 gallon water

1. Shake to combine ingredients (could use a ½ gallon mason jar and halve this recipe).
2. Depending on your hair thickness, use about ¼ cup to rinse hair right after using the borax-based shampoo. These two recipes should be used together.
3. Notes: substitute chamomile tea, rose water, orange blossom for some of the water.

Hair Detangler (adapted from www.happy-mothering.com webpage)

1:1 ratio of witch hazel to distilled water (may substitute apple cider vinegar for witch hazel)
1 tsp glycerin
15 – 20 drops essential oil such as lemon or grapefruit (use a nice scent combination)

Combine ingredients and transfer to a small spray bottle.

Conditioner-based Hair Detangler

Take ½ cup of your conditioner and add 2 cups of distilled water. Add to a spray bottle and use as a detangler.

Marshmallow Root Detangler

2 cups water
1/3 cup dried marshmallow root
1 Tbsp vinegar (may use lemon juice but it may lighten your hair)
2 tsp jojoba or almond oil
1 tsp glycerin
20 drops fragrant essential oil

1. Transfer water and marshmallow roots to a small saucepan over medium heat. Cook for 20 to 30 minutes until the mixture begins to thicken and form a gel, stirring frequently as it begins to thicken. When the mixture has thickened, turn off the heat and allow the mixture to cool.
2. Strain out the solids and add the vinegar, oil and essential oil.
3. You may use it as a thick gel or you may add to a spray bottle, adding enough water (or other liquid such as chamomile tea), to make it sprayable. Shake before each use.

Dry Powdered Shampoo https://mommypotamus.com/dry-shampoo/?fbclid=IwAR22_5v_LONGB0glAtgJ8Dlj2dnglELVneyb9duA9vM8aZBBaUOGzS_32eo

Blond / Light Hair	*Red Hair*	*Dark Hair*
¼ cup arrowroot powder	¼ cup arrowroot powder	2 Tbsp arrowroot powder
1 tsp cacao powder* (optional)	1 Tbsp cacao powder	2 – 3 Tbsp cacao powder
½ – 1 ½ tsp cinnamon	1 ½ tsp cinnamon	1 ½ tsp cinnamon
9 – 12 drops essential oils	1/8 tsp activated charcoal (optional)	up to 1 tsp activated charcoal
	9 – 12 drops essential oils	9 – 12 drops essential oils

Add all ingredients together and mix well. Store in airtight jar. Either use a makeup brush to apply to the scalp or a large-opening sugar shaker. Allow 10 minutes before brushing and styling.
*Eliminate if light blond or gray hair.

Chapter 42

Make laundry, hand soaps and deodorants

Powdered Laundry Soap

1 bar (4.5 oz) castile or Fels-Naptha, Ivory or Zote soap, grated
14 oz borax
14 oz washing soda
4 oz citric acid
1 cup dried lemon peel (just yellow and not white part)
Optional: Bleach granules (**see instructions**)

1. Add all ingredients to a high-speed blender and blend until it becomes a fine powder.
2. Store in an airtight jar and use 1 tablespoon per laundry load.
3. Add a teaspoon of bleach granules at the time of washing if you want to whiten a load of dingy whites and then dry outside on a line. Do not add the bleach granules to the entire recipe.
4. Add ½ to 1 cup of oxygen booster powder such as Oxy Clean to a load of heavily soiled laundry at the time of washing. Line drying on a sunny day is a great way to brighten whites.
5. You may also add a tablespoon or two of Bronner's Sal Suds for an extra boost.
6. When you first stain a piece of clothing, when possible, remove the clothing and immediately place in soapy water. Using a brush, apply borax and gently scrub to remove the stain. If the stain is a fruit-based stain, pour boiling water over the stain and it will go away. If blood-based, use hydrogen peroxide. Rust stains need a rust-remover liquid or powder.
7. Dry whites outside on a clothesline in bright sun to bleach and whiten your laundry, etc.
8. Notes: the purpose of washing clothes is to eliminate stains and odors. Adding scented oils and other "fancy" ingredients does not make sense. To add a scent to clothes, towels or sheets, make a spray using 1 oz of vodka or witch hazel and 50 to 100 drops of your favorite essential oil(s). Add to a pint-sized spray bottle and gently swirl for several minutes. Allow to rest for 15 minutes and add distilled water to within an inch of the top of spray bottle. Spray on clothes. ***WARNING***: *this may stain delicate fibers. Use on durable fabrics such as denim, sheets, towels, etc. If in doubt test a small piece of fabric first. Shake before each use. Bubbling cub soda for pre-treatment of fresh stains is another way to tackle stains.*

Liquid Laundry Detergent

1 Fels Naptha Soap Bar, grated
4 cups boiling water
4 cups borax powder / granules
4 cups washing soda powder
2 cups oxyclean powder
1 cup Epsom salt
1 cup fine grain salt
More hot water
2 cups dried lemon/orange peels (use only orange or yellow skins avoiding white pithy parts), blended
OR
20 – 30 drops lemon or grapefruit oil
¼ cup bleach granules (optional for whites)

1. Transfer grated soap and boiling water to a saucepan and dissolve over low heat.
2. Add remaining ingredients to a clean 5-gallon container along with 2 gallons of hot water, stir to dissolve solids. Add liquified soap bar and top off container with hot water, stirring until combined. Store and use ½ cup per load. May need to shake the container before using.

Liquid Stain Remover Options

- 7:1 ratio of water to Bronner's Sal Suds (add to a spray bottle or keep in a sealed mason jar).
- Dawn liquid dishwashing soap.
- Q-tip dipped in bleach and spot-used on whites.
- A small amount of lemon juice, rinse and then dry in the sun.
- Hydrogen peroxide for some stains, including blood stains, works well.

Liquid Hand Soap

1 cup grated castile, Fels-Naptha or Ivory soap
1 cup distilled water
1 Tbsp vitamin E oil
1 tsp citric acid
15 – 30 drops essential oils

1. Transfer all ingredients to a high-speed blender; allow to sit 10 minutes to soften before blending.
2. After waiting 10 minutes, blend on lowest setting for 10 – 20 seconds. Allow bubbles to dissipate.
3. Add to a glass jar equipped with a pump dispenser or a foaming soap pump.

Liquid Probiotic Underarm Toner

1 cup witch hazel
1 tsp baking soda
2 tsp bentonite clay
1 tsp willow bark extract or 2 capsules willow bark powder
5 – 10 drops essential oil (optional)
1 Tbsp hyaluronic acid gel
1 Tbsp aloe vera gel
Smallest pinch possible of *lacto bacillus* powder from an opened probiotic capsule of just *lacto bacillus* (optional)

1. Always thoroughly wash and scrub your arm pits and groin areas. These areas are rich in lymph nodes which constantly collect and release internal toxins to outside of the body.
2. Transfer witch hazel, baking soda, willow bark and essential oils to a small sauce pan over low heat. Heat just long enough to dissolve the solids. Remove and cool until just warm.
3. Stir in hyaluronic acid gel, aloe vera gel and a small pinch of lacto bacillus powder.
4. Apply to underarms using a cotton pad or spray bottle. Allow to dry before using other products.
5. Some may still need to use a natural deodorant, especially during hot months.
6. Store in an airtight container.

Natural Underarm Deodorant (results in a semi-solid deodorant, firmer if using shea butter and bees wax)

¼ cup baking soda
¼ cup arrowroot starch (avoid cornstarch)
1 Tbsp bentonite, kaolin, Brazilian, rose, French Fuller's, Moroccan or Rhassoul clay powder
½ tsp citric acid
¼ tsp vit E oil (optional; for preservation)
6 Tbsp coconut oil (melted)*, **
5 – 10 drops essential oils (e.g., tea tree, rose, lavender, rose, orange, lemon, cedar)

1. Always thoroughly wash and scrub your arm pits and groin areas. These areas are rich in lymph nodes which constantly collect and release internal toxins to outside of the body.
2. Combine dry ingredients in a small glass bowl and add then add oils. Stir/mash to combine.
3. Store in a glass wide-mouth airtight container. Apply using your hands or a cotton pad.
4. For a firmer product, *substitute half of the coconut oil with melted shea butter + 2 tsp melted bees wax. **Could sub 1 tablespoon castor oil for 1 tablespoon coconut oil (will be less firm).

Chapter 43
Make herbal bath bombs, sugar scrub and exfoliating paste

Herbal Bath Bomb

2 cups baking soda
1 cup arrowroot or corn starch
1 cup citric acid
1 cup Epsom salt
1 Tbsp bentonite clay
¼ cup dried citrus peel or combination of dried herbs
¼ cup almond oil
20 – 40 drops of essential oils
5 – 6 Tbsp water

1. Transfer dry ingredients to food processor fitted with an "S" blade and pulse several times.
2. Combine the oil, essential oil drops and the water; whisk and then drizzle into the food processor while pulsing. You want to minimize the amount of fizzing while adding the liquid ingredients.
3. The final mixture should look like wet sand.
4. Now take mixture and place in the bottom of mini muffin tins, gently pressing the mixture together.
5. Allow the bath bombs to completely dry and then store in an air tight container.

Sugar Scrub

1 ¼ cups white sugar (use fine grain brown sugar if you are using as a facial scrub)
1 – 2 tsp plant powder or finely ground coffee (for giving color)
1 tsp lemon juice (omit if using coffee powder)
¼ cup solid coconut oil
1 ½ Tbsp clear liquid soap
10 – 15 drops essential oil
1 tsp vitamin E oil
Optional: 1 Tbsp coffee grounds, 1 Tbsp ground mint leaves, 1 Tbsp ground lavender buds

1. Combine sugar, molasses and lemon juice; set aside.
2. Combine oil, essential oil drops and vitamin E oil.
3. Gently combine sugar mixture with oil mixture.
4. Store in an airtight glass jar.
5. Use once or twice per week (not daily)

Face Mask

1: ¼ avocado, mashed + 1 tsp rice flour. Combine and cover face.
2: 1 Tbsp cacao powder + 1 Tbsp ground coffee + 1 tsp rice flour + 1 tsp full fat coconut milk. Combine.
3: 1 piece fresh pineapple + 1 piece fresh papaya + 1 tsp rice flour. Mash together and cover face.

Gentle Exfoliating Paste

1 part liquid to 3 parts baking soda
5 – 10 drops essential oil
1 Tbsp coconut oil (a carrier oil for the essential oils)
1 tsp licorice root powder
1 tsp bentonite clay
1 Tbsp diatomaceous earth

Combine all ingredients and stir until you have a paste. You may need to add additional liquid by one teaspoon at a time. Liquids could include herbal teas, aloe vera, lemon juice, etc. Transfer to a sealable glass jar and use in the shower. **If you plan to use on delicate skin, leave out the diatomaceous earth.** If you want it to be creamier add a tablespoon of coconut oil. If it causes a skin reaction, discontinue using.

Herbal Detox Bath and Accompanying Beverage (warm to moderately hot, cooling to tepid)

Bath Formula
½ cup licorice roots and stems, simmered covered in 1 quart of water for 1 hour
Handful of fresh oregano, simmered covered in 1 quart of water for 1 hour
1 tsp copper sulfate
1 – 2 cups baking soda
2 cups Epsom salt
1 cup borax
½ – 1 cup clay (e.g., bentonite, kaolin, green)
20 drops oregano oil
20 drops tea tree oil

Simmer in a covered pan for 1 hour, licorice roots and stems and oregano in about 1 quart of water; when done simmering, drain and add to bath water right before you get in the tub. To prepare the bath water, add hot licorice water to your tub as it is filling with hot water. Add the bath formula components to hot bath water. When you have adjusted the water temperature for your body, get in and soak for 20 to 45 minutes. When you are ready to end your herbal detox bath, begin to drain the bath water, stirring the water to make sure the clay is in solution and won't leave behind a blockage in your plumbing. Run cold water after the tub as drained for several minutes to ensure no clay remains in the drain pipes. Also, don't allow loose herbs to go down the drain. For those with toenail fungus, after bathing, cover and soak your feet in 3% hydrogen peroxide for 30 to 60 minutes. This allows the oxygen to enter the body through dilated pores and it allows the oxygen to more easily access the nails and attack the fungus.

Accompanying Beverage Recipe (not too hot)
12 – 16 oz Chamomile tea
1 tsp honey
2 drops 2.2% Lugol's iodine
1 – 3 tsp diatomaceous earth (DE) or zeolytes or activated charcoal

Make tea as usual adding honey and lemon if desired and then add several drops of Lugol's iodine and one teaspoon of one of the three remaining ingredients (i.e., diatomaceous earth, zeolytes or charcoal).

Chapter 44

Make herbal mineral soaking water

King Xerxes is in the market for a new wife after his first wife, Vashti, refused to be publicly humiliated and paraded around naked. We pick up the story in the book of Esther chapter 2. The king requests the most beautiful virgins of his kingdom be recruited and readied for an audition to be the new queen. The women are identified and recruited to the king's residence. They spend the next 12 months, divided into two six-month periods, making various preparations to meet the king. Each aspect of their "purification" is supervised by Hegai, the king's eunuch. He is in charge of providing for their beauty treatments and making sure every detail of their preparation is perfect. During this time the women are treated to facials, mani- and pedicures, massages, and likely provided with herbal mineral baths and sweet-smelling oils. I can imagine they also received extensive instruction in their possible future role as queen. Nothing is overlooked as they prepare to stand before the king. A lovely orphan named Esther stood out among the young women. I'm sure you know the rest of the story... Esther's quiet demeanor and beauty impresses the king and she is crowned the new queen.

It is important to take care of our skin. Most of us are not going to be crowned a queen or a king. **However, we need to value our body enough to care for it and put forward the best version possible.** Esther's story provides us with some interesting insights into physical beauty. Not only is the skin the largest detox organ, it tells a story about how we take care of ourselves. Most of us do not have 12 months to spend on a purification program, but we can adopt habits which can fit perfectly into our daily and weekly routines.

There is another application of this story. We are all recruited by the King and given the opportunity to audition for His Kingdom. In fact, we are already part of His Kingdom. We are born into royalty. God made us in His image. We are meant to be handsome and beautiful. Esther was not only beautiful, she endured great hardship. She lost both parents. She was raised by her uncle, Mordecai, a devout Jew, who also raised Esther as a devout Jew. She lived as an exile in a country not her own, among people who desired to exterminate her race. She was not only beautiful on the outside, she was beautiful on the inside. Every person is invited by the Lord to go through the same "purification" process as Esther. The number of days or years we live is not the most critical aspect of our life. What is important is God chose us and now we must choose Him. It is through our conception we are born into the royal family of God (our justification to be part of His family through Christ's death on the cross). It is through conversion we begin the process of sanctification, the work of a lifetime. It is through sanctification, or the "purification" routine, we choose to live a holy life, acceptable unto the Lord.

However, after around 6,000 years of genetic load, we bear the marks of sin in both our outward appearance and our inward vitality. We are less resistant to chronic disease and degeneration. Instead of living 960 years and then dying, we are lucky to live three score and ten. Do we value our appearance on the inside as much as we do on the outside? It is perfectly normal to desire outward beauty. However, every single person on the planet is beautiful in God's eyes. **It is only humans who discriminate on the outward appearance.** Maybe we prefer black hair or blond hair. Maybe we prefer tall and lanky or short and compact. Some people look at a person's eyes while others are more concerned about the quality of their character. Be the person who sees beauty in everyone, no matter their skin, hair color, weight, no matter their crimes or their attitude, just see everyone as a child of God.

Herbal mineral bath. An herbal mineral bath is a means to infuse the skin with essential minerals such as magnesium, sulfur, silica, selenium, and others. Adding handfuls of freshly procured local herbs could include sage, rosemary, lavender, chamomile, roses, gardenia, parsley, dandelion, basil, and many others. Each herb brings special properties to the warm soaking bath. Lightly crush the herbs before adding or pre-heat them in simmering water and add to the bath. Most people prefer to not directly add herbs because of the potential for a messy bathtub and drain issues. However, there are extra-large tea strainers which could be used to keep flowers and herbs out of the drain. If using fresh herbs, place ½ cup of fresh herbs in a small cloth bag and add to bath water. Gently brush your skin while soaking.

For a stronger herbal brew, add fresh herbs to a covered pot of boiling water. Turn off heat and allow the herbs to infuse into the water for 20 minutes before adding to your bath water. When possible recycle the bath water to your garden or yard. Plants love magnesium and sulfate rich Epsom salt (in the right concentration). Clay-based minerals may also be beneficial to your vegetable garden.

- **Herbs and / or few drops of oils**: basil, calendula, chamomile, cleavers, clove, frankincense, grapefruit, helichrysum, lavender, lemon balm, mint, myhrr, orange, rose, rosemary, tea tree, thyme, parsley, sage, spruce, etc.
- **Minerals for soaking baths**: activated charcoal, borax, copper sulfate, diatomaceous earth (silica), epsom salt (magnesium / sulfur or MSM), bentonite clays, magnesium bath crystals, baking soda.
- **Add copper:** 5/8th tsp copper sulfate + 2 oz distilled water. Add 5 – 20 drops to bath water.
- **Other soaking options**: citrus rinds, rose petals (avoid rose bushes sprayed with chemicals), hydrogen peroxide, sea salt, etc.
- **Best water temp zone**: between 90°F and 110°F. Water should be warm but not uncomfortable.
- **Detox bath ideas**: baking soda, bentonite clay, charcoal, chlorella, copper sulfate, epsom salts, ginger, hydrogen peroxide, magnesium bath crystals, peppermint, rock sea salt, rose, borax, etc.
- **Heart**: Epsom salt, juniper berries, lavender, sea water, seaweeds, etc.
- **Rashes / poison ivy**: chamomile, Epsom salts, goldenseal, lemon balm, marshmallow, oats, licorice root, plantain, rose hips, etc.
- **Pain and soreness**: Arnica, epsom salt, frankincense, ginger, hops, juniper berries, lavender, MSM, parsley, rosemary, etc.
- **Infection**: borax, citrus, colloidal copper, silver, eucalyptus, oregano, rose hip, tea tree, yarrow, etc.
- **Fatigue**: basil, bergamot, camphor, cedarwood, cinnamon, frankincense, geranium, ginger, grapefruit, jasmine, lavender, lemon, lemongrass, lime, orange, oregano, peppermint, pine, rose, rosemary, spearmint, spruce, tea tree, etc.
- **Shower**: basil, eucalyptus branches, lavender sprigs, oregano sprigs, rosemary stems, etc.
- **Soaking time**: 15 – 20 minutes
- **Other additives**: coconut oil, almond oil, oatmeal, salts, baking soda, etc.
- **Contraindications**: if you have a heart or other major medical condition, if pregnant, consult your physician before beginning a new routine. Avoid baths if you are dehydrated, extremely fatigued, low or high blood glucose, cannot easily get out of the tub, etc.
- **Orally hydrate during bath time with**: cool water, cool herbal tea, elixir, etc.
- **Bulk bath salt recipe** (use 1 – 2 cups/bath): 4 C magnesium chloride + 4 C Epsom salt + 3 C MSM crystals + 2 C borax + 1 C baking soda + 1 C bentonite clay + ½ C sea salt + ¼ C copper sulfate + essential oils
- **Radiation exposure:** baking soda and salt.

Chapter 45

Make a salve, balm, ointment or liniment

To make an herbal salve

1. Different types of salves to make include: calendula, eucalyptus, lemon balm, pain relief cayenne and ginger, herbal salve, peppermint headache salve, burn salve, pine salve, etc.
2. To naturally infuse an oil with fresh herbs, flowers or roots, place the carrier oil with the rinsed fresh herbs in a sterile glass jar and place in a sunny window for up to 30 days, periodically shaking. At the end of this time, you are now ready to make an infused salve.
3. Black salve ingredients: 15 drops calendula oil, ½ cup castor oil, 3 tsp activated charcoal, 2 tsp beeswax, ½ cup coconut oil, 3 tsp bentonite clay, 1 tsp arnica oil, 5 drops andrographis, 1 tsp vitamin E oil, 20 drops lavender oil, 10 drops tea tree oil
4. Pine tar salve: herbal infused oil including pine tar, castor oil, lemon oil, beeswax, activated charcoal.
5. Natural bug repellants to add to a salve: blue cyprus, catnip, cedarwood, cinnamon, clove, eucalyptus, lavender, lemon, lemongrass, peppermint, rose geranium, rosemary, sage, sweet myrrh, tansy, tea tree, thyme, etc.
6. Combine 4 parts infused herbal oil with 1 part beeswax or carnauba wax.
7. Add wax to a double boiler over low heat until the beeswax melts. The beeswax gives the salve its consistency. More beeswax makes a firmer product and less beeswax makes a softer product.
8. Add herb infused oil to the melted wax and stir until combined.
9. Remove from heat and add essential oil.
10. Pour into tins or selected containers.
11. Cool before using.

Sample recipe for Activated Charcoal Drawing Salve

½ cup herb-infused olive oil (infused with calendula, plantain, lavender, rose, etc.)
2 Tbsp castor oil
3 Tbsp beeswax
1 Tbsp hemp oil
1 Tbsp activated charcoal powder
1 Tbsp bentonite clay
1 tsp psyllium powder
30 – 40 drops essential oil such as lavender
15 – 20 drops tea tree oil or frankincense

Directions: Transfer herb-infused olive oil and beeswax to the top section of a double boiler. Heat over low heat until the beeswax has melted. Remove from heat and add remaining ingredients. Stir until combined. Add more clay if you prefer a thicker salve. Transfer to salve container and seal.

To make a balm. Balms are an excellent way to moisturize and add therapeutic value to the skin. They are simple to make and are great for minor cuts, bruises and burns. **You can use on your skin or on your lips.** The ratio of beeswax to oil used to make a balm is 1:4. If you are going to make 100 grams or 3.5 ounces of a balm, you would use 20 grams of beeswax and 80 grams of oil. To assemble a balm, gently heat the beeswax and oil together on a double boiler until the beeswax melts and the two ingredients are combined. Dip a spoon in the mixture and remove. If it is not forming a thick balm-like texture, you may need to add more beeswax. If it is too hard, add more oil. Add no more than 2% to 3% of the total oil amount as essential oils. Transfer liquid to small glass or metal containers, a lip balm container and cool and cover. Best to store in the frig or a cool place.

Ingredients could include: white oak, calendula, marshmallow, burdock, sea buckthorn, chamomile, peppermint, thyme, yarrow, oak bark, arnica, mullein, black walnut, wormwood, etc.). Natural colorants could include powders of: annatto, beet, butterfly pea flower, avocado, calendula, carrot, elderberry, hemp, henna, hibiscus, orange beet, pomegranate, saffron, spinach, spirulina, turmeric, mica-containing powders, etc.

To make an Ointment. Commercial antibiotic ointments are essential for any first aid kit. They are used to keep an open wound covered and clean as well as prevent infection. This following recipe is adapted from https://joybileefarm.com/herbal-first-aid-ointment/ :

Ointment

4 oz herb-infused oil (almond oil, coconut oil, hemp, jojoba, etc.; herbs could include white oak, calendula, plantain, sea buckthorn oil, conifer resin, chamomile, peppermint, St. John's wort, yarrow, burdock, marshmallow, oak bark, arnica, goldenseal, olive leaf, thyme oil, mullein, black walnut, wormwood, vitamin E, etc.)
½ oz cocoa butter (or shea butter)
¼ oz beeswax
5 drops lavender oil
5 drops tea tree oil
5 drops myrrh oil
5 drops goldenseal oil
5 drops frankincense oil
5 drops helichrysum oil

1. Melt the herb-infused oil, cocoa butter and beeswax on low heat using a double boiler.
2. When melted, remove from heat source and add essential oils.
3. Stir and pour into glass, metal or lip balm containers. Seal with a lid and keep refrigerated until needed.

To make a Liniment. Liniments are similar to tinctures but are for external use only. Liniments with beneficial herbs may either be rubbed on the body or if in liquid form, they are sprayed on the body. Usually, liniments are rubbed on painful sore muscles, sprains, and bruises. Instead of using rubbing alcohol, substitute glycerin, witch hazel, aloe vera, lotion or cream. You may also add anti-inflammatory and pain killing herbals such as arnica, calendula, cayenne, chamomile, eucalyptus, ginger, lemon balm, menthol, lavender, licorice root extract, St. John's wort, willow bark, yarrow, etc.

Dimethylsulfoxide (DMSO) is an anti-inflammatory applied to the skin to reduce pain and swelling. It is not a natural substance, but is a byproduct of paper making. It is widely used in some circles. It is commonly used on animals such as race horses. Sometimes it is mixed with beneficial herbs and used as a carrier or delivery system. DMSO alone provides anesthetic properties but if you choose to use DMSO, it is critical to only use DMSO with pure products such as magnesium oil, arnica, etc. It transdermally transfers whatever is combined with DMSO (i.e., across the skin). Currently, the FDA has only approved DMSO for treating interstitial cystitis, a type of bladder infection. It is not listed as a carcinogen, although in 1965 it was banned because of possible changes in the refractive index of the lens in the eyes of research animals. It is advisable to consult with your physician or pharmacist before using DMSO or adding DMSO to things such as liniments.

Guidelines for using DMSO after consulting with your physician (https://baripharma.com/wp-content/uploads/2022/12/DMSO_Many-uses.pdf):

- Dental / oral cavity: 50% solution for swishing or direct gum rub (don't swallow)
- Eye drops: start with 10-20% DMSO concentration in solution.
- Ear drops: start with 40-50% concentration in drops
- Oral dosage: 1 – 2 teaspoons or 5 to 10 ml a day. Combine with tomato or grape juice to disguise its awful taste.
- Serious degenerative conditions (administered by qualified physician) via 'slow push' method: up to 20 cc DMSO which has been diluted to 25% DMSO concentration.
- Serious degenerative conditions (administered by a qualified physician) via slow IV drip method over 2-3 hour period: add 50-100 cc DMSO to a 500 cc glucose or saline solution, then dripped into a vein in the patient's arm.
- Sinuses: 25-40% concentration drops or diluted nasal rinse
- Topical applications should not exceed 80% solution of DMSO. The face and neck are more sensitive to topical DMSO compared to other body areas.

The liniment recipe is adaptable to the herbs of your choice. It is a liquid and can be sprayed on sore, swollen muscles and joints. If you do not have all the herbals, use what you have on hand. It is wonderful to have a good liniment for the times when you sprain your thumb or pull a muscle, etc.

Ginger Cayenne Liniment Recipe (warming and increases circulation; good for stiffness and aches)

2 oz fresh ground ginger
1 small fresh cayenne pepper, stem removed and cut in half
6 oz witch hazel

1. Combine all ingredients and store in a dark colored glass bottle in a dark cupboard.
2. Over a period of at least 2 weeks, shake the bottle several times a day, always returning to a dark cupboard.
3. After 2 to 4 weeks, strain out the solids and return the strained liquid to the dark bottle.
4. Store in a dark place and use as needed.

Therapeutic Liniment Recipe (external use only)

2 cups witch hazel
¼ cup licorice root tea
¼ cup dried willow bark tea
½ tsp cayenne pepper or 1 cayenne pepper, finely sliced
¼ cup fresh lemon balm leaves
1 inch fresh ginger, cut into thin rounds
1 sprig fresh rosemary
2 Tbsp dried yarrow
2 Tbsp dried comfrey or fresh comfrey (chopped)
2 Tbsp dried lavender
2 Tbsp dried arnica flowers (or use arnica tincture and add with St. John's tincture and peppermint oil)
1 tsp menthol crystals
1 tsp ascorbic acid powder
2 Tbsp St. John's wort tincture
20 drops peppermint oil

1. Transfer all ingredients except dried herbs, menthol crystals, ascorbic acid, St. John's wort tincture and peppermint oil, to a medium mixing bowl. Using a mortar and pestle, grind the dried herbs and add to the previous ingredients. Place in a glass jar and seal. Shake the contents.
2. Steep ingredients for 4 weeks. Shake several times a day.
3. When ready to use, strain out the herbs and add Menthol crystals, ascorbic acid powder, St. John's wort tincture, and peppermint oil.
4. Add to a spray bottle and spray on the affected area as needed. Keep refrigerated when not using.

Simple Ginger Cough Syrup

5 ginger tea bags
Enough water to make 1 cup of tea, about 5 oz
4 inch knob fresh ginger, juiced
2 Tbsp freshly squeezed lemon juice
½ – 1 tsp lemon zest
2 – 3 packets lipospheric vitamin C (optional)
½ cup honey

1. Boil 2 cups water and remove about 1/3 cup of the boiling water and place in a covered mug with the 5 ginger tea bags. Steep for 10 to 15 minutes.
2. After steeping the tea, add remaining ingredients, stir and store in an air-tight container in the fridge for up to 1 month.
3. To use, remove about 1 tablespoon, add to hot tea or a small amount of water and drink up to 5 times per day.

Chapter 46
Make lozenges and gummy swallows

Lozenges. Lozenges are hard, "medicated" tablets you place in your mouth and suck on while the therapeutic components in the lozenge slowly dissolve in your mouth. The tissue in your mouth is vascular and thin. It is rich in microorganisms and tends to reflect one's general health. **Pristine oral care is associated with less morbidity, including conditions such as heart disease, cancer, neurodegenerative conditions, etc.** Oftentimes, pathogenic microorganisms enter through the mouth and find their way into the back of the throat, feeling like a "little tickle." If the microorganisms multiply to a threshold level, they may infect the sinuses and possibly the lungs. If the infection remains in the sinuses, it is an upper respiratory infection. If it travels to the lungs, it is a lower respiratory infection. Perfect oral care and using lozenges during susceptible months are good methods to fend off respiratory infections. **Sucking on medicated lozenges ensures an almost continuous exposure of inflamed throats to soothing and therapeutic substances such as capsaicin, chamomile, cloves, coconut, echinacea, frankincense, ginger, goldenseal, honey, iodine, lemon, licorice root, myrrh, oregano, peppermint, rosemary, sage, slippery elm, turmeric, zinc, etc.**

Simple lozenges

½ cup honey (or table sugar)
1 cup soothing tea
1 Tbsp lemon or lime juice
½ – 1 tsp lemon or lime zest (optional)
1 Tbsp ginger juice
10 fresh mint leaves (optional; overblending may make mint bitter)
1 tsp licorice root powder
1/8 tsp activated charcoal powder (optional)
5 – 20 drops various essential oils (edible, food grade; see above)

1. Transfer all ingredients to a high-speed blender and blend.
2. Transfer blended ingredients to a small sauce pan and heat over medium heat.
3. Bring to a boil, frequently stirring. Monitor the temperature using a candy thermometer. As the mixture heats up it requires constant stirring.
4. When mixture reaches 300 to 302 °F, remove from heat, allow to cool for 3 to 5 minutes, and pour into silicone molds in the shape of what could be used as a small lozenge. Alternatively, take a metal half teaspoon and drop mixture onto a parchment lined baking sheet in form of small coins; allow to cool.

5. When completely cooled, remove from parchment paper and toss with tapioca starch, arrowroot starch or corn starch. Store in an airtight container, preferably in the refrigerator until time to use. They may also be kept in a metal tin in your purse or briefcase.

Gummy swallows. Gummies are a great way to convince your family to consume supplemental vitamins and minerals. The gelling and firming ingredient is not gelatin but plant-based agar. In fact, there are some important differences between agar and gelatin. Gelatin comes from skin, bones and connective tissues of cows, pigs, fish and chickens. Agar comes from red seaweed. Agar-thickened products have a firmer texture compared to gelatin-thickened products which are pliant and jiggly. Both thickeners work well for making gummies with the aim of delivering therapeutic compounds. It comes down to which ingredients you prefer to consume.

The ratio of agar needed for liquid is 1 teaspoon of agar powder to 1 cup of liquid. If you are using agar flakes, it takes about 1 tablespoon of agar flakes to 1 cup of liquid. In addition to binding ingredients, agar acts as a binder in the gut. It absorbs bile and other toxins, making even the thickener, a functional ingredient. Add interest to gummy swallows by varying the base juice(s) and the various add-ins.

To make vitamin and mineral containing gummy bears

1 cup fresh juice (lemon, lime, pomegranate, grapefruit, orange, blood orange, carrot, beet, greens, pineapple, mango, passionfruit, elderberry, etc.)
1 ½ tsp agar powder
2 – 3 Tbsp sweetener

Optional add ins:
- 4 Tbsp ascorbic acid (approximately 500 mg ascorbic acid per 100 units)
- Other vitamins and minerals (grind up in a coffee grinder)
- Herbal supplements (either grind up tablets or use powder in capsules, discarding the capsule)
- Herbs in powdered form (grind up in coffee grinder)

1. Transfer juice and sweetener to a small sauce pan. Simmer over low heat for 5 minutes.
2. Add the agar and continue to simmer for 3 to 5 minutes while continuously stirring.
3. Turn off the heat and add in the optional ingredients; stir just enough to mix in the ingredients.
4. Allow to cool for 5 minutes and then using a large kitchen syringe, fill up the gummy molds and cool in the fridge for 15 to 20 minutes or until the gummies are set up.
5. Store in an airtight container in the fridge.
6. Makes enough gummies for one person for a 30 to 40 days.

Chapter 47

Make a natural toothpaste and tooth wash

Foods which tend to protect your teeth:
- Apples
- Cheese
- Crunchy vegetables
- Leafy greens
- Nuts

Foods which tend to stain and / or demineralize** your teeth:
- Coffee
- Teas
- Citrus fruit / juices *#
- Soda
- Berries
- Tomato sauce *~
- Charcoal+
- Red wine
- Artificially colored candies and sweets
- Turmeric
- Balsamic vinegar*
- Soy sauce
- Sugar**

*May weaken tooth enamel
**May demineralize teeth
\# Use a straw to protect teeth
~Eat alkaline foods such as vegetables before and after
+Abrasive, avoid charcoal-based toothpaste

Good habits for healthy teeth and gums:
- Regularly brush your teeth (at least 2x/d).
- Non-fluoride toothpaste, use herbal / clay types, avoid those with antibacterials, soaps, surfactants.
- Always brush and floss before going to bed.
- Only floss the teeth you want to keep.
- Gently brush in small circular motions using an extra soft toothbrush.
- Avoid overly zealous, aggressive brushing.
- Use a soft toothbrush.
- Schedule regular visits with your dentist.
- Make sure you are healthy.
- Ensure optimal levels of essential nutrients.
- Limit intake of sugary foods, simple starches.
- Avoid soda and sugary drinks, even sugar-free.
- Avoid smoking and all tobacco products.
- Coconut oil pulling provides beneficial effects.
- Swish and swallow colloidal silver before bed.
- After you drink an acidic beverage, rinse your mouth with water.
- Xylitol based sugar-free gum (if you chew).
- Avoid using toothpaste containing silica or zirconium which are abrasive.
- Consult a biological dentist if you have amalgam fillings, root canals and before getting a crown.
- Adequate vitamin C to keep gums healthy.

Address Acidic Environment (may lead to gum recession). Dip toothbrush in baking soda and gently brush and rinse. Make mouthwash of ¼ tsp of baking soda + ¼ cup of water; swish for 2 minutes before bed.

Finishing Wash – 3% Hydrogen Peroxide. Dip your clean toothbrush in hydrogen peroxide. Gently brush around your clean teeth and leave the hydrogen peroxide on your teeth for 30 seconds. Rinse with water and spit out. Dipping your toothbrush in hydrogen peroxide will also keep it clean.

Finishing Wash – Aloe Vera. After brushing, dip your clean toothbrush in aloe vera and gently brush around your clean teeth. You may leave aloe vera on your teeth and gums.

Mouth wash. Heat 1 quart water + 1 cup mint leaves +2 Tbsp coconut oil (strain out mint). Add 1 Tbsp baking soda and store until time to use. To use, add 2 Tbsp to a cup + 1-2 tsp hydrogen peroxide. Swish and spit.

Herbal rinses (using powders, extracts, tinctures, teas, etc.). Aloe, amla, black walnut, bloodroot, calendula, chamomile, clove, echinacea, goldenrod, goldenseal, grapefruit seed extract, oregano, peppermint, sage, star anise, etc. Any of these herbs may be added to the mouth wash recipe above.

Salt water mouth wash: 1 tsp salt + ½ tsp baking soda + ¼ cup warm water. Swish and spit several times.
Gum poultices. Use a combination of the following: white oak bark powder, black walnut powder, willow bark powder, plantain, myrrh gum powder, licorice root powder, vitamin E, psyllium powder (binder), peppermint, hawthorne, ascorbic acid, etc. Add enough hydrogen peroxide or water to make a paste.
Prevent Dry Mouth (may be caused by deficiencies of biotin, vitamin B12, riboflavin or vitamin A) – 5,000 mcg biotin once or twice per week or as needed, daily B12, riboflavin and vitamin A.
Finishing Gargle and Swallow. Finish gargling with 1 tablespoon of 10 ppm colloidal silver water; gargle for 60+ seconds and spit or swallow.
Freshen breath. Chew 1 clove (spit out after chewing), chew a small piece of fresh parsley, etc.
Nutrients. All essential vitamins and minerals, 4 grams ascorbic acid, 100 – 300 mg CoQ10, 2 g omega 3 fatty acids, 600 – 1800 mg NAC, 300 – 600 mg lipoic acid, prebiotic foods, arginine, boron, coconut oil, etc.
Quick Tooth Paste: 1 tsp baking soda + enough hydrogen peroxide to make a paste.
Avoid buying toothpaste with these ingredients: fluoride, triclosan, sodium laurel sulfate, artificial colors, titanium dioxide, abrasive ingredients such as charcoal, glycerin.
Buy a dental tool pack: in addition to brushing and flossing, <u>carefully</u> use these instruments to keep the spaces between your teeth and gums healthy between dental appointments.

Minty Natural Toothpaste

½ cup coconut oil
¼ tsp vitamin E oil
2 – 4 Tbsp baking soda
2 tsp borax (100% borax only)
2 Tbsp xylitol (birch sugar; fights against cavities)
2 – 4 Tbsp white kaolin clay or bentonite clay
1 – 2 drops trace minerals

1 tsp licorice root powder (may prevent tooth decay and gum disease)
2 Tbsp microcrystalline hydroxyapatite (animal product) or 1 tsp calcium powder
¼ tsp pink or sea salt
5 drops each organic food grade myrhh and peppermint oil
2 – 4 Tbsp warm water

Optional Ingredients

- ½ tsp agar or carrageenan powder or 1 tsp psyllium powder (optional – makes it thicker)
- 2 drops of one of the following food grade organic essential oils: clove bud, ginger, lemongrass oil, myrrh, oregano oil, spearmint leaf, star anise, tea tree, Thieves oil, etc.

1. Transfer dry ingredients and powders to a small electric coffee bean ginder. Blitz to a fine powder. Using a beater, beat all ingredients until smooth and fluffy; store in a sealable glass jar.
2. Before brushing, floss your teeth.
3. Using a soft tooth brush, brush for 3 to 5 minutes.
4. After brushing your teeth, dip your brush in aloe vera gel, hydrogen peroxide, or **Teeth Wash** and gently go over your gums and teeth (spit and rinse after using hydrogen peroxide).
5. Leave out coconut oil, essential oils and water; substitute dried, powdered mint for a dry version.

Tooth Wash and Remineralizing Rinse

14 – 16 oz Milk of Magnesia (MOM; plain)
1 Tbsp white kaolin clay or bentonite clay
Pinch psyllium powder (optional)

2 drops food grade organic peppermint oil
½ tsp arginine powder

1. Transfer ingredients to a glass mason jar and shake to combine. Use to brush or rinse your teeth.
2. Notes: If you want a thicker wash, add 1 Tbsp of Instant Clear Jel or 1 tsp of psyllium powder. Neither Instant Clear Jel nor psyllium powder require heat to thicken. Combine Instant Clear Jel with bentonite clay before whisking into a small amount of MOM and then add remaining MOM.

Chapter 48
Make colloidal silver

Silver is a valuable, precious metal. It is used to make collectible coins, jewelry, silverware, silver embedded bandages, and medical instruments. Silver exhibits the highest electrical conductivity, the highest thermal conductivity and the highest level of reflectivity of any metal. Silver is used in a variety of electronics and other heat transfer products. There is up to a 10,000% mark-up on commercial colloidal silver. It is much cheaper to buy silver bars and make your own silver generator. It takes about $40 to $50 to get started, including the price of the silver bars, which runs around $30.

Silver, a mineral known as 'Ag' on the periodic table, has been used for millennia as a purifier. Silver cups were traditionally used to purify water, silver coins placed in milk bottles have been used to extend the life of milk before refrigeration was widely available and today, colloidal silver (CS) is used for hundreds of reasons. Silver is not the only metal with antibacterial effects but it is the most effective metal exhibiting no toxicity to human cells. When antibiotics were discovered in 1928, the use of silver diminished. With the emergence of antibiotic resistant strains of bacteria, silver has re-emerged as a viable and effective treatment for bacteria, viruses, fungi and even protozoa.

Regarding the increasingly widespread use of CS, some have observed a disconnect between allopathic medicine practitioners and CS users. Allopathic physicians almost never recommend CS, even for simple applications. However, if you talk to silver users, they energetically recommend CS for a wide range of applications. Many users make their own CS.

This information could literally save you money, aggravation, and lost time spent treating infections. Never underestimate the value of CS in boosting you back to health and preventing prolonged, miserable periods of illness. As a disclaimer, the information in this chapter is not intended to take the place of regular visits with your primary health care practitioner(s). As always, consult with your primary health care practitioner(s) before you begin any new therapy.

How does CS work? In part, the particle size of silver determines the basis of its cellular actions. Silver likely utilizes one or more of its unique properties as a nano-sized mineral to attack bacteria, viruses, fungi and other harmful organisms, while leaving useful cells intact (PMID: 29808627).

Korean researchers (PMID 18245232) demonstrated a silver ion solution significantly reduced *S. aureus* and *E. coli* bacteria concentrations after just 90 minutes of exposure to silver. Microscopic analysis of the silver-cultured bacteria indicated considerable changes in the integrity of bacterial membranes, which they attribute to bacterial cell death. The antibacterial effect of silver may be the result of silver's interactions with cellular amino acids and enzymes. Silver ions cause the release of potassium ions from bacteria, leading to membrane damage and eventually death. Silver inhibits bacterial growth. These same researchers also demonstrated the effectiveness of a silver ion emitting washing machine in preventing the transmission of bacteria and fungi via contaminated laundry, even in the absence of a detergent, silver ions significantly reduced E. coli. In another study (PMID 27899918), researchers showed silver nanoparticles to be a potent antibacterial agent. They proposed several mechanisms of action including inhibiting the growth of bacteria, interfering with bacterial gene expression, adhesion and penetration of the bacterial cell membranes, generating free radicals within microbial cells (leading to cell death), and altering signaling pathways. There is evidence demonstrating the smallest silver particles (in the nanometer range) are more effective than larger particles (possibly acting by adhering to virus' DNA).

In addition to silver's effects on bacteria and fungi, it is effective against viruses. For example, small nanoparticle sized silver has been shown in vitro, to inhibit replication of the HIV-1 virus and hepatitis B virus (PMID: 27036553).

On the human cell side of the equation, silver particles may modulate the human immune system by acutely upregulating the inflammatory response, which is another mechanism used to attack pathogenic microorganisms. Silver exhibits selective toxicity for pathogenic microorganisms while sparing healthy cells.

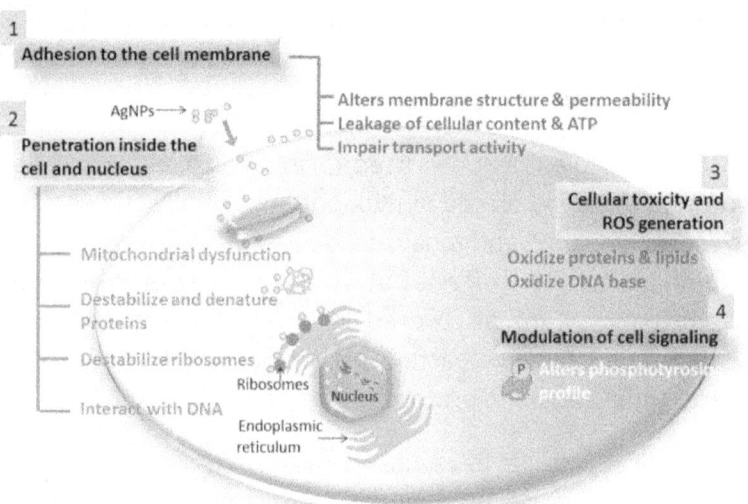

Colloidal Silver, Figure 1.
The four most prominent routes of antimicrobial action of silver nanoparticles

1. Silver nanoparticles adhere to microbial cell surfaces resulting in membrane damage and altered transport activity.
2. Silver nanoparticles penetrate inside microbial cells and interact with cellular organelles and biomolecules, thereby, affecting respective cellular machinery.
3. Silver nanoparticles cause an increase in reactive oxygen species inside microbial cells leading to cell damage.
4. Silver nanoparticles modulate cellular signaling systems causing cell death. (PMID 27899918).

To make colloidal silver, you need the following:
- Approximately 20+ inches of 8 gauge, 0.999% or 0.9999% pure silver wire.
- Distilled water
- Half gallon mason jar OR a new drip coffee maker glass carafe.
- Two alligator clips with metal clamps on both ends of each wire.
- One of the following power sources:
    - Method 1: 1 6-volt battery,
    - Method 2: 4 9-volt batteries connected in series, or
    - Method 3: 1 12-volt power supply or a 30-volt, 200 mA power supply
- Total dissolved solids (TDS) meter, used to confirm strength – you are aiming for 10 – 20 ppm.

To assemble, transfer 2 quarts distilled water into container. Bend tops of silver bars just enough so they rest on opposite sides of the glass jar. Silver bars should not touch each other. Attach each of the alligator clips to bent end of silver bars. Attach loose ends of the alligator clips, one to the positive anode and one to the negative cathode of your power source. If using AC, plug in the power source and start timer for 30 minutes. If using battery power (DC), you are now generating energy; the process has begun. Check concentration of silver in the water every 30 minutes using the TDS until desired strength is reached. As the process of electrolysis progresses, one bar usually remains silvery and the other bar looks fuzzy. Do not touch either bar until the process is complete. When completed, gently remove the silver bars and using a rubber sponge, clean the bars and store them in a dry place. Allow large pieces of oxidized silver to drop to the bottom and pour off the remainder of clear silver water for consumption. Store in clear or amber glass jars. Gently shake before using.

Chapter 49
Activated charcoal

Charcoal has a strong negative charge and binds molecules and compounds with a positive charge. Charcoal is a porous carbon skeleton network, with incredible surface area for a**d**sorption of toxins with a positive charge. A**d**sorption can be compared to a wet sponge which picks up dirt on your kitchen counter. The dirt adheres and you wash it out under running water. A**b**sorption is when you add water to cornstarch and the starch a**b**sorbs water and swells. Charcoal forms a stable toxin-charcoal complex which is large enough to avoid absorption in the gut and exits the body via the intestines.

Charcoal carries oxygen in its porous structure which also helps oxidize toxins drawn into the carbon network. Used in water filtration systems, charcoal is antimicrobial. Activated charcoal is produced with high temperatures, steam, CO_2, etc., to remove impurities and create small particles. One gram of activated charcoal has a surface area of 1,000 m^2 to 3,500 m^2 (PMCID: PMC1306980).

Another recently described mechanism of charcoal is the "mechanism of action including 'back diffusion' and disruption of enterohepatic loops (PMCID: PMC1306980)." Repeated charcoal doses prevent toxins that may enter the enterohepatic circulation (a route taking some compounds from the liver via bile acids to the small intestine and then reabsorption back into the body in the lower small intestine) from the systemic circulation by adsorbing the toxins and preventing their re-entry into the systemic circulation. The entero-hepatic loop is the only route of elimination for cholesterol, the precursor to making bile acids. Soluble fibers and charcoal bind bile acids and toxins which may be present in bile acids, and remove them from the body via the intestinal tract. Binders such as soluble fibers including psyllium husks, oats, apples, etc., and compounds such as bentonite clay and silica may aid in removing toxins via interrupting the enterohepatic circulation.

Timing: Take at least one hour before taking meds, supplements or meals; take two hours after a meal or meds.

Dosing: 1 – 2 grams for most conditions. 10 – 25 grams for therapeutic interventions, 50 – 100 grams as antidote for poisoning (10 – 25 grams for children). Take with at least 16 ounces of water.

Forms: powder, tablets, capsules.

Sources of activated charcoal: coconut shells, bamboo, wood, coal, petroleum, bone char, etc.

When to orally use activated charcoal (internal):
- Immediately after ingesting a suspected poison.
- Drug overdose (effective for some drugs) – only effective when the drug is in stomach.
- For inflammation.
- Indigestion, bloating, excessive intestinal gas.
- May lower high cholesterol when taken at high doses on a regular basis (first check w/ your MD).
- As one aspect of a detoxification protocol.
- Prophylactic use for animals – 1 teaspoon in food or water once or twice per month.
- Take during a cold or viral infection.

- Allergies, histamine sensitivity. For a peanut allergy after consuming peanuts, immediately consuming charcoal <u>may</u> form complexes with peanut proteins, binding them after accidental ingestion. **This should not be construed as permission to eat peanuts.** (PMID: 12847195)
- Neonatal jaundice (under care of a physician).
- Itchy skin.
- To reduce elevated serum levels of systemically absorbed drugs or poisons (only done under the care of a physician) (PMCID: PMC1306980).
- If required to get a vaccine(s), oral charcoal may help detox from vaccine adjuvants.
- Charcoal and glutamine are beneficial for chemotherapy-induced diarrhea (PMCID: PMC6247548)
- The liver aids the body in detoxification. It aids excretion of toxins via the kidneys and intestinal tract. Activated charcoal assists the liver in detox functions by removing toxins found in enterohepatic circulation.

Best poultice recipe (charcoal patch): 2 Tbsp activated charcoal, ¼ cup water, ½ tsp psyllium husk powder. Combine and stir for 1 minute. Place on sticky side up using press and seal plastic wrap, place charcoal mixture and another piece of plastic wrap on top; roll into a thin sheet, about ¼ inch thick and freeze for 15 minutes. Using some old cloth, secure the charcoal patch to the skin, placing another piece of cloth over the top. Secure with plastic wrap and an ace bandage. See this video for extended details not included here. https://charcoalhouse.com/psyllium-husk-powder-organic.html

When to use a charcoal poultice (external):
- Skin infections, for wound healing.
- Venomous bites (use as an adjunct and not as the primary treatment – you must seek immediate medical care if you have been envenomated by a poisonous vector).

Using charcoal in beverages and food:
- Charcoal combined with food is an anti-nutrient, meaning it reduces the absorption of some essential nutrients, prescription meds, herbals, and others.
- When charcoal is used as ingredient in beverages and / or food, it decreases the absorption of some nutrients such as calcium, which has a positive charge. When adding charcoal to food, avoid combining with highly nutritious foods. Keep in mind, a significant amount of ingested calcium is not absorbed. It is unclear whether combining charcoal with calcium and other mineral-rich foods significantly alters calcium and mineral absorption from usual levels, but it is prudent to avoid the potential for a negative interaction.
- Occasionally, small amounts of charcoal may be used to color beverages and food when used or in a targeted way such as charcoal lemonade, charcoal waffles, charcoal bread, etc.

Charcoal not useful for the following conditions:
- Whitening teeth – may damage teeth.
- Drug poisoning due to ingestion of: alcohol, heavy metals, cyanide, iron, lithium, potassium, acid or alkali poisonings, opioids, DDT boric acid, mineral acids, N-methyl carbamate, malathion, electrolytes, methanol, tolbutamide (PMCID: PMC1306980).
- Do not combine with sorbitol or magnesium citrate.
- Do not use orally with a person not able to swallow or who might choke or vomit including persons who are drowsy or semi-conscious. Avoid aspirating charcoal to the lungs. This risk is lessened with the use of charcoal tablets or capsules.
- People with variegate porphyria should not use charcoal.
- Severe constipation, bowel perforation or blockage, or holes in the bowel.

Chapter 50
Medicine cabinet herbs and other items

Herbal remedies have largely remained in the realm of unlicensed practitioners (which is mostly a good thing considering the cost of herbal remedies would skyrocket if it were possible to patent common plants and their uses). It is also good to keep nutrients and herbals available as over-the-counter options, as opposed to limiting their availability through licensed practitioners. They have not proven to be detrimental or toxic in commonly used doses. It is arguably better to accept the rare instance of a non-lethal over-dose on an herbal product rather than limit their availability, which would lead directly to much greater concerns related to their unavailability. This is in comparison to medical errrors related to prescription meds, where around 100,000 people die every year and 7 million are negatively impacted by prescription errors. In fact, severely restricting herbals is not possible because they are easily grown in one's backyard.

Allopathic medicine (i.e., Western medicine based on prescribing pharmaceuticals and performing life-saving measures to repair broken bodies and treat debilitating symptoms, etc.) has established deep roots in modern society. Many aspects of allopathic medicine are rooted in restoring health, but probably an equal number or more, result in a lower health index and not enhanced or better health. This trend may continue in its present form for decades to come. It is unknown how much naturopathic, nutritional, herbal and other natural approaches to restoring health may influence allopathic medicine in the future. However, herbal remedies and other natural approaches to restoring health and achieving wellness (e.g., nutritional, lifestyle, orthomolecular, naturopathy, integrative and functional approaches), are gaining in acceptance and may serve to enhance and positively modify allopathic approaches. For example, when diagnosed with cancer, many people are re-thinking the cut, burn, and poison philosophy of treating solid tumors. This is because of growing evidence of effective natural therapies. If the evidences were not there, we would never see people seeking out alternative cancer therapies. When natural therapies work, they are either dismissed as a false positive (i.e., it was never cancer to begin with) or the cancer would have regressed no matter the intervention. Just based on my experiences, allopathic practitioners are uncomfortable with accepting natural approaches outside of their scope of practice. Many consider energy medicine, homeopathy, herbs, orthomolecular approaches, and even lifestyle modifications to be either unnecessary or even harmful. This may be due to very different reading and study materials.

For more than two decades, it has been my philosophy, **to make the body so healthy it cannot harbor disease**. This philosophy drives my nutritional, integrative, functional and ortho-molecular practice. It is an essential aspect of how I approach and understand methods used to guide my clients to health. I view the restoration of health as a default type setting. If enough of the foundational and constitutional components of restoring health are put into place at roughly the same time, the body realigns itself to a higher level of functioning. Oftentimes, clients are surprised at the list of recommendations. Unfortunately, it takes an equal effort to restore health compared to the effort it took to destroy one's health. This is why every meal, every activity (or lack of activity), every lifestyle factor, every thought, every action matters. If your life includes frequent or chronic stress, poor food choices, poor lifestyle choices, negative thoughts, no time for spiritual reflection and prayer, energy imbalances (illustrated by under or over-weight), and other types of factors which tend to tear down and not build up your constitution, then you are likely faced with a long upward battle to regain your health. For some, restoration occurs relatively fast but for most, it takes commitment, perseverance and time.

Some things you cannot control. If your mother was malnourished, smoked or used drugs before and during your gestation (pregnancy), you may not achieve your full genetic potential or you may suffer from one or more chronic conditions as an adult. This is known as the Fetal Origins Hypothesis. This may show up as short height, heart disease, type 2 diabetes, etc.

It is not easy to choose a non-allopathic (complementary and alternative medicine options) treatment course when you are faced with serious illness. Most health care plans do not cover naturopathy or lifestyle-oriented programs. They certainly do not cover herbal remedies.

While it is not necessary to be a trained and licensed herbal medicine expert to take advantage of the hundreds, if not thousands, of plant-based remedies growing all over our incredible planet, it is a good idea to find people who have practiced and used herbal remedies for many decades to help guide your choices. <u>Always consult your regular healthcare provider before starting a new therapy</u>.

There are several ways to learn more about herbal therapies. You may enroll in an herbal and natural medicine degree. If you are not ready to get a degree in herbal medicine or naturopathy, you may read and learn about the various herbs and how they are used. Most herbalists are self-trained

Some Herbal Resource Books
- Principles and Practice of Phytotherapy, 2nd ed., By K. Bone and S. Mills, 2013.
- Medical Herbalism: the Science and Practice of Herbal Medicine by D. Hoffman, 2003.
- Textbook of Natural Medicine, 4th ed., by J.E. Pizzorno, 2012.
- Encyclopedia of Herbal Medicine by A. Chevaltier, 2016.
- The Modern Herbal Dispensatory: a Medicine-making Guide by T. Easley and S. Horne, 2016.
- Herbal Antibiotics by S.H. Buhner, 2012.
- Herbal Formularies for Health Professionals, Vol 1, Digestion and Absorption by J. Stansbury, 2018

and rely on tradition as well as newer scientific information. The simple concept of, "the dose is what makes the poison," is always relevant. Even water, when consumed in excess, is deadly. Almost every plant on the planet is toxic at a certain dose. This is why small amounts of herbs can be very effective when taken either singly or in combination with other herbs and essential compounds. This list is not inclusive of every single therapeutic herb. It is a starting point for collecting herbs to add to your Country Living Medicine Cabinet. ***<u>Disclaimer: These statements have not been evaluated by the Food and Drug Administration. Any product mentioned is not intended to diagnose, treat, cure or prevent any disease</u>.***

A – B

Agrimony (*Agrimonia eupatoria*). Member of rose family. Also known as cocklebur and liverwort. Flowering plant reaches 3 – 4 feet. Rhizome roots. Yellow flowers. Known for sore throat, stopping bleeding, sleep, boost immunity, diarrhea, gargle, bacterial infections, etc.

Alfalfa (*Medicago sativa*). <u>While alfalfa is a highly nutritious food, the seeds contain the amino acid canavanine. This amino acid competes with arginine and is associated with the development of lupus, kidney troubles, immune issues, and hemolytic anemia.</u> I have included it in this section to make it clear there are risks associated with **alfalfa seeds**. It may also cause severe issues for animals. Because of this, I urge caution in using alfalfa seeds. If you have found the alfalfa herb to be beneficial, you may make an infusion / tea, tincture, fluid extract, powder, sprouts. Fresh is best for internal use. Applications may include: lowering fever, detoxification, anti-stroke, neutralize intestinal carcinogens, lowers cholesterol, alkalization, balances blood glucose, hormone adaptogenic, promotes pituitary functions, diuretic, anti-fungal, anti-inflammatory, helps reduce bleeding, ulcers, skin disorders, digestive system, arthritis, improves appetite, reduces edema, etc. **Warning: Alfalfa contains coumarins and vitamin K, making it an effective anti-coagulant. Use with caution if you have anemia. Also, alfalfa contains saponin, which can cause GI distress in animals, especially horses and dogs. If allergic to pollen, use alfalfa in its pre-bloom state. Pregnant women (and really everyone) should avoid alfalfa seeds.**

Allspice (*Pimenta dioica*). Flavor profile similar to cinnamon, nutmeg and ginger. Berries dried and ground into a powder. Contains an anesthetic compound - eugenol. Use for toothache. Antioxidant.

Aloe vera (*Aloe barbadensis-miller*). Aloe vera is a plant which produces several types of gels and a latex coming from the leaves. It is 99% water and 1% solid content including over 75 vitamins and minerals. The outer 18 layers are composed of chloroplasts. Contains 10 various carbohydrates, including glucose, arabinose, xylose, mannose, galactose, etc. It may be used to make a tincture, made into a powder, and in found in pill form. Fresh is best for external use. Applications include: constipation, anti-bacterial, antioxidant, promotes skin healing, helps with burns, psoriasis, antifungal, laxative, improves circulation, speeds wound healing, acne, may reduce blood glucose, insect bites and stings, gastritis, hyperacidity, may reduce the harmful effects of exposure to radioactivity, etc. Interactions may include: Using with digoxin may cause toxicity. Warnings may include: Aloe latex, used to treat constipation, is likely unsafe in doses of 1 or more grams / day. Do not use during pregnancy or lactation.

Amla fruits (*Phyllanthus emblica*). Widely used in India. High in vitamin C. It is used as a powder, tea, tincture, etc. Applications are widely believed to include: cholesterol lowering, heartburn, diarrhea, nausea, hair growth stimulant, anti-aging, beautiful skin, improved eyesight, immune-stimulant, etc. Considered safe for short term usage up to 1,000 mg / day. Scientific literature does not support all claims. Warnings: may worsen constipation if inadequate water consumed. Avoid if bleeding disorder. May decrease blood glucose levels. Stop taking if pregnant, lactating, preparing for surgery.

Angelica (*Angelica archangelica*). Use root and leaf. Roots may be used to make a flour. May be prepared as an infusion, decoction, tincture, extract, or powder. Applications may include: improved circulation, warms the body, causes distaste for alcohol, stimulates appetite, anti-bacterial, relieves gas, helps with heartburn, arthritis, stroke, dementia, muscle spasms, stimulates kidney actions, good for gastro-intestinal tract, stimulates gastric juices, ulcers, vomiting, stomach cramps, intermittent fever, nervous headache, colic, general weakness, lung diseases, coughs, colds, fevers, runny nose, insomnia. Use externally for rheumatism. Warning: Avoid using large doses. Diabetics should avoid using angelica. Avoid direct sun exposure after using. May be confused with European water hemlock which is poisonous.

Anise (*Pimpinella anisum*). A mild spice known as an aphrodisiac. Anti-flatulence. Anti-spasmodic. Stimulates the pancreas. Affects hormones. Helps coughs, expectorant, thins mucus. Helps with insomnia.

Apricot kernels. An apricot kernel is the seed found inside of the seed of an apricot. This seed kernel is used to make pressed oils, amaretto biscuits, etc. The oil is rich in vitamin E. Also contains a compound known as amygdalin. It is known to contain small amounts of cyanide, a known toxin. Long-term exposure may lead to negative effects on the heart and brain (both central and peripheral nervous systems). Most retailers selling apricot seeds recommend consuming no more than 1 – 3 kernels per day and children should avoid. Always check with your physician for the best practice in consuming novel substances such as apricot kernels.

Arnica (*Arnica montana*). Use as a tincture (add to a footbath to relieve sore feet), cream, salve, pills (homeopathic is ok). Applications include: bruises, sore joints, sore muscles, sprains, acne, boils, etc. Warning: do not take internally, has an irritant effect on the stomach. Avoid putting on open wounds. Arnica can be unsafe taken by mouth, even though it is a flavoring ingredient. You can find homeopathic arnica pills in some health food stores. <u>Consult your physician before consuming arnica.</u>

Asafoetida (*Ferula asafoetida*). A common Indian spice. The powder is used in Indian cooking to add a distinct sour flavor. Also thought to stabilize mental health, calm nerves, reduce anxiety, reduce cholesterol, anti-flatulence, intestinal cramping, anti-parasite, insect bites, repel insects, coughing, etc. Pregnant women should avoid.

Ascorbic acid. Used in almost every situation to improve conditions related to out-of-control oxidative stress. Recommended intakes are 1,000 to 20,000 mg / day or to bowel tolerance.

Ashwagandha (*Withania somnifera*). Usually in the form of a powder or liquid extract. Considered an adaptogen and antioxidant. Used to address the following issues: fatigue, memory, blood glucose, stress, immunity, libido, strengthen immune system, as a mild sedative, increases vitality, may help regulate blood glucose, male fertility, reduce stress, stimulates the thyroid, Parkinson's, Alzheimer's disease, etc. Warnings: stop taking at least 2 weeks before surgery. May increase thyroid levels. Combine with rhodiola and tulsi for a tea.

Astragalus (*Huang chi*). Targets spleen, kidneys, lungs, blood. Use the root. Applications may include: lowering fever, improving digestion, improving immune system, aids adrenal functions, increasing metabolism, increasing blood supply, promotes healing, combats fatigue, insomnia, anti-viral, anti-bacterial, antinflam-matory, may increase telomerase activity (assoc with longevity), lowers blood glucose, lowers lipids, adaptogenic, improves heart function, increased metabolism, etc. Warning: high doses may suppress immune system, otherwise considered safe.

Bacopa (*Bacopa Monnieri*). Forms may include: capsules, tablets, etc. Applications may include: Alzheimer's disease, cognitive functions, anxiety, seizure disorders, insomnia, etc. Bacopa is serotonergic. May slow heart rate, reduced GI motility, could worsen lung conditions, etc. Avoid use during pregnancy and lactation.

Baking soda (sodium bicarbonate). Used as a powder, salve or body scrub. Add to food and water. Applications may include: natural anti-acid, treats acid reflux, apply to itchy skin, deodorant, may slow progression of kidney disease, soak produce in baking soda water to remove pesticides, alkalizing, exercise enhancer, alleviates urinary tract infections, gout, anti-fungal, anti-bacterial, exfoliator, itchy skin, etc.

Barley grass (*Hordeum vulgare*). Provides vitamins, fiber, beta-glucan, protein, vitamins and minerals.

Beet root powder (*Beta vulgaris*). Applications may include: aphrodisiac, good circulation, heart conditions, cognitive functions, etc. One tsp beet powder is roughly equivalent to eating one beet.

Bentonite clay similar to Fuller's earth (use food grade for internal consumption). Other clays include: French green clay, kaolin clay, Moroccan clay, Rhassoul clay, and sea clay. Healing clay, assumed to bind to toxins. Most bentonite clay comes from Wyoming. Regular bentonite clay contains lead and should not be consumed but may be used as a face mask, soaking baths, etc.

Bergamot (*Citrus bergamia*). A citrus fruit, native to South Asia, but also grows in Southern states where other citrus trees grow. Fruit is sour and bitter. Forms are essential oil, aromatherapy, extract, capsules. Applications may include: lowers cholesterol, used with UV light to treat skin fungal infections, preventive for lice and other parasites, psoriasis, reduces skin inflammation, scent may reduce anxiety, etc. Warnings: increases skin sensitivity to sunlight. Direct application may cause severe sunburn, rashes and blisters.

Bitters (e.g., artichoke, chamomile, gentian, milk thistle, motherwort, goldenrod, myrrh, dandelion, burdock). Bitters botanical formulas which are used as leaves, flowers, stems, roots, liquid, extract tincture, powder, pills, salve, etc. Use when the liver is under stress due to toxic exposures such as heavy metals, new carpet, formaldehyde, gasoline, kerosene, pesticides, solvents, adhesives, glues, fabric softener, cleaning agents, medications, etc. For example, the liver breaks down excess histamine. When the liver is under stress, it may not rapidly clear histamine. This may lead to symptoms. Bitters may improve the ability of the liver to naturally remove toxins. If you suffer from frequent heartburn, take bitters in water or tea before a meal. Applications: stimulates secretion of hydrochloric acid and bile production, improves digestion, lessens heartburn and reflux, heartburn, bloating, gas, etc. Warnings: avoid if you have gastritis, a peptic ulcer, gallbladder disease or kidney disease.

Black walnut (*Juglans nigra*). Applications may include: anti-parasite, insecticide, etc.

Black cohosh (*Cimicifuga racemosa*). Applications include: menstrual problems, recovery from childbirth, hot flashes. Warnings: do not take regularly for more than 6 months.

Blackstrap molasses. Blackstrap molasses is approx.-imately 10% minerals by weight. It is a great way to consume and replete minerals. It is good for anemia of pregnancy and iron deficiency anemia. If interested, read about the Boston Molasses Disaster in 1919. 13 tons of molasses burst out of a storage tower in Boston, killing 21, injuring 150 people.

Boron / borax (mineral). Forms: powder, tablet, etc. Applications may include: menstrual cramps, yeast infections, osteoarthritis, osteoporosis, baths, etc. Warnings: do not exceed 20 mg/d, avoid if kidney issues.

Bromelain. Group of enzymes found in pineapple flesh. The highest amount of bromelain is found in the pineapple stem and in fresh pineapple juice. Bromelain is anti-inflammatory. It is used post-operatively to ease the pain after surgery. The manganese in fresh pineapple juice is claimed to sharpen the outlines of internal organs on MRIs (33488688, 32832119, 15569640, 25245815).

Buckthorn (*Rhamnus frangula*). Forms include tea, oil, concentrates. Applications may include gastrointestinal, blood pressure, heart conditions, complements cancer therapies, boosts immunity, obesity, etc. Warnings: may act as blood thinner, may increase risk of bleeding. Interactions: may interact with meds used to treat GI disorders, arrhythmias, cancer and autoimmune disorders. Avoid using if pregnant or breastfeeding.

Burdock (*Arctium lappa*). Cultivated for its leaves and roots, tinctures, powder, tablets, etc. Considered invasive in some regions. Applications may include: treating poison ivy / oak, parasites, diuretic, sore throat, colds, diaphoretic, blood purifying agent, increases urine flow, increases sweating, useful in detox, reduces pain and swelling, treats burns, etc. Warnings: avoid if allergic to marigolds / ragweed, of child-bearing age, lactating, etc. <u>Do not confuse with poisonous rhubarb leaves.</u>

Butterbur (*Petasites hybridus*). Leaves, roots, flowers and stems used medicinally; found as a powder, pill, tea, tincture. Dosage: 50 to 75 mg twice/day. Functions as anti-spasmodic, anti-inflammatory, heart tonic, diuretic, diaphoretic, and leaves are analgesic. Used for: headache, emotional distress, eczema, itchy eyes, seasonal allergies, runny nose (rhinitis), nasal congestion. Warnings: compounds found in butterbur are toxic and cause liver damage. Consult your physician before using.

C – D

Calendula (*Calendula officinalis*). Forms: flowers, oil, salve, lotion, extract, soap, liniment, tinctures, ointments, washes, baths, balm. Functions: anti-inflammatory, promotes wound healing, anti-bacterial, anti-fungal, stimulates bile, stimulates menstrual flow, stimulates lymph, etc. Applications: promotes digestion, insect repellant, burns, rashes, ear infections, pressure ulcers, muscle spasms, reduce fever, skin inflammation, wound healing, gum inflammation, diaper rash, anal tears, etc. Warnings: avoid using if pregnant, lactating, avoid using if sensitive to ragweed.

Cannabis (*Cannabis sativa*). Forms: CBD and THC oil, etc. Applications may include: nausea and vomiting from chemotherapy, muscle spasms, chronic pain, stroke, weight gain, etc.

Caraway (*Carum carvi*). Forms include oil, fruit, seeds. Seeds used in cooking and baking. Applications may include: indigestion, irritable bowel syndrome, obesity, etc. May lower blood glucose. Interactions: caraway with peppermint oil may cause excessive burping, heartburn and nausea. May increase absorption of iron. Avoid using 2 wks before surgery.

Cardamom (*Elettaria cardamomum*). Member of ginger family. It is widely used in Indian cooking and baking. Functions may include: anti-spasmodic, antibacterial. Applications may include: reduce swelling, boosts immune system, may improve fatty liver, may lower blood glucose, may lower triglycerides, may lower blood pressure, may help with obesity, etc. Avoid during pregnancy and with gall stones.

Carob aka locust pods (*Ceratonia siliqua*). High content of isobutyric acid. Used to be a primary source of sugar until cane sugar became widely available. Used as a substitute for chocolate. Contains theobromine. Carob seeds were used by Romans as a weight comparison for gold. One gold coin weighed the same as a carob seed, hence the label of 24-carat or pure gold.

Castor oil (*Ricinus communis*). Castor oil is a unique vegetable oil, comprised mainly of ricinolenic acid. Forms include: poultice, salves, balm, oil, etc. Functions as: anti-inflammatory, antimicrobial. Applications include: laxative, improves the appearance of hair, improves immune system, stimulates lymphatic system, joint pain, induces labor, etc. Warnings: used to induce labor, so avoid internal use during pregnancy unless directed by your physician.

Catnip (*Nepeta cataria*). Form: leaves, young shoots, tea, tinctures, poultice. Applications may include: anxiety, relaxant, upset stomach, supports digestion, poultice may reduce swelling, bug repellant. Warnings: avoid if pregnant or lactating unless other-wiseadvised by your MD/DO.

Cats claw (*Uncaria tomentosa*). Form is extract, pills. Dose is 100 to 300 mg / day. May be used in the following applications: antiviral, antibacterial, anti-fungal, anti-proliferative, anti-inflammatory, good for intestinal support, promotes wound healing, osteoarthritis, rheumatoid arthritis, etc. Warnings: may cause headaches, dizziness, vomiting, over-stimulation of the immune system, decrease clotting, lower blood pressure, may worsen leukemia, stop taking 2 weeks before surgery. Avoid if pregnant/ lactating.

Cayenne pepper (*Capsicum annuum*). Truly a medicine cabinet essential. Usual forms utilized include: powder, whole pepper, extracts, Cool Cayenne 100,000 Heat-units, etc. Functions as an anti-inflammatory. Applications may include: pain, stabilizing arteries (i.e., spasms), clotting, improves circulation, aids digestion, increases metabolism, good for Raynaud's disease, arthritis, rheumatism, detoxification, improves immunity, increase fertility, anti-parasitic.

Chamomile (*Chamomilla recutita* or *Chamaemelum nobile*). Forms: tea, dried flowers, powder, tincture, elixirs, gargle, bath water, hair care, etc. Functions may include: anti-inflammatory, antioxidant, astringent, etc. Applications may include: promotes healing, relaxation, anti-cramping, toothache, ear-ache, neuralgia, swelling, anxiety, depression, eye infections, blocked tear ducts, for insomnia, may reduce nightmares, eczema, hemorrhoids, burns, itchy skin, psoriasis, indigestion. Warning: avoid if sensitive to ragweed.

Chaparral (*Larrea tridentata*). Has a terrible taste. Warnings: may lead to liver and kidney toxicity. **Limit to topical use only.**

Charcoal (see chapter on charcoal).

Chickweed (*Stellaria media*). Forms: ointments, decoctions, extracts, teas. Functions: anti-inflammatory. Applications may include: ulcers, abscess, edema, digestion, constipation, asthma, respiratory infections, weight loss. Warnings: avoid excess oral consumption, it causes toxicity at higher doses (including animals).

Chicory (*Cichorium intybus*). Leaves, seeds and roots used. Chicoric acid may be active ingredient. Applications may include mild laxative, increases bile, decreases swelling, osteoarthritis, high blood pressure, heart failure, constipation, liver disorders, gallbladder disorders, cancer, skin inflam-mation, poor appetite, upset stomach, etc. Source of beta-carotene. Warning: may cause gas, allergy (ragweed family), may lower blood glucose, stimulates bile production, stop taking chicory 2 weeks before surgery. No known severe interactions.

Cinnamon, Ceylon (*Cinnamomum zeylanicum* and *Cinnamon cassia*). Forms: bark, powder, extract, decoctions, tea, beverages, baking, cooking, etc. Functions include: antioxidant, antidiabetic, anti-microbial, antifungal. Applications may include: weight loss, increased metabolic rate, improved blood glucose control, improves colon functions, increases blood circulation, tissue regeneration, upregulates BDNF, may protect against Parkinson's disease, reduces plaque seen in Alzheimer's disease, aids insulin, helps maintain good blood pressure, etc. Warnings: if you consume cassia cinnamon, avoid more than 1 to 2 teaspoons or 9 grams / day due to high coumarin content. Use of cinnamon supplements can alter liver enzymes, thin the blood and change kidney functions (pharmacytimes.com). Ceylon cinnamon is lower in coumarins compared to more common *cassia* cinnamon.

Citric acid. Organic acid obtained from limes and lemons. Also referred to as alpha hydroxy acid. Chelates metals. May be used to soften hard water.

Citicholine (CDP-choline). May increase dopamine receptor densities. May elevate acetylcholine. May influence the hormones: luteinizing hormone, growth hormone, and thyroid stimulating hormone.

Colloidal silver (CS). Learn how to make your own CS using either a 6-volt battery, 4 9-volt batteries or an AC power supply. You need alligator clips, colloidal silver bars, distilled water and a glass jar. Colloidal silver may be used externally and internally. Nebulize it, drink it, spray it on your skin, drop it in your eyes, treat ear infections, etc.

Comfrey (*Symphytum officinale*). Forms: leaves and roots used to make salves, ointments, liniments, etc. Functions: expectorant. Applications: wound healing, wound healing, soothing to irritated tissues, etc. Warning: FDA banned manufacturers of dietary supplements from adding comfrey to supplements d/t danger of liver damage and possible role as a cancer-causing agent.

Dandelion (*Taraxacum officinale*). Forms: leaves, flowers, roots, extract, teas, tincture, decoctions, salads, baths, powders, poultices, beverages, etc. Functions as: anti-inflammatory, anti-itching, diuretic, blocks UVB sunlight. Applications may include: eczema, heartburn, gastrointestinal functions, edema, stimulates insulin production, etc. Warnings: avoid if sensitive to ragweed, chrysanthemums, marigold, latex. Pregnant and lactating women should avoid.

Diatomaceous earth/DE (fossilized remains of aquatic organisms known as diatoms; primarily composed of silica). Form: light powder. Applications may include: against bed bugs, cockroaches, crickets, fleas, ticks, spiders; expelling GI parasites; a source of silica, etc. Use only food grade DE for internal use.

DMSO – dimethyl sulfoxide. Forms: gel, lotion, IV. Functions: easily absorbed into skin. Applications may include: anti-inflammatory (NSAID), antioxidant, transdermal carrier, pain, analgesic, bladder infections, shingles, etc. Some advocate using DMSO immediately after a stroke to dissolve blood clots. Warnings: safe when prescribed by a physician. Avoid industrial grade due to possible contaminants. Readily permeates skin and carries whatever it is combined with including toxins. May cause dry skin, headache, dizziness, drowsiness, nausea, vomiting, diarrhea, constipation, breathing issues, vision issues, blood problems, allergic reactions, etc. May cause "garlic" breath and body odor.

Dong quai (*Angelica sinensis*). Forms: leaves and roots. Applications may include: hypertension, heart conditions, menopausal symptoms, etc. Interactions: Dong quai may heighten effects of other medications, especially anticoagulant and antiplatelet.

E – G

Echinacea (*Echinacea purpurea, angustifolia, pallida*). Forms: powder, capsules, teas, tinctures, juice, decoctions, etc. Applications may include: shortening period of cold symptoms, reducing severity of common cold symptoms, infections, anxiety, eczema, etc. Warnings. Some may experience temporary tongue tingling after consuming in a beverage, avoid if you have autoimmune disorder. Echinacea may decrease how caffeine is eliminated. Avoid taking echinacea with other medications.

Elderberries (*Sambucus nigra*). Forms: berries must be cooked, syrup, jam, candy, tea, extract, wine, etc. May function as: antioxidant, etc. Applications may include: flu, infections, headache, laxative, diuretic, lower lipids, lowers blood pressure, increase insulin secretion, gastric ulcers, anti-depressant, etc. Warnings: bark, unripe berries and seeds may cause stomach problems. Fresh berries contain small amounts of cyanogenic glycosides (can release cyanide). Cooked berries are not problematic. Be sure you have correctly identified the plant as American or European elderberry. Other elderberries are more toxic. Pregnant and lactating women should avoid.

Elecampane (*Inula helenium*). Forms: teas, tinctures, powder, pills, etc. May function as: anti-microbial, anti-spasmodic, demulcent, liver tonic. Applications may include: coughs, drowsiness, eruptive skin disorders, respiratory issues, etc. Warnings: Avoid if pregnant or lactating. Not indicated for dry, irritated coughs. Avoid if allergic to ragweed. Avoid if diabetic or take meds for high blood pressure. Quit using at least 2 weeks before scheduled surgery.

Epsom salts (magnesium sulfate). Form: salt, bath salt, etc. Applications: soreness, bruising, irregular heart rhythms, muscle cramps, etc.

Essential oils: Pick up a good encyclopedia of essential oils and use this for guidance.

Eucalyptus (*Eucalyptus globulus*). There are around 500 varieties of eucalyptus. Each variety has a unique phytochemical profile. Forms: oil, extract, diffused, steam inhaled, lotions, gels, shampoo, bath salts, etc. May function as: anti-fungal, antibacterial, anti-inflammatory, decongestant. Applications may include: itchy scalp, rejuvenate stiff / sore muscles, promotes healing, soothing, relieves pain, wounds, cuts, bites, dandruff, eliminate lice, cleaning agent / ingredient, relieves congestion, headache, etc. Warnings: Avoid if pregnant or lactating. High concentrations may cause skin irritation. Avoid eyes, inner ear, and other sensitive areas.

Feverfew (*Tanacetum parthenium*). Forms: Functions may include: anti-inflammatory. Applications may include: arthritis, constipation, diarrhea, difficulty in labor, dizziness, fever, headaches, menstruation, migraine prevention, rheumatism, tension headaches (natural serotonin inhibitor), etc. Warnings: No known serious side effects, but use caution about long term use, high quantity usage and usage if you are pregnant or lactating. May experience digestive problems, nausea, bloating, mouth irritation.

Foxglove (*Digitalis lanta*). The foxglove plant is used to make the prescription drug, digoxin. Digoxin is used to treat heart failure, fluid buildup, irregular heart beat (A-fib). Warnings: All parts of the plant are considered poisonous for self-medicating. Do not use this plant for anything other than for its visual beauty.

Frankincense (*Boswellia arteri, sacra, serrata*). May function as: anti-bacterial, anti-fungal. Applications may include: arthritis, asthma, good for improving gum health, pain, swelling, flatulence, wound healing, etc. Avoid using when pregnant.

Ginger (*Zingiber officinale*). Forms: raw, juice, powder, capsules, beverages, tinctures, decoctions, etc. Fresh ginger contains zingibain, a protease (with acetyl-cholinesterase inhibitory activity). May be used as a rennet substitute and used in making cheese. Applications may include: anti-nausea, prevents motion sickness, etc. Warnings: may cause heartburn, etc.

Ginkgo (*Ginko biloba*). Applications may include: lung problems, heart conditions, memory loss,

Alzheimer's disease, improves blood flow to brain, hemorrhoids, eye problems, etc.

Ginseng (*Panax ginseng/quinquefolius*). May function as: adaptogen. Applications may include: aphrodisiac, mood enhancer, improves immune functions, reduces cholesterol, slows aging process, good for adrenals, vasodilation, angiogenesis.

Glucose gel. For use with diabetics for suspected hypoglycemic events.

Goldenseal (*Hydrastis canadensis*). Dried root is used (contains berberine). May function as: antibacterial, anti-inflammatory, anti-fungal, etc. Applications may include treatment for: common cold, abnormal heart rhythms, digestive disorders, stomach pain, gastritis, peptic ulcers, hemorrhoids, diarrhea, constipation, urinary tract infections, internal bleeding, chronic fatigue, applied to the skin for rashes and infections, ringworm, cold sores, etc. Some people use as eyewash for pink eye. Interactions: May decrease how rapidly cyclo-sporine and digoxin are broken down. Goldenseal may change CYP450 system of metabolizing meds, possibly increasing side effects of the medication. Warnings: pregnant women, breastfeeding women and infants should avoid goldenseal.

Gymnema (*Gymnema sylvestre*). Forms: powder, tablets, capsules. Applications may include: may help restore insulin-producing capability of the pancreas' beta cells, reduces sugar cravings, may lower blood glucose, may promote weight loss. Interactions: may decrease blood glucose.

H – J

Hawthorn berries (*Crataegus monogyna L.*). Leaves, berries and flowers are used. Forms include: tea, raw berries, jams, desserts, wine, vinegar, supplements. Functions may include: antioxidant, anti-inflammatory, prebiotic, etc. Applications may include: used to treat heart conditions, treatment for blood pressure, may lower cholesterol, treats digestive issues, decreases intestinal transit times, may stimulate hair growth, may reduce anxiety, etc. Warnings: may cause mild nausea or dizziness. Interactions: may interact with certain heart, blood pressure and cholesterol medications.

Helichrysum (*Helichrysum italicum*). Forms: oil, tincture, extract, etc. Functions may include: anti-inflammation, anti-microbial, anti-fungal. Possible applications: anti-malarial, digestive issues, hemorrhoids, mental stress, lower insulin, addresses insulin resistance, wound healing, burns, wounds, etc. Warnings: Does not display significant levels of cytotoxicity or genotoxicity. May be slight changes in liver activity of CYP, and there is always potential for allergic reactions.

Holy basil, aka tulsi (*Ocimum tenuiflorum*). Forms: capsules, tinctures, powders, tea, etc. Contains: eugenol, ursolic and rosmarinic acid, apigenin, lutein, ocimumosides A and B. May function as: adaptogenic, anti-inflammatory, antioxidant, adaptogen, etc. Applications may include: anxiety, stress, high chol, insomnia, venomous bites, metabolic syndrome, mercury poisoning, may increase testosterone, etc. **Warnings: Avoid during pregnancy/lactation. Warnings: May lower blood sugar level. May affect thyroid hormones. High doses may damage the liver. May cause nausea, diarrhea, rapid heartbeat and seizures. Stop using at least 2 weeks before scheduled surgery.**

Homeopathic remedies: aconite for shocking and bad news, allium cepa for common cold with nasal discharge, apis for insect bites, arnica for pain due to injury, arsenica album for anxiety and loneliness, Bach's rescue remedy, arsenicum for food poisoning, belladonna for migraines and sunstroke, carbo vegetabilis for heartburn, calendula for cold sores and mouth ulcers, chamomilla for sound sleep, gelsemium for flu, hypericum for nerve injury, Ignatia for acute grief / depression / anxiety, kali phosphoricum for mental / physical exhaustion / anxiety, magnesia phosphorica for cramps, nux vomica for too much alcohol or overeating, oscillococcinum for flu, pulsatilla for women and children, rhus tox for sprains / strains, sulphur for itchiness, zinc metallicum for restless leg syndrome, etc.

Hops (*Humulus lupulus*). Forms: used to make beer, powder, pills, tincture, etc. May function as: anti-inflammatory, anti-anxiety, analgesic, anti-cancer. Applications may include: athero-sclerosis, hot flashes, insomnia. Warnings: may cause tiredness, may cause allergic cross-reaction in people allergic to birch pollen, people with depression, breast cancer, endometriosis, stop taking 2 wk before surgery.

Hydrogen peroxide (H_2O_2). Applications include: any bite, wound or sore – apply immediately and keep immersed until bubbles stop rising to the top. Soak feet with toenail fungus in hydrogen peroxide once per day for 30 to 60 minutes. Use for ear infection.

Hyssop (*Hyssopus officinalis*). Forms: oil, extract, tincture, fragrance, etc. Functions may include: anti-inflammatory, immune regulation. Applications may include: anti-convulsant, digestive aid, hoarseness, insecticide, intestinal issues, gastroprotective, respiratory infection, circulation, skin problems, etc. Warnings: Not implicated in causing liver injury. Avoid during pregnancy and lactation.

Iodine (iodine, iodate, iodide). Use for infections, detox, chronic conditions, etc. Consult with your physician about the best form and dosage. Avoid if iodine allergy.

Juniper berry (*Juniperus communis*). Used as a condiment, flavoring ingredient and extract oil. May function as: antioxidant, anti-inflammatory, anti-diabetic, antibacterial, antifungal. Applications may include: upset stomach, decrease swelling, diuretic, joint and muscle pain, wounds, bloating, heartburn, etc.

K – M

Lavender (*Lavandula angustifolia, stoechas, latifolia, intermedia*, etc.). Forms: fresh, dried, oil, diffused, etc. Functions may include: antiseptic, anti-inflammatory. Applications may include: anti-convulsant, anxiety, depression, improved mood, pain, restless-ness, tremor, etc. Warnings: lavender taken per oral may cause constipation, headache, increased appetite. (PMID: 23573142)

Lemon balm (*Melissa officinalis*). Forms: fresh, extract, tea, tincture, decoctions, powder, pill, etc. Applications may include: anxiety, cold sores, dementia, indigestion, insomnia, stress, etc. Warnings: may lower blood glucose in diabetics, discontinue use 2 weeks before surgery, may interfere with thyroid functions.

Lichen (*Usnea*). Forms: whole lichen, powder, pills, tincture, extract. Applications may include: promotes immune system, promotes healthy urinary tract system. Warnings: avoid during pregnancy and lactation.

Linden (*Tilia spp.*). Forms: tea, etc. May function as: a diuretic, etc. Applications may include treating: colds, headache, insomnia, itchy skin, reduce mucus production, relieve anxiety, etc. Warnings: frequent use of linden tea has been associated with heart damage, but this is rare. Avoid if pregnant or breastfeeding. If taking lithium, consult your healthcare provider before using linden.

Licorice root (*Glycyrrhiza glabra*). Forms: leaves, roots, powder, tea, decoction, tincture, lotions, salves, cream, candy, sweetener (50X sweeter than table sugar). Licorice contains more than 300 natural chemicals conferring various benefits. May function as: anti-inflammatory, antiseptic, antiviral. Applications may include: inflammation, redness, itching, eczema, skin infections, indigestion, heartburn, stomach ulcers, etc. Warnings: too much may lower potassium levels leading to abnormal heart rhythms, high blood pressure, swelling, and lethargy. Pregnant / lactating women should not consume licorice. Those with high blood pressure should not use licorice. Those with electrolyte issues should not consume licorice.

Magnesium spray. Magnesium chloride flakes dissolved in water (not oil). Used to relieve local pain and redness.

Mallow (*Malva neglecta*). Forms: may eat the leaves, make tinctures, decoctions, elixir, salves, etc. May function as: laxative, expectorant, emollient, demulcent, diuretic astringent, etc. Applications may include treatments for: ulcers, soothe GI tract, boosts immune system, good for insomnia, anxiety, for numbing, respiratory illnesses, pain, skin infections, burns, etc. Warnings: large doses may cause diarrhea.

Marshmallow (*Althaea officinalis*). Mucilaginous leaves may be chopped and added to salads or as a garnish. Functions may include: anti-inflammatory, antibacterial, anti-pain, diuretic, etc. Applications may include treating the following conditions: common cold, skin irritation, wound healing, digestive aid, soothe and repair the gut lining, support heart health, etc. Warnings: Avoid using if pregnant, breastfeeding, if diabetic, if you have a scheduled surgery (for 2 weeks prior).

Meadowsweet (*Spirea ulmaria*). Applications may include: colds, heartburn, pain, arthritis, swelling, bladder infections, etc. Interactions: may be similar to aspirin and magnesium trisalicylate. May interact with narcotics. Warnings: pregnant women should not use due to increased risk of miscarriage. May cause lung spasms and possibly worsen asthma.

Melatonin (N-acetyl-5-methoxytryptamine). Forms: pills, food, lotions, creams. Applications may include: insomnia, jet lag, sleep disorders, endometriosis, high blood pressure, temporomandibular disorders, pre-surgery anxiety, low platelets (thrombo-cytopenia), sunburn (external) hormone-dependent cancers, etc. Warnings: avoid using if on medications which influence blood clotting, if depressed.

Milk thistle (*Silybum marianum*). Forms: capsules. Applications may include: protecting liver, mild liver detox, speeds recovery from hepatitis, alcoholic cirrhosis, serves as adjunct for some types of poisoning / toxicities, etc. Dose is 140 mg Silmarin, 3 times per day. Warning: side effects rare.

Minerals: 250 mcg - 50 mg iodine, 12.5 mg Iodoral, Lugol's iodine, 100 mcg selenium, 15 – 45 mg zinc, 3 mg copper, boron, magnesium, calcium, blackstrap molasses, liquid trace mineral formulations containing 70+ trace minerals, etc.

Mistletoe (*Viscum album*). Mistletoe is poisonous but as always, it is the dose which makes a substance poisonous. At low doses, there may be benefits. Only European mistletoe is used therapeutically. Forms include: tea, etc. Applications may include treatment for following conditions: seizures, headaches, meno-pause symptoms, inhibits cancer cell pro-liferation, kills existing cancer cells, used as adjunct for chemo-therapy, boosts immune system, relieves depression and anxiety, improves heart health, used as complementary therapy for cancer treatments, etc. Warnings: may cause nausea, vomiting, diarrhea, low blood pressure, inflammation (at injection site if injected), dizziness, pain, etc. **ONLY EURPOEAN mistletoe is considered safe to use in low doses. American mistletoe is poisonous and may cause vomiting, seizures, slow heart rate and even death.** Interactions: may interact with heart disease and blood pressure meds, anticoagulants, antidepressants, etc.

Moringa (*Moringa oleifera*). Forms: fresh leaves, Ben oil, decoctions, tea, powder, etc. Functions: anti-inflammatory, galactagogue, anti-paralytic, antiviral, analgesic, hypo-glycemic, anti-dyslipidemic, etc. Applications may include: diabetes, infections, joint pain, heart health, cancer, inflammation, etc. Avoid during pregnancy. Warning: roots contain spirochin, a nerve paralyzing compound – avoid consuming moringa roots.

Motherwort aka Lion's Tail (*Leonurus cardiaca*). Forms: because it is a bitter herb it should be combined with something sweet or sour such as honey or lemon. Use as a tea, shrub, elixir, etc. May function as: anti-inflammatory, anti-oxidant, etc. Applications may include: heart tonic, relaxes blood vessel walls, depression, paradoxically may encourage uterine contractions, regulate of menstrual periods, anxiety, lower blood pressure, heart palpitations, over-active thyroid, etc. Warnings: may cause diarrhea, drowsiness, sedation, altered heart rhythms, low blood pressure, uterine bleeding and contractions, increase sensitivity to the sun (when applied to skin), etc. Do not use with bleeding disorder, taking Coumadin, sedative meds, a scheduled surgery, with low blood pressure, if pregnant/breastfeeding, etc.

Mullein (*Verbascum thapsus*). Forms used: flowers, leaves, roots, tea, extract, powder, capsule, elixir, oil, etc. Contains polyphenols, saponins, flavonoids, phenylethanoid glycosides, iridoids, etc. Functions may include: anti-inflammatory, anti-bacterial, antiviral, etc. Applications may include: help with difficult breathing, asthma, cough, common cold, bronchitis, COPD, earaches, eczema, sleep tuberculosis, etc. Interactions: mullein + amantadine has been shown to be a good treatment against the flu.

Myrrh (*Commiphora myrrha*). Forms: sap-like resin from a tree. Oil, tincture, mouthwash, toothpaste, ointments, soaps, etc. Functions as: anti-bacterial, anti-fungal. Applications may include: reducing blood sugar, oral infections, immune stimulant, gingivitis, Bechet's disease (inflammatory disorder), wound healing, edema, headache, rheumatoid arthritis, etc. Warnings: Avoid taking greater than 2 to 4 grams per day. Pregnant and lactating women should avoid. Stop taking at least 2 weeks before scheduled surgery. Avoid consuming in high doses. Consult physician before consuming myrrh.

N – P

NAC (N-acetyl cysteine). Powerful antioxidant in form of a powder, capsules, may be inhaled. Dose is 600 mg twice per day. Precursor to glutathione, the antioxidant naturally found in highest concentration in human body. Used for following: counteract some poisons (e.g., acetaminophen, CO poisoning, some heavy metals, some X-ray dyes, phenytoin), upper and lower respiratory infections, ear infections, relieve hangovers, Lou Gehrig's disease, heart disease, lowers cholesterol, improves side effects of some cancer treatments, anti-viral, antibacterial, helps with polycystic ovary syndrome, improves energy and vitality, may improve psych conditions such as depression and bi-polar, Alzheimer's disease, Parkinson's disease, autism, cystic fibrosis, reduces lung mucus, etc.

Neem (*Azadirachta indica*). Forms: powdered, liquid, soap, shampoo, lotions, creams, etc. Applications may include leprosy, intestinal parasites, skin ulcers, heart conditions, fever, gum disease, liver. Pregnant women avoid.

Nettle (*Urtica dioica*). Nettle contains formic acid, the same compound found in stinging ants, serotonin, acetylcholine, 5-hydroxy-tryptamine which lends it its characteristic stinging quality. If you want to read more about nettle: https://www.botanical.com/botanical/mgmh/n/nettle03.html
Forms include: infusion, dry, tinctures, boiled and eaten, powdered, juice, etc. Functions may include: astringent, expectorant, tonic, anti-inflammatory, diuretic, etc. Applications may include: goiter, weight loss, diuretic, hair tonic, anti-asthmatic, venomous bites and stings, hemlock poisoning, diabetes, benign prostatic hyperplasia, etc. Warnings: mild GI distress, allergies, etc. Consult a physician before using nettle.

Niacin. 500 – 3,000 mg dose of niacin may lead to a niacin-induced flush which can be part of an effective detoxification regimen.

Normal saline (0.9% sodium chloride). Form: liquid. Applications: fluid & electrolyte replacement.

Olive leaf (*Olea europaea*). Forms: whole leaf, tincture, powder, tea. May function as antioxidant.

Oregano (*Origanum vulgare*). Forms: gel caps, oil, tincture, fresh, dried, etc. Functions as: antibiotic, antifungal, antioxidant, anti-parasite, etc. Applications may include: lower cholesterol, yeast infections, improves gut functions, leaky gut, pain, wt loss, etc. Warnings: consult MD before using.

Papain. Papaya (*Carica papaya*) contains a proteolytic enzyme known as papain. It also contains benzyl isothiocyanate. It is used to break down protein into small protein segments or amino acids. Also used to treat digestive issues, pain, inflammation and swelling. May also be effective with cardiovascular issues, parasitic infections, diarrhea, and allergies. May relieve fever and malaria. If eating the whole fruit, always eat fully ripe fruit. Unripe papaya may cause smooth muscle contractions and should be avoided by pregnant women. Papaya seeds may be dried and substituted for black pepper.

Pau d'arco (*Tabebuia impetiginosa*). Forms: powder, cream, tincture, decoction, tablets, etc. Functions as: anti-inflammatory, antioxidant, anti-cancer, antiviral, antimalarial, anticoagulant. Applications may include: insect bites, eczema, athlete's foot, fever, colds, liver disease, Parkinson's disease, leukemia, yeast infections, etc. Pregnant women should avoid.

Peppermint (*Mentha piperita or balsamea*). Used as fresh leaves, tea, tincture, oil and in pill form. Contains menthol, which activates cold-sensitive receptors in the skin and mucosa. Applications may include: relieving tension and migraine headaches, freshens breath, insomnia, relieves indigestion, healthy respiratory functions, bug repellant, muscle aches, itching, etc. Oral use of peppermint should not exceed 140 mg of the peppermint constituent, pulegone. Peppermint oil should be diluted and limited to a few drops if taking per oral or applying directly to the skin. Too much taken internally may cause heartburn. Do not apply directly to skin without diluting in a carrier oil. To repel insects on plants, combine 16 oz water and ½ cup witch hazel with 1 Tbsp peppermint oil and spray on plants.

Pine, fir and spruce needles. Use needles to make a tea. Fir and spruce needles taste citrusy. They are a source of vitamin A, high in vitamin C and anti-oxidants, B vitamins. To make a tea, let needles steep but not boil in hot water for 20 minutes. Applications may include: antioxidant, anti-depressant, anti-bacterial, antiviral, anti-tumor, anti-inflammatory, arthritis, coughs and colds, immune booster, improves heart functions, respiratory infections, sore throat, tea can be used as antiseptic wash, etc. Historically added to mattresses to aid in rheumatism. Warnings: Spruce tea may act as an abortifacient. **Avoid ponderosa pine needles which are both abortifacient and toxic. Avoid Norfolk Island pine and Yew needles, brewing can make them toxic.** In general, if trying to get pregnant, if you pregnant or lactating, avoid using pine needles.

Pine tar soap. Use for poison ivy exposure.

Poppy (*Papaver somniferum, P. rhoeas*). Forms: whole seed, tea, etc. Applications may include: sleep aid, smooth muscle relaxant, diarrhea, abdominal cramping, sedative analgesic, antitussive. Interactions: none well documented. Warnings: the outer surface of the poppy seed contains morphine (drinking poppy seed tea may concentrate the morphine, leading to death), noscapine, codeine, papaverine, and hebaine; eating large amounts may block the bowel; avoid if allergic to poppy seeds.

Probiotics. Forms: pills, yogurt, etc. Functions: According to NIH, health information, probiotics are identified by their specific strain. Seven strains used most frequently, includes: *lactobacillus, Bifidobacterium, bacillus, saccharomyces, streptococcus, enterococcus escherichia*. Probiotics target gut. Used to influence bacteria composition in gut, known as the microbiome. Collective activities of the microbiome are thought to influence various aspects of human health and disease. Each bacterium is different with widely ranging and different "origins." Some probiotic bacteria are found in soil, human and animal guts, female vagina, etc. For example, *bacillus subtilis*, is a spore-forming, rod-shaped, gram-positive, facultative aerobe. It thrives in temperature range of 77°F to 95°F. This bacterium has ability to produce and secrete antibiotics. It is possible this bacterium may prevent buildup of alpha-synuclein, associated with Parkinson's. *Lacto bacillus acidophilus*, commonly lives in intestines and vagina. *Lacto bacillus acidophilus* is associated with reduced risk of atopic dermatitis. This area of research is active and needs more study before making broad recommendations for universal use. There are times when probiotics are indicated. Consult MD to guide in use of selected probiotics.

Psyllium (*Plantago ovata*). A single plant can produce up to 10,000 psyllium seeds. Rich in vitamins and minerals. It's seed coat, made from mucilage, absorbs water. This allows seeds to swell up to 1,000 times its original weight. Applications may include: diarrhea, stool softener, improves gastrointestinal functions, hemorrhoids, constipation, lowers cholesterol, may protect gut from external toxins, etc. Psyllium possesses digestive properties. Always use psyllium with a LOT of water. Take 1 tablespoon of psyllium with 12 – 24 ounces of water. Stir psyllium into the water and immediately drink. Psyllium powder does not have the same therapeutic potential for gut as psyllium husks.

Puerarin (*peuraria lobata*). Wild leguminous plant promotes angiogenesis and increases endothelial progenitor cells. Improves coronary microcirculation. (https://doi.org/10.1155/2022/8831750)

Q – S

Quinine (*Cinchona officinalis*). Forms: bark contains quinine. Functions: anti-malarial, secretagogue, anti-septic. Applications may include: malaria treatment, stimulate flow of saliva, stimulates secretion of stomach hydrochloric acid, low appetite, leg cramps, hemorrhoids, varicose veins, muscle cramps, stimulates hair growth, etc. Warnings include: possibly slowed heart rate, ringing in ears, deafness, rash, visual disturbances are possible. Do not use if you are pregnant or lactating, if you have stomach ulcers, if you are preparing for surgery (stop at least 2 weeks before scheduled surgery), do not take if using quinidine, be cautious with carbamazepine, anticoagulants, antiplatelets, phenobarbital, antacids, H2 blockers, proton pump inhibitors, etc.

Red raspberry leaf (*Rubus idaeus, Rubus occidentalis*). Forms: tea. Functions may include: uterine tonic, increases blood flow to uterus. Applications may include: uterine contraction, uterine relaxation, may prevent postdate pregnancy, may reduce need for forceps during delivery, lower blood pressure. Drink 1 – 3 cups of tea during last 2 pregnancy trimesters.

Rhodiola (*Rhodiola rosea*). Forms: capsules, tea, tincture, etc. Applications may include: adaptogen, stress, anxiety, fatigue, depression, boost brain function (nootropic), improved exercise performance, may lower blood glucose, etc. Take in the morning and not evening, it acts as a mild stimulant. Combine rhodiola, ashwaganda and holy basil (tulsi) for an anxiety-reducing tea. Interactions: avoid using or consult your physician before using if you are taking antidepressants, high blood pressure meds, CNS stimulants, liver meds, phenytoin, warfarin, etc. Best to avoid during pregnancy and lactation.

Rose hips (*Rosa canina, R. gallica, R. Rugosa, R. villosa*). Forms: small pod, tea, freezer jam, tincture, decoction. Contains vitamin C, flavonoids. Functions may include: antioxidant. Applications may include: may reduce capillary fragility, varicose veins, promotes vascular health, etc.

Rosemary (*Rosmarinus, officinalis*). Forms: fresh, tincture, oil, dried powder, salves, etc. Functions may include: anti-inflammatory, antioxidant, anti-microbial, diuretic, etc. Applications may include: treats headache, improves memory, relieves muscle pain and spasms, stimulates hair growth, supports circulatory and nervous systems, increases menstrual flow, abortifacient, indigestion, etc. Warnings: large doses of rosemary oil and fresh rosemary may cause miscarriage, nausea, vomiting, spasms, coma, pulmonary edema. May interfere with ACE inhibitors. Use caution if taking lithium.

Sage (*Salvia officinalis*). Forms include: fresh or dried leaves, tea, decoctions, extracts, tinctures, powder, etc. Functions include: anti-inflammatory, antioxidant, antifungal, anti-bacterial, preservative. Applications may include: digestive aid, relieves cramps, anti-diarrhea, dries up phlegm, poor appetite, heartburn, reduces swelling, skin salve, excessive sweating, poor blood flow to brain, Alzheimer's disease, improves memory, painful menses, sore mouth / throat / tongue, swollen nasal passages, inhale for asthma, etc. Warnings: sage contains the plant chemical, thujone. If you consume high amounts for long enough, thujone may accumulate and damage the liver or nervous system and possibly cause seizures. Avoid high doses over long periods. Avoid during pregnancy and lactation. Stop using sage 2 weeks before scheduled surgery.

Saw palmetto berries (*Serenoa repens*). Applications include: enlarged prostate, cachexia, wasting, promotes return of strength after illness, increased libido for men. Dosing: 160 mg, twice per day.

Shatavari root (*Asparagus racemosus*). Forms: powder, extract, etc. May function as: adaptogen, antioxidant, anti-anxiety, anti-depressant, galactagogue, tonic, immunomodulatory, etc. Applications may include: aphrodisiac, female hormonal imbalances, polycystic ovary syndrome, boosts milk supply during lactation, may help with hot flashes and night sweats during menopause, diuretic, may help maintain blood glucose levels, relieve coughs, diarrhea, good for liver, ulcers, etc. Warnings: found to be safe but always use caution and consult your health care provider before using.

Shilajit. Natural, sticky black substance, mainly composed of fluvic acid, found in the Himalayas. May block tau self-aggregation, an aspect of brain physiology related to Alzheimer's disease (PMID: 22482077). Multiple benefits to human health.

Slippery elm (*Ulmus rubra, Ulmus fulva*) Forms: lozenge, powder, tea, decoction, tincture, poultice, etc. Functions may include: anti-inflammatory, stimulates mucus secretion, astringent, diuretic, emollient, etc. Applications may include: bladder infections, cold sores, colic, constipation, cough, diarrhea, hemorrhoids, irritable bowel, sore throat, tapeworms, UTIs, etc. Warnings: avoid if pregnant or lactating.

Spikenard (*Aralia racemose*). In the same family as valerian. Mentioned in the Bible. Highly fragrant. The root is used to sweeten beverages.

Spirulina (*Spirulina platensis*). Blue green algae found in water. Rich in vitamins, minerals, and antioxidants.

Star anise (*Illicium verum*). Contains anethole, gallic acid, linalool, limonene, quercetin and shikimic acid.

Stevia (*Stevia rebaudiana*). Leaves contain stevioside, a glycoside. It is up to 300 times sweeter than sugar.

St. John's Wort (*Hypericum perforatum*). Forms: powder, capsules. Applications may include: mild to moderate depression. Dose is 600 to 1,800 mg / day. Warnings: may cause stomach upset, decreases effectiveness of birth control pills. Widely interacts with other drugs. <u>**Check with your physician before adding 5-HTP or St. John's Wort to your routine!**</u>

T – W

Tea tree (*Melaleuca alternifolia*). Form: Functions include: anti-bacterial, anti-viral, anti-fungal. Applications include: skin infections, colds, viruses, acne, arthritis, lice, warts, eczema. Do not take orally.

Turmeric (*Curcuma longa*). Forms include fresh root, powder, extracts, tinctures, etc. Taking with black pepper increases its absorption. Functions as: anti-inflammatory, anti-oxidant, anti-viral, boosts BDNF. Applications may include: aids digestion, improved brain function, reduced heart disease risk, may slow spread of cancer, address Type 2 diabetes issues, improve Alzheimer's disease, arthritis, reduce PMS symptoms depression, may slow down the aging process. Warnings: avoid with gallstones, bile duct obstruction, bleeding issues, may lower blood glucose in type 2 diabetes. Too much may lead to heart arrhythmias. It also stains everything it contacts. When using turmeric, whether in the kitchen or consuming as a supplement, take care to avoid getting turmeric on clothing and other textiles.

Uva ursi (*Arctosaphylos uva ursi*). Use as diuretic, urinary antiseptic, weight loss, kidney remedy, for PMS, wound healing, cold sores. When consumed it may turn urine a dark green (it's considered normal). Pregnant women should avoid.

Valerian (*Valeriana officinalis, wallichii*). Used in following forms: extracts, beverages, powder, pills, essential oil, aromatherapy. Dosing varies, start here: 500 mg to 1,000 mg. Applications include: promoting sleep, insomnia, anxiety, menopause, depression, dysmenorrhea, PMS, stress, etc.

Vinegar (acetic acid). Made by fermenting anything containing sugar or made from diluted alcohol. Use vinegar-soaked paper bag to cover poison ivy rash and draw out toxin.

Vitamins: B complex 50/100, vitamin C, Vitamin D3/K2, Vitamin E, biotin, folate and beta-carotene from food, methylcobalamin, etc.

Vitex (*Agnus-castus;* aka, chaste tree). Commonly used forms include decoctions added to sitz baths, extracts, tea, pills, capsules. Applications target women and monks including: PMS, mood upsets, reducing sexual desire, amenorrhea, dysmenorrhea, endometriosis, female infertility, fibrocystic breast disease, headache, menopause, menorrhagia, menstrual difficulties, nausea, premenstrual syndrome, fever, dyspepsia, colic, catarrh, diarrhea, hemorrhoids, hemicrania, etc. Studies show this herb stimulates release of luteinizing hormone and inhibits the release of follicle stimulating hormone, having a progesterone-like effect. Some undesired side effects may include: upset stomach, nausea, itching, rash, headaches, weight gain, insomnia, acne. Warnings: do not use if pregnant or lactating, have a hormone-sensitive condition, or participate in *in vitro* fertilization, have Parkinson's disease or schizophrenia, may cause stomach upset, headache, heavy menstrual flow.

Vodka. I am not advocating for drinking vodka, but if it is available, there are several legitimate medicinal uses for having vodka in the medicine cabinet. Historically, it has been used as an antiseptic and anesthetic. Used to disinfect wounds. It is also used to make tinctures and extracts.

Wheatgrass (*Triticum aestivum*). Contains significant amounts of vitamins, minerals and fiber.

Wild dagga aka Lion's tail (*Leonotis leonuris*). Leaves and flowers are commonly used. Leonotis Leonuris is commonly known as "wild" cannabis. Is not used as a hallucinogen. Smoking it may lead to calming effect, mild eupohoria, visual changes, dizziness, nausea, sweating, sedation, and light-headedness. It is used as a decoction both topically and orally. May function as a mild narcotic and sedative. Applications may include: boils, eczema, epilepsy, headache, hemorrhoids, itching, rashes. Phytochemical is marrubiin. An antioxidant with cardio-protective properties. Toxic at high doses. Not be legal in all countries.

Klip dagga aka or lion's ear (*Leonotis nepetifolia*). Flowers brewed as tea to relieve anxiety and as sleep aid. Used as a treatment for snake bite. Mild narcotic. Anti-inflammatory, hypo-glycemic, heart tonic, etc.

Wild quinine or wild feverfew (*Parthenium integrifolium*). Forms include: leaves, paste, poultice, etc. Flowering tops used to make infusion containing quinine sulfate. Used as a substitute for the quinine-producing Cinchona tree. Functions as: anti-inflammatory, anti-periodic, emmenagogue, kidney stimulant, lithontripic, etc. Applications may include: external burn treatment (as a poultice), dysentery, fatigue, respiratory infection, etc. Warnings: plant may become invasive, check with local agriculture extension. Only root and flowers are edible; avoid the plant.

Wild yam root (*dioscorea composite, villosa*). Known for diosgenin, a compound used to make steroid hormones, tinctures, extracts, creams.

Witch hazel (*Hamamelis virginiana*). Liquid tonic water, containing tannins, for face and skin. Its uses include: acne, bruises, burns, hair, redness, insect bites, pain and commonly used to shrink pores and cleanse the skin. Warnings: not for internal use.

Wormwood (*Artemisia absinthium*). Form: the entire herb is used – root, stems, leaves, and flowers. It is a strong, bitter taste. May be used as a tea, essential oil, powders, pills. Applications may include: expelling worms /parasites, insect repellant, anti-inflammatory, may be useful in treating jaundice, may increase libido. Warnings: avoid too much or you may experience diarrhea. Some have claimed wormwood is effective for treating or preventing malaria, but the NIH has not yet seen substantiating evidence proving this. It has been proposed as an adjuvant for treating Covid-19.

X – Z

Yarrow (*Achillea millefolium*). Forms include: poultice, etc. Functions: antimicrobial, antiseptic. Applications may include: external used to stop bleeding, wound healing, infections, skin redness, diarrhea, gas, asthma, colds, runny nose, arthritis, wounds, skin healing, liver disorders, MS, gingivitis, IBS, fever, etc. Warnings: yarrow contains thujone which may not be safe but if taken in tested amounts found in medicine it is likely safe. Do not take during pregnancy, if you have a bleeding disorder, are allergic to ragweed, scheduled for surgery within 2 weeks. Interactions: do not take if you taking an anticoagulant or antiplatelet medication, lithium, barbiturates, antacids, H2 blocker, proton pump inhibitors.

Ylang (*Cananga odorata*). Flowers are the source of the essential oil (Complete ylang ylang). Inhaled, if applied to body use a carrier oil to dilute.

Applications may include: reduce anxiety and tension, increased alertness and attentiveness, lowers blood pressure. Warnings: avoid using excess ylang it may cause headache or nausea.

Zeolite clinoptilolite / heulandite / chabazite. Naturally occurring aluminosilicate minerals; contain oxygen and other metals. Porous structure. Contains magnesium, potassium, calcium and sodium. Strong negative charge of aluminum attracts positively charged environmental pollutants. Calcium, magnesium and phosphate are exchangeable (displaced from zeolites) cations for other known positively charged toxins. Zeolites used to detox mercury, lead, tin, cadmium, arsenic, aluminum, antimony, iron and nickel. Zeolites are used in QuikClot as a hemo-static agent. It is safe and nontoxic at most commonly used levels.

Different preservation methods are used to retain the health-giving and healing properties of medicinal plants. When first using a new product, first test it using a small amount. For example, if using essential oils, do a patch test first before broadly applying the oil. To do this, take a small amount of the oil and apply directly to your skin. If you notice redness or swelling, you may be sensitive. You either need to avoid this oil or possibly dilute the oil in a carrier oil such as coconut oil or jojoba oil.

Below are a few lists of various herbs and their reported actions (not all compounds on these lists is in the Country Living Medicine Cabinet List):

Possible anti-viral herbs and others: andrographis, astragulus, basil, black walnuts, coconut oil, echinacea, dandelion, elderberries, fennel, garlic, ginger, ginseng, green tea, lemon balm, licorice, milk thistle, olive leaf, oregano, pau d'arco, peppermint, rosemary, sage, St. John's wort, turmeric, wormwood, etc.

Possible anti-bacterial herbs and others: ascorbic acid, boric acid, cinnamon, clove, cranberry juice, echinacea, eucalyptus, garlic, ginger, goldenseal, grapefruit seed extract, green tea, H2O2, honey, horseradish, lavender, lemon, moringa, onions, oregano, pineapple, tea tree, turmeric, etc.

Possible anti-fungal herbs and others: aloe vera, berberine, biotin, castor, cedar, chamomile, cinnamon, coconut, echinacea, eucalyptus, garlic, geranium, grape seed extract, lavender, lemon balm, lemongrass, mint, myrrh, olive oil, oregano, Oregon grape, rosemary, sage, tannins (tannates), tea tree, thyme, etc.

Anti-inflammatory herbs and others: aloe vera, calendula, cat's claw, cayenne (capsaicin), chamomile, chlorophyll, cinnamon, cloves, frankincense, ginger, green tea, holy basil, licorice, omega-3s, pycnogenol, rosemary, turmeric, white willow bark, etc.

Herbs promoting angiogenesis after heart attack (article ID: 8831750): *Salvia miltiorrhiza* bunge extracts, *carthamus tinctorius* extracts, *Pueraria lobate* extract, *Astragulus* extracts, *Panax ginseng* extracts, *Panax notoginseng* extracts, *Cinnamon cassia* extract, *Rehmannia glutinosa, Leonurus japonicus, Scutellaria baicalensis,* and *geum macrophyllum.*

Soothing herbs and others: ashwagandha, borage, CBD, chamomile, ginger, holy basil (tulsi), hops, kava, lavender, lemon balm, licorice, passion flower, peppermint, rose, St. John's wort, turmeric, valerian, etc.

Potential uses for hydrogen peroxide H2O2 (3% food grade hydrogen peroxide, NOT 35%): clean countertops, sanitize kitchen sponge, sanitize toothbrush, remove clothing stains such as blood (do a test patch first), surface disinfectant, whiten laundry, white porcelain sinks, spray in dishwasher to keep away pathogenic micro-organisms, vegetable rinse, kill mold, sprout seeds, dilute and use as a gargle, disinfect any scratch or wound that punctures the skin, use diluted to gradually lighten hair, clean toilet bowl, add to bathwater, add to humidifier, get rid of L'aeu du skunk, diluted soak for toe nail fungus, remove ear wax, treat canker sores, whiten teeth, teeth wash, etc.

Bible verses: Exodus 30:23, 34; Job 30:4; Psalm 51:7; Isaiah 38:21; Song of Solomon: 4:14; Ezekiel 47:12; Revelation 22:2

Plant Research Databases and Resources:
https://www.nccih.nih.gov/health
https://www.medicalnewstoday.com
https://www.herbwisdom.com/
https://www.webmd.com/
https://www.friendsofthewildflowergarden.org/
https://cb.imsc.res.in/imppat/home
https://phytochem.nal.usda.gov/phytochem/search
http://faculty.iiitd.ac.in/~bagler/webservers/Phytochemica/index.php
http://envis.frlht.org/
http://www.theplantlist.org/
https://www.tropicos.org/home
http://bioinf-applied.charite.de/supernatural_new/index.php
https://www.ibscreen.com/natural-compounds
http://www.herbgarden.co.za/ (South Africa)
https://www.herbco.com/c-2-bulk-herbs-spices.aspx

Herbals
- Peterson Field Guide to Medicinal Plants and Herbs by Steven Foster & James A. Duke Houghton Mifflin Harcourt, 3 ed., 8 April 2014
- Rosemary Gladstar's Medicinal Herbs, A Beginner's Guide
- Rosemary Gladstar's Herbal Recipes for Vibrant Health
- Encyclopedia of Herbal Medicine by Andrew Chevaltier
- Medicinal Plants and Herbs by Steven Foster and Christopher Hobbs
- The Earthwise Herbal by Matthew Wood
- Herbal Antibiotics by Stephen Harrod Buhner
- Herbal Antivirals by Stephen Harrod Buhner

Essential Oil Reference Books
- https://learningherbs.com/herbmentor/
- https://scienceandartofherbalism.com/the-fine-art-of-making-herbal-tea-2/

Resources
https://www.bulkapothecary.com/

Educational videos
https://www.youtube.com/watch?v=UUtWgVZ9VwE (harvesting fresh herbs and flowers for tinctures and teas)

https://www.youtube.com/watch?v=EM81V9sgdos Wild edibles with Sergei Boutenko

Chapter 51

Basic medical equipment to have on hand

1. **128 Hz tuning fork**: used to detect large fiber neuropathy and the possible presence of a vitamin B12 deficiency.
2. **500 lb quick litter.** Used for patient transfer.
3. **Abdominal binder.**
4. **Adaptive eating devices.**
5. **AED – automated external defribrillator.** Use to restart heart during a cardiac emergency.
6. **Alligator clips**: used to make colloidal silver.
7. **All terrain walker.**
8. **Alternating air pressure mattress.**
9. **Bandages.**
10. **Batteries (various sizes)**: needed to make colloidal silver.
11. **Bibs (reusable).**
12. **Bleeding control measures.** Quick clot, etc.
13. **Blood electrification**: delivery of low power electrical pulses.
14. **Blood glucometer and strips**: used to test blood glucose.
15. **Blood pressure monitor**: measures BP
16. **Casting materials.**
17. **Castor oil.**
18. **Choking rescue device / portable airway assist device.**
19. **Compression socks.**
20. **Cool mist humidifier**: keeps moisture in air.
21. **CPR rescue mask.**
22. **Crutches.**
23. **Dehumidifier**: removes excess moisture from the air.
24. **Diffuser**: used to distribute small particles of essential oils to the air within a room.
25. **Disposable pads, underpants, etc.**
26. **Distilled water**: used to make colloidal silver, nasal washes, etc.
27. **EKG (1 – 12 leads)**: used to detect abnormal heart rhythms.
28. **Electrolyte powders.**
29. **Epi-pen or equivalent**: injectable epinephrine used to treat anaphylaxis.
30. **Foam rolls and wedges.**
31. **Gel packs.**
32. **Gloves**: non-latex gloves used to provide protection against pathogenic micro-organisms.
33. **Grabber.**
34. **Grinder (small).**
35. **HAM radio with antennas.**
36. **Head lamp**: a flashlight attached to a headband and used for a variety of purposes, including hands-free examinations during night time.
37. **Hearing aids.**
38. **Heating pads (various types).**
39. **Hot water bottle**: used to apply heat.
40. **Ice bags.**
41. **Inflatable bathtub, washing sink, etc.**
42. **Ketone strips**: used to test urine and degree of ketosis and ketones in urine.
43. **Knee braces.**
44. **Lifting straps.**
45. **Masks**: various sizes and types.
46. **Massage table**: foldable massage table.
47. **Microcurrent**: treat chronic pain, etc.
48. **Mini exercise bike.**
49. **Minor surgery kit**: a kit containing scalpels, sutures, forceps, scissors, local anesthetic, etc. An Army Medic kit could work.
50. **Moist heat packs.**
51. **Motion sickness devices.**

52. **Nasal irrigation**: devices used to irrigate the nasal passages.
53. **Nebulizer**: a device producing a fine spray of liquid droplets used to transfer drugs to the lungs.
54. **Neck traction device and stretcher.**
55. **Needles and syringes.**
56. **NOAA emergency weather alert radio.**
57. **Otoscope.** Used to examine ears and provide a view of ear canal and drum.
58. **Oxygen concentrator**: used to deliver oxygen.
59. **Pen light**: a small medical flashlight
60. **Personal protective equipment**: gloves, gowns, shoe coverings, masks, hair covers, eye glasses, etc.
61. **pH strips**: small strips of paper which change color based on pH
62. **Pill cutter.**
63. **Pill organizer.**
64. **Portable soaking tub.**
65. **Pulse oximeter with perfusion index**: detects percent oxygen saturation of blood flowing through the tip of your finger. Perfusion Index is the ratio of pulsatile blood flow to non-pulsatile blood in peripheral tissue.
66. **Razors, scalpels, etc.**
67. **Reading glasses of various strengths.**
68. **Red light**: decreases skin redness, improves skin tone, may have additional benefits. 620 – 700 nm wavelengths.
69. **Rice bag**: externally heated and used as a heating pad.
70. **Scale (macro and micro)**: used to weigh a child or adult; micro-scale used to weigh amounts in the grams and up to several pounds.
71. **Scenar**: Class IIa medical device. Non-invasive interactive self-controlled adaptive regulator. Used to establish a bio-feedback link with body, continuously changing properties of applied electric impulses in response to how the body is reacting. Used as an active reflex biofeed-back device and helps achieve homeostasis and initiate healing processes. Exhibits general and local effects on skin, blood vessels, muscle, nervous, endocrine and immune systems.
72. **Scrubs.**
73. **Sheepskin mattress.** Prevents bedsores for those who are bedbound.
74. **Silver bars**: used to make colloidal silver.
75. **Sitz bath.**
76. **Splints.**
77. **Stethoscope**: used to listen to heart and bowels.
78. **Stretch bands.**
79. **Surgical kit / equipment.**
80. **TENS unit (portable).** Muscle stimulator. For treating sore muscles, etc.
81. **Textbooks.** First aid, field survival, basic surgical, etc.
82. **Thermographic camera**: used to examine thermatomes and detect early changes related to temperature differentials.
83. **Thermometer**: detects body temp.
84. **Thermophore heating pad**: moist heating pads, come in several sizes.
85. **Timer**: audible alert based on programmed time.
86. **Transfer bench.**
87. **Ultra violet sanitizing light (UV-C)**: form of electromagnetic radiation with the wave-length 100 - 290 nm used to disinfect and kill microorganisms by destroying their cells' nucleic acids.
88. **Urinal bottle.**
89. **Venom desensitizer / VenomX**: small electronic device used to desensitize venomous bites and stings.
90. **Video monitoring system**: cameras used to remotely monitor a space / outdoors.
91. **Walking canes.**
92. **Water pick.**
93. **Water purification options.**
94. **Wheelchair.**

Section 6

Country Living Land and Homes

Chapter 52
Find and evaluate the land and the location

When God sends you on a mission, He opens the doors for you. When it seems like you may never find the right property, He gives you eyes to see a diamond-in-the-rough type of property. Your "Goshen" or "Promised Land" may be overlooked by everyone else because it is perfect for you. You are the buyer with a vision, you have a plan for the land, you desire to be a blessing to others. This type of walk is known as faith. Faith is knowing with certainty God has provided for you. As these perilous times unfold, it is imperative we all learn to operate on faith. A little faith begets more faith. Sometimes people transitioning from the city to the country fail to recognize country property with potential. Pray God opens your eyes to His will and desire for your life as you search for a suitable property. This is an exciting journey. Humility, genuineness, sincerity, friendliness, and honesty may open many doors which might otherwise be closed. Never be afraid to share your faith and motivation for moving to the country. Your witness may spark soul searching and a spiritual awakening in others. It's not too late to make the transition. Be patient. It is worth the wait to find the "perfect" property.

This chapter addresses potential issues which may arise as you scout for land in the country. It is impossible to address every issue that could arise, but this chapter provides information to stimulate a conversation with your real estate agent or with the locals in or around your target destination. You may identify additional issues.

Jon Sailer, Unsplash.com

It is important to know about potential neighbors. Drive around the area. Talk to the neighbors. Neighbors can make your life pleasant or miserable. Are the potential neighbors normal or wacky, clean or messy, do they maintain their property, are they loud and noisy, etc.? Do they drive vehicles with loud mufflers? Do they park junk cars all over their property? Do they allow dangerous animals to roam their property (e.g., pit bulls)? Do their dogs bark all night? Fewer neighbors, as far away as possible is ideal. Get to know potential neighbors. There is a reason for the old adage, "Good [high] fences make for good neighbors." This does not have to be a literal fence, but enough space to neutralize the potential negative neighbor. Hopefully, potential neighbors are respectful and eager to be of service. Either way, be sure you understand the basic character and temperament of potential neighbors.

An equally important question is, "What type of neighbor am I?" Are you the type of neighbor who respects others, keeps your property clean and appealing, keeps noise to a minimum, avoids obnoxious behaviors, etc.? Do you take care of your home in a way that enhances the neighborhood or makes it look rundown and dirty? Would clean and tidy people want to live next door to you? When you move onto a property, does it go downhill or do you maintain it and even upgrade it to make sure it stays clean and pristine?

On the flip side, sometimes I think we are "plagued" with bad neighbors because the Lord wants us to cooperate with heaven in securing their salvation. We may be able to reach out to our "unruly" neighbors in a kind and generous fashion to demonstrate by actions, how a Christian treats difficult people. Recently, a friend in Arkansas told me about his neighbor. Just the two of them share the end of a cul-de-sac. His neighbor parked all kinds of broken down and ugly cars at the end of the cul-de-sac, almost blocking access to my friend's driveway. Being a former Marine, he had a man-to-man conversation with his neighbor and, unfortunately, the situation did not turn out well and even escalated. But being a Christian Marine, even though they got off to a rocky start, he decided instead of further confronting his neighbor, he would pray for him and help him around his property. Sixteen months later after our Marine friend had regularly helped his neighbor keep up his property and after his neighbor lived through two heart attacks, one day he woke up and all the cars blocking the cul-de-sac were gone. His neighbor, instead of being a foe, is now a friend.

In addition to good neighbors, it is important to evaluate the state and location of interest. Over the course of 2020, we have seen some states under a severe authoritarian rule and other states with minimal to no intervention in the everyday lives of its residents. Even if your state is one of the relatively "free" states, it may not remain in that category as leadership changes. An online site with a tool to evaluate your ideal location is at https://www.freedominthe50states.org/ . This site has a tool known as the State Freedom Index which interactively helps you choose the best state for the values you hold. Plug in your variables and it provides a listing of states based on your preferences.

As of this writing, some cities and states in the USA still offer FREE land. To find these deals, go to the internet and search the term, "Free land in the United States of America." This website has videos and details about finding free land in the USA. https://gokcecapital.com/free-land/ According to this site, the federal government no longer issues free land but several cities and states, hoping to gain new businesses and / or residents, may offer free land, but with stipulations. In addition, some cities may own land which has deteriorated and has become more of an upkeep burden than a benefit. They may be willing to sell small parcels for the price of doing the transaction. I have a friend in Texas who bought a lot from the city for $75. This lot could be developed to house a business or even a residence. Keep in mind all transactions require two parties. If you are pathetic, weak, dishonest, disingenuous, or less than straightforward, you may not be seen as someone who would be an asset to the community. If you are clean and well-kept person who keeps their word, works hard, has marketable skills, it is more likely you will be seen as a potential asset and not a risk. No one is going to give you free land if you are planning to put an old trailer on it or allow junk and trash to accumulate on the property. **Be an asset, not a liability.**

How you present yourself is critical. Keep your needs before the Lord. Do your part in cooperating with Heavenly principles such as the 10 commandments, the Golden Rule, hygienic factors, choices which lead to health and vitality and not sickness and debility, etc. Instead of having your hand out, give back to the community. Talk is cheap; our actions speak louder than words. Join a local church, feed the homeless, do random acts of kindness, etc. Be the best sincere and genuine "do-gooder" you can be. Remember, as Christians, we are God's emissaries on earth to those who do not know Him. Non-Christians observe how we live, comport ourselves, transact business, whether or not we disregard the environment **and the lives of animals**, etc. Oftentimes when they see hypocrisy, it convinces them they are better off without Christianity. We dishonor God, when by our lives, we fail to convince others there is a better way of living. Christians have access to the greatest power in the universe through praise, claiming God's promises, practicing the Golden Rule, personal testimony, and personal prayers.

There is no perfect place, but in the final analysis, when you have made your decision to purchase a piece of land, the most important thing you do is to dedicate your family and property to the Lord. When you use your land to glorify God and to help others, it is evidence you are cooperating with God's purposes. If this means you share produce from your crops, or you allow others to park their RV on your land, or whatever the Lord has asked you to do, this honors the Lord. Take the time to go over this list and then use it to optimize your search process.

Below are three generic hypothetical plans for moving to the country with limited funds. While they may lack detail, the plans target purchase of essential items to get you situated. At a minimum, you need some land, a structure providing you with living spaces, a source of water, electricity and a septic system. Obviously, additional funds are needed for ongoing improvements, etc. This assumes you have employment and a regular income. Hypothetical plans will never completely fit your circumstances, but they can give you some ideas for what might work.

Plan A: Less than $10,000 budget. Assuming you have some level of regular income and you have $10K to spend, buy 1 to 2 acres for no more than $2,000. At the end of this chapter is a list of resources. Visit each resource to learn how to bid on inexpensive properties or purchase property at an auction, etc. Once you have your property, buy a shed, travel trailer or 5th wheel for no more than $5,000. Park the travel trailer or 5th wheel on the property. This may be temporary until you can get an income stream established and build a home. For $3,000 get electric (or a generator), for heat you can get a wood burning stove (or use the generator), water and a rudimentary septic system on the property. If the property already has one or more utilities, set aside at least $1,000 for an emergency fund. Now you are in the country and can start gardening and saving money to build a modest home on the property. In the future, you could purchase small sheds to place on the property. In most cases, sheds do not need a building permit and can serve as a storage unit, a bunk house, an outhouse, or even a kitchen. If you do not have a truck to pull the travel trailer or 5th wheel, pay to have it towed to your property. Hopefully, once it is on the property, you may not need to move it for a while. If you don't have $10,000 then find someone living in the country who agrees to trade your valuable services for a place to park a travel trailer or 5th wheel. This could include property maintenance, care for farm animals, managing a greenhouse or farm operation, working on cars and other equipment, book keeping, child care, etc.

Plan B: Less than $35,000 budget. Assuming you have some form or regular income, buy one to five acres for no more than $10,000. Buy a travel trailer, 5th wheel or geodesic dome tent for no more than $10,000. Park the travel trailer or 5th wheel on the property. For $3,000 to $5,000 install electric, water and a small septic system on the property. For around $1,500 purchase a large hoop house to start gardening in as well as plant an outdoor garden. Set aside the remaining money as an emergency fund.

Plan C: $100,000 budget. Assuming you have some regular form of income, buy 1 to 10 acres for no more than $15,000. Spend no more than $40,000 to build a metal building. Spend $5,000 to $10,000 to install electric, water and septic. For around $1,500 purchase a large hoop house to start gardening in as well as plant an outdoor garden. Set aside remaining money as an emergency fund.

YOUR PLAN

Your crew:
Your budget:
Your location:
Your needs:
Reliable monthly income stream:
Emergency fund:
Time line:

Needed tools: car mechanic tools, various flashlights, various batteries, solar charger, alligator clips, various knives, chainsaw, axe, sledge hammer, various hammers, mallet, stud finder, nail gun, nails, screws, washers, bolts, electric drill and drill bits, wrenches, socket wrenches, alan keys, clamps, weed eater, tractor, mowers, shovels, rakes, hoes, screw drivers, pliers, various nails and screws, rubber hoses, rubber washers, various glues, various types of tape, various lubricants, indoor / outdoor paint (white, gray, black, etc.) spray paint (purple, white, pink, black, clear), various stains, paint sprayer, various masks, respirator, brushes, lifts, voltage tester, multi-meter, various PVC pipe sizes and joints, hinges, brushes, tarps, stakes, various sizes of wood, various sizes of aluminum, chicken wire, barbed wire, trowel, measuring tapes, laser, plumb line, wire cutters, level, grinder, compound snips, vise, zip ties, caulk and caulk gun, chisels, circular saw, various other saws, extension cord, gardening tools, ladder, dry wall knife, caliper, funnel, metal files, staple gun, crowbar, spackle spatula, sanding paper, cord / rope, bunge cords, safety glasses, scissors, shop vac, square, wire strippers, magnetic tip finder, etc.

Solar / Wind / Hydroelectric: panels, racks, turbine (wind), powerhouse flow generator (hydroelectric), battery bank, inverter, meter / control panel, power optimizers, etc.

Work Sheet for Finding and Evaluating Potential Land and Property

Should I move to the country?

1. Has God called me to move out of the city?
2. How has God opened the door for me to move?
3. What barriers, if any, are keeping me from moving to the country?

Where should I live?

4. Ideally, where do you want to live?
5. Where is God leading you and your family?
6. Has Satan has hijacked your effort to move to the country? If yes, in what ways?
7. How do you know God has paved the way for you to move to this location?
8. What if you move and it doesn't work out, will you blame God?
9. Have you asked God to be with you, even when you make a mistake?
10. Do you want to live near specific family members, friends, a church, a school, etc.?
11. Do you know the country, region, state, county, city where you prefer to live?
12. What drives your motivation to search for a property in this area?
13. If you live in the city, would you be able to access this property using only one tank of gas?
14. If you work in a city, what is the maximum practical distance to get to your country property?
15. Calculate your potential drive times to school, work, church, grocery store, shopping, airport, medical offices, etc.
16. Do you prefer hilly, flat, rolling pastures, clear, with trees, a combination of cleared land and forests, water feature(s), grazing land, structures or just land, a view, etc.? It is usually a good idea to avoid low-lying swampy land or land prone to flooding.

How much land do I need?

17. Do I have the funds to put a minimum of 20% down payment on a property? If you have the funds, then you need a current bank statement or a letter of pre-approval for up to a certain amount of money. It is ideal to outright purchase the property and not have debt.
18. How much land do you want / need to meet your goals and objectives for moving to the country?
19. How much land can you afford? Do you have readily available earnest money to reserve the land?
20. Will this be a fulltime or a seasonal residence?
21. What types of agriculture are you planning? If you are planning an orchard, greenhouse, or large garden, you will need to factor the number of trees, access to water, type of soil, etc.
22. What types of animals will you have? If you want to have farm animals, you will need to factor a location to fence and prepare for the animals.

23. Do you have enough wooded land to provide for timber to use as heating fuel? Is the timber good for burning?

What are some sources of land for sale?

24. Go to www.realtor.com , www.landandfarm.com , www.landwatch.com , www.landsofamerica.com , www.loopnet.com , www.reonomy.com , www.land.com , www.land.us , www.landandwildlife.com , www.hudhomesusa.org , www.landsearch.com , www.craigslist.com , www.landleader.com , www.crexi.com , Bank owned land, check with local and national banks for land they want to sell.
25. City and county owned land – check with city or county clerk.
26. Foreclosures – check with foreclosure web sites.
27. Land auctions – check online for upcoming auctions in the area of interest.
28. Tax delinquencies – contact the tax assessor's office at the courthouse and find out if there are any delinquent properties which might be willing to sell to avoid tax collection and wage garnishment.
29. Run-down properties with a double wide or dilapidated dwelling. At a minimum, you can tear down the structure and you do not need to put in electric, possibly gas, water and septic. This can be a big savings, even though you may have to pay for hauling away demolished waste. Sometimes there is usable lumber and other assets. Old barns usually have valuable barn wood which can be used in new builds or in other ways.
30. MLS listings; frequently check for new MLS listings.
31. Look at rental property and explore rent-to-own option with the owner.
32. Mining, timber and drilling companies may be selling land which has been previously worked.
33. Facebook marketplace and Craigslist are other potential sources for buying property.

Look up historical records on properties of interest

34. When you find several properties you are interested in, go to the county office and look up the property using the owners name. You will be able to tell who is taxing the property, school district and other valuable information.

Water Issues

35. Is there a year-round source of water on the property (e.g., creek, spring, river, lake)?
36. Will it meet your needs?
37. Will the water provide for your gardening needs?
38. What is the average annual rainfall?
39. If you plan to collect rain water, what structures will you use / need?
40. Is it legal to collect rain water in this state / county?
41. If you are going to drill a well, check local drilling records for information about well depth, flow rate, seasonal changes, etc. Get a well log of surrounding properties to determine how deep your neighbors dug to find water.
42. If there is a well, what is the flow rate (a minimal flow rate could be a concern)?

43. Is the water contaminated with heavy metals (e.g., arsenic, manganese, iron)?

44. Always test the water for contaminants. Does water have sulfur or metallic taste?

45. Also check with the water district and / or local irrigation district to determine availability and costs.

46. If you want to use city water it may cost several thousands of dollars to tap into municipal water.

47. Keep in mind, if the well freezes or the pump breaks, you will not have water unless you have a backup system.

48. Water restrictions and water rights. There are various types of water rights to understand. Be sure you understand any type of water rights or restrictions associated with a potential property. There are rights to surface water, riparian rights (land which abuts a river or stream), littoral rights (land which abuts an ocean, bay, delta, sea, lake), and possibly other types of common law rights to water. Be sure to understand irrigation water rights if this applies to your situation. All this needs to be researched before you purchase a property with water. People may be able to access your land along rivers and streams for the purpose of fishing and hiking.

49. If you rely on a pond or lake for water, is it located above, at same elevation, or below where you plan to build or where the home is located? Will you need to pump your water or will you be able to use gravity flow to access water? Is there a water source near the building site? Where is it located in relation to the building site (i.e., above, on same level, below)? Calculate psi at ½ pound for every foot of elevation above the building site / home. If a creek is present, calculate the flow – gallons / minute.

50. Will you share the water feature with other land owners? What are the restrictions for lake use? Some restrictions might include use of motor craft? Wakes generated by motor craft may cause erosion of private property bordering lakes and rivers. What types of water craft are allowed? Are there additional fees associated with living on the waterfront? Taxes, water inspections, etc.?

Suitability of the property

51. If you have small children, are there dangerous features intrinsic to this property? If yes, how would you deal with them?

52. Is electricity available at site? Is natural gas available or do you need propane? City water / sewer?

53. Are you planning to be off the grid?

54. Is the land / property in your preference area rocky, clay, or does it have good soil? Has top soil washed away? What is the slope of the land? Is it too steep to farm?

55. Do you want land near federal lands or do you want to be relatively close to non-federal outposts?

56. How far from a major highway do you want to live?

57. Is this an area where the forest is being cut down / cleared or is it grazing pastures? Does the property around your property of interest have timber rights clauses?

58. If there are trees, are there enough to use for winter fuel for the next 10 to 20 years?

59. If the land is wooded or partly wooded, is there a lot of undergrowth to the trees? If so, there is greater risk of severe fire.

60. Are people wanting to move to this area, possibly negating reason for moving to a secluded area?

61. What is the orientation of the property? If it is hilly or mountainous, forested or cleared, which direction does it face? This may determine how you heat the house, garden, set up a solar array, etc.
62. What is the elevation of the property?
63. How far do you want to live from the nearest town / city? Super market? Auto Zone? Tractor Supply? Costco? Hospital? Doctor's office (especially if you have small children)?
64. How far away do you want to live from the nearest large metropolitan center? Airport?
65. What do you like about the location?
66. What do you dislike about the location?
67. What is the level of poverty in this location?
68. What is the education level, income level, etc.?
69. What about crime? Who patrols the area? City or county law enforcement? Does 911 work in your area? Look at online at this site: https://www.bjs.gov/ , https://www.statista.com , https://www.fbi.gov, state crime commissions, city statistics and other sites may help you determine the level and types of common crimes. Check out this website for sexual offender registry websites: https://www.fbi.gov/scams-and-safety/sex-offender-registry . <u>You may not want to live next to a convicted child molester or rapist</u>. You can find this information online. Data bases provide addresses, names and the nature of the conviction.
70. Describe what you know about weather events for the location? Check out what the Farmer's Almanac writes about the location.
71. Are there structures on the property? A house, barn(s), workshop, etc.? What is their condition?
72. How close are the nearest neighbors? Are they visible from the property of interest?
73. Are your neighbors planning to sell the property, subdivide, develop, etc.? Find out if they are willing to offer purchase rights to you first before putting their property on the market.
74. Do neighbors dump hazardous materials into local ponds, creeks, etc., which could show up in your water?
75. Do neighbors have a vacation rental business, which could bring lots of people into the area?
76. If you want to have a vacation rental business, is it allowed, or do ordinances prevent it?
77. In some areas, there are local pockets of people who are a law unto themselves. When a new-comer moves into the area and begins to make changes or ask local law enforcement to enforce laws on the books (previously ignored), they like to take matters into their hands, which may result in defacing your property and might even result in personal harm threats. Find out if such an element exists in the area of interest. This might explain why the property is cheap and the seller is eager to unload the property.
78. Are there potential business opportunities related to the land (e.g., retreat, commercial crops, orchards, vineyards, valuable rocks, rock climbing, air strip, horseback riding trails, wilderness survival training, canoeing, kayaking, boating, etc.)?
79. How likely is it the land around would be built up within the next 10 years?

80. Will you have year-round access to the property or will snow and / or rainy season limit access? Sometimes just a 20-minute drive can make a big difference in the amount of snow accumulation.

81. Who is responsible for snow plowing the roads?

82. What is the condition of the roads?

83. Who does road maintenance? If there are pot holes they will only get worse over time.

84. Will you need to purchase different vehicles to safely use the back roads? How long is the rough road? Are you willing to invest in more durable tires or do you enjoy frequently changing tires?

85. Are you able and willing to invest in land maintenance country living equipment such as bush hogs, tractors, road grading equipment, tilling equipment, etc.

86. Is there a nearby casino?

87. Is the property near an Indian reservation?

88. Is there a dormant dump site on or near the property?

89. Talk to the locals as well as several local real estate agents about the property to find out subjective and objective information which may be otherwise difficult to locate.

90. Do you like the school district?

91. Does potential property border Forest Service land? How frequently do Forrest Service personnel survey and patrol the area around your property?

92. What are the potential seasonal issues such as flooding, hurricanes, tornadoes, seasonal / summer vacationers, hikers, kayakers, campers, outdoor concerts, etc.

93. What is your attitude toward the second amendment of the USA constitution regarding gun ownership, gun usage, and defending your property? Become familiar with local law enforcement and their attitude toward gun usage laws. Be sure you understand state gun laws, concealed carry, etc.

94. Look at GIS (geographic information system) maps for topography, dirt roads, cabins, neighbors, etc. Look for hidden industries such as poultry farming, cattle farming, mining, etc.

95. What is the growing season / climate? Check the USDA Hardiness Zone Map (see Figure 1). See more detailed maps of the USA and Canada at the end of this section. You can find information about temperatures, rain totals, seasonal peculiarities, etc.

96. What is the average length of the growing season. Some places with long growing seasons allow for planting 2 or 3 crops, while colder climates usually only allow for one summer crop plus fall and spring crops. For every 1,000 feet rise in elevation the temperature drops by an average of 3.5 °F.

97. Get the legal address of the property including the county and go to county website, property appraisal page, and see how the property is zoned. If it does not list the word "agricultural" then you may not be able to farm and homestead. Check all zoning restrictions. Research municipal zoning codes for locations of interest.

98. Are there valuable natural resources on the land?

99. Check to see if property is in the 100-year flood zone. Also, determine if the property is in an area that is subject to frequent flooding. Avoid purchasing land and buildings in washes and gullies.

100. Can you subdivide the property?

101. Are HOA fees associated with the property?
102. Check code of ordinances. What types of businesses / industries can move into neighborhood?
103. Noise ordinances.
104. Drone ordinances.
105. There may be restrictions on placing an RV on the land. Some restrictions are based on square footage. If it is your plan to put an RV on the property, check with local ordinances to ensure this is legal and copacetic.
106. Is it level enough for an RV? Is there septic, electric, water at the site?
107. Are there protections for specific species of animals and / or fish?
108. Are there limitations on wood-burning fireplaces, etc.?
109. Warranty deed – be sure you have this.
110. Title insurance. Be sure the title is clean and clear. Start by requesting pre-title insurance. This gets the title research process initiated and makes it easier when a closing date is set to ensure the title is free and clear.
111. Are there covenants associated with the property? Covenants are legal conditions associated with the use and ownership of the land. Covenants are in place regardless of the owner. Covenants may affect the value and desirability of the land. It is critical to research whether or not the potential property is governed by covenants. Covenants could include cell tower lease, architectural, residential vs. commercial use, etc.
112. Mineral rights (above- and in-ground).
113. Easements can be tricky. The title company does research for deeded easements affecting the property, including property access. If you do not have access to your land via an easement, it may not be what you want. Surrounding land owners must cooperate, otherwise it is a good idea to pass on a property with no access. Be sure you precisely understand which companies, property owners, and others have legal access to your property and vice versa. Sometimes deeded easement roads are required for property access.
114. Local industries may have claims to land use such as a timber clause made by the previous owner.
115. Do ATV trails cross over or near the land? What are use guidelines. Are there a lot of trails indicating heavy use? Seasonal or year-round use?
116. Are there restrictions for other types of buildings?
117. If the property abuts a national park or federal land, do not build or cut down trees on these lands.
118. Are there restrictions on the type of housing allowed on property?
119. What types of wildlife are commonly seen on the land? Is it a migration route? Rocky land may increase the likelihood of finding snakes and scorpions.
120. Is hunting allowed on the land or local properties? Some land owners may request hunting rights be retained even after the sale of the property.
121. Contamination of natural resources, such as copper mining next to a river, local dumps, etc.

122. Ask about local gatherings, conferences, etc.
123. Find out how the community gets together in the neighboring area for concerts, swap meets, etc.
124. The buyer should opt for a property survey. It is essential. If possible, walk the property line before buying.
125. Has a PERC test been done? If yes, how recent? Was it done near building site or septic area?
126. Is there a septic system? How old is the septic system? Older systems may not meet existing requirements. Rocky land may increase difficulty in digging and laying septic field lines. If there is an existing septic system, how often does it need to be pumped? Are you be required to get an aerobic system? Are their restrictions for aerobic septic systems?
127. Are trees dying on the property? This indicates potential drought or even poisoning issues.
128. Is the property rocky, clay soil, no topsoil? These may seriously impact your gardening plans.
129. Has the property been fracked, mined? If yes, test ground water for contamination.
130. Can you build using geothermal heating on this property?
131. Are there poisonous plants on the property? Poison ivy and oak can be a problem. Are there other poisonous plants such as giant hogweed, hemlock, etc.
132. Is property level, sloped, mountainous, etc.? Is there enough level space to build and garden?
133. Does the property have a pest problem (e.g., bears, big cats, wild boars, snakes, scorpions)? Will it be difficult to protect domesticated pets and livestock?
134. How close are essential services?
135. Is property on or near fault lines? Tornado alley? Hurricane area? Flood zone? Nuclear plant?
136. Is the property near high voltage wires, a large cell phone tower or a rail road track or crossing?
137. Check out weather trends for past 30 years.
138. If property is not fenced, how difficult, how expensive would it be to fence in the property?
139. How complicated is the permit process for building a home and other structures? What kind of inspections are required?
140. What about cell phone signal? Find out what company the neighbors use? WIFI signal? Find out which internet provider neighbors use. What about the presence of 5G towers? Are you comfortable being in an area without cell phone coverage?
141. How much would insurance run?
142. Other potential issues:
143. _____.

Resources

Finding and Buying You Place in the Country by Les & Carol Scher, ISBN: 0793141095 / ISBN-13: 978-0793141098

Land & Property Research in the United States by E. Wade Hone, ISBN: 159331325X / ISBN-13: 978-1593313258

https://www.youtube.com/watch?v=2qcsWajivnl
https://www.landwatch.com/
https://www.landcentury.com/under-1000-land-deals
https://cheaplands.com/
https://ruralvacantland.com/
https://www.land.com/
https://www.landsofamerica.com/
https://www.landandfarm.com/
https://www.governmentauction.com/default.aspx
https://lowcostland.com/
https://www.landzero.com/
https://www.landflip.com/
https://americanforestmanagement.com/
https://momsmakecents.com/free-land/
https://ebay.com – look under land and real estate
https://www.google.com/earth/
https://www.homestead.org/frugality-finance/how-to-buy-land-very-cheaply/
http://www.classiccountryland.com/properties/government-land-for-sale

Discussion questions

1. What other considerations should we make in evaluating a potential land purchase?
2. How close in proximity do you want to be to other like-minded believers?
3. Have you ever used googleearth.com to look at land from above?
4. What buying mistakes have you previously made?
5. Do you feel it is a good idea to live communally?

Chapter 53

Evaluating the homestead and other structures

Over the years and as a single woman, I have bought five houses and looked at hundreds. The first house I bought was beautiful and perfect except for one small detail: it was pathologically close to a railroad crossing. I developed a sleep disorder and only lasted 18 months living at that address. The second house was in a perfect location and was awesome. I hated moving to relocate to a different state. The third house was a well-built custom home and also a great buy. The fourth house I bought, tragically turned out to be a money pit. It took years to recover from the trauma of this home. I keep the huge stack of receipts from all the expenditures on this home as a reminder to avoid making a similar mistake. Even though I lost money on this home, I learned many important life lessons. The last house I bought was lovely. It was on several acres in the country, surrounded on three sides by spring-fed creeks. It had been outfitted with an expensive de-humidifying system before I bought it which kept the relative indoor humidity below 55%. Because of the nearby water features, it attracted snakes and tended to cause minor flooding to the driveway area but not the house. Overall a great experience. Three out of five homes were good purchases (60%). If I had used a checklist, I might have avoided purchasing the two difficult homes and saved myself a lot of time and money. This is why it is important to write down your "must have" features and the "nice to have" features.

Recently, I looked at an out-of-state property with a small cabin on 8 acres. The property was 18 miles outside of a town with a population of about 5,000. It was 8 miles off of a two-lane highway. The last 2 miles were on a gravel / dirt road. The scenery along the drive to the cabin was spectacular. I had to cross a beautiful river as I got onto the gravel part of the road. I was excited to see the property. When I drove up, I knew this was the place! I loved it! I left telling the owner I would likely submit an offer as soon as possible. However, upon returning home, I prayed about it. Almost immediately, I couldn't believe it when the answer seemed to be, no, not this property. After many discussions with the owner, an inspection, and obtaining additional information, I decided to drive the 700 miles round trip to take a second look at the property.

The second time I looked at the property, I noticed a lot of things I had missed the first time. The land was beautiful, but was heavily wooded. I didn't have much of a view or a place for a garden and hoop house. The price was reasonable, but upon reading the deed, I found all the timber and mineral rights in the area were owned by a multi-national company. There was a significant easement with a road on the edge of the property. The cabin was built within feet of the property line on one side and on the other side of the narrow strip, the neighbor's property was visible, as well as a large trash pile. I never knew you could buy a place and not own the timber. This was an important lesson to learn. Even though the property was on 8 acres, it was a narrow strip of land, meaning there would be little to no privacy. According to nearby neighbors, the next-door neighbors were somewhat noisy and random. The cabin on the property was 25 years old and needed a significant amount of updating. There was mold underneath the house and there were huge rivulets all along the driveway, making it extra challenging to navigate, even with a

4-wheel drive vehicle. What initially seemed so attractive turned out to be much more problematic after an inspection and a second visit. There was also a nudist colony about a mile up the road.

Avoid the mistake of committing early and falling in love with a property without having enough useful information upon which to base a decision. Ultimately, it is important to pray about these decisions and then consider the surrounding circumstances and facts. Get a home inspection! Consider the inspector's findings? What are the hard facts regarding the property? How does the property compare against your checklist? Is prayer about the property giving you a contrary answer?

Another mistake to avoid is purchasing property with other families. While this might initially seem like a great idea, sometimes plans change and now the finances, commitment and original plan can fall apart. Instead of jointly purchasing a property, it is better to buy properties in close proximity or buy a common piece of land and divide it. Communal living might sound like a good idea, but there are enough examples of how this has spectacularly failed, to seriously consider other alternatives.

If money is an issue, consider buying land and then placing a large shed on the property. You can add a wood stove, a couple of beds and a rudimentary kitchen and the shed can serve as a temporary shelter until permanent housing is built. Usually, sheds do not need a building permit, nor do they need an inspection (always check local ordinances). A shed can be converted back to a storage building from a small cabin when you finish building a cabin or other type of living structure on the property.

How much land do you need to minimize noisy neighbors? I did a little research and found a wide range of answers, but the minimum amount of property, depending on the size and shape of the property as well as the topography, is around 50 acres. Hundreds of acres are better. One site recommended an eight-mile by eight-mile property to ensure minimal bothersome influences (1 square mile = 640 acres). This is 64 square miles, a lot of land to find and afford to purchase. This might be why many people prefer to buy land which abuts to a national forest or is more mountainous in nature. Finding property near a stream or river may help minimize certain types of noise. Even the ambient noises of horses and cattle may help.

Most people are not able to afford 50+ acres in the country. Pray for spiritual eyesight to see a good deal when it becomes available, regardless of size. Even one acre without close neighbors can be a blessing and provide a productive mini-farm. If you are entrepreneurial, buy 15 or more acres and place RV pads on ½ acre lots. An RV pad includes electric, septic, water, parking spaces and a fenced in area for pets. Assuming you have well water, an RV pad would cost anywhere from $3,000 to $7,000 to build. If you buy 30 acres and half of it is usable, this gives you 30, ½ acre RV sites. If you buy the land for $50,000 to $70,000 and then build 30 RV sites at $5,000 per site, that is a $220,000 investment. Assuming you charge $500 to $1,000 per site per month, this is a monthly income of at least $15,000. At this rate, it may take you just over a year to break even. RV pad sites are usually gravel (4 – 6 inches deep; #57 or #2 washed gravel) or concrete. Pads should be at least 45 feet long by 10 to 15 feet wide. While there is an initial investment in the property and RV pads, you may easily make a rapid return on your investment plus a profit within the first year or two. Once you pay off the RV pads and land, plan to build several hoop houses as a community garden and then build a large metal building which could serve as a community center, school, church, craft room, etc. This brings together a small community while allowing each family to live independently. Be sure to establish strict rental guidelines and get everything in writing (i.e., a contract), so there are no misunderstandings. Issues such as quiet hours, domesticated animals, number of people and cars allowed per site, trash disposal, hygiene factors, guests, etc., should all be codified and strictly enforced for the general welfare of everyone. This is just one example of how small groups may come together for a common purpose and allow families to live inexpensively while saving money to buy their own land.

It is best to choose a property you can afford, if not outright purchase. Better to slowly improve the property as funds become available than to buy an expensive property and be a slave to the bank. You may qualify to purchase a property but what happens if you lose your job or become disabled? Now you own a property you cannot afford which may be difficult to sell. You may have to take a loss. Again, buying a property you must finance adds a huge variable which is not always within your control.

Get everything, every agreement, every detail in writing and into the contract. **NEVER trust an oral agreement or a handshake**. This may occasionally work, but more often than not, it is a recipe for disaster. If there is a "surprise claus" in the contract, ask for a day or two to review it. Take several days to pray and go over the contract before signing. Take time to understand every aspect of the contract. Do not be afraid to call off signing a contract if you are unsure it is the right decision or if the other party includes a "surprise" clause. If you have any doubt, take several different friends to the property to look for potential downsides. Never pre-commit to a property, no matter how appealing the initial deal may appear, until you have thoroughly examined it, especially if the property is run down. Always get a contractor to inspect it and give you repair estimates for all needed repairs.

Checklists provide a way to improve decision-making, especially when your checklist is composed before you begin the search process and appropriately modified during the process. Take a few minutes or even days to write down everything you desire in a country property. This way, when you see the property, you will know it is the right property. The next few pages contain items to include on your checklist. Not all the items are relevant to everyone. If you have experience buying properties, you may not need this checklist. If you are not knowledgeable about property and structures, take someone with you who can point out their strengths and weaknesses.

In the final analysis, a beautiful property and a modest home on the land should be a happy place, full of comfortable surroundings, with logical flow, lots of natural light, proximity to garden and flower beds, a place to work and a place to rest, lots of great smells including the smell of fresh bread baking in the oven, the heady fragrance of mixed flower bouquets, family pictures on the walls, height chart markings on the door jamb, your favorite artwork hanging on the walls, and a couple of domesticated animals happy to just hang out with you and your family. Not everyone is lucky enough to have a nuclear family, so count your blessings when you have a close-knit family and a loving network of friends and colleagues. You are blessed!

Jack

My companions

Speckles 1

Shelby

Major issues regarding the land and living structure(s)

1. Can I afford this property? If not, can the property be subdivided to a smaller more affordable parcel? You may be able to get a loan for the property but this does not mean you can afford it. Affording something implies you are also able to fund and pay for the rest of your needs such as nutritious food, car upkeep and maintenance, children's schooling, annual vacation / breaks, health insurance, medical bills, utilities, etc. A good rule of thumb when purchasing a property is to avoid payments that exceed 25% of your take home pay after taxes and tithe and offerings.

2. Do I want a mortgage? The bank owns your home until the mortgage is paid off. How many months can you afford to make mortgage payments if your income is interrupted? Even if you pay cash for the home and own it, you still owe yearly taxes. If you can, pay your property taxes several years in advance. If you are 60 or older, you may qualify to freeze property tax increases.

3. Is this property offered at an appropriate value? If it is over-valued, will the owner come down on the price or be offended if you make a significantly lower offer?

4. Look into obtaining a USDA rural development loan to purchase a property in rural areas. These loans are for low- and very-low income applicants. You may be able to purchase a country home for as little as $1,000 down.

5. I recommend avoiding all properties with Home Owners Association (HOA) fees. The fees may seem reasonable but you are at the mercy of the HOA as far as future increases go. The HOA may also govern how you keep up your yard, what can be kept on your front porch, the color of external paint, mailboxes, etc. It is best to just avoid purchasing property when an HOA is involved.

6. Location!!! This is usually the first consideration. A great property can be all wrong if it is near a dairy or poultry farm, a sewage treatment plant, a prison, rail road tracks, a race track, a retreat where there are large annual gatherings, a shooting range, large illegal crops, lots of ATV trails, near a river that seasonally floods, chemical dumping, etc. Personally, I prefer to be as far away as possible from rail road tracks. I like to sleep with an open window and train whistles potentially interfere with my sleep. I also prefer to be where there are no artificial bright lights. Talk to locals and look at satellite images to see what is near the property under consideration. One exception to the location principle, might be when you need to live in a certain area or place to be near family and / or a job. Some things are more critical than finding the ideal location, but even if you are limited to a specific geographic location, you may still be able to optimize the location of where you buy and build. Also, it may not be located near a sewage treatment plant, but there might be future plans to build a sewage treatment plant on adjacent land. Find out if there are future plans for development.

7. Does the property appear to be well-maintained? If possible walk the property, send up a drone to look at the property, look at satellite images of the property, etc.

8. Is the house directionally suited for the climate or location? If the house is in a hot climate, a southern or western facing living area may easily warm up and be difficult to cool. If you are purchasing in a cold climate zone, you want a south-facing home where the sunlight warms the house during the day.

9. Are there large trees shading the structure? Are there bushes right next to the structure? Both trees and bushes near the structure may be fire hazards and may be fall hazards during severe rain and wind storms as well as contributing to dampness and darkness. Sunlight and fresh air work great together to cleanse the home and promote a hygienic environment.

10. Does the property have water? Well(s), creeks (seasonal or all year), rivers, lakes, ponds, waterfront, etc.? Is the water source above the house, level with the house or below in elevation to the house? This will determine how you move water to the house. Is the water clean / pure? Is it hard or soft?

11. Does it have high levels of heavy metals? If you live in an area where there are manganese deposits, you may have toxic levels of manganese in the water. This can lead to a LOT of health issues for the entire family (which may be overlooked by most healthcare practitioners). Will you need a whole house filtration system? Hard water may affect your pipes, depending on the material. Get a water test to know what you are dealing with. There are simple home testing kits and additional testing can be done by the county.

12. Neighbors are critical! If you have neighbors nearby, you have no control over their activities. Things such as outdoor lighting, the noise levels, is there a registered sex offender living next door, their frequent visitors, how they dispose of trash, how many pit bulls they allow to roam free, etc. There is a national sex offender registry where you can enter an address and it shows how many sex offenders live in a specific zip code. It even provides their exact address. Before buying a property, plan on spending a good part of at least 1 week day and 1 weekend day watching the neighbor's activities. It is advisable to also see how they handle evenings and nights. Do you suspect they use alcohol? Drugs?

13. Disclosures are important. They should be thorough and complete. As part of the inspection, determine whether or not a house has previously been infested with termites, scorpions, snakes, etc. Is there previous damage due to water, fire, tornado, mold, etc.? Asbestos? Lead paint? What type of insulation is used? Other hazards? Always examine the crawl space under a pillar post type house for standing water, mold, floor joist issues, foundation issues, etc.

14. Regarding structures, the type of foundation is worth considering. Do you prefer a slab foundation or pillar post? Cracks in the walls and ceilings may indicate foundation issues as well as windows which won't easily open and shut and uneven floors. Foundation cracks may also be seen in the slab. Sometimes you can see how the foundation has settled or sunk too much. Kitchen cabinets separating from the wall may indicate foundation issues. Are large nearby shrub or trees roots buckling the foundation (and potentially interfering with plumbing), is there clay in the soil which may cause the ground to contract and expand based on weather; this issue does not resolve on its own. These are just some of the foundation issues to examine.

15. If the house is pillar-post, what is the condition of the floor joists and the crawl space?

16. Make sure the wood under the house is not rotten or termite damaged. Always get a termite inspection from a highly reputable termite inspector. Get a guarantee on the termite inspection and sign up for regular termite control visits. Termites can cause thousands of dollars of damage if not eradicated and then annually treated with preventive measures. Do not take the word of the seller on termites.

17. What is the roof's condition? What type of roof? Does the roof sag? Is it missing pieces? How old is it? Does it leak? Does it have a warranty? Hail damage? Other types of damage? Condition of the attic fans? Physically inspect the roof. While looking at the roof, check out the gutters? First, are there gutters? Do the gutters go around the entire edge of the roof or are they just in specific areas? If there are gutters, are they clean and in working order? How do they drain? Are they functional?

18. What direction does roof face (generally a south-facing roof is good for solar panel placement)?

19. What is the capacity of the AC / heating system? How old? How soon does it need replacement? Is it energy efficient? Run the system for an extended amount of time to find out if it works.

20. Check out the water heater. How old is it? What is the capacity? Has it been regularly cleaned (i.e., is it full of silt on the bottom)? If the hot water runs out right away, it probably has not been cleaned. Does it have a warranty? If it needs to be replaced, ask for a reduction in price to compensate for a replacement.

21. Does the house have decks? If yes, what is the condition of the deck(s)? Have they been kept up or ignored? Do they need to be repaired or replaced? Decks can be expensive to repair and replace. Are they wood or composite materials? Do they need to be re-stained?

22. Bathrooms and kitchens need to be carefully inspected. Are faucets in working order? Filtration systems working? Test all of the faucets, lights, look at the built-in medicine cabinets? Is it rusted? Does it need to be replaced? Is the tub / shower in good shape or does it need major repairs? Is the shower door cracked? Is there mold in the shower? Let the water run and see if the drain backs up. I have actually seen plants growing out of the shower drain. This is not a good sign. Flush the toilet a bunch of times. Look in the tank on the back of the toilet. Is it clean or not? Check the seal around where the toilet meets the floor. Examine for potential leaks.

23. Is outdoor water drainage adequate, is a French drain needed? Loss of topsoil? What is the predominant type of soil? Are there large rivulets around the perimeter of the house? This indicates water is removing the top soil and damaging driveways which requires leveling and new gravel.

24. Is there standing water in the basement, watermarks on the floor / walls / ceilings? Are the ceiling and walls crumbling? This is a terrible sign and should never be ignored.

25. Look for black mold in and under the house; moist and potentially moldy basements; what is the humidity level? A constant relative humidity of 55% or higher leads to mold. Mitigating mold usually takes time, money and long-term investment. If you want to avoid mold issues do not buy properties in areas where high humidity is an issue.

26. Is the property in a flood zone? If the property is in a flood zone, you may not have enough top soil for immediate gardening needs, although if you decide to purchase the property, you can still plant a garden. It usually requires amendments and lots of organic material to build up the soil.

27. Where is the nearest fire station? Can a fire truck access your property and home? If you are outside of the protection of the local fire department, how does this impact home owner's insurance rates? This information is on the property tax statement. If there is no itemized cost for fire protection you are not covered or you may be under protection of Bureau of Land Management (BLM).

28. Lots of trees close to house and covering the roof may lead to mold, increased fire hazard, etc. If you have to pay someone for tree removal, be sure you get estimates before you buy. In some areas, this can be a significant expense.

29. If the house has well water, make sure you understand what is involved in having a well, etc. If the water is mineral rich, this may impact the condition of the plumbing pipes. If there is hard water, are you able to install a water purification / filtration system?

30. Plumbing is a large ticket item if it needs repairs or updating. If necessary, get a plumber to evaluate potential issues. Be sure to look at basement plumbing as well as how plumbing connects to city or well water, are there large trees in the path of the plumbing, test for slow leaks by watching the meter, listening for leeks, cameras, etc. Also, determine plumbing pipe material. Is it copper or

plastic? What is the interior condition of the pipes that contain your drinking water? This can be absolutely frightening and can affect your family's health.

31. Electrical issues, get an electrician to evaluate the safety of the electrical system, look at outlets for modern wiring, etc. Determine if there are added sections to the house and if electricity in all areas is up to the same grade. Is the electric box outdated and dangerous or is it safe and solid? Do you want to automate your electricity? Do you want to connect to solar or other types of electricity generators?

32. Examine integrity of all the wood found in the kitchen, around the sinks, bathrooms, around the toilets, outside wood, floor joists, indoor wood, make sure there is no wood rot, look for termites, look for wasp damaged wood, etc. Is damage superficial or problematic in nature? If there is wood along the roofline, get up on a ladder and inspect the condition of the wood. Also make sure there are no unprotected openings into the house. This allows wild animals and other pests to freely enter and leave the home.

33. Thoroughly examine attic for presence of leaks, condition of attic fans, condition of wood, insulation sufficiency, rats and other pests. If rats are present, you may also have snakes and other critters. This reminds me of a friend who, while she carried a box of decorations down a ladder from the attic, she felt something move and a snake tumbled out of the box. She almost fainted and fell off the ladder along with the snake. Needless to say, her husband had to immediately leave work to eliminate the reptile. Where there are mice and / or rats, there may be snakes.

34. If the house has a basement, spend time in the basement looking for water damage, drainage, mold, pest invasion, structural issues, plumbing issues, support beams, etc. Ask the owner if there is a drainage system (e.g., French drain) to keep water out of the basement or from walls which are low lying and possibly in the path of water draining from a higher point to a lower point.

35. Make sure the floor is level – this can be a major irritation if you fail to recognize it, especially if this is in the kitchen, bathroom, etc. Take a golf ball or a level to determine if the floors [and walls] are level. Sometimes adding heavy tile to a weak wood floor causes the floor to buckle and changes the elevations, up to a 5 or 6 inch differential.

36. Do you like the layout of the rooms, size of the rooms, specific laundry room area, butler's pantry (area to store canned and preserved food), etc. Where would you place kitchen appliances (e.g., dehydrators, blenders, mixers, juicers, freezer, additional refrigerator)? Do you want a main floor master bedroom or is an upstairs master bedroom ok? Are children's rooms near enough to the master bedroom? Are children's rooms safe and not easily accessed from outside? If you entertain and need a large dining room area, make sure you have a large enough space for this function. Make sure the house has the rooms you need to function or space which can be modified to include these areas. Do not rely on the possibility of adding on to the structure. This may or may not materialize. Evaluate just the structure as it stands and not the possibility of future additions. This doesn't mean you won't eventually add on to the house, but it takes into consideration that add-ons take time and money and do not usually happen in a timely manner.

37. Are there enough storage areas in the home?

38. Do you prefer a home with or without a second floor? At what age do you think you might not want to go up and down one or more flights of stairs? If you plan for this home to be your "forever" home, consider how you might prefer a one floor ranch style home over a two-story farmhouse home. If the master bedroom is on the main floor, a two-story home might be a good option.

39. Make sure all windows work, move up and down, lock, etc. Are there cracks or gaps in the window sill, doors, etc.? Windows which are stuck or have large cracks in the fittings may indicate foundation issues.

40. Would you need to remove or build a wall inside the home? Is the wall a simple dry wall composition or is it plaster, which is much more difficult to remove? Is it a support wall or not? This may determine whether or not you can easily remove or modify the wall.

41. Is there a place for a wood burning stove? Determine where you would install a wood burning stove if the house does not already have one.

42. Condition of the fireplace bricks / stones. Check the outer bricks and the inner bricks. Does the chimney need to be cleaned? Is there creosote buildup in the chimney?

43. Attached vs. detached garage vs. carport, place to put tools, etc. It is important to have a garage or a dedicated area for tools, woodworking equipment, etc. Does it have a shed(s), what is the condition of the shed, etc.?

44. Does the property have a steep driveway / lawn area? If the driveway is steep, it can be a hazard for driving in cold and icy conditions. It may also be a hazard for young children, who like to run and bike up and down the driveway and play in the yard. This also means the lawn will be more difficult to mow, etc.

45. Condition of pavement, outside walls, are they crumbling, are there missing bricks etc.? If they are in the crumbling phase, they may need immediate repair.

46. Do large trees need to be removed? I recommend removing large trees within a 20 to 50 foot radius of the outside of the house, especially trees which appear to be leaning toward the house or play areas. Small fruit-bearing trees or Japanese maples might be less problematic while still offering some shade and heat relief. Certainly, trees near water lines and septic tanks should be removed or their roots may destroy plumbing and septic pipes.

47. Quality of indoor workmanship for kitchen cupboards, bathrooms, windows, etc. Do doors close and seal? Are cupboards laminate or solid wood? Are the handles cheap or durable and sturdy?

48. Is the dryer vent against an outside wall? This makes venting easier and it is less of a fire hazard. Avoid laundry rooms which are in the interior of the house. This requires a long venting system and may need an annual inspection and cleaning.

49. Do you like the external looks of the house? If you hate it, this may not change and could ruin your home-buying experience. If it is just the matter of changing the paint color or adding landscaping, it could be considered minor, but if you hate the large bay window or don't like spindly pillars, these are major issues.

50. If the previous owners have added rooms or sections to the original home, be sure to compare the foundation, types of materials used, sturdiness and workmanship of the addition. If they did not get a permit, this could be an issue.

51. If the home has an in-ground pool, I highly recommend having a pool expert examine the integrity of the pool and its related equipment.

52. Is the condition of the floor adequate for immediate living? Does it need repair, refinishing, new carpet, etc.? Personally, I don't like carpet or linoleum flooring. They are made of petroleum products and generally off-gas some pretty toxic chemicals over a relatively long period of time. Carpet retains dirt, pollen, pollution, hair, skin, and lots of other disgusting microscopic things. I have

known people who have lived in a house with carpet and never had it cleaned. This may be a legitimate source of allergens and even mold.

53. Speaking about black mold, check every corner, every wall, every bathroom, check the A/C vents, A/C filter, basement, pull up carpet in areas with water pipes, etc., to check for black mold. This can be a serious issue which may negatively affect your health for decades.

54. If the house is partially built into a hillside, be sure there are no mold or drainage issues.

55. I recommend buying a home warranty at the time of purchase. This ensures replacement of appliances which may break down within the first year or two of purchase. I have used this enough to believe it is worthwhile. It is usually purchased by the seller at the buyer's request.

56. If the house uses a septic system, get all the details about access, location of field lines, last date of cleaning, which service to use, etc. Is the septic tank functional and adequate? This likely requires a site inspection by a septic tank expert.

57. If there are other structures on the property, be sure to inspect them as well. You may be assuming they have inherent value, but upon close inspection, they do not add value, but represent a potential hazard.

58. Find out if the outer buildings come with the purchase. Sometimes the seller takes their metal shed or greenhouse with them. This is usually spelled out in the contract, but it is good to have this information as you are considering the purchase.

59. Where will you place a small to large garden and accompanying structures? What is the condition of the soil? If you do soil testing before purchasing, what amendments does the soil need?

60. I have known of properties which have a small grave on them. This may mean strangers have access to the property from time to time. Something to consider.

61. Does the property have a storm shelter or a safe room? This is a good thing to know in case the property is located in tornado alley.

62. If there is a large gun safe on the property, be sure to find out if it goes with the property or will it be removed. If it stays be sure to get the code to open the safe at the sale of the house. Some safes are so large and heavy it is better to leave them behind than to move them.

63. If you want to install solar panels, where would you install them and where would you store batteries?

64. Confirm which appliances and / or other items are included with the purchase of the property. This could include refrigerators, freezer, dishwasher, gas stove tops, ovens, washer, dryer, garbage disposal, lighting, chandeliers, animals, sheds, wood, stained glass, door knockers, etc. Confirm light fixtures and everything which is included in the purchase. Sometimes, certain light fixtures are removed and not included in the purchase.

65. What equipment, if any, goes with the purchase of the property? This could include mowers, tractors, watercraft, mailboxes, gates, signs, jacuzzi, sauna, extra building materials, rocks, etc.

66. Confirm what happens with the dog(s) and / or cat(s) living on the property. Be sure to get a forwarding address and / or contact information in case you need to contact the previous owners.

67. Determine if the property comes with security cameras. If there are security cameras on the property, be sure you know their location, monitoring costs and how to access the feeds.

68. Also, in this digital era, it is important to sweep for hidden electronic monitoring devices. You can easily purchase a relatively inexpensive device to detect hidden cameras, microphones, etc. I strongly urge you to purchase such an item for use when traveling and using public hotels and even private homes, and of course to use before moving into a new home.
69. Others:_____.
70. _____.
71. _____.
72. _____.

Minor issues

1. Paint color.
2. Ceiling popcorn.
3. Is the garbage disposal adequate and functional?
4. Does septic tank need cleaning? Do you know where the septic clean-out lines are?
5. Is there a fence? What is the condition of the fence? Locks on the fence?
6. Are bushes too close to the house?
7. Is there an outside clothes line? Condition?
8. Will all plants and bushes remain? Are there lots of tree stumps in the yard area?
9. Are windows and door frames adequately sealed? Do the doors fit into the door frames?
10. How is internet service? Sometimes a metal roof interferes with telephone and internet signals.
11. How does the lawn look? Is there sparse grass, lots of weeds, rickety fence, no fence, minimal landscaping, trash around the yard, no top soil, etc.?
12. Is there a security system? If so, be sure to get instructions, codes, etc.
13. Is there a sprinkler system? If so, be sure to get instructions, codes, etc.
14. Is there a phone landline and if yes, where is the jack?
15. Be sure to find out usual monthly utility costs for garbage, sewer, electricity, gas, water, etc.
16. Sometimes there is upgraded lighting, outdoor lighting, gates, water features, garden beds, fixtures, plug and switch covers, bee hives, chicken coops, etc. Find out if these will be left behind or replaced with cheaper versions.
17. Other potential issues:_____.
18. _____.
19. _____.
20. _____.

Resources
https://www.hudhomesusa.org/welcome.html
https://www.youtube.com/watch?v=bOOXmfkXpkM

Discussion questions

1. Are there some issues that you would move from minor to major or vice versa?

2. What additional issues should be considered?

3. What experiences have shaped your home purchasing experiences?

Section 7

Potential Country Living Income Streams

Index for Section 7

Apple or peach orchard, p 400
Appliance repairs, p 401
Art / pottery studio for the public, p 401
Assist others with exercise, p 398
Baalams Donkey, p 395
Bake bread, p 398
Bee keeping, p 400
Blog, p 401
Bookkeeping, p 401
Canning kitchen, p 401
Carrots, p 400
Chicken coops, p 402
Child care, p 402
Citrus fruit, p 400
Clean gutters, p 398
Commercial kitchen, p 401
Computer tutoring and repairs, p 402
Darkfield microscopy, p 399
Deep weeds, p 393
Division of labor, p 393
Doggie daycare and grooming, p 399
Dog sit, p 400
Eggs, p 400
Elderly day care, p 399
Elderly well-checks, p 399
Equipment repair, p 401
Estate sales, p 398
Exercise classes, p 398
Farm equipment rentals, p 401
Feed farm animals, p 400
Florist and flower arranging, p 400
Flower growing, p 399
Food truck, p 399
Garlic, p 400
Goat rental, p 400
Gourds, p 400
Grapes and scuppernong vineyards, p 400
Greens, p 400
Health clinic, p 399
Health coach, p 402
Home organizer, p 401
Home visits, p 398
Housekeeping and cleaning, p 402
Hydrotherapy, p 401
In the weeds, p 393
John 12, p 397
Latin words for lazy, p 393

Light the fire, p 393
Local attractions tour organizer, p 401
Matthew 25, p 394
Meals on wheels, p 399
Microgreens, p 400
Mise en place, p 393
Moral development of children, p 397
Mushrooms, p 401
Music lessons, p 401
Numbers 22, p 395
Outdoor lights, p 401
Pack and move, p 398
Paint homes, p 401
Photography, p 399
Plan of salvation for animals, p 396
Plant nursery & sell seeds, p 401
Pool maintenance, p 399
Pools and hot tubs, p 399
Pottery barn, p 401
Produce stand, p 401
Remodel RVs, p 402
Retaining walls, p 402
Revelation 14, 15, 22, p 396
RV pad sites, p 401
RV transport, p 402
Seamstress, p 401
Science and math classes, p 401
Sheds and tiny homes, p 401
Shooting range, p 401
Small building projects, p 399
Spring water, p 400
Stop smoking classes, p 402
Teach, p 402
Technology assistance
Tree / Christmas tree farm, p 401
Tutoring, p 402
Unusual fruits, p 400
Unusual vegetables, p 400
Vanilla bean vines, p 400
Wedding coordinator, p 400
Weddings, p 400
Window washing, p 401
Woodworking, p 401
Writing and editing, p 401
Yard cleaning, p 399
Yard care and sprinklers, p 399

Chapter 54
Monetize your country home

Thriving, and not just surviving, is the goal. The sooner you learn how to thrive and not just survive is the day you become independent. This is a journey and not something that happens overnight. During the process, your extended family and friends may express serious doubts about your decisions, but as long as you and your family are working hard and following Biblical principles, you should succeed. The following list of questions may help you focus on important aspects of monetizing your homestead. There may be other important issues you will identify specific to your endeavors.

There is another virulent 'virus' in addition to Covid-19, infecting more and more people every day. It is an epidemic. The Latin name for this virus is *disidiam recesseras*. Other Latin terms include *"piger," "iners," "ignavus," "segnis," "desidiosus," "cussilliris," "lentus," "supinus,"* and *resupinus."* These Latin words are commonly translated as "lazy" or "laziness." When laziness is allowed in young people or people of any age, it only multiplies. It is not "cured;" it must be reverse engineered through deliberate and difficult choices. When laziness takes hold, one finds many excuses to avoid work.

Moving to the country is a good first step in reverse engineering this novel virus. Ideally, it must be avoided at all costs. If this means limiting internet time to "X" number of minutes, then do it! Instead of one person making dinner and cleaning up after dinner, everyone needs to be engaged. Streamlining the process of preparing food can be done. One person can "mise en place," a French term for 'gathering the needed ingredients and equipment in one place,' usually on a tray or cart. Food can be prepared "a la minute." This means to prepare recipes from scratch up to a certain point and then when needed, the final preparation steps are easy and quick. Another fun culinary term is, "light the fire." This means it is time to start cooking! The final culinary term, "in the weeds." Means you are behind. If you are in "deep weeds," you are overwhelmed with orders / tasks. To keep Mom from being in the "deep weeds," everyone should pitch in and help with meal preparation and clean-up. After the meal, one person puts away leftover food. Another person washes dishes, and another person sweeps and mops the floor. Every person in a household must be responsible for a list of daily jobs. Rotate the jobs on a regular schedule so everyone is familiar with every job. This keeps the order of the house in right proportion. One person is not doing all the work while the rest of the family members relax and disappear; out of sight, and usually out of touch. Even guests should be given tasks and expected to contribute. Another common tactic is talking. Some people consider talking to be a task and cannot multi-task while talking. If someone is just standing around and talking while others are working, give them several tasks to do and always follow-up on how they completed the task(s). If you run into a chronically work-resistant person, it may be time to consider other options.

Division of labor is good for specialized tasks, but there are some jobs which everyone should learn. Jobs such as taking care of the animals, tending the garden, making bread, doing laundry, washing the dishes, preserving and canning food, engaging in security measures, adding and maintaining the oil levels in mechanized farm equipment, etc. If just one person knows how to do essential tasks, this limits the functioning effectiveness when that person is out of town or unavailable.

Essential tasks must be accomplished before chitchatting and relaxing activities occur. Having animals, crops to tend, fences to repair, tractors to keep oiled, and errands to run are just a few things which oppose this novel virus. In reality, it is not novel and it is not new. It has been around for millennia. Think back to the flood. For 120 years, Noah preached and built the ark. While he was busy building a mammoth ship, the local city folk were eating, drinking and entertaining themselves. Sound familiar? We read about a related story in Matthew 25. Think about the 10 virgins waiting for the Bridegroom to arrive. How many had done the essential tasks before the Bridegroom arrived? Boredom is not an option while living in the country and depending on your outputs (i.e., work and essential tasks) for survival. This is why monetizing your county living lifestyle is critical. Even children as young as 5 years old can be taught to add more money to the family's living expenses as well as boosting their allowance.

Determine what needs exist within your immediate family and within the local community. Maybe you can monetize activities in your current routine. For example, if you love chickens and goats, build a large chicken coop for egg-laying hens and build a large outdoor area with a shelter for keeping goats. You can gather and sell eggs and milk the goats and make goat cheese and sell their milk and cheese. This is useful if you are planning a community-based business. If you are only interested in online customers then a community-based assessment may not be necessary. Specialize in something you love to do. Do you have marketable essential skills or do you have one or more products to market? If you love to cook, start a food truck or catering business. If you enjoy quilting, start a quilting or tailoring business.

Check with your local city or county department of commerce for laws pertaining to business in your city or county. Be sure to list your services in the local telephone book as well as provide a list of your services to all the local businesses. If possible, have a presence on the internet and social media. If you have a business, make sure you register an account for your business on: Gab, WhatsApp, Messenger, WeChat, Instagram, Linked In, Facebook, Twitter and Snap Chat. Use one or more of these media venues to advertise specials and new services.

Referrals are one of the best ways to gain clients. When you begin a business, open up a business account at a local reputable bank. This helps you keep track of your transactions. Also, enlist the aid of a bookkeeper or someone who can help you keep track of your income and expenditures. They also help track and manage data. Be sure to pay yourself an income, save some money, pay bills related to the business, put away money to pay required taxes, and return tithe and offerings. Allocate your income in whatever proportions you have predetermined - every day you do business you need to receive an income. Even if you cannot initially afford a bookkeeper, you can purchase inexpensive bookkeeping software and do it yourself until you can afford a bookkeeper.

Think about how you might advertise. Some small towns use local radio stations to advertise services or a classified newspaper. You may be able to rent a billboard or place flyers around town. Who are your clients? Who is your competition? What, if any, are the threats to this type of business? How much money do you want to make? How much money do you need to make? Is it possible to make enough money using this business model? How long before you to reach your financial goals? Who will cover for you when you take a vacation or need time off? What are the initial and ongoing investments? Can this also be a ministry? Is this business compatible with Christian principles? These are just a few questions you need to contemplate with your family or business partner(s).

Branding your products and / or services is critical. This is an important topic and deserves a significant amount of time and attention. Branding involves a marketing approach which puts your services / product at the forefront of your customers mind. Branding involves marketing, pricing, promotions, advertising, labeling, critical statistics about the community, business cards, window dressing, slogans, colors, a logo, specific fonts, etc. Avoid gimmicks and misleading advertising. Once you have lost a valued customer, you may lose more than just one customer. A dissatisfied customer on average, tells 11 other people about their bad experience. With social media, the negative influence can extend even further. Examine successful similar businesses for their branding and marketing techniques. Use what makes sense to your specific situation.

Make it a point to give more than what people expect. This keeps your business honest. Give a percentage of your profits back to the community. This gives the community extra incentive to use your goods and services.

Maybe you daydream about having a large property to rescue all kinds of animals. Maybe you have always loved miniature cows or you have always enjoyed cooking or playing an instrument. Think about turning your avocation into an income stream. How does your business glorify God?

Rescuing animals fulfills the command to have a lovely dominion over the animals. Remember when Balaam began to beat his donkey because the donkey would not follow his commands. The donkey actually turns around and speaks to Balaam. Let's join the story beginning in Numbers 22:21-35 (NIV):

"Balaam got up in the morning, saddled his donkey and went with the Moabite officials. But God was very angry when he went, and the angel of the LORD stood in the road to oppose him. Balaam was riding on his donkey... When the donkey saw the angel of the LORD standing in the road with a drawn sword in his hand, it turned off the road into a field. Balaam beat it to get it back on the road. Then the angel of the LORD stood in a narrow path through the vineyards, with walls on both sides. When the donkey saw the angel of the LORD, it pressed close to the wall, crushing Balaam's foot against it. So, he beat the donkey again. Then the angel of the LORD moved on ahead and stood in a narrow place where there was no room to turn, either to the right or to the left. When the donkey saw the angel of the LORD, it lay down under Balaam, and he was angry and beat it with his staff. <u>Then the LORD opened the donkey's mouth, and it said to Balaam, "What have I done to you to make you beat me these three times?"</u> Balaam answered the donkey, "You have made a fool of me! If only I had a sword in my hand, I would kill you right now." <u>The donkey said to Balaam, "Am I not your own donkey, which you have always ridden, to this day? Have I been in the habit of doing this to you?"</u> "No," he said. Then the LORD opened Balaam's eyes, and he saw the angel of the LORD standing in the road with his sword drawn. So, he bowed low and fell facedown. The angel of the LORD asked him, "Why have you beaten your donkey these three times? I have come here to oppose you because your path is a reckless one before me. <u>The donkey saw me and turned away from me these three times. If it had not turned away, I would certainly have killed you by now, but I would have spared it.</u>" Balaam said to the angel of the LORD, "I have sinned. I did not realize you were standing in the road to oppose me. Now if you are displeased, I will go back." The angel of the LORD said to Balaam, "Go with the men, but speak only what I tell you."

The talking donkey story illustrates several beautiful points about our dominion of animals. It is a partnership. God saved the animals in the Ark. Even the 10 Commandments includes animals in the 4th commandment – to rest on the Sabbath day. Our partnership with animals is not meant to be harsh and cruel. Animals provides us with many important benefits and in return we feed and care for them.

God speaks and is understood by the animals.

God cares about how we treat the animals.

God's tender loving mercy extends to the animals and possibly beyond what is even afforded to mankind.

Just like God sent the animals into Noah's Ark, there is a plan of salvation for the animals.

When we provide loving care for the animals within our influence, God extends to us an extra measure of mercy as the story of Balaam and the talking donkey beautifully illustrate God's love for animals.

Back to the subject of this chapter, monetizing your country home, consider the following statements? Take time to ponder what gives you the greatest satisfaction and fulfillment in life. If your only goal is to make lots of money, you may fail or you may succeed. However, if your goal is to follow Christ and be a light for Jesus in the community, you will succeed. Revelation 22:17 says, "And the Spirit and the bride say, Come." **This means to invite others to follow Jesus.**

Revelation 14 and 15 give us the Angel's messages to earth's occupants. The first Angel proclaims: "Fear God and give glory to Him, for the hour of His judgment is come: and worship Him that made heaven and earth, and the sea and the fountains of waters." The second Angel's message is: "Another angel followed, saying, 'Babylon is fallen, is fallen, that great city, because she made all nations drink of the wine of the wrath of her fornication.'" The third Angel's message reads as follows: "Then a third angel followed, saying with a loud voice, 'If man worship the beast and his image, and receive his mark in his forehead or in his hand, the same shall drink of the wine of the wrath of God, which is poured out without mixture into the cup of his indignation…' Here is the patience of the saints: here are they that keep the commandments of God and the faith of Jesus" Rev 14:6-10a, 12.

A few more angels follow the first three angels. In Revelation 14:15, a 4th angel follows the 3rd angel out of the temple, "… crying with a loud voice to him that sat on the cloud, Thrust in thy sickle, and reap: for the time is come for thee to reap; for the harvest of the earth is ripe." Verse 17, "And another angel [5th] came out of the temple which is in heaven, he also having a sharp sickle." Verse 18, "And another angel [6th] came out from the altar, which had power over fire; and cried with a loud cry to him that had the sharp sickle, saying, Thrust in thy sharp sickle, and gather the clusters of the vine of the earth; for her grapes are fully ripe. And the angel thrust in his sickle into the earth, and gathered the vine of the earth, and cast it into the great winepress of the wrath of God." Revelation 15:1, "And I saw another sign in heaven, great and marvelous, seven angels having the seven last plagues; for in them is filled up the wrath of God." We live in momentous times. Your best contact with people may be through your business. This is why it is critical to maintain honest and polite business practices. When others see how you conduct business, they should see a true Christ follower at work. Always provide more than you promise and never miss an opportunity to lift up Christ, "And I, if I be lifted up from the earth, will draw all men to me." **John 12:32**

Now is the time to invite others to follow Jesus. It is time to consider the context of our times, to keep the Gospel at the forefront, and to warn others of Christ's soon return. As we wrap up our time on earth, it becomes more and more difficult to deny we are living in the days before Christ's return. What a privilege and responsibility we are given. Make sure each family member hears about what Jesus has done for us! Make sure each person is welcome to your country home where our characters are refined and where we find the Gospel written on every leaf, every drop of morning dew, how we protect our young, where we observe how animals provide for their young, and how form and function in nature combine to unite us and point us to the Creator. If you care for someone, help them make the transition to the country. If they choose to remain in the city, pray for them and continue to stay in contact with them.

Use your business and your homestead to glorify God and to create an opportunity to invite others to follow Him. **Pray God gives you spiritual eyesight to discern how you can monetize your country home AND bring others to Christ.** This provides the greatest reward in life. It also provides a way to move forward in your desire to move to the country.

Take an inventory of your skills and the things you are passionate about. If you love to cook, explore ways to monetize cooking. If you repair engines, explore ways to monetize a repair shop. If you love to write, find ways to monetize your writing skills. If you love babies and small children, monetize a business in caring for babies and small children. If you love animals, house and keep farm animals such as cows, horses, goats, etc., on your property. If you are age 65 or older, you may qualify for a homestead property tax exemption. Forty states offer this type of tax relief. In some cases, even the school taxes, which are a large chunk of local taxes, are waived if the property owner is 65 years of age or older. This may be something to consider when buying a property. Check with your state for which criteria meet the definition of a residence "homestead."

Lastly, consider how your activities and thoughts are tied to your moral development. Discipline is required for children's moral development. Children raised without discipline oftentimes fail to morally advance. Manual labor is another important aspect of moral development. With manual labor, little time exists for indulgence and useless amusements. Enduring hardship is another aspect necessary for moral development. Growing up in the lap of luxury with every want and desire satisfied, poisons one's moral powers. Engaging in any aspect of intemperance also weakens moral powers. Moral development occurs from the first breath we take and is shaped by our experiences as small children and throughout our lifetime. Remember Hannah and her son Samuel? She dedicated him to the Lord and from a very early age, his moral development was foremost in his mother's actions. If parents provide for every want and desire without purposefully shaping their children's life experiences, then moral development is overshadowed by an increasing appetite for amusement and pleasure. Beginning with small children, as young as 5 years old, children can be taught skills and learn to make money, even start their own business. This teaches so many important life lessons as their industriousness contributes to the family's well-being.

Here are just a few ideas which may help you in planning your way forward. The list below is not comprehensive, but it may be used to stimulate more ideas for a small town, country living business.

1. **Bake 10 – 20 loaves of bread, 3 or 4 days a week**. Make a different type of bread each day. Initial investment might be a 30- or 40-quart commercial floor mixer (may be able to find a used one for $1,500 to $2,000), commercial ovens (around $2,000 to $3,000 for used ovens) and pans ($200 - $400). The ingredients for a large loaf of bread usually do not exceed $1.00 to $1.50 unless you are adding nuts, seeds and / or dried fruit. It takes about 3 – 5 hours to make bread, including baking times and clean-up. You sell 20 loaves for $5 per loaf, which is roughly an $80 profit. If you make $80 three times per week, which is $240 per week for just 12+ hours of work. Add granola bars, breakfast cookies, chocolate chip cookies and brownies to the queue and you have not hugely extended the amount of time needed – you can make up cookie dough and brownies while the bread is rising and then sell extra-large cookies and brownies for $1.50 each to local coffee shops. This increases your profits by almost double. Now you are making about $500 per week. Not too bad for about 15 to 20 hours of work per week and an initial investment under $5,000. Other options could include: muffins, decorated cakes, etc. As long as you are making fresh bread, buy a grain grinder and grind grain to sell fresh flour to local farm stands, markets, bakeries, and individuals.
2. **Help people pack and move**. Packing and moving is a miserable experience. Extra help makes a huge difference. Most people are happy to pay for good labor to help with packing, lifting and moving heavy furniture and pianos. This might require investing in a pick-up truck and maybe a covered trailer. Add a few young kids eager to earn money and now you have a small moving company.
3. **Organize estate sales**. If you are an organized and methodical person, advertise to run estate sales. These usually happen during the week with a finale sale on one weekend day. It is a privilege to help, usually older people, go through their treasures and help them find new homes. Estate sale agents charge a percentage of the sales. The hours can be long, but some people enjoy the time spent getting to know people and they feel good about helping others.
4. **Consignment shops**. If you have access to a commercial space, consider opening a consign-ment shop. You can be open as many days and hours as you desire. Maybe you only want to resell antiques or old cars – you determine the hours and days and what you want to sell.
5. If you are a nurse or physician, offer your services as a **home-visiting nurse / doctor**. Offer weekly packages of 1 to 5 visits a week. Provide a report of your findings and leave it for the family (**see appendix for a reporting form**). This package could include a 30 minute or 60-minute visit. During this time, take blood pressure, pulse oximeter (O2 saturation), temperature, provide a 5-minute neck and shoulder massage, wash their hair, trim nails, prepare a meal, etc.
6. **Clean home gutters and windows.** With just a ladder and a few other tools you can go around and clean out leaves and other debris from gutters.
7. **Exercise with others**. Some people pay to have you walk with them. This gives them the incentive to get outside and exercise. Charge by the hour or mileage. A great way to introduce people to Jesus.
8. **Exercise classes** – do something that is unique and different such as take people through a par course, agility exercises, core exercises, exercises with purpose such as chopping wood, building things, etc.
9. **Well checks on the elderly**. Offer weekly packages of 1 to 5 visits a week for 30 minutes, one hour, or two-hour visits. During this time, clean, cook, run errands, etc.
10. **Elderly day care**.
11. If you like to cook, offer **meals on wheels** service. Provide a large plate of food including a large portion of protein (enough to last for at least 2 meals), a large amount of carbohydrate (rice, potatoes, bread), delicious vegetables (both cooked and fresh), a bag of chips, a soup (or a soup packet), and a fruit and / or dessert. If you stick to plant-based proteins, you may be able to make a meal for around $2.50 and sell it for $5 to $10.

12. **Darkfield microscopy and medical** counseling for blood samples (for medical professionals). Takes significant investment in equipment and special training classes, but it can be a rewarding endeavor.
13. Start a **small health clinic**, for licensed medical professionals only.
14. **Food truck**. You can remodel a trailer as a food truck. First, determine the menu and then add the appropriate equipment. Food trucks can be great way to make good money in a small amount of time. For example, recently while traveling, I had stopped to get gas and food. I decided to check out a food truck which had just pulled into the parking lot where I was parked. It turned out to be a food truck that made 1,500 to 2,000 huge fresh donuts on site and sold them hot, dripping in a delicious glaze. People lined up and waited in line to buy these $2 donuts. They made the dough in advance, refrigerated it and then let it rise and then they notified their buyers of their location via social media. When the dough is gone, they are done for the day. It might take 3 to 6 hours, but it is a nice profit. Works best for limited menus (e.g., donuts, crepes, smoothies, desserts, food bowls).
15. **Photography**. Learn how to take beautiful pictures of engagements, birthday parties, anniversary parties, weddings, etc.
16. **Doggie daycare and grooming**. If you have the land and are willing to fence in at least an acre or so, keep it free of ticks and fleas, preferably with a water feature, trees and an optional indoor space for rainy days, start a doggie daycare business. Charge by the half day and be reasonable. This allows you to expand your business. This gives dogs a chance to socialize and it gives conscientious owners another option for their lonely dogs, especially on long work days. Add grooming as an extra service while caring for the dogs.
17. **Yard clean-up service**. Many homes have messy yards. If your family is willing to help clean up the mess, you could make some money. Always take precautions when cleaning up people's junk. You usually need a dumpster on the site and maybe other equipment as well. Check local ordinances about burning certain types of trash. This can make a huge difference in the neighborhood, when a yard goes from junky to trash free.
18. **Mowing, yard care and sprinkler installation**.
19. **Plant and maintain gardens** for others. Gardens include vegetable gardens, herb gardens, flower gardens, pollinator gardens, etc.
20. **Small building projects** such as fencing, decks, cement slabs, etc.
21. **Build in-ground pools and hot tubs**.
22. **Pool care and maintenance**.
23. **Grow bearded iris', dahlia, etc. – sell the bulbs**. Many bulb-based flowers divide, making more bulbs and more flowers. If you are into growing bulb type flowers, you may be able to make a business selling the bulbs. I have known several people who have made good money in the spring selling flower bulbs. It's not something you can do year-round, but it works well for seasonal income. Sell your bulbs at the local gardener's club or farm and garden supply store.
24. **Grow market crops**. High value market crops include mushrooms, garlic, greens, fruits, etc. You can expect around $5 per square foot of income from your garden. Plan the size accordingly.
25. **Grow microgreens**. For a minimal investment, you can grow microgreens to order, for restaurants, markets, individuals, etc. Pea shoots and sunflower microgreens are high return crops.
26. **Grow fresh greens**. If you have a green house or orangerie, you can grow greens such as lettuces, radicchio, arugula, and fresh herbs all year long.
27. **Sell eggs**. If you have chickens or other types of birds, sell their eggs. Take standing orders and sell to local produce stands and markets.
28. **Grow garlic**. You can pretty much plant garlic almost any time of the year, except in colder zones.

29. **Grapes, scuppernongs** – U pick. Sell your grapes to local markets or offer a you-pick period of time. If you offer you-pick option, be sure to have additional retail items available such as grape jelly, fresh juice, etc.
30. **Sell pure spring water** from spring water sources on your property.
31. **Plant a nut orchard and see the nuts both in the shell and cracked.** Nuts make a great seasonal crop. Pecans, walnuts, pine nuts, etc.
32. **Grow carrots for a juice bar**. Plant large sections of your garden to make juices.
33. **Grow unusual fruits** such as kiwi, passionfruit. Kiwi and passionfruit are both perennial vines, which may be sensitive to sub-freezing temperatures, but the roots usually survive lower temps. A heated greenhouse could be kept to grow fruit all year long.
34. **Grow citrus fruit**. Mandarins, lemons, limes, tangelos, oranges, grapefruit are all excellent fruits to grow if you are in the right zone.
35. **Flowers, flower arranging**. Grow, arrange and deliver flowers for anniversaries, birthdays, weddings, engagements, etc.
36. **Weddings**: decorate, cater, plan, rent out your barn, etc.
37. **Wedding coordinator**.
38. **Grow usual and unusual vegetables** to sell.
39. Grow a variety of sweet potatoes and **sell sweet potato starts.**
40. **Grow gourds** – make birdhouses and other gourd-based items.
41. **Apple or peach orchard**. Sell your excess crop to locals.
42. Dog sit – set up an indoor room and dog runs so guest dogs **can be part of your family.**
43. **Feed farm animals** while others are on vacation. Farmers rarely take vacations because of their daily obligations. If you understand farm animals and their nutritional and social needs, you could consider starting a feeding business.
44. **Rent out your goats** to clean up fields and overgrown lots.
45. **Keep bees and sell honey.**
46. **Vanilla bean vines.** Vanilla beans are an expensive commodity. If you have a green house or orangerie, vanilla bean vines might be a great way to earn extra money. Grow vanilla:
    https://www.youtube.com/watch?v=QV9ukZ2wWd0
    https://www.youtube.com/watch?v=A99bqKvyeEs ;
    https://www.youtube.com/watch?v=KyCi4UB-Jjg
    https://www.youtube.com/watch?v=Nhju7wj-LnI ;
    https://www.youtube.com/watch?v=2H0jdVv0fZ0 ;
    Make vanilla. See this video: https://www.youtube.com/watch?v=My74LL1qYE4
47. **Small trees, Christmas trees**, etc. Grow trees to sell.
48. **Bookkeeping**. If you have some accounting classes in your background, consider bookkeeping as a possible income avenue.
49. **Sew / knit aprons, curtains, valences, place mats, etc.**
50. **Paint homes.**
51. **Commercial kitchen for the public** to rent to use for special events, canning, etc.
52. **Art / pottery studio for the public.** Sell and give art classes.
53. **Set up a pottery barn.**
54. **Help people organize their home and lives**.
55. **Organize tours** of local attractions, the USA and even foreign destinations such as a Bible tour of Israel, Greece and Turkey, a Reformers tour of Europe, a chocolate tour of Europe, etc.
56. If you are trained in English and grammar, take up **writing and / or editing**.
57. Teach **science or math classes** for home schooled kids.

58. Teach **music lessons** for piano, flute, clarinet, horn, etc.
59. **Set up a hydrotherapy room**: float tank, hot tub, jacuzzi, sauna, etc.
60. Road side **produce stand**.
61. **Grow mushrooms**.
62. **Window washing service**.
63. **Put up outdoor lights (Christmas)**.
64. Set up several **RV pad sites** and charge by the week / month.
65. **Shooting range**.
66. **Blog, monetize** your blog.
67. **Sell seeds, bulbs, rhizomes, seedling plants, plants, trees, vines**.
68. Set up a **canning kitchen** for the public from May to November.
69. **Metal storage building** to rent out storage for farm equipment.
70. Car and farm **equipment repair**.
71. **Appliance repairs**.
72. **Woodworking**.
73. **Build sheds, tiny homes**.
74. **Remodel RVs**.
75. **RV transport**.
76. **Tutoring**.
77. **Child care**.
78. **Teach classes** at the local community college or at your place.
79. **Teach stop smoking classes**.
80. **House-keeping and cleaning**.
81. **Computer tutoring and repairs**.
82. **Health coach**.
83. **Technology assistance**.
82. **Chicken coops**. Build, clean, maintain, etc.
83. Build **retaining walls, raised beds, etc.**
84. Many others!

Passive income ideas:
1. **Rent out** personal items of rental value.
2. Buy and maintain a **vending machine**.
3. Buy and manage a **laundry mat**.
4. Invest in **CDs**.
5. **Drop shipping**.
6. **YouTube channel**.
7. **Affiliate marketing**.
8. **Rent a room**.
9. Sell an **e-book**.
10. Create an **app**.
11. Create / sell an **online course**.

Your ideas:

Bible verses: Leviticus 19:35-36; Proverbs 14:23, 16:1, 22:1, 31; 1 Corinthians 6:10; Revelation 13:17

Resources

- https://www.youtube.com/watch?v=CTW0_s8YP0A – My 5 most profitable crops.
- https://www.youtube.com/watch?v=9-JoxKte1yQ - Mushroom farming
- https://www.youtube.com/watch?v=ksf6KBymnLo - $200,000 on 1 acre in second season, in NC.

Discussion questions

1. How does this endeavor glorify God and point others to Him?
2. Am I more interested in making money or helping others? What is the best balance?
3. How will I deal with those who cannot afford my services?
4. How motivated am I to start and succeed in monetizing my country home?
5. What do I love to do?
6. What are my strongest skills?
7. What are your passions?
8. What do I dream about doing?

Section 8

Country Living Gardens and Landscaping

Chapter 55

Am I ready to garden?

If you are new to gardening, take the time to read the following list of questions. This ensures a better return on your investment of time and money.

Pre-considerations for planning your garden?
1. Determine your growing zone and what can be grown during which months of the year.
2. What is your water source and how will you get water to the gardening areas?
3. Determine what you want to grow.
4. Draw a rough map of your potential gardening spaces. This could include flower beds, side yards, pots, a patch along a fence, greenhouses, raised beds, etc.
5. Determine how many plantings you want to make over the year (i.e., early spring, late spring, late summer, fall, winter).
6. Determine the health of your soil? Get a professional soil test done. In the long run, this saves time, energy and money.
7. How unpredictable is the weather during the growing season (e.g., hail, winds, floods, pestilence) and how might this affect where and what you plant?
8. Do you primarily want a chef's garden or a large vegetable garden?
9. Do you want a rose garden?
10. Do you want an herb garden?
11. Do you want an experimental garden?
12. Determine if you want to use flower beds for edible landscaping.
13. Do you want to grow from seeds or small plants?
14. Where do you get seeds / plants?
15. Is organic important to you?
16. Inventory usable spaces, square feet, dimensions, etc.
17. Do you plan to use bulbs / rhizomes?
18. Do you have refrigerator space to store bulbs and harden off seeds?
19. Determine the amount of space you need for non-edible flowers.
20. Do you want to include a water feature in the garden?
21. Make sure paths between rows are adequate. Wide paths allow plants to spill onto the path.
22. Check for compatibility between plants near each other and between near trees and vines.

Psychological fitness for gardening?
23. Do you have the energy and motivation to garden? Match your energy to garden dimensions.
24. Do you have the support of your friends and family?

Appropriate equipment and supplies available?
25. What equipment do you own?
26. What equipment do you need?
27. Do you compost?
28. Do you have access to leaves, pine needles, mulch, etc.?
29. Do you understand the concept of garden tunnels and when to use?
30. Do you have a hoop house, greenhouse, walipini, or orangerie?
31. If you do not have a hoop house, green house, or orangerie, are you interested in building one?

Available outside labor for gardening needs?
32. Do you need help? If yes, whom do you plan to use?
33. What scale of gardening is appropriate for your physical constraints (if present)?

Does your schedule allow for adequate time to spend gardening?
34. Do you have an extended summer vacation planned?
35. How will you cover time away from your garden?

Appropriate soil, location and property to garden on for what you want to grow?
36. Do you have gardening restrictions where you live?
37. Do you have rocky or clay-based soil?
38. What soil amendments are you likely to need?
39. How do you plan to amend your soil?
40. Do you need a soil test?
41. How do you plan to adjust pH?
42. How do you plan to water your beds?
43. Are you using raised beds or in-ground beds?
44. Do you need trellises?
45. Do you need other supports?
46. Are your beds exposed to high winds?
47. Determine if you have space to plant trees bearing edible fruits and / or nuts.
48. Do you have space for a small "orchard" or "vineyard?"
49. Determine if you want to use space against the house for a trellis.
50. Determine how many container / pots you want to use.
51. Determine how many hanging pots you want to use for edibles.

Plans for preserving the harvest?
52. How interested are you in growing and preserving your own food?
53. Do you have neighbors you can share crops with?

What is your level of gardening experience?
54. What type of gardening methods do you use?

What might possibly interfere with your garden?
55. What "hard" landscape features do you need to work around (e.g., paths, sundial, gates, etc.)
56. Do domestic animals have access to garden?
57. What wild animals do you deal with in your area? Do wild animals have access to your garden areas? How do you plan to deter these animals?
58. How do you plan to deter squirrels and birds?
59. How do you plan to deter snakes?
60. Determine space available for shade-loving plants and sun-loving plants.
61. Vacation plans – if you plan to be gone all summer, vegetable gardening may not work.
62. Weather phenomena which may impact your growing season and gardening?

Discussion questions

1. What can I do in advance to improve the chances of a successful season of gardening?
2. How do you think your pre-planning activities improve your gardening outcomes?

Chapter 56
Basic gardening terminology and techniques

Learning profession-specific language is one of the first steps to attaining a new skill or trade. This holds true with gardening and farming. When you understand the meaning of words, an entire new vista of opportunity opens. Read through the following words and their definitions and see how many words and their definitions you know. This list is not exhaustive to gardening and farming but it may get you started on your new journey. Many of the definitions are compiled from Wikipedia. You are going to find regional variations of some of the definitions.

Abscisic acid: plant hormone that inhibits germination.
Acidic: having a pH between 0 and 7.
Aeration: loosening the soil to allow air and oxygen to access soil microorganisms.
Aerobic: organisms which require oxygen.
Alkaline: having a pH between 7 and 14.
Anaerobic: organisms not requiring oxygen to live.
Annual: plants which complete their lifecycle in one or less year.
Anti-nutritional factors: naturally occurring chemicals known to either prevent germination or toxins with variable toxicity. Phytic acid, found in seeds coats and the germ of plant seeds, forms insoluble or nearly insoluble compound with essential minerals, reducing their physiological absorption. In some cases, sprouting the seeds slightly reduces phytic acid content.
Aquaponics: agricultural method combining hydroponics with raising aquatic fish in a symbiotic environment.
Baby greens: young, leafy vegetables harvested when they are no taller than 4 to 6 inches.
Bare root: buying a plant with developed roots but with little to no accompanying dirt.
Biennial: plant that lives for 2 years, producing leaves the first year and flowers the second year.
Biodynamic gardening: avoid using synthetic fertilizers and pesticides. Plant in cooperation with moon cycle, weather, etc. Soil health is important.

Blood and bone: amend the soil by adding nitrogen; promotes green growth, and encourages microorganisms
Bolt: premature flowering and going to seed.
Bone meal: adds phosphorus to the soil.
Boron deficiency: needed for many plant processes, for pollination and seed production. May show up as brown spots, brown stripes, or internal brown areas.
Bulbs: rounded underground storage organ; dormant over the winter.
Calcium deficiency: misshapen new leaves, stunted growth. Dead leaves on young plants. Leaf curling. Death of terminal buds and root tips. Initially, the new growth is affected. Blossom end rot in tomatoes and zucchini. Browning in cabbage and Brussels sprouts. Amend by adding lime to soil.
Calvin cycle: light-independent biosynthetic reactions. Produces sugars for the plant to use.
Canavanine: toxic compound found in alfalfa and other leguminous seeds and sprouts; may cause toxicity for animals consuming large amounts of alfalfa. It's effects (arginine antagonist; it substitutes for arginine) are magnified in protein malnutrition. Consumption of alfalfa seeds and sprouts is linked to lupus-like symptoms in humans and if enough is consumed, it is toxic. Horses consuming high amounts of canavanine, are at risk of death, especially vulnerable horses.

Metabolically, canavanine is structurally similar to arginine and may inhibit the nitric oxide pathway, affect peristalsis, and destroy vitamin B6. Removal of alfalfa from the diet usually corrects the symptoms if they are not advanced. Canaline is the toxic metabolite of canavanine.

Cation exchange capacity (CEC): a measure of how many nutrients soil can hold and release to growing plants over time.

Chelation: a bond formed between an organic compound and a metal.

Chlorophyll: green plant pigment.

Chlorosis: yellowing of plant leaves due to lack of chlorophyll, usually related to nutrient deficiency(ies).

Cold climates: areas which experience freezing temperatures, usually USDA zones less than or equal to 9.

Cold frame: raised bed with a clear top and able to provide a higher ambient temperature for seeds and plants.

Companion planting: maximize combining plants that grow well together. Use plants which repel pests or attract butterflies, pollinators, etc.

Composting: Kitchen scraps (excluding meat, fish, dairy, citrus, banana peels, human and animal waste), eggshells, grass clippings, leaves, coffee grinds, etc., may be added to a compost bin and allowed to heat up and decompose.

Conventional gardening: gardening techniques using chemical fertilizers, herbicides and pesticides.

Copper deficiency: copper is a component of many plant enzymes. Copper deficiency manifest by brown spots on leaves, death of shoot tips and death of the plant. One remedy is copper sulfate solution.

Corms: rounded underground storage organ; solid stem bases, a type of bulb.

Cotyledons: first set of "leaves" on a tomato plant coming from the seed; not true leaves.

Cover crops: include different types of plants with various features. Legume cover crops are used for their nitrogen-fixing properties. This provides large amounts of nitrogen to the soil. Winter cover crops include clover, field peas, hairy vetch and clover. Summer legume crops include clover, soybeans, etc. Alfalfa, rye, oats, buckwheat are all good cover crops.

Crop rotation: shifting crops to different locations.

Cultivar: a specific species bred for distinct features. It is a cultivated variety requiring human intervention. Cultivars are sometimes propagated using stem cuttings and not necessarily from seed. This ensures the plant is similar to the parent plant for one generation. A cultivar may be a hybrid plant and in which case, the seeds of the cultivar are not reliable. For example, a tomato cultivar is cross between two tomatoes, usually to bring together two or more desirable traits seen in the parent tomato plants. Once the cultivar is stabilized and has been around for 50 or more years, it is considered an heirloom variety.

Cultivating: preparing the soil for planting.

Damping off: occurs when young seedlings are attacked by a fungus and wilt and die. Usually the result of too much water.

Dappled shade: areas where there is a mixture of shade and sun, partial shade.

Days to emerge: number of days it takes for the first stem of section of a plant to emerge.

Days to harvest: number of days from sowing or transplanting to harvest.

Deadheading: removing dead flowers off of plants to encourage additional blooms.

Deciduous: shrubs and trees which lose their leaves in fall and winter.

Deep shade: needing less than 2 hours of sun per day.

Determinate: tomato plants which produce most of their fruit within a 2- or 3-week period. Good for canning tomato sauce, etc.

Dioecious: refers to plant reproduction where there are distinct female and male plants needed to produce fruit.

Direct seed: plant seeds directly into the ground / their final location.

Disease resistance: a variety or cultivar with greater ability to thrive and avoid plant stressors.

Disease tolerant: usually able to fend off common plant diseases.

Dolomite: clay-busting mineral. Source of magnesium. Use when magnesium deficiency is indicated.
Dormancy: the period of time a plant rests from the growth cycle.
Drought tolerance: ability to survive in low water conditions.
Endosperm: the internal seed material which nourishes and provides for growth material as the seed germinates and grows.
Espalier: a tree or bush whose branches are trained to grow flat against a wall.
Etiolation: characteristics of a plant grown in low or no light conditions such as pale, limp, weak, etc.
Fertilizer: organic matter added to the soil to improve nutrient content. Organic matter may be added by amending minerals, plant material and animal material.
Filler: plants used toward the front to the middle of a bed or container connecting the spillers to the thrillers.
Fishmeal: adds nitrogen and phosphorus.
Foliar fertilizing: applying organic matter in liquid form directly to plant leaves.
Full shade: less than 4 hours of direct sun per day.
Full sun: six or more hours of sunlight.
Fulvic acid: fluvic acid is formed when plants and animals die and decompose. It is natural substances such as soil, peat, coal and shilajit. Fulvic acid is a component of humus.
Genetically modified organism (GMO): variety manipulated in a laboratory at the gene level.
Genus: part of the scientific name given to each plant.
Germinate: to soak or otherwise place seeds in water or directly in the soil.
Germination rate: how many seeds of a particular plant species are likely to successfully germinate over a given period.
Gibberellin: plant hormone which ends seed dormancy.
GMO: genetically modified organism, usually modified to gain a desired, beneficial function.
Green manure: a crop grown to incorporate into the soil to improve soil quality.
Gypsum: used on alkaline soils to break up heavy clay content. Does not increase pH. Rich in calcium and sulfur.
Gynoecious: a plant bearing predominantly female flowers.
Habit: structure of a plant. Habits may be climbing, clumping, mounded, spreading, trailing, upright, etc.
Hardening off: acclimating plants started indoors or in a greenhouse to transferring them outside while nighttime temperatures may drop low but not below freezing.
Hardiness zone: temperature zones based on the lowest average temperature each area is expected to receive during the winter.
Hardy: can withstand exposure to frost without protection.
Head space: space between the top of the soil and the top of the container.
Heat tolerant: plants that do well in hot temperatures.
Heavy soil: poorly drained soil, usually with a high amount of clay.
Heirloom: an open pollinated plant variety 50 plus years old.
Humus: decomposed plant matter; dark, aerated, nutrient rich soil.
Hybrid: F1 hybrid is a first generation made by cross-pollination with two parent varieties.
Hydroponics: growing plants in nutrient rich water instead of soil
Indeterminate: tomato varieties which produce fruit from mid-summer until the first frost.
Iron deficiency: iron is needed as a catalyst for chlorophyll production. When iron is deficient, plant leaves lose their color and turn pale yellow or white. Soil needs iron chelates.
Keyhole garden: a garden space with a center section devoted to a large compost pile and plants surround the compost pile. The compost section is covered with a mesh and then watered, allowing nutrients trickle down to the plants in the periphery.
Lasagna gardening: this method used to reduce weeding frequency. Clear the ground, and layer with cardboard, newspapers, straw manure, leaves, finishing with dirt on top.

Lime: soil amendment to increase the pH.
Loamy soil: equal parts sand, silt and clay. Loamy soil is ideal for food crops. It is good for root vegetables.
Magnesium deficiency: central constituent of chlorophyll. Used for many vital plant processes. Beets, potatoes and tomatoes most affected by magnesium deficiency. First sign is yellowing of leaves between the veins of older leaves. Leaves may curl and become brittle.
Manganese deficiency: regulates mineral metabolism and certain enzyme activity. Deficiency symptoms similar to iron deficiency (e.g., yellow leaves on young plants), sunken spots on leaves, stunted growth, elongated holes between veins.
Manure: waste product of animals which is composted and added as a soil amendment. Contains nutrients, microorganisms, and helps encourage earthworm activity. Healthy soil can take 10% to 20% manure by volume.
Medium: material plants grow in.
Medium height: 10 – 24 inches
Microgreen: plants harvested when they are roughly 2 to 4 inches in height.
Mineral chelation: as seeds sprout the minerals merge (chelate) with the plant proteins, giving them metabolic function.
Molybdenum deficiency: reduces nitrates to ammonia. Deficiency leads to reduced plant growth and rolled, pale leaves.
Monoecious: a plant producing both pollen-producing and pollen-receiving parts.
Mulch: organic matter such as wood chips or leaves, used as a soil covering and provides nutrients as it breaks down.
Nitrogen deficiency: upper leaves turn light green while lower leaves are yellow. Bottom and older leaves are yellow and shriveled.
NPK: N=nitrogen, P=phosphorus, K = potassium. The macronutrients of soil.
Open pollinated: genetically stable varieties which reliably reproduce a stable cultivar.
Organic gardening: avoid using synthetic fertilizers and pesticides; use compost and cover crops.

Parthenocarpic: plant produces fruit without fertilization / pollination. Good for greenhouses.
Part sun / part shade: plants that need 3 to 6 hours of sunlight.
Perennial: a plant which lives for 2 or more years, usually surviving over the winter months.
Permaculture: self-sustainable garden with native and other plants, water features, etc. Insect houses, bees, and pollinators are encouraged.
Pet friendly: does not poison pets or farm animals.
pH: when soil is too acidic you may have major nutrient deficiencies. When soil is too alkaline, you may find trace element deficiencies. Neutral pH is usually optimal for plant growth. Nitrogen, phosphorus, potassium, sulfur, iron, manganese, boron, copper, zinc, calcium and magnesium are in perfect balance.
Phosphorus deficiency: leaves are darker than normal, maybe slightly purplish; loss of leaves. Stunted roots.
Photoperiodism: related to the length of the day and refers to flowering by plants in relation to daylight hours.
Photosynthesis: plants convert light energy into chemical energy, which is stored in plants as carbohydrate molecules. This equation represents photosynthesis: $6CO_2$ (carbon dioxide) + $6H_2O$ (water) in combination with light yields $C_6H_{12}O_6$ (sugar) + $6O_2$ (oxygen)
Pinch: using either your soft finger tips or the finger nails to remove a portion of a plant.
Pollination: fertilization of flowering plants by wind, flying pollinators, etc.
Pollinator: a vector which transfers pollen between plant flowers.
Potash: supplies minerals. Good for fruiting vegetables. Sulfate of potash is high in sulfur.
Potassium deficiency: essential for healthy plants. Needed for difficult growing conditions such as high or low temperatures, lack of water, etc. Pushes fruit production, but keep in mind, too much potassium slows fruit production. Speeds up the composting process, improves drainage and water retention.
Proteinase inhibitors: substances which inhibit the activity of proteins and enzymes such as trypsin, chymotrypsin, carboxypeptidase, elastase, and alpha amylase (digestive and other types of enzymes found

in the plant kingdom). Found in legumes, cereal grains, potatoes and tomatoes. Six percent of proteins in soybeans are proteinase inhibitors. Heat generally inactivates proteinase inhibitors.
Prune: drastic removal of stems and branches to rejuvenate the plant.
Rhizomes: underground stems (not roots).
Riparian zone: interface of land bordering a river or stream and extending about 100 feet or more. Vegetation with greater water requirements is able to grow in riparian zones.
Rock phosphate: crushed rock high in phosphorus. Aids with a slow up take of phosphorus.
Root bound: roots which have taken up most of the space within a pot.
Root rot: when roots are destroyed by a fungus, usually due to overwatering.
Row covers: lightweight material used to cover plants, excluding pests or used to retain heat near the ground. May also be used in constructing low tunnels.
Scarification: nicking or barely scratching the exterior shell or surface of a seed to allow moisture or water to penetrate.
Seaweed fertilizer: good source of micronutrients and trace elements.
Selenium deficiency / toxicity: selenium may be deficient in acidic soil and areas of high rainfall. Toxicity may result in stunted plant growth.
Self-sow: seeds drop from a plant, remain dormant in the ground and begin to grow the next season.
Semi-determinate: produce one larger crop with lesser amounts produced until frost.
Shilajit: a sticky, black substance made from decomposed plants found in Himalayan rocks, also known as mineral pitch.
Short height: ≤ 10 inches
Side dressing: working fertilizer into the soil around a plant.
Soil bag gardening: plant directly into a soil bag. May plant 1 or 2 plants per soil bag.
Soil elements: soil and the atmosphere provide oxygen, hydrogen and carbon.
Soil macronutrients: required by plants in relatively large amounts and includes: calcium (Ca), magnesium (Mg), nitrogen (N), phosphorus (P), potassium (K), and sulfur (S).

Soil micronutrients: required by plants in relatively minute amounts and includes: boron (B), chlorine (Cl), cobalt (Co), copper (Cu), iron (Fe), manganese (Mn), molybdenum (Mo), nickel (Ni), zinc (Zn).
Soil microorganisms: there are different types of soil microbes: bacteria, actinomycetes, fungi, protozoa, nematodes, algae, bacteriophages. Bacteria (e.g., cyanobacteria, azobacter, brady-rhizobium, agrobacterium, bacillus) are active in the final stage of breaking down nutrients and releasing them to the roots of plants. Actinomycetes (e.g., actinomyces, nocardia) can have a positive or negative effect on plants. On the positive side, they act as plant antibiotics. Fungi (mycorrhiza; e.g., Trichoderma, aspergillus, fusarium, alternaria) live in the rootzone and also provide nutrients to growing plants. Protozoa interact with bacteria to provide nutrients to plants. Nematodes break down organic matter, providing nutrients to plants.
Spiller: plants placed along the edge of a bed or container to trail or spread out along the ground or down the container.
Spore germination: emergence of cells and subsequent growth from resting spores.
Sprouting: process by which seeds or spores germinate and send out roots and shoots. On established plants, sprouting involves producing new leaves or buds.
Square foot gardening: planting in one square foot sections.
Stratification: some seeds require special conditions to exit dormancy and germinate. The most common is cold stratification. This requires placing seeds in a soil-filled pot and then placing pot in the ground so the seeds spend winter in the pot, exposed to cold temperatures. Sometimes it's possible to place the seeds in the fridge for a period of time and then plant them. One stratification process places sand in a sealable plastic bag, add seeds, seal bag and refrigerate for up to 1 month before planting.

Straw bale: add planting mix and plant in straw bales.

Succession planting: serial plantings to ensure a near continuous supply of a particular type of fruit or vegetable. For example, you may want more than one type of strawberry or raspberry to ensure the availability of fresh strawberries and raspberries over the summer.

Sulfur deficiency: deficiency shows up as yellow leaf edges and veins. Youngest leaves affected first.

Tall height: ≥ 24 inches in height.

Tap root: straight root extending deep into the soil.

Tender perennial: perennials hardy only in USDA zones 7 and higher.

Thinning: removing seedlings to achieve proper spacing between plants.

Thriller: plants placed in the middle to the back of a bed used to add drama and height.

Tilth: physical qualities of soil.

Top soil: the upper layer of soil, usually rich in nutrients from decomposed leaves and other organic matter. Easily washed away by heavy rains and flooding.

Trace elements in soil: chromium, copper, iron manganese, molybdenum, selenium

Tubers: starchy outgrowth root vegetables; includes potatoes, sweet potatoes, Jerusalem artichokes, groundnuts, yams.

Untreated seeds: seeds not conditioned or treated with a fungicide.

USDA hardiness zone: geographic regions sharing similar weather characteristics such as average, low and high temperatures.

Variety: a variety is grown from seeds which remain relatively stable over generations if not cross pollinated. A variety is a sub category for the taxonomic category of species. It is a subspecies designation specific to certain characteristics. For example, a Brandywine tomato is a variety of a tomato plant. Brandywine is considered to be an heirloom vegetable because it has been around for well over 50 years. Specific plant varieties may be legally protected.

Vermicomposting: use of red worms to convert food scraps into worm castings; high quality organic matter.

Vernalization: cold treatment necessary to produce flowers in some varieties.

Vivipary: occurs when seeds within a fruit or vegetable begin to sprout before detachment from the parent plant.

Volunteer: a plant that emerges from a seed which over-wintered in the ground or was left by an animal.

Wet feet: plants which stay wet and do not dry out between watering. Some plants do not like "wet feet" such as lavender.

Worm castings: worm poop from the consumption of vegetable matter, compost, animal waste, soil, etc. Contains bacteria, enzymes, humus, and remnants of plant matter. pH of worm castings is neutral.

Xeriscaping: Using local and low maintenance, low-water requiring plants in the landscape.

Zinc deficiency: zinc is needed in the production of chlorophyll. When zinc is deficient the leaves discolor and plant growth is stunted.

A Description of Commercial Seed Starting Greenhouse-based Operation (see chapter 59 for home gardener)

For almost a year, I have volunteered at an organic farm to learn about commercial greenhouse operations. This is not a comprehensive description of a commercial operation, but a brief synopsis, limited by space available (this has been added to later editions of this book). The greenhouse operation includes three large greenhouses, a soil mixing and seed planting station (an outdoor covered area), a walk-in incubator (in the barn) with fans for use during cold months, a temperature and humidity-controlled room for storing seeds, pot storage, a large composting area, a pole barn for storing equipment, an outdoor sink area to wash used pots and equipment, an outdoor 'clean' sink area to wash greens and produce along with commercial spinners to dry the washed greens, an office and staff kitchen area, a barn to store equipment and to package edible flowers, greens and microgreens for commercial sale, and another large barn with a commercial kitchen and an area for cooking classes and small weddings and celebrations. Around the greenhouses are raised beds with all kinds of various herbs and unique plants. In addition to the large commercial greenhouses, there are several large high tunnels, and there are multiple outdoor growing fields which include onions, strawberries, eggplant, squash, zucchini, tomatoes, cucumbers, etc. There are also around 50 large blueberry bushes along with some raspberry and blackberry plants. There are several large fig trees. Not all the outdoor fields are used every year. Some are planted with cover crops to restore their nutrient content.

Topics for further study include: soil mixing and recipes to make seed starting mix, potting mix, arid mix, etc.; temperature and humidity control in the greenhouse; watering; how to address germination issues; plant pricing; personnel management, etc.

The greenhouses grow plants to use on the farm as well as to sell to the local community. Fruits and vegetables grown on the farm (both outdoors and in the greenhouses) are part of a CSA program and are taken to several local Farmer's Markets during the week and on the weekend. Restaurants also contract with the farm to grow specific crops such as microgreens, edible flowers as well as fresh mixed greens.

Greenhouse #1 houses microgreens, edible flowers, large succulents, small bay trees, non-edible plants, etc. This is also where many of the sprouted seed trays start out. Greenhouse #2 is where the transplants grow until they are big enough to sell. Greenhouse #3 houses larger plants, small trees, bushes and 'mother' succulents and succulent pots. These divisions are specific to the goals and objectives of the farm. A different farm might have a greenhouse dedicated to citrus trees, vines, etc. This farm is mostly dedicated to edible plants, herbs, vines, fig trees, flowers and landscaping plants.

To start large numbers of seeds, you need to identify reliable sources of large quantities of seeds. Once you have established reliable sources of seeds, you will need to collect shallow trays for planting the seeds. Gardening trays come in many sizes but a good standard size 10" x 20" (aka, 1020 trays), 1020 web trays, 1020 nesting trays, shallow germination trays, propagator trays (small plugs), plug flats, 3-inch insert trays, 4-inch insert trays, 1 quart pots, 1 gallon pots, round pot carrying trays of various sizes, etc. Almost any 2 to 4 inch deep plastic container can be modified to use for seed planting (add holes to the bottom of the plastic trays).

The greenhouse director as well as the director of outside crops and staff meet late in the year, usually in October / November / December to determine what sold well in the past year and to decide which seeds and how many to plant for the next year. Decisions about how many seeds to plant (take into consideration the germination rate of each seed packet which you will not know until you receive the seeds) is critical. It is important to understand the planting process for each seed. Group seeds together that require surface sowing and group seeds together that require arid planting mix, etc.

To start seeds, read the directions. Some seeds will need surface sowing while other seeds will need a soil topping. Some seeds require cold stratification and should be kept in the fridge for up to 1 month. Typically, ultra small seeds are surface sown while larger seeds need to be planted anywhere from ¼ inch to maybe ½ inch deep. Use chopsticks or a similar type instrument to make holes in soil packed plug trays, 3- and 4-inch trays, etc. Certain types of greens may be started in plug trays while tomatoes, peppers, eggplant, etc., can be group sown with up to several hundred seeds started in a 1020 shallow tray.

Resources
- Vegan grows 200 fruit trees in urban garden in Phoenix, AZ. https://www.youtube.com/watch?v=bQ93DLOXaKc
- Sheer Total Utter Neglect (STUN) Farming https://www.youtube.com/watch?v=RePJ3rJa1Wg
- Treating the farm as an ecosystem with Gabe Brown, part 1, soil health https://www.youtube.com/watch?v=uUmIdq0D6-A
- Grossing $350,000 on 1.5 acres of High Intensity No-Till Vegetable Production on Neversink Farm https://www.youtube.com/watch?v=u5IE6lYKXRw ; https://www.youtube.com/watch?v=jCVSIIanSvI ; https://www.youtube.com/watch?v=lPZng8VJk_w
- Sunken greenhouse wraps home and feeds suburban antifragile co-op https://www.youtube.com/watch?v=9jbLZxwWudk
- Back to Eden no-till gardening videos
- Late Bloomer Urban Garden, Los Angeles https://www.youtube.com/watch?v=Guf4jbIv7Hs
- How to plant potatoes for a great yield. Simple Living Alaska. https://www.youtube.com/watch?v=t_DwM91jGKY
- First year garden potato harvest – the biggest spuds we've ever seen! Growing potatoes in Alaska https://www.youtube.com/watch?v=B_TUoG5Jktg
- Lasagna gardening, simple living Alaska https://www.youtube.com/watch?v=z0J79cU8D8o&list=PU3FHvW16m_i117IqPnb0nmA&index=6
- July garden tour in Alaska, how we plan to eat all this food. Simple Living Alaska. https://www.youtube.com/watch?v=y16js5b3OJQ
- Agri Supply – a website to purchase farm equipment at wholesale prices https://www.agrisupply.com/

Chapter 57
Long-term gardening and outdoor planning

If you have never lived in the country and have just purchased several acres in the country, the thought of where to begin can be overwhelming. It is advisable to devise a 1- to 5-year plan to reach your goals. A written plan ensures a more organized and methodical approach to setting up a homestead, a farm-related business, and / or an off-the-grid arrangement. It is likely you will modify the plan; make one anyway. After living on the property for a year, you may delete some projects and add others. There is no perfect plan, but if you have no plan, you might as well plan to maintain the status quo. Even a poorly executed plan is better than no plan. **In addition to a 5-year plan, keep a homesteading / farming journal.** I buy black and white $0.50 college composition notebooks to keep notes on almost all of my projects and use them to journal as well. This allows you to reference critical information without the bias which comes with the passing of time.

This chapter includes a 5-year gardening and land improvement plan. Read over the list and modify it to fit your needs. As you begin to plan for your garden, determine which activities are important and then prioritize them by year. This plan focuses on the outdoor aspects of homesteading, work flow, gardening, play and entertainment areas. Highlight projects in green which you want to do the first year. Use an orange highlight pen for projects you want to do the second year and so on, giving each year a different color. Planning also takes into consideration the potential for income earning projects. This particular project does not cover home improvement aspects of a newly acquired property, only the outdoor spaces.

As you design your property, take the time to formulate goals. These goals usually guide your objectives. Objectives are the steps needed to achieve one or more goals. You may choose the goal of being 75% self-sufficient. This goal would likely include objectives such as purchasing a generator to charge your batteries when wind / solar fail, installing solar power and a battery bank, a water well, installing a large propane tank, etc. Consider geothermal for cooling your home. The ground temperature at 4 to 6 feet below the surface is 55 °F year around. As far as food goes, near self-sufficiency requires large garden plots and ideally some egg-laying chickens. Maybe your goal is to just can several hundred quarts of tomato sauce, green beans and other fresh produce. This requires a much smaller garden space compared to 100% self-sufficient garden. **Space estimates for near self-sufficiency are around 1,200 square feet of garden space per person in the household.** This is roughly six or seven 50-foot rows of plants per person (with 2 – 4 feet between each row).

Maybe one of your goals is to generate an income. This might involve planting a U-pick scuppernong vineyard, a 25-acre blueberry farm, growing culinary herbs or microgreens for local markets and restaurants. Several years ago, I heard about an entrepreneur in Dallas, Texas who lived on one acre in the middle of the city. **He planted various garlic varieties all over his property. Over the years, his business grew to grossing more than $60K per year selling gourmet**

garlic to Dallas restaurants and farmer's markets. When you grow enough of one or more crops to be a reliable source, restaurants may prioritize your products.

Establish a budget to buy supplies thereby laying the groundwork for your projects. Make a bulletin board dedicated to organizing your projects. Hang your multi-year calendar on the bulletin board and place receipts in an envelope tacked to the board, etc. First, do a rough drawing of your property, including all structures and even potential structures. Add in all the various outdoor components you want to design and build. Make sure there is good flow and functionality between each component. For example, the compost pile should be close to the kitchen and close to gardening areas and not in a place easily accessible to domestic and wild animals. If the compost pile is at the farthest corner of your property, it may not be convenient enough to use on a daily basis and wild animals might mess with it.

If you have one or more water features, make sure you maximize the placement of your home, garden, playground area, etc., to take advantage of a beautiful view as well as supply home and garden water needs, etc. Make sure you maximize the placement of your home to view the water feature. Even an ugly water feature can be turned into a beautiful asset with some planning and hard work. If your house faces away from a view of your water feature, you have lost a degree of connectedness with the land and it may negatively affect your home and its re-sale value. If your house is above the water feature / source and you plan to use the water for your house and watering the garden, you will need to pump the water.

Using a rough map, place each component of your plan on the drawing and then put it away for several weeks. After you have had a week or two to contemplate the plan, return to the map and re-evaluate the plan and layout. Make necessary modifications. When you have a good drawing, write out a list of all the projects you want to complete over a 5-year period.

Prioritize the projects and then divide them into 1-year periods. Next, estimate the costs for each project. Some projects may only require your labor while others require some level of investment. Be sure to include each project into your yearly budget. You may also put some projects on your wish list and when funds become available, the project can be added to the calendar. Obviously, you may come up with projects not listed here. This is to be expected. Each person comes with their own set of priorities and desires. Personalize this project to meet your needs. Finally, dedicate your plan to the Lord. He will direct your steps.

Years one and two are usually the most intense in regards to time and expense. Pull out a multi-year calendar and schedule each project. **Early planning pays off in huge dividends in the later years.** Initially, you may not be able to plant all the privacy trees or plant the entire orchard but any amount you can accomplish is a huge step forward. You may want to spend your vacation time and money the first few years after purchasing a new place, on making solid improvements to your property. Most kids living on a farm, work hard. If this is the case, set up an awesome play area for the kids to escape for a few minutes. It could include a tree house, a swinging bridge, a dock at the pond, slides, bars, a zip line, a natural pool, or whatever makes sense for your situation. Be sure to join them on their play adventures when possible. It teaches them the importance of hard work and play.

Children grow up fast. In the blink of an eye, they often leave the parental nest in a glorious fashion. They go to college, they move for a job, they meet and marry a sweetheart, they travel the world – they are gone! Make each moment of their home life memorable (in the positive sense). **Country living provides a great backdrop for memorable moments.** For one thing, it tends to limit the options for getting away from the family. This means more games, more meals together, more funny moments, shared moments of awe and amazement as you lie on your backs and watch the brilliant stars move in their paths against the backdrop of illimitable dark space, etc. **Kids never forget the horror mixed with great excitement and uncontrollable laughter the moment dad accidentally launches himself off the roof while trimming a large tree branch (without sustaining major injuries) or the time mom "accidentally" added salt instead of sugar to her rhubarb pies – these are just a few of the indelible moments which make up an unforgettable childhood and family life.** As parents, be sure you schedule fun times with your family. Vacations are a great way to see and learn about the world. A change in scenery, whether vicariously reading books together or in real time visiting new places and forming great memories, is always highly anticipated. Vacations are a great way to make family memories, establish new traditions, and learn the art of togetherness. Just like we make time for God, make time for your family. **The best investment you make is time spent with God and your family!**

Fence the property – barbed wire is good. Clearly demarcate your property lines. If you have a large property in a popular hunting area, be sure you clearly mark the property as a non-trespassing and non-hunting zone by spraying purple paint on trees or fence posts along your property line. There is a shade of purple known as "No Hunting Purple," although any shade of purple serves this purpose.

Determine if and where you want privacy trees and hedges. Do this within the first year of moving to the country. Usually, fall is the best time to plant trees. This allows the roots to grow during cool weather and when spring comes, the energy is diverted to leaves and fruit. Most people do not know how to properly plant trees. Usually, they are planted too close to each other or too close to driveways, structures, gardens, etc. Thoroughly study the types of trees you intend to plant and their growing habit. Plant accordingly. You may want to look into the "blueprint" method of planting trees, described in the chapter on "Orchards." You may want to supplement the privacy hedge trees with vines, shrubs, perennials and annuals as the trees grow. The chapter on hedgerows includes rapidly growing trees, vines and shrubs which are ideal for privacy barriers.

It is important to identify a good source of organic matter, usually manure. Collect fresh manure for composting. Determine a source for the manure, a schedule to collect the manure, and a location to compost the manure, preferably near the mulch, wood chips and other compost areas. Be sure to animal-proof compost bins where left-over food is composted. Better yet, give left-over vegetables to the chickens who process it into highly desirable chicken manure for composting.

Autumn is also a good time to collect leaves and other organic material for composting over the winter. Leaves provide a rich source of carbon to balance the nitrogen in the soil. They also aerate the soil making it more attractive to earthworms and beneficial microbes. Collect your neighbors' garbage bags full of leaves and then mow over them. This reduces their volume and helps them decompose faster. Mix the leaves with other organic matter and place in a large pile; cover with a tarp if necessary. If you are interested in getting wood chips as a mulch, consult with local city managers and garden centers about getting free mulch delivered to your place. Get as many loads as they are willing to bring. Pile this up somewhere outside of the fenced-in garden area and use it as needed. Mulching with wood chips, leaves, or hay significantly reduces the amount of water needed to keep the soil moist and your plants happy.

Speaking about water, determine how you plan to water your garden and if close proximity to a water source is necessary. Can you water from a pond or a well? What type of equipment does your watering system require? How frequently do you need to water? Watering methods include using sprinklers, drip system, well water, rain water towers, pumps, etc. Watering with well water saves on paying for city water. **On average, every square yard of garden requires 6 gallons of water per week, or about one inch of water.** If it regularly rains, you may not have to water as frequently, if at all. **Mulching also reduces the need for water and in some locations, gardens need very little if any additional water.**

Choose your garden location. Consider the amount of sunlight, proximity of trees / shade, usual wind direction, etc. Now double to quadruple the size and plan to secure or fence in this area. This keeps deer and other wildlife from foraging in your garden. Put up a sturdy fence with a gate large enough to drive a truck or tractor into the area. If you are going to use a hoop house or greenhouse, enlarge the fenced area to accommodate this as well. If you live in a cold hardiness region where temperatures drop significantly below freezing, consider building a greenhouse into the side of a sloped area (a walipini) or find a way to heat the greenhouse. Plan an area near the greenhouse or your garden to mulch leaves and other material for composting.

Determine whether to plant directly into the ground or build raised beds. If you are going to sow directly into the soil, you need to prepare the ground. If you want basic raised beds, you need to build them and fill with soil. Determine the best area(s) for a garden plot and the type of fencing you need for the area. If you are planting a garden to use for canning and for long-term use, experts recommend designating a minimum of 1,000 to 1,200 square feet of garden space per person. This is the equivalent of a 10' x 100' plot or a 20' x 50' plot per person. Decide the location of the garden based on the amount of full sun during summer months, drainage, convenience, soil quality and other features, etc. Roughly outline each garden area and if possible, begin planting the perennial plants. Even if you are only able to plant four or five perennial plants in the medicinal garden, this is a good start. Add plants as you find them until you have reached your goal.

The German word, hügelkultur, is used to describe a large mound or hill culture. These beds are a valuable addition to your garden. If you are planning several large hügelkultur beds, you need to spend some time to assemble them. A hügelkultur bed is a type of raised bed, whether it is in an enclosed bed or mounded up. If making in a raised bed, fill the bottom with rotting wood, wood, wood chips, dirt and top soil (this is not a traditional hügelkultur bed but some people refer to this as a hügelkultur bed).

Usually a hügelkultur bed is assembled on the ground and raises up several feet. It increases the planting surface area. Rotting wood logs are used at the base and core of the bed. As they decompose, they provide a rich ecosystem for keeping the soil healthy. Dirt, grass clippings, compost, leaves, etc., are piled on top of the logs and on top of this you place good composed soil. Plants keep the soil from washing away. Over a period of several years, a hügelkultur bed will take on a life of its own. Not all types of wood will work in a hügelkultur bed. Avoid trees with strong alleopathic effects (i.e., a biological phenomenon where one plant inhibits the growth of another) and rot resistant wood and twigs from the following sources: American elm, black locust, black walnut, cedar, eucalyptus, firs, goldenrod, manzanita, pepper tree, pines, red oak, sugar maple, sycamore, etc.

Depending on when you purchase the property, the first years' garden may be small. **Even if you cannot plant a large garden, plant enough to provide for a modest harvest.** The second year you can plan for a larger garden with greater variety. If possible, plant the following: 10 heirloom tomatoes, 4 cherry tomatoes, 4 paste tomatoes, 1 keeper tomato, 50 beets, 50 onions, 2 20-foot rows of carrots, 2 20 foot rows beans, 4 eggplant, 4 zucchini, 4 yellow squash, 5 pumpkins, 5 assorted winter squash, 2 jalapeno, 10 red bell peppers, 2 – 4 Swiss chard, 2 kale, 4 celery, 2 cucumber, 2 cantaloupe, 4 watermelons, 4 basil, 2 parsley, 2 oregano, 2 thyme, 2 sage, 2 chives, 10 Egyptian walking onions, 50 garlic, 2 red-veined sorrel. Also consider planting several potato towers or rows of potatoes.

Consider where to put up a hoop house, a minimum of 45 feet long and 20 feet wide. You will not regret building the biggest hoop house you can afford. I recommend using a hoop or green house to get a more controlled environment for both spring, summer, fall and even winter gardening. If you want citrus or tropical trees, then be sure you have enough height in your hoop house for these trees to grow. To choose the best location, look for a relatively level plot which gets at least 6 to 8 hours of full sun per day. Avoid low lying areas which tend to stay wet.

Determine where to put a chicken coop if you opt for one. You need to plan for at least 3 to 5 square feet per chicken for the chicken house and 8 to 12 square feet per chicken for the grazing area.

Determine where to plant a small apple or other type of orchard. Choose a space where you could expand if desired. If you want additional fruit trees such as pears, fuyu persimmons, pomegranates, apricots, plums, figs, etc., be sure to plan appropriately for including additional trees. The first year or two of living in a new country location is the best time to plant the fruit-bearing and privacy trees you need. Check with the local agricultural extension for the best varieties to plant in your area. Determine where to plant the nut trees. Be sure to plant walnut trees as far away from other trees and the garden as possible. Pecan trees are large and need a lot of room to grow. Other nut trees are smaller and less imposing.

Determine where to plant grape and other types of vines. Grape vines need several years to establish and start producing a good amount of fruit. Find out which grapes do well in your area and start with those. I suggest starting with a minimum of 10 to 12 vines. If you have the space, plant as many as you can afford. You may want to plant two or more varieties. You will not regret having an abundance of grape vines. You may want to consider planting scuppernong varieties as well. They are large, delicious, and highly desirable. Other types of vines include passionfruit, dragon fruit, and kiwi.

Determine where to plant berry bushes such as blueberry, raspberry and blackberry bushes. Each type of berry needs different considerations. Blueberries may need to be protected from deer and other wildlife. I have known people who have built a 40' x 40' fence around their blueberries and then covered the top with netting. Your set-up may be different, but think about how wonderful fresh blueberries taste and then decide how many bushes you want. When it comes to raspberries, there are varieties with various levels of difficulty. I suggest starting with easy to grow varieties. Check with your local agriculture extension office or nursery for suggestions. As far as blackberry bushes, they are usually planted and then they prefer to be ignored. You have the option of planting thornless blackberries or the usual ones with thorns. If you want to protect a certain area, planting blackberry bushes with thorns may prove to be a deterrent, but there is no guarantee.

Determine how big and where to plant your herb garden. Herb gardens near the kitchen are more user friendly and convenient. This makes it simple to dash out and gather a few sprigs of fresh herbs without burning what's on the stove. Many herbs are perennials and provide year-round fresh herbs. Depending on your growing zone, some are perennial, dying back during the winter and re-growing in the spring. Lemon balm is a good example. Some herbs are annuals and require yearly plantings. Basil tends to self-seed and grow back from seed every year. It's nice to have several types of basil plants. They grow rapidly; be prepared to harvest and preserve basil over the course of the summer months. Some kitchen herbs are also medicinal and can be combined with a medicinal garden.

A medicinal garden may overlap with a chef's herb garden, but most of a medicinal garden is different. Check out the chapter on medicinal plants and determine if this is something you want. Obviously, you may not be able to plant every known medicinal plant. Do some research on some of the following varieties and determine which varieties might meet your needs and grow best in your area.

> Some plants a medicinal garden might include are: *agrimony, aloe vera* (laxative*), angelica* (phytoestrogen*), ashwagandha, astragulus, bay laurel, bilberry, bitter orange, black cohosh, black mustard seed, borage, burdock, calendula, cannabis, castor oil bean, catnip, cats claw, cayenne, centaury, chamomile, chaparral* (exercise extreme caution*), chaste berry, chickweed, chicory, cinquefoil, curry plant, echinacea, elderberry, elderflowers, elecampane, eucalyptus, eyebright, fennel, fenugreek, feverfew, fleabane, foxglove* (cardiac glycoside digitalis*), ginger, ginkgo, ginseng, goldenseal, gotu kola, great yellow gentian, hawthorn, henna, hibiscus, hollyhock, holy basil, horseradish, horsetail, hyssop, juniper, lambs ears, licorice root, lemon balm, lavender* (terpenes*), lichens* (specific ones*), marigold, marsh-mallow plant, milk thistle, mugwort, mullein, neem, nettle, nigella sativa, oregano, parsley, passion flower, peppermint, plantain, poppy* (alkaloids morphine and codeine*), purslane, red raspberry leaves, rhubarb* (anthraquinone glycosides; DO NOT EAT THE LEAVES*), rose hips, rosemary, sage, sea buckthorn, self-heal, senna* (anthraquinone glycosides; laxative*), skull-cap, slippery elm, star anise* (shikimic acid*), St. John's wort, sweet gum tree* (sap, leaves, bark, and seeds contain shikimic acid and sap / storax used to treat skin problems, coughs, ulcers), tea tree oil, thistle, thyme* (thymol antiseptic and antifungal*), turmeric, uva ursi, valerian, verbena, vetiver, watercress, white willow, witch hazel, woodruff, yarrow, yellow dock, yerba santa.* Other medicinal plants such as dandelion, plantain, etc., are naturally occurring "weeds" and usually do not need to be formally planted or given space in a medicinal garden.

Plant an asparagus garden in a raised bed area in the first year. Ten to twenty, one-year asparagus crowns do not produce much but by the third year, they are much more productive. Plant 12 to 15 asparagus crowns per person or around 50 asparagus crowns for a family of four. Asparagus plants are perennial and provide you with up to 20 years of asparagus harvests. Plant several varieties.

Don't forget the flower beds. A garden without several flower beds is incomplete. I like a rose garden, a zinnia garden intermingled with snapdragons and dahlias, and a cacti garden. I also enjoy ornamental alliums, lilac trees, honeysuckle, jasmine, and salmon colored hyacinth bean vines. If you want to grow orchids, you may need a dedicated spot in a greenhouse or in your bathroom.

During cool fall and winter months, take the time to work on small projects such as building several small raised beds with covers to grow lettuce and delicate crops in the early spring months. You can salvage old used glass doors and windows attached to hinges as tops for the raised beds.

Learn to preserve what you grow. This may involve canning, dehydrating, making powders, freezing, root cellar storage, etc. This saves money and frees up resources to do other things.

During fall and winter months, make a list of things you want to grow and raise and do not want to buy. The list could include things like: eggs, asparagus, potatoes, figs, lemons, grapes, onions, garlic, strawberries, blackberries, blueberries, corn, fresh herbs, flowers, jam, pecans, teas, etc. Once you know what you want to grow, make plans for how much and which varieties to grow. December through February are good months to order seeds and pre-order plants.

The off season is a great time to schedule small gardening projects such as setting up a potting shed or bench. This could hold clean empty pots, soil amendments, gardening tools, gloves, fertilizers, etc. Build tomato cages or a permanent system to stake up and support sprawling tomato plants.

Tree-planting projects may influence your plans for the months of September through December because autumn is the ideal time to plant most trees. Break down each task into discrete time units, such as 16 hours, 2 days or 4 half days. This way you can accurately schedule the task. I have found most tasks take at least double the amount of time initially estimated.

If you are business minded and plan to monetize one or more aspects of your homestead or small farm, develop a business plan. There are many formats available on the web. Search for a business plan that fits your needs. A business plan might include a mission statement, goals and objectives, current inventory, desired inventory, number of acres in development, operating budget, anticipated growth, SWOT (i.e., strengths, weaknesses, opportunities and threats) analysis, etc.

In summary, if possible, complete the planting of privacy and fruit-bearing tree plantings within the first year. Hoop houses are relatively cheap and can be erected in a day or two. Identify your gardening areas, build the needed structures, and plant them (e.g., asparagus bed, flower garden, herb garden, medicinal garden, vineyard, orchard). Identify your watering and weed control methods. Plan to save seeds from the fruits and vegetables you want to plant again. Be aware, if you planted hybrids, the seeds may not be viable. If you planted heirloom seeds and plants, they should be viable seeds. Join a seed exchange group. Get to know the people at the local agricultural extension in case you have questions. If one of your goals is to establish an income crop, do your research and make sure you have planted several varieties to evaluate. Cut down dead trees or living trees you may need for winter fuel. Keep your eyes open for a wood splitter. Clean your tools, oil equipment, change the oil in tractors and mowers, sharpen blades. If you have water features such as a small pond or a fountain, consider adding a gallon of homemade colloidal silver once per month.

It is critical to set up a loving and caring relationship with your animals, both domesticated and farm animals (including birds). One way to demonstrate a beautiful, heavenly dominion with the animals is to care for their needs, including their social needs, nourishment needs, and their health needs. Be sure to keep their hair combed and clean. Always take measures to prevent ticks and fleas, heart worms, parasites, sores, etc. If you have horses, make sure they are not having to deal with excessive fly issues during warmer months by providing them with face and eye protection. Keep them warm in the wintertime with coats and cozy barns with lots of hay to keep their bellies full. **Be sure they have enough grass to eat during winter months and if necessary, supplement their grazing with additional food sources.**

In the second year, continue planting privacy and fruit-bearing trees as needed. Adjust your plans based on your first year's experiences. Consider making gravel, stone or wood walk-ways between your garden plots. This negates having to deal with muddy pants and boots. If you are considering a root cellar, start collecting different designs. If you want a strawberry tower or a trellised walkway, this might be a good year to consider a project. If you want to supplement your energy usage with solar power, this would be a good year to examine your options and get some bids or do it yourself. You may also want to consider building your own solar furnace if you have a basement. Cut down any dead trees or trees you may need for winter fuel. Walk your property and cut away any vines from trees. Do poison ivy control if needed. Thin out wooded areas if needed. Repair fencing if needed. It is a good idea to do a water test at least once per year to make sure your water remains pure and safe to drink. Always take time to praise God for your blessings!

Year three is a good time to reflect on the first two years of country living and again, tweak what is working and change or cull what is not working. Continue planting privacy and fruit-bearing trees as needed. Adjust your plans based on the first two year's experiences. You may want to add one or two building projects such as a solar dehydrator or more raised garden beds, fencing, etc. This might be the year to consider monetizing your outdoor efforts if you have not already done so. If you have an area of land you could set up several RV sites for friends and family. You may be able to rent the sites for a modest income. Clean around the outside perimeter of your home and property line. Trim bushes and trees. This helps demarcate your property and communicates to your neighbors, you are in charge of your property and keeping it up. Repair roads, grade and re-gravel if necessary.

The first two to three years of setting up a homestead in the country are busy and full of new chores and tasks. Hopefully you and your family easily adapt to this new lifestyle. If you are too busy to take a vacation the first two years, you definitely should consider taking one during the third year. Plan and save to get away and enjoy time together as a family. Farming and country living, while full of blessings and beauty, can also wear you down if you don't get away. Children especially need to get away and experience different scenery. If your family enjoys active vacations, plan something active. If your family is more cerebral, plan an educational tour of the east coast or a foreign country. If your family is into music, plan a vacation around visiting famous musicians' home towns and their countries. Be sure some aspect of your vacation is special for each family member, including the parents! It is a good idea to take as much time as possible for a vacation. A minimum of two weeks is good, but a month

Is even better if possible. If you plant a large garden, your vacation times need to be scheduled in the off season, between October and March. Identify who can farm-sit for you during your vacation dates; plan at least 6 months in advance. Single people can be a great resource for house- and farm-sitting. They may have a more flexible calendar and appreciate a change in their routine. Be sure they have spent several weekends or even weeks with you before you take off for Greece! Have a back-up plan in place if something changes at the last minute. When you make plans to leave on vacation, do not broadcast it to the community. You may trust your friends, but you never know who might hear about your trip and sneak onto the property and steal your equipment, etc.

The fourth year is a good time to do a thorough inspection of your home, out-buildings and property. What needs repair? Inspect the roof, attic and basement for leaks. Inspect windows and doors for tight seals and drafty openings. Clean the fire place and wood-burning stove. Touch up the walls and ceilings if necessary. Add a few more raised beds if you need them. If you have had underground pests, take care of them to ensure they do not continue to make your life miserable. Make a list of needed projects and repairs. Prioritize and get them done during the off season when possible.

As the fifth year arrives, take time to reflect as well as look forward. Maybe the past four years have been incredibly hectic but a routine is setting in. Your hard work is paying off. Instead of feeling panic-stricken when it rains too much or doesn't rain enough, you know the Lord is caring for you and your family. It is both a humbling and intensely satisfying realization. **You have enough. In fact, you have enough to reach out and help others.** You have learned the differences between wants and needs and now it is time to give back to the community and the less fortunate. **Galatians 5:13**, "For you were called to freedom, brothers. Only do not use your freedom as an opportunity for the flesh, but through love, serve one another." "It is like a mustard seed that a man took and sowed in his garden. It grew and became a tree, and the birds of the sky nested in its branches" **Luke 13:19**. "Still other seed fell on good soil. It came up and yielded a crop a hundred times more than was sown" **Luke 8:8**.

There are various avenues to give back. Start a local small farmers club or support group. Volunteer to speak at schools and for other groups. Build alliances with restaurants, businesses, other farmers, churches, home school groups, etc. Learn about wild edible plants in your area and how to use them. Helping others be successful also helps you. Table 1, is a worksheet for long term planning.

A word about crop rotation. Planting a garden utilizes nutrients in the soil which need to be replenished. Regularly adding organic matter to garden beds is essential. Organic additives can be seasonal. During the fall, add mulched leaves. In the winter add wood mulch. During the spring, add composted organic matter. During the summer add humic and fulvic acid teas, worm castings, rock dust, compost tea, green weed tea, comfrey tea, grass clipping tea, nettle tea, dandelion tea, yarrow tea, fertilizers, vegetable scraps, and bone meal as determined by soil testing, etc.

Planting legumes (nitrogen fixers), fixes nitrogen and prepares for crops which are high nitrogen utilizers. Nitrogen fixing plants: peas, beans, peanuts, alfalfa, lupins, clover, vetch, sweet pea flowers.

Green leafy vegetables require high amounts of nitrogen. If you plant green leafy vegetables where legumes grew as the previous crop, the green leafy vegetables will do very well. The green leafy vegetables will go crazy but plants that produce a flower (fruit) will not do as well.

Flowering plants produce fruit require less nitrogen and more phosphorous for high production. Plants needing phosphorous: cucumber, eggplant, melons pepper, potato, squash, and tomatoes. These plants are "lighter" feeders than other groups. Plants that utilize and need potassium (K) and even extra potassium: root plants such as carrots, parsnips, beets, garlic, onions, radishes.

Long-term Garden and Outdoor Planning for Your Homestead, Table 1
Plan your projects for greater success!

Project	Year 1	Year 2	Year 3	Year 4	Year 5
Airplane landing strip for those owning a private plane					
Asparagus beds – start with 1- or 2-year bare root plants					
Barn – regular or pole barn					
Bee hives for honey production					
Berry patches: raspberry, blackberry, blueberry					
Bird feeders – various types for specific birds					
Blog / journal about your experience					
Bread / pizza oven					
Building projects:					
Building projects:					
Building projects:					
Building projects:					
Building projects:					
Building projects:					
Burn pile or a burn barrel					
Butterfly garden					
Cacti garden					
Chicken coop					
Clean up: garden beds, sheds, pots, animal areas, hoop house, green house, etc.					
Clear areas around the house / property perimeter					
Clothesline					
Collect large rocks for landscaping or design features					
Compost bin / area / system					
Corral (fenced area for horses or cows to gather)					
Cover crops: plant					
Crop rotation program / plan					
Cut back unwanted vines/poison ivy during the winter					
Cut down dead trees and mulch if possible					
Edible wild plant foraging area					
Enhance / enlarge pet enclosures / yard area and farm animal areas, grazing areas, etc.					
Espalier fruit and other types of trees					
Experimental garden areas					
Fence: garden areas, orchard, etc.					
Fence: perimeter, purple spray paint, etc.					
Fire pit, fire place, wood burning stove (clean/maintain)					
Firewood shed / area					
Flower beds: roses, dahlias, zinnias, etc.					
Gardening beds, preparation, etc.					
Gas tank (for storing gas used by farm equipment)					
Generators: gas, propane, etc., for emergencies					
Grain crop growing area(s)					
Greenhouse(s)					
Grind wheat and other grains (buy grinder)					
Hanging decorative and / or edible plants					
Hay: cut and store in barn					

Project	Year 1	Year 2	Year 3	Year 4	Year 5
Hedgerows					
Herb garden					
Hoop house					
Hydroelectric energy generator					
Hydroponic growing towers					
Inspect: attic, basement, roof					
Inspect: windows, doors, skylights					
Level the ground					
Maintenance: fireplace, wood stove, etc.					
Maintenance: gates, fences, etc.					
Maintenance: orchard, grafting, new trees					
Maintenance: plumbing, drains, water line					
Maintenance: sharpen blades, change oil					
Maintenance: tools, power equipment, etc.					
Maintenance:					
Maintenance:					
Manure, collect					
Medicinal garden					
Mulch leaves for composting					
Mushroom log area					
Off grid modifications					
Orangerie					
Orchard: fruit trees					
Orchard: nut trees					
Order equipment:					
Order seeds, bulbs, rhizomes and plants:					
Order (other):					
Outdoor kitchen					
Outdoor shooting range					
Outhouse / composting toilet system					
Painting project:					
Par course					
Paths and walkways					
Perennials, plant and tend					
Pest deterrence					
Pest management: gophers, etc.					
Plant trees (fruit, nut, etc.)					
Playground / area for kids					
Pollinator home / garden area					
Potato barrels / patch					
Potting bench / shed					
Privacy hedgerow plantings (best to plant asap)					
Propane tanks – may need a larger size or replacement					
Purple spray paint non-hunting areas					
Rainwater collection: barrels, tanks, etc.					
Raised beds					
Repair: equipment					
Repair: roads and walkways					
Repair:					
Rocket mass heater for greenhouse					
Root cellar					

Project	Year 1	Year 2	Year 3	Year 4	Year 5
RV site with hookups, septic, etc.					
Sauna					
Security features					
Seed starting					
Shed					
Sheer animals					
Signage					
Solar dehydrator					
Solar furnace using the basement					
Solar-heated black water barrels					
Solar operated gate					
Solar operated outdoor lights					
Solar oven					
Solar power, battery banks					
Solar water heater					
Sound system					
Sports areas: croquet, volleyball, mini-golf, frisbee, etc.					
Spring cleaning					
Strawberry beds					
Summerize					
Treehouse					
Tomato cages, build					
Tornado shelter					
Trellises					
Trim bushes and trees					
Tune up pets / farm animals: clean teeth, trim nails, etc.					
Tunnels: high					
Tunnels: low					
Vegetable garden					
Vineyard: grapes, scuppernongs, etc.					
Vineyard: other					
Walipini					
Water safety and adequacy					
Water: dig a well and build well house					
Water: supply to garden areas					
Water: supply to outbuildings					
Water: supply to house					
Water feature(s)					
Water feature: pool, hot tub, etc.					
Water feature: fountain					
Water feature: pond					
Water feature: trough					
Windmill, wind energy					
Winterize your home, barn, equipment					
Wood chips: collect, spread, etc.					
Wooded areas, thin out					
Wood splitting, wood chipper, lumber/saw mill					
Worm farm					
Workshop					
Zip line					

Chapter 58

What and how much to plant?

Fruits and Vegetables for _____ People

1. **Fruit bushes** (e.g., blackberries, blueberries, currants, gooseberries, lingonberries, raspberries, strawberries)
   A. 5 ea biloxi, bluecrop, Brightwell blueberries D.   G.
   B.   E.   H.
   C.   F.   I.
   Notes: _____

2. **Fruit and Nut Trees** (e.g., almond, apple, apricot, Asian pear, banana, cherry, chestnut, chinquapin, citrus, crabapple, fig, goji berry, guava, hazelnut, hickory, jujube, loquat, mayhaw, mulberry, nectarine, olive, pawpaw, peach, pear, pecan, persimmon, pinenut, plum, pomegranate, quince, walnut)
   A. 5 Blenheim apricot trees   I.   Q.
   B. 5 Arkansas black apple trees   J.   R.
   C.   K.   S.
   D.   L.   T.
   E.   M.   U.
   F.   N.   V.
   G.   O.   W.
   H.   P.   X.
   Notes: _____

3. **Fruit Vines** (e.g., grapes, kiwi, passionfruit, melons, dragon fruit, vanilla beans)
   A. 5 Moondrop grape vines   C. 5 crimson seedless grape vines   E.
   B. 5 concord grape vines   D.   F.
   Notes: _____

4. **Grain Crops** (e.g., amaranth, barley, buckwheat, corn, emmer, millet, wheat)
   A.   B.   C.
   Notes: _____

5. **Animal Feed and Cover Crops** (e.g., clover, rye, barley, cowpeas, alfalfa, hairy vetch, fava beans, radishes, turnips)
   A.   B.   C.
   Notes: _____

6. **Lettuce & Leafy Greens** (e.g., arugula, bok choy, chard, collards, endive, kale, lettuce, mustard greens, radicchio, cress)
   A.   E.   I.
   B.   F.   J.
   C.   G.   K.
   D.   H.   L.
   Notes: _____

7. **Nightshade Crops** (e.g., tomatoes, potatoes, eggplant, peppers)
   A.   F.   K.
   B.   G.   L.
   C.   H.   M.
   D.   I.   N.
   E.   J.   O.
   Notes: _____

8. **Non-starchy Vegetable Crops** (e.g., artichoke, broccoli, Brussels sprouts, butternut squash, cabbage, cauliflower, celery, collards, green onions, kale, leeks, mushrooms, okra, peppers, pumpkins, squash, spinach, zucchini)
   - A.
   - B.
   - C.
   - D.
   - E.
   - F.
   - G.
   - H.
   - I.
   - J.
   - K.
   - L.
   - M.
   - N.
   - O.

   Notes: _____

9. **Root Vegetables** (e.g., beets, carrots, garlic, jicama, kohlrabi, onions, parsnips, radishes, rutabaga, shallots, sweet potatoes, turnips)
   - A.
   - B.
   - C.
   - D.
   - E.
   - F.
   - G.
   - H.
   - I.
   - J.
   - K.
   - L.

   Notes: _____

10. **Asparagus and / or Strawberry Bed**
    - A.
    - B.
    - C.

    Notes: _____

11. **Herbal / Medicinal Garden** (e.g., balm, basil, chives, dill, mint, oregano, parsley, rosemary, sage, savory, tarragon, thyme)
    - A.
    - B.
    - C.
    - D.
    - E.
    - F.
    - G.
    - H.
    - I.
    - J.
    - K.
    - L.
    - M.
    - N.
    - O.

    Notes: _____

12. **Flowers** (e.g., borage, calendula, dahlias, dianthus, lavender, marigold, nasturtium, pansy, rose, sunflowers, viola, zinnias)
    - A.
    - B.
    - C.
    - D.
    - E.
    - F.
    - G.
    - H.
    - I.
    - J.
    - K.
    - L.
    - M.
    - N.
    - O.

    Notes: _____

13. **Barrier / Privacy Trees and Bushes** (e.g., arborvitae, bamboo, cypress, hydrangea, forsythia, juniper, lilac, privet)
    - A.
    - B.
    - C.
    - D.
    - E.
    - F.
    - G.
    - H.
    - I.

    Notes: _____

14. **Others**
    - A.
    - B.
    - C.
    - D.
    - E.
    - F.
    - G.
    - H.
    - I.
    - J.
    - K.
    - L.
    - M.
    - N.
    - O.
    - P.
    - Q.
    - R.
    - S.
    - T.
    - U.
    - V.
    - W.
    - X.
    - Y.
    - Z.
    - AA.

    Notes: _____

Chapter 59
High yield, fast-growing fruits and vegetables

'God designed plants to deliver nutrients' -Bob Iacono. "And God said, Behold, I have given you every herb bearing seed, which is upon the face of all the earth, and every tree, in the which is the fruit of a tree yielding seed; to you it shall be for food." **Genesis 1:29**. There were many beautiful plants and trees bearing edible fruit. Genesis 1:29, tells us every seed-bearing plant was made for man. The only exception in the garden of Eden was the tree of knowledge of good and evil. The above verse possibly indicates this tree bore fruit but had not seeds.

In a second look at creation, **Genesis 2** (RSV), provides additional insight into the garden. Starting with verse 4, "In the day that the Lord God made the earth and the heavens, when no plant of the field was yet in the earth and no herb of the field had yet sprung up – for the Lord God had not caused it to rain upon the earth, and there was no man to till the ground; but a mist went up from the earth and watered the whole face of the ground – then the Lord God formed man of dust from the ground, and breathed into his nostrils the breath of life; and man became a living being. And the Lord God planted a garden in Eden, in the east; and there he put the man whom he had formed. And out of the ground the Lord God made to grow every tree that is pleasant to the sight and good for food, the tree of life also in the midst of the garden, and the tree of knowledge of good and evil." Verse 8, describes how the Lord God formed man from the dust of the ground and verse 9, describes how God made the plants to grow out of the ground. Verse 19, "So out of the ground the Lord God formed every beast of the field and every bird of the air, and brought them to the man to see what he would call them; and whatever the man called every living creature, that was its name." The Lord God deviated when he made woman. He used Adam's rib as the starting material. Verse 21, "So the Lord God caused a deep sleep to fall upon the man, and while he slept took one of his ribs and closed up its place with flesh; and the rib which the Lord God had taken from the man he made into a woman and brought her to the man. Then the man said, 'This at last is bone of my bones and flesh or my flesh; she shall be called Woman, because she was taken out of Man.' Therefore, a man leaves his father and his mother and cleaves to his wife, and they become one flesh."

The ground, what we know as dirt or soil, formed the basis for the creation of plants, animals and humans. Unfortunately, the word, "dirt" has been hijacked to mean something worthless. However, on this planet, dirt is the medium for many reactions essential to life on earth. Soil is formed when rocks disintegrate, leaving behind minerals and organic matter decomposes. Removing rocks from gardens may eventually lead to mineral depletion of the soil. Organic matter is formed when plants, insects and animals decompose. When organic matter fully breaks down, it leaves behind humus and fulvic acid. Healthy soil is loose and contains air pockets, allowing oxygen to interact with soil components including living microorganisms, earth worms, etc. This is why clay soil does not work well for rapidly growing edible plants. Soil-based living organisms such as insects, lichens, and others, take up the minerals and release them as organic material into the soil. Nutrients such as nitrogen, phosphorus, potassium, magnesium, calcium, sulfur and many additional trace minerals are needed by plants. When it rains, organic matter combines with water and the nutrients dissolve and are taken into the plant's roots. The dissolved minerals, using capillary action, are distributed throughout the plant, including the edible portions of the plant, and then eaten and transferred to humans. Humans use minerals as building materials, for nerve transmission, muscle contraction, as co-factors, to make hormones such as thyroid hormones, for growth, energy production, etc.

Plants provide vitamins, fibers, macronutrients, electrons, water, and many other valuable components. Each component of edible plants contains phytochemicals which make up the vast array of plant colors and structural components. Plant pigments exist together in an infinite combination of colors. Just like snowflakes, no one plant is exactly the same as another plant of the same species. Edible plants have remarkably similar nutritive values or they would not be able to grow and produce an edible carrot, or assemble an asparagus stalk, or form a perfect apple. There are slight variations in nutrients based on growth medium and other factors, but by definition, edible plants must have enough nutrients to form a carrot or it will not grow into a carrot.

High Yield, Fast Growing Fruits and Vegetables, Figure 1. Heme (haem b) and chlorophyll structures. Haems and chlorophylls: comparison of function and formation by GAF Hendry and OTG Jones, 1980.

Chlorophyll is the green pigment of grasses, shrubs, vines and trees. Every living green plant contains this unique compound, we know as chlorophyll. It is the plant equivalent of human hemoglobin. Hemoglobin is also a pigment found only in animals and humans. It is the red pigment which gives blood and muscle its color.

Chlorophyll and hemoglobin have similar structures (see Figure 1). Hemoglobin is a large molecule built around an iron (Fe) core and chlorophyll is a large molecule built around a molecule of magnesium (Mg). Plants use energy from the sun to manufacture sugar, starch and proteins. This process builds plants and provides food and nutrition for animals and humans. Humans use three primary pigments to make every color used in an artist's palette: blue, yellow and red. **Nature produces its own palette of pigments, each with its unique composition, which combine to make** gorgeous colors unique to every plant. More than 1,000 naturally occurring versions of chlorophyll have been identified. Each different type absorbs a different combination of wavelengths. Carotenoids are usually present with chlorophyll and as the days become shorter in the fall, the chlorophyll fades and the carotenoids become prominent, giving us beautiful fall colors. Scientists have identified more than 500 naturally occurring carotenoids and more than 3,000 flavonoids.

Pigments are a colored substance produced by a plant. They absorb visible radiation between 380 nm (violet) and 760 nm (red). The absorption spectrum is the radiation wavelengths a pigment absorbs. Chlorophyll absorbs red and blue wavelengths but not green wavelengths. This makes chlorophyll-containing plants appear green. **Plant pigments are roughly divided into fifteen general pigment colors plus an additional light-emitting compound:** 1. green (chlorophyll), 2. purple (flavonoids including anthocyanins), 3. blue (anthocyanadins, indoles, bilichrome), 4. blue-green (phytochrome), 5. red (carotenoids, lycopene, betalains, anthocyanins), 6. red-violet (betacyanins, phytochromes), 7. pink (anthocyanins, canthaxanthin), 8. orange (carotenoids, betaxanthins), 9. yellow (carotenoids, flavonoids, betalains, betaxanthins, xanthophylls, lutein, zeaxanthin), 10. orange-yellow (flavins), 11. beige (proanthocyanidins), 12. reddish-brown (theaflavin), 13. white (flavonols, flavones, anthoxanthins), 14. brown (tannins), 15. black (melanin, tannins) and 16. light-emitting luciferin, a bioluminescence found in some species of mushrooms. Each color category contains dozens of slightly different color variations. According to the Science and Technology Encyclopedia, flamingoes and goldfish contain similar plant-related carotenoid pigments giving them their distinct pink and orange colors, respectively. https://www.youtube.com/watch?v=yZRdLIKd3Y0

South Korean researchers, J. H. Lee, et al., published an article about plants exposed to low levels of short-term ultraviolet-A light (at wavelengths of 370 and 385 nm). This stimulates certain plant genes and increases the growth and overall antioxidant and pigment content of phenolic compounds. As the atmosphere surrounding the earth has changed over millennia, it is possible the amount of UV-A has been filtered out; this may have negatively impacted plant growth and possibly nutrient composition.

A few plant pigments are sensitive to heat, light, and / or pH. **For example, some anthocyanins, when exposed to heat, disappear.** This happens when purple beans or purple cauliflower is steamed or cooked. The anthocyanins bleach out and the white and green pigments become visible. However, most purple pigments (anthocyanins) are not heat sensitive including those found in blueberries, figs, plums, etc. Foods with the highest anthocyanin content include blueberries, blackberries, red cabbage, cherries, cranberries, pomegranate, purple sweet potatoes, etc.

Green grass is underappreciated. It is rich in protein, sugar, vitamins, minerals and fiber. It is consumed by millions of animals. The nutritional value of one ounce of wheat grass is remarkable (see Figure 2)! Most animals are true herbivores, consuming only plants. A horse consumes about 1% of its weight in grass or hay on a daily basis. **A horse consuming just enough kilocalories to maintain health needs to eat around 15,000 kcalories per day. A moderate working horse needs to consume approximately 25,000 kcalories and a heavy work horse needs 33,000 kcalories.** These kcalorie levels seem astronomically high, but when you look at the weight of ahorse and the nutritive value of grass, it is realistic for horses, cows and other animals to live on green grass. A horse eats anywhere from 10 to 20 or more pounds of grass and / or hay per day. This is why you usually see horses with their heads down and grazing on grass. It is critically important for grazing animals have enough green pasture land to consume a nourishing diet. This is more challenging in cold, winter months. Supplementing their diet may be necessary. As you can see from Figure 2, grass is excellent at mobilizing and storing nutrients from the soil below. When we cut the grass and send it in plastic bags to the dump, we are wasting a valuable resource which could be composted and returned to the earth. Just in case you think it might be a good idea to give grass cuttings to your neighbor's horses, be sure to check with their owners first to make sure your grass is acceptable and does not have potentially harmful weeds and seeds.

Discussing the nutritive value of grass reminds me of a Bible character who ate grass for 7 years. King Nebuchadnezzar, the greatest king who ever lived, boasted about his accomplishments to God and was forced out of his kingdom and into the fields where he, along with oxen, grazed on grass. At the end of 7 years, he regained his "right mind" and praised God. He returned as the king of Babylon. From a modern perspective, one could make the argument, Nebuchadnezzar followed a vegan diet, but it really goes beyond what we under-stand even today, in the age of modern science and medicine. If we assume the kings calorie require-ments were at least 2,500 calories (alternatively we could assume he needed to consume 1% of his body weight, assuming a weight of 175-185 lb, this would be 28-30 ounces of grass), and he ate enough grass equivalent to providing 2,500 kcals. If this is the case, he consumed supra-physiological levels of vitamins and minerals. He would have needed 21 ounces of wheat grass to consume 2,500 kcals. Using a multiplication factor of 21 to apply to the nutrition data in Figure 2 (which is based on 28 grams or 1 ounce), the amount of

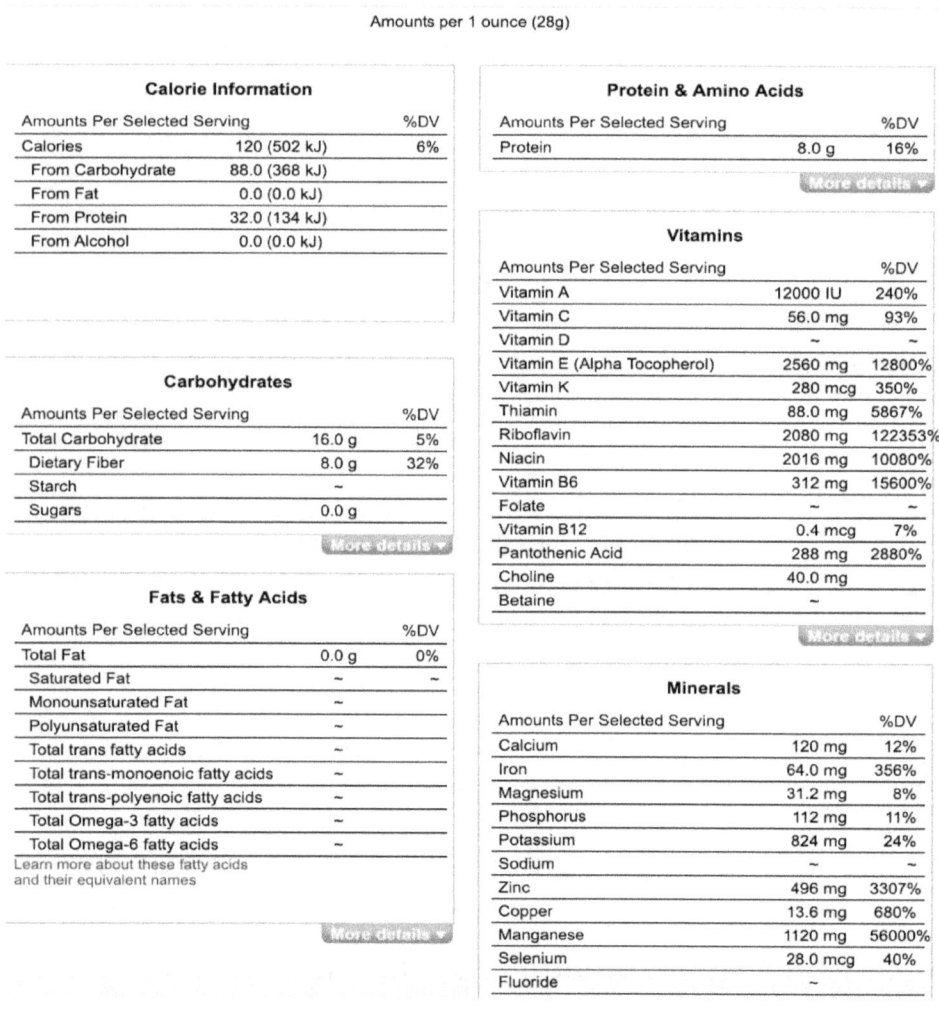

Figure 2. Nutritional data for 28 grams wheat grass. Self Nutrition Data.
https://nutritiondata.self.com/facts/custom/900675/2

wheat grass providing 2,500 kcals would also provide: 336 g of carbs, 168 g protein, 168 g fiber, 252,000 IUs Vit A (in form of beta carotene), 1,176 mg Vit C, 53.8 g Vit E, 5.9 mg Vit K, 162.6 g thiamin, 43.68 g of riboflavin, 2.5 g calcium, 1.3 g iron, 10.4 g zinc, and 23.5 g manganese, etc. From a nutritionist's perspective, this is mind boggling. Even if he only consumed half this amount of kcalories, the potential for mineral toxicity from the perspective of what we know about minerals in the 21st century, is almost certain.

The King Nebuchadnezzar story gets even more interesting as new research emerges. In an article published in 2014 by the Journal of Cell Science (Chen Xu, et al; PMID: 24198392), researchers describe how mammalian (animals and humans) mitochondria capture light (as photons) and synthesize ATP when chlorophyll is present. ATP is the body's energy currency. For example, if you want to lift a finger, your body requires an exchange of ATP. In effect, when we consume green plants and are subsequently exposed to sunlight, certain mammals are able to synthesize ATP. Chen Xu, et al, found that mice, rats and swine, when fed a chlorophyll rich diet and upon subsequent sunlight exposure, were able to capture light and synthesize ATP. They suggest the mechanism for this is through catalyzing the reduction of coenzyme Q. This is groundbreaking research. Let me state this another way. Theoretically speaking, when animals consume green plants, in which the chloroplast has captured energy from the sun and converted it to glucose, the mammalian generated dietary metabolites of chlorophyll retain the ability to absorb light in the visible spectrum at wave-lengths which can superficially penetrate into animal tissues. Plants also contain significant amounts of water. This group showed dietary metabolites of chlorophyll can enter the circulation and are present in tissues and can be enriched in the mitochondria. Their findings, if accurate, have huge implications for how we age, our lifestyle, and our diet. In fact, this may partially explain Nebuchadnezzar's 7-year grass diet and his subsequent return to sanity and his re-establishment as the king of Babylon. In addition, chlorophyll and its metabolites also bind toxins such as dioxins, heterocyclic amines, polyaromatic hydrocarbons, and aflatoxin as well as binding heavy metals. https://doi.org/10.1002/mnfr.202000761

Light wavelengths of 670 nm may penetrate the human body.

The study goes on to describe how 670 nm light wavelengths penetrate the human body, yielding ~ 43 kcal/mol (1.18 X 10^{-22} kcal / photon). Based on chlorophyll concentrations in the body and photon flux at 670 nm (duration, intensity, amount of exposed skin), each chlorophyll metabolite would be expected to absorb a few photons per second, a negligible amount of additional energy but if there was a light-capturing chlorophyll "antenna" system in place, the photon capture could be greater. The significance of this and other similar studies is the small increase in ATP synthesis. How much of an increase is biologically significant? Even small increases in experimental mammals contributed to an increased lifespan. This study demonstrates in addition to sun exposure producing sulfated vitamin D (the best kind), the sun's photons may also interact with chlorophyll metabolites in vivo and optimize oxidative phosphorylation by increasing ubiquinol, generated from the photoreduction of CoQ, protecting against long-term oxidative damage. Yikes! <u>If that sounded a little too scientific, it basically means, hypothetically when we consume fresh greens and then spend time outdoors in the sunlight, we are potentially able to capture a small amount of energy from the sun's photons interacting with metabolites of green plants in our superficially located blood vessels.</u>

Light creates energy in biological tissues. Green plants soak up sunlight and this starts their molecular motors and photosynthesis commences. Photosynthesis drives growth. The first step in photosynthesis is to split water (H_2O) into H^+ OH^-. When the positive and negative charges are separated, they have potential electrical energy. Negatively charged 'water' represents potential energy to do biological functions in the cell. This is responsible for healthy functional cells. Light, with the most effective wave-lengths being in the infrared range, provides energy to organize and orchestrate energy flow in the body by forcing charge separation, much like you see in a battery. Professor Gerald Pollack, studies negatively charged water, $H3O2$, and has described it as the 4th phase of water, which he labels as semi-crystalline water or EZ water (exclusion zone).

Researchers in Dr. Pollack's lab have shown focusing light on physiological tissues, causes charge separation and this represents potential energy. Water absorbs light and light organizes the water in biological tissues and this contributes to energy. It is for these reasons and others, **the green smoothie and time spent outdoors are two of the best things you can do to recover and stabilize your health.** Incorporate as many activities that charge your body and your cells including: eating high water foods (fruits and vegetables), coconut water, greens, green juices and smoothies, sunshine, outdoor work, time spent in nature, earthing, etc.

Back to Nebuchadnezzar and his seven-year period of eating grass. Let's look at a small slice of his story in the Bible.

> While on the roof, the king said, "Look at Babylon! I built this great city. It is my palace. I built this great place by my power. I built this place to show how great I am." The words were still in his mouth when a voice came from heaven. The voice said, "King Nebuchadnezzar, these things will happen to you: Your power as king has been taken away from you. You will be forced to go away from people. **You will live with the wild animals and eat grass like an ox.** Seven seasons will pass before you learn your lesson. Then you will learn that God Most High rules over human kingdoms and gives them to whomever he wants." These things happened immediately. Nebuchadnezzar was forced to go away from people. **He began eating grass like an ox. He became wet from dew.** His hair grew long like the feathers of an eagle, and his nails grew long like the claws of a bird. Then at the end of that time, I, Nebuchadnezzar, looked up toward heaven, and I was in my right mind again. **Then I gave praise to God Most High. I gave honor and glory to him who lives forever. God rules forever!** His kingdom continues for all generations. God does what he wants with the powers of heaven and the people on earth. No one can stop his powerful hand or question what he does. *ERV: Holy Bible: Easy-to-Read Version*

Unfortunately, it is impossible to do an accurate "post-mortem" on Nebuchadnezzar's 7-year diet. There are too many unknowns to be accurate, other than to say, this is indeed a remarkable diet for human survival.

In addition to chlorophyll (green) pigments and their metabolites capturing photons, the human body gives off a pulsating glow, with a mean intensity in the range of up to a few ten-thousand photons per second per square centimeter. This is known as "cellular glow" or "ultra-weak bioluminescence, another potential method of communicating cellular information (Popp FA, et al., (1984); Bischoff M, Frölich).

Grass is not only nutritious, it protects the dirt, and provides a covering or a barrier, preventing valuable components of the dirt from washing away. Grass protects soil from drying out, from shifting and washing away every time it rains, and it provides a hospitable environment for soil physiology to take place. As organic matter breaks down, it produces carbon dioxide. Grass takes up carbon dioxide and produces oxygen. Grass also participates in photosynthesis. Other plants also produce oxygen, forming a symbiotic relationship with the soil. Healthy soil produces healthy grass and edible plants.

Mulch is an excellent material to use in the garden. Most gardeners pull grass and other weeds from the soil immediately surrounding their edible plants. This allows edible plants to use large amounts of the soil's nutrients. However, because there is no grass on top of the soil (kind of like a roof on top of a house), the soil is vulnerable to drying out, washing away, and the grass is not providing a ready source of oxygen. In some ways, placing a thick layer of mulch around the plants, allows the soil to maintain most of its healthy functions. Mulch is made from wood chips, bark, leaves, grass clippings, straw, hay, pine needles, and even seaweed. At least 6 to 8 inches of mulch is needed to block the growth of weeds, protect delicate soil physiology, and maintain soil moisture. Keep in mind, the type of mulch may impact your plant's growth. Avoid wood chips containing black walnut trees.

Compost is a great way to add organic material to your garden. Organic matter includes food scraps (excluding animal flesh, dairy products, fats, and citrus fruits), leaves, grass clippings, manure, etc. Micro-organisms in the soil consume organic matter and their by-products are rich in nutrients. When using manure, allow the manure to fully compost before adding it to your garden beds, other-wise, the manure may "burn" delicate, rapidly growing plants. There are many composting methods. Find a method that works best for your situation. If you have farm animals, you have access to lots of fresh manure and the ability to produce rich composted organic matter. Take advantage of the resources at hand!

Every component of edible plants supports human life with one exception, vitamin B12.

Vitamin B12 is the only nutrient not transferred from soil into the plant and subsequently made available to humans eating the plant. If vitamin B12 is found in a [or on the plant] plant, it is either due to contamination with the by-products of soil-based microorganisms, or it is one of several analogue forms of the vitamin, which are believed to be non-functional (and actually compete for absorption with the real vitamin B12). As far as the plant kingdom goes, vitamin D is found only in mushrooms but it can be obtained by sun exposure, consuming fortified foods and consuming animal products.

If you are new to gardening, do some basic research about the types and specific varieties and cultivars of fruits and vegetables you want to grow. Most of what we choose to grow is what we love to eat. Some gardeners like to experiment and grow unusual and even rare fruits and vegetables. Be sure you understand your climate and the requirements of the fruits and vegetables you plan to grow.

Most edible plants are easy to grow but others may require pruning and special treatments. Some plants attract bugs and other plants are susceptible to rust and blight. Every year you spend in the garden brings new insights and revelation. However, nature never ceases to surprise and amaze even the most prolific and experienced gardener.

Harvest perfectly ripe produce early in morning.

This chapter provides basic information in the form of lists about growing fruits and vegetables. This information is easily accessed on the web but it is also nice to have it in one location. Modify these lists to match your experience. For example, there is a list of fruits and vegetables deer usually avoid. This does not preclude the fact that sometimes deer eat just about anything growing in your garden. I have read about people spending hundreds of dollars to plant flower and vegetable gardens only to have voles dig it up within a few days. It is important to remember there are underground predators as well as above the ground predators.

God gave man dominion over the earth, including plants and animals. This dominion was never intended to be threatening, harsh, murderous, sadistic, devoid of compassion, or a humiliating dominion. As humans, we have an obligation to care for the environment, including domesticated animals and even non-domesticated animals. There is every indication in the Bible our earthly animals will be in Heaven.

Living in the country, comes with certain Biblical obligations to take care of the animals, especially the ones within your sphere of influence. Most animals are social. Isolated animals oftentimes feel anxiety and act out in irregular animal behaviors such as chewing, biting, destroying furniture, digging, urinating inside, etc. Animals also can detect whether or not people like them. Cohabitation with animals in the country is a real blessing. They provide many benefits to humans including companionship, protection, security alerts, rodent and snake deterrence, protection from predatory animals, etc. Some farm animals provide eggs and others provide milk. Farm animals provide a ready source of manure which can be composted and used in the garden or to enrich the soil immediately surrounding your homestead.

Animals have needs just as we do. They need socialization, co-habitation with other animals, food, clean water, love and affection. They need to be monitored for fleas, ticks and heart worms. Their nails need to be trimmed and their ears need to be regularly cleaned. They need to be bathed and brushed on a regular basis. They need a comfortable bed, protection from the elements, a nice yard to run and play and they need socialization with other animals, preferably of their kind. Occasionally, animals need additional care by a veterinarian. It is important to include animal care in your family budget.

How we treat animals is a window to the soul. We should never treat them harshly, isolate them, or use and discard them without concern for their health and well-being. They should NEVER be tied up and kept in small spaces with minimal human contact. People who shun the command to have dominion over the animals will answer to God. Animals are sentient, have familial ties, they are social and in need of love and affection, just like every single human. Animals can also provide insight into how God loves us. Most dog owners attest to their canine's unconditional love. We can learn a lot about love from the animals we care for and treat with tenderness. This does not mean all animals are loving, but there are many ideals to learn from animals, how they care for their young, and how they socialize. Spend time in nature studying the birds and animals for amazing insights into God's kingdom.

Compassionate gardeners and farmers plant enough food to provide for the wild animals. Maybe this means placing a few pear trees or grape vines at the edge of your property or planting delicious cover crops for grazing animals. No matter how animal-friendly your property, if you live in the country you usually have critters competing for your crops. This does not make them your enemy. It makes fences and hoop houses essential for protecting crops you plan to harvest.

Revelation 22:2 provides insight into Heaven's gardens. The Tree of Life yields 12 fruits, a different fruit for each month. The leaves act as a medicine to heal our infirmities as well as nationalistic pride. The fruit from the Tree of Life is a rapidly maturing fruit, assuming a 30-day month (although this assumption might be too simplistic for what may likely be a very different reality).

Photo Credit: Bonnie Kittle at Unsplash.com

In reality, most fruit and vegetable plants rapidly grow and provide high yields. The plant cycle begins with planting a dormant seed in warm soil and barely covering the seed with soil. Germination begins by adding a little water, exposure to oxygen and some warmth from the sun. The optimal temperature range for seed germination is 75 °F – 90 °F (23 °C – 32 °C). The sun and water provide enough energy to break open the seed and send down a root. Loose soil allows enough oxygen to contact the seed. As the seed opens and the root grows, the stem of the plant emerges. The metabolic blueprint and supporting machinery are now in place for the plant to grow and produce edible fruits and vegetables. As the seed sprouts, the nutrients multiply. Sometimes the shell surrounding the seed is hard and dry. Slightly nicking it may improve the chances of a successful germination. This is may be done for individually hand-planted seeds and not seeds that are directly broadcast to the soil.

1 acre = ~43,500 square feet

When it comes to mushrooms or fungi, a spore is the microscopic "seed" that finds its way to a moist, dark area via wind currents. Mushroom spores commonly "germinate" in loose, moist soil, at the base of trees, in sawdust or woodchips, compost, etc. As the spore lodges at the base of a tree or in moist soil, it sends down a root and also sends up a hyphae, which forms the body of the mushroom. **You can purchase mushroom spore plugs and drill holes in large tree branches or trunks and grow a variety of mushrooms.** Mushrooms prefer cool weather, and grow between 45 to 60 ° F. They also prefer darkness or low light. Some mushrooms grow rapidly while others take up to several years to mature. Mushrooms, a hot culinary commodity, are low in calories checking in at about 125 calories per pound.

Mushrooms make a unique contribution to human physiology. The human gut contains the enzyme, trehalase, which targets foods containing the little-known natural sugar, trehalose. Trehalose is produced and used by a few plants, including mushrooms, and animals. It allows some plants to completely dry out and subsequently rehydrate, coming back to life.

This reminds me of Ezekiel's vision of the valley of dry bones. In the vision Ezekiel sees a big pile of dry bones and God directs him to tell the bones that God is going to breathe life into the bones. In this vision, the bones grow flesh and became an army. **Trehalose is found in: mushrooms (e.g., shiitake, maitake, nameko), sunflower seeds, baker's yeast, honey, vinegar, and sea algae.** Mushrooms contain up to 20% trehalose, allowing them to dry out and re-hydrate. Trehalase is also found in plasma and in the kidney, meaning trehalose can be injected into the bloodstream and break down to glucose without harm. For those who are technical, trehalose is two glucose molecules, with the alpha 1,1 linkage. (Trehalose, a new approach to premium dried foods by Bruce Rosner in Trends in Food Science & Technology, July 1991).

Gardening brings surprises. Some years are better than others. The yield estimates below are averages. Some farmers are able to maximize these numbers while others are lucky to come close to these yields. The yield numbers are to be used as a general guide. If your yields are low, do some research to discover what you could do to improve your yields. Adding organic matter adds additional carbon, nitrogen and phosphorus as well as trace minerals. This is usually the best way to improve yields along with earthworms which keep the soil loose and add back organic matter. Heavy mulching allows the soil to retain water while discouraging weeds.

Seed starting
1. Know your time zone and the date of last frost / freeze.
2. If you have an indoor grow room or greenhouse, you may start seeds one to two months before the date of the last frost.
3. Read about each seed type you plant. Read other people's experiences with that specific seed type. Check out online seed stores for ideas and tips. Add this information to a gardening or planting journal.
4. Do the seeds need cold stratification? This means they need to be stored in the refrigerator for a period of time specific to that type of seed, bulb or rhizome.
5. Some seeds need to be scratched or nicked to encourage germination. Older seeds may also need a slight nick to germinate.
6. For seeds which are germinated indoors before transplanting to warm soil, germinate on an unbleached wet paper towel covered with plastic wrap or in small containers with seed starting soil and under a grow lamp and a grow mat underneath.
7. Most seeds are directly sown into warm soil and then lightly covered. With the application of water and sunlight, the seed rapidly germinates and growth begins. Some seeds have longer germination periods and it may seem they might never germinate; it is specific to certain seeds.
8. Decide which type of containers you are going to use. This varies depending on how many seeds you plant. Some seeds can be planted in a large container and when they germinate and put out a primary root below and a stalk above, the plant can be transplanted to an individual container or straight into the ground.
9. As the seed is watered and warmed up with sunlight, it swells and ruptures. This is when the seed sends out a root and stem. Some seeds need specific wavelengths of light while others do not germinate if exposed to light.
10. During germination the seed expands and the early seedling growth is initiated. Germination is stimulated by gibberellin while dormancy is related to the concentration of abscisic acid (prevents germination). It is the balance between gibberellic and abscisic acids which determines when the seed, also given other variables, will germinate.

11. As germination proceeds, the sugars, starches and amino acids in the seed are utilized and the seed turns into a seedling with a root and primary shoot or stalk.
12. The seedling must be "established." Early in the process, the seed's DNA is repaired if necessary and growth proceeds.
13. As the plant grows, it "hardens" off in the environment where it remains. This includes exposure to cool nights, wind, morning dew, sunlight and other variables.

Ideas for acquiring plants
1. Seeds: buy, trade, collect from actual fruits and vegetables, etc.
2. Roots: divide and propagate
3. Rhizomes: ginger, turmeric, dahlias, etc.
4. Bulbs: usually planted in the fall or early spring, depending on location.
5. Corms
6. Tree cuttings / grafting
7. Vine cuttings
8. Spore seeding
9. Others

High yield, fast-growing fruits and vegetables
Table 1. High Yield Fruit and Vegetables (100 foot row yields)

Asparagus: 50 roots, 80 – 100 lb	Onions: 220 lb
Basil: plant 6 – 12 inches apart, ~ 75 – 100 lb	Parsnips: 100 lb
Beans (lima beans): 32 lb	Peanuts: 40 lb
Beans (snap): 30 lb	Peas (southern): 20 lb shelled
Beets: ~ 75 lb	Peas (English): 40 lb
Blackberries: 24 gallons	Peas (snow): 65 lb
Broccoli: 50 plants, ~ 80 – 100 lb	Peppers (bell): 125 lb
Brussels sprouts: 50 plants, ~ 80 –100 lb	Peppers (hot): 200 lb
Cabbage: 70 – 100 plants, ~ 150 – 200 lb	Potatoes (Irish and sweet): 200 lb
Cabbage (Chinese): 200 – 300 lb	Pumpkins: 150 lb
Carrots: 100 – 150 lb	Radish: 50 lb
Cauliflower: 50 – 75 plants, ~ 80 lb	Rhubarb: 25 – 30 plants, ~ 150 – 200 lb
Celeriac: 200 plants, ~ 100 – 150 lb	Shallots: 35 bunches
Collards: 175 lb	Spinach: 40 – 60 lb
Corn: 100 – 150 lb	Squash (summer): 80 lb
Cucumbers: 200 lb	Squash (winter): 200 lb
Eggplant: 50 – 75 plants, ~ 100 – 200 lb	Strawberries: 170 lb
Garlic: 350 heads	Swiss chard: 85 lb
Jerusalem artichokes: 150 lb	Tomatoes (cherry): 450 lb
Kale: 100 lb	Tomatoes: 250 lb
Kohlrabi: 100 lb	Turnips: 100 – 120 lb
Lettuce: 25 – 30 lb	Watermelon: 200 – 300 lb
Okra: 175 lb	Zucchini: 70 lb

Most calories per acre (roots / tubers account for 30% of cultivated land; commercial production)
- Amaranth – 1 lb of amaranth = 1,696 calories, 1 acre yields ~ 10 tons or 33,920,000 kcals
- Bananas – 10,665,000 calories / acre / year
- Beans – 2,600,000 calories/ acre
- Corn, 12,000,000 - 15,000,000 million calories / acre
- Eggs – 670,00 calories / acre
- Elderberries – 12,000 lb / acre or 4,800,00 calories / acre

- Fruit trees – variable yields
- Jackfruit (in the tropics) – 38,400,000 calories / acre
- Lentils – 2,100,000 calories / acre
- Nut trees – variable yields
- Peas – 3,317,000 calories / acre
- Potatoes – 17,800,000 calories / acre
- Quinoa – 1,000 lb / acre and 1,696 calories / pound = 1,696,000 calories
- Soybeans – 2,100,000 – 6,200,000 kcals / acre
- Sugar beets – 195 calories / lb and 18 – 32 tons / acre = 7,020,000 – 12,480,000 calories
- Sugarcane – 17,000,000 – 37,000,000 calories / acre
- Sunflower seeds – 4,300,000 calories / acre
- Sweet potatoes – 31,000 calories / acre (multiple crops)
- Wheat (winter) – 4,100,000 - 6,400,000 calories / acre

Fast growing fruits and vegetables
- Arugula: 30 days. Sow seeds every two weeks for continuous harvesting.
- Beets: 35 to 60 days.
- Bok choy: 35 - 45 days. 30 days (immature) and 45 days (mature) leaves. Prefers cool weather.
- Bush beans: 50 to 60 days
- Garden cress: 14 days
- Green onions (scallions): 21 days, cut back to base and they will grow back.
- Kale: 30 days. Cut throughout growing season. Avoid cutting the central bud / leaf.
- Microgreens: 10 to 25 days
- Radishes: 24 to 30 days, plant every other week for a constant harvest
- Spinach: 30 days, plant every other week for continuous harvesting.
- Sprouts: 3 to 5 days
- Swiss chard: 30 days. Cut throughout growing season. Avoid cutting young center leaves.
- Tatsoi: 25 days (immature) to 40 days (mature). Cool weather vegetable; plant every 14 days.
- Turnips: 30 to 55 days.
- Zucchini: 40 to 50 days.

High yield, fast-growing fruits and vegetables		
Table 2. Nutrient Dense Plants (in alphabetical order)		
Amaranth leaves	Green onions	Seaweed
Arugula	Green peas	Seeds
Avocado	Kale	Spinach
Beet greens	Legumes	Sweet bell peppers
Broccoli	Lettuce	Sweet potato leaves
Carrots	Mushrooms	Swiss chard
Chinese broccoli	Mustard greens	Watercress
Collards	Nuts	Winter squash
Dandelion greens	Parsley	
Garlic	Quinoa	

Come and cut again all-season plants: amaranth leaves, arugula, asparagus, basil, beet greens, bok choy (outer leaves), broccoli, carrot greens, celery leaves, chives, dill, green onions, kale, lettuce, mint, parsley, radicchio, oregano, rosemary, sage, sorrel, spinach, sunchokes, Swiss chard, turnip greens, etc.

Plant and ignore. Apples, beets, blackberries, carrots (only need to be thinned), chives, garlic, grapes, green beans, kale, lettuce, onions, potatoes, radishes, rhubarb, strawberries, Swiss chard, zucchini, etc.

Plants deer love. Apples, beans, beets, blueberries, broccoli, cabbage, cauliflower, carrot tops, corn, kohlrabi, lettuce, peas, pears, plums pumpkins, raspberries, spinach, strawberries, sweet potato, etc.

Plants deer usually ignore. Artichoke, asparagus, carrot, chives, dill, eggplant, fennel, fig, garlic, lavender, lemon balm, marjoram, mint, onion, oregano, parsley, pawpaw, rhubarb, rosemary, sage, tarragon, thyme

Plants deer typically do not eat but may eat if hungry. Anise, basil, bok choy, borage, Brussels sprouts, cilantro, cucumber, currants, horseradish, kale, melons, okra, olive, pepper, potatoes, radish, serviceberry, squash, Swiss chard, tomatoes, etc.

Perennial vegetable plants. Artichoke, arugula, asparagus, black salsify, bunching onions, capers, cardoon, chicory, elephant garlic, fennel, garlic, garlic scapes, ginger, groundnut, horseradish, Jerusalem artichokes, kale, multiplying leeks, radicchio, red veined sorrel, thicket bean, watercress, etc.

Perennial fruit plants. Blackberries, blueberries, currants, goji berries, grapes, huckleberries, kiwi, passion fruit, raspberries, rhubarb, scuppernongs, strawberries, etc.

Lady bug and butterfly garden. Angelica, blue bottle flowers, blue button or corn flower, butterfly weed, calendula, caraway, chives, cilantro, coreopsis, cosmos, dandelions, dill, fennel, feverfew, garlic, marigold, mint, parsley, scented geraniums, statice, sunflower, sweet alyssum, tansy, wild carrot, yarrow, etc.

Bee garden. Keep in mind the following when planting a pollinator garden: spraying flowers with pesticides may harm pollinators. You may control the damaging pests but you may also harm and kill the pollinators. Bees are wildly attracted to colors such as blue, purple, orange and yellow. Keep a water source available for pollinators. single flowers provide more nectar and pollen than double or pom pom type flowers. Bees love the following plants: apple tree, aster, basil, berry plants, black eyed Susan, borage, cherry tree, chives, citrus trees, coneflower, cosmos, cucumbers, day lilies, echium, foxglove, goldenrod, Joe Pye weed, lavender, lemon balm, liatris, milkweed, mint, Meyer lemon tree, oregano, pansy, peach tree, pear tree, penstemon, peony, phlox, pumpkins, sage, salvia, scarlet beebalm, sedum, snapdragon, squash, sunflower, tomatoes, zinnia, zucchini. Trees include: ash, black locust, crab apple tree, dogwood, elm, false acacia, maple, pear tree, red horse chestnut, sumac, sycamore, willow, etc.

Pollinator garden. Bee balm, begonia, bleeding heart, butterfly bush, canna, cardinal flower, century plant, clematis, cleome, columbine, coral bells, crape myrtle, crimson bottlebrush, evening primrose, giant hyssop, dame's rocket, delphinium, fire pink, four o'clocks, foxglove, fuchsia, geranium, gladiolus, glossy abelia, hollyhocks, honeysuckle, impatiens, iris, lantana, liatris, lily, lobelia, lupine, nasturtium, nicotiana, onion, paintbrush, penstemon, petunia, phlox, red hot poker, sage, salvia, scabiosa, scarlet sage, sweet William, verbena, yucca, zinnia, etc.

Black edible plants. Basil, beans, bell peppers, carrots, chili peppers, corn, eggplant, radish, salsify, sorghum, soybeans, sprouting radishes, tomatoes, wheat, etc.

Blue edible plants. Acai, blackberry, blueberry, corn, elderberry, grapes, plums, potato, tomatoes, etc.

Brown (or beige) edible plants. Beans, cauliflower coconut, dates, figs, garbanzos, ginger, kiwi, mushrooms, onions, parsnips, passionfruit, peppers, potatoes, pumpkins, shallots, tomatoes, etc.

Green edible plants. Apple, arugula, asparagus, avocado, banana, beet greens, bitter melon, Brussels sprouts, cabbage, cucumber, fennel, grapes, green beans, guava, honeydew melon, jackfruit, kale, kiwi, leeks, lettuce, limes, mustard greens, onion, pear, pepper, plum, spinach, Swiss chard, watercress, watermelon, zucchini, etc.

Orange edible plants (pigments include: carotenes, lutein, zeaxanthin, neoxanthin, violaxanthin and antheraxanthin) Apricots, bell peppers, cantaloupe, carrots, chili peppers, eggplant, grapefruit, ground cherries, kiwano, kumquat, lemons (some Meyer lemons), loquats, mandarins, mango, mushrooms (chanterelle), nectarines, oranges, papaya, peaches, persimmon, pumpkins, raspberries, squash, sweet potatoes, tangerines, tomatoes, watermelon, etc.

Pink edible plants. Apricots, banana squash, cabbage, carrots, chard, dragon fruit, figs, lychees, peaches, pomegranates, radishes, raspberries, rhubarb, tomatoes, watermelon, etc.

Purple edible plants. Amaranth (purple), apples, asparagus, artichoke, banana, basil (purple), beans (purple), beets (bull's blood), bell peppers, black berries, blood orange, blueberries, borage, broad beans (purple), broccoli (purple), brussels sprouts, cabbage, cacao, carrots, cauliflower (purple), cayenne, chili peppers, chives, corn, currants, dragon tongue bean, eggplant, elderberries, figs, garlic, grapes, jalapeno, kale (purple), kohlrabi, lavender, lettuce, muscadines, mustard, olives, onion, orach, passionfruit, peach ("Blackboy"), plums, potatoes, podded peas, pumpkin, radicchio, radishes, radish sprouts, raspberries, rose, shallots, shisho, spinach, sugar cane (purple), sugar snap beans, sweet potato, thistle, tomatillo, tomatoes, turnip, ube, violets, watermelon, wonderberries, etc.

Red edible plants. Apples, beans, bell peppers, beets, berries, carrots, cherries, chili pepper, currants, grapefruit, hibiscus, hot pepper, pomegranate, pear, potatoes, pumpkin, radishes, rose, strawberries, tomatoes, watermelon, etc.

White edible plants. Bananas, beans, cauliflower, coconut, fennel, garlic, jicama, kohlrabi, leeks, mushrooms, onions, parsnips, pears, peppers, potatoes, pumpkins, radishes, tomatoes, etc.

Yellow edible plants. Apples, bananas, beans, beets, cape gooseberries, carrots, corn, bell pepper, grapefruit, hot pepper, kiwi (yellow), lemon, passionfruit, pears, pineapple, potatoes, pumpkins, rutabagas, squash, sweet potatoes, tomatillo, tomatoes, watermelon, etc.

Plants you can propagate and grow from your grocery store (must be raw, not roasted or heat treated). Basil (place in water to root), beans, beet greens, black cumin (Nigella sativa) seeds, bok choy (place root side in soil), dill seeds, fennel seeds, garlic, ginger, green onions, mustard seeds, peas (dried), pepper seeds, popcorn, potatoes, quinoa, sweet potatoes, tomatoes seeds, whole grains, etc.

Bible verses about animals. Genesis 1:20-21, 26-28, 30-31, 2:15-19, 6:19-20, 7:1-15, 8:1, 9:9-10; Exodus 20:10, 23:5-12; Deuteronomy 22:4-10, 25:4; Job 12:7-10; Psalm 8:4-8, 23, 36:6, 50:10-11, 104:24-25147:9, 150:6; Proverbs 12:10, 27:23; Isaiah 11:6-9, 32:20-24, 40:11, 65:25; Job 12:7, 38:41; Ezekiel 34:11; Nehemiah 9:6; Jeremiah 2:7; Jonah 4:11; Hosea 2:18; Matthew 6:25-30, 10:29; Luke 12:6-24, 14:5; John 1:3; Rom 8:22; 1 Corinthians 9:9; Colossians 1:16; James 3:7; 1 Timothy 5:18; Revelation 5:13

Bible verses about gardening. Genesis 1:29, 2:7, 2:15, 3:24, 26:12; Ezekiel 17:5; Job 40:15; Isaiah 40:8; Psalm 104:14-15; Matthew 6:25-34, 12:1-50, 13:3-9, 13:23; Mark 4:20; Luke 8:6-15; John 12:3, 15:5; Rev 22:1-2

References and resources
- FB page: Amazing fruits and vegetables – Strange fruit; That pumpkin is too big_Most Amazing Fruits and Vegetables; Peaceful village with amazing orange farm – my dream life; Lost in a giant vegetable garden_Amazing Agriculture; The wealth of Chinese agriculture – Amazing agricultural farming; The most perfect garden I have ever seen – Amazing Farm; Such a Beautiful and Colorful fruit Garden when my old…; Amazing labor that creates values for life_Amazing Agriculture Farm; Growing and harvesting strawberries using a hydroponic method; Strange fruit garden in the snow; Visit the wonderful cherry garden in china; Such a beautiful & Yummy Sugarcane Farm_Yummy Fruit.
- https://humaneherald.files.wordpress.com/2019/05/calories-and-protein-produced-per-acre-1.pdf
- http://www.gardeningplaces.com/articles/nutrition-per-hectare1.htm
- https://www.quora.com/What-crop-including-tree-crops-produces-the-most-calories-per-acre
- https://www.youtube.com/watch?v=i-T7tCMUDXU

Chapter 60

A word about tomatoes

Have you ever known anyone with OCD, aka, obsessive compulsive disorder? Some people wash their hands a lot, others mop their floors several times per day, and then there are those who plant lots of tomatoes! I fall into the latter category. For many years I have been obsessed with growing tomatoes.

It probably dates back to my childhood. I used to spend a large part of every summer at my grandmother's home in the country where she and grandpa always had a huge garden covering about an acre. The best part of the garden was the fresh tomatoes. We ate tomato sandwiches on freshly made bread, put tomatoes on pizza, made spectacular tomato sauce, and awesome juicy tomato salads. She also grew watermelons, cantaloupe, lima beans, black eyed peas, Swiss chard, peas, corn, onions, leeks, and many other fruits and vegetables, but the tomato was king! Those memories of grandma's fresh summer tomatoes were so awesome. Unfortunately, as I grew older I spent less time at her house over the summers. At some point in young adulthood as I left home and went to boarding academy and then college and grad school, I decided I didn't like tomatoes. It took moving to Southern California and finishing up grad school before I returned to my first love, home grown fresh tomatoes.

Store-bought tomatoes are almost never a real culinary representation of a home-grown, freshly picked tomato. When I started gardening on my own, I decided to include some tomatoes as a tribute to my grandmother's garden, even though I didn't like them. What happened next, revolutionized my life. I realized all along, the store-bought tomatoes had deceived me into believing I didn't like tomatoes. **Once the real tomato was back in my life, I have never let it go!** This was the beginning of a beautiful obsession with tomatoes.

My tomato obsession began innocently enough by buying tomato plants and transplanting them into warm, moist fertile Southern California soil. Every summer I was rewarded with enough tomatoes for my household and plenty to share. When I moved back to Texas, I vigorously added composted organic matter to newly constructed garden beds full of heavy clay soil and once again with significant time and effort, I had the perfect yard and soil for gardening. It was during this time, I branched out and started buying tomato seeds. This is when my love for tomatoes became an obsession. I learned about heirlooms, hybrids, experimental tomatoes, cross breeding for various characteristics, etc. The picture above includes one of the most unusual tomatoes I have grown. It is known as Voyage or Brain Tomato. It consists of multiple lobes of cherry tomatoes fused together. It even tasted decent. After adding a greenhouse to the back yard, growing tomatoes became a year-round obsession. Most years I planted between 500 to 1,000+ tomato seeds. It required elaborate notes, labeling methods, etc. Most of the plants I gave away but I usually planted about 50 to 60 tomatoes everywhere around my yard, in pots, and in the flower beds.

It is impossible to claim a favorite. I love cherry tomatoes almost as much as beefsteak tomatoes. I love Cherokee Purple as much as I love Wapsipinicon peach, a beautiful pale yellow, almost white tomato. I might have said I didn't have a favorite, but Juane Flamme would be a contender. It is one of the most beautiful tomatoes I have ever seen and its taste matches its beauty. Juane Flamme is a French tomato with the most unique combination of colors including yellow, gold, salmon, pink and red. Another contender for a favorite is Momotaro. It is the most perfect red tomato with outstanding flavor. Brandywines are also hard to beat, especially the pink, orange and yellow varieties. Tomatoes are in the nightshade family, *Solanacea*. This means most of their growth and flowering occurs overnight. They contain the highly beneficial phytochemical, lycopene.

The tomato world reminds me of how God loves us. He doesn't pick favorites but when we cooperate with and shine for Him, we please him. Tomatoes come in all colors, shapes and sizes. Some are sweet and some are tart. Some are a combination of sweet and tart. Some tomatoes prefer to be the star of the meal while other tomatoes make a great supporting cast. I hope you come to love tomatoes as much as I do and enjoy the hundreds if not thousands of different cultivars available to gardeners. Figure 1., lists a few tomatoes in each category by their outward coloring. Use this list as a starting point to choose varieties to grow. Keep a notebook and learn how to save seeds. Add new varieties as you consult with others.

Tomato resources

Baker's Creek Tomato Seeds	https://www.rareseeds.com/store/vegetables/tomatoes
Tradewinds Fruit Tomato Seeds	http://www.tradewindsfruit.com/tomatoes/
Sand Hill Preservation Center	https://www.sandhillpreservation.com/
Tomato Fest	https://www.tomatofest.com/
Seed Savers Exchange	https://www.seedsavers.org/category/tomato
Totally Tomatoes	https://www.totallytomato.com/category/85

Discussion questions

1. What is your favorite flower, fruit or vegetable and how does it reflect God's love for us?
2. How many genes does a tomato have and how does this compare to humans?
3. Do you think God intended for man to manipulate genetic traits?
4. Look up artificial selection (selective breeding) vs. genetic engineering?
5. How does this apply to making new types of tomatoes?
6. How do you like to eat tomatoes?

A word about tomatoes
Table 1. Tomatoes by Color

Black tomatoes	Dester	Chocolate stripes
Black beauty	German lunchbox	Copia
Black brandywine	German pink	Get stuffed (keeper / stuffer)
Black cherry	Henderson's pink ponderosa	Gold medal
Carbon	Hungarian heart	Green zebra
Chestnut chocolate	Mortgage lifter	Hillbilly
Chocolate pear	Mushroom basket	Lucky tiger (Roma)
Japanese black trifele		Orange jazz
		Pineapple
	Purple tomatoes	Pink Berkeley tie-dye
Blue tomatoes	Cherokee purple	Pink boar
Blue beauty	Paul Robeson	Pink bumble bee (cherry)
Blue berries (ch: cherry)		Solar flare
Blue cream berries (cherry)		Striped Roman (paste)
Brad's atomic grape (cherry)	**Red tomatoes**	Sunrise bumble bee (cherry)
Indigo apple	Abe Lincoln Original	Tiger cherry Roma mix
Wagner blue green	Amish paste	Vernissage art colors (cherry)
	Anna Russian	Vintage wine
	Bonny best	Violet jasper
Green tomatoes	Brandywine OTV	
Aunt Ruby's German green	Brandywine Sudduth	
Emerald evergreen	Carmello	**White tomatoes**
Green doctors (cherry)	Chadwick cherry (camp joy)	Cream sausage
Green giant	Celebrity	Grandpa's white wax
Green zebra (green stripes)	Costoluto Florentino	Great white
	Cor de boi	White beauty
	Minibel (cherry)	White currant
Orange tomatoes	Momotaro	White Tomesol
Amana orange	Principe Borghese (cherry)	
Azoychka	Red beefsteak	
Dad's sunset	Roma	**Yellow tomatoes**
Dr. Wyche's yellow	Rutgers	Barry's crazy cherry
Isis candy (cherry)	San Marzano	Blondkopfchen (cherry)
Juane Flamme	St. Pierre	Hugh's
Kellogg's breakfast	Sunset's red horizon	Ildi (cherry)
Kentucky beefsteak	Tappy's heritage	Dr. Wyche's yellow
Orange icicle		Wapsipinicon peach
Orange brandywine		Yellow brandywine
	Striped tomatoes	Yellow gooseberry (cherry)
	Anana's noire	Yellow pear (cherry)
Pink tomatoes	Berkeley tie-dye	Yellow ruffled
Anna Russian (heart shaped)	Big rainbow	
Brandywine	Blue fire (cherry)	

Chapter 61
Edible plants, bushes, vines and trees

Adam and Eve could trace the skill and glory of God in every spire of grass, and in every shrub and flower. The natural loveliness which surrounded them reflected like a mirror the wisdom, excellence, and love of their heavenly Father. And their songs of affection and praise rose sweetly and reverentially to heaven, harmonizing with the songs of the exalted angels, and with the happy birds who were caroling forth their music without a care. There was no disease, decay, nor death. Life was in everything the eye rested upon. The atmosphere was filled with life. Life was in every leaf, in every flower, and in every tree.

The Lord knew that Adam could not be happy without labor; therefore, He gave him the pleasant employment of dressing the garden. And, as he tended the things of beauty and usefulness around him, he could behold the goodness and glory of God in His created works. Adam had themes for contemplation in the works of God in Eden, which was heaven in miniature. God did not form man merely to contemplate His glorious works; therefore, He gave him hands for labor, as well as a mind and heart for contemplation. -Confrontation, by E. White, page 11

This chapter provides you with an alphabetic listing of many edible plants, including trees and vines found in North America. Included are a few flowers which may or may not be edible, but are common to country gardens.

By some estimates, 94% of all edible plants are extinct. Modern agriculture promotes cultivars which do well commercially, oftentimes, at the expense of valuable heirloom varieties which fail to meet size, appearance, productivity and other expectations. When I visited Romania in 2001 for an extended stay, we frequently feasted on watermelon. We either gathered the melons from the garden, or if we were out, we would purchase 10 or so melons for the group. Sometimes they were the only food we ate for a meal. During the course of traveling around the country, we ate several different types of melons. Each one had a unique size and flavor. Since that time, the European Union has sought to limit the types of melons grown in Romania to just several varieties. This potential loss of diversity may have unintended consequences. Unless there is small scale production and seed saving of lesser popular varieties, they eventually become extinct.

Seek out unique varieties of seeds for planting. When possible, save seeds for planting the next year. When you visit a grocery store, look for fruit and vegetables which are unique and when possible, save their seeds. I have planted numerous hot peppers and tomatoes by saving seed from organic fruits and vegetables. Take a picture of the fruit or vegetable and save the seed in paper or other appropriate envelopes, labeling the envelope with the picture and a written label. The following pages contain a brief description of almost every edible farm-grown type plant grown in North America.

Edible plants, bushes, vines, trees and a few flowers

A

- **Acorn squash** (Honey Bear, etc.). Yields up to 24 lb per vine. Yields up to 5 fruits per plant. Each fruit feeds 1 to 3 people.
- **Agastache.** Flowering perennial with aromatic leaves and beautiful flowers.
- **Alfalfa**. Used as a cover crop and for sprouts.
- **Alliums**. Plant bulbs in the fall in full sun to partial shade.
- **Almond tree**. Trees bear in 3 to 4 years and each tree typically yields 20+ lb of almonds.
- **Aloe vera**. Can be grown in pots or in the ground. Highly medicinal and edible.
- **Amaranth**. Yields ¼ to 4 lb / plant. 7' – 10" between plants, 10" – 12" between rows.
- **Anaheim pepper**. Yields 30 - 50 pods/plant.
- **Angelica**. 6' plant. Stems and leaves edible.
- **Anise**. Sow seeds directly into warm soil. Prefers full sun. Attractive, ornamental plant about 2 feet tall.
- **Apple tree**. Miniature trees yield ¼ to 1 bushel. Dwarf apple trees yield 1 to 5 bushels of fruit and semi-dwarf trees yield 5 to 10 bushels of apples and standard trees yield 8 to 20 bushels. A bushel weighs 40 pounds. Plant mature trees 25 to 35 feet apart, semi-dwarf trees 15 to 20 feet and dwarfs 7 to 10 feet apart. 10 acres is minimum size for an apple orchard. Plant 300 to 400 dwarf trees / acre.
- **Apricot tree**. Yields 500 apricots / tree.
- **Aronia berry**. See chokeberry.
- **Arrowroot**. Edible tubers are grown for their starch.
- **Artichoke** (Imperial Star, Green Globe, Violetta). Yields 3 to 12 buds or artichokes / plant; 1 to 2 plants / person, plant 18" apart; 30 to 50 crowns / household of 4 people; 24" to 36" inches between rows.
- **Arugula**. Recommend 5 plants / person; space 6 inches apart.
- **Ashwagandha**. Small woody shrub. Plant one or two per family.
- **Asian beans**. Yields 120 beans for every 1 bean planted.
- **Asian pear tree**. Fruit can be stored for months.
- **Asparagus crowns** (wild, Connover's Colossal, Guelph millennium, Apollo, UC-157, Jersey Giant, Jersey Knight, etc.). Each crown yields 20 spears or ½ pound. Plant crowns 15 inches apart to fill in to form a 24 inch wide bed. A bed of 25 mature plants produces about 10 pounds of asparagus per year. Grow 30 to 50 crowns for a four-person household. Yields 3 to 4 pounds per 10 foot row. An asparagus bed produces for up to 20 years.
- **Autumn olive berry.** Fruiting shrub which produces huge amounts of edible red berries. It can be an aggressive plant so plant it accordingly. Berries grown in full sun may be sweetest. Make great berry tarts.
- **Avocado tree**. On average, trees yield 150 avocados (about 60 pounds) but may produce as many as 500 (200 + pounds) avocados in one year.

B

- **Banana tree.** Each pseudostem produces 25 lb to 40 lb of fruit. Each banana tree can produce up to 240 bananas a year.
- **Banana pepper**. Yields are 25 to 30 pods / plant.
- **Barley**. Prepare field and scatter 20 to 25 seeds / square foot. A 10 x 10 square foot bed requires ½ to ¾ pound of seed and can produce 5 lb to 15 lb of grain.
- **Basil**. Yields ½ to 1 pound / plant. Yields 10 pounds / 10 foot row of basil.
- **Bay tree or Bay Laurel**. An evergreen bush / tree whose leaves are used to flavor soups and sauces. One of the herbs in *bouquet garni*. Leaves also repel pests and can

- be placed in cupboards and sealed food bags. Plant in full sun location. Can be propagated through seeds or softwood cuttings.
- **Beans, pole.** Yields 1 pound per plant. A 25' row of pole beans planted 4" – 6" apart provides about 40 lb of pole beans. Grow 4 to 8 plants per person. Row 2 to 3 feet apart.
- **Beans, bush.** Yield is around ½ pound / plant. Plant bush beans 2" – 4" inches apart and thin to 6 inches apart. One ounce of seeds plants a 25 foot row and yields 20 – 30 pounds of bush snap beans (approximately 2 to 3 lb / plant). Expect about 1 ½ pounds of dry beans from a 25 foot row. Plant 15 bush bean plants / person and 2 to 4 pole beans / person. 18" – 24" btwn rows.
- **Beets.** Each seed yields one beet plus greens; 5 to 20 plants / person; 4 to 6 pounds / 10 foot row; 3 inches apart for roots and 1 inch apart for greens, rows 12 inches apart.
- **Bell pepper.** Yields 6 to 8 peppers per plant, 2 to 4 plants per person, yields 5 to 18 pounds / 10 foot row. Space plants 18 to 24 inches apart in rows 28 to 36 inches apart. 15 plants / 25 foot row and 60 plants / 100 foot row.
- **Bergamot / bee balm.** Medicinal and attracts butterflies, bees and hummingbirds.
- **Bergamot orange tree.** Small citrus tree that blooms during winter. Produces sour fruit.
- **Betony.** Medicinal herb. Great pollinator. Treats migraines to stimulating blood circulation.
- **Bitter melon.** Grow on trellis, plant 2 to 4 plants / person.
- **Blackberry bush.** There are several types of blackberry bushes: erect, semi-trailing and trailing. Some are thornless, most have thorns. Each bush produces 10 to 20 pounds of fruit per bush. You need about two pounds per pie and about 6 pounds for 2 to 3 pints of jam.
- **Blackeye peas.** Need full sun. 70 days to maturity. Vines require trellises or support. Plant seeds 1 inch deep, 2 inches apart, rows 3 feet apart.
- **Blueberry bush.** Blueberry bushes yield 2 – 4 pounds or 5 – 7 pints of blueberries (some bushes produce much higher).
- **Bok choy** (Black Summer, Feng Qing, White Flash, Joy Choi, Win-win Choi). One seed yields one plant. 12" btwn plants.
- **Borage.** Thin to 1' apart and rows 1' apart. Plant borage with strawberries to bring bees and increase yields.
- **Boysenberry.** Cross between a European raspberry and a European blackberry.
- **Brahmi** (Bacopa Monnieri). Medicinal herb. Thrives in substandard conditions. Prefers consistently moist soil.
- **Breathe wild mint.** Vigorous plant, strong medicinal breath cleaning properties. Grows up to 2'. Spreads via rhizomes.
- **Broad beans.** Plant 2" deep and about 9" apart. Usually 8 to 10 beans / pod and 15 to 20 pods / plant.
- **Broccoli** (broccolini, Raab, Italian, Heading, etc.). Different varieties include large-headed, sprouting, Romesco and raab. Yields 3 lb / plant; 3 to 5 plants / person, 18" to 20" apart, rows 2' to 3' apart; 4 lb to 6 lb / 10 foot row
- **Brussels sprouts.** Single plant may produce up to 3 lb of sprouts. Recommend 18" to 24" between plants and 30" to 36" between rows. Grow 2 to 5 plants / person. Yields 3 lb to 7.5 lb / 10 foot row.
- **Buckwheat** (high quality protein; grows well in poor soil). To harvest, gently cut stems near the ground and transfer to a sheet or tarp. Beat the vines with a broom to loosen the seeds then transfer seeds to a container. A box fan blows away most of the chaff. Now grind the seeds to make buckwheat flour.
- **Buffalo berry.** A 6 to 12 foot shrub producing small tart berries. Grows up to 12 feet tall. Requires a male and female plant in proximity to produce berries (i.e., meaning the plant is dioecious).
- **Bunching onions.** Non-bulbing perennial onion which grows stalks that divide from the base. Cold hardy to -30 °F.
- **Burdock root.** Yields 6 to 17 lb / 100' row.

- **Bush cherries.** Needs full sun. Makes a nice hedge bush. Not always self-fertile, plant 2+.
- **Butterfly pea flower.** To grow from seed, gently nick or file off part of the outside seed coating. Soak overnight in room temperature water. Sow directly into warm soil. Plant 12 inches apart and 24 inches between rows. To make butterfly pea flower powder, pick the flowers and dehydrate for about 5 hours or until completely dry. Remove the blue section and add to a coffee grinder. Grind until a fine powder. Store in airtight container.
- **Butternut squash.** Each squash weighs ~ 1 lb and each plant produces 3 or 4 fruit.

C

- **Cabbage.** Cabbage comes in various colors and shapes including green, red, savoy, pointed heads, and Napa. Yields 4 to 8 plants per person, yields 10 to 25 lb a 10 foot row; space plants 16 to 30" apart. Smaller varieties may be spaced 12" apart. Yield is usually around 1 lb per foot of row. Grow 4 to 8 plants per person. Three pounds of cabbage per person for spring and summer and 4 pounds per person for fall to make sauerkraut.
- **Calendula.** Use petals either fresh or dry.
- **Canna.** Plant the eye in springtime in full sun. Will perennialize.
- **Cantaloupe.** With adequate water, each plant produces 4 to 8 melons. Plant 36 to 42 inches apart or if using an 8 foot trellis, plant 12 inches apart.
- **Caraway.** Biennial herb. Space plants 8 inches apart, thin to 12 to 18 inches and space rows 18 to 24 inches apart. Grow 6 caraway plants for everyday use and 12 plants for preserving seeds.
- **Cardoon.** Cardoon grows up to 4' tall and 2' wide. Plant 1 or 2 cardoons / family member. Plant cardoon 24" apart and space rows 36 to 48" apart. Even though cardoon is a perennial, is it usually grown as an annual.
- **Carob tree** (locust tree; St. John's bread, Egyptian fig, *Ceratonia siliqua*). Carob pods grow up to 12 inches long and are somewhat sweet and contain only small amounts of bitter flavonoids (compared to chocolate). Large subtropical ornamental tree. Begins producing pods within 10 years. The tap root goes down 75 to 125 or more feet mobilizing mineral and rare earth elements. Grows as high as 30 to 45 feet. Maybe planted as an ornamental. In the story of the prodigal son, he desired to eat the carob pods which were fed to the pigs. DOI: 10.5923/j.fph.20130306.06
- **Carrots.** Types include: Nantes, Chantenay and Ball (or miniature), Imperator, and Danvers. Sow 2 inches apart and thin to 4 to 6 inches apart; 3 to 5 pounds per 10 foot row. Space rows 10 inches apart. Grow 30 to 200 plants per person (depending on whether you want juicing carrots). Nantes carrots are good for juicing because they tend to be the sweetest and have fewer compounds which may give juice a slightly off flavor, but generally all carrots work!
- **Cauliflower.** Types of cauliflower include: early cauliflower and main season cauliflower. General seeding dates are: 30 May in Maine, 15 June in New York, 1 July in Kentucky, 15 July in Alabama, 15 October in Arizona. Plant 24 inches apart. 2 – 4 plants per person.
- **Cayenne pepper.** The more you pick cayenne peppers, the more peppers you harvest. Usually one plant provides enough peppers for one family.
- **Celeriac.** Sow directly. Plant 3 to 4 inches apart and thin to 6 to 8 inches apart, rows 24 to 30 inches apart. Germination is tricky and may take up to 2 weeks.
- **Celery.** 5 to 10 plants per person (depending on whether you want enough for juicing needs). Yields 6 to 8 stalks per plant, space plants 6 to 12 inches apart, rows 2 feet apart.
- **Chamomile** (Roman). Medicinal herb used to make a soothing tea.

- **Chayote** (mirliton, choko). One vine for 1 to 4 people. Vines 10' apart; train to trellis or sturdy wall.
- **Cherokee long ear corn**. Usually 2 cobs / plant. Makes great popcorn. Relatively small kernels. Plant 3 to 4 inches apart and space rows 2 to 3 feet apart. Thin to 1 foot.
- **Cherry tomatoes**. Yield 10 to 15 pounds / plant (some significantly more).
- **Cherry tree**. One semi-dwarf tree yields about 30 to 60 quarts of cherries / year. Dwarf tree yields 10 to 15 quarts.
- **Chestnut tree**. Each tree averages 20 lb of chestnuts per tree.
- **Chickpeas, garbanzos, ceci beans**. Yields ½ to 2 lb / plant; 1/10 to ½ lb dry / plant; 4 - 6 lb / 10' row; 4 - 8 plants / person, 3" to 6" apart, rows 24" to 30" apart.
- **Chicory**. Yields 1 to 2 plant / person, 6 to 12 inches apart in rows 2 to 3 feet apart.
- **Chinese cabbage**. 6 to 8 heads / person. Space plants 4" apart in rows 24" to 30" apart.
- **Chives** (Chinese flowering leek, garlic chives, etc.). Plant chives in a contained bed as they are a perennial and will multiply. Use the chive flowers as an edible garnish.
- **Choke or aronia berries**. Produces dark blue, almost black, sour (astringent) berries with high medicinal value.
- **Cilantro / coriander**. Plant in 3 wk intervals for a near continuous supply of fresh cilantro over the summer. Plant 1 – 2" apart and space rows 12" apart. To harvest the seeds, cut off the seed heads when the plant begins to turn brown. Place in a paper bag or other container. When the seed heads dry out the seeds fall off. Store in an airtight container.
- **Clary sage** (aka eye bright). Flowering herb, native to the Mediterranean region. Contains linalool, a brain enhancing nootropic.
- **Clover** (red and white). Clover flowers are edible. Usually served as a tea.
- **Cloudberry** (*Rubus chamaemorus*). Grown in northern regions. Fruit and flowers are edible.
- **Cockscomb & celosia**. Used as medicinal herb.
- **Coffee tree**. California and Hawaii grow coffee but large-scale production is not feasible. However, the home gardener could grow a tree. There is a Kentucky coffee tree, which produces seeds which may be roasted and used as a coffee substitute. However, be careful, the unroasted seeds are toxic. Roasted chicory and dandelion root make nice coffee substitutes.
- **Collards**. Recommend 3 to 5 plants / person. Yields 4 lb to 8 lb / 10' row. Space plants 15" to 18" apart in rows 3' apart. Tree collards are a unique variety of collards and provide a year around source of collard leaves and lives up to 20 years.
- **Comfrey**. One plant should be adequate. It is invasive.
- **Corbaci sweet pepper**. Prolific plant, produces up to 100 pepper pods / plant.
- **Corms** (Dasheen, Eddoe, Konjac, Taro, Water Chestnut). Tropical vegetable. Eddoe is considered to be tropical potatoes. Edible plant stems and roots. Usually dug up.
- **Coriander**. Sow directly every 3 weeks from late March until early September.
- **Corn** (Sweet, Dent, Heirloom, Flint/ndian/Pod, Popcorn; Golden Bantam, Blue Hopi, Stowell's Evergreen, etc.). 12 to 20 plants / person, yields 1 to 2 ears / plant, 10 to 12 ears / 10' row. Plant 4" to 6" apart in rows 2' to 3' apart. There are on average, 36 kernels of corn / cob. If you have space, freeze as many ears of corn as possible for use throughout the year or remove kernels from cob and freeze. 50 cobs / person for canning and freezing.
- **Cowpeas**. Do well in the south where summers are hot and humid. They are vining plants. Sow 2" to 3" apart and thin to about 4" apart. Leave 3' to 5' btwn rows. 1 oz of seed sows from 15' to 45', depending on the type of seed. Deer love this plant.
- **Crabapple tree**. Holds fruit thru winter.
- **Cubanelle sweet pepper**. Plant 18" apart and space rows 24" apart.

- **Cucumber**. Different types of cucumbers include: American slicing, pickling, Asian, greenhouse, horned (e.g., kiwano, jelly melon) and others. Grow 2 to 4 plants / person, grow 3 to 4 plants / quart pickling, yields 8 to 10 pounds per 10' row, space plants 8" to 10" feet apart in rows of 3' to 4' apart.
- **Cucumbers** (vining). Each plant yields around 10 lb per plant.
- **Cumin**. Plant seeds 8 to 10 inches apart.
- **Cupid Culver's Root**. This is a beautiful perennial purple flowering plant. Bulbs are planted in the spring. Attracts butterflies and hummingbirds.
- **Currants** (black, red, white). Cold hardy bush reaching up to 6' tall. Shade tolerant.

D

- **Daikon** (Japanese minowase, long, red, watermelon, white icicle). A type of radish. Plant in full sun. Direct sow. Sow 1 seed per inch and rows 12 to 18 inches apart. Thin seedlings to 4 to 6 inches apart.
- **Dandelion roots**. Yields 7 to 41 pounds per 100 foot row. Add dandelion flowers and leaves to fresh salads.
- **Dahlias**. Plant dahlia bulbs in garden beds and around your home for beautiful cut flowers. Petals and tubers are edible.
- **Date palms**. Grows in hot and dry climates such as desert California, Middle east, and Mediterranean regions. Bear first crop at 5 to 8 years. Early crop trees produce from 15 to 20 pounds of fruit. By age 13, trees produce between 130 to 175 lb. Peak production occurs between 30 to 35 years, when a healthy tree produces up to 200 pounds of fruit per year.
- **Dill**. Dill is a popular host plant, attracting Anise Swallowtail Caterpillars. Plant a few seeds to feed the caterpillars and plant one or two seeds to have fresh dill. Dry some of the dill to use during the winter.
- **Dittany of Crete**. Medicinal herb used for digestive issues, snake bite, anti-convulsive, easing childbirth pain, etc.
- **Dragon fruit**. Sub-tropical fruit. Prefers full sun. Optimal temperatures are between 65 °F to 80 °F. Can be grown in pots. One plant can produce for 20 to 30 years. One plant produces every 12 to 18 months, providing 20 to 60 pounds of fruit per plant.

E

- **Earth pea tuber**. Sweet tuber. Perennial. Can be trellised. Prefers full sun but tolerates some shade. Cold hardy to -25 °F. Best in cooler climates.
- **Echinacea**. Yields 5 lb to 32 lb per 100' row.
- **Eggplant**. 2 to 3 plants / person, yields 8 fruits / Italian oval varieties, yields 10 to 15 fruits / Asian varieties. Space plants 24 to 30 inches apart in rows 3 feet apart.
- **Elderberry**. Grow 6' to 12' high. High in vit C.
- **Endive and escarole**. Grow 2 to 3 plants / person. Yield 3 to 6 pounds per 10 foot row. Space plants 6 to 12 inches apart in rows 2 to 3 feet apart.

F

- **Fava beans**. 6 to 8 oz of beans / plant; 4 to 8 plants / person. Space 4 - 5 inches apart in rows 18" to 30" apart.
- **Fennel**. If planting fennel for its seeds and herbal culinary uses, one plant will do. If planting fennel for using its bulb, plant 6 to 8/ family. Harvest bulbs before the flowers bloom. Many people enjoy nibbling on the raw fronds. Do not plant near dill. Best to plant fennel away from most other plants.
- **Feverfew**. Reduces fever and known to relieve migraines.
- **Figs** (Green, Brown, Purple; Magnolia, Little Ruby, Brown Turkey, Celeste, etc.). A mature fig tree produces 50 to 250 figs / tree. Plant 5 or more fig trees for a bumper crop of figs!

- **Flax seeds.** Plant one tablespoon of flax seeds per 10 square feet.

G

- **Garlic.** Grow 12 to 16 plants / person. Yield 10 to 30 bulbs / 10-foot row. Space cloves 3" to 6" apart in rows 15" apart. Garlic may be planted with onions and leeks in the same bed.
- **Garlic scapes.** Garlic scapes are harvested before they flower so the garlic plant can direct all its energy into producing garlic bulbs. Dice up and add to soups, vegetable dishes, entrees.
- **Germander.** Medicinal perennial. Ground cover with small blooming flowers. Has a slight garlic aroma.
- **Ginger.** Grow ginger in pots or in the ground. Prefers filtered sunlight in hot climates and full sun in cooler regions. Sprout rhizomes before planting. Plant about 3 pounds per 10 foot row. Ginger yields extensive new roots about one year after first planting.
- **Ginko biloba tree.** Takes about 10 years to produce fruit.
- **Goji berry.** 18 to 24" bush. Considered to be both a fruit and an herb. Part of the nightshade family. Grows in shade or sun.
- **Good King Henry.** Tiny nitrogen-fixing tubers that grow underground like a string of pearls. Vines grow to be about 6 feet tall.
- **Gooseberry.** Beautiful shrub producing various colors of gooseberries. From seed to producing berries takes 3 years. Grows up to 8 feet tall and 6 feet wide.
- **Goumi berry.** Berries high in vitamins & minerals.
- **Gourds.** Gourds are great for making bird houses, pots, sponges and decorative items. They are not edible, but are fun to grow. The edible version of a gourd is squash.
- **Green beans.** 6 beans/pod and 20 pods/plant.
- **Grapes.** On average, 1 vine produces up to 7 lb of fruit. Each wine bottle takes ~ 2.6 lb of grapes.
- **Ground cherries** (Dwarf Cape Gooseberry, Strawberry Tomato). Plant seeds or plants 3' apart and rows 3' to 4' apart. Each plant produces up to 300 fruits, bearing non-stop until frost. Eat fresh or process into jam, preserves, sauces, tarts.
- **Groundnut.** Perennial vine that is nitrogen fixing and produces potato like tubers.
- **Guava.** Bears around 3 years. A mature 10 year old guava tree yields up to 200 or more lb of fruit.

H

- **Habanero pepper.** Grows 24" to 36" tall. Plant 18" apart. Produces up to 200 pods / year.
- **Haskaps berries** (aka, honeyberries, edible honeysuckles, blue honeysuckles, sweet berry, Canadian honey berry). Cold hardy, huge, healthy, tart and makes a great jam.
- **Hazelnut tree.** A mature tree produces up to 25 lb of nuts / year.
- **Helichrysum** Augustifolium / Italicum (some-times called curry plant). 2' to 4' bushy perennial produces small yellow flowers. Daisy family. Extracted oil is medicinal.
- **Hemp.** 1 plant yields 1 lb of hemp flowers.
- **Henna.** Shrub/tree like. Prefers dry conditions.
- **Hibiscus** (Roselle). Space plants 3' apart and rows 5' apart. Produces 1 to 2 lb of calyxes / plant.
- **Hickory tree.** Slow bearing, takes a long time to begin producing nuts but when ready, produces for many years.
- **Hollyhock.** A classic cottage garden flower. They grow up to 8 feet tall and should be direct sown into warm soil. The flowers are not poisonous but the stems and leaves may be skin irritants.
- **Holy basil.** Perennial herb; grown as an annual in most zones. Adaptogenic herb.

- **Honeyberry.** Cold hardy shrub producing large elongated smooth purple berries. Needs to cross pollinate with a different variety. Native to Russian, Japan and North America. Shrub reaches 6 feet in height and needs 6 feet of spacing.
- **Honeydew melon.** Plant 36 to 42 inches apart. Each plant produces 3 to 6 melons.
- **Horehound.** Perennial medicinal herb.
- **Horseradish.** Grow 1 plant per person. Space plants 30 to 36 inches apart.
- **Huckleberry.** Takes up to six years before first major huckleberry production. Plant for long-term use.
- **Hyssop.** Lovely varieties include: Korean 'Golden Jubilee,' anise hyssop, apricot sprite, Arcado pink, mint rose, mosquito plant, Texas hummingbird, mint heather queen, Navajo sunset, etc. A perennial used to flavor soups, salads, beverages, etc. Also used medicinally. Plant 12 to 24"apart and space rows 12 to 24"apart. Harvest hyssop stems and leaves and store whole. To dry, tie cuttings together and hang upside down.

I - J

- **Indian celery.** Flower buds, seeds, stalk and cooked roots are edible. May grow up to 8 feet tall. **Do NOT confuse this plant with similar looking poisonous hemlock.**
- **Iris.** Plant bulbs in the spring in full sun. Will perennialize.
- **Jalapeno.** 25 to 35 jalapenos per plant; 3 to 5 plants per person.
- **Japanese black sticky corn** (waxy or glutinous corn). This corn produces kernels high in amylopectin.
- **Jasmine flowers.** Good for teas, infusions, etc.
- **Jerusalem artichoke.** Tubers are edible, raw or cooked. May be ground into flour. Contain inulin.
- **Jicama.** 1 to 6 pounds of tubers per plant.
- **Jimmy Nardello Italian pepper.** Plant 12 to 24 inches apart. Reaches about 24 inches in height. Some recommend limiting pods to 3 to 4 per plant for the largest size; others do not recommend pruning.
- **Joe Pye weed.** Great medicinal herb and pollinator. Pink and lavender flowers make this herb a standout in the herb garden or in landscaping. Grows up to 6 feet tall. Butterfly attractor.
- **Jujube tree.** Plant 10 to 15' apart. Grow to be about 20 feet tall but may grow as tall as 50'. Can be grown in a container. Mature trees annually produce 40 to 100 pounds of fruit.

K

- **Kale** (kalettes, Russian red, scarlet, red Ursa, Nero, toscana, blue, dwarf, thousand head, tronchuda, walking stick, etc.). Grow 4 to 5 plants per person. Yield 4 – 8 pounds / 10-foot row. Space plants 12" – 18" apart in rows 2' apart.
- **Kiwi.** A single, mature (3 to 4 year old vine sometimes up to 7 years) kiwi vine yields 50 to 100 pounds of fruit.
- **Kohlrabi.** Grow 4 to 5 plants per person. Yield 4 to 8 pounds per 10-foot row. Space plants 4 to 6 inches apart in rows 12" – 24" inches apart.
- **Kumquat** (Meiwa, Nagami, etc.). Mature trees yield 200 or more fruits.

L

- **Lavender** (Irene Doyle, W. G. Doyle, L. Lady, Twickle Purple, Dwarf Blue, Hidcote, Royal Purple, Loddon Blue, etc.). Plant 24 to 36 inches apart and rows 30 to 36 inches apart. Propagated by cuttings, layering and root division.

- **Leeks**. Grow 12 to 15 plants per person. Yield 4 to 6 pounds per 10-foot row. Space plants 2 to 4 inches apart in rows 6 to 10 inches apart.
- **Lemon balm**. Plant as part of edible landscaping. Plant as many as you can fit into your garden. They smell great! Grows into a 2 foot mounding shape. Dies back in the winter and comes back in the spring. Makes great beverages. Medicinal uses. Bee attractor.
- **Lemon grass**. Plant 36 inches apart and space rows 36inches. Lemon grass is used in edible landscaping. Perennial grass used to flavor beverages, stir-frys, soups and Asian dishes.
- **Lemon tree**. A mature lemon tree produces more than 100 pounds of lemons per year.
- **Lemon verbena**. If you only plant one you may wish you had planted more. Smell is fabulous.
- **Lettuce** (Boston, Butter, Romaine, Garnet Rose, Ice, Little Gem, Merlot, Merveille Des Quatre Saisons, Oak Leaf, Celtuce, etc.). Grow 6 to 10 plants per person; plant succession crops with each harvest. Yield 4 to 10 pounds per 10 foot row. Space loose leaf lettuce 4 inches apart and all other types 12 inches apart in rows 16 to 24 inches apart. Sow up to 5 times per season to have a continuous supply of lettuce. Plant 12" apart.
- **Licorice**. Requires a 3 to 4 year growth cycle. Grow in a field to get a mature root.
- **Lilac tree**. Lilac flowers are edible
- **Lily**. Plant bulbs in full sun.
- **Lima or butter beans**. 6 to 8 ounces per plant or 4 to 8 lima bean plants per person; 4 to 6 pounds per 10 foot row; 3 to 6 inches apart, rows 24 to 30 inches apart, increase distance for pole limas.
- **Lobelia cardinalis**. Perennial. Hummingbird attractor. Needs moist soil.
- **Loganberry**. Hybrid between a North American blackberry and a European raspberry. Produce 2 harvests.
- **Long beans**. 120 beans per plant or 20 pods per plant; 4 to 8 plants per person; 1 to 3 inches apart in rows 2 to 3 feet apart
- **Loquat**. Mature loquat trees yield from 35 to 300 pounds of fruit per year.
- **Lotus root**. Unusual root, usually eaten cooked, boiled, fried, etc.
- **Lovage**. Perennial celery-esque culinary herb. Eat stems and leaves. Seeds can be ground and used as salt. Pollinators love.
- **Luffa** (sikwa, patola, kabatiti). Harvest young and eat like a summer squash. A sponge gourd used in cooking. High in fiber and nutrients.

M

- **Mandarin tree**. A mature mandarin yields up to 135 lb of fruit / year.
- **Manioc** (yucca, cassava). Sweet tuber similar to potatoes.
- **Marigold**. Plant 8 to 18 inches apart in all directions. Height is 6 to 18 inches.
- **Marionberry**. Type of blackberry. Vigorous vine producing canes up to 20 feet long.
- **Marjoram**. Prefers full sun. Cold sensitive. Usually grown as an annual, but it is a perennial in some climates. One to 2 foot bush, plant 8" to 12" apart.
- **Marshmallow**. All parts of plant are edible / medicinal. Produces white and pink flowers. Prefers moist soil. Reaches up to 6' tall. Roots harvested in 2 to 3 yr.
- **Mayhaw tree**. 6-year old trees produce 10 lb to 20 lb of fruit / year; 9-year old tress produce up to 25 lb to 40 lb / year. Space 15' apart with 20' btwn rows.
- **Melon**. Grow 4 to 8 plants / person. Yield 2 to 3 melons / vine. Space plants 3' to 4' apart in rows 3' wide.
- **Meyer lemon tree**. May begin to produce within 2 years. Trees grow to 15' tall and 12' wide. Prefer full sun. May produce all year but there are 2 distinct blooming times: fall and early spring. A mature Meyer Lemon tree produces 100 to 200 pounds of lemons / tree.
- **Milk thistle**. Vigorous plants. Butterfly attractors. Include in landscaping areas.

- **Milkweed**. Grow milkweeds for Monarchs. Include as part of edible landscaping.
- **Millet**. Plant seeds 2" apart. Rows 12" apart. Harvest when seeds turn golden brown.
- **Mint**. Plant loses productivity within 3 to 4 years. Grows best in virgin soil. Rotate crop.
- **Moringa tree**. Leaf fresh weight yield is 2 to 10 pounds per tree per year.
- **Mulberry tree**. Young trees yield 7 to 15 pounds in the first 2 to 4 years. Mature trees produce over 500 pounds per tree.
- **Muscadine grapes** (Sugar gate, Supreme, Black Beauty, Dixie, Cowart, Nesbitt, Noble, Sweet Jenny, Summit, Fry, Granny Val, Carlos, Scuppernong, etc.). 16 to 20 feet between vines and 10 to 12 feet between row. Yield 75 to 100 pounds / vine; female vines produce 50 to 80 pounds.
- **Mushrooms.** Grow your own gourmet mushrooms using pre-inoculated mushroom spore logs or do it yourself.
- **Mustard**. Grow 6 to 10 plants / person. Yield 3 to 6 pounds per 10' row. Space plant 6 to 12" apart in rows 15 to 30 inches apart.

N

- **Nasturtium** (Alaska Mix, Alaska Red, Bloody Mary, Dwarf Jewel, Jewel Peach, King Theodore, Orchid Cream, Tall Trailing Mix, Tip Top Alaska Salmon, Yeti, etc.). Leaves and flowers are edible, tastes slightly peppery. Save seeds, dry and replant in the spring.
- **Nectarine tree**. Miniature tree yields ¼ to 1 bushel, dwarf yields 2 to 3 bushels and standard yields 3 to 5 bushels.
- **Nopal**. Type of edible cactus.

O

- **Oats** (good cover crop and Out-compete weeds). Yield 66 bushels per acre.
- **Oca**. Perennial tuber, similar to a potato.
- **Okra**. Yield is around 1 lb / plant, 3 to 4 plants / person, yield 5 lb to 10 lb / 10' row. Space 12" to 18" apart in rows 2.5' to 4' apart.
- **Olive tree**. Depending on size, tree produces between 100 to 500 (or more) lb of olives. 220 lb or 100 kg of olives yields approximately 20 liters of olive oil.
- **Olallieberries**. Large blackberry. Hybrid between a blackberry and a youngberry.
- **Onion** (Spanish, Sweet, Red, Brown, Globo, Bunching, Red of Florence, Yellow, etc.). Yields 7 lb to 10 lb per 10' row. Space onion sets or transplants 4" to 5" apart in rows 8" – 12" apart. Plan for 60 lb to 70 lb of onions for a year or 15 lb / person
- **Orach**. Alternative to spinach. Green, purple and red varieties. Grows up to 6' and spreads out to 1.5'. Tolerates some frost.
- **Orange bell pepper**. Yield is ~ 3.5 to 5 lb or 6 to 8 fruits / plant.
- **Oregano**. Best to prune back 1/3rd of plant early in season so plant becomes bushy.

P

- **Painted mountain corn**. One seed grows a stalk which yields 300 to 700 kernels / plant.
- **Pansy**. Pansies are edible and add a pop of color to landscaping.
- **Papaya**. Each tree yields up to 75 to 300 pounds of fruit over a season. Dehydrate the seeds and use in the place of black pepper.
- **Parsley**. Plant parsley every 4 inches. It is ready to harvest in about 3 to 4 weeks.
- **Parsnip**. 10 plants per person. Yield 10 lb / 10' row. Space plants 4" to 5" apart in rows 24" apart.
- **Passion fruit** (aka Maypop Vine). One perennial passion fruit vine can yield 35 to 45 fruits and up to 50 lb of fruit per season. Fruiting within 1 to 3 years of planting.

- **Pawpaw Tree**. True Native American tree, indigenous to eastern half of USA. Some claim deer avoid this tree but not always. Produces largest edible fruit native to North America.
- **Peach tree**. Miniature tree yields ¼ to 1 bushel, dwarf yields 1 to 3 bushels, standard yields 3 to 6 bushels.
- **Peanuts**. Each plant produced between 25 to 50 peanuts. Each plant is around 18 inches tall. Plant 18 - 24 inches apart.
- **Pear tree**. Asian varieties of a dwarf yield 2 to 3 bushels, standard yields 4 to 6 bushels. European varieties of a dwarf yield 1 to 3 bushels and standard yields 3 to 6 bushels.
- **Peas**. Grow 30 plants per person. Yield 2 to 6 pounds per 10 foot row. Space plants 2 to 4 inches apart in rows 2 feet apart, 5 feet apart for vining peas.
- **Pecan tree**. A single pecan tree may produce up to 50 pounds of nuts per tree in the 10th year and 100 pounds in the 15th growing season. Plant 12 to 48 trees per acre. Can produce 1,000 pounds per acre.
- **Pepperoncini pepper**. Average plant produces 1 to 3 pounds of peppers.
- **Pepper tree** (black, red, white). Yields are based on tree size.
- **Perilla / Japanese shiso**. Plants grow to 3 or 4 feet. All leaves are edible.
- **Persimmon tree** (Fuyu, Hachiya). May take up to 7 years before yielding fruit. Hachiya trees are larger than Fuyu trees. The Fuyu fruit is hard and sweet. Hachiya fruit is soft and sweet.
- **Pimento pepper**. Plant seedlings 18 inches apart and space rows 30 inches apart. Large fruited plants bear 5 or 6 fruits and small fruited plants bear 30 to 70 peppers.
- **Pinyon pine**. The source of pine nuts! Bear after 25 years. Grow to be 15 to 60 feet. Plant 10 to 20 feet apart.
- **Plum tree**. Japanese dwarf varieties yield ½ to 2 bushels, standard yields 2 to 4 bushels. European dwarfs yield 1 to 2 bushels, standards yield 3 to 6 bushels.
- **Poblano pepper**. Plant seedlings 24 to 36 inches apart and space rows 24 inches apart. Plants grow up to 5 feet but are usually about half that size. Plants are productive.
- **Pomegranate**. Trees begin bearing in the 3rd year but become mature in the 6th year. Mature trees produce between 100 and 250 fruits or 50 to 75 lb / year.
- **Potatoes**. 1 plant yields 5 to 10 potatoes. Yields 10 to 20 pounds per 10 foot row. Space potatoes 8" – 12" apart in trenches 24" – 36" apart. Plan for 75 lb of potatoes / person for a year.
- **Psyllium plant** (*Plantago psyllium*). Annual herb grows to a ht of 12 to 18 inches. Plants flower in 60 days.
- **Pumpkin** (Sugar Pie). Yields 1 to 2 pumpkins/plant. Yield 10 to 20 lb per 10 foot row. Bush pumpkins 24 inches apart in rows 3 feet apart. Set 2 to 3 vining pumpkins on hills 6 to 8 feet apart.

Q - R

- **Quince tree**. Dwarf varieties yield ½ a bushel. Standard varieties yield 1 bushel.
- **Quinoa**. Plant 3" – 6" apart and thin plants to 18". Plants reach up to 4' to 8'. Each plant yields 6 oz of quinoa seeds.
- **Radicchio**. Grow 5 to 6 plants/person. Plant 6" apart in rows 18" apart.
- **Radish**. Grow 15 plants/person. Yield 2 to 5 lb per 10 foot row. Space plants 1 inch apart in rows 12 to 18 inches apart.
- **Ramps or wild leeks**. Related to onion. Emerges in spring, found in the south. Leaves and bulbs are edible. Grow in a shady place, under trees in moist loam.
- **Raspberry vines** (everbearing, summer bearing). Yields for summer-bearing red raspberries for a 20' row are 50lb - 70 lb of raspberries. Yields for primocane-fruiting raspberries per 20' row are 30 lb to 40 lb. Yields for 20' row of black raspberries are 15 lb to 25 lb. Raspberry plants spread and can be propagated.

- **Red marconi pepper**. Grows up to 3' tall. Space plants 24" to 36" apart. Productive.
- **Rhubarb**. Grow 2 to 3 plants / person. Yield 1 lb to 5 lb / plant, plant 3' to 6' apart.
- **Root beer plant**. Perennial plant grows up to 6' tall. Fruit provides a strong, spicy licorice flavor to root beer. Shade loving. Wild turkeys love it. Used for jelly-making.
- **Rose bush**. Leaves, buds and petals are edible and many rose bushes produce edible rose hips. Rose petals can be used to make syrups and rose water, a refreshing spritz for face and body.
- **Rose hips**. Rose hips are found on rose bushes which produce single or semi-double blooms. All rose hips are edible. Some are tastier than others. Pick after the first frost, usually late August through October.
- **Roselle**. See hibiscus.
- **Rosemary**. Rosemary can be trailing or may grow up to 6 feet tall. Plant different varieties of rosemary around your yard, both as part of edible landscaping and in your herb garden. I like to plant rosemary at door entrances.
- **Rutabaga** (neeps). Grow 5 to 10 plants per person. Yield 8 lb to 30 lb / 10' row. Space plants 4" to 6" apart in rows 15" to 36" apart.

S

- **Sage** (Pineapple, Scarlet, Grape-scented, Common, Purple, Golden, Tricolor, Berggarten, etc.). Plant as edible land-scaping. Could plant an entire bed with different sage varieties. Incompatible with cucumbers.
- **Salad burnet**. Beautiful plant with a slight cucumber flavor.
- **Salal berries**. Bush grows up to 6 feet. Produces small dark colored berries. Bears fruit at 2 to 3 years of age.
- **Salmon berries**. Reach about 6 feet in height and width. Bears berries all summer long in the Pacific northwest. Begin bearing 2 to 3 years after planting.
- **Salsify**. Grow 10 plants / person. Space plants 3" to 4" apart in rows 24" to 30" apart.
- **Samphire**. Succulent, salt tolerant plant grows along the coast, usually pickled.
- **Saskatoon fruit tree**. Saskatoon fruits are used in making wine, sauces, pies, jam. Does well in cool climates. Cold hardy to 50 °F. Grows 15 ft tall, 15 ft wide.
- **Savory** (summer, winter). Summer savory is an annual and winter savory is a perennial. Winter savory is slightly bitter. Uses are similar to sage.
- **Scallions**. Yield 1½ lb / 10-foot row. Spaces onion sets or plants 2 inches apart for scallions or green onions.
- **Scarlet runner beans**. Most grow as ornamentals, but the beans as well as the flowers, young leaves and tubers are edible when cooked.
- **Schisandra berry vine**. Grow on a strong fence or trellis. May grow 20 to 60 feet. Shade tolerant. Cold hardy to -30 °F. May require a male and female but not always. Fruits in 4 years of planting.
- **Sea buckthorn or sea berry**. Nitrogen fixing tree producing healthy berries. Super long thorns. Plant accordingly.
- **Sea kale**. Usually grown as ornamental plant, it may grow as large as 3 feet tall.
- **Serviceberry tree**. Produces fruit which ripen from red to blue with the perfect balance of sweet and tart. Trees usually grow to 20 feet tall and 15 feet wide. Cold hardy to -40 F.
- **Shallot**. Yield 2 to 12 cloves / plant. Space plants 5" to 8" apart, rows 2' to 4' apart.
- **Sesame**. Plants are 12 to 24 inches. Produces white to purple flowers. Grown for the seeds. When seed pods mature, they burst open, giving us the phrase, "open sesame."
- **Shishito pepper**. Space plants 14 to 16 apart and space rows 24 to 36 inches apart. Each plant yields 30 to 50 pods.
- **Shisho** (perilla). Leaves are used in cooking.
- **Skullcap**. Medicinal herb. Grows in wild bogs and near creek beds.

- **Snake bean.** Grows up to 60 inches long. Use like beans or squash.
- **Snapdragon.** Snapdragon flowers are a beautiful addition to a flowerbed or even a corner of your vegetable garden. They make a great cut flower and bloom all summer.
- **Snap peas.** Plant 1 to 1.5 inches deep and 2 to 3 inches apart. Leave 1 to 2 feet between rows for dwarf varieties and 3 feet for other varieties. Rows 6 feet apart. Plant early and late varieties. Best to pick before peas are fully mature.
- **Sorghum.** Four seeds yield about three uniform stalks and heads. Plant one seed every four inches on rows spaced 30 inches apart. On average one head of sorghum yields about $1/10^{th}$ of a pound of grain.
- **Sorrel** (Red Veined, Blond de Lyon). Grow 3 plants per person. Space plants 12 inches apart in rows 18 inches apart.
- **Soy beans.** Approximately 30 to 50 pods per plant, 2.5 beans per pod, about 125 to 150 beans per plant; 4 to 8 plants per person, 2 in apart, rows 2 to 3 ft apart.
- **Spaghetti squash.** Each plant produces up to 3 fruit. Allow plenty of space for plants. Plant on hills, with 3 or 4 transplants per hill. Allow 3 feet btwn each hill.
- **Spanish mammoth pepper.** Plants grow to around 3 to 4 feet tall. One plant produces 3 to 10 peppers. Plant 6 to 12 plants if you are a big fan of peppers and plan to use in preserves or 3 to 6 plants for fresh eating.
- **Spinach.** Grow 15 plants / person. Yield 4 to 7 pounds / 10 foot row. Space plants 3 to 4 inches apart in rows 1 to 2 ft apart.
- **Squash, summer** (scallop, Romanesco, crookneck, straight neck, etc.). Grow 1 to 2 plants per person. Yield 10 to 80 lb per 10' row. Yields 20 to 30 squash blossoms per plant. Space plants 2 to 4 feet apart in rows 5 feet apart. Plant radishes around squash hills to deter pests.
- **Squash, winter** (delicata, cushaw, banana, kabocha, etc.). Grow 1 plant / person. Space at least 2 or more ft apart.
- **Strawberries** (3 types include June Bearing, everbearing, day-neutral). June bearing strawberries produce between 0.5 to 1 lb of strawberries / foot of row during the 2nd and 3rd years of life. Everbearing strawberries produce between 0.25 and 0.5 lb of strawberries / foot of row, during both 2nd and 3rd years of life. Day neutral strawberries produce between 0.25 and 0.74 lb of strawberries / foot of row during the 1st year of life and expected harvest increases to 0.5 to 1.5 lb per row foot for the 2nd and 3rd years.
- **Stevia.** Space 6" to 8" apart, 30" btwn rows. Perennial, harvest for 3 to 5 yrs.
- **Stinging nettle.** Perennial. Yields 4 lb to 12 lb / 10' row. Number may double or triple at higher elevations. High in minerals.
- **St. John's wort.** Vigorous perennial plant. Spreads by rhizomes.
- **Sunchokes.** Grow 5 to 10 plants/person. Space plants 24" apart in rows 36" to 40" apart. Edible tubers.
- **Sunflower.** Grow 1 plant / person. Yield 1 lb to 2½ lb of seed / flower. Space plants 8" to 12" apart in rows 30" to 36" apart.
- **Sweet peas.** Plant enough sweet peas to keep a bouquet in every room of your house. Not edible, just fragrant & pretty.
- **Sweet potato.** One tuber produces up to 30 slips. Plant slips 12 to 18 inches apart. Grow 5 - 10 plants per person. One plant produces at least one pound of sweet potatoes. Yield 8 to 12 pounds per 10-foot row. Space plants 12 inches apart in rows 3 feet apart.
- **Swiss chard.** Grow 3 to 5 plants / person. Yield 8 to 12 lb per 10-foot row. Space plants 12 inches apart in rows 18 to 30 inches apart.

T - V

- **Tangelo tree**. fruit ripens in the winter. Juicy and sweet. Hardy to 20 °F.
- **Tansy**. Medicinal herb. Use caution.
- **Tayberry**. Cross btwn a blackberry and red raspberry. Developed in Scotland.
- **Thicket bean** (Wild Bean, Wild Kidney Bean). Perennial, native to North America. Similar to lima bean. May grow up to 20 feet tall.
- **Thimbleberry**. Both young shoots and berries are edible. Bush grows to 6 feet and needs 2 to 3 feet between other plants. Self-fertile, bears second year from seed.
- **Thyme** (breckland, common, creeping, elfin, lemon, lime, orange balsam, pink chintz, wild, wooly, etc.). Plant several types to supply needs throughout the year. Perennial but need to be replaced about every 3 yr.
- **Tiger nut**. Type of tuber. High in fiber.
- **Tomatillo**. Grow 1 to 2 plants / person. Yield 1 lb to 2 lb / plant. Space plants 10" apart in rows 2' apart.
- **Tomato, cherry**. Grow 1 to 4 plants/person. Space plants 3' apart, rows 35" to 45" apart.
- **Tomatoes, heirloom**. 10 lb to 20 lb / plant. Plant 2 to 4 plants / person.
- **Tomato, raw / eating**. Grow 3 to 6 plants of each variety; this yields 8 to 10 quarts of tomato sauce. Space plants 42 in apart in rows 40 - 50 in apart.
- **Tomato, paste**. Depending on the type of tomato plant, you can reasonably expect 10 pounds of paste tomatoes / plant and possibly up to 30 pounds, depending on growing climate. If you want to put away 10 pounds of tomato paste, you need to grow about 4 paste tomatoes. If you want to make 50 quarts (or 100 lb) of tomato sauce or salsa, you need about 15 to 20 paste tomatoes, considering some will be used for immediate needs.
- **Tomato, keepers**. Yield 7 lb to 10 lb/ plant. Keeping tomatoes usually stay good for up to several months after removing from vine. Plant 2 plants/family of four for 2 to 3 months of coverage after the first frost.
- **Tomato, slicing**. Grow 2 to 4 plants per person. Space plants 42 inches apart; rows 40 to 50 inches apart.
- **Toothache plant**. All parts above the ground are medicinal. Slightly numbing and stimulates saliva flow.
- **Truffles**. Purchase tree trunk inoculated with truffle spores.
- **Turkish rocket** (Skirret or Perennial Broccoli). It is not a brassica and does not have pest issues related to brassicas. The broccoli heads are very small but prolific and tasty.
- **Turmeric**. Takes 10 months from planting until harvest. Start indoors in large pots. When warm transplant outdoors. Plant 1 to 2 rhizomes /person.
- **Turnip**. Grow 5 to 10 plants / person. Yield 8 - 12 lb / 10' row (turnips weigh about 1 lb each). Space plants 5 - 8 inches apart in rows in rows 15 - 24 inches apart.
- **Turpentine bush**. Tolerates heat and drought as well as temps down to 10 °F. Deer & rabbit repellant. Medicinal plant.
- **Valerian**. Plant several plants/family, more if you enjoy their foliage. Valerian is a highly aromatic, beautiful perennial flowering plant does well in an herb garden or edible flower bed. Flowers may be red, pink or white. Drought tolerant. Propagates by root divisions in spring or fall. Thought to stimulate growth of neighboring plants by stimulating phosphorus and attracting earthworms. Leaves high in minerals.
- **Vanilla bean vine** (Madagascar, Mexican, Indonesian, Tahitian, Indian, Tonga, etc.). This is a high profit plant. Best to purchase plants. Plants take 3 to 5 years before they produce. Plant produces flowers on short racemes. Each raceme produces 6 to 20 flowers. For home use, 5 plants should work. Do better in a greenhouse with constant temperature and humidity. Pods are ready 9 months after hand pollination. A single vine may grow to 300 feet, but shorter vines are the norm. Vine's lifespan is 10 years.

- **Vervain**. Butterfly attractor / pollinator.
- **Violets**. Violets are edible. Sometimes they are crystallized and used in baking.

W – Z

- **Walnut tree**. A 5 to 7 year old tree produces 15 to 25 pounds of nuts. Older trees produce between 65 to 350 pounds of nuts, just not every single year (the higher range).
- **Wasabi**. Grows in cool, shady conditions. Prefers high humidity and shade during summer months. Takes up to 18 to 36 months to reach maturity. Difficult to grow. In N. America, grows best along Pacific NW coastal regions and Blue Ridge mountains in North Carolina and Tennessee. Prepared wasabi comes from rhizome; all parts edible.
- **Watercress**. Best grows in cooler weather. Propagate from cuttings.
- **Watermelon**. 2 to 4 melons / plant. Grow 2 to 4 plants / person. Depending on size, yield is 8 to 40 lb per 10' row. Space plants 4' apart, rows 4' wide and 8' apart.
- **Wheat** (emmer, white Sonora). 80% germination. On average, there are 22 seeds per head and 5 heads per plant, or 110 seeds per plant. 15,000 seeds per pound, 900,000 seeds per bushel. 1.5 bushels per acre. 1,000 square feet produces 1 bushel of wheat. A bushel of wheat equals 60 pounds of grain, enough to make 90 loaves of bread.
- **Wild rye**. Grows at edges of open woodlands, along streams, in prepared beds. Seeds are ground into flour. Perennial plant. Grows up to 5 ft tall. Plant 6 - 12 inches apart.
- **Winter squash** (pumpkin, spaghetti squash, acorn, etc.). Harvest when mature. Outer skin is a tough rind. Fruit is eaten cooked.
- **Witch hazel shrub**. Reaches 10' to 12' high. Produces small yellow flowers. Bark and leaves used to make an external tonic.
- **Woad**. Contains a blue dye chemical, Indigotin. Medicinal. Biennial, grows the 1st year and then flowers and produces seeds the 2nd year. Invasive. Best to plant in pots.
- **Wormwood** (artemisia). Wormwood has many uses; it is toxic at high levels.
- **Yacon**. Grows over 6' tall. Related to the sunflower. Produces tubers with a texture similar to apples. Can be dehydrated, pickled or canned. Grind into flour to add to baked products, etc.
- **Yams** (Chinese Yams, Ube). Propagate by roots, bulbils and cuttings.
- **Yardlong beans**. Slender, long beans with red or black seeds.
- **Yarrow**. Perennial flower. Be careful, while a valuable herb, it is toxic to cats, dogs, horses.
- **Yellow monster pepper**. Plant 24 to 36 inches apart, space rows 36 inches apart. Plants are about 3 feet tall. Each plant produces 5 and 20 peppers. Most peppers exceed one lb. Plants need support.
- **Yuzu**. A citrus tree, cold hardy to 10 °F.
- **Zatar**. Culinary herb.
- **Zinnia petals**. Zinnias are prolific flowers and add visual interest to a garden, yard or flower bed. Keep cutting the flowers and they rebloom until frost.
- **Zucchini**. Plant zucchini 28 inches apart and 36 inches between rows. Zucchini can grow up to 2 inches per day. One zucchini plant yields 3 to 10 lb.

Resources

Vegetable production chart (1 page): https://www.canr.msu.edu/uploads/files/Table%204.pdf
https://www.youtube.com/watch?v=lSUxcsJDgJM
https://www.canr.msu.edu/grapes/uploads/files/GrapeGuide-PDF-final2020.pdf
https://www.canr.msu.edu/resources/an_introduction_to_blueberries
https://www.canr.msu.edu/resources/beekeeping_for_pollination_and_honey
https://www.canr.msu.edu/resources/plant_based_enterprises
https://permacultureapprentice.com/resources/#PERMACULTURE_DESIGN
http://www.adventistonline.com/video/mountain-media-ministries-planting-by-the-blueprint
https://nativefoodsnursery.com/
https://www.rareseeds.com/
http://www.sampleseeds.com/
https://www.tradewindsfruit.com/
https://www.sandhillpreservation.com/
https://www.dahlias.com/
https://www.forestfarm.com/
https://www.seedman.com/
https://www.superseeds.com/
https://www.seedsavers.org/
https://territorialseed.com/
https://www.richters.com/
https://thegrowers-exchange.com/collections/rare-and-unusual-herb-plants
https://www.selectseeds.com/rare-antique-heirloom-flowers/
https://store.underwoodgardens.com/Rare-Herbs/products/43/
https://www.chilternseeds.co.uk/unusual-varieties
https://www.fieldstonegardens.com/
https://www.gardencrossings.com/
https://www.highcountrygardens.com/perennial-plants/unique-plants
https://www.johnnyseeds.com/
https://www.logees.com/
https://www.plantdelights.com/
https://www.plant-world-seeds.com/
https://www.prairiemoon.com/
https://www.selectseeds.com/
https://www.roughwoodtable.org (sign up to be a grower)
https://www.southernexposure.com/
https://www.youtube.com/watch?v=uZeN48rjTgY&fbclid=IwAR2F_U1Z8SOzWbAhgjyZyJY8315LQjvK-IDKkVJHTM_F0J2Zx6_INdP2o9k – Low maintenance backyard food forest produces amazing food all year
https://www.youtube.com/watch?v=RkLLnyvQTwg – So you want a food forest? Bushes – my top 6.
https://www.starkbros.com/

Chapter 62
Edible Wild Plants

Identification and consumption of wild edible plants has been gaining in popularity for decades. It has been a small, slow movement, but one which has steadily gained in numbers and may be surging in interest with the recent rise of prepper groups and the trend toward moving to the country. I remember while teaching at a small private university in Southern California during the 1990s and 2000s, once a week, we shared our class-room space with a community-based edible wild plants class. I enjoyed watching them bring in huge plants, roots and all, into the classroom and spreading them out on the tables. I wished for more time to be able to join them. Over the years, I collected a number of their handouts and enjoyed studying them. This rather vicarious introduction to wild edible plants while mostly theoretical, has contributed to appreciating the value of learning to forage for edible wild plants.

Reading about edible plants is very different than actually foraging and consuming them. It is essential to have a theoretical knowledge as well as a practical, experienced-based knowledge of edible wild plants. If this topic interests you, take steps to formalize your training with experts in this field. Check for local clubs and community groups, edible wild plant walks, etc.

Below are a few basic guidelines for your consideration. They target those who wish to gain a greater knowledge of edible wild plants. I hope this chapter stimulates your interest and pushes you toward practical experiences in foraging. It is a great way to spend time in nature, learn to appreciate the various seasons, and fellowship with others who have similar interests.

1. Only eat plants you positively identify as 100% safe and edible.
2. What might be a safe level of intake for an adult, may not be "safe" for a child or for an adult with a compromised liver, or other medical issues.
3. Make sure you are not eating plants contaminated or treated with chemicals.
4. Learn which parts of the plant are edible, medicinally used, etc.
5. Understand the best time of the year to harvest the plants.
6. Do not use plants from the side of the road, where car exhaust and other chemicals are released.
7. Purchase several reference books with pictures of edible plants.
8. Harvest just enough to use, no more than 15% to 20% of what is available. This allows for sustainability and for propagating additional plants.
9. Learn the wild edibility rule for testing unknown plants.

It is important to get a trustworthy, credible wild edible plant book for positive plant identification. As a disclaimer, do not take any information on edible wild plants (including information in this book) as 100% accurate. Always verify any information related to consuming edible wild plants.

Choose several plants common to your geographic location and learn everything about them. Once you have mastered several plants, it is easier to learn more. Exercise great caution and then once you have developed your skills, you may reap many benefits related to safe identification of edible plants and how to use and prepare them.

Keep in mind, even people with decades of experience and considered to be experts in the field of edible wild plants, may have small disagreements with other experts. This is due to plant and human variabilities. Consult several authoritative sources before you move forward with consuming wild plants.

Mushroom identification is another discipline which absolutely requires expert training and input. I strongly advise against consuming any wild mushroom without 100% positive identification and confirmation by a trained expert (i.e., a mycologist). Some mushrooms are so poisonous, even a small bite may lead to rapid death. The most lethal mushrooms are in the genus, *Amanita phalloides* and the genus *Cortinarius*. The names of the mushrooms are: the death cap (commonly grows in B.C. Canada and the Pacific Northwest and is expanding into Northern California), destroying angel, and the fool's mushroom. Their names alone should instill fear into any amateur mushroom forager. According to the British Columbia Medical Journal in an article written by Moor-Smith, et al., (Vol 61, No 1, Jan/Feb 2019), the death cap mushroom is responsible for 90% of the world's mushroom-related fatalities, leading to multi-system organ failure, coma and then death within 4 to 9 days after consumption. It is easily mistaken for edible mushrooms such as the puffball and paddy straw mushroom. None of the amatoxins are destroyed by heat, drying or freezing.

If you have recently consumed a wild plant or mushroom and end up with gastrointestinal issues, seek immediate medical care and be prepared to describe and even provide a sample of the plant in question. Immediate medical care may be the difference between life and death.

The U.S. Army Survival Manual describes a Universal Edibility Test. It is listed below. Perform this test at your own risk.

1. Test only one part of a potentially edible plant at a time.

2. Separate the plant into its basic parts - leaves, stems, roots, buds and flowers.

3. Smell the food for strong or acid odors. Remember, smell alone does not indicate a plant is edible or inedible.

4. Do not eat for 8 hours before the test.

5. During the 8 hours you abstain from eating, test for contact poisoning by placing a piece of the plant part you are testing on the inside of your elbow or wrist. Fifteen minutes is enough time to allow for a reaction.

6. During test period, take nothing by mouth except purified water and the plant part you are testing.

7. Select a small portion of a single part and prepare it the way you plan to eat it.

8. Before placing the prepared plant part in your mouth, touch a small portion (a pinch) to the outer surface of your lip to test for burning or itching. If after 3 minutes there is no reaction on your lip, place the plant part on your tongue, holding it there for 15 minutes.
9. If no reaction, thoroughly chew a pinch and hold in mouth for 15 minutes; don't swallow.
10. If no burning, itching, numbing, stinging, or other irritation occurs during the 15 minutes, swallow.
11. Wait 8 hours. If any undesirable effects occur during this period, induce vomiting, drink water, and take charcoal.
12. If no ill effects occur, eat ¼ cup of the same plant part prepared the same way. Wait 8 hours. If no ill effects occur, the plant part as prepared is safe for eating.
13. Try a tablespoon or two mixed into a suitable recipe. If no negative side effects it should be ok.

Next is a partial listing of edible wild plants. Each geographic region has its own specific edibles. There are blank spaces for you to add species specific to your geographic region. Be careful and bon appetit.

Edible Wild Plants Common to North America

Always confirm a wild plant is an edible plant with an expert as well as a picture identification. Plants on this list are considered to be edible in variable amounts. Too much of any edible plant may be toxic. Not all parts of an "edible wild plant" are edible. The author of this list takes no responsibility for accidental consumption of a poisonous plant. If you are pregnant or lactating, most edible wild plants are not recommended. This list is a starting point to use for additional research.

A - C

- **Acorns** (*Quercus*). Do not eat raw acorns, the tannins must be removed before consuming. Leach out the tannins by soaking shelled acorns in water. Soak, drain off water and repeat until soaking water is clear. Do the same for acorn flour.
- **Alfalfa** (*Medicago sativa*). Leaves and young shoots are the only parts which may be eaten raw. Contains phytoestrogens including spinasterol, coumestrol, and coumestan. Raw seeds and sprouts may be a source of canavanine (toxic to humans and animals).
- **Allium** (*Allium canadense*). In the same family as chives, onions, leeks, garlic, etc. Considered to be an invasive weed.
- **Aloe vera** (*Aloe barbadensis miller*).
- **Amaranth** (*Amaranthus retroflexus*). Leaves, flowers, stems and seeds are edible. Seeds may be ground into flour. Accumulates nitrates and may contain oxalates.
- **Arrowhead** (*Sagitaria latifolia*). Grows in shallow freshwater swampy areas. Tubers edible when roasted or boiled. Best in fall and early spring. High in starch.
- **Asparagus** (*Asparagus officinalis*). Wild asparagus has a thinner stalk.
- **Bamboo** (*Acidosasa*). Bamboo shoots are the edible portion but not all bamboo species are edible.
- **Barrel cactus fruit** (*Ferocactus wislizeni*). Dehydrate and use in soups and stews. Seeds can be dried and ground into flour.
- **Beech leaves** (*Fagus sylvatica*). Beech nuts are edible (avoid eating large amounts which may cause poisoning). The leaves are also edible. Avoid if pregnant or lactating.
- **Birch catkins.** High in protein but they reportedly do not taste good. Boiling improves palatability. Some species of birch leaves are edible.
- **Blue verbain** (*Verbena hastata*). Leaves, seeds and roots are edible.

- **Broadleaf plantain** (*Plantago major*). Entire plant is edible. Young leaves are best eaten raw.
- **Bull thistle** (*Cirsium vulgare*). Leaves and roots are edible. Remove prickles from leaves before consumption.
- **Burdock** (*Arctium lappa*). Young roots and interior of the flower stalks are edible. Older leaves are better cooked. Do not confuse with cocklebur.
- **Canadian white violets** (*Viola canadensis*). Young leaves and flower buds are edible raw or cooked. Used for mucilaginous properties to thicken soups.
- **Catnip** (*Nepeta cataria*). Young leaves and flowers are edible. Tastes like mint.
- **Cattail** (*Typha latifolia*). Shoots, roots, leaves and flowers are edible. Only use roots from clean water; roots are used to filter our contaminants.
- **Chanterelles** (*Cantharellus cibarius*).
- **Chickweed** (*Stellaria media*). Stems, leaves, flowers and seeds are edible. A nice salad ingredient.
- **Chicory** (*Cichorium intybus*). A member of the dandelion family. Pretty blue flowers. Leaves can be eaten raw. Roots are only edible if boiled.
- **Chokecherry** (*Prunus virginiana*). Red and black berries are edible but do not eat the cyanide-containing pits.
- **Cleavers** (*Gallium aparine*). Leaves and stems are edible, but sticky.
- **Cloudberry** (*Rubus chamaemorus*). Salmon-colored berries with 3 leaves. Found in the northern boreal regions. Similar looking plants may be poisonous.
- **Clover** (*Trifolium pretense*). Avoid white clover in warm climates. Crimson and red clover are edible. See **Red clover**.
- **Coltsfoot** (*Tussilago farfara*). Flowers may be eaten raw or processed into jelly or a tea. Leaves may also be eaten. Avoid if pregnant.
- **Common violet** (*Viola sororia*). Eat leaves and flowers.
- **Coneflower** (*Echinacea purpurea*). Leaves and petals are edible.
- **Creeping Charlie** (*Glechoma hederacea*). Young leaves may be eaten raw.
- **Cup plant** (*Silphium perfoliatum*). Medicinal value.
- **Curly dock** (*Rumex crispus*). Consume only small amounts of the young leaves. Avoid over-eating due to high oxalic acid content.
- Others:_____
_____

D - F

- **Daisy fleabane** (*Erigeron annuus*). Raw leaves are edible. Contains caffeic acid.
- **Dandelion** (*Taraxacum*). The entire plant is edible. Young plants in shaded areas are milder than mature plants in full sun.
- **Downy yellow violet** (*Viola pubescens*). Flowers and leaves are edible.
- **Dulse.** Reddish seaweed attached to rocks.
- **Echinacea** (*Echinacea purpurea*). Leaves and flowers are edible.
- **Elderberry** (*Sambucus nigra*). Large heads of white flowers turn to purple. Flowers may be used, berries used to make syrup / jelly.
- **Evening primrose** (*Oenothera biennis*). Roots are edible and succulent-like. May be eaten raw or cooked. Flowers are edible and added to salads. Young seed pods are also edible and a source of gamma linolenic acid (GLA).
- **Fern leaf yarrow** (*Achillea filipendulina*). Leaves are edible and eaten raw or cooked. Consume in small quantities.
- **Fiddleheads** (*Matteuccia struthiopteris*). Harvested and eaten while the fronds are still rolled up. Cook (boil or steam) before consumption. Some ferns are poisonous.
- **Field pennycress** (*Thlaspi arvense*). Leaves and seeds are edible.
- **Fireweed** (aka willow herb; *Chamerion angustifolium*). Peel stem and eat raw. Tastes like asparagus. Too much causes laxative effect.

- **Forget me not** (*Myosotis arvensis*). Flowers are edible.
- Others:_____
_____

G – K

- **Garlic mustard** (*Alliaria petiolata*). Entire plant is edible.
- **Ginkgo** (*Ginko biloba*). Wrinkled fruit on the ground is ripe. Remove skin and there is a nut on the inside. Stir fry the nut and it pops like popcorn; a small green nut comes out.
- **Grass.** Most grasses are edible.
- **Green briar shoots** (*Smilax rotundifolia*). Long vines with sharp thorns. The edible part is the soft new growth above the first thorn. Eat raw or cooked. Taste similar to green beans.
- **Harebell** (*Campanula rapunculoides*). Leaves are edible.
- **Henbit** (*Lamium amplexicaule, purpureum*; aka dead nettles). Leaves, flowers and stems are edible.
- **Herb Robert** (*Geranium robertianum*). Fresh leaves and flowers are edible.
- **Hibiscus** (*Hibiscus syriacus*). Flowers and leaves are edible.
- **Hosta.** All are edible but the ones with the best taste are: *h. fortune, h longipes, h. montana, h. sieboldiana*. Used for tempura, salad, pan fried, stir fry, etc.
- **Jerusalem artichoke** (*Helianthus tuberosus*). Root is edible as raw or cooked.
- **Joe Pye weed** (*Eutrochium purpureum*). Entire plant is edible.
- **Juniper** (*Juniperus communis, drupacea, phoenicea*). Evergreen tree. Berries are edible raw or sun dried.
- **Kelp.** Most seaweed is edible but best to harvest from water and not the seashore. Freshwater blue-green algae is poisonous.
- **Knapweed** (*Centaurea nigra*). Rosette flowers are edible. Considered invasive.
- **Kudzu** (*Pueraria montana*). Edible and may be used for other non-eating purposes. Leaves and roots are edible. Good for salad or pot herb. Flowers make a great jelly.
- Others:_____
_____

L – P

- **Lamb's quarters** (wild spinach; *Chenopodium album*). Leaves and seeds are edible; usually boiled. Avoid consuming too much as it may interfere with absorption of other nutrients.
- **Lichen** (*Usnea*). Soak in water to remove strong elements. Eat raw, boiled or dried.
- **Linden tree** (*Tilia Americana*). Flowers, shoots, young leaves and sap are edible.
- **Lotus flower** (*Nelumbo nucifera*). Root is edible.
- **Mallow** (*Malva neglecta*). Leaves are edible and mucilaginous. Immature seed pods are edible.
- **Maple seeds.** Larger seeds are more likely to be bitter and smaller seeds are sweeter. If bitter, boil to release the bitter flavonoids. Seeds may be cooked and eaten or dried and ground into a flour. Young maple leaves are edible as well as the maple sap used to make syrup (from certain *Acer* series such as *saccharum*).
- **Mayapple** (*Podophyllum peltatum*) Low growing plant with 7 leaves and a small apple like fruit. Only eat the ripe apples if you can find them before the wildlife eat them. Do not touch the root – may cause dermatitis. Leaves are poisonous.
- **Meadowsweet** (*Filipendula ulmaria*). Leaves, flowers and tuberous roots are edible. Contains salicylates, flavonoids, tannins, etc.
- **Milk thistle** (*Silybum marianum*). Edible parts include young stalks, leaves, roots and flowers. May be eaten raw or cooked. Remove sharp spines first. Liver protectant. The primary antidote to amanita mushroom poisoning along with high dose vitamin C.
- **Milk weed** (*Asclepias curassavica*). All parts are edible. Flower and seed pods are taste amazing.

- **Miner's lettuce** (*Claytonia perfoliata*). Found in Western regions. Found in April and May. Entire plant is edible, but may be high in oxalates, as is spinach.
- **Morels** (*Morchella*). Type of wild mushroom high prized in the culinary world. There are "false" or poisonous mushrooms which look similar to morels.
- **Moringa tree** (*Moringa oleifera*). Leaves used to make tea. High in calcium and phosphorus.
- **Mulberries** (*Morus alba, rubry*).
- **Mullein** (*Verbascum thapsus*). Leaves and flowers are edible. Some are allergic to the small hairs on plant.
- **Nettle** (*Urtica dioica*). Leaves are edible after blanching in boiling water.
- **Partridgeberry** (*Mitchella repens*). Leaves and berries are edible. Berries are somewhat bland but are highly medicinal.
- **Peppergrass** (*Lepidium virginicum*). Leaves and flowers used. Leaves are pot herb.
- **Pickerelweed** (*Pontederia cordata*). Seeds and young leaves and stalks are edible. Boil older weeds before consuming.
- **Pickleweed** (*Salicornia europeae*). Top parts of the stems are edible.
- **Pineapple weed** (*Matricaria matricariodes*). Flowers and leaves are edible.
- **Pine tree.** All parts are edible. Some parts taste like turpentine. Inner bark eaten raw. Cones have nuts, roast in fire and crack open.
- **Plantain** (*Plantago major*). Leaves taste like collard greens. Broad and narrow leaf plantain. Eat young leaves raw, older leaves need to be boiled. Do not mistake young lily plants for broadleaf plantain.
- **Prickly pear cactus** (*Opuntia compressa* or *humifusa*). The broad flat pads and red to purple fruit are edible. Remove the prickles. Eaten raw.
- **Purple deadnettle** (*Lamium purpureum*). Entire plant is edible.
- **Purslane** (*Portulaca oleracea*). Succulent type plant. Entire plant is edible. Contains omega-3 fatty acids.
- **Others**:_____
_____

Q – Z

- **Red clover** (*Trifolium pratense*). All parts are edible but only consume in early spring; fall clover contains high amounts of alkaloids. Pregnant women should not consume.
- **Roses** (*Rosa virginiana*). Petals and rose hips are edible.
- **Saltwort** (*Salicornia rubra*). Large group of plants which grow along the seashore and in salt marshes. Saltwort grown in gardens is not salty.
- **Sassafras** (*Sassafras albidum*). Boiled roots make a nice tea. May repel mosquitoes, used to thicken stews. May induce drowsiness. Avoid large doses.
- **Sheep sorrel** (*Rumex acetosella*). Lemony mild taste. Good for nibbling.
- **Shepherd's purse** (*Brassicaceae bursa-pastoris*). All parts can be used. Contains tyramine, histamine, choline, acetylcholine, rutin, saponins, tannins, carotenoids, etc.
- **Sow thistle** (common). Leaves, flowers and roots are edible.
- **Spring beauty** (*Claytonia caroliniana*). Leaves and stems can be eaten raw. Roots may be eaten raw or cooked.
- **Staghorn sumac** (*Rhus typhina*). Not to be confused with poisonous sumac with white berries. Red berries are edible.
- **Stinging nettle** (*Urtica dioica*). Perennial plant with stinging hairs which inject histamine and other chemicals that cause a burning sensation. Cooking the leaves de-activates the stinging chemicals.
- **Sunflower** (*Helianthus*). Entire plant is edible.
- **Sweet birch, silver birch** (*Betula pendula*). Young leaves may be steamed or sautéed. White birch bark may be ground into flour.
- **Sweet gale or bog myrtle** (*Myrica gale*). Grows near bogs. Has flat long leaves. The fruit and leaves are edible. Acts as insect repellant.

- **Tea plants:** bee balm, birch, creeping Charlie, dandelion, nettle, pine needles, raspberry leaf, red clover, spruce tips, sumac, etc.

- **Teasel** (*Dipsacus fullonum*). Young leaves are edible. Avoid spiny hairs. Contains inulin and a scabiocide (ediblewildfood.com)
- **Thistle** (*Cirsium edule*). Before it flowers, scrape off thorns and cook. May also use after it flowers, but it may taste stronger. Leaves, roots and unopened flower buds are edible.
- **Toothwort** (*Dentaria diphylla*). Leaves and roots are edible.
- **Vervain mallow** (*Malva alcea*). Flowers, leaves and seeds are edible.
- **Watercress** (*Nasturtium officinale*). Leaves, stems and flowers are edible.
- **Water lily.** Roots and tubers are edible.
- **Wild apple** (*Malus*). A small edible sour fruit.
- **Wild bergamot** (*Monarda fistulosa*). Makes a great tea. Leaves and flowers are edible.
- **Wild black cherry** (*Prunus serotina*). In the rose family. Fruit can be made into jelly and beverages but the rest of the tree contains amygdalin, a toxic compound.
- **Wild garlic** (*Allium ursinum*).
- **Wild ginger** (*Asarum caudatum, canadense*). Rhizomes and leaves are edible. Too much may have laxative effect.
- **Wild grape vine** (*Vitus riparia*). Wild grapes can be eaten but taste better after first frost. Leaves are edible. Beware: there is a similar plant known as *menispermum canadense* which is poisonous. Become familiar with each habitat.
- **Wild leeks, ramps or ramsons** (*Allium tricoccum*). Mild onion taste. Usual harvest May thru July. Eat in small amounts as larger volumes may cause nausea, vomiting, diarrhea. Contains sulfides. Looks similar to Lily of the Valley which is poisonous.
- **Wild mustard** (*Sinapis arvensis*). Leaves, seed pods, flowers and roots are edible. Potency of plant varies by geographic location. Best to consume small amounts to avoid stomach irritation.
- **Wild onion** (*Allium bispectrum, canadense*). Many versions of wild onions, however, there are wild onion doppelgangers as well; avoid those. Edible wild onions should smell oniony while the poisonous ones do not have an onion smell.
- **Wild rose** (*Rosa spp.*). Flower with 5 pink petals and produces rose hips. Petals, rose-buds, young shoots and leaves are edible.
- **Wild violet** (*Viola sororia*). Leaves and flowers are edible. Mucilaginous.
- **Wood lily** (*Lilium philadelphicum*). This is specific to orange flowers with purple spots. The flowers and seeds are edible. Not all lily varieties are edible.
- **Wood sorrel** (*Oxalis stricta*). Looks similar to clover. Not related to garden sorrel. Sour weed containing oxalic acid. All parts of wood sorrel are edible.
- **Yaupon holly tea leaves** (*Ilex vomitoria*). Do not eat the red berries – they will make you vomit, but the caffeine-containing leaves are edible when prepared as a tea.
- **Yarrow, common** (*Achillea millefolium*). Small amounts of bitter yarrow used medicinally may be safe for humans, but not for dogs, cats, horses, etc. In some cases, yarrow may cause severe allergic skin rashes. Some yarrow may contain thujone, which is not safe.
- **Yaupon holly** (*Ilex vomitoria*). Leaves are high in caffeine. Do not eat red berries. To prepare leaves, roast in a skillet until they turn brown. Brew in hot water, strain out leaves and you have a caffeinated beverage. Always confirm edibility of new foods.
- **Yuca** (*Manihot esculenta*). Root of cassava. Rich in vitamins and minerals. Leaves may also be eaten. All parts of plant msut be boiled before consumption. This deactivates the hydrocyanic acid content.
- **Yucca** (*Yucca guatemalensis*). Flowers, buds, fruit and stalks are edible. Flowers taste wonderful, similar to cucumbers. Use in small amounts.

- Others:_____
  _____
  _____

Poisonous plants include but are not limited to: amanita mushrooms, autumn crocus, azalea, bella-donna, buttercups, caladium, death angel, castor bean, daffodil, death camas, deadly nightshade, elephant ear, foxglove, giant hogweed, goldenrod, holly, horse nettle, iris, jack in the pulpit, Jerusalem cherry, jimsonweed, lady slipper, lantana, lily of the valley, mayapple (immature), mistletoe, moonseed, morning glory, mountain laurel, oleander, peace lily, pennyroyal, philodendron, poison hemlock, poison ivy, poke weed, poison oak, poison sumac, pothos, rhubarb leaves, rosary pea, skunk cabbage, spurges, tobacco, water hemlock, wild parsnip, and yew.

Good site for reading about edible wild plants, contains pictures and short descriptions. https://www.ediblewildfood.com/

Websites
- https://www.ediblewildfood.com/wild-food-recipes.aspx
- https://www.ediblewildfood.com/dessert-snack-recipes.aspx?fbclid=IwAR2pHH7W_2tzAnAP7OGB9ElPA57wjGHmrHClbI7xTTafpRsY6PxgLmjl9V4
- https://www.ediblewildfood.com/free-wild-food-files.aspx

Books
- The Official U.S. Army Illustrated Guide to Edible Wild Plants by Roman & Littlefield Department of the Army, 1 February 2019
- Wild Edibles by Sergei Boutenko (Random House)
- The Complete Guide to Edible Wild Plants, Mushrooms, Fruits, and Nuts: How to Find, Identify and Cook Them, by Katie Letcher Lyle (Lyons Press)
- Peterson Field Guide to Edible Wild Plants by Lee Peterson (Houghton Mifflin Company, 1999)
- Book: Stalking the Wild Asparagus by Euell Gibbons

Videos
- Out of the cities: the sequel in practicum, Intro to wild edibles in your backyard, by Jasmene and Thomas Rhem. https://www.youtube.com/watch?v=3DXxrRFWIrw
- How do we leave the cities? A response to one of the most frequently asked questions. https://www.youtube.com/watch?v=cmoMGwqfiIQ

Plants which may be processed (i.e., washed to remove bitterness and / or dehydrated and milled) and used as a partial flour substitute: acorns, almonds, amaranth, cattails, chestnuts, clover, coconut, dandelions, dock seeds, hazelnuts, mesquite pods, millet, wild parsnips, plantain seeds, quinoa, rice, sunchokes, zucchini, etc.

Chapter 63

The herb garden

20 Essential herbs

Herb gardens are a great joy! They provide loads of fresh herbs to the gourmet chef while adding important nutrients, including antioxidants. There are 20 basic herbs essential for a chef's herb garden. They are a mixture of annuals and perennials. As a bonus, some of the herbs also produce edible flowers.

Gardens, vineyards, orchards, and herbs are mentioned throughout the Bible. Solomon built complex beautiful gardens. **The King's garden in Jerusalem provided food as well as a place to meet and congregate. Plants of all types and sizes dotted the gardens not only providing heady fragrances but beautiful colors and textures as well as food and nourishment.** Herbs were used as medicine, preservatives, flavorants, etc. **Herbs mentioned in the Bible include: aloes, anise, balm, bitter herbs, calamus, caraway, cassia, castor bean, cedar, cinnamon, citron, coriander, cumin, cypress, date palm, dill, frankincense, galbanum, garlic, grape, hyssop, juniper, mandrake, mint, mustard, myrrh, myrtle, nard, olive, onycha cistus, onion, pomegranate, rue, saffron, sage, spikenard, stacte, thistle, thyme, and wormwood.**

This chapter includes 20 herbs for planting in an herb garden. To plant the 20 herbs listed below, you might consider a space about 12 x 12 feet or 8 x 15 feet, larger if planting multiples of the herbs (e.g., planting 10 basil plants). You may want to plant additional herbs such as basil, thistle, rosemary and thyme, in your land-scaping, around gates and entrances, pots, and even indoors. Ideally, the location of your herb garden is close to your kitchen, making it easy to access.

Frequently harvest flowering herbs.

An herb garden is a year-round type garden. The annuals die off in the fall after the first frost, but, depending on your location, the perennials may provide herbs throughout the year. **If you have the space, make your herb garden a little larger than you think you might need. You may want to add other unusual herbs once you establish a basic herb garden.**

20 Essential herbs!

1. **Balm, lemon**
Lemon balm, in the mint family, deserves a place in every herb garden. It smells great and while it does die back when cold weather arrives, it returns to make an even more spectacular mound of lemony minty smelling green leaves. There is also a variety that produces striking yellow leaves (Golden Lemon Balm, Aurora and Variegated). Lemon balm makes a great tea or addition to salads. Plant several together, about 15 inches apart and enjoy them all summer long. Plant this cottage herb and enjoy for may years. Also consider Bee Balm, or Bergamot; they produce pretty pale pink flowers.

2. **Basil**
Sweet basil is the standard used for making pesto, adding to pasta dishes, soups and salads. However, there are many other types of basil you may want to explore. These include: Genovese, Purple Ruffles, Cardinal, Mammolo, Holy Basil, Thai, Mammoth, Lettuce Leaf, Persian, Lemon, Fino Verde, Greek Dwarf, Blue Spice, Persian, Licorice, Lime, Dark Purple Opal, Red Freddy, Siam Queen Thai, Spicy Globe, and Cinnamon basils. Each cultivar has a distinct basil fragrance and flavor but with a slight added twist. Plant several varieties and use in your flower arrangements as well as your cooking. Basil is also an insect repellant. I like to plant 5 to 10 basil plants. You should not be disappointed, especially at the end of the summer when your plants grow huge and you harvest enough basil to make several quarts of pesto – enough to use throughout the winter.

3. **Bay leaves**
A small bay leaf plant eventually becomes a tree. This is a great tree to have. It will provide you with a lifetime of bay leaves to use in cooking and also to keep pests out of your cupboards.

4. **Chervil**
Chervil, also known as French parsley, is one of the ingredients used to make fines herbes – chervil, tarragon and chives. It is added to delicate soups, egg dishes, and salad dishes. It is a pretty, fern-like plant which produces small white flowers. This herb is not common but is worth growing in your herb garden.

5. **Chives**
Chives are one of my favorites. They produce a small white or purple flower and have a hint of garlic or onion smell. They are great on potato dishes, in salads and used as a garnish. Chives are perennial and are a beautiful addition to any herb garden. Allow several square feet for the chives to take over.

6. **Cilantro / Fresh Coriander / Seed**
Cilantro is the fresh part or the leaves and stems of the coriander plant. The seeds are known as the spice, coriander. The seeds and the fresh leaves are not used interchangeably. Cilantro is best grown in cooler climates, as it bolts as soon as the weather warms up. However, slow-bolt cultivars are available for southern gardens. The cilantro plant is not that big. One plant usually provides enough cilantro for several batches of salsa. Plant in succession if you want to have cilantro available throughout the growing season. Harvest before it bolts. Technically, the leaves and stems are known as coriander, but the seeds of the cilantro plant are known as coriander. Allow the plant to dry and then harvest the seeds from the dried plant.

7. **Cumin**
Cumin is an essential herb for most chefs. It is added to Mediterranean, African, Indian, Mexican, Italian and many other types of cuisines. The cumin plant is a beautiful plant, producing large heads of small white flowers. To harvest the seeds, remove the seed heads and allow them to dry. Collect the seeds and grind into a fine powder.

8. Dill

    Dill is a huge plant producing large yellow flower heads and feathery foliage. Seeds follow the blossoms. It attracts all kinds of pollinators, including the parsley caterpillar which morphs into a beautiful Swallowtail butterfly. Plant one or two dill plants just for the caterpillars and plant another one in your herb garden.

9. Fennel

    Fennel is an absolute essential. There are two types of fennel: bronze and Florence. Bronze is a beautiful reddish-brown color and the Florence cultivar is a beautiful green. Fennel looks and grows like dill, although they are quite different in flavor. Fennel root is used in Italian cooking.

10. Fenugreek

    An annual, grown for its seeds and leaves (known as "methi"). Seeds are used in formulating curry powders. They may also be used to make a tea. Small amounts of fenugreek are safe but consuming large amounts should be avoided.

11. Lavender

    Lavender is a novel culinary herb as well as a familiar fragrance. It is one of the herbs used in Herbs de Provence. It is added to soaps and perfumes for its magnificent fragrance. Lavender is a beautiful addition to any herb garden. It tends to prefer dry soil, but grows in most well-drained gardens. Use in sparingly in cooking – a little goes a long way! It is also great for garnishing sweets and adding visual interest to culinary dishes such as scones, biscuits, cheesecake, beverages, sorbets, tarts, etc.

12. Marjoram

    Low growing herb, with floral woodsy flavor notes is a staple kitchen herb used to flavor rice and beans, Mediterranean foods, tomato-based dishes, and added to fresh salads. It's a nice plant to grow around larger herbs.

13. Mint

    Many variations are available. Peppermint, orange mint, chocolate mint and others. Find a mint which meets your needs and plant it in a corner or place where it does not crowd out other herbs.

14. Oregano

    One of my top seven or eight go-to fresh herbs. Goes well with Mediterranean, Italian, Indian and other cuisines. Add to soups, sauces and salads. Once established it is a lovely perennial addition to any herb garden.

15. Parsley

    Several varieties of parsley include flat leaf and curly parsley. Parsley does not have a strong smell or flavor but is full of nutrients. Parsley is also good for including in mild detoxes. Plant several parsley plants for a continuous supply of fresh parsley all summer long.

16. Rosemary

    Rosemary scent is associated with improved memory and recall. This alone is a great reason to plant in your herb garden. Several rosemary cultivars are known to grow in the US. Certain ones produce small blue flowers and others do not usually bloom. Rosemary is added to soups, sauces, entrees, and many other dishes. Plant several different types of rosemary in your herb garden and enjoy the lovely scent.

17. Sage

    Numerous types of sage plants exist. They grow well in Mediterranean type regions but are adapted to most regions of North America. Sage leaves make a lovely tea and are great added to savory dishes.

18. Savory

    A small delicate looking bushy herb which produces small lilac colored flowers in summer. It is one of the herbs found in Herbs de Provence mixture.

19. Tarragon

    A perennial sweet, slightly bitter herb used by chefs. Several versions include French, Russian, Mexican and Texas tarragon. It is one of four herbs found in fines herbes a mixture of used to flavor fish dishes, soups, sauces, entrees, etc.

20. **Thyme**

   An aromatic perennial herb used to flavor soups and sauces. A low-growing herb which usually graces every herb garden. It makes a beautiful garnish as well as an addition to soups and sauces.

   Notes: _____

Non-essential herbs which are also nice to grow if space allows:

- **Anise** – Flowering plant lending the flavor similar to star anise, fennel and licorice.
- **Bee balm** – Also known as wild bergamot and known for its pretty flowers. Used medicinally.
- **Borage** – This is a lovely plant with soft hairy spines and deep purple or white blooms. They can grow quite large and in many locations such as North Texas, are considered wild.
- **Caraway** – Pretty flowering plant whose seeds are used to flavor Mediterranean, Indian and Middle east dishes.
- **Comfrey** – easily grown and is used externally for some issues.
- **Curry plant** – other than its name, this plant has nothing to do with curry powder or turmeric. It belongs to the *Helichrysum Italicum* genus and species. It has an intense fragrance produces small yellow flowers. It is used to extract the essential oil, Helichrysum.
- **Eucalyptus** – One year I picked up a "Eucalyptus" herb at a Mennonite farm in Tennessee. It had elongated leaves and did not resemble the traditional eucalyptus tree. It was a lovely herb and I wish I could find it again.
- **Garlic scapes** – Scapes are the long green shoots that grow from hardneck garlic bulbs. They are used in a wide range of dishes to lend a subtle garlic flavor and they make a great pesto.
- **Ginger** (*Zingiber officinale*; root rhizome) – the root is widely used as a spice and also as a folk medicine.
- **Lemongrass** – Lemongrass is a stand-out herb. It is a grass and grows to be almost 3 feet tall and spreads out to 3 feet. Be sure to give it plenty of room to grow when placing lemongrass in your herb garden. Could also be planted as an ornamental landscaping plant around your home.
- **Lovage** – Lovage is an unusual plant, with leaves growing off a main stalk. The leaves, stem and roots are edible. It produces small yellow flowers.
- **Paprika** – dried red bell peppers, Aleppo, and any mild red pepper can be dried and ground into a culinary powder.
- **Pineapple sage** – plant for the lovely fragrance and the pollinators.
- **Red pepper flakes** – Any hot pepper such as cayenne and jalapeno, contain pepper seeds. Dry long, thin-walled cayenne peppers, remove the seeds and using an herb grinder, grind the dried flesh of the cayenne pepers and add to the dried seeds. Use as red pepper flakes.
- **Telegraph plant** – leaves move and respond to light. It's a fun plant to grow and children love it.
- **Turmeric root** – grow your own fresh turmeric root to make juices, curries, etc.

Notes: _____

Bible verses about herbs and beautiful gardens

Genesis 1:29-31, 3:21, 9:3; Exodus 30:34; Esther 1:5, 7:7; 2 Kings 25:4; Song of Solomon 4:12-16, 5:11-13, 6:11, 8:13; Proverbs 15:17; Psalm 51:7; Ecclesiastes 11:5; Nehemiah 3:15; Ezekiel 4:9; Jeremiah 29:5, 28, 39:4, 52:7; Amos 9:15; Matthew 26:36-46; John 18:1-2, 19:41, 20:15; Revelation 21:1, 22:2

Chapter 64
Flower gardens

Flowers serve to point us to the Creator, who gives us an endless variety of colors, shapes, and scents for our enjoyment. Many flowers are functional because their blossom precedes the formation of a fruit or vegetable. Pineapples are a great example of how a flower becomes a fruit. Over the course of about a year, multiple flowers fuse together to form a pineapple. Botanically speaking, if a plant flowers, it is considered a fruit. This would make tomatoes and zucchini a fruit and not a vegetable. However, most of us go by the common culinary distinction of fruits and vegetables. While some flowers are functional, others are just beautiful and meant for our pleasure.

A young pineapple in flower.
Wikipedia (2020).

What you may not know is there are unproven and even proven health benefits to gardening and having flowers in your life. **Women oftentimes associate positive memories with the men who bring them flowers over the ones who fail to do so.** Some of the potential benefits of flowers include:

- Demonstrating your romantic intentions.
- Affirming romantic relationships.
- Flower therapy. Flowers can heal you. Their presence in a room may speed up healing and recovery (could be psychological or physical phenomenon).
- Improved memory and recall.
- Improved formation of new memories.
- Improved concentration.
- Improved mood.
- Helps with relaxation; reduces stress.
- Flower gardening puts us directly in touch with the benefits of the earth including electron transfer and even the earth's magnetic field.
- Gardening and planting flowers demonstrate our obedience to the command to have dominion over earth by caring and tending for God's creation.
- May improve sleep.
- May improve productivity.
- Chemicals in flowers may have positive effects on health parameters such as lowering blood pressure and cholesterol levels.
- Flowers add a gourmet touch to scones, desserts, beverages, salads, sandwiches, etc.
- Edible flowers can be added to tea for extra interest and nutrition.
- We show others we care about them by giving them flowers on their birthday, anniversary, new job, new baby, and even at the death of a loved one.

Many flowers are famous for their unique chemical cocktail of scents. The first scents I can remember are from the magnolia, gardenia and rose. These flowers grew in our yard and even today, when I smell these flowers, they invoke powerful childhood memories. The heady fragrance of orange groves in bloom reminds me of living in Southern California. I could never get enough of their scent and nothing compares to the real blossom.

Flowers produce unique mixtures of chemicals responsible for their lovely fragrance. Over 1,700 different scent compounds have been identified in flowers. These heady flower scents draw insect and bird pollinators to their nectar while sometimes their chemicals are meant to repel predators. Nevertheless, once the flower has been pollinated, a hormone is produced inside the bloom which inhibits another chemical, methyl-benzoate, responsible for producing the scent. This in turn makes the flower less desirable for pollinators.

Scents are combinations of terpenes and other types of chemicals. Each flower scent has a unique fingerprint, including a vibration or frequency (hertz or Hz). Scientists have identified over 400 chemicals from over 150 rose species which lend roses their distinctive fragrance. Roses have the highest known vibrational frequency of any flower, resonating at 320 Mhz. Rose oil and extracts are used for formulating soaps, lotions, perfumes, etc. Only the Idaho Blue Spruce, a fragrant tree, has a higher resonance, coming in at 580 MHz.

For millennia, chemists have combined various scents to make emotion-evoking scents. Some perfumes sell for thousands of dollars per ounce. Chanel Grand Extrait sells for $4,200 (2020) for one ounce. However, this Chanel fragrance is not the most expensive perfume. DKNY combined their perfume with a container studded with 2,909 precious stones which sells for $1,000,000.00 (luxhabitat.ae). Some scents are so rare it takes up to a ton of the fresh flowers to extract their powerful scented oils. Today many perfumes are made from synthetic chemicals but it is the natural fragrances which are the most in demand and command the highest prices.

Christians may see the most expensive perfume as the one Mary used to anoint Jesus' feet two days before the Passover and the Feast of Unleavened Bread. His death and resurrection were imminent. **John 12:3** reads, "Then took Mary a pound of ointment of spikenard, very costly, and anointed the feet of Jesus, and wiped his feet with her hair: and the house was filled with the odor of the ointment." The cost of the oil was equivalent to two years of wages. Judas Iscariot, observing her benevolent act toward Jesus, was quick to criticize her for "wasting" the oil on Jesus' feet and not selling it and giving the money to the poor. Judas feigned concern for the poor to make himself look better in the eyes of the men present. However, he failed to see the beauty in the act itself. Just a few days later, Jesus would wrap a towel around his waist and wash his disciples' feet, including Judas Iscariot's feet. Judas' eyes only saw dollar (i.e., denarii) signs and not a loving and devoted act of humility and affection. However, in verse 7,

Christ quickly defends Mary saying to Judas, "Leave her alone, she was intended to keep this perfume to prepare for the day of My burial. The poor you will always have with you, but you will not always have Me." In case you are wondering, spikenard is a flowering plant from the valerian family. It grows in the Himalayas, China and India. Mary purchased this and is inspired to anoint the feet of Jesus, even though she knew she would be criticized. How many would be willing to give Jesus 1 to 2 years of our wages to publicly anoint his feet? Table 1, provides Bible verses mentioning flowers and how they were made for our pleasure and enjoyment.

Flower preferences are personal. I am partial to the flowers I saw growing in my grandmother's flower beds. She lived in Mt. Pleasant, Texas, a small town in East Texas. Every summer, the local flower club had weekly flower arranging competitions. She brought home many blue and red ribbons over the years. She preferred unusual, asymmetrical arrangements which included things such as tree twigs, bark, vegetable plants, and anything she saw on her small farm that would fit in a vase. During the summer she would round up several tumbleweeds and keep them in the barn until Christmas time. She decorated them with sugared gummy candies and small twinkling lights. We eagerly anticipated seeing the tumbleweed tree, as well as her other trees and decorations.

Some flowers serve a dual purpose – they are great for cut flower arrangements and they have medicinal value. Agastache, alliums, amaranthus, angelica, begonia, bergamot, black cohosh, blood root, butterfly weed, calendula, California poppy, carnation, chrysanthemum, corn flower, daisy, dandelion, echinacea, foxglove, gardenia, hibiscus, honeysuckle, hyssop, jasmine, lavender, lilac, lobelia, lotus, mallow, nasturtium, peony, pineapple sage, plum flowers, roses, snapdragon, sunflower, thistle, yarrow and others are just a few examples of flowers which are beautiful (visual therapy) and have fragrant (olfactory) benefits, medicinal and / or nutritional value. Maybe you have used Bach flower therapy, flower essences combined into a homeopathic preparation and used to address emotional suffering.

Many flowers are edible. Adding flowers to a salad, dessert, beverage or even an entrée adds interest and flavor. Most flowers are not strongly flavored. They tend to taste similar to how they smell. Table 2 provides a list of edible flowers.

Safety is a primary consideration. To be on the safe side, only use flowers from an organic source or a flower bed which has not been sprayed with herbicides, fungicides and / or insecticides. If you have hay fever, asthma or allergies, it is advisable to avoid eating edible flowers. When picking a flower to use fresh or in cooking, be sure to thoroughly clean it and check for small pests. It is important to positively identify all wild flowers and plants before you prepare to eat them. If you have never eaten a certain flower, take a small bite and wait for 30 minutes. If your stomach has not rebelled, then eat a slightly larger amount and wait another 30 minutes. If no signs of upset, then probably a small amount of the flower is edible and not toxic. Keep in mind, in all cases, the dose makes the poison. Even water is toxic if you consume enough. Another caution to note is, just because the flower is edible does not mean the rest of the plant is edible. Just because one person can eat a wild plant does not mean another person or child will tolerate it. Leaves, seeds, bark, stems and roots need to be independently confirmed as edible before consuming. Another concern is that some edible flowers such as Queen Anne's Lace looks very similar to poisonous Hemlock. **This would be a tragic mistake to make.** If in doubt, leave it out! When it comes to small children, only let them eat a few common flowers such as rose petals, violets or squash blossoms. They should be educated to identify the edible flowers and to always consult their parents first before eating wild flowers.

The most poisonous flower in North America is the oleander flower, which is a common flowering bush frequently seen in the southern states. It is found in back yards, along the roadside, office landscaping and in the wild. If children are encouraged to eat flowers they may not discriminate and might consume a potentially deadly flower such as the oleander flower.

When it comes to the most poisonous plant in North America, it is water hemlock. A hint that a plant might be dangerous is the slight smell of almonds. This indicates the plant may contain the toxin, cyanide. Again, collecting and eating wild edible plants should be done alongside people familiar with edible plants and an edible plant reference book with pictures and with people who can identify harmful and deadly plants. Otherwise, stick to known edible plants you can retrieve from your local market.

A lovely bush is the old-fashioned bridal wreath spirea. It is a shrub that reaches almost 8 feet high and is covered in white flowers. Because of its spiny stems, it also makes a great addition to a privacy hedge and butterflies love it.

The flower list in Table 3 is limited to my favorites and includes either flowers I have grown or am planning to grow. Most of the flowers on my favorites list make great cut flowers in combination with others or they can stand alone. When arranging cut flowers, I like to add twigs, pine cones, grasses, and fresh herbs if they are available such as thyme, basil, rosemary, etc. Flower beds can take various shapes and sizes. Plan several flower beds to accent your yard. I like to have a rose bed, with various types of roses, a zinnia and snap dragon bed, a cacti bed, and bed for planting various bulbs such as dahlias, lilies, canna, etc. Bougainvillea was a staple in my yard while living in Southern California, but it does not survive colder climates. Look at Pinterest and various flower catalogs to identify which flowers appeal to you.

Planting a beautiful flower garden reminds us one day we will occupy a beautiful heavenly garden. This garden will be a joy to tend. There will be an infinite variety of beautiful flowers to enjoy and experience. Plant a colorful flower bed and enjoy the many benefits of having cut flower arrangements, beautiful scents wafting through your home and even take advantage of having a few edible flowers with a meal.

Flower Gardens Table 1. Bible verses mentioning flowers

Genesis 1:12	Song of Solomon 2:1-2, 12	Isaiah 40:6 – 8
Exodus 25:31-36	Song of Solomon 4:16	Hosea 14:4-7
Numbers 17:8	Song of Solomon 5:13	Matthew 6:28-30
1 Kings 6:18	Song of Solomon 6:2	Luke 12:27-2
Psalm 103:15-16	Isaiah 35:1-2	

Flower Gardens Table 2. Edible flowers*

- Agastache
- Allium blossoms
- Angelica
- Apple blossoms
- Arugula flowers
- Banana blossoms
- Basil flowers
- Bachelor's buttons
- Bee balm
- Begonia
- Bergamot
- Blue porterweed
- Borage
- Butterfly pea flowers
- Calendula
- Camelia
- Carnation petals
- Chamomile
- Cherry blossom
- Chervil flowers
- Chive blossoms
- Chrysanthemum
- Cilantro flowers
- Citrus blossoms
- Clover
- Corn flower
- Cosmos sulphureus
- Dahlia
- Dandelion
- Day lily
- Dianthus (fringed)
- Dill
- Elderflower
- English daisy
- Fuchsia
- Gardenia
- Garlic mustard
- Ginger flowers
- Gladiolus
- Hibiscus
- Hollyhock
- Honeysuckle
- Hyssop
- Impatiens
- Jasmine
- Johnny jump up
- Kale blossoms
- Lavender
- Lemon verbena
- Linden flowers
- Lilac
- Magnolia
- Marigold
- Marjoram flowers
- Nasturtium
- Okra flowers
- Orchid
- Pak choy flowers
- Pansy
- Passion fruit flowers**
- Pea flowers/tendrils (edible peas)
- Peanut flowers (perennial)
- Peony
- Phlox (perennial)
- Pineapple guava
- Pineapple sage
- Pomegranate flowers
- Prickly pear cactus flowers
- Primrose
- Pumpkin blossoms
- Purslane
- Queen Anne's lace *(looks similar to poisonous hemlock)*
- Quince flower
- Radish blossoms
- Redbud tree flowers
- Rose
- Rose of Sharon
- Rosemary flowers
- Safflower
- Sage flowers
- Savory flowers
- Scarlet runner bean flowers
- Scented geraniums
- Snapdragon
- Squash blossoms
- Spiderwort
- Strawberry blossoms
- Stock
- Sunflower
- Sweet olive flowers
- Sweet woodruff
- Tulip petals
- Violet
- Wapato
- Water lily
- Yucca flower petals *(not Y. filamentosa)*
- Violet
- Zinnia petals
- Zucchini blossoms

*INDEPENDENTLY CONFIRM EDIBILITY OF ALL FLOWERS ON THIS LIST. Be sure to thoroughly clean and remove dirt and debris. Avoid using flowers which have been sprayed with herbicides or pesticides.

**Avoid consuming large amounts.\

Flower Gardens Table 3. My favorite flowers

African violets	Delphiniums	Mallow
Agapanthus	Echinacea	Nasturtiums
Agastache	English daisy	Orchids
Alliums	Floss flowers	Pansy
Alyssum	Foxglove	Pelargonium (geranium)
Amaranthus	Fuschia	Peony
Amaryllis	Gardenias	Plumeria
Begonia	Geraniums	Poinsettia
Blue bonnets	Ginger	Poppies
Borage	Gladiolus	Protea
Bougainvillea	Hibiscus	Queen Anne's lace
Bromeliads	Hollyhock	Ranunculus
Butterfly bush	Honeysuckle	Rose
Cacti, flowering	Hydrangea	Runner bean
Calendula (pot marigold)	Indian paintbrush	Snapdragon
Canna	Irises	Staghorn fern
Cardoon	Jasmine	Succulents
Chrysanthemum	Larkspur	Sunflower
Clematis	Lavender	Sweet peas
Cockscomb	Lilac	Thistle
Coleus	Lilys	Veronica (Speedwells)
Coral bells	Lobelia	Yarrow
Cyclamen	Lotus pods	Water lily
Dahlia	Lupine	Wisteria
Day lily	Magnolia	Zinnia

Discussion questions

1. Why did God make flowers?
2. Is it possible the chemical profile in spikenard oil had a therapeutic effect on Jesus?
3. What do flowers symbolize and what do the different colors represent?
4. Are flowers also functional?
5. What are the occasions we send flowers and why do we send flowers?
6. Are flowers essential?
7. How do you think Adam and Eve felt after when they saw the first flower wilt and die?
8. What are your favorite flowers and why?
9. What effect do scents have on your mood?

Chapter 65
Orchards

Landscaping is a part of every home, office building, mall, campus, etc. Landscaping includes flower beds, bushes, trees and other accents. **In a world where food security is not universal, it is useful to consider planting edible plants, bushes, vines and trees in your landscaping projects.** Even planting an orchard of fruit or nut bearing trees as part of a landscaping plan, provides a yearly harvest of valuable fruit or nuts for employees and visitors. It also conveys environmental bona fides to those concerned about preserving the original intention of the earth – bringing forth fruit! Fruit- and nut-bearing trees produce hundreds of beautiful flowers and then go on to produce their fruits or nuts. Planting edible landscaping plants makes sense. Trees, vines, and plants provide food and beauty. **Edible landscapes make food for both humans and wild animals. How wonderful it is to provide for the wild animals. This sounds like a lovely dominion over the animals described in the first few chapters of Genesis.**

Some great landscaping plants, vines and trees include: alliums, amaranth, artichokes, basil, bay laurel tree, beets, blueberries, cardoon, cherry or currant tomatoes, chives, dill, eggplant, elderberries, fennel, fig, garlic, grapes, hyssop, kale, lavender, leeks, lettuces, onions, orach, peppers, potatoes, rhubarb, runner beans, sage, sorrel, Swiss chard, dwarf and regular size fruit trees, persimmon trees, loquat and kumquat trees, etc. If you want to see examples of beautiful edible plants, the Baker Creek Heirloom Seeds webpage, www.rareseeds.com, provides some of the best pictures of these plants. I do not have any kind of beneficial relationship with Baker Creek, but have over many decades appreciated their high-quality seeds and commitment to excellence.

Orchards are a great way to grow large amounts of fresh fruits or nuts. An orchard is generally a grouping of 5 or more of the same types of fruit- or nut-producing trees. Orchards may include 150 trees per acre up to 9,000 trees per acre. Orchards usually require a significant investment and most require ongoing upkeep. Consider this before you plant an orchard. Orchards require planting, watering, pruning, cross pollination in some cases (for female and male trees), propagation, fertilizing, pesticide control, etc. These tasks must be done every year or the orchard may fail to bear quality fruit.

An orchard can be a grouping of bushes, dwarf trees, espaliers, potted trees, or trees in the ground. It is not the same as a vineyard, which is a grouping of vines. Trees are usually spaced 10 to 12 feet apart and rows are 15 feet apart. Some nut trees such as pecan and walnut, need more space. Most small farm orchards are around 10+/- acres, but this is only a general guideline. This may represent the maximum size a single family can manage, without dedicating a significant amount of time and money into managing the orchard. Measure the land where you want to plant the orchard. Draw the area to scale and see how many trees can be planted in the available space.

If you have not heard of the Blueprint Method for planting trees, it is advisable to study this method. This method is not quick and easy but if you follow the blueprint method you will be more than rewarded with robust and healthy trees. There are excellent resources found on the internet and listed below. But in case you do not have access to the internet the following is a brief summary of how to use this method for planting trees (www.timeandbeing.com/application/CountryLiving/EGWTreePlanting.pdf, and https://www.azurefarmlife.com/farm-blog/tag/planting+by+the+blueprint). This method has been written out by master gardener Lynn Hoag (see the first video resource listed below). This webpage (see above) has visuals of the process. You need the following materials: 1 tree, a large tin can, 6 cubic feet of compost, 6 cubic feet of leaf mold and gopher wire.

1. Dig a 3' x 3' x 3' hole, setting the top soil to one side and the sub soil to another pile.
2. Mix the soils. Mix the top soil with compost, 20 lb soft rock phosphate, leaf mold and 4 cups of gypsum (in dry areas) or 4 cups of dolomite (in wet areas).
3. Put a 4-inch "breather" pipe in bottom of the hole, surrounded on bottom and ends by small rocks.
4. Fill the bottom third of the hole with the mixed soils and compact it by walking on it. You need about 3 cubic feet of topsoil, 3 cubic feet of compost and 3 cubic feet of leaf mulch and half the contents of the soil mixture.
5. Place a layer of rock on top of the soil. At this point you may wish to install gopher wire to prevent gophers from digging from under the newly planted tree and eating the tender roots.
6. Fill the next third of the hole with just top soil.
7. Now it is time to plant the tree. Prune any broken roots. Keep roots moist at all times before planting.
8. Fill remainder of the hole with the rich soil mixture. If available, add some earthworms to this layer.
9. Place 1 - 3 inches of compost mulch around the tree.
10. Place protection around the tree trunk (tin can cut to fit).
11. Place 2 to 3 inches of leaf mulch on top of the compost.
12. Create a small berm around the tree to hold in water and fertilizer. Deeply water and watch it grow!
13. Additional instruction on this method found here:
14. Lynn Hoag video: https://www.youtube.com/watch?v=zRGmBBn3s_o
    https://www.azurefarmlife.com/farm-blog/tag/planting+by+the+blueprint
    https://www.youtube.com/watch?v=dUaviX9xuwo;
    https://www.youtube.com/watch?v=bJUadb3UYK4;

Depending on the type, orchards may not bear fruit for 3 to 7 years. This means you may be tending to the orchard long before it begins providing a harvest and an income. Contact your local agricultural extension office to research which varieties grow best in your area. Some trees are self-fertile and others are not. **Orchard management includes selecting varieties, planting, replanting, fighting off pests and diseases, fertilizing, protecting from wildlife, protecting from weather, thinning fruit, harvesting, washing and polishing fruit, finding buyers, selling the produce, transporting produce, hiring and training labor, upkeep of equipment and machinery, pruning trees, etc.** These activities may be manageable with several trees but a 20-acre orchardis an entirely different challenge.

Pollination strategies must be in place for an orchard. Planting ornamental crab apple trees has been beneficial for some. Also planting comfrey plants and other types of pollinators in or around your orchard can improve pollination and yields. This will provide a food for pollinators as well as send deep roots into the soil. It can be harvested / cut down several times a year and will grow back. Another pollination strategy is keeping a colony of bees near the orchard. This ensures you will always have pollinators on your property.

A watering method is essential, especially for larger orchards. Methods include sprinklers, sprayers, trickle irrigation, impact, overhead, flood, surface vs subsurface systems, etc. Ensure you have a proper watering method in mind before you proceed with planting an orchard.

Identify a section of your property to devote to an orchard. You can start small and expand as you have time and resources. A mixed orchard includes more than one type of tree. Groupings of 5 or more such as apple, pear, peach, plum, pomegranate, fuyu persimmon, kumquat, fig and pecan trees, provide you with several small orchards capable of feeding your family and providing extra produce for selling at a roadside stand or farmer's market. Once established, an orchard provides years of food and enjoyment.

Table 1 Types of orchards	
Almond	Mulberry
Apple	Olive
Apricot	Orange
Avocado	Papaya
Cherry	Peach
Date	Pear
Fig	Pecan
Grapefruit	Persimmon
Hazelnut	Pistachio
Kumquat	Plum
Lemon	Pomegranate
Lime	Tangelo
Loquat	Tangerine
Mandarin	Walnut

Bible verses: Genesis 1:11-12; Genesis 13:18; Exodus 37:1-5; Deuteronomy 20:19; Joshua 24:26; Judges 9:9; 1 Kings 10:11-12; Psalm 1:3; Psalm 52:8; Isaiah 6:13; Isaiah 41:19-20; Isaiah 60:13; Isaiah 65:22Ezekiel 17:5-6; Jeremiah 1:11-12; Amos 7:14; Acts 5:30; Romans 11:24; Revelation 22:1-4, 14

Resources
- Transforming this land into a home orchard. Simple Living Alaska. https://www.youtube.com/watch?v=69V-l3izyyU
- https://www.youtube.com/watch?v=3gCrf6oGa4M – grafting video
- http://www.timeandbeing.com/application/CountryLiving/EGWTreePlanting.pdf
- The blueprint planting method: https://irp-cdn.multiscreensite.com/78bb8ef4/files/uploaded/Gl2M56X2S7GZwW5AumDq_Ellen%20G.%20White%20Tree%20Planting%20Method_NEW.pdf

Discussion questions

1. Read Ecclesiastes 2:1-6. What do these verses tell us about planting vineyards and orchards?
2. What does the Bible say about the type of fruit the Tree of Life produces?
3. What do trees in the Bible represent?

Chapter 66
The vineyard

Vineyards evoke a picture of gently rolling hills with neat rows of vines stretching into the distance. Vineyards remind me of Tuscany, Italy and Northern California. But Northern California has recently had to share its reputation for beautiful vineyards with almost every other state in the US, including Illinois, Michigan, New York, North Carolina, Oregon, Pennsylvania, Texas, Virginia, and Washington leading the pack.

Vineyards are not exclusive to grapes. Other types of atypical vineyards include aloe vera, dragon fruit, kiwi, muscadines, passion fruit, and scuppernongs. Each one of these plants is unique and provides a potential income stream within the first year or two. While grape vineyards have become common-place, other types of vineyards are more unique. These types of vineyards are a welcome addition to small farms and the communities they serve.

Aloe vera farms are popping up in many southern states. They are used to grow aloe vera for commercial purposes. These plants do not need a lot of water and they grow with very little labor and investment compared to other types of vineyards. Aloe vera contains unique carbohydrates and phytochemicals.

Vineyards do not necessarily translate into a winery. Most people consume whole grapes and not processed grapes as juice or wine. In the USA, several varieties of grapes dominate the market. Black grape varieties include blue / black seedless, ribier, exotic, niabell, fantasy / marroo, and others. Red grapes include red seedless, flame / ruby / emperatriz, crimson, and others. Green grapes include perlette, Thompson, sugarone, autumn, and green seeded. Muscat grapes, red globe grapes, concord grapes, and champagne grapes round out the list of common grape varieties in the USA. However, there are hundreds of grape varieties, each with a slightly different flavor profile.

Grapes around the world provide a dizzying array of flavors. Some taste like candy, while others have a flower-like flavor. Their flavor components, embedded in their cool, succulent flesh, contribute to the unique flavor profile of each variety. Each part of the grape, including the skin and the different sections of flesh (i.e., the central, intermediate and peripheral zones), provide a slightly different nutrient and flavor profile. The skin and seeds contain compounds not found in the flesh. There are variable levels of sugars found in grapes, which depend on picking time, maturity level, storage time, etc.

Naturally occurring phytochemicals in grapes include flavonoids such as catechins, epi-catechins, procyanidins, quercetin, and petunidin. Phenolic acids include coumaric acid, caffeic acid, ferulic acid and gallic acid. Stilbenes in grapes include resveratrol, piceatannol and pterostilbene. Carotenoids, anthocyanidins and other plant-based pigments give grapes their unique color.

Grapes have been consumed for millennia. Grapes are mentioned more than any other fruit in the Bible. Experts have touted the health benefits of 5 to 9 servings daily of fruits and vegetables; grapes are a great way to eat fruit.

Some experts recommend consuming 1 to 2 glasses of wine for heart health benefits. However, today's wine is vastly different from wine in Biblical times. In fact, some Biblical experts differentiate the term "new wine" to refer to the freshly squeezed grape juice and not it's fermented counterpart.

The Bible describes wine: "Wine is a mocker and strong drink is raging: and whosoever is deceived is thereby not wise" Proverbs 20:1.

Biblical texts warn against the dangers of alcohol including the following passages. "Be not winebibbers, or among gluttonous eaters of meat" **Proverbs 23:20**. "And the Lord spake unto Aaron, saying, Do not drink wine nor strong drink, thou, not thy sons with thee, when ye go into the tabernacle of the congregation, lest ye die: it shall be a statute forever throughout your generations: and that ye may put difference between holy and unholy, and between unclean and clean; and that ye may teach the children of Israel all the statutes which the Lord hath spoken unto them by the hand of Moses. **Leviticus 10:8-11**. "They shall not drink wine with a song; strong drink shall be bitter to them that drink it" **Isaiah 24:9**. "Do you not know that the unrighteous will not inherit the kingdom of God? Do not be deceived; neither the immoral, nor idolators, nor adulterers, nor sexual perverts, nor thieves, nor the greedy, nor drunkards, nor revilers, nor robbers will inherit the kingdom of God" **1 Corinthians 6:9-10** (NRSV).

Jeremiah 35 describes the Rechabites, descendants of Rechab. He commanded his family to abstain from drinking wine, not to build houses, not to plant vineyards, and to dwell in tents for their entire lives. For 300 years, the Rechabites were known for their fidelity to these commands. However, when Nebuchadnezzar besieged Jerusalem, the Rechabites living in the countryside just outside of Jerusalem, were forced to move into the city, although they still lived in tents. It was during this time, they were invited to the temple and offered wine, but they refused to drink it, remaining faithful to Rechab's commands. **It was a reproof to the Jews and evidence that abstaining from alcohol can be an acceptable lifestyle choice.** "And Jeremiah said unto the house of the Rechabites, Thus saith the Lord of hosts, the God of Israel; because ye have obeyed the commandment of Jonadab your father, and kept all his precepts, and done according unto all that he hath commanded you: therefore, thus saith the Lord of hosts, the God of Israel; Jonadab the son of Rechab shall not want a man to stand before me for ever" **Jeremiah 35:18-19**. To this day, there are nomadic tribes in the Middle East who claim to be the descendants of the Rechabites and refrain from drinking alcohol.

There are a few things you should know about wine and why it might not be the healthiest adult beverage. Most wine contains toxins just like most other processed foods contain variable amounts of toxins. The issue with wine is the labeling. The only nutrition-related information required on a wine label is the percent of alcohol and the presence of sulfites. Most modern vineyards also spray the vines and surrounding area with pesticides, herbicides, fungicides, and chemical fertilizers; these chemicals are not mentioned or required to be on the label.

Chemicals found in wine could include the weed killer Roundup (glyphosate is the active ingredient). It is not sprayed directly on the vines but is sprayed on the ground and surrounding areas. Some research has associated this chemical with some forms of cancer and Parkinson's disease. The International Agency for Research on Cancer (IARC) has categorized glyphosate as a probable human carcinogen (2015), but the USA-based EPA has not agreed with this classification and consider glyphosate to be non-toxic to the nervous and immune systems, although children may be more sensitive. It has also been shown to perturb honey bees, a major contributor to pollination of many crops. It has been approved for use in the USA since 1974 under the trade name, Roundup (manufactured by Monsanto). Recently (2019), EcoWatch tested wine and beer for glyphosate contamination and 19 out of 20 test products contained glyphosate, including organic beverages. Levels detected were below EPA risk standards but studies have shown even very low amounts of glyphosate are associated with interrupting the endocrine system and stimulating the growth of certain types of cancer. Testing has even found glyphosate in pharmaceutical testosterone preparations using soy oil as a base. Even small amounts can add up with additional exposures found in common household foods, animal products, general anesthetics such as soy-based propofol, pharmaceuticals, etc. According to the National Pesticide Information Center (www.npic.orst.edu), glyphosate is found in over 750 products. This number increases every year. A recent report published by Food Democracy Now! And the Detox Project, Glyphosate: Unsafe on any plate, found alarming levels of Monsanto's glyphosate in hundreds of commonly consumed foods, including almost all commercial oat products except for the Whole Foods 365 Oats. General Mill's Cheerios, with one of the highest amounts of glyphosate of any cereal, checks in with around 1,125.3 ppb. Just 0.1 ppb glyphosate altered the gene function of over 4,000 genes in the livers and kidneys of rats. The permitted level of glyphosate in tap water in the European Union is 0.1 ppb compared to 700 ppb in the USA.

When it comes to wine labels, the FDA requires 9 pieces of information: brand name, name and address of grower, varietal designation, name of origin, alcohol content, vintage date, net volume, sulfite declaration, and a health warning. Wine producers may add up to 76 FDA-approved additives, (only 38 of which are generally recognized as safe (GRAS) by the FDA), without disclosing their presence on their label. These chemicals include purple and red dyes, sugar, sulfur dioxide, dimethyl decarbonate, fish bladders, commercial yeast, acetaldehyde, albumin (from egg white), ammonium phosphate, ascorbic acid, defoaming agents (poly-oxyethylene 40 monostearate, silicon dioxide, dimethyl-poly-siloxane, sorbitan monostearate, glyceryl mono-oleate and glyceryl di-oleate), gelatin, milk, oak chips / particles, soy flour, tartaric acid, cork, etc.

It is not necessary to consume wine to get the benefits attributed to consuming wine. **You can get the same benefits of wine from consuming fresh whole grapes and grape juice, especially freshly squeezed grape juice.** Grape juice contains antioxidants, flavonoids, and many other amazing phytochemicals associated with reduced risk of heart disease. Researchers at the University of Wisconsin in Madison (1999), asked people with coronary artery disease (CAD) to drink grape juice every day for 2 weeks. After the experimental period, blood tests showed improved oxidation of LDL (bad cholesterol) and improved arterial blood flow compared to their baseline levels. A recent study including almost 400,000 participants (Biddinger KJ, Emdin CA, Haas ME, et al., Association of habitual alcohol intake with risk of cardiovascular disease, in Cardiology, 25 March 2022), showed alcohol consumption at all levels is associated with risk of cardiovascular disease. There is added risk even at alcohol consumption levels considered to be acceptable consumption amounts.

To make wine, grapes are fermented to produce alcohol. When alcohol (i.e., ethanol) is consumed, it breaks down in the body to acetaldehyde, a toxin known to damage DNA. As with almost any substance, the dose or the amount consumed is what makes the toxin. But even at lower consumption levels, alcohol is associated with increased risk for breast and bowel cancers. Liver disease is positively associated with alcohol intake. There seems to be an alcohol consumption threshold, which when exceeded, leads to permanent liver damage. The impact on society, families and employment is huge. **Oftentimes, alcohol addiction splits up families, wreaks havoc on mental health, and causes loss of income due to frequently changing jobs and job loss.**

In a recent publication by the NY Times, an article "Moderate drinking has no health benefits, analysis of decades of research finds" (based on a meta analyses published on 23 March 2023 publication by the Journal of the American Medical Association, *AMA Netw Open.* 2023;6(3):e236185. doi:10.1001/jamanetworkopen.2023.6185) the concept of benefits associated with 'moderate drinking' have been overstated. According to the article, most studies showing a benefit with moderate drinking were observational and not able to prove cause and effect. These same studies failed to account for healthy habits and other protective factors of study participants. In fact, the meta analysis, re-examining the findings of over 4 million study participants, found elevated risks for former drinkers above those of lifetime abstainers and female drinkers have greater all cause mortality risk compared to male drinkers but especially when drinking 25 or more grams of ethanol per day. "There is significantly increased risk of all cause mortality among female drinkers who drank 25 or more grams per day and among male drinkers who drank 45 or more grams per day." Translated, this means, "low volume alcohol drinking is not associated with protection against death from all causes," which was for many decades thought to be true and has influenced the habits of millions of people not only in the USA but internationally as well.

Regular alcohol consumption may be associated with Wernicke-Korsakoff's syndrome. Wernicke is associated with encephalopathy – a condition that goes along with alcoholism and poor intake of B vitamins, specifically Thiamin. Wernicke is also associated with malnutrition and alcoholism. Korsakoff syndrome is due to alcoholism. Wikipedia states: "This neurological disorder is caused by a lack of thiamin in the brain and is exacerbated by the neurotoxic effects of alcohol." (accessed on 10 Mar 2021). Other problematic behaviors associated with alcoholics include: confabulation (chronic lying), short-sightedness, memory loss, blackouts, etc.

Alcohol is known to exert negative effects on frontal lobe functions. Alcohol causes physical changes to the frontal lobes, including decreased utilization of glucose (the primary fuel in the brain) and reduced cerebral blood flow. Alcohol related damage to the brain is not limited to the frontal lobes. It damages neurotransmitters and contracts brain tissue. Alcohol related effects include poor short-term memory, lack of creative thinking, neutered emotions and hyper-emotional behaviors, decreased attention span, impulsivity, disinhibition, poor motivation, issues with problem solving, etc. Most of these alcohol-related behaviors are consistent with damage to the frontal lobes.
https://doi.org/10.1093/alcalc/36.5.357

The safe amount of alcohol consumption is zero. If you choose to drink wine, most health experts recommend low alcohol wines over regular ones. Another common wine ingredient is sugar. Wine manufacturers are not required to list the amount of added sugar.

In some cases, wine can be a significant source of sugar. Studies have shown that food products with the highest sugar content sell better than similar products with less added sugar or no added sugar, making sugar a critical ingredient for selling their product. Evidence suggest women are more likely to crave sweets compared to men. This may also translate to women's preferences for sweeter alcoholic beverages, including sweeter wines.

Sulfites are almost always added to preserve flavor. Some people are sensitive to sulfites and end up with various symptoms such as a rash, flushing, dizziness, abdominal cramping, diarrhea, etc. Sometimes symptoms are progressive and may lead to life-threatening conditions such as an asthmatic reaction and even anaphylactic shock. You may tolerate sulfites one day and a week later, have a reaction to consuming them.

Alcohol generates free radicals known to damage blood vessels. **It is the grape components of wine which primarily confer the heart healthy benefits and not the alcohol.**

In addition to the potential for consuming wine-containing toxins, consider the price of most wines. Wine and other types of alcohol related consumption can add significant cost to your food budget while potentially causing significant issues. Consider your specific situation as well as your Biblical beliefs before you decide to regularly imbibe. One of the best ways to immediately improve your life and your wellness quotient is to quit drinking alcohol.

In addition to the phytochemical attributes of grapes, their physical shape and perfect packaging, may cause problems for young children. **Whole grapes can be a choking hazard for small children and even adults with swallowing issues.** Keep in mind, kids under the age of 5 are prone to choking on food. The top three foods responsible for causing choking in children include hot dogs, candy and whole grapes! Just because grapes are healthy doesn't mean they are not problematic for small children. Parents or an adult should always supervise children as they eat grapes. Cherry tomatoes may also be problematic. Grapes and cherry tomatoes should be cut in half before serving them to children or adding to a salad which is be served to children.

The following table provides a list of how you can use healthy and delicious grapes in cooking and food preparation:

Vineyards		
Table 1. Creative Ideas for Using Grapes in Raw Eating, Food Preparation, and Cooking		
Fresh or frozen	Grape butter	"Chicken" salad
Juices / other beverages	Icees	Stuffing
Milkshakes	Popsicles	Grape salad
Syrup	Granita	Savory salads
As a sweetener in a recipe	Cereal topping	Fruit salad
Stovetop preserves, jelly, jams	Salad ingredient	Fruit kabobs
Conserves	Sweet bruschetta	Ice cream
Confit, chutneys, etc.	Roasted	Galette / pie / tart
Raisins	Mezza tray	Pudding, bread pudding

Bible verses: Genesis 40:10-11; Numbers 6:3; Numbers 13:20; Numbers 13:24; Numbers 23:24; Deuteronomy 8:8; Deuteronomy 24:21; Deuteronomy 28:30; Deuteronomy 32:32; Judges 8:2; Judges 9:27; Nehemiah 13:15; Song of Solomon 2:15; Song of Solomon 7:7; Micah 4:4; Isaiah 5:1-6; Isaiah 17:6; Isaiah 24:13; Jeremiah 8:13; Jeremiah 25:30; Jeremiah 35:18-19; Jeremiah 49:9; Hosea 9:10; Amos 9:13; Obadiah 1:5; John 15:2; Rev 14:18

References and resources

- https://www.youtube.com/watch?v=AJ-GqrSRcyY – 5 tips to grow a ton of passionfruit from ONE passion fruit
- https://www.youtube.com/watch?v=4woqw1zicfk – Passion fruit vine ('Frederick') / Old vs. New Trellis Systems / Nutritional Value / Propagation
- Association between daily alcohol intake and risk of all-cause mortality, A systematic review and meta-analyses by Jinhui Zhao, Tim Stockwell and Tim Naimi. https://jamanetwork.com/journals/jamanetworkopen/fullarticle/2802963

Discussion questions

1. How would a vineyard benefit your family?

2. Why do you think grapes are the most frequently mentioned fruit in the Bible?

3. What do grapes in the Bible symbolize?

4. How were grapes consumed in the Bible?

5. What is your favorite Bible story including grapes?

6. Does the Bible recommend consuming wine (i.e., is wine use in the Bible a description or a proscription)?

7. Do you think Isaiah 24:13 has an application to the time before Jesus' return?

8. Have you considered planting grape vines? If you have grape vines, can you share your methods with others and help others plant a vineyard?

Chapter 67

Experimental, demonstration and test gardens

Most people have probably never heard of an experimental garden. It is likely I might not have heard of them except for living close to the Fort Worth Botanic Garden and also for many years, living close to Huntington Gardens in Pasadena, California, both of which have experimental or demonstration gardens. The experimental garden can be located in a greenhouse or might be a designated raised bed or area of your yard.

The experimental or test garden in Fort Worth, Texas is a concentric series of raised beds around a central gazebo. **The experimental garden is a place to experiment with new varieties and various combinations of plants together.** It is also a place to grow out a species and collect its seeds for larger future plantings. This type of garden may be used to generate different characteristics with a specific cultivar. Can the variables be manipulated? Which conditions affect plant growth the most? These are the types of issues which can be addressed with an experimental garden bed.

A demonstration garden is used to educate people about a specific variety or demonstrate how to grow various crops. Test gardens allow the public to collect seeds when available. Public demonstration gardens schedule regular educational sessions for the public including school children and garden clubs.

Huntington's experimental garden, Ranch Garden, is primarily an educational garden demonstrating urban gardening. It targets children and adults. It's rambling vegetable rows and rapidly growing vegetable plants are a sharp contrast to the carefully planted and neatly organized main Huntington Gardens. It is not perfectly trimmed but when taken together, it is a 15-acre "lovely mass of colorful edible delights." It is designed to educate city dwellers about the benefits of incorporating edible plants into their landscape. Edible plants can be added to patios, back yards, porches, front yards, side yards and basically anywhere there is dirt.

If you are interested in testing a specific variety or cultivar to determine whether or not you want to use it in your garden, set up a small experimental garden area where you can plant novel bushes, vines and even trees. You may want to contain an invasive plant.

Maybe you collected seeds from a wild edible plant and now you want to determine if it is invasive or how it might grow in your area. Do you have unidentified seeds and want to grow them? Plant them in the experimental garden. This is its purpose. You may also use a test garden to educate others about a specific variety or cultivar.

Another use of a test garden is to grow different wheat or corn varieties. For example, you may want to test various types of corn for viability. Set up several different test areas to plant and grow corn. If you plant more than one type of corn each variety needs to be planted at least 250 feet apart and ideally 400 to 500 feet apart to avoid cross pollination. Otherwise, depending on the variety, if you are going to use some of your corn as seed for the next year, all of your corn may look the same. Sweet corn cross pollinates in the current year and if you are saving seed to plant again, other types of corn may show up in the following years' crop. If you know other farmers in the area, each farmer could grow a different corn variety (or cultivar) and share their seeds. Experimental gardens are fun and provide you and your family some interesting and even educational insights into gardening. Maybe even start a blog about your experimental garden.

Resources

Read about Washington state's demonstration gardens here:
https://mgfkc.org/resources/demonstration-gardens
https://www.thehenryford.org/collections-and-research/digital-collections/expert-sets/105228/
Read about using chamomile extract to prevent damping off of seedlings in this experiment garden:
https://homeroofdesign.com/experimental-gardens-unusual-plants-and-landscaping-ideas/
Read about roof gardens on this website:
https://anexperimentalgarden.com
Read about this experimental garden in Indiana which explores plants that were common before corn crops took over in America:
https://exploreari.org/experimental-gardens/
Horticultural students at Colorado State University grow and maintain experimental gardens to research cultivars best suited to Colorado's harsh environment and weather conditions.
https://exploreari.org/experimental-gardens/
Check out the 172 acres of Blandy's Experimental Farm in Virginia and be sure to read about their stunning grove of gingko trees in the fall that turn bright yellow and drop sticky, stinky fruit.
https://blandy.virginia.edu/content/state-arboretum-virginia
Learn about what 5th graders at this school are doing with their experimental gardens:
https://growing-minds.org/planning-an-experimental-garden-5th-grade/
List of demonstration gardens in Florida:
https://sfyl.ifas.ufl.edu/lawn-and-garden/demonstration-gardens/

Discussion Questions

1. What aspects of a demonstration garden intrigue you?
2. How could a demonstration or experimental garden function for your family?
3. What types of plants would you grow in a demonstration garden?
4. Was the Garden of Eden a type of 'demonstration garden?'
5. What lessons can we learn about how to keep our demonstration garden pure and protected from cross pollination?

Chapter 68

Green houses, orangeries, hoop houses, walipinis, high and low tunnels

Enclosed gardening structures give your plants' a much better chance of success compared to 100% dependence on whatever conditions dominate your growing season. You may have a cool, rainy summer or you may live in the south where hailstorms can take out your crops. Grasshoppers could invade your area. An enclosed gardening structure ensures you have more control over light, water, temperature and air flow.

Think about your location, the surroundings, weather, types of nearby plants, and other structures, etc. Is your growing season long or short? How much produce do you want to grow? Are you considering commercial crops? Do you need a large protected structure or a small shed-type structure? Gardening structures such as greenhouses, hoop houses, walipinis, orangeries and tunnels provide an array of options for extending the growing season and protecting crops from extreme weather as well as wandering deer and other hungry wild animals. Do you want to build a walipini, a functional high tunnel, or cobble together materials using old windows, wood pallets, and spare building parts to make a small greenhouse?

A few years ago, Dad built me a 10 x 14 foot greenhouse using only materials from his garage he had collected over the years. He had the 2 x 4 lumber, some aluminum, clean painting tarps, screen, nails, etc. The only cost incurred in the construction of the greenhouse was $0.99 for buying more staples. It lasted for years until I moved. One winter season it held 10 inches of snow and never ripped or caved in.

It was a lean-to greenhouse, meaning it was attached to the side of the house on two sides (see above picture). If you have space and a few easily located materials, you can build a greenhouse. Dad built my greenhouse early in October (in NE Texas) which meant I could transfer some of the plants from the garden into pots and over-winter them in the greenhouse. The pictures show the construction phase and the pots in the greenhouse after it was finished. It housed garlic, peppers, tomatoes, lettuce, sorrel, lemons, spinach, Swiss chard, herbs and even edible nasturtiums over the winter. The annual plants eventually died but the perennials lived until I could move them out of the greenhouse in the spring. It also allowed me to start planting seeds in January and February.

When you move to the country, consider which type of structure for extending the growing season best fits your family and interests. You may be building a home on the property and decide to add an orangerie, a window-rich room which allows at least 6 hours of natural light per day to fill the room with the sun's rays.

Use the following brief descriptions to choose a compatible structure for extending and augmenting your gardening activities. Research your options and discuss with seasoned farmers before deciding on an option.

Orangerie – A room or part of a building or estate home dedicated to growing citrus trees, fruits and vegetables all year long. It may have a dining room area and a sitting area. Sometimes an orangerie or sun room has floor to ceiling windows as well as roof windows. This allows for full sun exposure which is defined as 6 or more hours of full sunlight per day. High ceilings allow for trees and vines to thrive. An orangerie may be open to the house or sealed off from the rest of the house. Trees and plants create their own climate and humidity. Orangeries were popular in the 17th through the 19th centuries. Other names for an orangerie include greenhouse and conservatory.

Greenhouse – Greenhouses are usually stationary and built to last for decades. They may have venting, a watering system, doors, a potting area, raised beds, a heater, fans, and window openings. Greenhouses are made from many different types of building materials. When you walk into a greenhouse you can feel the quality of air is much different compared to outside air. During wintertime, it is a great feeling to walk into a warm, humid greenhouse, teeming with beautiful plants, flowers and trees. A greenhouse traps the sun's solar energy during cold days and nights and plants thrive while outdoor temperatures are cold and harsh. You can plant your own seeds and avoid the use of common pesticides and even growth inhibiting or stimulating plant hormones. Greenhouses are not just for traditional edible plants but also for flowers, vines and trees. Novel plant ideas include vanilla bean vines, kiwi vines, dwarf citrus trees, and banana and papaya trees.

Walipini or pit greenhouse - Temperatures six to eight feet below ground are a constant 50 °F to 60 °F. Farmers take advantage of this by digging into the side of a sloped area of land, preferably a south-facing location. Inside materials are built using stone or mud, preferentially dark colors, which better absorb and retain heat. Sometimes black plastic barrels are filled with water and placed where sunlight warms them during the day and they release their heat as temperatures drop throughout the night. Sometimes a heat source such as a wood stove is used.

Hoop house – A hoop house is a hybrid of a greenhouse and a high tunnel. They are usually smaller than a high tunnel and rounded at the top and may or may not have constructed lower walls.

High tunnel – High tunnels usually are larger and taller than traditional greenhouses. They are large enough to allow the use of tractors and other types of large farm equipment. High tunnels usually have a single layer covering which extends the growing season. The season can start early with the use of high tunnels and can be extended past the first frost, protecting tender crops. They are adjustable and movable for convenient use.

Low tunnel – Low tunnels are similar to high tunnels except they are closer to the ground while not touching the crop. They are just high enough to protect their crops. They are moveable for convenience and protect delicate crops from frosts.

Resources

- Alaska garden harvest and high tunnel update. Simple Living Alaska. https://www.youtube.com/watch?v=D52z0gxJ084&list=PU3FHvW16m_i117IqPnb0nmA&index=9
- High tunnel prep. Simple Living Alaska. https://www.youtube.com/watch?v=4qN4vjG-jrI
- Walipini https://www.youtube.com/watch?v=fJLKKOratSU
- Greenhouses for cold climates: https://insteading.com/blog/underground-greenhouse/?fbclid=IwAR27orm_S1oDYKcDWqAhM-tSPS-2MfSmqpltB9wsHhwOLzUwU_aq9gjWT8
- https://www.youtube.com/watch?v=Qvk7Sszh6fg&feature=youtu.be&fbclid=IwAR1S5AllNHxCQvV1yaZakK6OME6d4nr0BFOflJ1lvKDUBvp9SvUuVqdAsQI – constructing a walipini

Chapter 69
Great plant combinations

Asparagus	Basil, cilantro, marigolds, nasturtiums, oregano, parsley, peppers, sage, thyme, tomatoes. AVOID: garlic, onions, potatoes.
Beans	Beets, cabbage, carrot, cauliflower, celeriac (small to moderate amounts), celery, corn, cucumbers, marigold, summer savory. AVOID: chives, fennel, garlic, gladiolus, leeks, onion, peppers, shallots.
Beets	Broccoli, brussels sprouts, bush beans, cabbage, cauliflower, chard, kohlrabi, lettuce, onions. AVOID: pole beans.
Borage	Squash, strawberries, tomatoes.
Broccoli	Beets, buckwheat, calendula, carrots, chamomile, dill, hyssop, marigolds, mints, nasturtiums, onions, rosemary, sage, thyme, wormwood.
Br. sprouts	Beets, buckwheat, calendula, carrots, chamomile, dill, hyssop, marigolds, mints, nasturtiums, onions, rosemary, sage, thyme, wormwood.
Cabbage	Broccoli, brussels sprouts, celery, chard, spinach, tomatoes.
Cauliflower	Broccoli, brussels sprouts, celery, chard, spinach, tomatoes.
Cantaloupe	Corn
Carrots	Cabbage, chives, early potatoes, leeks, lettuce, onions, peas, radish, rosemary, sage, salsify, tomatoes, wormwood. AVOID: coriander, dill, parsnips.
Chives	Apples, berries, carrots, grapes, peas, roses, tomatoes.
Comfrey	Makes everything thrive. Large plant and may spread and be invasive unless kept in check. Natural green fertilizer. Grows in shade and under trees.
Corn	Beans, broad beans, cucumbers, early potatoes, melons, peas, pumpkins, soybeans, squash, zucchini.
Cucumbers	Beans, cabbage, celery, corn, dill, early potatoes, lettuce, marigold, nasturtium, peas, radishes, sunflowers. AVOID: aromatic herbs such as sage.
Dill	Broccoli, brussels sprouts, cabbage, cauliflower, cucumber, lettuce, onions.
Eggplant	Green beans, peppers, potatoes, tomatoes.
Garlic	Cabbage, cane fruits, fruit trees, roses, tomatoes.
Green beans	Broccoli, brussels sprouts, corn, cucumber, marigold, nasturtium, peas, potato, radish, rosemary, summer savory. AVOID: beets, onion family.
Kale	Buckwheat, cabbage, marigolds, nasturtiums.
Kohlrabi	Cabbage, cauliflower.

Lettuce	Beans, beets, broccoli, carrot, corn, marigold, mint, parsnip, peas, radish, strawberries.
Marigolds	All
Mustard	Fruit trees, grapes, legumes.
Nasturtiums	All
Onions	Beets, cabbage family, carrots, chamomile, lettuce, parsnip, tomatoes. AVOID: asparagus, beans, peas.
Parsnips	Onions, radishes, wormwood.
Peas	Beans, carrots, corn, cucumbers, early potatoes, radishes, turnips. AVOID: onions.
Peppers	Basil, carrots, eggplant, onions, parsley, spinach, tomatoes. AVOID: beans.
Pole beans	Corn, marigolds, potatoes, radishes.
Potatoes	Basil, beans, cabbage family, corn, eggplant, flax, hemp, marigolds, peas, squash.
Radishes	Beets, carrots, cucumber, kale, lettuce, melons, peas, nasturtiums, onions, root crops, spinach, squash.
Rosemary	Beans, cabbage, carrots.
Sage	Cabbage family, carrots, tomatoes.
Soybeans	Corn, potatoes.
Spinach	Celery, cauliflower, eggplant, or strawberries.
Strawberries	Borage, bush beans, lettuce, pyrethrum, spinach.
Sunflowers	Cucumbers
Swiss chard	Bush beans, kohlrabi, onions.
Tomatoes	Asparagus, basil, carrots, celery, gooseberries, lettuce, mustard, onions, parsley, sage, spinach, stinging nettles. AVOID: beets, cabbage, corn, cucumbers, dill, fennel, potatoes, rosemary.
Zucchini	Beans, corn, dill, marigolds, peas, radishes. AVOID: Potatoes.

Notes:

Chapter 70
Privacy hedgerows: flowers, shrubs, vines and trees

Hedgerows composed of vines, trees and bushes offer fresh produce, beauty, privacy, biodiversity and much more! Hedgerows add interest to a landscape and value to a property. They provide privacy, and in some cases, a noise and wind barrier. Hedgerows may be used to demarcate property lines and if dense enough, they may act as fencing. Hedgerows include both annual and perennial plantings. A hedgerow is usually at least 40 feet if not much wider. Hedgerows may be as deep or shallow as you desire.

Plant a privacy hedgerow soon after purchasing a property. This ensures curious and even prying eyes on the ground do not have easy access to viewing your property. Another term for a type of hedgerow is food forest. It may be food for wild animals and birds or it may provide food for your family. It may include trellises, fencing, gates, walkways, stepping stones, water features, bee hives, rock gardens, cacti, bird baths, bird houses, bird feeders, etc. You may even want to build a maze or small orchard as a hedgerow.

The list below has both fruiting and non-fruiting privacy shrubs and trees. Combine these trees with edible vines, flowers and plants to add interest and functionality to your privacy hedgerows. Before you plant, confirm each plant is compatible with other nearby plants. For example, black walnut trees produce a chemical known as jugulone. This chemical is toxic to many plants and causes them to wilt and die. There are a few plants which are impervious to jugalone, including Jerusalem artichoke, Joe Pye weed, lamb's ear, ostrich fern, peppermint, violets, wild ginger, peach, nectarine, cherry, pear, black raspberry, quince, beans, beets, carrots, corn, melons, onions, parsnips and squash.

Make a list of your favorite vines, shrubs and bushes from reading their descriptions on the next pages. Pick a mixture of fast-growing and slower-growing plants. Be sure to add some flowering shrubs and vines as well as some food-producing trees and plants for the wildlife. If you can propagate cuttings it will reduce your planting costs.

Enjoy your newfound privacy and enjoy your hedgerow for many years to come.

Privacy Hedgerows, Vines and Trees Table 1. Privacy / barrier trees, vines and bushes

- American Arborvitae. The one drawback is deer also love to nibble on this tree.
- Austree Willow. Grows 10 – 15 ft/yr.
- Bamboo. Bamboo is fast growing and when planted in bunches creates a privacy screen. Can be considered invasive.
- Bay leaf tree. Bushy tree bearing culinary fragrant leaves which perform double duty by repelling insects in pantry and cupboard areas.
- Berberis. Prickly hedge producing flowers and non-edible berries. Many varieties. Colorful. Thrives in poor conditions.
- Blackberries. A blackberry thicket creates a low-lying protective barrier.
- Black locust (false acacia). Beautiful ornamental tree; fragrant flowers. Grows up to 50' tall, 25' wide.
- Blue pea vine. Can be used as a fast-growing screen. Flowers and seeds are edible.
- Boston ivy. Grows up to 30 feet. Well-behaved climbing vine; does not destroy masonry.
- Bridal wreath. Easy to grow. Fast growing up to 8 feet. Requires regular pruning. Hardy. Tolerates partial shade. Easily survives harsh winters and summers within its hardiness zones.
- Butterfly bush. These bushes make beautiful additions to any hedgerow or privacy fence. They produce long purple or blue flowers which attract butterflies and pollinators.
- Camellia sinesis. This bush produces tea leaves. Makes a beautiful hedge with pretty white flowers.
- Cherry laurel. Grows 5 to 20 feet high and creates a thick bushy barrier.
- Chilean glory vine. Attracts hummingbirds. Fast-growing vine, with gorgeous flowers in pink, orange, red, and yellow.
- Coffee tree. Grow in tropical or subtropical areas. Tree's foliage is beautiful and scented.
- Concolor Fir. Reaches height of 40'x20' wide. Good for large properties but maybe not in south.
- Crabapple. Bunched together this tree makes a nice barrier, even an outdoor room with the added benefit of edible fruit.
- Crepe myrtle. Beautiful blooms in the summer.
- Dawn Redwood. Grows more than 2 feet per year until reaching mature height.
- Deodar Cedar. Fast growing large, evergreen, elegant cedar. Reaches a height of 40 to 70 feet and a spread of 20 to 40 feet. Known to grow up to 2 feet per year.
- Douglas Fir. Grows to 40 to 80 feet tall and 20 feet wide. Attractive.
- Eastern Red Cedar. Grows to 40 to 60 feet and 10 to 20 feet wide. Plant 20 feet away from power lines, neighboring homes, etc.
- Eastern White Pine. Grows to 60' tall and 30' wide. Not good for humid south. Blocks out vast views when mature.
- Edgeworthia. Shrub with beautiful yellow winter flowers.
- Elder. Fast-growing tree.
- Elderberry. Makes a great addition to a hedgerow.
- Elecampine. Perennial bush (or large plant) w/ gorgeous spikey yellow flowers. Grows up to 8' tall. Plant as part of a privacy hedgerow and as a bonus, it keeps away deer. Roots are medicinal.
- Emerald Green Arborvitae. Reaches a mature height of 14 feet. Grows around 6 to 9 inches a year. Width range is 3 to 4 feet in rows.
- False Cypress. AKA white cedar, medium to large evergreen shrub (DO NOT EAT THE FLOWERS).
- Feijoa. Unusual looking tree bearing red spikey flowers producing pineapple guava egg-shaped fruit.
- Flowering Dogwood. Reach a height of 25 feet and have a width range of 15 to 25 feet.

- Flying dragon. Covered in long thorny spikes and produces a bitter orange fruit. May reach up to 20 feet in height with a 10 – 12 foot spread but most are 6 x 6 feet. Hardy to -10 °F.
- Forsythia. Good for bright yellow spring color, pollinators love this bush.
- Fragrant Tea Olive Shrub. Flowering shrub whose fragrance lasts up to 4 months.
- Golden Flowered Agave Century Plant. By itself, this is not a privacy tree, but it goes well in a hedgerow or as an accent to a privacy row. Native to Arizona but grows in mountain areas up to 6,900 feet. Heat and cold hardy. Beautiful clumps of yellow flowers. Rapidly grows to 30 feet. It is not a privacy tree but makes a great addition to a hedgerow providing color and interest.
- Golden mop cypress. Shrub which grows up to 5 or 6 feet; wide at the bottom and pointy tip.
- Goldspire Ginkgo. Height is 14 to 16 feet. Width range is 5 to 6 feet. Beautiful yellow fall foliage.
- Gooseberries. Thorny brambles producing edible berries.
- Gorse hedging. Bright yellow flowers make a striking hedge.
- Green Giant Thuja (Arborvitae). Fast growing. Survives many climates. Not affected by many pests or diseases. Annual growth around 3 to 5 feet. Grow to 40 feet, with a width range of 5 to 8 feet.
- Hazelnut. Rapidly growing, up to 20 inches / year, nut-producing tree.
- Hybrid Willow. Fast growing tree, growing at a rate of 6 to 12 feet per year. Reaches mature height in 5 years. Good as a windbreak. Great for drying out swampy soil. Reach 35 to 45 feet in rows and 75 feet alone. Width range is 20 feet. Plant 5 feet apart for a privacy fence.
- Hydrangea. Makes a beautiful addition to a privacy hedge. Produces large, lovely flower heads.
- Idaho Blue Spruce. Good for northern locations.
- Japanese False Cypress. Reaches about 6 feet tall but much higher in the wild. Pyramidal form.
- Kumquats. Bushy citrus tree bearing fragrant small orange fruit. Fruit remains viable for months.
- Lawson Cypress. Reaches 40 feet at maturity with a 20 foot spread.
- Leighton Green (cupressocyparis leylandii). Fast growing and easily trained into privacy hedge.
- Lemon Myrtle. Can be trained into a tall hedge. Leaves have culinary uses.
- Leyland Cypress. Fast growing. Can reach 50 feet in height in 15 years and up to 70 feet when completely mature. Create an impenetrable mass of branches to block wind and even noise. Width range is 15 to 20 feet, 30 feet alone.
- Lilac. Lovely smelling bushes which send out suckers and propagate to fill in gaps.
- Lilly Pilly (Cascade). Hedge bush bearing beautiful pink berries.
- Mock Orange. Fast growing bush with dense busy structure. Can be planted in tight groups to form a privacy hedgerow and the flowers in the spring release a lovely fragrance.
- Murraya. Grows quickly, pest and disease resistant. Grows up to 12 feet high.
- Natal Plum. Evergreen with beautiful blossoms and small red fruit.
- Norway Spruce. May grow to 60' tall but usually less; 25 to 30' wide. Pendulous growth hangs down.
- Orange tree. Grow in warmer climates for the lovely smell of orange blossoms and the fruit.
- Orangeola Japanese Maple. Stunning orange fall leaves. Heat resistant. Beautiful form. Fastest growing of the small Japanese maples.
- Ornamental Cherry. Bunched together this tree creates a barrier.
- Ornamental Pear. Bunched together this tree creates a barrier.
- Osage Orange. Commonly used as a tree row windbreak. When dried, wood has highest BTU content of any wood. Fruit may deter spiders, cockroaches, boxelder bugs, crickets, fleas, etc.
- Passionfruit. Plant a couple of vines along your privacy hedge and several months later, enjoy!
- Pittosporum Tenuifolium. Small evergreen tree, grows up to 35 feet.
- Pomegranate. Bush or tree shape, bearing edible fruit.

- Princess Flower Bush. Produces beautiful purple flowers.
- Privet. Fast growing. Needs to be pruned. Produces sweet smelling flower in the spring.
- Queen's Wreath. Climbing vine with pendulous lavender blue flowers. Grows up to 40 feet.
- Quince. A nice addition to a hedge row which produces beautiful blossoms and edible fruit.
- Red Cedar. Mature ht is 30'. Plant 8' apart. Prickly foliage keeps out invaders. Drought resistant.
- Red Dragon Japanese Maple. Dramatic accent tree. Sun and drought tolerant.
- Rose (climbing). Add color and interest to a privacy hedge.
- Rosemary. Once established, rosemary grows in and makes a beautiful low-to-the-ground hedge.
- Sasanqua Camellia. Beautiful addition to a hedge. Produces flowers. Hedge may grow up to 15' high.
- Silverberry. Nitrogen fixing plant. May grow up to 30 inches / year.
- Snowball Viburnum Bush. Produces hundreds of huge white flower heads.
- Spartan Juniper. Grows to 15' high, width of 3' to 5'. Serves as barrier and even as a windbreak.
- Sweet Viburnum. Vigorous grower forms a dense hedge. Requires frequent pruning.
- Thuja Occidentalis (Arborvitae). Reaches mature height of 20 to 30 feet and 10 feet wide.
- Upright Juniper. Grows 40 to 50 feet tall, some mature at half this height.
- Viburnum Odoratissimum. Fast growing hedge plant.
- Vitex. Similar to the butterfly bush, with clusters of lovely clustered long purple flowers.
- Weeping Podocarpus. Woody evergreen. Reach a mature height of 35 to 45 feet and have a width range of 10 to 20 feet. Drought tolerant.
- Weeping Yoshino Cherry Tree. This is a stunning tree which needs its own location to make a statement. A hedgerow of just these trees would be stunning.
- White Bower Vine. Rapid growth; flowers several times during summer. Grows beautifully among trees.
- Wisteria. Perennial vine, growing to 25 or more feet. Produces many violet blue flowers.
- Witch Hazel. Vase-shaped shrub/tree, bright yellow winter blossoms.
- Yew. Grows anywhere from 2 to 60 feet tall.

Protective border plants. Cacti, blackberry vines, common holly, giant rhubarb, pyracantha, etc.

Indoor plants known to remove pollutants and airborne toxins. Aloe vera, Amstel king ficus, areca palm, Boston fern, Benjamin ficus, bromeliads, Chinese evergreen, dracaena, dragon tree, English ivy, mother-in-law tongue, mums, pothos, peace lily, philodendron, rubber plants, spider plants, weeping fig, etc.

Resources
Propagate elderberries https://www.youtube.com/watch?v=kYYBlU4gbCA

Discussion questions

1. Why is privacy important?
2. On a scale of 1 to 10, with 1 being least important and 10 being most important, how important is privacy to you and your family?
3. What measures are you willing to implement to attain privacy for your property / residence?
4. How do you feel about planning for privacy in the future, even if it is not a current priority?
5. What types of privacy barriers interest you?
6. Have you heard about forest bathing?
7. Plants and trees naturally release chemical compounds that enhance health and well-being. How do you feel after spending time hiking in nature?

Chapter 71
Plants for repelling pests

The Creator made plants for our enjoyment. Plants mobilize and synthesize nutrients, antioxidants and chemicals (i.e., phytochemicals) for their protection and for our enjoyment. Some chemicals protect them from pests, predators, scorching sunlight, etc. A few insect repelling phytochemicals include citronellol, geraniol, camphor, menthol, coumarins, and hundreds of others.

Some chemicals are released as volatile oils into the air while others are released upon consumption. Many plant chemicals attract pollinators and repels pests. Below is a list of plants and the pests they are known to repel. Not every plant works every time. Sometimes plant chemicals need to be released into the air to repel undesirable insects. Gently walking among the scented plants may improve their ability to repel undesirable insects. Insects also use plant scents to navigate to food. If you grow plants with pungent scents, it may deter them from other desirable plants with delicate scents. Use this list to address potential pest issues in your garden, around and even inside your home.

PLANT	REPELS...
Achillea moonwalker	Ants
Agapanthus (pink)	Fleas, mosquitos, snakes
Agastache cana	Mosquitoes
Alliums	Broad-spectrum natural insecticide; repels slug, aphid, carrot fly, cabbage worm
Andrographis p.	Snakes
Basil	Asparagus beetle, carrot fly, flies, mosquito, snakes, tomato hornworm, whitefly
Bay leaves	Flies, roaches
Bee balm	Mosquitos; attracts butterflies, hummingbirds and bees
Bergamot	Mosquitos
Borage	Tomato hornworm
Castor bean	Moles
Catnip	Ants, aphids, cabbage looper, Colorado potato beetle, deer, flea beetle, Japanese beetle, mice, mosquitos, rats, roaches, squash bug, stink bug, weevils; may attract cats, 10X more powerful repelling mosquitos than DEET (2 cups catnip muddled + 1 qt vinegar)
Cedar / cedarwood	Aphids, fleas, flies, spiders, ticks
Chamomile	Flies, mosquitos, ticks
Chives	Ants, aphids, carrot flies, flea beetles, Japanese beetles
Chrysanthemums	Pyrethrins repel roach, ant, Japanese beetle, tick, silverfish, lice, flea, bedbug, spidermite (Dry and crush the flowers and sprinkle on pets. Instantly kills flying and crawling insects.)
Citronella	Mosquitoes, spiders; may deter cats
Clove	Bed bugs, snakes
Coriander	Aphids, Colorado potato beetle, spider mites
Crown Imperial	Mice, moles, rabbits, squirrels, voles
Dahlias	Nematodes
Dill	Aphids, cabbage loopers, squash bugs, spider mites, tomato hornworms
Eucalyptus citriodora	Aphids, bed bugs, cabbage looper, Colorado potato beetles, head lice, ticks
Fennel	Aphids, slugs and snails

PLANT	REPELS...
Feverfew	Ants, bedbugs, cockroaches, flies, mice, mites, mosquitoes
Floss Flower	Flowers contain coumarin which repels mosquitoes
Garlic	Bean beetle, fruit tree borers, Japanese beetles, June bugs, peach tree borer, rabbits, roaches, maggots, snakes, spider mites, stink bugs, weevils
Geranium, scented	Gnats, mosquitoes, ticks, etc.
Horse radish	Colorado potato beetle
Hyssop	Cabbage looper / moths, flea beetles (don't plant near radishes)
Lavender	Ant, bed bug, flea, flies, mosquito, moth, scorpion, spiders, ticks, water scorpions
Leeks	Carrot flies
Lemon balm	Mosquitoes
Lemongrass	Ants, flies, gnats, mosquitoes, snakes, stink bugs, ticks
Lemon thyme	Mosquitoes
Lettuce	Carrot flies
Marigold	Aphids, asparagus beetle, mosquitoes, nematodes, rabbits, snakes, white flies
Mint	Indoor ants/bugs, cabbage maggot/moth, flea beetle, flea, fly, mice, mosquito
Mother-in-law tongue	Snakes
Myrrh	Mosquitos
Mountain tobacco	Use dried and crushed as a pesticide base for the garden
Narcissus	Moles
Nasturtiums	Aphids, beetles, cabbage loopers, squash bugs, stink bugs, whiteflies
Oregano	Many pests
Osage orange	Boxelder bugs, cockroaches, crickets, fleas, spiders
Parsley	Asparagus beetles
Pennyroyal (fleabane)	Ants, fleas, flies, gnats, mosquitoes, ticks
Peppermint	Ant, spider, aphid, beetle, caterpillar, flea, flies, mice lice, mosquito, moth, snake
Petunias	Aphids, asparagus beetles, leafhoppers, tomato hornworms, squash bugs
Radish	Cabbage maggot, cucumber beetles, stink bugs
Rosemary	Beetles, cabbage moth, carrot fly, flies, mosquitoes, slugs, snails, stink bugs, ticks
Rue	Deer, flea beetles, fruit flies, rabbits, slugs, snakes
Sage	Beetles, cabbage moths, carrot flies, flea beetle, flies, snails, ticks
Scented geraniums	Leafhoppers and certain geraniums repel mosquitoes
Shoo-fly plant	Flies, white flies
Snakeroot	Snakes
Spearmint	Ants, aphids, beetles, cabbage looper, rodents, squash bugs
Summer savory	Bean beetles
Sweet Annie	Gnats
Sweet Woodruff	Moths
Tansy (toxic to animals)	Ants, beetles, cabbage white, cutworms, flies, mosquito, small white, squash bugs
Tea tree	Mosquitos
Thyme (lemon)	Bed bugs, cabbage loopers, cabbage maggots, corn earworms, mosquitoes, small whites, stink bugs, ticks, tomato hornworms, whiteflies, etc.
Tobacco	beetles, carrot flies
Walking onions	Cabbage looper, moles, moths, rabbits, small white
Wormwood (invasive)	Snakes
Zinnia	Cucumber beetle and tomato hornworm

Section 9

Country Living

Small Building Projects for Consideration

Chapter 72
Small building projects for consideration

It is a good idea to do things right the first time. So often, we want to do a project but don't have the time or money to do it the right way or the way we envision doing it. We quickly pull together something which may work, thinking, we will do it better or improve on it when we have time. However, this type of thinking usually leaves us only with the initial quickly completed project. If it is working, why take the time to improve on it? So, it is better to do it right the first time, because it is likely the version you will be living with for a long time.

Activities and tasks specific to artisanal farming and homesteading include but are not limited to: acquiring additional land / property, establishing alternative energy sources, animal husbandry, aquaculture, caring for ponds and small bodies of water, assisting neighbors and those in need, baking and cooking on a wood-fired stove / oven, baling hay, barn work, bartering, bee keeping, asparagus and berry beds, blogging and video, bread making, canning and preserving food, chopping wood, construction projects, cooking for large groups, decks, electrical, fences, fire-prevention measures, foraging, gardening, general repairs, greenhouses and high tunnels, growing food, hardwood floors, HVAC, long-term planning, INCOME GENERATION, making butter / cheese / yogurt from cow's and goat's milk, making curtains, managing and eliminating pests / snakes / insect critters, milking cows / goats, milling whole grains into flour, mowing, mulching, mushroom cultivation, preparing natural products and remedies, plumbing, propane, protecting property, raising chickens for eggs, raising children, mechanics, repairing farm equipment, root crops, seed swapping, seed preservation, sewing and repairing clothing, septic, small construction projects, spinning wool into yarn, storing food, tapping maple / birch trees, transporting things (hay, horses, animals, equipment), welding, well water / pump house, wood working / milling wood, etc.

When it comes to homesteading and country living, schedule several planning sessions with your family and involved friends. Find out what aspects of country living are important for each member of the team. It may be important for one person to have several horses and another person may want a large garden with a green house. These projects need to be planned and coordinated. Rank the projects from high to low priority projects. If you promised your kids they could choose some farm animals, this is an important promise to keep. As you go through each project, use a calendar and a map of your homestead to plan for and schedule projects. Emphasize how each person is essential to completing the projects. Everyone chips in and helps out, even if it is not their pet project.

These planning meetings give credibility and motivation to each person and provide a way to make the transition to the country meaningful and significant. Start out by giving several examples of projects which are essential and non-essential. Then give other members the opportunity to provide input. Discuss each project then assign it a priority listing, including not only time required to complete the project, but the location and costs involved.

You can find extensive resources on the internet, books at the library and conversations with those who have completed similar projects. In some cases, you can even buy a chicken coop or horse trough instead of constructing your own, however, you will likely save significant money if you complete the project yourself, oftentimes with materials you already own.

This chapter provides ideas for possible small farm projects. There are hundreds of projects and many projects are specific to your situation. Some projects you may complete with materials on hand. Other projects require significant investment of time and resources. If you have good skills and experience, you may likely do better choosing more complex projects. If you are new to building and construction, you may want to begin with easy projects. Consult with your handy man / handy woman friends to determine the actual scope of projects you find interesting. Below are just a few ideas to consider. Most of the videos are found at YouTube. If you go to the YouTube website and then pull up the search bar, you only need to type in the letters and numbers (usually 9 to 12 or so characters) after the word "**watch?v=**": HVvbjnf08xw

Project ideas could include building, planting or establishing: apple grinder / press, barn, bat house, bee hives, bench, bird house, cacti garden, chicken coop , compost bins, decking, dock for a pond, dog bathing area, driveway, exercise track / par course, feeding trough, fencing, fire pit, French drain, garden beds, garden pathways, gazebo, goat pen, greenhouse, hand pump, hydroelectric generator, outdoor kitchen / canning kitchen, outdoor shower, outhouse, permanent glamping tent, picnic tables, pizza oven, playground, pond, rainwater collection, rocket stove, rock garden, RV site with hookups, shooting range, spring or wellhouse shed, storm cellar, swing, tree house, wood fired hot tub, wood working shop, etc.

- Apple grinder and cider press
  https://www.youtube.com/watch?v=HVvbjnf08xw
  https://www.youtube.com/watch?v=7fD3yTDCMMk (not in English but good techniques)
  https://www.youtube.com/watch?v=kTARNR2xjZQ
- Barn
  https://www.youtube.com/watch?v=sHvPNhZPoqM
  https://www.youtube.com/watch?v=VM0CN6esA3Y
  https://www.youtube.com/watch?v=9q_x6Ta6u1U
  https://www.youtube.com/watch?v=v_DlgC7Ke9I
- Bat house
  https://www.youtube.com/watch?v=dbyPyWV-VgM
- Bee hives
  https://www.youtube.com/watch?v=rt2AC9U-fhY
- Benches
  https://www.youtube.com/watch?v=EzxTiHZI_VU
  https://www.youtube.com/watch?v=CNS6f4QqBts
  https://www.youtube.com/watch?v=R1vQZf8wKjA
- Bird house with feeder
  https://www.youtube.com/watch?v=EF0nuiz-YYs
  https://www.youtube.com/watch?v=vvMM62-pqMg
- Cacti garden
  https://www.youtube.com/watch?v=sD47cdC2FlYhttps://www.youtube.com/watch?v=ejdl8l8-1Yw
- Chicken coop
  https://www.youtube.com/watch?v=Ll9vPN60nJ0
- Compost bins and worm farms
  https://www.youtube.com/watch?v=bGRunDez1j4
  https://www.youtube.com/watch?v=UaajjQ0FhM4https://www.youtube.com/watch?v=l698hczXpMM
- Decking
  https://www.youtube.com/watch?v=rxqdwHTHEKU
- Dock for pond / lake (includes floating dock)
  https://www.youtube.com/watch?v=vBTcDtKEoqU
  https://www.youtube.com/watch?v=iusA-zLwGAg

- https://www.youtube.com/watch?v=kW2aipuCzPw
- Dog bathing station
  https://www.youtube.com/watch?v=LMeFyb6M2pc
  https://www.youtube.com/watch?v=KkMu0GyMLXI
  https://www.youtube.com/watch?v=ylnORx0iaX0
- Driveway
  https://www.youtube.com/watch?v=oZVWci31NlM
  https://www.youtube.com/watch?v=ey_NEoM2SpM
- Dutch bucket hydroponic gardens
  https://www.youtube.com/watch?v=nXy32Dr4Z4A
  https://www.youtube.com/watch?v=gcS0lcwWIUg
- Exercise track / par course
  https://www.youtube.com/watch?v=8QaBr1oYYKo
  https://www.youtube.com/watch?v=fpUVflGBT-0
  https://www.youtube.com/watch?v=j3JbfZrb_U
  https://www.youtube.com/watch?v=K5NkG3_0jEE
- Feeding trough
  https://www.youtube.com/watch?v=EZthRfDDBxQ
- Fencing
  https://www.youtube.com/watch?v=AOg8FJvYfyI
  https://www.youtube.com/watch?v=tCFI_63oowU
  https://www.youtube.com/watch?v=1YyvDtivSBw
  https://www.youtube.com/watch?v=LrK5KHwevB4
  https://www.youtube.com/watch?v=ODH_Xj3RrGQ
- Fertilizer
  http://seattlegardenfruit.blogspot.com/2017/04/how-to-turn-rinsed-rice-water-into.html
  https://www.motherearthnews.com/organic-gardening/milk-and-molasses-magic-zbcz1402
- Fire pit
  https://www.youtube.com/watch?v=zcZHeSZIC6Q
  https://www.youtube.com/watch?v=vmFUNIC3ZnQ
- French drain
  https://www.youtube.com/watch?v=izzIAlOaXpo
- Gardening areas and beds
  https://www.youtube.com/watch?v=YtnArAl617k
  https://www.youtube.com/watch?v=0zTqkiLBAEQ
  https://www.youtube.com/watch?v=ef_TS19TRQg
- Garden pathways
  https://www.youtube.com/watch?v=2cq0yFT1mBA
  https://www.youtube.com/watch?v=c4Dsqvad8FI
  https://www.youtube.com/watch?v=D0iQ-Rwf5dY
  https://www.youtube.com/watch?v=wRr5BLdVVQQ
- Gazebo
  https://www.youtube.com/watch?v=0Ge4hrUSmJs
  https://www.youtube.com/watch?v=3pJmVLQyd6U
  https://www.youtube.com/watch?v=GAhqK_D6Xck
- Goat pen https://www.youtube.com/watch?v=ZT42AjP-IXU
  https://www.youtube.com/watch?v=fURAGnAz_V0
- Greenhouse
  https://www.youtube.com/watch?v=Dd-FOj7cuLc
  https://www.youtube.com/watch?v=Eg-A8_L2N30
- Hand pump
  https://www.youtube.com/watch?v=Vm422bfrjws
- Hay feeders
  https://www.youtube.com/watch?v=8zvFxW3C1RU
- High tunnel
  https://www.youtube.com/watch?v=GvfDUaKbej0

- Horse corral
  https://www.youtube.com/watch?v=Uq-VeicDJDI
- Hydroelectric power generator
  https://www.youtube.com/watch?v=1KyL1-0A0Gw (bad language warning)
  https://www.youtube.com/watch?v=ZmHY9DkD1Hw
  https://www.youtube.com/watch?v=Xb6TIWub6KU
- Outdoor kitchen
  https://www.youtube.com/watch?v=b1zCK1RLxDU
  https://www.youtube.com/watch?v=DTPc9p34sKA
- Outdoor shower
  https://www.youtube.com/watch?v=klviM3Jd-No
- Outhouse
  https://www.youtube.com/watch?v=-gHnQ0JYGZo
- Permanent glamping tent
  https://www.youtube.com/watch?v=Kl5an169N18
- Picnic table
  https://www.youtube.com/watch?v=nyB8mFXZdEI
  https://www.youtube.com/watch?v=DSliTVOxKlc
- Pizza oven
  https://www.youtube.com/watch?v=0Qno-XJwPKw
- Planters (concrete)
  https://www.youtube.com/watch?v=Nfj31YrRj70
- Playground
  https://www.youtube.com/watch?v=BpeQat3cmQw
  https://www.youtube.com/watch?v=wKQNlxALeU0
- Pond
  https://www.youtube.com/watch?v=DiHNBja4G8g
  https://www.youtube.com/watch?v=DiHNBja4G8g
  https://www.youtube.com/watch?v=6dtTl5IduVQ
  https://www.youtube.com/watch?v=gWPpKCv7S74
  https://www.youtube.com/watch?v=sdeAKZ2toAM
  https://www.youtube.com/watch?v=cNqMak84Z1g
- Rain water collection
  https://www.youtube.com/watch?v=5_0zfjrRmyk
  https://www.youtube.com/watch?v=tDMbhmna2iI
  https://www.youtube.com/watch?v=kazEAzGWuIc
  https://www.youtube.com/watch?v=I5Y2vCGz2k4
  https://www.youtube.com/watch?v=P-e6oOyrQ04
- Rocket stove
  https://www.youtube.com/watch?v=gQyU4lokVe4
  https://www.youtube.com/watch?v=B9BQGamXLMk
- Rock garden
  https://www.youtube.com/watch?v=SjZ95sGaD-k
- RV site with hookups
  https://www.youtube.com/watch?v=2Xw83_o1tg8 (pad only)
  https://www.youtube.com/watch?v=8kk8S9mjU9g
- Farm animal scratching post
  https://www.youtube.com/watch?v=SmIRrCcwPt0
- Septic system
  https://www.youtube.com/watch?v=udBaGyzJyU8
  https://www.youtube.com/watch?v=ynCR0C9B-Do
  https://www.youtube.com/watch?v=Qbf6r3CL8Fg
  https://www.youtube.com/watch?v=e8YpYmGTigI

- Shooting range
  https://www.youtube.com/watch?v=aVNpkQJZ0lc
- Small water feature
  https://www.youtube.com/watch?v=nBeHAyJJiPM
  https://www.youtube.com/watch?v=VvnHZwukk5I
- Solar projects
  https://www.youtube.com/watch?v=5i3AN-lHMk4
  https://www.youtube.com/watch?v=tOpoupq7DRI
  https://www.youtube.com/watch?v=Sc78nueDQ64
- Solar furnace
  https://www.youtube.com/watch?v=a62mZMIMpc0
- Solar oven
  https://www.youtube.com/watch?v=mzoL-Rjjg6A
- Solar panel array
  https://www.youtube.com/watch?v=ov7ArKkm07c
- Spring or well house
  https://www.youtube.com/watch?v=IGecgmobpEE
  https://www.youtube.com/watch?v=hKxdAesHk9M
  https://www.youtube.com/watch?v=Viu4JEsXRJc
- Storm cellar
  https://www.youtube.com/watch?v=0tsqK5pbxcs
- Swing
  https://www.youtube.com/watch?v=PKhHpPy7wNs
- Treehouse
  https://www.youtube.com/watch?v=qaIDV8wH9ag
  https://www.youtube.com/watch?v=HkgY9JaIACE
- Walipini
  https://www.youtube.com/watch?v=Qvk7Sszh6fg
  https://www.youtube.com/watch?v=9jbLZxwWudk
  https://www.youtube.com/watch?v=X0-gxjok2Mc
  https://www.youtube.com/watch?v=EysR2mlhSmQ
  https://www.youtube.com/watch?v=5SYBfG74VC4
  https://www.youtube.com/watch?v=TynzRWHsZOI
  https://www.youtube.com/watch?v=ucqjXN0omIU
  https://www.youtube.com/watch?v=W25IWtHOHWA
  https://www.youtube.com/watch?v=dsWCscCdBQM
- Water filtration system
  https://www.youtube.com/watch?v=kazEAzGWuIc
  https://www.youtube.com/watch?v=232xA2e8RiQ
  https://www.youtube.com/watch?v=0DlnAq5UAqY
- Water sprinklers
  https://www.youtube.com/watch?v=axS3eIfTpoA
  https://www.youtube.com/watch?v=-hfIMgxZpVQ
  https://www.youtube.com/watch?v=Eg-A8_L2N30
  https://www.youtube.com/watch?v=bKYX2GLSbZU
- Well
  https://drillyourownwell.com/
  https://www.youtube.com/watch?v=5rYPRMm8Arw
  https://www.youtube.com/watch?v=1Ue2DkG64r8
- Windmill, wind generator
  https://www.youtube.com/watch?v=MDb6HEY-uR4
  https://www.youtube.com/watch?v=wlMlEkR704U
  https://www.youtube.com/watch?v=THkiIaeTLPE
  https://www.youtube.com/watch?v=qSWKoPGfx3w
- Wood-fired hot tub
  https://www.youtube.com/watch?v=6WhwQ-u0Q9I
- Wood working shop
  https://www.youtube.com/watch?v=ovFBGKop4Sw
  https://www.youtube.com/watch?v=e9GSTO-4Txo
  https://www.youtube.com/watch?v=p299Gs9qZIU
  https://www.youtube.com/watch?v=7kErNwKA-Ao

Discussion Question / Activity

1. Assign each family member / team member the task of researching and choosing one or two building projects. Then determine what each chosen project says about that person.

Chapter 73
Solar and Wind Energy

Solar and wind energy options allow your country home to either be off the grid and completely energy independent (i.e., off-the-grid) or to be on the grid with the option of paying for energy when solar and wind are inadequate or receiving credit when solar and wind power exceed your usage (i.e., grid-tied). Both options can provide loads of energy but they are not always reliable and steady. The sun doesn't always shine and the wind doesn't always blow. As you contemplate your energy options, it is might be a good idea to consider a scenario of no electric utilities (i.e., energy) for a month or two time period. During this time, you would have no idea when your electricity might be restored. Potentially you could initially use up most of the contents of the fridge, but what about the food in your freezer(s)? Electric service and food have monetary values, but do they have more than just monetary value? When you see the cost of adding a large solar panel array, it is expensive and may not fit into your budget. However, if you can't heat or cool your home, your family may suffer. Not having the basic ability to light your home at night time can be a huge inconvenience. Instead of just comparing solar installation to your bills, put a value on having a steady supply of electricity. When you take the value of electricity into consideration, an off-the-grid solution such as solar may seem like an excellent option. While solar and wind energy can be initially expensive to implement and the return on investment may take decades, the value and peace of mind that go along with energy independence may make alternative energy options a much better option. Keep in mind, once you have invested in a solar array or a windmill or both, it makes it less likely you will want to relocate in the future.

There are several types of solar panels: monocrystalline, polycrystalline and thin-film. Monocrystalline is the most efficient but also the most expensive. Polycrystalline is low cost but along with lower costs are lower efficiency. Thin-film solar is portable and lightweight but is also the lowest efficiency. New solar configurations are coming out with increasing frequency. Soon, roofs may use solar tiles instead of composite roofing materials. Some solar panels are in the shape of a large flower, which opens during day time hours and follows the sun on a dual axel, improving efficiency and lasting until the sun sets. The "flower" then closes and opens again the next day. It detects high winds and closes to protect the solar panels. Some solar arrays target electric car-recharging while others power home systems.

The sun's energy in the form of photons, hits the solar array panel. The panel is made up of conductive elements such as silicon, cadmium telluride, amorphous silicon, and copper indium gallium selenide. Glass covers the conductive surface and electrodes are placed both on the front and back of the surface to capture electrons, the electrical current. Current is then transferred via electric cables to a battery bank where the energy is stored until used. Batteries deliver direct (continuous) current (DC) but most home appliances take alternating current (AC) which has a 60 hertz (Hz) or cycles per second. An inverter box is placed between the battery bank and the line feeding power to your home. The inverter box is equipped to do several things. It converts DC to AC. Some are designed to provide you with information about the operation of your system, including the ability to improve the system's efficiency. There are three types of inverters: string inverters, microinverters and power optimizers. Each system has its own advantages and disadvantages. String inverters are the most common, but micro-inverters and power optimizers allow for monitoring power production of each panel. Take the time to study each component and determine which system best fits your needs.

A solar system consists of the following components. Study each piece to understand how it fits into a working unit. Solar panels, solar array mounting racks, tracking mounts, array DC disconnect, solar inverter (e.g., micro-inverter, string inverter, power optimizers), battery pack, solar meter, charge controller / charge regulator, breaker panel, back-up generator (for use with off-grid systems), wiring (size is important) and fuse box connections, utility power meters (for grid-tied systems), etc. Take the time to learn and understand each component as you are considering whether or not solar is an option.

If there is shade on your solar panels and the panels are all connected, the efficiency of each solar array does not exceed the panel with the lowest output. Newer systems address this issue in several ways. String inverters connect several panels and then connect to a central string inverter. These work best for solar arrays which have full sun all the time. String inverters may also be paired with power optimizers which address the partial shade issue.

Power optimizers may be used on each panel to minimize energy losses due to shading. Each panel is connected to a power optimizer. It sends power to a string inverter and has the effect of minimizing overall system power losses due to shading. The string converter then converts DC to AC and sends the energy to a central inverter. This addresses the shade issue. This allows the user to monitor the activity of each panel separately.

Microinverters may be installed on each panel to address shade issues as well. Each panel converts DC to AC and then sends the energy to your home without needing a separate central inverter.

Central inverters are similar to string inverters but they are used for larger arrays. In this system, the string inverters all meet at the central inverter where the current is converted to AC. The type of inverter also deserves consideration. It is vital to the success of a robust solar system.

Battery based inverters and chargers are used where bi-directional energy is important. This means the energy can be stored for later use or the excess energy beyond what is stored in the battery pack, is put back into the grid. These systems may be stand alone or be interactive (share energy back into the grid). Large systems provide greater than 10 KW of energy storage, usually enough to run a large home or a small business.

Charge controllers are used for off-grid systems. They direct the flow of energy (i.e., electrons) from high to low voltage. When the sun is high and electricity is coming into the system, the charge controller sends the power to the battery bank. As the battery bank gets charged up, the charge controller will lower the amount of electricity going to the batteries to just enough to keep them charged. It also automatically disconnects the flow of energy to the battery bank when the voltage is low, preventing overcharging the batteries. Keep in mind, there are different types of charge controllers. Take the time to explore different charge controllers and read about their features.

If you are just starting out with solar, you may want to start with a small system which would be just enough to power a computer and a few lights. This system would cost in the range of $200 to $500. It could work for someone who wishes to be off the grid or possibly live in a van. It would not power appliances. If you need more energy but are not able to invest tens of thousands of dollars, you could set up a system for around $2,500 to $3,500 that would power a few appliances, a computer and lights.

Going to the larger systems which range from 3 kW or more costs around $2.90 to $3.30 per watt, or starting around $9,000. If you are eligible for a rebate, the cost is less. Depending on your location and several other factors, you should be able to run a small home with 1 to 3 people.

It is simple to calculate your usage – check your electric bill. The bill gives you the cost of electricity per kilo watt hours (kWh) and how many kWh you use in a month. The cost per kWh runs from $0.10 to $0.35+ per kWh. The average American home uses around 1,000 kWh of electricity per month. If you are interested in setting up a solar system, first you need to determine the average number of hours per day that you would be able to generate solar energy. For example, if you live in a sunny location, you may be able to generate at peak transfer for 6 hours a day. Multiply 6 hours per day X 30 days per month and this is 180 hours per month. To generate 1,000 kWh per month: 1,000 kWh per month / 180 hours per month = 5.6 kW system. However, if you live in a place which is not sunny all year, you must take into effect a different set of parameters. For example, if you are only assured an average of 3.2 hours of sunlight per day and you use 1,400 kWh per month, your numbers may look like this: 1,400 kWh per month / 96 hours per month = 14.6 kW system.

Adding battery backup capabilities also adds to the cost of a solar system, typically running from $200 to $800 / kW. Several types of batteries are used to store solar energy. Lead acid batteries have been used for decades. They are inexpensive but do not last as long as lithium batteries and they also have lower depth of discharge compared to most other batteries. Lithium batteries require no maintenance and operate at low temperatures without affecting capacity. They are safer than lead acid batteries. Some lithium batteries have a cycle life of 10,000+. Lithium batteries weigh less than lead batteries, making them good choices for RVs, marine and other mobile operations.

In addition to capacity, a battery has a power rating. This is the amount of kW the battery can deliver at one time. A battery with low capacity and a high power-rating could run an entire home for a few hours. A battery with a high capacity and a low power rating could deliver a small amount of electricity for a long time.

Depth of charge is the amount of a battery's capacity which can be used before it needs to be recharged. Round-trip efficiency describes how much energy is used in storing energy in the battery vs. how much is available to use. Take your time to research solar energy. Talk with others who have done it and learn from their successes and mistakes.

Harnessing energy from the wind uses some of the same concepts of solar power but instead of using the sun's photons, wind energy requires wind and some type of wind mill. The spinning windmill generates electricity which spins a generator, which creates electricity. Electricity is then used to power a house or it is stored in a battery bank for later use. Components of a wind system include: tower, rotor blades, nacelle, low-speed shaft, high-speed shaft, gearbox, generator, controller, yaw controlling mechanism, pitch system, anemometer, braking system, some type of foundation.

Hydroelectric energy is similar to wind energy except it requires water to flow at a certain minimum rate and requires a minimum drop in feet. This spins a generator and sends electricity to the home for immediate use, or it is stored in a battery bank for later use. The more energy generation strategies you implement the greater the possibility you can be 100% energy independent. This lifts the burden on paying expensive utility rates for electricity. You may still need to purchase water and natural gas or propane, but your electric needs are fully met by one or more off the grid solutions.

Having recently survived a week of sub-freezing temperatures, including several nights of sub-zero-degree (F) weather in Texas (February 2021), along with two back-to-back snow storms, it is important to realize alternative energy systems may be inadequate for extreme weather conditions. In February 2021, snow along with ice and sub-freezing weather blanketed Texas for one week, all the way from the most northern borders in the panhandle to the furthest southern tip. Every single county in Texas was impacted by this deadly polar vortex. Solar and wind power (as well as other types of power) were negatively impacted. Keep this in mind as you plan for supplying power to your home. If your solar, wind and hydroelectric power are unavailable, how would you keep your family warm and keep all electric-powered appliances (including cars) supplied with electricity? What happens when your well pump freezes? How do you keep your wind or water turbines from damage when the water freezes and temps are near zero degrees fahrenheit? Consider having several gas-powered generators on hand for extreme weather conditions.

In the meantime, there are a number of habits, when implemented, reduce your reliance on electricity. These habits are usually simple things such as drying your clean clothes on a clothesline, towel drying your hair for 10 to 15 minutes before blow drying it, using LED lights, turning off lights when not in use, wearing an extra sweater in the wintertime and using evaporative cooling during the summertime, using blackout shades to keep your home cool in the summer, using a toaster oven instead of your full-size oven when possible, etc. There are many ways to conserve energy. This makes your off-the-grid system more efficient and extends its life.

The discussion questions below are meant to provide each participant with critical information needed to consider whether or not solar and other alternative energy systems are necessary and reasonable.

References and sources
https://www.nrel.gov/docs/fy19osti/71714.pdf
https://www.energysage.com/solar/solar-energy-storage/what-are-the-best-batteries-for-solar-panels/

Discussion / Activity

1. Each person / family should bring their electric bill with usage data. Use this as a starting point to determine the output needed to cover 100% of electric needs.
2. What types of activities could be reduced or eliminated to reduce electric use?
3. What is the cost of the system needed to provide 100% off the grid capabilities?
4. What is the length of time needed for a return on investment?
5. Describe each of the components of a solar system.
6. What are the components of a wind turbine system?

Chapter 74
Build a root cellar

Root cellars are a great way to preserve the fall harvest. A well-designed root cellar can spare freezer space and extend the period you can benefit from your harvest. They work because they are relatively cold and the high humidity helps prevent or slow the release of ethylene gas. This slows down enzyme reactions and stops the growth of microorganisms. Curing winter squash and pumpkins is relatively easy and ensures your harvest will keep well into the winter months. Curing is similar to dehydration but without cutting into the squash or pumpkin. It allows the excess moisture to evaporate and it slows down the plant's respiration processes. Evaporation concentrates the sugars making cured squashes and pumpkins sweet and delicious.

Root cellars may be large and complex or small and simple. Look for a design which fits your need for space, outward appearance, storage requirements, etc. You may need more than one type of cellar to preserve both fruits and vegetables. Sometimes a designated place in your home such as a cool basement or crawl space may also work. Below is a listing of the various types of root cellars. Do research into root cellars and see which type of design fits your budget and needs. Below are brief descriptions of different types of root cellars:

1. Above ground root cellar: many designs, rock or stone construction is good.
2. Attics.
3. Basement root cellar.
4. Built into hillside root cellar.
5. Cabbage clamp: dig holes in hard ground to store cabbages and root vegetables. Cover with thick layer of straw and then dirt to protect from frost. Then cover with a straw bale.
6. Clamp: compact heap or mound of root crop vegetables. Excavate a shallow rectangular depression and stack crops into the base up to a height of 6 or so feet. Cover crop with several inches of earth, stray and old hay to protect from rain. Keeps produce fresh for months.
7. Closets: a dark closet in a cool room might be a perfect place to store some kinds of produce.
8. Concrete block root cellar: built below ground level.
9. Dresser or chest of drawers: an old dresser or chest may be converted into root crop storage.
10. Earth berm: at ground level or partially above ground.
11. Garages: a dark cool corner of the garage might be a perfect storage place.
12. Garbage can root cellar: bury a galvanized garbage can and store beets, carrots, potatoes, etc.
13. Hole in the ground root cellar: a hole in the ground may be the perfect place to keep root crop.
14. Larder: cool area for storing food prior to use, usually with cold stones and on north side of house. Window with wire mesh and not glass.
15. Leaf bucket "cellar" – use a 5 gallon bucket to make a simple root cellar for carrots.
16. Partially underground root cellar.
17. Pit house – large house in the ground used as a shelter and doubles as a root cellar.
18. Potato barn or potato house.
19. Sheds.
20. Spring houses: small building constructed over a spring. Keeps a constant cool temperature throughout the year.
21. Zeer pot: one small clay pot inside a larger clay pot with sand between the two pots and water added to promote evaporative cooling.

Root crops should be put into storage in late fall. They can withstand light frosts but not freezing. Handle sweet potatoes carefully. They should cure and then be put into storage containers at harvest time. Important factors contributing to long-keeping are: temperature, humidity, airflow, presence of pests, and ethylene gas. Designate a crisper drawer for non-ethylene sensitive fruits and vegetables.

Below are some of the basic requirements for long term fruit and vegetable storage:

- **Vegetables which must be cured before storage**: onions, potatoes, pumpkins, winter squash.
- **Produce which benefits from paper wrappings**: apples, pears.
- **Can be packed in damp sand, peat moss or sawdust (not touching)**: beets, carrots, radishes, rutabagas, turnips. Celery can be stored upright with roots in sand.
- **Produce that needs darkness**: potatoes.
- **Can be replanted in a bucket or bag of moist soil**: brussels sprouts, cabbage.
- **Can be kept in dry, unheated space or may be stored in shallow baskets no more than two layers deep**: garlic, onions, shallots.
- **Can be kept in unheated basement**: pumpkins, sweet potatoes, winter squash.
- **Refrigerator storage**: root crops (but not potatoes, sweet potatoes, onions or garlic). Refrigerate roots and tubers in plastic bags.
- **Leave in ground covered with mulch until ground freezes**: beets, carrots, potato, radish, turnip.
- Do not store or display ethylene (plant ripening hormone released as a gas) sensitive fruits and vegetables together in the refrigerator, root cellar or at room temperature next to or in proximity with ethylene producing fruits and vegetables.
- **Ethylene producing fruits include**: apples, avocados, bananas, apricots, cantaloupe, figs, green onions, grapes, honeydew, kiwi, mango, nectarines, papaya, passion fruit, peaches, pears, persimmons, plantains, plums, potatoes, quince, tomatoes.
- **Ethylene sensitive foods include**: asparagus, Belgian endive, blackberries, broccoli, brussels sprouts, cabbage, carrots, cauliflower, chard, collards, cucumbers, eggplant, garlic, green beans, kale, leeks, lemons, lettuce, limes, okra, onions, peas, peppers, raspberries, spinach, squash, strawberries, sweet potatoes, unripe bananas, watercress, watermelon.
- **Fruits and vegetables not sensitive to ethylene gas**: blueberries, cherries, beans (snap) garlic, grapefruit, oranges, pineapple, potatoes, raspberries, strawberries, tomatoes, yucca.
- Do not store ethylene producing fruits with vegetables in plastic bags. This traps the ethylene gas and causes the fruits and vegetables to ripen faster and possibly go to waste.
- When it comes to bananas, much of the ethylene is produced from stem area. Some may see a small benefit if you wrap the stems with plastic wrap or foil, to increase the shelf life of your bananas.

Cold (29 °F – 31 °F) and damp (90% to 95%) storage: pears, etc.
Cold (32 °F – 42 °F) and damp (90% to 95% humidity) storage: apples, beets, broccoli, brussels sprouts, cabbage, carrots, Jerusalem artichokes, leeks, parsnips, potatoes, rutabaga, turnip, winter radish, etc.
Cold (40 °F – 45 °F) and damp (90% to 95% humidity): potatoes, etc.
Cool (50 °F – 60 °F) and dry (60% to 70% humidity) storage: beans (dried), garlic, onions, pumpkins, squash, sweet potatoes, tomatillos, tomatoes.
To cure potatoes: harvest, brush off excess dirt, remove any bad potatoes, store in slatted boxes in dark room with 45 °F to 60 °F and 85% to 95% relative humidity. Small nicks and bruises may heal during curing. After 2 weeks, remove any wrinkled or bad ones and then store in boxes or trays.
Cure before storing: beans (dry on plant), garlic (hang where good air flow for 2-3 wk), potatoes, squash.
Store separately: apples, broccoli, cabbage, citrus.

On this page and the next is a description of each type of fruit or vegetable which may be stored for use during fall and winter months.

Apples: individually wrap or keep in plastic bag and store separate from other fruits and vegetables. They produce ethylene gas which accelerates ripening of other produce. Store around 32 °F – 40 °F, high humidity. Immediately remove bad apples.
Beans, dry: cool and dry (32 °F to 50 °F), 60% to 70% relative humidity. After drying beans, shell them and either refrigerate them at 0 °F or below for 3 or 4 days or heat them in the oven at 180 °F for 15 minutes.
Beets: cold and moist (32 °F to 40 °F), 90% to 95% relative humidity. Layer with straw or moist sand.
Brussels sprouts: cold and very moist (32 °F to 40 °F), 90% to 95% relative humidity. 3 to 5 weeks.
Cabbage: cold and very moist (32 °F to 40 °F), 90% to 95% relative humidity. Wrap. Store from late fall through early to midwinter. 3 to 4 months.
Carrots: cold and very moist (32 °F to 40 °F), 90% to 95% relative humidity. Layer in a box with moist sand, peat or moss. 4 to 6 months.
Cauliflower: cold and very moist (32 °F to 40 °F), 90% to 95% relative humidity. Store for 6 to 8 weeks.
Celery: cold and very moist (32 °F to 40 °F), 90% to 95% relative humidity.
Garlic: 50 °F and 50% humidity.
Grapefruit: cold and very moist (32 °F to 40 °F), 80% to 90% relative humidity.
Grapes: cold and very moist (32 °F to 40 °F), 80% to 90% relative humidity, do not store with vegetables.
Horseradish: cold and moist (32 °F to 40 °F), 90% to 95% relative humidity. May be left in ground until needed. Cover with thick layer of mulch.
Jerusalem artichoke: cold and very moist (32 °F to 40 °F), 90% to 95% relative humidity. Best to leave in the ground until needed. Cover with thick layer of mulch.
Kale: cold and very moist (32 °F to 40 °F), 80% to 90% relative humidity. Sealed in fridge, unwashed.
Kohlrabi: cold and very moist (32 °F to 40 °F), 80% to 90% relative humidity.
Leeks: cold and very moist (32 °F to 40 °F), 80% to 90% relative humidity. Pull up with roots allow roots to remain while in storage.
Onions: to cure onions, harvest after several days of dry weather, remove excess soil, do not cut off their stems. Cure for 2 wk. Place in a warm, dry well-ventilated location (i.e., window screens), not touching each other or hang upside down. After curing, trim off brown leaves, store in a cold and moist location (32 °F to 35 °F), 60% to 70% relative humidity. Store through fall and winter.
Oranges & citrus: cold and very moist (32 °F to 40 °F), 80% to 90% relative humidity, do not store with vegetables.
Parsnips: cold and very moist (32 °F to 40 °F), 90% to 95% relative humidity.
Pears: cold, very moist (29 °F to 40 °F), 80% to 90% relative humidity, don't store with veg.
Peas: need an airtight container. cold and moist (32 °F to 50 °F), 60% to 70% relative humidity.
Potatoes: Cure in a dark place for 1 to 2 weeks at 45 °F to 50 °F. Store at 38 °F to 40 °F in cold and moist place with 80% to 90% humidity. There are many ways to store potatoes, discuss with others and read internet. 5 to 8 months.
Pumpkins: Leave stem on the pumpkins and cure for several weeks either in a dry field or in a dry warm greenhouse or sunroom for 2 wk. After curing, store around 50 °F to 55 °F and 50% to 75% relative humidity. Do not store pumpkins in outdoor cellars or pits.
Radish: cold and very moist (32 °F to 40 °F), 90% to 95% relative humidity.
Root crops (not potatoes): Keep in the ground. Cover any part of vegetable protruding above ground with dirt or mulch, hay, leaves, etc. Dig out when you need them. Cold temps increase sugar content, making them sweeter.
Tomatoes: Right before the first frost, pick all tomatoes, even the green ones. Store in a cool dark place on newspaper and not touching each other. Several days before using, place the tomato on the window sill and allow it to ripen. Some tomato varieties keep well for up to 3 months, even when

almost ripe. Also, some cherry tomatoes can be kept on the vine and the vine hung in the basement. Green tomatoes on the vine eventually ripen and may be used. Long keeping tomato varieties include: Garden Peach, Long Keeper, Reverent Morrows Long Keeper Winter Storage, etc.

Turnips: cold and very moist (32 °F to 40 °F), 90% to 95% relative humidity.

Winter squash (banana, buttercup, butternut, delicate, hubbard, kabocha, spaghetti): harvest before a hard freeze. Leave stem on to cure for 10 to 14 days at 75 °F to 85 °F. Store in moderately dry and warm location, between 50 °F to 60 °F and humidity between 50% to 70%. Do not store squashes on a shelf or rack or in outdoor cellars or pits.

You may need to plan several storage spaces based on what you plan to store. The later the crop matures (i.e., closer to fall and cooler temperatures), the better it stores in a root cellar. Never store fruits with vegetables. They need separate storage areas. For some vegetables, storage improves their sugar content. Be sure to trim off green tops to about one inch or more above the root. Make sure the produce you store is not bruised, nicked or pierced. This shortens its storage life. It is critically important for you to vent your root cellar so dangerous gases can escape. Vegetables such as cabbage and turnips may require separate storage areas so other produce does not absorb their strong odors. Never allow produce to freeze and re-thaw, this ruins it unless you use it right away. You may want to choose a few vegetable cultivars known to be suited for long term storage. Root vegetables should be cured immediately after picking (but not left out in direct sun) and then placed in the root cellar.

This site is an excellent site providing information on the types of root cellars and storage tips.

- The Old Farmer's Almanac, Root Cellars: Types and Storage Tips https://www.almanac.com/content/root-cellars-types-and-storage-tips
- Large family pantry tour, food storage challenge https://www.youtube.com/watch?v=zMMG5oA36YU
- Earthbag root cellar build, off grid food storage, part 1 https://www.youtube.com/watch?v=xtDdf1K73j0&list=PU3FHvW16m_i117IqPnb0nmA&index=8
- Earthbag root cellar build, off grid food storage, part 2
- https://www.youtube.com/watch?v=hucNE7732jM&list=PU3FHvW16m_i117IqPnb0nmA&index=2
- Earthbag root cellar, part 3 https://www.youtube.com/watch?v=IG9va-Gn5aI&list=PU3FHvW16m_i117IqPnb0nmA&index=11
- Did our food supply last through the winter? https://www.youtube.com/watch?v=CYk4bXYWziU
- Great website for finding gardening tools: https://www.gardeners.com/home

Discussion questions

1. What are some reasons to build a root cellar?
2. How much space do you think you will need?
3. What are potential hazards of root cellars?
4. Are there ideal climates for needing and using a root cellar?
5. Are there one or more spiritual insights to be learned from using a root cellar?

Chapter 75
Build a solar dehydrator

Dehydration removes moisture from food. This prevents bacteria, yeast and mold from growing on food. Drying food also slows the ripening process.

Several physical aspects are necessary to successfully dehydrate food. They are low humidity, air circulation, and heat. A clean and hygienic dehydrating environment is also critical. If flies and bugs have access to dehydrating food, it may become contaminated. Dehydrating in direct sunlight also takes advantage of UV rays and their sterilizing properties. Sun drying and solar drying utilize the sun's energy to heat the food and remove moisture. Electronic options include ovens and dehydrators.

Dehydrating food is a sound method to preserve it for later consumption. Many fruits and vegetables are easily dehydrated to preserve a large harvest. Apples can be sliced and dehydrated and added to granola, lunch bags, etc. Tomatoes can be dehydrated and used in a variety of recipes.

Many fruits and vegetables are easily dehydrated. I like to dehydrate kale rubbed in cashew cheese sauce. This makes tasty kale chips. Thinly sliced dehydrated mangoes make a great snack as do apricots, grapes, plums and many other fruits. **One of the prettiest dehydrated fruits is pineapple.** Remove the outer bumpy layer and thinly slice into rounds. Dehydrated, it looks like a beautiful flower and tastes great! Dehydrated food works well for camping and backpacking as most of the moisture is removed and food can be rehydrated at the campsite to save precious space and weight in backpacks and camper trailers.

Many vegetables are easily dehydrated. For example, heat and air circulation are used to completely dehydrate beets and then dehydrated beets can be pulverized to make beet powder for using in smoothies or dehydrated beet pieces may be added to soups. Garbanzo beans may be seasoned and then dehydrated as a delicious snack or used in salads. If you want to keep dehydrated food "raw," keep dehydrating temperatures between 105 °F (41 °C) and 121 °F (49 °C).

Dehydrators range in price from around $20 to $1,000 or more. If you want to buy a dehydrator, I like Excalibur, although this tends to be one of the more expensive models. Excalibur models cost between $130 and $300. Most models have timers and you can fine tune the dehydrating temperatures.

Not all dehydrators are electronic. Dehydrators can be built at home and be 100% solar driven or may incorporate a heating element and fan. Either way, if you are handy, consider building your own dehydrator.

You can build it to size and to fit the needs of your specific situation. This page includes several examples and web page links for learning how to build a useful and inexpensive food dehydrator.

Solar Drying

https://nchfp.uga.edu/how/dry/sun.html

https://www.instructables.com/id/A-Radiant-Solar-Food-Dehydrator-that-doesnt-fight-/

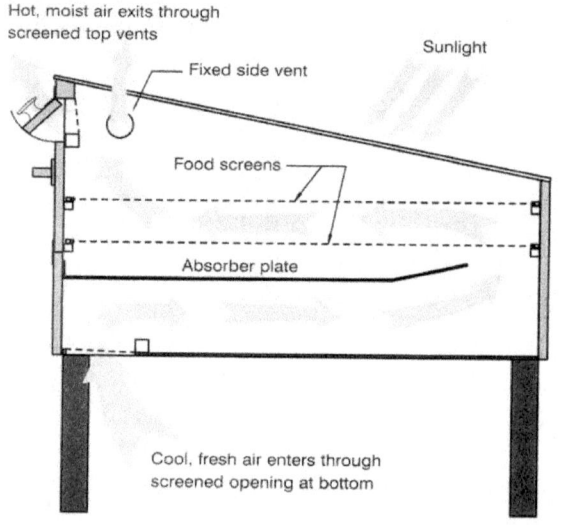

https://www.motherearthnews.com/diy/solar-food-dehydrator-

How to Build a Food Dehydrator
How to construct a food dryer powered by the sun, a stove or electricity; including materials, diagrams for assembly.
https://www.motherearthnews.com/diy/build-a-food-dehydrator-zmaz93fmztak

Sun Drying by the National Center for Home Food Preservation
Outdoor drying racks / solar drying.
https://nchfp.uga.edu/how/dry/sun.html

6 Ways to Build a Food Dehydrator at Home – DIY Electric and Solar
Types of DIY food dehydrators
https://dehydratorlab.com/how-to-build-a-food-dehydrator-diy

Food Dehydrator – Simple and Cheap
12 Components for electric dehydrator
https://hackaday.io/project/27724-food-dehydrator-simple-and-cheap

Discussion questions

1. What are the main advantages to dehydrating fresh produce?
2. How might dehydration contribute to less food waste?
3. Would dehydration concentrate or dilute the flavor and nutrients?

Chapter 76
Build raised beds with or without covers

When you decide to build a raised garden bed(s) you have likely seen a design you like. This short section devoted to building raised beds is not comprehensive. Entire books are devoted to building raised garden beds. This section is to get you thinking about the general idea of raised garden beds.

Garden bed. Photo credit, Markus Spiske, Unsplash.com

Here are a few items to consider. When you have determined a location and narrowed down your ideas about aesthetics, size, height, number, etc., then you may want to consult someone with building skills. The links below provide information for beginners and may be adequate for most people wanting to get started.

1. Determine the type, size, numbers and ideal location for your raised garden bed(s). Maybe you want parallel beds or maybe a U-shaped bed area.
2. Prepare the area
3. Purchase materials (e.g., wood and other hardware)
4. Build the beds (watch "how-to" videos)
5. Fill the beds with various types of dirt, soil amendments, branches, leaf mulch, etc.
6. Plant the beds. Determine what you want to grow in the beds and plant them. Be sure to mulch them to keep weeds from growing and taking over.
7. Water the beds
8. Maintain the beds

It is important to make a few early decisions such as the following?
- What is your budget?
- How expensive are raised bed materials to build, fill, and set up with automatic watering?
- What do you want to plant in the beds?
- What seasons do you plan to use the beds?
- Do you want to build the beds in a greenhouse or outside?
- Will you build the beds against another structure or will they be free-standing?
- Do you want beds on the ground or above the ground?
- Are you ok with leaning over or kneeling to garden, pull weeds, pick produce, etc., or would you rather do these tasks while standing?
- How high do you want the beds?

- Do you want the beds to look basic or fancy?
- Do the beds need to match any other aspect of the planned space(s)?
- Do you want automatic or manual watering?
- How do you plan to protect the beds from animals such as dogs, cats, deer, birds, etc.
- Others:

Once you have settled on a basic plan, set up a schedule to complete the plan. Some people use the materials they have on hand and others spend some time planning and preparing. Whatever your style, this is a great project and it deserves consideration for your gardening spaces.

How to build raised garden beds
https://www.familyhandyman.com/garden-structures/how-to-build-raised-garden-beds/

Raised Garden Beds (with several videos)
https://learn.eartheasy.com/guides/raised-garden-beds/

The Basics: Gardening in Raised Beds
https://www.gardeners.com/how-to/raised-bed-basics/8565.html

The complete raised bed gardening video
https://www.youtube.com/watch?v=YlvSMlwRua0

Discussion questions

1. What are the advantages of raised garden beds for you?

2. What types of designs appeal to you?

3. What did it mean when God cursed the ground right after Adam and Eve sinned?

4. How do you plan to enrich the soil in the immediate future and over many seasons?

Chapter 77
Build a strawberry bed or tower

In the southern United States, strawberry plants are considered to be perennials. The plants bear fruit for up to five years but even when the original plants die, each year, runners make new plants. This is a perfect crop to plant in either a bed or a tower.

There are three types of strawberries: June-bearing (one large crop in June), everbearing (two crops), and day-neutral (requires temperatures less than 75 °F). Strawberries can be started from seeds, bare roots or seedlings. As the strawberries begin to bloom in the first year or the first crop, you want to pluck off all the blooms. This means no strawberries if you are growing June-bearing strawberries which yield only one crop. But the second year, the strawberry plants reward you with bigger and better berries and lots of them. If you are growing everbearing strawberries, prune the first crop and harvest the second one.

It's a good idea to grow the plants in a protected place. Otherwise eager children, wild animals and birds may find the berries first. Beds can be covered with chicken wire framed with wood supports, bird netting, or grown in beds covered with screens. Do some online research and talk with seasoned gardeners about the best planting and propagating methods. There are novel ways to build strawberry beds off the ground. A strawberry tower is a fun way to vertically grow strawberries. However, their runners do not propagate as easily as when they are grown on the ground. Another novel way to grow strawberries is in tubs, pots, raised beds, hanging pots, repurposed rain gutters, hay bales, etc.

When you are harvesting and eating fresh, juicy strawberry shortcake, or making strawberry jam or a heaping strawberry pie, you may wish you had planted twice as many berries. This also allows you to avoid store-bought berries which are sprayed with herbicides and pesticides. In addition to planting strawberries, plant other types of berries which bear right away so you don't have to be sad about not having strawberries the first year.

During cold winter months and after the first several frosts, trim the strawberry plants back to about 1 inch (when the temperature drops to 20 °F). Mulch them with 4 to 6 inches of mulch, which could include straw, pine needles, wood chips, leaves, etc. When spring arrives, carefully remove the mulch and watch them grow!

In addition to building a strawberry patch, you may want to build or designate an area to plant raspberry or bramble plants. Raspberries need full sun and must be pollinated by bees and other pollinating insects. They need to be annually pruned and should be protected from roaming rabbits during dormant months.

The types of raspberries available to the home gardener have exploded! You can find red raspberries, purple or black raspberries, orange raspberries, yellow raspberries and even white raspberries. Their roots are perennial so they only need to be planted once and usually bear fruit for 10 to 15 years unless they get a virus in which case they must be destroyed.

Some raspberries grow upright without needing support but it is usually recommended to put up a simple trellis for raspberries to use during the growing season. Raspberries need lots of sun and good circulation but not necessarily a windy location. Follow the directions for each type of raspberry you plant. Each type of raspberry may have slightly different spacing requirements.

Discussion questions

1. How many people in your household would enjoy fresh strawberries?
2. What are the health benefits of fresh strawberries?
3. How would you prepare your strawberries or would you eat them fresh?
4. What types of strawberry plants would you grow?

Chapter 78
Build a chicken coop

Over the past several decades, chicken coops have become urban status symbols. Many small cities have modified their bylaws and ordinances to allow a certain number of backyard chickens. This has been a good thing for both chickens and families. Chickens are loved and small children learn to care for farm animals and fresh eggs are the best!

If you desire to have chickens, they become part of your family. They are not a disposable commodity, to be used and discarded when the weather gets cold or they are no longer needed. God commanded man to care for the animals. Ask yourself how you think God would want you to care for farm animals. Every animal, no matter how small, ugly or feeble, matters!

If you are serious about having chickens, check out a book or two about chickens from the library. Be sure you have thoroughly researched this topic before you dive in and buy them. If you plan to raise chickens for their eggs, then you may want to consider the following:

Photo credit: The Brewers, Hunter Valley, NSW, Australia at Unsplash.com

- Local ordinances and codes regulating chickens.
- How many chickens can you have?
- How many chickens do you want?
- Which types of chickens?
- Where will you build a chicken coop?
- What size coop do you need?
- Can you afford to keep chickens?
- Is selling eggs be a potential small business?
- What will you feed them?
- Are you committed to their well-being and caring for them when they get ill and have minor or major medical needs?
- Are you prepared to deal with their issues? De-worming them, etc.?
- Are you prepared to deal with their predators such as snakes, possums, raccoons, foxes, dogs, birds of prey, etc.?
- How will you care for them when you are away from home on vacation?
- Who will be responsible for cleaning their coop on a daily basis?
- Will keeping chickens complicate your life or will it enhance your life?
- Are you prepared to treat them with respect and kindness?
- Do you realize if they are not properly cared for they may be become diseased?

Building a coop is not necessarily a simple proposition like building a raised bed or even a solar dehydrator. A chicken coop takes some planning and consideration. It is a small shed which must include nesting areas, feeding and watering areas, a protected outdoor area, heating options (for those in cold weather climates but some say chickens do not need additional heat source), etc. Below are some links to webpages dedicated to showing you how to build a chicken coop. There are hundreds of similar type pages. Do the research and pray for wisdom and guidance before you take on this added responsibility.

https://www.thehappychickencoop.com/chicken-coop-plans/

https://www.thespruce.com/free-chicken-coop-plans-1357113

https://modernfarmer.com/2015/09/how-to-build-a-chicken-coop/

Discussion questions

1. Am I prepared to care for and take into consideration the welfare of my chickens or do I just want chickens because it is a fad and my friends are doing it?

2. What does it mean to have "dominion" over the animals? Four Hebrew words are translated as "dominion." The first is "radah." This word is often translated as "rule" or "have dominion over." This word implies dominion for the sake of the animal and not the human. Additional insight comes from the second Hebrew verb used to modify dominion, "abad" a word meaning "servant or serve," or "bring to pass," or work," or "worship." The third word is "Shamar" suggesting "keeper," or "observe," or "preserve." The fourth word is kabash. This word may be understood in the context to mean, "subduing something in line with its nature." See this page/source for additional insight: https://kgsvr.net/xn/discussion/radah2.html

3. How would God want us to treat the animals he created on the same day he created man?

4. Are you prepared to do what is best for your chickens as far as keeping the safe, sheltered from the elements, etc.?

5. Are you prepared to do in depth research into the needs and requirements of keeping chickens?

6. Who is able to care for your chickens when you go on vacation?

Chapter 79

Build a small chapel on your property

Most people do not own a church or chapel. We prefer to get in the car and drive to church where we fellowship and study the Word with others, where kids play together, we eat together, we sing together and we contemplate the awesome God we serve. No wonder most of us never thought about building a small chapel on our property.

However, there may be times where you just want to be in God's presence or get away from your familial obligations for a brief respite. Having a chapel on site is the perfect get-away for personal prayer time, contemplation, study and meditation on the Word. If you are interested in such a project, check out pictures and plans for building "tiny house" chapels.

Photo Credit: Mor Shani at Unsplash.com

https://tinyhouseblog.com/tiny-house-concept/tiny-churches/

https://www.foxnews.com/us/minister-builds-tiny-chapel-to-hold-really-small-weddings

https://homehacks.co/320-sq-foot-chapel-tour/

Discussion questions

1. Jesus spent a lot of time both in the temple and in nature, contemplating the scriptures. Is it important to have a physical place dedicated only to worship at home or can one worship anywhere at any time?

2. Would a small chapel on your property positively contribute to your family's spiritual development?

3. If a small chapel is not on your building agenda, is there a way to designate a space on your property for worship?

Section 10

Civil Unrest, Local and National Emergencies

Chapter 80

Make plans for civil unrest, local and national emergencies

Natural disasters occur with regularity all over the planet. Civil unrest is commonplace in many countries around the world. In the 1980s, I spent almost 2 months on an art and history tour of Europe. Our tour group was just barely ahead of widespread violence which occurred all over Europe that summer. I remember visiting Spain in 1997 and getting caught up in a violent demonstration in downtown Barcelona, protesting the mafia-style death of a beloved politician who was kidnapped, shot, and unceremoniously dumped from a moving car in the middle of Barcelona. African countries are known for near constant violent uprisings and conflicts as well as widespread civil wars. Famine, pestilence, drought, earthquakes, tornados, hurricanes, floods, and fires while devastating and tragic, are all considered part of life. Now it looks like the USA must add pandemics, civil unrest, brazen shoplifting, and the threat of martial law to the list of possible modern-day disasters.

In 2020, the year the world faced an international pandemic as well as widespread civil unrest, many were unprepared for what unfolded. One of the most surprising elements of 2020 was widespread civil unrest and violence against the backdrop of volatile political debate. Many of us expected law and order to be quickly restored, but it never happened. The violence continued almost unabated. Authorities refused to stop rioting and wide-spread property destruction. Many suffered material losses, physical injuries and even death at the hands of dissidents and rioters. Those living in large cities and poor neighborhoods experienced greater risks and losses. Losses for the year 2020 were in the billions of dollars, surpassing all previous natural disasters.

Martial law is the suspension of existing laws and implementation of targeted laws to address issues such as out-of-control violence, an act of war, or even a devastating natural disaster, etc. Most of us have not lived through a state of martial law. During a national emergency such as martial law, lines of communication may not work, gas, food and essential supplies may be rationed, and the military may be mobilized to enforce draconian measures such as forced vaccination, removing children from 'uncooperative' parents, etc. We have come to heavily rely on cellular communication modes to stay in touch with our friends and loved ones. However, in a time of national emergency, we may not have access to cellular communications and even the internet. How would you communicate with your loved ones if you could not use cell phones or the internet? Do you have a landline phone? Can you operate a HAM radio? Does your family have a meet-up place both local and distant if you cannot unite together at the same time? What is your plan and does everyone in your family / group know what to do???

Civil unrest motivated many who had been on the fence about moving to the country to purchase country properties. Real estate agents across the country claimed, "The telephone did not stop ringing in 2020." This is particularly true for real estate agents in rural areas of every state. Maybe you are one of those families who has transitioned from the city to the country. If so, congratulations!

This section is about being prepared. While it may be impossible to prepare for every possible scenario, positive outcomes favor those who prepare. It is a good idea to at least contemplate possible scenarios. This section is designed to provide you with some resources to use during a national emergency (forms are found in the appendix).

The resources in the appendix are designed based on some of the following questions:

- Who is your team?
- Where will you go?
- How will you get clean water?
- How long can you survive if the food supply is disrupted? How long will your food last?
- Are you in good enough physical shape to walk 20 to 50 or more miles? Walking shoes in car?
- How will you get there to where you need to go (if you are unable to stay in your home)?
- What will you do if the internet goes down?
- Do you know basic first aid? CPR? Minor surgical procedures such as stitching?
- Do you have a distant family meeting place should the event be mainly local?
- What happens if you are arrested?
- How will you prove ownership of your possessions in case of squatters or otherwise?
- How long will your "supplies" last?
- What will you do if you are required get numerous vaccines to travel?
- How will you care for aged parents?
- What happens if your vehicle breaks down and you need parts which are not available?
- What will you do if you cannot get prescription medications?
- In the event of a power outage, how long will your battery supply last?
- Who is in charge of making decisions? Who is second in 'command?'
- What if your pre-planned escape route is blocked?
- Are your vehicles going to be an asset or liability? What happens to them if there is an EMP?
- What will you do if you cannot fill up your vehicles with gas?
- What will you do if cell phone service goes down?
- Who will you join with to weather the event or a difficult time period?
- What will you do if the transportation infrastructure goes down?
- What happens if your children are removed from you?
- What happens if the water supply is disrupted?
- What if you are out of state or out of the country when civil unrest occurs?
- Do you keep enough gas in your car at all times to get out of town (if you live in town)?
- What happens if you are separated from your family?
- What happens if you cannot find your family members?
- When your cell phone battery runs out, how will you access important phone numbers?
- How will you gather family members to a "safe" place if they are spread out at work, etc.?
- If you want to be incognito, do you know about potential "tracking" elements found in your phone, computer, vehicle, etc.? Do you know how to escape a large violent crowd?
- If something happens and your family is separated, who should stay put and who should go find the rest of the family members?
- Does each family member know what to do in a worst-case scenario?
- Would an electric bike or motorcycle be useful for you and your family?
- Do you keep a "bug out" backpack in case you need to go on foot?
- Do you know techniques for getting out of a dangerous mob or riot situation?
- What happens if you get bit by a wild animal or a venomous insect or snake?
- Many other questions! Add your questions to this list.

The appendix contains forms to help you prepare for emergencies.

Appendix

Section 1: Spiritual Preparation
God Given Tasks, 534
Country Living Personal Skills Inventory (PSI), 535
A Collection of Scripture Promises, 543
Types of Cognitive Biases, 552
The Holmes-Rahe Life Stress Inventory, 558

Section 2: Country Living Health and Lifestyle
Hydrotherapy Methods and Techniques, 559

Section 3: Country Living Nutrition
Histamine Intolerance, 564
Risk Factors for 9 Common Conditions, 568

Section 4: Country Living Plant-based Culinary Arts

Section 5: The Country Living Medicine Cabinet and Essential Skills

Section 6: Country Living Land and Homes

Section 7: Monetize Your Country Home
Care Giver Daily Activity and Progress Note, 569

Section 8: Country Living Gardens and Landscaping
12 Months of Gardening Tasks, 571

Section 9: Small Building Projects for Consideration

Section 10: Civil Unrest and Local and National Emergencies
Age Appropriate First Aid Kits, 573
Emergency Services Contact Numbers and Locations
- Construction, Fire, Local Utilities, Neighbors, Police, 575
- Church and Clergy, 576
- Friends and Relatives, 576
- Websites and News Outlets, 576
- News Outlets: Radio Stations, TV Stations and HAM Radio Operators, 576
- Medical and Emergency Type Services Directory, 577

Emergency Supply List, 578
Contingency Group Plans, 581
Vital Document Checklist, 582

| My Daily God-given Tasks | Date: |

Big stuff for today and this week...
1. _____
2. _____
3. _____
4. _____

What keeps me going...

I'm inspired by....

I'm excited about....

Anonymous kind acts...

Kind acts toward animals...

Breakfast

Lunch

Dinner

My steps today:

Activities & times:

Cups of water:

1 2 3 4
5 6 7 8
9 10 11 12
13 14 15 16

Today's accomplishments
- _____
- _____
- _____
- _____
- _____
- _____
- _____
- _____
- _____

Today's to do list
- _____
- _____
- _____
- _____
- _____
- _____
- _____
- _____
- _____

What today might look like (my appointments)
- _____ : _____
- _____ : _____
- _____ : _____
- _____ : _____
- _____ : _____
- _____ : _____
- _____ : _____
- _____ : _____
- _____ : _____
- _____ : _____
- _____ : _____
- _____ : _____
- _____ : _____

Motivational quote or Bible verse:

Gratitude for:

Notes:

Self-care / reward Ideas:

Country Living Personal Skills Inventory (PSI)
for Group Projects and Community Living Arrangements

Date: _____

Name of Person Being Evaluated: Completed by:

My Briggs-Myers Temperament Type (if known):

Skills or Traits	Ranking	Notes
Area 1: Christian walk with God	1=no, not at all; 10=absolutely, yes	
1. I love the Lord so much He is all I think about all day.	Yes / No	
2. I spend daily time with God in prayer and Bible study.	1 2 3 4 5 6 7 8 9 10	
3. Overall my faith is increasing based on my walk with God.	1 2 3 4 5 6 7 8 9 10	
4. I have complete confidence God is leading in my life.	Yes / No	
5. I have a passion for winning souls to Christ.	Yes / No	
6. My family is my most important mission field.	1 2 3 4 5 6 7 8 9 10	
7. I spend quality time with my family in worship, praise, prayer, ministry, and the study of God's word.	1 2 3 4 5 6 7 8 9 10	
8. I believe in and support the 10 commandments.	Agree / Disagree	
9. I am a Bible-based Christian, not here to promote the ministry or beliefs of another person or organization, but only the ministry of Jesus. ONLY CHRIST SHOULD BE LIFTED UP.	Agree / Disagree	
10. I do not plan to promote any specific person, excessively refer to a specific person by name, or promote any organization while working as part of this group or within this community.	Agree / Disagree	
11. I seek to unite God's people based on Christian virtues of love, patience, kindness, long-suffering, etc.	Yes / No	
12. I seek out and promote controversial beliefs which tend to divide the Christian community.	Agree / Disagree	
13. All of my religious beliefs are 100% correct.	Yes / No	
14. It is my way or the highway when it comes to religious dogma.	1 2 3 4 5 6 7 8 9 10	
15. One or more of my beliefs significantly diverges from my chosen religious tradition (i.e., church affiliation, organization).	Yes / No	
16. I believe that which unites us as Christians is more important than the small issues which may divide us.	Agree / Disagree	
17. I believe in the equal calling and ministry of all people.	Agree / Disagree	
18. My fears tend to drive my thoughts and actions.	1 2 3 4 5 6 7 8 9 10	
19. I maintain high moral behaviors beyond reproach of the law and moral code.	1 2 3 4 5 6 7 8 9 10	
20. I am frequently judgmental of others.	1 2 3 4 5 6 7 8 9 10	
21. I frequently insert myself into the personal lives of others.	1 2 3 4 5 6 7 8 9 10	
22. I expect life to be completely fair.	1 2 3 4 5 6 7 8 9 10	
23. I expect life to be completely fair or my view of God is altered.	1 2 3 4 5 6 7 8 9 10	
24. I fold up and check out when life gets difficult.	1 2 3 4 5 6 7 8 9 10	
25. I often help others, even if it comes with a personal cost.	1 2 3 4 5 6 7 8 9 10	
26. I discuss personal lives of others without their knowledge / approval.	1 2 3 4 5 6 7 8 9 10	
27. I prefer to associate w people who improve my social standing.	1 2 3 4 5 6 7 8 9 10	
28. I am a "safe" person to know.	Agree / Disagree	
29. On a scale of 1 to 10, my health can be described as:	Excellent Average Poor	

Skills or Traits	Ranking	Notes
30. I am not "detached" from reality nor mentally ill.	Agree / Disagree	
Area 2: My health and wellness philosophy 1=nonexistent/poor/no/low/bad; 10=great/yes/high/excellent/good		
31. I am physically in tip top shape.	1 2 3 4 5 6 7 8 9 10	
32. I do some type of physical activity for 45 or more minutes, on how many **days** per week?	0 1 2 3 4 5 6 7 **days**	
33. I can run / walk 5+ miles without stopping in < than 90 min.	Yes / No / It's close to 90 min	
34. I am into health and wellness.	1 2 3 4 5 6 7 8 9 10	
35. I am careful about how I live and what I put into my body.	1 2 3 4 5 6 7 8 9 10	
36. I feel vital, energetic, and full of energy.	1 2 3 4 5 6 7 8 9 10	
37. My energy lasts all day long; I rarely need a nap.	1 2 3 4 5 6 7 8 9 10	
38. I get adequate sleep.	Yes / No	
39. I am outside for at least 30 or more minutes per day.	Yes / No	
40. I perform all tasks necessary for 100% independent living.	Yes / No	
41. I am reliant on one or more prescription medications to maintain or treat one or more health condition(s).	Yes / No	
42. Prescription medications I use alter my physical or mental condition requiring a change in my routine.	1 2 3 4 5 6 7 8 9 10	
43. I am mentally healthy.	1 2 3 4 5 6 7 8 9 10	
44. I require special dietary modifications.	Yes / No	
45. I consume just enough calories to maintain a healthy and desirable weight for my height and gender.	Yes / No	
46. I perform an adequate amount of activity / exercise to maintain a desirable and healthy body weight.	Yes / No	
47. Number of pounds I need to lose to feel and look better and to achieve better health.	0 5 10 15 20 25 25-50 50–75 75–100 100+	
48. How motivated are you to make positive health changes?	1 2 3 4 5 6 7 8 9 10	
49. How many meals, including snacks do you eat in a day?	1 2 3 4 5 6 7+ meals	
50. I do not eat between meals.	Agree / Disagree	
51. I am open to fasting one or more days per month?	Agree / Disagree	
52. I prefer to eat wholesome and minimally processed food.	Agree / Disagree	
53. I need special modifications for my home or apartment.	Yes / No	
54. I have a disability.	Yes / No	
55. I have adapted to my disability and do not need extra care.	Yes / No / Not applicable	
56. I have a disability and need significant alterations to my living environment.	Yes / No / Not applicable	
57. I bathe every day and take steps to limit body odor.	1 2 3 4 5 6 7 8 9 10	
58. I brush my teeth at least 2X/day and take steps to limit bad breath.	1 2 3 4 5 6 7 8 9 10	
59. I care about my oral health and daily take steps to maintain good oral health and avoid cavities and gum disease, etc.	1 2 3 4 5 6 7 8 9 10	
60. I clean my face and nose on a daily basis.	Yes / No	
61. I care about how I look and present myself to others.	1 2 3 4 5 6 7 8 9 10	
62. I prefer not to discuss my health issues with others outside of my immediate family.	Agree / Disagree	
63. I tend to live a chaotic life.	Agree / Disagree	
64. I tend to live an ordered, well-planned life.	Agree / Disagree	

Skills or Traits	Ranking	Notes
65. I feel it is inappropriate to discuss personal health issues with friends and acquaintances.	Agree / Disagree	
66. I believe my friends enjoy hearing about my health issues.	Agree / Disagree	
67. I feel it is important to avoid sharing personal health information with others, especially gender specific issues.	Agree / Disagree	
68. I do not have questionable, uncomfortable or inappropriate conversations with others.	Agree / Disagree	
69. I have never been accused of gender bias, inappropriate conversations, or inappropriate behaviors.	Agree / Disagree	
70. I have a medical condition which leads to being overwt / obese.	Yes / No	
71. I am overweight / obese because I eat too much.	1 2 3 4 5 6 7 8 9 10	
72. I am overweight / obese because I don't exercise enough.	1 2 3 4 5 6 7 8 9 10	
73. I am motivated to lose weight.	1 2 3 4 5 6 7 8 9 10	
74. I am underweight or too thin to be healthy and vibrant.	1 2 3 4 5 6 7 8 9 10	
75. I am frequently fatigued and out of breath.	1 2 3 4 5 6 7 8 9 10	
76. I need frequent rest periods and / or naps during the day.	Agree / Disagree	
Area 3: Work commitment and area(s) of expertise		
77. Hours you are able to participate in light manual labour.	0 1 2 3 4 5 6 7 8 hrs	
78. Hours you are able to participate in medium manual labour.	0 1 2 3 4 5 6 7 8 hrs	
79. Hours you are able to participate in hard manual labour.	0 1 2 3 4 5 6 7 8 hrs	
80. Do you have a defined skill set such as mechanics, farming, wood working, farming, construction, electrical, plumbing, etc.	Agree / Disagree	
81. Do you have a defined skill set such as healthy food prep, baking, sewing, cleaning, ironing, farming, gardening, education, etc.	Yes / No	
82. If you have a skill set, how many years have you worked in area?	1 2 3 4 5 6 7 8 9 10+	
83. Are you a medical professional with a current license or registration and experience in a specific area?	Yes / No	
84. If you are a health / medical professional, how many years have you worked in this area?	1 2 3 4 5 6 7 8 9 10+	
85. How many hours per day are you willing to work in your area of expertise or in areas which are needed?	0 1 2 3 4 5 6 7 8 9 10+	
86. Do you usually do things right the first time?	Yes / No	
87. Do you make efforts to solve problems before requesting help?	Yes / No	
88. Do you frequently generate new problems to be solved?	Yes / Sometimes / No	
89. Is it ok to fudge a little bit or make up information when communicating with others?	Yes / No	
90. I am able to establish and maintain healthy boundaries.	1 2 3 4 5 6 7 8 9 10	
Area 4: Work ethic		
91. When asked to do a task, do you do it right away or do you procrastinate or give an excuse to do it later?	1 2 3 4 5 6 7 8 9 10 1 = procrastinate; 10 = do immediately	
92. Are there jobs you won't do or will complain about doing?	Yes / No	
93. Are you a hard worker or do others work longer and harder?	1 2 3 4 5 6 7 8 9 10 1 = lazy; 10 = hardest	
94. Consistently speaking, when do you report for a job?	Early / on time / late / never	

Skills or Traits	Ranking	Notes
95. How frequently do you access and use your phone while working?	Never Life & death emergencies only. Once or more per shift.	
96. Do you need frequent reminders to complete assigned tasks?	1 2 3 4 5 6 7 8 9 10 1 = always; 10 = never	
97. Do you find yourself making excuses to get out of doing hard or difficult work?	1 2 3 4 5 6 7 8 9 10 1 = always; 10 = never	
98. What is the quality of your work?	1 2 3 4 5 6 7 8 9 10 1 = poor; 10 = excellent	
99. Do you shun unpleasant jobs such as cleaning the toilet, unclogging the toilet, cleaning shower drain, changing a tire?	Yes / No / Sometimes	
100. Do you avoid getting your hands or nails dirty?	Yes / No	
101. Do you feel entitled to receive something you have not earned or worked for?	Yes / No	
102. Do you disappear when difficult tasks need to be done?	Yes / No	
103. I am a national treasure and should be treated better than others.	Yes / No	
104. How industrious are you?	Very / somewhat / not at all	
105. Are you a creative problem solver?	1 2 3 4 5 6 7 8 9 10 1 = poor; 10 = excellent	
106. Are your contributions showy and artificial vs. substantive and goal / group oriented?	1 2 3 4 5 6 7 8 9 10 1 = artificial; 10 = substantial	
107. I have addictions which affect my work ethic.	Yes / No	
108. Do you pick up after yourself as you work?	Yes / No	
109. Do you expect others to clean up for your as you work or after you have completed a job?	Yes / No	
110. Do you complete a job or leave it partially undone (e.g., cleaning, putting things away, communicating about the project with appropriate people)? (circle one)	Complete the job Partially complete the job Usually leave a mess	
111. Would your co-workers and supervisor say you are reliable?	Yes / No	
112. Have you ever been violent or aggressive toward someone?	Yes / No	
113. Have you ever intentionally physically harmed someone else?	Yes / No	
114. Do you tell questionable jokes or stories while working?	Yes / No / Sometimes	
115. Has anyone ever complained you exhibit inappropriate behaviors or comments toward others?	Yes / No	
116. Do you believe women and men are of equal value?	Yes / No	
117. Do you treat opposite gender with respect and consideration?	Yes / No	
118. Do you show basic consideration and respect to those of different nationalities, skin color, etc.?	Yes / No	
Area 5: Attitude toward work and others 1=no, not at all; 10=absolutely		
119. Do you consider yourself a good conversationalist?	Yes / No	
120. What would make you a better conversationalist?		
121. Do you think you know it all?	Yes / No	
122. Do you make excuses as to why you cannot work?	Yes / No	
123. Are your conversations with others lopsided, where the other person spends more time listening to you than speaking?	Yes / No	
124. Do you find yourself telling your story over and over, even to the same person(s)?	Yes / No	

Skills or Traits	Ranking	Notes
125. Do you complain about your friends, what they have done, what they did to hurt you, etc.?	Yes / No	
126. Are you careful to always uplift others, even your enemies?	Yes / No	
127. Are you careful to effectively use other people's time and not waste their time with your personal issues, especially if they are there to help you?	Yes / No	
128. Do you understand if you refuse to learn new relational skills to accommodate growth in your relationships (marriage, friendship, etc.) they will stagnate, your friends may drift away, your family may spend less time with you, and ultimately you will be owned by the skills you refuse to develop or refine?	Yes / No	
129. When someone comes to help you do you have things ready when they arrive or are you disorganized and not ready?	Yes / No	
130. Do you take longer to do tasks which others do in half or significantly less time?	Yes / No	
131. Do you like to talk about yourself, your past, your accomplishments, your history with others?	Yes / No	
132. Do you spend more than 30 seconds telling others how you are doing when asked, "How are you doing?"	Yes / No	
133. Do you repeat same stories over and over to family / friends	Yes / No	
134. Do you find yourself discussing others' affairs, gossiping, spreading facts and falsehoods about others or involving yourself in their affairs without their knowledge or invitation?	Yes / No	
135. Do you sometimes esteem yourself and your work to be better than others?	Yes / No	
136. Do you allow your spouse to do difficult work while you are on your phone, the computer, or pretending to be busy?	Yes / No	
137. Do you help your spouse with cooking and cleaning and other household chores or do you leave your spouse to do chores while you go golfing, shopping, watch sports, etc.?	Yes / No	
138. Do you make excuses about the quality or quantity of your work or your behaviors?	Yes / No	
139. When faced with a difficult job, do you persist until done?	Yes / No	
140. When faced with a difficult job, do you give up easily?	Yes / No	
141. Are you frequently asked to redo your tasks?	Yes / No	
142. Do you expect others to do things for you?	Yes / No	
143. Do you feel entitled not to work or materially contribute and yet be part of a group?	Yes / No	
144. Compared to others, your material contributions to group gatherings or projects are none to very minor.	Yes / No	
145. Do you say you will work but your actions prove otherwise?	Yes / No	
146. I am always kind to others, including animals.	Yes / No	
147. I believe we have an obligation to care for the environment.	Yes / No	
148. I believe we have an obligation to care for the animals.	Yes / No	
149. I easily forgive others when they hurt or offend me.	Yes / No	
150. I hold grudge sagainst others, even when they ask forgiveness.	Yes / No	
151. Do you make people feel good about themselves?	Yes / Usually / No	
152. Do people like to be around you?	Yes / Usually / No	
153. Do you make other people feel inferior to you?	Yes / Sometimes / No	

Skills or Traits	Ranking	Notes
154. Are you a complainer / whiner?	Yes / Sometimes / No	
155. Are you mostly pleasant or grumpy?	Pleasant / Grumpy	
156. Are you more of an optimist than a pessimist?	Yes / No	
157. Are you more of a pessimist than an optimist?	Yes / No	
158. Are you more of a realist than an optimist or pessimist?	Yes / No	
159. I prefer to talk about myself more than listening to others.	Yes / No	
160. I am a good listener and prefer to hear more about others than I prefer to talk about my life.	Yes / No	
Area 6: Work relationships 1=nonexistent/poor/no/low/bad; 10=great/yes/high/excellent		
161. How good are you with taking guidance from others?	1 2 3 4 5 6 7 8 9 10	
162. It is easy to make time for leisure activities while essential chores and tasks tend to go undone?	Yes / No	
163. Do you work well as a team member?	1 2 3 4 5 6 7 8 9 10	
164. Do you prefer to work alone?	Yes / No / Depends	
165. Are you comfortable with being supervised?	Yes / No	
166. Do you frequently criticize your supervisor?	Yes / No	
167. Do you have a prince or princess complex?	Yes / No	
168. Are you collaborative, seeking to find common ground when working as part of a group?	Yes / No	
169. If you are a leader, do you lead by example or do you prefer to sit back and tell others what to do?	Lead by example Like to sit back and direct	
170. Would you rather chat with others than work?	Yes / No	
171. Do other people enjoy working with you?	Yes / No / Mostly	
172. Do people try to get out of working with you?	Yes / No	
173. Do you frequently ask others for help before you attempt to solve the problem by yourself?	Yes / No	
174. Have you ever purposefully sabotaged a project?	Yes / No	
Area 7: Attention to detail, ability to follow instructions		
175. How well do you read instructions, follow orders, understand directives?	1 2 3 4 5 6 7 8 9 10 1 = never read; 10 = always	
176. People tend to get more work done than I do in a similar amount of time?	1 2 3 4 5 6 7 8 9 10 1 = always; 10 = never	
177. Are you a problem solver?	Yes / No	
178. What is your influence on others?	1 2 3 4 5 6 7 8 9 10 1 = negative; 10 = positive	
179. Is your language reflective of Christian values?	Yes / No	
180. Is your lifestyle reflective of Christian values?	Yes / No	
181. Do you take God's name in vain?	Yes / No	
182. I am the person who makes everyone else laugh.	Yes / No	
183. Is it ok to take questionable shortcuts to complete a job?	Yes / No	
184. I have addictions which could affect my moral influence on others, especially young people.	Yes / No	
Area 8: How will your health or lack thereof affect your ability to contribute?		
185. I need to have frequent breaks?	Yes / No	

Skills or Traits	Ranking	Notes
186. I need to snack between meals?	Yes / No	
187. I need to be frequently absent from work and obligations.	Yes / No	
188. I need others to frequently assist me.	Yes / No	
189. My lack of health and vitality may keep me from working?	Yes / No	
Area 9: What tangible and intangible things do you bring to a job site or a working team?		
190. Are you going to eat more food and consume more resources than the value you can contribute?	Yes / No	
191. Are you able to spend your own money to purchase necessities, food, clothing, housing, etc.?	Yes / No	
192. Are you able to make significant contributions to overall living expenses such as fuel, food, equipment, supplies, etc.?	Yes / No	
193. Do you help clean up / put things away without being asked?	Yes / No	
194. I show gratitude to others by helping out, giving monetary gifts, or giving useful items to those in need, etc.	Yes / No	
195. I am able to support myself and do not need assistance.	Yes / No	
Area 10: Your children's habits and attitudes toward work		
196. Are your kids well-behaved?	Yes / No	
197. Do your kids exert a positive influence on other children?	Yes / No	
198. Do your kids exert a negative influence on other children?	Yes / Possibly / No	
199. Are your kids willing to work hard and be industrious?	Yes / No	
200. Are your kids lazy, preferring to play video games or watch TV?	Yes / No	
201. Are your kids honest and truthful?	Yes / No	
202. Do your kids enjoy personal Bible study and devotions?	Yes / No	
203. Are your kids honest and truthful?	Yes / No	
204. Are your kids adverse risk takers, a potential safety hazard?	Yes / No	
205. Do your kids follow instructions?	Yes / No	
206. Do your kids interfere with your work schedule?	Yes / Sometimes / No	
207. How often do your kids interfere with your scheduled work time?	All the time Frequently Infrequently Never	
208. Do your kids almost always work independently?	Yes / No	
209. Will your children be in the way or disrupt others?	Yes / No	
210. Do your kids play quietly or scream and holler a lot?	Play quietly Scream and holler	
211. Do your kids lie and tell falsehoods?	Yes / Sometimes / No	
212. Do your kids dress provocatively?	Yes / No	
213. Are your kids sexualized, do they easily converse about sex, drugs, and inappropriate subjects for their age?	Yes / No	
214. Do your kids curse and / or take God's name in vain?	Yes / No	
215. Do your kids have addictions such as computer games, phone time, junk food, drugs, etc.?	Yes / No	
216. Can your kids successfully follow detailed instructions?	Yes / No	
217. Overall, considering time management, safety, influence on others, legitimate skills, a high worth ethic, the ability to start and finish tasks - my kids will make significant positive contributions and few if any negative ones and be an asset for this project.	Yes / No	

Skills or Traits	Ranking	Notes
Area 11: Real, established skills I have and am willing to perform on a regular basis – write the number of years you have spent doing each of the following tasks you check below, in the notes column.		
218. Accounting, book keeping	1 2 3 4 5 6 7 8+ hr/day	
219. Manager, I lead by example	1 2 3 4 5 6 7 8+ hr/day	
220. Director, I place people in the best positions for their skills	1 2 3 4 5 6 7 8+ hr/day	
221. Construction: general, cleaning the site, etc.	1 2 3 4 5 6 7 8+ hr/day	
222. Construction: cement work, brick laying, etc.	1 2 3 4 5 6 7 8+ hr/day	
223. Construction: electrical	1 2 3 4 5 6 7 8+ hr/day	
224. Construction: painting, caulking, sanding, etc.	1 2 3 4 5 6 7 8+ hr/day	
225. Construction: plumbing, septic	1 2 3 4 5 6 7 8+ hr/day	
226. Construction: wood working, cabinets, etc.	1 2 3 4 5 6 7 8+ hr/day	
227. Construction: other:	1 2 3 4 5 6 7 8+ hr/day	
228. Heavy equipment operator	1 2 3 4 5 6 7 8+ hr/day	
229. Land surveyor	1 2 3 4 5 6 7 8+ hr/day	
230. Fencing, digging posts, moving ground / dirt, etc.	1 2 3 4 5 6 7 8+ hr/day	
231. Energy mgmt: electric, solar, wind, hydro, propane, gas, etc.	1 2 3 4 5 6 7 8+ hr/day	
232. Mechanic: heavy equipment	1 2 3 4 5 6 7 8+ hr/day	
233. Mechanic: cars and trucks	1 2 3 4 5 6 7 8+ hr/day	
234. Appliance repairs	1 2 3 4 5 6 7 8+ hr/day	
235. Greenhouse, tunnels	1 2 3 4 5 6 7 8+ hr/day	
236. Plowing, planting, harvesting, tending	1 2 3 4 5 6 7 8+ hr/day	
237. Farming, general	1 2 3 4 5 6 7 8+ hr/day	
238. Architect, design, drafting	1 2 3 4 5 6 7 8+ hr/day	
239. Grounds maintenance: mowing, small repairs, landscaping, water features, signage, fencing, septic, etc.	1 2 3 4 5 6 7 8+ hr/day	
240. Marketing and selling farm produce	1 2 3 4 5 6 7 8+ hr/day	
241. Growing and selling microgreen crops	1 2 3 4 5 6 7 8+ hr/day	
242. Chef or line cook	1 2 3 4 5 6 7 8+ hr/day	
243. Kitchen worker with food handler or ServSafe certificate	1 2 3 4 5 6 7 8+ hr/day	
244. Maid: cleans floors, dusts, cleans windows, polishes, scrubs walls, bathtub, sinks, cleans dirt, laundry, irons, etc.	1 2 3 4 5 6 7 8+ hr/day	
245. Other:	1 2 3 4 5 6 7 8+ hr/day	
Area 12: Skills I have and am willing to perform on a regular and long-term basis		
	1 2 3 4 5 6 7 8+ hr/day	
	1 2 3 4 5 6 7 8+ hr/day	
	1 2 3 4 5 6 7 8+ hr/day	
	1 2 3 4 5 6 7 8+ hr/day	

Notes

A Collection of Scripture Promises

1. **Claim God's promise to Abraham to be part of His nation.** And the angel of the LORD called unto Abraham out of heaven the second time, and said, By myself have I sworn, saith the LORD, for because thou hast done this thing, and has not withheld thy son, thine only son: that in blessing I will bless thee, and in multiplying I will multiply thy seed as the stars of the heaven, and as the sand which is upon the sea shore; and thy seed shall possess the gate of his enemies; and in thy seed shall all the nations of the earth be blessed; because thou has obeyed my voice. Gen 22:15-18

2. **I am the Lord your God! I will take care of you.** And I will take you to me for a people, and I will be to you a God: and ye shall know that I am the LORD your God, which bringeth you out from under the burdens of the Egyptians. Exodus 6:7

3. **The Lord fights for us.** The LORD shall fight for you, and ye shall hold your peace. Ex 14:14

4. **We have nothing to fear.** It is the LORD who goes before you; he will be with you, he will not fail you nor forsake you; do not fear or be dismayed." Deuteronomy 31:8

5. **God's words are always true.** And now, O Lord God, thou art that God, and thy words be true, and thou hast promised this goodness unto thy servant: therefore, now let it please thee to bless the house of thy servant, that it may continue forever before thee: for thou, O Lord God, has spoken it: and with thy blessing let the house of thy servant be blessed forever. 2 Samuel 7:28-29

6. **God's mercies toward us endure forever.** O give thanks unto the Lord; for he is good; for his mercy endureth forever. 1 Chronicles 16:34

7. **Repent and turn away from sin – he is faithful to forgive and heal us.** If my people, which are called by my name, shall humble themselves, and pray, and seek my face, and turn from their wicked ways; then will I hear from heaven, and will forgive their sin, and will heal their land. 2 Chronicles 7:14

8. **The joy of the Lord is your strength.** Nehemiah 8:10

9. **His favor surrounds us like a shield.** For you bless the godly, O Lord; you surround them with your shield of love. Psalm 5:12

10. **The Lord is our refuge.** The Lord also will be a refuge for the oppressed, a refuge in times of trouble. Psalm 9:9

11. **He shields us when we take refuge in Him.** God's way is perfect. All the Lord's promises prove true. He is a shield for all who look to him for protection. Psalm 18:30

12. **The law of the Lord is perfect**, converting the soul; the testimony of the Lord is sure, making wise the simple. Psalm 19:7

13. **God comforts and leads us.** Even when I walk through the darkest valley, I will not be afraid, for you are close beside me. Your rod and your staff protect and comfort me. Ps 23:4

14. **We have nothing to fear.** The Lord is my light and my salvation; Whom shall I fear? The Lord is the strength of my life; of whom shall I be afraid? Psalm 27:1

15. **The Lord is the only one who never forsakes us.** For my father and my mother have forsaken me, but the LORD will take me up. Psalm 27:10

16. **God is our hiding place.** For you are my hiding place; you protect me from trouble. You surround me with songs of victory. Psalm 32:7

17. **God teaches us**. The Lord says, "I will guide you along the best pathway for your life. I will advise and watch over you. Psalm 32:8

18. **Blessed are we when we take refuge in the Lord**. Taste and see that the Lord is good. Oh, the joys of those who take refuge in him! Psalm 34:8

19. **When we seek the Lord, we lack nothing**. Even strong young lions sometimes go hungry, but those who trust in the Lord will lack no good thing. Psalm 34:10

20. **The Lord hears us**. The Lord hears his people when they call to him for help. He rescues them from all their troubles. Psalm 34:17

21. **God delivers us**. Then call on me when you are in trouble, and I will rescue you, and you will give me glory. Psalm 50:15

22. **God will not let the righteous fall**. Give your burdens to the Lord, and he will take care of you. He will not permit the godly to slip and fall. Psalm 55:22

23. **God grants favor and honor**. For the Lord God is our sun and our shield. He gives us grace and glory. The Lord will withhold no good thing from those who do what is right. Psalm 84:11

24. **God's love abounds toward us**. O Lord, you are so good, so ready to forgive, so full of unfailing love for all who ask for your help. Psalm 86:5

25. **Psalm 91**.

26. **God's love endures forever**. For the Lord is good. His unfailing love continues forever, and his faithfulness continues to each generation. Psalm 100:5

27. **He satisfies our desires with good things**. He fills my life with good things. My youth is renewed like the eagle's! Psalm 103:5

28. **God's love fills the earth**. O Lord, your unfailing love fills the earth; teach me your decrees. Psalm 119:64

29. **God helps us in our time of need**. I look up to the mountains – does my help come from there? My help comes from the Lord, who made the heaven and earth! Psalm 121:1-2

30. **He will not let us stumble**; the one who watches over you will not slumber. Psalm 121:3

31. **The Lord himself watches over us!** The Lord stands beside you as your protective shade. Ps 121:5

32. **God protects us 24/7**. The sun will not harm you by day, nor the moon at night. Ps 121:6

33. **The Lord preserves us from evil**. The Lord keeps you from all harm and watches over your life. Psalm 121:7

34. **The Lord watches over us**. The Lord keeps watch over you as you come and go, both now and forever. The Lord shall preserve your comings and goings from now to evermore. Psalm 121:8

35. **Our help is from the Lord**, who made heaven and earth. Psalm 124:8

36. **Trust in the Lord!** They that trust in the Lord are as secure as Mount Zion; they will not be defeated but will endure forever. Just as the mountains surround Jerusalem, so the Lord surrounds his people, both now and forever. Psalm 125:1-2

37. **God cares for those who mourn**. Those who plant in tears will harvest with shouts of joy. Ps 126:5

38. **God protects us.** Unless the Lord builds a house, the work of the builders is wasted. Unless the Lord protects a city, guarding it with sentries will do no good. Psalm 127:1

39. **He gives us sleep.** It is useless for you to work so hard from early morning until late at night, anxiously working for food to eat; for God gives rest to his loved ones. Psalm 127:2

40. **Lo, children are a gift of the Lord**; they are a reward from him. Psalm 127:3

41. **We are blessed when we fear the Lord.** How joyful are those who fear the Lord – all who follow his ways. Psalm 128:1

42. **We shall eat the labour of our hands.** You will enjoy the fruit of your labour. How joyful and prosperous you will be! Psalm 128:2

43. **God cares about marriage.** Your wife will be like a fruitful grapevine, flourishing within your home. Psalm 128:3

44. **We have hope in the Lord!** O Israel, hope in the Lord; for with the Lord there is unfailing love. His redemption overflows. Psalm 130:7

45. **We are redeemed from our sin.** He himself will redeem Israel from every kind of sin. Psalm 130:8

46. **Shout for joy!** May your priests be clothed in godliness; may your loyal servants sing for joy. Ps 132:9

47. **We can live in harmony with others.** How wonderful and pleasant it is when brothers live together in harmony! Psalm 133:1

48. **His faithful love endures forever.** Psalm 136

49. **God saves us from our enemies.** Though I am surrounded by troubles, you will protect me from the anger of my enemies. You reach out your hand, and the power of your right hand saves me. Ps 138:7

50. **God is compassionate and good.** The Lord is good to everyone. He showers compassion on all his creation. Psalm 145:9

51. **The Lord helps us when we fall.** For your kingdom is an everlasting kingdom. You rule throughout all generations. The Lord always keeps his promises; he is gracious in all he does. The Lord helps the fallen and lifts those bent beneath their loads. Psalm 145:13

52. **The Lord is near to us.** The Lord is close to all who call on him, yes, to all who call on him in truth. Psalm 145:18

53. **He guides our paths.** Trust in the Lord with all your heart; do not depend on your own understanding. See his will in all you do, and he will show you which path to take. Prov 3:5-6

54. **His banner over me is love.** He escorts me to the banquet hall; it's obvious how much he loves me. Song of Solomon 2:4

55. **God gives us strength and power.** He gives strength to the weary and power to the weak. Isaiah 40:29

56. **God renews our strength.** But those who trust in the Lord will find new strength. They will soar high on wings like eagles. They will run and not grow weary. They will walk and not faint. Isaiah 40:31

57. **I have summoned you by name; you are mine.** O Israel, the one who formed you says, "Do not be afraid, for I have ransomed you. I have called you by name; you are mine. Isaiah 43:1

58. **When we pass through deep waters He is with us**. When you go through deep waters, I will be with you. When you go through rivers of difficulty, you will not drown. Isaiah 43:2

59. **When we walk through the fire, we will not be burned.** When you walk through the fire of oppression, you will not be burned up; the flames will not consume you. Isaiah 43:2

60. **God is with us.** For I am the Lord, your God, the Holy One of Israel, your Saviour. I gave Egypt as a ransom for your freedom; I gave Ethiopa and Seba in your place. Others were given in exchange for you. I traded their lives for yours because you are precious to me. You are honored, and I love you. Isaiah 43:3-4

61. **God never forgets us**. Never! Can a mother forget her nursing child? Can she feel no love for the child she has borne? But even if that were possible, I would not forget you. See, I have written your name on the palms of my hands... Isaiah 49:15-16

62. **God's love for us is not shaken**. For the mountains may move and the hills disappear, but even then, my faithful love for you will remain. My covenant of blessing will never be broken, says the Lord who has mercy on you. Isaiah 54:10

63. **No weapon formed against us will prosper**. But in that coming day no weapon turned against you will succeed. You will silence every voice raised up to accuse you. These benefits are enjoyed by the servants of the Lord; their vindication will come from me. I, the Lord, have spoken! Isaiah 54:17

64. **God's plans for us**. No longer will you need the sun to shine by day, nor the moon to give its light by night, for the Lord your God will be your everlasting light, and your God will be your glory. Your sun will never set; your moon will not go down. For the Lord will be your everlasting light. Your days of mourning will come to an end. All your people will be righteous. They will possess their land forever, for I will plant them there with my own hands in order to bring myself glory. The smallest family will become a thousand people, and the tiniest group will become a mighty nation. At the right time, I, the Lord, will make it happen. Isaiah 60:19-22

65. **God proclaims freedom for us!** The Spirit of the Sovereign Lord is upon me, for the Lord has anointed me to bring good news to the poor. He has sent me to comfort the broken-hearted and to proclaim that captives will be released and prisoners will be freed. Isaiah 61:1

66. **He adorns us with a crown of beauty for the of ashes for mourning**. To all who mourn in Israel, he will give a crown of beauty for ashes, a joyous blessing instead of mourning, festive praise instead of despair. Isaiah 61:3

67. **We are called oaks of his righteousness**. In their righteousness, they will be like great oaks that the Lord has planted for his own glory. Isaiah 61:3

68. **God comforts us**. I will comfort you there in Jerusalem as a mother comforts her child." Isaiah 66:13

69. **God has plans for us and hears our prayers**. For I know the plans I have for you, says the LORD. They are plans for good and not for disaster, to give you a future and a hope. In those days when you pray, I will listen. Jeremiah 29:11-12

70. **God's love is everlasting**. Long ago the Lord said to Israel: I have loved you, my people, with an everlasting love. With unfailing love, I have drawn you to myself. Jeremiah 31:3

71. **God's mercies are new each morning**. Yet I still dare to hope when I remember this: The faithful love of the Lord never ends! His mercies never cease. Great is his faithfulness; his mercies begin afresh each morning. I say to myself, "The Lord is my inheritance; therefore, I will hope in him!" So, it is good to wait quietly for salvation from the Lord. Lamentations 3:21-27

72. **God gives us a new heart**. And I will give you a new heart, and I will put a new spirit in you. I will take out your stony, stubborn heart and give you a tender, responsive heart. Ezekiel 36:26

73. **God will pour out his Spirit**. Then, after doing all those things, I will pour out my Spirit upon all people. Your sons and daughters will prophesy. Your old men will dream dreams, and your young men will see visions. Joel 2:28

74. **There is one true God worthy of our worship**. But you, O Lord my God, snatched me from the jaws of death! As my life was slipping away, I remembered the Lord. And my earnest prayer went out to you in your holy Temple. Those who worship false gods turn their backs on all God's mercies. But I will offer sacrifices to you with songs of praise and I will fulfill all my vows. For my salvation comes from the Lord alone. Jonah 2:7-9

75. **God is our refuge**. The Lord is good, a strong refuge when trouble comes. He is close to those who trust him. Nahum 1:7

76. **God removes our shackles**. This is what the Lord says: "Although they have allies and are numerous, they will be destroyed and pass away. Although I have afflicted you, Judah, I will afflict you no more. Now I will break their yoke from your neck and tear away your shackles." Nahum 1:12 – 13.

77. **Jesus is with us when we mourn**. God blesses those who mourn, for they will be comforted. Matt 5:4

78. **Seek his kingdom first and everything else will fall into place**. So, don't worry about these things, saying, 'What will we eat? What will we drink? What will we wear?' These things dominate the thoughts of unbelievers, but your heavenly Father already knows all your needs. Seek the Kingdom of God above all else, and live righteously, and he will give you everything you need. Matt 6:31-33

79. **God gives good gifts**. Do not judge others, and you will not be judged. Matthew 7:1

80. **Jesus gives us rest**. Then Jesus said, 'Come to me, all of you who are weary and carry heavy burdens, and I will give you rest. Take my yoke upon you. Let me teach you, because I am humble and gentle at heart, and you will find rest for your souls.' Matthew 11:28-29

81. **Nothing is impossible with God**. For the word of God will never fail. Luke 1:37

82. **Our names are written in heaven**. But don't rejoice because evil spirits obey you; rejoice because your names are registered in heaven. Luke 10:20

83. **God's love comes to us through Jesus**. For the law was given through Moses, but God's unfailing love and faithfulness came through Jesus Christ. John 1:17

84. **We have eternal life!** For this is how God loved the world: He gave his one and only Son, so that everyone who believes in him will not perish but have eternal life. John 3:16

85. **Jesus is the light of the world. Whoever follows Jesus will never walk in darkness**. Jesus replied, 'I am the bread of life. Whoever comes to me will never be hungry again. Whoever believes in me will never be thirsty.' John 6:35

86. **Jesus is the light of the world**. Jesus spoke to the people once more and said, 'I am the light of the world. If you follow me, you won't have to walk in darkness, because you will have the light that leads to life.' John 8:12

87. **We are set free**. So, if the Son sets you free, you are truly free. John 8:36

88. **We belong to God.** Anyone who belongs to God listens gladly to the words of God. But you don't listen because you don't belong to God. John 8:47

89. **We have abundant life.** The thief's purpose is to steal and kill and destroy. My purpose is to give them a rich and satisfying life. John 10:10

90. **No one can snatch us from God's hand.** I give them eternal life, and they will never perish. No one can snatch them away from me. John 10:28

91. **Jesus is the resurrection and the life.** Jesus told her, 'I am the resurrection and the life. Anyone who believes in me will live, even after dying.' John 11:25

92. **Jesus is preparing a place for us.** There is more than enough room in my Father's home. If this were not so, would I have told you that I am going to prepare a place for you? When everything is ready, I will come and get you, so that you will always be with me.' John 14:2-3

93. **God's peace is with us.** I am leaving you with a gift – peace of mind and heart. And the peace I give is a gift the world cannot give. So, don't be troubled or afraid. John 14:27

94. **God remains in us.** Remain in me, and I will remain in you. For a branch cannot produce fruit if it is severed from the vine, and you cannot be fruitful unless you remain in me. John 15:4

95. **Our joy is complete in Christ.** I have told you these things so that you will be filled with my joy. Yes, your joy will overflow! John 15:11

96. **God chose us to bear fruit.** This is my command: Love each other. John 15:17

97. **The Holy Spirit guides us to truth.** When the Spirit of truth comes, he will guide you into all truth. He will not speak on his own but will tell you what he has heard. He will tell you about the future. John 16:13

98. **Jesus has overcome the world.** I have told you all this so that you may have peace in me. Here on earth you will have many trials and sorrows. But take heart, because I have overcome the world. John 16:33

99. **Jesus is the way, the truth and the life.** Jesus told him, 'I am the way, the truth, and the life. No one can come to the Father except through me. John 14:6

100. **We have the righteousness of Christ.** We are made right with God by placing our faith in Jesus Christ. And this is true for everyone who believes, no matter who we are. Romans 3:22

101. **We are under grace.** Sin is no longer your master, for you no longer live under the requirements of the law. Instead, you live under the freedom of God's grace. Romans 6:14

102. **We are not condemned.** So now there is no condemnation for those who belong to Christ Jesus. Rom 8:1

103. **We are children of God.** So, you have not received a spirit that makes you fearful slaves. Instead, you have received God's Spirit when he adopted you as his own children. Now we call him, "Abba, Father." For his Spirit joins with our spirit to affirm that we are God's children. Romans 8:15-16

104. **God works for our good.** And we know that God causes everything to work together for the good of those who love God and are called according to his purpose for them. Romans 8:28

105. **If God is for us, who can be against us?** What shall we say about such wonderful things as these? If God is for us, who can ever be against us? Romans 8:31

106. **We are more than conquerors.** No, despite all these things, overwhelming victory is ours through Christ, who loved us. Romans 8:37

107. **Nothing can separate us from God's love.** No power in the sky above or in the earth below – indeed, nothing in all creation will ever be able to separate us from the love of God that is revealed in Christ Jesus our Lord. Romans 8:39

108. **God provides a way out of temptation.** The temptations in your life are no different from what others experience. And God is faithful. He will not allow the temptation to be more than you can stand. When you are tempted, he will show you a way out so that you can endure. 1 Corinthians 10:13

109. **We have victory over death!** Then, when our dying bodies have been transformed into bodies that will never die, this Scripture will be fulfilled: "**Death is swallowed up in victory!**" 1 Corinthians 15:54

110. **God's promises are "yes" and "amen."** For all of God's promises have been fulfilled in Christ with a resounding "Yes!" and through Christ, our "Amen" (which means "Yes") ascends to God for his glory. 2 Corinthians 1:20

111. **We are a new person in Christ.** This means that anyone who belongs to Christ has become a new person. The old life is gone; a new life has begun. 2 Corinthians 5:17

112. **God blesses us.** And God will generously provide all you need. Then you will always have everything you need and plenty left over to share with others. 2 Corinthians 9:8

113. **Christ redeemed us.** But Christ has rescued us from the curse pronounced by the law. When he was hung on the cross, he took upon himself the curse for our wrongdoing. For it is written in the Scriptures, "Cursed is everyone who is hung on a tree." Galatians 3:13

114. **The fruits of the Spirit are God's gifts to us.** But the Holy Spirit produces this kind of fruit in our lives: love, joy, peace, patience, kindness, goodness, faithfulness, gentleness, and self-control. There is no law against these things! Galatians 5:22-23

115. **Principle of sowing and reaping.** Do not be deceived; God is not mocked, for whatever a man sows, that he will also reap. Galatians 6:7

116. **Remain faithful, do not give up**. So, let's not get tired of doing what is good. At just the right time we will reap a harvest of blessing if we don't give up. Therefore, whenever we have the opportunity, we should do good to everyone – especially to those in the family of faith. Galatians 6:9-10

117. **Spiritual blessings abound.** All praise to God, the Father of our Lord Jesus Christ, who has blessed us with every spiritual blessing in the heavenly realms because we are united with Christ. Eph 1:3

118. **We are saved through grace.** God saved you by his grace when you believed. And you cannot take credit for this; it is a gift from God. Salvation is not a reward for the good things we have done, so none of us can boast about it. Ephesians 2:8-9

119. **God is finishing the work he began in us.** And I am certain that God, who began the good work within you, will continue his work until it is finally finished on the day when Christ Jesus returns. Phil 1:6

120. **Jesus is the way!** Therefore, God elevated him to the place of highest honor and gave him the name above all other names, that at the name of Jesus every knee should bow, in heaven and on earth and under the earth, and every tongue declare that Jesus Christ is Lord, to the glory of God the Father. Philippians 2:9-11

121. **The hope of glory.** To whom God would make known what is the riches of the glory of this mystery among the Gentiles; which is Christ in you, the hope of glory: whom we preach, warning every man, and teaching every man perfect in Christ Jesus: whereunto I also labor, striving according to his working, which worketh in me mightily. Colossians 1:27-29

122. **We are chosen, holy and dearly loved.** Since God chose you to be the holy people he loves, you must clothe yourselves with tenderhearted mercy, kindness, humility, gentleness, and patience. Col 3:12

123. **God protects us from the evil one.** But the Lord is faithful; he will strengthen you and guard you from the evil one. 2 Thessalonians 3:3

124. **We have a spirit of power and love.** For God has not given us a spirit of fear; but of power, and of love, and of a sound mind. 2 Timothy 1:7

125. **We receive grace and peace.** May God our Father and the Lord Jesus Christ give you grace and peace. Philemon 1:3

126. **God's peace is with us.** I always thank my God when I pray for you, Philemon, because I keep hearing about your faith in the Lord Jesus and your love for all of God's people. And I am praying that you will put into action the generosity that comes from your faith as you understand and experience all the good things we have in Christ. Your love has given me much joy and comfort, my brother, for your kindness has often refreshed the hearts of God's people. Philemon 4:4-7

127. **Give thanks!** I always thank my God when I pray for you. Philemon 4:19

128. **God promises His people a special rest.** So, there is a special rest still waiting for the people of God. Heb 4:9

129. **God's Word is powerful.** For the word of God is alive and powerful. It is sharper than the sharpest two-edged sword, cutting between soul and spirit, between joint and marrow. It exposes our innermost thoughts and desires. Hebrews 4:12

130. **God blesses the bold for Christ.** So, let us come boldly to the throne of our gracious God. There we will receive his mercy, and we will find grace to help us when we need it most. Hebrews 4:16

131. **God's blessing to Abraham extends to us.** Saying, Surely, blessing I will bless thee, and multiplying I will multiply thee. Hebrews 6:14

132. **God gives us wisdom.** If you need wisdom, ask our generous God, and he will give it to you. He will not rebuke you for asking. James 1:5

133. **Every good and perfect gift is from above.** Whatever is good and perfect is a gift coming down to us from God our Father, who created all the lights in the heavens. He never changes or casts a shifting shadow. James 1:17

134. **God comes near to us.** Come close to God, and God will come close to you. Wash your hands, you sinners; purify your hearts, for your loyalty is divided between God and the world. James 4:8

135. **God cares for us.** Give all your worries and care to God, for he cares about you. 1 Peter 5:7

136. **God makes us strong and resolute.** In his kindness God called you to share in his eternal glory by means of Christ Jesus. So, after you have suffered a little while, he will restore, support, and strengthen you, and he will place you on a firm foundation. 1 Peter 5:10

137. **We have life and godliness.** By his divine power, God has given us everything we need for living a godly life. We have received all of this by coming to know him, the one who called us to himself by means of his marvelous glory and excellence. 2 Peter 1:3

138. **Jesus is faithful and just to forgive us when we ask.** But if we confess our sins to him, he is faithful and just to forgive us our sins and to cleanse us from all wickedness. 1 John 1:9

139. **Perfect love casts out fear.** Such love has no fear, because perfect love expels all fear. If we are afraid, it is for fear of punishment, and this shows that we have not fully experienced his perfect love. 1 John 4:18

140. **Walk in truth.** From John, the old elder of the church. To: that dear woman Cyria, one of God's very own, and to her children whom I love so much, as does everyone else in the church. Since the truth is in our hearts forever, God the Father and Jesus Christ his Son will bless us with great mercy and much peace, and with truth and love. How happy I am to find some of your children here and to see they are living as they should, following the truth, obeying God's command. And now I want to urgently remind you, dear friends, of the old rule God gave us right from the beginning, that Christians should love one another. If we love God, we will do whatever he tells us to. And he has told us from the very first to love each other. Watch out for the false leaders – and there are many of them around – who don't believe that Jesus Christ came to earth as a human being with a body like ours. Such people are against the truth and against Christ. Beware of being like them and losing the prize that you and I have been working so hard to get. See to it that you win your full reward from the Lord. For if you wander beyond the teaching of Christ, you will leave God behind; while if you are loyal to Christ's teachings, you will have God too. Then you will have both the Father and the Son. If anyone comes to teach you and he doesn't believe what Christ taught, don't even invite him into your home. Don't encourage him in any way. If you do, you will be a partner with him in his wickedness. 2 John 1-11

141. **Only God is good.** Dear friend, don't let this bad example influence you. Follow only what is good. Remember that those who do what is right prove that they are God's children; and those who continue in evil prove they are far from God. 3 John 11-12

142. **God is able to keep us from falling.** Now all glory to God, who is able to keep you from falling away and will bring you with great joy into his glorious presence without a single fault. All glory to him who alone is God our Saviour through Jesus Christ our Lord. All glory, majesty, power, and authority are his before all time, and in the present, and beyond all time! Amen. Jude 1:24-25

143. **Our prayers reside in God's throne room.** And when he took the scroll, the four living beings and the twenty-four elders fell down before the Lamb. Each one had a harp, and they held gold bowls filled with incense, which are the prayers of God's people. Rev 5:8

144. **Probation is closed, the time is near.** He that is unjust, let him be unjust still: and he which is filthy, let him be filthy still: and he that is righteous, let him be righteous still: and he that is holy, let him be holy still. And, behold, I come quickly; and my reward is with me, to give every man according as his work shall be... Blessed are they that do his commandments that they may have right to the tree of life and may enter in through the gates into the city... For I testify unto every man that heareth the words of the prophecy of this book, if any man shall add unto these things, God shall add unto him the plagues that are written in this book: and if any man shall take away from the words of the book of this prophecy, God shall take away his part out of the book of life and out of the holy city and from the things which are written in this book. He which testifieth these things saith, surely I come quickly. Amen. The grace of our Lord Jesus Christ be with you all. Amen. Rev 22:11-12, 14, 18-21

Types of Cognitive Biases and Logical Fallacies

	Cognitive Bias	Description
1.	Affect heuristic	The tendency to rely upon current emotions when making quick, automatic decisions.
2.	Ambiguity bias	The tendency to prefer options that are known or familiar to us.
3.	Anchoring bias	The tendency to rely more heavily on first impressions or the first piece of information or evidence introduced when making decisions or future plans. Tendency to hold onto first thing we learn about something and it becomes difficult to let go of this opinion.
4.	*Animal bias*	The tendency to see some animals as having high value while seeing other animals as objects of appetite or recreational pleasure (e.g., hunting) and not seeing them as sentient animals who have families, form relationships and are part of a larger ecological animal community.
5.	Anthropocentric bias	The tendency to use human comparisons as a baseline for reasoning about animal and other biological phenomena.
6.	Association bias	A tendency to judge people based on their associations (e.g., church, political party).
7.	Attentional bias	The tendency to focus on some things while completely ignoring relevant others.
8.	Authority bias	The tendency to trust and be influenced by the opinions of authority figures.
9.	Automation bias	The tendency to rely on automated systems, sometimes trusting too much on automated data even ignoring contradictory evidence, when it is correct. The tendency to rely on automated systems may lead to erroneous automated information, overriding correct human decisions.
10.	Availability cascade	Tied to our need for social acceptance. Collective beliefs gain more plausibility through public perception if it appears the majority of people believe a certain way. If you repeat something often enough for long enough, it will become true.
11.	Availability heuristic	The tendency to rely on immediate examples which come to mind while making judgments instead of carefully considering all angles of a situation. Sometimes a quick decision or judgment is required, but a quick assessment and decision may lack correctness and foresight for the situation at hand.
12.	Baader-Meinhof phenomenon	As new information comes to your attention, it subsequently appears this new person, new information, new idea is everywhere, when in reality your brain is processing and filtering this information differently.
13.	Backfire effect	Arguing hard against someone makes them more hardened in defending their position.
14.	Bandwagon effect	The tendency to support opinions as they become more popular. Ideas, fads and beliefs grow as more people adopt them, whether or not they are sound ideas based on fundamental knowledge or widely held beliefs. Most people are followers and are easily swayed by the opinions and actions of others.
15.	Base rate fallacy	The tendency to rely on event-specific information over statistics. This is almost universal among most people. Statisticians and epidemiologists keep us honest!
16.	Belief bias	Tendency to judge an argument's strength not by how strongly it supports the conclusion but how plausible the conclusion is in our own minds. If someone says something that supports our beliefs, we more easily adopt their other ideas/opinions.
17.	Ben Franklin effect	We like doing favors and we are more likely to do another favor for someone if we have already done a favor for them than if we had received a favor from them.
18.	Berkson's paradox	The tendency to misinterpret statistical experiments involving conditional probabilities (the measure of the probability of an event occurring, given that another event has already occurred).
19.	Biderman effect	Extreme attempts to manipulate others using a variety of pervasive tactics. Used on prisoners, by abusers, perpetrators of violence and fear, etc. As a result of these manipulative events, one is more likely to exhibit intense concern for self, be afraid of resistance, feel dependent, be concerned only about their immediate condition, develop the habit of compliance, feel anxiety and despair, exhibit weakened mental and physical abilities, etc.
20.	*Blind spot bias*	The tendency to believe we do not have certain biases; we see it in others more than ourselves.
21.	Bottom dollar effect	The tendency to be dissatisfied with a lower cost item than we otherwise would be.
22.	Bounded rationality	Our decisions may not be optimal because they are limited by time, information and mental capacity.
23.	Bundling bias	The tendency to favor individual purchases over a bundled purchase.
24.	Bystander effect	The more people around the less likely we are to help a victim.

Cognitive Bias	Description
25. Cashless effect	The tendency to spend and pay more when no cash is involved in a transaction.
26. Category size bias	The tendency to label some brands, people, attitudes, companies, etc., based on our perceptions and stereotypes. Something is more acceptable if it is recognized and part of a large category than if it is obscure and in a small category.
27. *Chaos effect*	The tendency to introduce enough external chaos into a situation so it overshadows our personal issues and chaotic personality.
28. Cheerleader effect	The tendency to see people in a group as individually more attractive than in isolation.
29. Choice overload	The tendency to have difficulty making decisions when faced with too many options.
30. Choice-support	The tendency to remember one's choices as better than they actually were.
31. Clustering illusion	The tendency to find patterns and "clusters" in random data.
32. Cognitive dissonance	The tendency to reject correct information which contradicts or does not support our beliefs.
33. Commitment bias	The tendency to support past ideas, even when provided with information and evidence they were wrong.
34. Compassion fade	The tendency to be more compassionate toward a small group of victims compared to a large anonymous group of victims.
35. Confirmation bias	The tendency to find and remember information which confirms our existing beliefs and perceptions, while ignoring and even mocking contrary information.
36. Congruence bias	The tendency to test hypotheses exclusively through direct testing instead of testing possible alternative hypotheses.
37. Courtesy bias	The tendency to give a more socially correct opinion than one's true opinion.
38. Cross-race effect	The tendency to not identify with people of a different race.
39. Cryptomnesia	This happens when the occurrence of new thought appears to be original, but in reality, it is not a novel thought or event.
40. Curse of knowledge or the curse of expertise	The tendency to assume everyone else has the same knowledge and understanding, when in reality, everyone has a different grid of knowledge combined with experience and belief. Assuming others have the background to understand.
41. Decision fatigue	When faced with making many decisions in a short and stressful time frame, the ability to make rational decisions is reduced.
42. Declinism	The tendency to romanticize the past and view the future negatively, believing that societies and institutions are in decline.
43. Decoy effect	The tendency of the third inferior option to change how we decide between two similar-in-value options.
44. Default bias	The tendency to generally prefer to keep our situation as it currently exists (even when it is a less than desirable situation). When given a choice between a default position and a new option, the tendency is to choose a default option.
45. Defensive attribution	The tendency to agree more with those with whom we share characteristics or we relate to better. If a person attacks another person, we are more likely to help the person we relate to, whether it is the victim or the perpetrator.
46. Denomination effect	Tendency to spend more money when it is in small denominations rather than spending larger denomination bills.
47. *Derangement syndrome*	The tendency to completely destroy your life, lose friends and see things through a highly distorted lens. When a situation or condition so totally takes over your life that you no longer are able to be objective about a specific event or person. The mind that alters, alters all (William Blake).
48. Digital amnesia	The tendency to forget or not memorize information which is easily found on the internet. This effect makes people overestimate their intelligence.
49. Distinction bias	The tendency to view two options as more distinctive when we evaluate them simultaneously than separately.
50. Dunning-Kruger effect	The less you know, the more confident you are. The more you know, the less confident you are.
51. Echo chamber bias	The tendency to want to hear the opinions of others only when they coincide with yours.
52. Empathy gap	The tendency to mis-predict behaviors based on your emotional state.
53. End-of-history illusion	The belief one will change less in the future then one has changed in the past.
54. Endowment effect	The tendency to value your possessions more highly than the possessions of others.

Cognitive Bias	Description
55. Escalation of commitment	The tendency to invest more in things which have a cost us something rather than altering our investments, even if we face negative outcomes.
56. Exaggerated expectation	The tendency to expect or predict more extreme outcomes than what actually happens.
57. Experimenter's expectation	Researchers tend to believe, certify and publish data which agrees with their expectations of the outcome. The tendency to disbelieve, discard or downgrade data which appears to conflict with expectations.
58. Extrinsic incentive bias	Some people are more motivated by extrinsic or external incentives than other people.
59. False consensus	The tendency to believe more people agree with us than is true reality.
60. False memory	The tendency to mistake imagination for real memories.
61. False uniqueness bias	An attributional type of cognitive bias in which people tend to view their personal attributes and qualities as unique, when in reality, they are not. People tend to believe they are more unique in regard to their desirable traits.
62. Focusing effect	The tendency to place too much importance on one aspect of an event.
63. Forer effect	We easily attribute our personalities to vague statements, even if they can apply to a wide range of people. "You really understand me."
64. Framing effect	The tendency to draw different conclusions from the same information depending on how it is presented.
65. Functional fixedness	It is oftentimes difficult to see "off label" uses of common tools or objects besides their standard use.
66. Fundamental attribution error	We judge others on their personality or fundamental character, but we have a different standard for ourselves or for those close to us, which allows us to judge ourselves based on the situation and not necessarily our true character.
67. Gambler's fallacy	The tendency to believe future possibilities are affected by past events.
68. Gender bias	Implicit biases which discriminate against one based on their gender.
69. Google effect	The tendency to forget information which can easily be accessed on the internet.
70. Groupthink	The tendency to make irrational decisions to minimize conflict and maintain harmony and conformity within a group. Usually results in irrational, dysfunctional decisions while suppressing dissenting views.
71. Halo effect	The tendency to see a person as having a positive trait, which spills over into other aspects of their personality and character, even when serious flaws are evident.
72. Hard-easy effect	The tendency to overestimate our ability to do something considered difficult and underestimate our ability to do something considered easy.
73. Herd mentality	Do what others are doing based on emotions and not independent analysis.
74. Hindsight bias	The tendency to see unpredictable events as predictable after they occur. "I knew it all along."
75. *Holier than thou bias*	If I quote the Bible enough on the points I agree with, I can ignore the ones which make me uncomfortable or come up with my own version of interpreting scriptures.
76. Hostile attribution	The tendency to interpret others' behaviors as having hostile intent, even when the behavior is benign and harmless.
77. Hot-hand fallacy	The tendency to interpret and perceive a series of positive outcomes for random events, leading us to predict future outcomes will also be positive.
78. Humor effect	Humorous items are more easily recalled than non-humorous items.
79. Hyperbolic discounting	The tendency to value small immediate rewards more than larger long-term rewards.
80. Identifiable victim effect	The tendency to identify with and help specific groups even though others need help as well.
81. Ikea effect	The tendency to place a higher value on things we partially create for ourselves.
82. Illicit transference	Treating everyone in a group the same when in reality each individual of the group is different.
83. Illusion of control	The tendency to overestimate our ability to influence events.
84. Illusion of validity	The tendency to be overconfident of our ability to predict future events.
85. Illusory correlation	The tendency to assume a correlation between two variables when there is no association.
86. Illusory truth effect	The tendency to believe something is true if it is repeated enough times.
87. Incentivization	The tendency to be more motivated when perks and rewards are involved.

Cognitive Bias	Description
88. In-group favoritism	The tendency to favor people who are in our "in-group" or tribe as opposed to an "outside group" or someone you don't interact with as often. The people in my church are much better people than the rest of my friends.
89. Insensitivity to sample size	The tendency to under-expect variation in small samples. Variation is more likely in smaller samples.
90. Interoceptive bias	The tendency to interpret external factors based on our internal state (e.g., being well-fed, well-rested).
91. Irrational escalation or commitment	The tendency to increasingly commit to a belief or decision even when a significant amount of new evidence points to the contrary.
92. Just world hypothesis	The tendency to believe the world is just, therefore, we assume moral acts are rewarded and acts of injustice are punished and deserved.
93. Lag effect	The tendency to take more time to process information than anticipated. Ultimately, we do not want to change course, or we not remember or have the opportunity to assimilate new information.
94. Law of the instrument	The tendency to use a skill / tool / instrument in any given situation. When you have a hammer in your hand, everything looks like a nail.
95. Law of triviality	The tendency to give disproportionate weight to trivial issues, often while spending very little time with more complex issues.
96. Less-is-better	The tendency to prefer the smaller or lesser alternative.
97. Leveling & sharpening	The phenomenon of how we lose certain details of our memory and why other memories stand out.
98. Levels-of-processing effect	Why repetition improves memory retention. Episodic memory is better for information which is conceptual versus shallow perceptual processed memories.
99. Look-elsewhere effect	When an apparent statistically significant observation, blatant event, or person is overlooked on purpose. When an apparent statistically significant finding is actually due to chance because of the size of the parameter.
100. Loss aversion	Why the pain of losing is felt twice as powerfully compared to equivalent gains. The more losses one experiences the more loss-averse they become.
101. Mass formation psychosis (hypnosis)	When society uncouples from its historical values and definitions in combination with free-floating anxiety, it is swept up by events and accepts previously unlikely and even dangerous behaviours.
102. Mental accounting	The tendency to treat one's money differently. We see money spent in one category as different than money spent in another category.
103. Mere exposure effect	Simple exposure to a person or idea or concept makes us view that thing or person more positively.
104. Moral credential effect	Occurs when someone who does something good, gives themselves permission to be less good in the future, knowing that they have a certain amount of good will based on their previous actions.
105. Moral luck	Better moral standing happens due to a positive outcome, worse moral standing happens because of a negative outcome. The best team won (even though they cheated).
106. Motivating uncertainty effect	Rewards of an uncertain size or amount tend to motivate us more than known rewards.
107. Naïve allocation	The tendency to prefer evenly spreading out limited resources across all the options.
108. Naïve cynicism	The tendency to believe we observe objective reality and that other people have a higher egocentric bias than they actually do in their intentions and actions. "The only reason this person is doing something nice for me is they want something from me."
109. Naïve realism	Tendency to believe we observe objective reality and that other people are irrational, uninformed or biased. "I see the world accurately and everyone else is an idiot."
110. *Narcissistic bias*	Tendency to only see your needs and desires as important while marginalizing the needs of others.
111. Narrative fallacy	The tendency to like stories and relate to them. The person or situation with the better story is more believable than someone without a story or a poor narrative. The pastor with a heart-wrenching testimony is more believable.
112. Negativity bias	Negative occurrences tend to have a greater impact on our psychological state than positive ones.
113. Neglect of probability	The tendency to completely disregard probability when making a decision, given uncertain circumstances.
114. Noble edge effect	The tendency to favor brands which show care to societal issues we care about.
115. Normalcy bias	Refusal to plan for or react to a disaster which has never happened before.
116. Nostalgia effect	The tendency to view past experiences as positive and to anticipate future events will not be as positive. Viewing the past through rose-colored glasses.

Cognitive Bias	Description
117. Nuance bias	The inability to see fine nuances within a certain situation or between situations, which may be significant. The tendency to believe one thing and when subtle or even overt changes occur, the tendency is to ignore nuances.
118. Observer effect	The presence of observers may consciously or unconsciously affect the behaviors of the observed.
119. Omission bias	Tendency to strongly react against harmful actions leading to tendency to omit information which may lead to subsequent poor decisions. Leave out negative but relevant info in decision making.
120. Optimism bias	The tendency to be over-optimistic about achieving a positive outcome.
121. *Ostrich effect*	The tendency to avoid dangerous or negative information.
122. Outcome bias	The tendency to retroactively judge a decision based on its eventual outcome and not the quality of the decision at the time it was made.
123. Outgroup homogeneity bias	The tendency to perceive non-group persons as homogenous and the tendency to perceive our preferred groups and associations as more diverse.
124. Overconfidence bias	A false sense of skill, talent, self-belief which may lead a person to believe an event will happen because they want it to happen.
125. Overton window	To only pursue ideas and policies that are widely accepted throughout society. Avoid ideas and policies that are not widely accepted and embraced.
126. Pareidolia	Tendency to see random events as significant such as seeing images in clouds, hearing messages from outer space, messages on records played in reverse, etc.
127. Paternal argument / benevolent dictator	Using the argument of higher educational attainment, position, and influence to convince others you are right and they must follow your advice, ignoring the fact that most people have enough innate intellect to do what is in their best interest when they are given two distinct choices.
128. Peak – end rule	The tendency to judge an experience on how we felt at its peaks and at its end.
129. Pessimism bias	The tendency to overestimate the likelihood of a bad outcome.
130. Placebo effect	The tendency to believe a treatment will work, and the possibility it will have a small or significant impact even if the effect is merely psychological leading to a physiological effect. What is mental may become physical.
131. Plan continuation bias	The failure to recalibrate plans and goals as the situation changes.
132. Planning fallacy	The tendency to underestimate the time needed to complete a task.
133. *Plant blindness*	The tendency to ignore plants, underappreciate their contributions to their local environment and even needlessly destroy plants in their environment.
134. *Pot calls kettle black*	The inability to see our personal deficits while we readily point out similar deficits in others.
135. Primacy effect	Information presented first is more easily recalled than the rest of the information.
136. Priming effect	When presented, some ideas prompt other ideas later on without our conscious awareness that we were primed by something someone previously said or had done.
137. Projection bias	The tendency to believe our current preferences will stay the same in the future. We overestimate how much our future selves share our current preferences, leading to sub-optimal choices.
138. Publication effect	Higher probability of publishing results showing a significant finding.
139. Pygmalion effect	When expectations of others, affects the target person's performance. If we have low expectations of others, they will usually underperform.
140. Reactance	The tendency to do the opposite of what we are told, especially when we perceive a threat to personal freedom. We resist attempts to constrain freedom of choice.
141. Reactive devaluation	The tendency to devalue proposals made by people considered to be adversarial, in a different category, at a different education level, etc.
142. Recency illusion	When you become aware of something and see it as new when in fact, it is a long-established fact.
143. Regret aversion	The tendency to choose the option which minimizes regret, even if it is not ideal.
144. Representativeness heuristic	Occurs when people believe two objects are similar and they are correlated with each other.
145. Response bias	Responses to a survey or experiment can be inaccurate based on how they are asked or framed.
146. Restraint bias	The tendency to overestimate control over impulsive behaviors.
147. Rose-colored-glasses retrospection	The tendency to only remember the positive elements of our past.
148. Rhyme-as-reason	The tendency to see rhyming statements as more truthful.
149. Risk compensation	The tendency to take more risks as perceived safety increases.

Cognitive Bias	Description
150. Salience bias	The tendency to focus more on items or information which are more prominent and ignore less prominent information.
151. Scarcity bias	Assume scarce items are more valuable than things that are abundant.
152. Self-serving bias	The tendency to see our failures as situational but our successes are directly due to our hard work and taking responsibility for lives. We tend to overestimate our contribution to an outcome.
153. Semmelweis reflex	The tendency to reject new evidence which contradicts an established paradigm.
154. Sexual over/under-perception	The tendency to over- or underestimate the sexual interest of another person.
155. Social comparison bias	The tendency to favor potential candidates who do not compete with your particular characteristics.
156. Social desirability bias	The tendency to over-report socially desirable characteristics or behaviors in oneself and under-report socially undesirable characteristics or behaviors.
157. Social norms bias	The tendency to act in similar ways as the communities we identify with.
158. Source confusion	Why we forget where our memories come from and thereby lose our ability to distinguish reality or likelihood of each memory.
159. Spacing effect	Information learned repeatedly is better retained when learned at different time points than all at once.
160. Spotlight effect	The tendency to overestimate how much people pay attention to our behaviors and appearance.
161. Status quo bias	The tendency to prefer things to stay the same. Changes that occur from our baseline are considered to be a loss.
162. Stereotyping	Tendency to adopt generalized beliefs that members of a group will have certain characteristics despite not having specific information about the individual.
163. Strategic incomprehension	You don't understand what is happening because you still operate in a different 'world,' a different time with different values.
164. Subjective validation	Assigning perceived connections between purely coincidental events.
165. Suggestibility effect	The tendency of children to mistake ideas suggested by a questioner for actual memories.
166. Sunk cost fallacy	When facing increasingly negative outcomes, one continues their behavior instead of altering course.
167. Surrogation	Losing sight of the goal and focusing only on the objective(s) or the construct or measure which is under consideration.
168. Survivorship bias	The tendency to focus on those things which survived a process and overlook ones that failed. We misjudge groups by only looking at specific group members.
169. Tachy-psychia	Tendency of perceptions to shift over time depending on trauma, drug use, and physical exertion.
170. Telescoping effect	Recent events seem to be longer ago than they actually were and remote events are seen as being more recent in time.
171. Third person effect	The tendency to believe others are more affected by mass media consumption than we are.
172. Transfer of allegiance	The tendency to assign virtue or blame to a person or group based on their previous associations. Ideas associated with one cause or person, while justified, are automatically transferred when this person or group accepts a new idea or position.
173. Unit bias	Focusing on a unit instead of recognizing a fraction of a unit might be a better option.
174. Weber-Fechner law	Difficulty in comparing small differences in large quantities.
175. Women are wonderful effect	The tendency to associate more positive attributes with women than with men.
176. Zelgaarnik effect	The tendency to remember incomplete tasks more than completed ones.
177. Zero risk bias	The tendency to reduce small risks to zero, even if we can reduce more risk overall with another option. In other words, we prefer to eliminate one category of risk entirely, even if doing so increases overall risk.
178. Zero sum bias	Assumes one person gains at the expense of another person losing. I win, you lose mentality.

https://en.wikipedia.org/wiki/List_of_cognitive_biases; *biases in italics are original*

It is ok to have biases but it is not ok to allow personal biases to interfere with your friendships, ability to lead, wildly altered personal perceptions (*The mind that alters, alters all.* W. Blake), etc. Everyone should be aware of the types of bias inherent to their personality and temperment. This understanding can greatly expand one's ability to see different perspectives and thus to build more bridges instead of blowing up bridges and relationships.

The Holmes-Rahe Life Stress Inventory
The Social Readjustment Rating Scale

Instructions: Mark down the point value of each of the listed life events which has happened to you during the previous year. Total the points and then match up to the assessment at the end.

Life Event	Points
1. Death of spouse	100
2. Divorce	73
3. Marital separation from spouse	65
4. Detention in jail or other institution	63
5. Death of close family member	63
6. Major personal injury or illness	53
7. Marriage	50
8. Being fired at work	47
9. Marital reconciliation with spouse	45
10. Retirement from work	45
11. Major change in health or behavior(s) of a family member	44
12. Pregnancy	40
13. Sexual difficulties	39
14. Gaining a new family member	39
15. Major business adjustment	39
16. Major change in financial state	38
17. Death of a close friend	37
18. Changing to a different line of work	36
19. Major change in number of arguments with spouse	35
20. Taking on a mortgage (home or business)	31
21. Foreclosure on a mortgage or loan	30
22. Major change in responsibilities at work	29
23. Son or daughter leaving home	29
24. In-law troubles	29
25. Outstanding personal achievement	28
26. Spouse beginning or ceasing work outside the home	26
27. Beginning or ceasing formal schooling	26
28. Major change in living condition	25
29. Revision of personal habits	24
30. Trouble with the boss	23
31. Major changes in working hours or conditions	20
32. Change in residence	20
33. Changing to a new school	20
34. Major change in usual type or amount of recreation	19
35. Major change in amount of church activity	19
36. Major change in social activities	18
37. Taking on a loan	17
38. Major change in sleeping habits	16
39. Major change in number of family get-togethers	15
40. Major change in eating habits, surroundings, etc.	15
41. Vacation	13
42. Major holidays	12
43. Minor violations of the law	11

Add up the points on the lines you circled:

< 150 points: a relatively low amount of life changes and a low susceptibility to stress-induced health problems.

150 to 300 points: at risk (about a 50% chance) of a major stress-related health problem within the next 2 years.

> 300 points: at risk (about an 80% chance of having a major stress-related health problem within the next two years.

Source: adapted from Thomas Holmes and Richard Rahe. Holmes-Rahe social readjustment Rating Scale, Journal of Psychosomatic Research, Volume 11, 1967.

Hydrotherapy and Hydropathic Techniques and Methods

See www.traditionalhydrotherapy.com for specific instructions for some of techniques listed here.
See hydrotherapy and other helpful videos here: www.youtube.com/@preparingforthetimeoftroub8279/videos

Hydrotherapy Techniques	Brief Description
Ablutions	Cooling friction. Washing the body to cool and stimulate it. Used to stimulate nerve endings, increase muscle tone, cause vasodilation, increase heat loss from skin, deepen respiration. www.traditionalhydrotherapy.com
Air bath	Wear loose clothing and no shoes while working outside. End with dip in cool water.
Animal hydrotherapy	Many of the same hydrotherapy techniques for humans may be successfully used for animals.
Aquatic exercise	Aqua jogging associated with reductions in waist circumference and body fat and improvement in aerobic fitness and quality of life.
Bakera	An herbal steam bath prepared with various plants and plant oils used for recuperation after child birth. Soothes heaviness in limbs, edema, etc. (PMID: 17293070)
Balneotherapy or Egyptian bath	Balneotherapy defined as the use of bath minerals at a temperature of at least 20 °C and a mineral content of 1 gram/liter. Iodine is usually one of the minerals used. Fulvic and humic acids are also used. Used for sleep problems and other conditions such as inflammation, fibromyalgia, ankylosing spondylitis, pain, tiredness, fatigue, etc. Waters contain minerals including S, Na, Ca, Mg, etc. In addition to mineral rich bathing water, may use mud packs, inhalations, irrigations, therapeutic beverages, high pressure underwater jets or water hose, and massage. Thought to activate healing processes. Low amounts of sulfur in water and steam may break up mucous and activate normal breathing. (PMID: 29882782)
Bathing	The act of applying water to the body to clean, relax or stimulate.
Body shampoo	Day spas may offer body shampoo services. Great for exfoliating the body and achieving super soft skin. Only down side is you are completely naked and body scrubbed by stranger.
Brand bath	Anti-pyretic bath, especially for typhoid fever. www.traditionalhydrotherapy.com
Bubble baths	A good recipe might include castile liquid soap or Sal Suds, Epsom salts, a small amount of full fat coconut milk, and some essential oils.
Clay soak	Add 1 to 2 cups bentonite clay powder to your bath (more for a deep detox bath). Use with hot bath water. Add premixed clay water to bath and soak for up to 30 minutes. Stay hydrated during the soak. Do not allow large clumps of clay to go down your drain, follow-up with lots of running water. Water outdoor plants or lawn with clay bath water.
Cold compress	Local therapeutic "bath" using a cold cloth soaked in ice water.
Cold mitten friction	Used to stimulate circulation, increase rate of blood flow, increase white blood cell activity and antibody production, stimulate neuromuscular tone, reduce a fever, and as a vasomotor tonic. Friction applied to skin using a combination of salt or sugar + oil. Use loofa or hand mitts for friction in place of salt. Demarginates white blood cells. www.traditionalhydrotherapy.com
Cold sheet therapy	Wrap patient in a sheet which has been dipped and wrung out in ice cold water. Have them lie down on a bed covered with a plastic sheet and then a cotton sheet. Cover them with several blankets, a cold towel on their forehead and a hot water bottle near their feet. Cover the patient, bedding and all, with a plastic cover to protect from dampness. Allow the patient to sweat, keeping a fresh cool cloth on their forehead at all times.
Cold shower	Stimulates central nervous system. Improves immunity, lymphatic functions, heat stress, circulation, digestion, improved productivity, etc. Don't use on young children unless acclimated. Used as potential treatment for depression (PMID: 17993252).

Hydrotherapy Technique	Brief Description
Cold water immersion	Sends overwhelming amount of electrical impulses from peripheral nerve endings to the brain. Analgesic effect. Reduced muscle fatigue and recovery after exercise. Use a snorkel to immerse the head in an ice-cold water bath.
Cold water plunge	The therapy will alter various physiological parameters based on water temperature, ambient air temperature, time of immersion, amount of body area immersed, etc. Improves metabolic rate and gastrointestinal functions.
Contrast therapy	Also known as hot/cold immersion therapy. Part of the body or the entire body is immersed in ice water and then immediately immersed in warm water. Repeat several times. Decreases plasma lactate concentration after intense anaerobic exercise. Improves muscle soreness. Assists in exercise recovery. Demarginates WBCs and may improve WBC numbers.
Cool bathing	Good for recovering from hikes, bike rides, vigorous physical activity, etc.
Cool sponge bath	Good for fevers.
Cryotherapy	Cold water treatment. Yet to demonstrate efficacy. Promotes vasoconstriction.
Effervescent bath (aka Nauheim bath)	Uses carbonated salt water. Used for those with heart failure, cardiac insufficiency, cardiac enlargement, valvular disease, renal inactivity, chronic nephritis, etc. Go to www.traditionalhydrotherapy.com to read about specific indications and specific steps and recipes for bath water. Simplest formula: 2 – 3 kg sodium chloride, 400 – 700 g sodium bicarbonate, 400 g muriatic acid. Completely dissolve salts in 5 cm of water in a tub. Fill bath so it is 30 °C – 34 °C. Mix acid with 1 liter of water and then distribute into water, thoroughly mixing the acid in with the salt water. Begin with 8 minutes up to 15 minutes over time. Place cooling compress on head and precordial compress. Do not rub the patient, 3 baths per week for 3 to 4 weeks. Never more than 20 baths. Only do this under supervision by an experienced and trained hydrotherapist.
Enemas	Various types of enemas are used to achieve colon dynamic effects. The coffee enema is used in various detox regimens. Other types of enemas include cold enema, graduated enema, hot enema, warm enema, etc. Some enemas are medicated and are used at the direction of your physician.
Epistaxis (nose bleed)	Hot packs to face, ice pack to upper spine and occipital area, hands in ice water, hot foot bath, etc. www.traditionalhydrotherapy.com
Eucalyptus steam shower	Place a fresh stem of eucalyptus leaves in your shower and take a hot shower. The eucalyptus will help clear your sinuses.
Fan bath	Fans are directed to patient while staff rub the patients' body.
Far infrared sauna	Heats your body without warming the air around you. Uses radiant heat from heat lamps, etc. Broad spectrum infrared waves create heat in your body, causing you to sweat and release stored "toxins."
Fomentations	Applying hot packs to heat up the chest or any area of the body. This improves circulation, enzyme action, removal of toxins, etc. See www.traditionalhydrotherapy.com for detailed instructions.
Float tank with Epsom salts	Benefits are incredible, including reduced stress, pain relief, improved skin, improved cardiovascular functions, better sleep, reduced anxiety, etc.
Full body immersion tanks (aka, Hubbard tank)	Immerse affected limb in a tank at a specific water temp with circulating water or not. Used to debride tissue. Water buoyancy supports weight and eliminates shock and effects of gravity on system and need to balance.
Graduated tub bath	Antipyretic. Use when a cold bath is contraindicated. Gradually lowers the water temperature while constantly rubbing. Once a favorable reaction is achieved (lowered temperature), maintain temperature. See www.traditionalhydrotherapy.com
Half bath	Immersing only the lower half of your body in a hot bath. Used for upper body congestion and pain relief.

Hydrotherapy Technique	Brief Description
Head bath	Calms the nervous system, may reduce inflammation.
Heat compress	Applying heat through a hot cloth. Usually the hot cloth is applied and then covered to retain heat.
Herbal mineral bath	Soothing and relaxing. Herbal extracts or the actual herbs and minerals (usually Epsom salts) are added to warm bath water.
Hot and cold tub bath	Hot bath for several minutes followed by a cold tub bath with friction for 1 minute. Sprinkle hot water over body after cold bath.
Hot-cold compress	Good for muscular soreness, breast engorgement pain, etc.
Hot Roman bath (thermae)	In Roman times, bathing was a community ritual and not a private affair. Roman baths generally included an oil rub, lounging, steam room, hot bathing, skin scraping, a cooling off time, and then more oils and perfumes.
Hot soaking	Japanese use hot soaks to treat muscle and joint pain, improve sleep, decrease stress, manage pain. Some soaks use minerals and produce a mild detox effect. There are natural soaks at various places around the world where the water has a slight effervescence.
Hot springs	Water usually contains a variety of minerals, including calcium and sodium bicarbonate. Promotes blood circulation, sleep, reduces stress, etc.
Hydrogen peroxide bath	Add up to 4 cups or 1 liter of 3% hydrogen peroxide to your usual bath. It is assumed your body will absorb oxygen (no studies have been done to prove this true or false). You may experience slight "negative" side effects due to "detoxing." See this website for additional detail: www.using-hydrogen-peroxide.com and www.waterbenefitshealth.com
Hydro-massage (Watsu)	Form of aquatic exercises used for relaxation and as passive therapy. Involves stretching, massage and acupressure.
Hyper-thermic immersion induced fever therapy	Used to bring the core body temperature to a certain point with the goal of killing cancer cells. This is not a proven cancer therapy. This procedure requires training and a certain skill set. **See your local naturopath for assistance.**
Ice bath	Ice bathing is associated with many amazing benefits including improved cognitive functions and mood, weight loss, improved stress response, less inflammation, improved immunity, better looking skin, increased energy, improved concentration and more! Going from an ice bath to hot shower and back, may help flush out toxins and it will certainly improve circulation. Avoid using with small children.
Ice massage/facial	Ice used to soothe skin, treat swelling / inflammation, reduce eye puffiness, etc.
Ice pack	Treats pain, inflammation, swelling. Good for decreasing circulation if necessary.
Irrigations	Various body parts may be irrigated including the bladder, ears, eyes, mouth, rectum, stomach, urethra, vagina, etc. Specific irrigations may be suggested by your physician.
Ice water immersion	Treatment for exertional heatstroke, hyperthermia, etc. Can immerse face in ice water using a snorkel.
Infrared sauna	Outstanding benefits including reduced inflammation, stress, stiffness, soreness, improved circulation, sleep, relaxation, etc. Also used as part of detox regimens.
Iodine-Grine	Adding thyroid responsive minerals to bath water including iodine.
Mud bath	Mud baths are usually heated. Contain a combination of minerals, volcanic ash and hot spring water.
Mustard bath	Used as a skin stimulant. 60 g freshly ground mustard in 1 liter hot water. Add to tub bath. www.traditionalhydrotherapy.com
Neutral tub bath	Soaking in water 93 °F (34 °C) to 99 °F (37 °C). Used for insomnia.
Ozone hydrotherapy	Ozone oxidizes bacteria, viruses, yeast spores, mold and almost every bad pathogen. Believe it or not, dog spas commonly use ozone spa baths.
Pine needle bath	Skin stimulant for cardiac insufficiency, chronic nephritis. 94 °F. www.traditionalhydrotherapy.com

Hydrotherapy Technique	Brief Description
Pool exercise	(Halliwick 10-point aquatic therapy for rehab injury and disability.
Private luxury baths and massage	Spas around the world use their proprietary techniques, minerals, equipment, herbals to make for a world class experience in relaxation and stress reduction. May also include mani- and pedicures, hair styling, etc.
Sauna	Uses dry heat, usually from hot rocks or a closed stove. Many positive health effects.
Scotch applications	Similar to alternating applications except the heating stage is shorter and hotter, the cold application is shorter and there are always 3 changes. Scotch applications include: Scotch compress, Scotch douche, Scotch shower, simultaneous Scotch douche. www.traditionalhydrotherapy.com
Scots hose	Deep muscle massage with a high velocity water hose.
Scots shower	Hot shower that ends with at least a minute of icy cold water.
Sea bath	A bath in any natural body of water, 3 to 30 minutes. Exercise while in water. After leaving water, vigorously dry off with towel.
Sebastian Kneipp	Use of various herbals and minerals in water of various temperatures to treat a variety of conditions. Immersion in Dead Sea salt water produces significant decreases in blood glucose for type 2 diabetics.
Shallow bath (tonic)	Tub bath in cool water. While sitting in bath, attendants vigorously rubs back and hips while patient rubs arms, legs and chest. Patient then lies in the bath and rubs chest and abdomen while attendant rubs legs. Very short bath.
Shiver therapy	11 minutes / week of shivering are associated with significant health benefits.
Sitz bath	A bath / soak for the fanny area. Alternates hot and cold water in different basins. Some basins may have water jets. May benefit anal-rectal disorders.
Sponge bath	May use hot, tepid and cold water. May include a mustard sponge bath.
Steam sauna	Steam rooms are heated and filled with hot steam from boiling water.
Sun bath	Used in chronic disease. Expose as much skin as possible to sunlight. Start at 5 minutes on each side of body, working up to 30 minutes on each side. Highly therapeutic.
Surge bath	Very brief (15 – 20 seconds) cold bath, precede with warming treatment. Use for a healthy and robust patient.
Swiss shower	Shower of multiple jets sprayed all over the body. May be vertical or horizontal.
Vichy shower exfoliations	Water massage. Large quantities of water are sprayed over the entire body while the patient lies in a shallow wet bed with a drain.
Tepid tub bath	Immerse up to shoulders. Antipyretic. Water temperature 88 to 92 °F.
Thalassotherapy	A pool, bath or whirlpool bath using sea water and / or seaweed containing the minerals Mg, K, Ca, Na, I – hot sea water, sand and mud wrapping. Gurney's Montauk Yacht Club & Resort is one of a few thalassotherapy sites in the USA.
Turkish baths (hammam)	Steam rooms are heated and filled with hot, dry air to promote perspiration. Move to a second hotter room. Then finish washing in cold water. Turkish massage involves vigorous kneading, twisting and joint cracking.
Underwater massage	Use of hands or hose to target and improve muscle functions, treat pain and injuries, relieve stress. Used to elongate muscle fibers, oxygenate, decrease muscle lactate, improve circulation, etc.
Underwater treadmill	This form of therapy or training reduces stress on joints and body. Also used to treat injuries and rehab after serious injuries.
Visceral douches	Hot, cold or neutral douches applied to various body areas for various time frames to achieve specific end points. Types of douches include: articular, cerebral, cerebrospinal, cardiac, enteric, gastric, genito-urinary, hepatic, muscle, pulmonary, renal, splenic, steam, vapor, etc. https://www.traditionalhydrotherapy.com/Techniques/VisceralDouches.html

Hydrotherapy Technique	Brief Description
Wim Hof Method	A combination of ice baths, breathwork and meditation used to improve health. Cold exposure for 2 to 3 minutes may mitigate inflammation and improve arterial health. Boosts immunity and benefits those with autoimmune disorders.
Wraps	Hot and cold wraps; increase circulation to a specific area or limb.
Warming socks	Treatment warms up the feet, increasing circulation in the upper respiratory passages while decreasing congestion in the head. Some report improved sleep quality and quantity. Stimulate the body's natural healing mechanisms.
Warm water soaks	Good for colonic spasms.
Water birthing	Labor scores are lower for water births. Decreased labor time from 2 cm dilation onward. Reduces the use of an epidural.
Water walking	Increases activity of muscles along the spinal cord (erector spinae) and activates rectus femoris (one of four quadriceps muscles); great for after exercise activity to delay onset of muscle soreness.
Wet sheet pack	Place a plastic covering over a bed. Place another sheet over the plastic sheet. Wrap the patient in a wet sheet while they are lying on the bed so almost every square inch of the body is touching the wet sheet. Be sure to wrap the sheet in a way that no air can enter around the neck area. Place dry blankets over the patient. The patient will go through 3 physiological stages during this treatment. The 1st stage is cooling. This occurs as the body brings the wet sheet to body temperature. The 2nd stage is when the wet sheet reaches skin temperature. The 3rd stage is the warming stage when the wet sheet causes the skin temperature to rise. This causes superficial blood vessels to dilate and draw blood away from congested organs. It is important to keep the feet warm during the entire procedure. See this website for specific instructions. (www.traditional hydrotherapy.com)
Whirlpool: arm, leg, hip	Hydrotherapy using fast moving water at a specific therapeutic temperature. Leg immersion before exercise improves markers of muscle damage.
Zephyr therapy	Uses heated air jets to massage the body.

Histamine Intolerance

Histamine sensitivity has been recognized since the mid 1900s. It was originally described as scromboid fish poisoning but today is simply known as histamine intolerance or sensitivity. Under normal conditions, histamine is used to activate the immune system when the body perceives a "threat." It is released and the threat is subdued. You may consume histamine and you may consume the precursor amino acid to histamine, histidine. You may consume foods which cause the release of histamine. Most people are able to consume the histamine precursor, histidine, without experiencing symptoms, but up to 3 % of the population show histamine sensitivity. These people may be unable to normally metabolize histamine, resulting in sensitivity to normal or even low levels of histamine. In addition, tolerance threshold for histamine can be a moving target, sometimes high and sometimes low.

Diagnosis of histamine sensitivity is difficult due to low specificity of symptoms and a wide range of variability, even in the same person. Some medical experts suggest histamine intolerance is related to liver and maybe kidney "congestion" possibly due to excessive intake of "toxins." The average person with histamine sensitivity presents with 11 symptoms. Those with histamine sensitivity are often perceived to be emotionally unstable and even a hypochondriac. Histamine is involved in stimulating gastric acid secretion, inflammation, smooth muscle cell contraction, vasodilation, cytokine production, etc. It is also a neurotransmitter.

Those with histamine sensitivity may have low levels of certain enzymes. There are two known metabolic pathways which use histamine: the diamine oxidase (DAO) and the histamine-N-methyl-transferase (HNMT) pathway. DAO is a **copper dependent enzyme**. The HNMT pathway requires **S-adenosyl methionine (SAM-e)** as a methyl donor. DAO is found in the small intestine, ascending colon, placenta and kidneys. The HNMT enzyme is found in the kidneys, liver, spleen, colon, prostate, ovaries, spinal cord, trachea and respiratory tract. DAO protects the body against exogenous histamine sources. HNMT enzyme is more protective against endogenous histamine. DAO supplementation usually improves symptoms.

Those with histamine intolerance may have less gut microbiome diversity. This may even be a causative element. Histamine forming bacteria are found in the large intestine and may include: *Hafnai aluei, Morganella morganii, Klebsiella pneumonia, lactobacillus hilgardii, Lactobacillus buchnerii, Lactobacillus curvatus*, and *Oenococcus oeni* as well as certain strains of *Entero-bacteriaceae*. This underscores the importance of a healthy microbiome. It is for this reason (and others), I do not recommend the regular use of probiotics. There may be more problematic bacteria than mentioned above. For many, it is better to consume pre-biotic foods than to take probiotic supplements, unless specifically advised by your physician or nutritionist.

When it comes to assessing for histamine intolerance, a food diary is an invaluable resource. This helps target specific foods and circumstances associated with histamine intolerance. For those with severe symptoms, a 6- to 12-month low histamine diet may improve and even completely resolve the symptoms. The gut is critical to achieving success. It is important to limit to 2 to 3 meals and no snacks. This gives the gut a break from digestion and absorption. Fresh food is usually best. Avoid refrigerated leftovers and reheating food over and over. Hygienic food preparation is also critical.

On the next page is a list of histamine intolerance symptoms broken down by body system. You may have a few or many of the listed symptoms. <u>Discuss your symptoms and potential solutions with your healthcare provider.</u>

Histamine Intolerance Symptoms
(and histamine receptors*)

Cardiac & Circulatory (H1/H2)
Arrhythmias
Chest pain
Circulatory collapse
Dizziness
Fluttering Rapid beating
High blood pressure
Hypotonia
Low blood pressure
Rapid heart beat (tachycardia)
Shivers and chills (constant)
Tiredness (excessive)
Temperature fluctuations
Tissue swelling

Gut (H1/H2/H3/H4)
Bloating (abdominal distention)
Constipation
Diarrhea
Flatulence
Food sensitivities
Heartburn
Hunger (excessive)
Indigestion
Irritable bowel
Nausea
Pain (abdominal, general)
Postprandial fullness
Reflux (acid reflux)
Stomach ache / cramps
Vomiting

Neuro / Psychological (H2/H3)
Anxiety
Brain fog
Depression
Headache (chronic)
Inattentiveness
Inflammation
Irritability
Lack of concentration
Mood swings
Motion sickness
Stress
Thirst (excessive)
Vertigo

Respiratory (H1/H2/H3)
Anaphylaxis
Asthma
Chronic cough
Congestion
Difficulty breathing
Insect stings (severe reaction)
Nasal congestion
Runny nose (rhinitis)
Shortness of breath
Sneezing (excessive)

Skin (H1/H2/H4)
Acne
Eczema
Flushing
Hives
Itchy skin / eyes
Psoriasis
Rashes
Rosacea / redness
Swelling
Temperature fluctuations

Miscellaneous
Adrenal fatigue
Bone / joint pain
Edema (eyes, throat)
Fatigue
Fibromyalgia
Headaches
Insomnia
Migraines
Muscle pain
PMS (severe)
Wine intolerance

Histamine Receptor Family (H1, H2, H3, and H4)*

H1 receptors = activated in the heart and central nervous system.

H2 receptors = stimulates gastric acid production, regulates gastric motility and intestinal secretions.

H3 receptors = expressed in the peripheral and central nervous system; affects release of dopamine, GABA, acetylcholine, noradrenaline, histamine and serotonin.

H4 receptors = expressed in bone marrow, white blood cells and the mouth.

Use the following list on the next page to find out if you are sensitive to histamine. If you avoid foods on the high histamine list, your symptoms may subside. On the next page, you may notice the low histamine list, the high histamine food list and then a list of foods which do not necessarily contain histamine but may cause the release of histamine. The last list contains foods which may block the DAO enzyme, the enzyme which effectively reduces and 'neutralizes' histamine.

Table 1, contains information published in Biomolecules, 2020 Aug; 10(8):1181 (PMID: 32824107), and is useful in providing insight into histamine sensitivity; an abbreviated list is provided below. It is interesting to note that, according to this source <u>most</u> fruits, nuts, legumes, fresh meat and un-ripened cheeses have no detectable amount of histamine. Some of this contradicts the following compiled lists. I have been unable to reconcile why some foods are on the high histamine food lists while the Encyclopedia of Food Safety textbook claims the same foods do not contain histamine (unless they block DAO or there is another avenue of expression). Some have claimed the degree of ripeness, maturity, or even the lack of hygienic preparation can affect histamine tolerance. It is possible there is more than just histamine sensitivity in play. Other factors which may raise histamine include alcohol, estrogen, exercise, extreme temperatures, low oxygen, medications, over-ripe fruits, stress and certain toxins. References and sources: PMID: 10779289, 8376104, 32824107.

Table 1. Histamine content in different food categories adapted from the Encyclopedia of Food Safety, Volume 2					
Food	Number tested	Mean (SD)	Median	Minimum	Maximum
Fruits	136	0.07 (0.2)	ND	ND	2.51
Nuts	41	0.45 (1.23)	ND	ND	11.86
Vegetables	98	2.82 (7.43)	ND	ND	69.72
Legumes	11	ND	ND	ND	ND
Cereals	28	0.12 (0.33)	ND	ND	0.89
Chocolate	25	0.58 (0.44)	0.17	0.16	0.56
Spices	12	ND	ND	ND	ND
Beer	176	1.23 (2.47)	0.70	ND	21.60
Red wine	260	3.81 (3.51)	1.90	0.09	55.00
White wine	83	1.24 (1.69)	0.45	0.10	13.00
Fresh fish	136	0.79 (0.71)	ND	ND	36.55
Canned fish	96	14.42 (16.03)	5.93	ND	657.05
Semi-preserved fish	49	3.48 (3.37)	2.18	ND	34.90
Fresh meat	6	ND	ND	ND	ND
Cooked meat	48	0.30 (0.26)	ND	ND	4.80
Cured meat	23	12.98 (37.64)	0.80	ND	150.00
Dry fermented sausage	209	ND	8.03	ND	357.70
Unripened cheese	20	ND	ND	ND	ND
Raw milk cheese	20	59.37 (106.74)	18.38	ND	389.86
Pasteurized milk cheese	20	18.05 (38.23)	4.59	ND	162.03
ND: not detected; PMID: 32824107					

Foods which do not necessarily raise histamine

- Almond butter
- Butter
- Carob
- Chia seeds
- Coconut oil
- Coconut sugar
- Coffee
- Cream cheese
- Dates, date sugar
- Eggs – fully cooked
- Fish: freshly caught, cooked
- Flax seeds
- Foods with no additives
- Fresh fruits except plantains
- Fresh herbs and spices
- Fresh veg's except: *eggplant, spinach, tomato*
- Fruit (fresh)
- Gluten free grains
- Greens
- Goat milk
- Hemp seeds
- Herbs (fresh)
- Honey
- Maple syrup
- Milk: plant based
- Mineral water
- Molasses
- Monk fruit
- Mozzarella
- Nuts and nut butters
- Palm sugar
- Sheeps milk
- Tea: herbal varieties

High histamine foods

- Alcohol* (beer, wine, champagne, liquor)
- Anchovies
- Artificial sweeteners (sugar alcohols)
- Avocado
- Banana
- Beer
- Berries
- Breads**
- Buttermilk, sour cream, soured milk
- Cacao, chocolate, cocoa
- Cake decorations
- Canned foods
- Cashews
- Cheese
- Cherry
- Citrus
- Condiments: *catsup, pickles*
- Cranberry
- Dairy
- Dry dessert mixes
- Eggplant
- Fermented: *kefir, kimchi, kraut, yogurt*
- Flavored syrups
- Food colorants
- Frosting, icing
- Gelatin
- Kombucha
- Leftovers / refrigerated food
- Legumes, beans* ^
- Lentils
- Meat: *cured, deli, leftover, processed, smoked*
- MSG
- Nitrites
- Nuts including peanuts
- Olives
- Pickles and relish
- Pineapple
- Plantain
- Plums, prunes
- Prepared desserts
- Preservatives: *hydrolyzed lecithin, BHA, BHT*
- Pumpkin
- Raisins
- Ready meals
- Rice
- Seafood
- Seasoning packets
- Soda
- Soy products
- Spices: *anise, cayenne, chili, cinnamon, cloves, nutmeg*
- Spinach
- Spoiled foods
- Strawberries
- Sugars
- Sulfites
- Tea: black, green, mate
- Tomatoes
- Vinegar
- Yeast

Histamine-releasing foods

- Alcohol
- Bananas
- Chocolate
- Citrus
- Kiwi
- Legumes
- Milk (cow's)
- Nuts including peanuts
- Papaya
- Pineapple
- Plums
- Preservatives***
- Shellfish
- Strawberries
- Tomatoes
- Vinegar
- Wheat germ

Foods which block diamine oxidase (DAO) enzyme

- Alcohol (impairs histamine clearance)
- Black tea
- Energy drinks
- Tea: Green and mate tea
- Yogurt (depends on cultures)

* Eliminate for the first two weeks of following a low histamine diet. Then you may add back the like items on the "safe" list.
**May have a total of one slice of gluten free bread per day, gluten free pasta, gluten-free grains.
***Benzoate, sulfites, nitrites, glutamate, food dyes, etc.
^ Limit beans to ½ cup per day

Risk Factors for 9 Common Conditions

Autism	Snacking	Heart attack, stroke	Coronary artery disease
Low birth weight, premature	Bedtime bottle	Hormonal factors	Excessive alcohol
Smoked during pregnancy	Inadequate brushing	Peer pressure	Genetics
Male	Dry mouth	Hypothyroidism	**Neurological**
Vaccines, aluminum, mercury	Heartburn w/ reflux	Major life events	Overweight / obese
Endocrine disruptors	Purging / vomiting	Death of a loved on	Diabetes, high sugar diet
Mold, mycotoxins, toxins	Tooth abscess	Disturbed sleep	Metabolic syndrome, insulin
Maternal drug use	Difficulty chewing	Genetics, family history	Abdominal obesity
Family history	Failure to floss	Chronic pain	High blood pressure
C-section birth	Eating acidic foods	Single	Low HDL
Maternal antibodies	**Dementia**	**Diabetes**	Elevated lipids
Air pollution	Age > 65	Overweight / obese	B Vitamin deficiencies
Cancer	Smoking	Age 45+	Unrelenting stress
Smoking / Tobacco	Alcohol abuse	Family history	Head trauma
Second hand smoke	B Vitamin deficiencies	African American	Poor diet / nutrition
Radon gas	Females, loss of estrogen	Alaska native	Chemotherapy
Toxic exposures	Stress	American Indian	Surgery / anesthesia
Family history	Head trauma	Hispanics, Asians	Radiation
Depression	Obesity (controversial)	Pacific Islander, Hawaiians	Family history
Inflammation, chronic	Poor diet	Liver disease, fatty liver, etc.	Alcohol / drug abuse
Hormones	Lack physical activity	Sugar, elevated insulin	Hypothyroidism
Immunosuppression	Atherosclerosis, high sugar diet	High blood pressure	Oxidative stress
Infectious agents	Mild cognitive issues	Low HDL	Vaccines
Overweight / obese	High blood pressure	History gestational diabetes	Poor sleep patterns
Radiation	Diabetes, elevated insulin	Sedentary	Toxin(s) exposure
Sedentary lifestyle	Flu vaccine (controversial)	Depression	Poverty
Inflammatory bowel dz	Family history, genetics	History heart disease	High, prolonged fever
Night shift work	Elevated homocysteine	History of stroke	Metabolic disorders
Diet, alcohol consumption	Vitamin B12 deficiency	Polycystic ovary syndrome	Hypoxia
Hormone therapy	Hypothyroidism	Acanthosis nigricans	Genetic
Oral contraceptives	**Depression**	Virus at early age	Down syndrome
Radiation therapy	Disturbed sleep pattern	Live in cold climate	Lack social engagement
Vaccines	Illness, chronic pain, etc.	Unhealthy diet, mineral def.	Atherosclerosis
Sugar, Fructose, Insulin	Abuse: physical, emotional	Triglycerides ≥ 250	**Suicide**
Stomach problems	Female gender	Drinking cow's milk	Feeling hopeless, trapped
Liver cirrhosis	Lack social support	**Heart disease**	Guilt, poor diet/lifestyle
Coffee	Post partum	Age 55+	Burden to others
H. pylori infection	B vitamin deficiencies	Being male	Unbearable pain
Epstein-Barr virus	Alcohol / drug abuse	Family history	Increased use alcohol/drugs
Certain occupations	Multiple medications	Minority race	Increased use of drugs
UV light exposure	Retiring, retirement	High blood pressure	Social withdrawal, isolation
Atypical moles	Moving	Sedentary lifestyle	Serious health problem
Caries / Cavities	Job stresses	Overweight / obese	Depression, anxiety, fatigue
Toothache / pain	Family problems	Diabetes	Prolonged stress, irritability
Tooth sensitivity	Unemployment	Diet	Humiliation, agitation, rage
Temp sensitivity	Separation / divorce	Waist > 35 inches	Trauma (past / present)
Holes or pits in teeth	Excessive social media	Vitamin / mineral deficiencies	Friend commits suicide
Brown staining	Chronic, unrelenting stress	Elevated lipids; low HDL	Previous suicide attempt
Pain when biting	Poor nutrition	Fructose and elevated insulin	Mental disorder, family hx
Sugary foods / drinks	Mineral deficiencies	Hypothyroidism	Talk about suicide
Sticky, gummy sweets	Abuse	Atrial fibrillation	No reasons to live

Care Giver Daily Activity and Progress Notes

Date: _____ Care Giver Name & Telephone: _____

Patient Name: _____ Gender: ☐F ☐M   Ht: _____ Wt: _____ Wt Hx: _____

Diagnosis(es): 1. _____ 2. _____ 3. _____

Special Needs/Health Concerns:

Date/Time	Progress Notes
	Vital Signs: BP _____ / _____ , Temp: _____ Respirations: _____ Heart Rate: _____
	Vital Signs: BP _____ / _____ , Temp: _____ Respirations: _____ Heart Rate: _____
	Vital Signs: BP _____ / _____ , Temp: _____ Respirations: _____ Heart Rate: _____
	O2 Saturation: _____%; Dehydration / Tenting : ☐Y ☐N ; Dry Mouth: ☐Y ☐N
	Walking: ☐ No Issues ☐ 1-2 Falls ☐ 3+ Falls Falls: ☐ Forward, ☐ Backward, ☐ Sideways
	Oriented to time / place / people:
	% Time: Resting in bed _____ Sitting _____ Walking _____ Other _____
	Concerns:
	Needs assistance with:
	Interesting comments by patient:
	Plans for tomorrow:
	Community services / referrals:
	Supplies needed:
	Daily report to family:

Social Interactions (supervised / initiated by the caregiver)	
Visitors	
Phone calls	
Outing(s)	
Appointments	

Mental Stimulation (to be initiated by the caregiver)

☐Music   ☐Reading   ☐Played a game(s)   ☐Hobby   ☐Other:

Physical (initiated by the caregiver)

☐Stretching   ☐Walking   ☐Exercise   ☐Active hobby   ☐Other:

Spiritual Care (initiated by the caregiver)

☐Prayer   ☐Bible study   ☐Uplifting messages   ☐Other:

General Assessment Scale: 0=none;   1= a little;   2=moderate;   3=average;   4=above average;   5=high

Pain level 0 1 2 3 4 5	Happiness level 0 1 2 3 4 5	Engaged 0 1 2 3 4 5
Energy level 0 1 2 3 4 5	Sleep quality 0 1 2 3 4 5	Coherent / lucid 0 1 2 3 4 5

Activity of Daily Living Functions

Personal Hygiene	☐Bath/shower ☐Bed bath ☐Washed face ☐Clean glasses ☐Washed hair ☐Styled hair ☐Clean underwear ☐Dressed	Mouth / teeth care ☐am ☐noon ☐pm
Toilet Times and Comments	A=urine; B=bowel movement; C=diarrhea; D=high volume diarrhea; E=dark urine; F=blood in urine; G=incontinent; H=parasites; I=other:_____ 1 2 3 4 5 6 7 8 9 10 11 12 noon 1 2 3 4 5 6 7 8 9 10 11 Midnight	
Turns or Transfers Comments / Times	AM: 1 2 3 4 5 6 7 8 9 10 11 12 Noon PM: 1 2 3 4 5 6 7 8 9 10 11 12 Midnight	
Nap / Sleep Times Comments	AM: 1 2 3 4 5 6 7 8 9 10 11 12 Noon PM: 1 2 3 4 5 6 7 8 9 10 11 12 Midnight	

Food and Liquid Intake

Meal	Time	Food	Amount	Appetite	Comments
Breakfast					
Lunch					
Dinner					
Snacks					

Water Intake ounces	☐8 oz ☐16 ☐24 ☐32 ☐40 ☐48 ☐56 ☐64 ☐72 ☐80 ☐88 ☐96+
Other Liquids oz/ml	☐___ oz / ml _____ ; ☐___ oz / ml _____ ; ☐___ oz / ml _____

Describe feeding assistance if needed:

Rx Medications, Over-the-Counter, Vitamins, Minerals, Herbals, Other (attach separate sheet if necessary)

Name	Dose	Frequency	Delivery Route	Recommended Times	Time Meds Were Given	Special Instructions

Final comments:

Have a beautiful day! Your caregiver: _____ Shift time period: _____ am/pm

12 Months of Gardening Tasks

Tasks	Jan	Feb	Mar	Apr	May	Jun	Jul	Aug	Sep	Oct	Nov	Dec
Order seeds, bulbs and plants												
Clean/sharpen garden tools												
Clean/sterilize garden equipment												
Sharpen mower blades												
Deal with leaves, branches, etc.												
Protect plants from weather												
Make plant labels												
Clean ponds and water features												
Weed and mulch												
Collect organic matter (e.g., leaves)												
Collect wood chips												
Clean greenhouse / hoop house												
Plant greenhouse / hoop house												
Clean cold frames												
Plant cold frames												
Maintain root cellar												
Prune fruit trees and rose bushes												
Add compost / amend garden beds												
Plant cool weather vegetables												
Plant bulbs												
Dig up and cold store bulbs												
Prune flowering shrubs												
Monitor for pest invasion												
Deadhead flowers and shrubs												
Deep water trees and shrubs												
Divide self-propagating plants												
Save seeds												
Reseed lawn / bare spots												
Store and protect bulbs for winter												
Soil testing												
Remove dead trees / bushes												
Harden off seedlings												
Plant tropical trees: banana, papaya												
Set out strawberry plants												
Direct sow seeds												
Build garden beds, fill with dirt												
Vacation: plan for coverage												
Determine best days for planting												
Plant in containers												
Feed / fertilize plants												
Set up composting system												

Tasks	Jan	Feb	Mar	Apr	May	Jun	Jul	Aug	Sep	Oct	Nov	Dec
Mow												
Plant seeds indoors												
Plant trees												
Plant vines												
Refresh perennial plants												
Maintain watering systems												
Clean greenhouse / hoop house												
Maintain high and low tunnels												
Lawn maintenance												
Weed control measures												
Layout vegetable garden												
Harvest												
Support plants with stakes												
Order hay / straw / wood chips, etc.												
Feed and water wildlife, birds, etc.												
Maintain/repair garden furniture												
Maintain/repair fences, decks, etc.												
Plant bare-root trees												
Plant potatoes												
Harvest potatoes												
Plant raspberry/blackberry canes												
Plant garlic, shallots, onions												
Repot indoor and patio plants												
Maintain herb garden												
Harvest/process medicinal plants												
Set out asparagus crowns												
Harvest and process herbs (e.g. basil)												
Plant containers, hanging baskets												
Protect sensitive plants from sun												
Stake tall perennials/annuals												
Mow/trim lawn												
Mulch / prune strawberry plants												
Transfer indoor plants outside												
Bring outside plants inside												
Paint yard / garden features												
Stakes: prepare and maintain												
Take measures to prevent mold												
Improve garden / yard drainage												
Make your own planting soil mixes												
Seed exchanges												
Fertilize fruit and nut bearing trees												
Cold stratify seeds, bulbs, etc.												

	Age Appropriate First Aid Kits	
Ages 2 – 5	☐Aloe vera (roll-on) ☐Assortment of band aids ☐Assortment of sterile gauze pads ☐Co-flex bandages ☐10 cotton balls ☐Lavender oil (roll-on) ☐Masks (age appropriate) ☐Flashlight + batteries ☐Gloves (assorted sizes, kid sizes) ☐Moist hand wipes ☐Paper pad ☐Paper Tape (medical grade)	☐Pencil ☐Rubber bands ☐Straws, rigid (wrapped and sterile) ☐Tweezers ☐Vinegar (roll-on) ☐Whistle ☐_____ ☐_____ ☐_____ ☐_____
Ages 6 – 10	☐**Above items** ☐Absorbent compress dressings ☐ACE bandages, flat emergency trauma dressing ☐Bowl, collapsible ☐Charcoal tablets or salve ☐Cold compresses ☐Fire starter material ☐Flat emergency trauma dressing ☐Flexible measuring tape ☐Forehead thermometer ☐Liquid soap ☐Magnifying glass ☐Mirror (compact)	☐Pen light + batteries ☐Scissors ☐String / cord ☐Water bottle, full ☐Water filtration straw ☐_____ ☐_____ ☐_____ ☐_____
Ages 11 – 17	☐**Above items** ☐Alcohol prep wipes ☐Antibiotic cream ☐Antiseptic fluid ☐Bandages (3- and 4-inch rolls) ☐Betadine wipes ☐Bleach (small amount) ☐Bulb syringe ☐Bunge cord (various sizes) ☐Cotton swabs ☐Dental floss / tape ☐Elastic bandages ☐Eye pads ☐Eye wash solution/cup ☐First aid instruction booklet ☐Goggles (eye protection) ☐Glycerin ☐Iodine, liquid ☐Hydrogen peroxide ☐Lip balm	☐Nail clippers ☐Poison ivy wipes ☐Popsicle sticks / splints ☐Safety pins ☐Sterile rags (in a zip lock bag) ☐Sterile saline solution ☐Surgical masks and / or N95 mask ☐Trash bags ☐Waterproof containers ☐Waterproof matches ☐Zinc oxide ☐Zip lock bags (assorted sizes) ☐Zip ties ☐_____ ☐_____ ☐_____ ☐_____ ☐_____

Adults, 18+	☐ **Above items** ☐ Anti-acids ☐ Antifungal cream ☐ Anti-nausea medication ☐ Arm sling ☐ Aspirin, other pain reducing meds ☐ Benadryl (anti-histamine) ☐ Biodegradable soap ☐ Blood stop powder ☐ Breathing barrier / resuscitation mask ☐ Burn gel ☐ Butterfly closure strips ☐ Calamine lotion ☐ Castor oil ☐ Cayenne capsules ☐ Collapsible water sink / basin ☐ Cough medicine ☐ Duct tape and other types of tape ☐ Ear plugs ☐ Electrolyte solution / powder ☐ Emergency space blanket ☐ Emetics to induce vomiting ☐ Epi-pen or equivalent ☐ Epsom salt (for constipation, soaking water) ☐ Glucose gel / tablets ☐ Glucose meter with test strips ☐ Hammock ☐ Headlamp ☐ Helichrysum oil ☐ Herbal teas (variety of therapeutic teas) ☐ Hot water bottle ☐ Hydrocortisone ointment ☐ Hyfin® vent compact chest seal, twin pack ☐ Imodium (anti-diarrhea) ☐ Insect repellant ☐ Laxatives / stool softener ☐ Lighter ☐ Liquid band aid	☐ Magnesium citrate ☐ Medical gloves (S/M/L) ☐ Mercury thermometer ☐ Mini and maxi pads ☐ Moleskin ☐ Multipurpose knife ☐ Nasopharangeal airway 28F with lubricant ☐ Needle decompression kit ☐ Otoscope (ear exam) ☐ Oximeter (oxygen saturation) ☐ Pain meds (strong, Rx strength) ☐ Pepper packets ☐ Personal locator beacon ☐ Petrolatum gauze pads ☐ Plastic wrap ☐ Press and seal wrap ☐ Psyllium powder ☐ Reflective blanket / tent ☐ Salt packets ☐ Save a tooth kit ☐ Silver infused bandages ☐ Smelling salts (ammonium carbonate) ☐ Solar power strip ☐ Sphygmomanometer ☐ Stethoscope (monitoring heart and gut) ☐ Stop bleeding (hemostatic) bandages ☐ Sugar packets ☐ Surgical kit with extra sutures ☐ Syringes and needles (assorted sizes) ☐ Tampons (for puncture wounds) ☐ Tea tree oil ☐ Tourniquets (CAT, SWAT-T, NAR Gen 7 CAT, etc.) ☐ UV light (battery operated) ☐ Venom desensitizer (venomous bites and stings) ☐ Vodka (small flask) ☐ _____ ☐ _____
Emergency Contact Numbers	Fire / Police: Call 9 – 1 – 1 Poison Control Center: 800 – 222 – 1222 Primary Care Physician: Specialized Physician: Dentist: Other: Other: Other: Other:	**Family Contacts** Mother: Father: Sibling 1: Sibling 2: Sibling 3: Child 1: Child 2:

Contact Numbers (include satellite numbers when possible) and Locations
Construction, Fire, Local Utilities, Neighbors, Police, Utilities Contact Information

Emergency Contacts	Phone Number	Address	E-mail
Contractor 1			
Contractor 2			
Electrician 1			
Electrician 2			
Employer 1			
Employer 2			
Equipment rental co.			
Fire department			
Fire department			
Gas station 1:			
Gas station 2:			
Gas station 3:			
Hardware store			
Hardware store			
Heavy equip operator			
Insurance, home			
Insurance, cars			
Landlord			
Locksmith			
Neighbor 1			
Neighbor 2			
Neighbor 3			
Neighbor 4			
News channel			
News channel			
Police			
Police			
Plumber 1			
Red Cross			
Tree services			
Utility: electric			
Utility: gas			
Utility: internet			
Utility: phone			
Utility: water			
Volunteer agencies			

Contact Numbers and Locations
Church and Clergy Contact Information

Church and Pastor	Phone	Address

Emergency Contact Numbers and Locations
Friends and Relatives Contact Information

Name	Phone	Address	Email

Contact Numbers and Locations
Websites and News Outlets: Newspapers, TV Stations, etc.

News Outlet	Phone	Web Address

Contact Numbers and Locations
Radio Stations (local and national) and HAM Radio Operators

Local Radio Call Name	FM or AM frequency	Local Area	Telephone Number

Emergency Services Contact Numbers and Locations
Medical and Emergency Services Directory

Emergency Service	Contact Name	Telephone Number	Location, Address, etc.
All Emergencies in USA		9 – 1 – 1	
Non-emergency Police or City		3 – 1 – 1	
Poison Emergency		1-800-222-1222	
Airport, international			
Airport, local			
Animal Shelter			
Center for Disease Control			
Child Protective Services			
Daycare			
Dentist			
Emergency Medical Services			
Environmental Protection Agency			
FEMA			
Fire Department			
Fire Protection Contractor			
Food bank / co-op			
Forrest Department			
Hazardous Material Clean-up			
Helicopter Transport Services			
Highway Patrol			
Hospital 1:			
Hospital 2:			
Infectious Disease Specialist MD			
Jail (local)			
Local City Hall			
Local Police Dept			
Local Red Cross			
Maritime Rescue Operations			
Orthodontist			
Periodontist			
Pharmacy			
Physician 1:			
Physician 2:			
Public Health Department			
School 1:			
School 2:			
State Environmental Agency			
US Forrest Service (report fires)			
Veterinarian			
Water Rescue Operations			

Emergency Supply List
Adapted from FEMA.gov

Yes	Emergency Supply Items
	Car Supplies
	Bible, inspirational reading, wild edible book, first aid book, music, hymnal, harmonica, etc.
	Flashlight(s) with extra batteries, glow sticks, small glow-in-the-dark orange traffic cones, headlamps.
	Important phone numbers on paper (copies for all family members).
	Family check-in procedure(s) with contact person(s) / number(s) and one or two alternative non-home "distant" staging locations with maps and coordinates.
	Emergency contingency plan on paper (copies for all family members).
	Car phone charger, extra battery and solar charger, walkie talkies, short wave radio, Ham radio.
	Battery operated (with extra batteries) or solar NOAA radio.
	Fire extinguisher, fire dousing liquid, fire blanket, waterproof matches.
	Dust mask, plastic sheeting, duct tape (used to seal off space from dust and contaminated air).
	First aid kit, first aid book, essential oils, charcoal, surgical kit, duct tape, epi pen, etc.
	Whistle, flares, emergency light, small mirror, flint, compass, waterproof matches in container, etc.
	Extra cash on hand, at least around $200 in small bills, small silver coins, valuable trading items.
	Extra reading or prescription glasses, prescription meds, sleeping aids, etc.
	One or two water filtration straws, iodine tablets / drops, water purification tablets.
	If you have warning of a coming storm or event, fill car(s) and extra containers with gas.
	Food supplies such as honey, granola bars, nuts, seeds, dried fruit, etc.
	Large bag pet food, collar, leash, tags, long lasting flea collar, dog bed, etc.
	Multi-function knife, small tools.
	Change of clothes and hiking shoes, rain coat, hat, underwear.
	Sleeping pad, sleeping bag, yoga mat, inflatable mattress, hammock, tent, large tarps, etc.
	Roll of colored plastic non-stick tape for marking a trail.
	National, state and local maps, paper, pencils, compass, etc.
	Extra fuses, car tools, head lamps, locking gas cap, at least two liters car oil, other fluids, etc.
	Jumper cables, air pump, etc, battery charger.
	Blanket, wool cap, extra socks.
	Car 12-V beverage heater.
	Pictures of close family members, friends and pets.
	Car 12-V heated blanket, hand and feet warmers.
	Home Supplies
	Boxes in the garage • Wrench or pliers to turn off utilities (keep required tool at each location). • Fire extinguisher. • Dust mask, plastic sheeting, duct tape (used to seal off from dust and contaminated air). • Whistle, flares, emergency light, small mirror, flint, compass, waterproof matches.
	Fire extinguisher (kitchen, garage, etc.).
	Box in Kitchen • Vitamin/mineral supplements, prescription meds, extra prescription / reading glasses. • Three gallons of water per person in your household along with water purification system (best to store water in a cool place where it can be refreshed every 3 – 6 months).
	First aid kit, charcoal, surgical kit, duct tape, epi pen, automated external defibrillator, etc.
	Extra cash on hand, at least $1,000 in small bills.
	One water filtration straw for each person in your household (a few extras are a good idea).
	If you have warning of a coming storm or event, fill car with gas, fill extra gas cans.
	If you have warning of a coming storm or event, fill zip lock plastic bags with water and freeze.

Yes	Basic Emergency Supply Items
	3-day supply of food (e.g., energy bars, dried fruit, honey, nuts, seeds, salt, sugar, etc.)
	For infants: diapers, wipes, formula, electrolyte water, medications, blankets, clothes, hat, etc.
	For young children: books, games, reading, balls, Frisbee, stuffed animals, blankets, etc.
	For older adults: comfortable seat, blanket, reading glasses, books, denture supplies, transfer belt, etc.
	Pet food and supplies (food, water, glow in dark collar, leash, rabies tag, lost tag, pictures, etc.).
	Kitchen tools: knives, can opener, utensils, paper towels, dish soap, bar soap, etc.
	64-ounce growler (insulated thermos).
	Several collapsible silicon containers (mixing bowl, small sink size, drinking, etc.).
	Moist towelettes, various size zip lock bags, various size garbage bags.
	Personal items: toothbrush, toothpaste, feminine hygiene products.
	Household items: spray vinegar, chlorine bleach, liquid dropper, hydrogen peroxide, etc.
	Small outdoor cooking stove with several camping pans and propane.
	Tent large enough for your family with sleeping bag, blankets, pads, etc.
	Clothes and shoes for three days.
	Natural bug repellant spray or essential oils.
	First aid book, survival book, edible plants wild plants book, devotional book (Bible), others.
	Important family documents: house deed(s), home insurance, car titles, birth certificates, social security cards, passports, drivers' license, car insurance, bank info, credit card info, etc.
	Back up of your computer hard drive.
	Spare non-phone digital camera.
	Personal protection unit: side arm with ammo, stun gun, etc. (keep with you when legal).
	Roll of colored plastic non-stick tape for marking a trail.
	Folding, battery powered bicycle.
	Purse / Wallet
	Several $200 gas cards in wallet
	Several $50 phone cards in wallet or pre-paid flip phone
	Copies of important family documents: house deed(s), home insurance card, car title, birth certificate, social security card, passport, drivers' license, car insurance, bank info, credit card
	Pictures of family members, pets
	Office Supplies
	First aid kit
	Moist towelettes, toilet paper, feminine hygiene products, beach towel, sleeping pad
	Three-day food supply such as granola bars, nuts, seeds, dried fruit, tea, etc.
	Blankets
	Change of clothes and extra pair shoes, hat, socks
	National, state and local maps, paper, pencils, etc.
	Back up of your computer hard drive
	Spare non-phone digital camera

Contingency Group (CG) Plans – Identify Your Group Members

CG's may include 18 or more people (including children) and may be networked to other CG's

CG Number (If CG is part of a larger network of CG's): _____ of _____

Distant Check-in Names and Telephone Number(s):

Name	Contact Information	Role(s) / Possible Location(s)
1.	Home / Cell: Work/School: Address:	Role(s): Possible locations:
2.	Home / Cell: Work/School: Address:	Role(s): Possible locations:
3.	Home / Cell: Work/School: Address:	Role(s): Possible locations:
4.	Home / Cell: Work/School: Address:	Role(s): Possible locations:
5.	Home / Cell: Work/School: Address:	Role(s): Possible locations:
6.	Home / Cell: Work/School: Address:	Role(s): Possible locations:
7.	Home / Cell: Work/School: Address:	Role(s): Possible locations:
8.	Home / Cell: Work/School: Address:	Role(s): Possible locations:
9.	Home / Cell: Work/School: Address:	Role(s): Possible locations:
10.	Home / Cell: Work/School: Address:	Role(s): Possible locations:
11.	Home / Cell: Work/School: Address:	Role(s): Possible locations:
12.	Home / Cell: Work/School: Address:	Role(s): Possible locations:
13.	Home / Cell: Work/School: Address:	Role(s): Possible locations:
14.	Home / Cell: Work/School: Address:	Role(s): Possible locations:
15.	Home / Cell: Work/School: Address:	Role(s): Possible locations:
16.	Home / Cell: Work/School: Address:	Role(s): Possible locations:
17.	Home / Cell: Work/School: Address:	Role(s): Possible locations:
18.	Home / Cell: Work/School: Address:	Role(s): Possible locations:

Vital Document Checklist			
Vital Document	Owner Name	Number / Identifier	Additional Information (address, telephone, etc.)
Airplane ownership documents			
Banking documents			
Birth certificates			
Boat registration and documents			
Business license(s)			
Car registration, license plate #s			
Car titles			
Cash			
Contact and telephone info lists			
• Church, clergy, elders			
• Construction, fire, police, etc.			
• Family			
• Friends			
• Medical emergency			
• Radio / HAM op stations			
• Websites & news outlets			
Court orders			
Credit card numbers and info			
Driver's licenses'			
Education records			
Professional license's			
Evacuation directions, hotels, maps			
• Main road plans			
• Back road plans			
Eye glass prescription(s)			
Family communication plan			
Family meet up plan			
Family photos (preferably on DVD)			

Vital Document	Owner Name	Number / Identifier	Additional Information (address, telephone, etc.)
Financial institution account #s			
401K plan and contact info			
ATM / debit car pin and numbers			
Brokerage statements			
Bonds			
Important contact information			
Contracts			
Insurance documents			
Firearm permits			
Investment documents, broker info			
Legal documents not listed here			
Loan documents			
Maps (state and country)			
Marriage certificate			
Medical insurance cards / numbers			
Dental records			
Medical records (critical ones)			
Immunization records			
Military records / documents			
Over-the-counter meds			
Passports (number, expiration, copies)			
Password list			
Payroll stubs			
Pet records			
Prescription meds			
Professional licenses			
Property deeds			
Recent family and animal photos			
Rental agreements			
RV / trailer registration / documents			
Social security cards			
Spare keys / lock codes			
Tax records			
Trust fund info.			
Wills, living wills, etc.			
Other:			
Other:			
Other:			
Other:			
Other:			

www.ingramcontent.com/pod-product-compliance
Lightning Source LLC
Chambersburg PA
CBHW080832230426
43665CB00021B/2820